HOUGHTON MIFFLIN SOCIAL STUDIES

America Will Be

U.S. Custom House, 1805.

 yes,

I say it plain,

America never was America to me,

And yet I swear this oath—

America will be!

An ever-living seed,

Its dream

Lies deep in the heart of me.

Langston Hughes

Beverly J. Armento
J. Jorge Klor de Alva
Gary B. Nash
Christopher L. Salter
Louis E. Wilson
Karen K. Wixson

America *Will Be*

Houghton Mifflin Company • Boston

Atlanta • Dallas • Geneva, Illinois • Princeton, New Jersey • Palo Alto • Toronto

Consultants

Program Consultants

Edith M. Guyton
Associate Professor of Early
  Childhood Education
Georgia State University
Atlanta, Georgia

Gail Hobbs
Associate Professor of Geography
Pierce College
Woodland Hills, California

Charles Peters
Reading Consultant
Oakland Schools
Pontiac, Michigan

Cathy Riggs-Salter
Social Studies Consultant
Hartsburg, Missouri

Alfredo Schifini
Limited English Proficiency Consultant
Los Angeles, California

George Paul Schneider
Associate Director
  of General Programs
Department of Museum Education
Art Institute of Chicago
Chicago, Illinois

Twyla Stewart
Center for Academic Interinstitutional
  Programs
University of California—Los Angeles
Los Angeles, California

Scott Waugh
Associate Professor of History
University of California—Los Angeles
Los Angeles, California

Teacher Reviewers

David E. Beer (Grade 5)
Weisser Park Elementary
Fort Wayne, Indiana

Jan Coleman (Grades 6–7)
Thornton Junior High
Fremont, California

Shawn Edwards
  (Grades 1–3)
Jackson Park Elementary
University City, Missouri

Barbara J. Fech (Grade 6)
Martha Ruggles School
Chicago, Illinois

Deborah M. Finkel
  (Grade 4)
Los Angeles Unified
  School District,
  Region G
South Pasadena,
California

Jim Fletcher (Grades 5, 8)
La Loma Junior High
Modesto, California

Susan M. Gilliam
  (Grade 1)
Roscoe Elementary
Los Angeles, California

Vicki Stroud Gonterman
  (Grade 2)
Gibbs International
  Studies Magnet School
Little Rock, Arkansas

Lorraine Hood (Grade 2)
Fresno Unified School
  District
Fresno, California

Jean Jamgochian
  (Grade 5)
Haycock Gifted and
  Talented Center
Fairfax County, Virginia

Susan Kirk-Davalt
  (Grade 5)
Crowfoot Elementary
Lebanon, Oregon

Mary Molyneaux-Leahy
  (Grade 3)
Bridgeport Elementary
Bridgeport, Pennsylvania

Sharon Oviatt
  (Grades 1–3)
Keysor Elementary
Kirkwood, Missouri

Jayne B. Perala (Grade 1)
Cave Spring Elementary
Roanoke, Virginia

Carol Siefkin (K)
Garfield Elementary
Sacramento, California

Norman N. Tanaka
  (Grade 3)
Martin Luther King Jr.
  Elementary
Sacramento, California

John Tyler (Grades 5, 8)
Groton School
Groton, Massachusetts

Portia W. Vaughn
  (Grades 1–3)
School District 11
Colorado Springs,
  Colorado

ISBN: 0-395-54892-6
  89-VH-97 96

Development by Ligature, Inc.

Acknowledgments

Grateful acknowledgment is made
for the use of the material listed below.
The material in the Minipedia is
reprinted from *The World Book* *Encyclopedia* with the expressed permission of the publisher. © 1993 by World
Book, Inc.

–Continued on page 652.

From Your Authors

*T*he hunters shiver as an icy wind blows across the empty land. It is flat and treeless here, covered only with moss and small shrubs. Far away, the hunters can see a tall range of mountains covered with ice and snow.

So begins an imaginary account of the first humans who ever crossed over the ice from Asia to North America. For periods of time during the Ice Age long ago, a land bridge connected the two continents. Historians think musk ox crossed over first, and hunters looking for game followed them. In Chapter 4 of this book, you will have the chance to read more about the ancestors of present-day Native Americans.

Most of the people you will meet in this book lived long ago in places that may seem very far away from home. But they all had feelings just like yours and faced many of the same challenges you will face in your life. And whether they were great leaders or ordinary people, their decisions and actions helped shape your nation and your world.

As you read about these people, places, and events, we hope you will ask many questions. Some questions may be about history: "What caused these people to make the decisions they did?" or "How do we know about these events?" Other questions may be about geography: "What are the land and weather like in that place?" or "Why did people choose to settle there?" Still other questions may be about economics: "How did people meet their needs for food and shelter?" or "How did people work out ways for using limited resources?"

Most of all, we hope you catch the excitement of thinking, questioning, and discovering answers about your world—now and in the 21st century.

Beverly J. Armento
Professor of Social Studies
Director, Center for Business and
Economic Education
Georgia State University

Christopher L. Salter
Professor and Chair
Department of Geography
University of Missouri

Louis E. Wilson
Associate Professor
Department of Afro-American Studies
Smith College

J. Jorge Klor de Alva
Professor of Anthropology
Princeton University

Gary B. Nash
Professor of History
University of California—Los Angeles

Karen K. Wixson
Associate Professor of Education
University of Michigan

Contents

About Your Book xii
Map and Globe Handbook G1

Unit 1 1 **The United States: Past and Present**	**Chapter 1** 2 *A Nation of Many Peoples*	Lesson 1 *A Tale of One City*	4
		Lesson 2 *A Land of Immigrants*	12
		Lesson 3 *A Country of Many Cultures*	17
	Chapter 2 28 *This Land of Ours*	Lesson 1 *Understanding Geography*	30
		Lesson 2 *Regions of America*	34
		Lesson 3 *Studying Globes and Maps*	41
		Lesson 4 *Stories Maps Tell*	49
	Chapter 3 56 *Clues to Our Past*	Lesson 1 *What Is History?*	58
		Lesson 2 *What Does a Historian Do?*	63
		Lesson 3 *Why Study History?*	70
Unit 2 76 **Exploring and Settling America**	**Chapter 4** 78 *The First People of the Americas*	Lesson 1 *People Come to the Americas*	80
		Lesson 2 *Four American Indian Cultures*	86
		Lesson 3 *Life in an Iroquois Village*	94
	Chapter 5 102 *The Age of Exploration*	Lesson 1 *Europe in the Age of Exploration*	104
		Lesson 2 *Portuguese and Spanish Exploration*	109
		Lesson 3 *French, Dutch, and English Voyages*	118
	Chapter 6 126 *Settling a New World*	Lesson 1 *Spanish and French Colonization*	128
		Lesson 2 *English Settlement in the South*	132
		Lesson 3 *English Settlement in New England*	138
		Lesson 4 *English Settlement in the Middle Colonies*	143
Unit 3 152 **Life in the English Colonies**	**Chapter 7** 154 *The Southern Colonies*	Lesson 1 *A New Settlement in Virginia*	156
		Lesson 2 *Rebellion in Virginia*	163
		Lesson 3 *Slavery in the Southern Colonies*	167
	Chapter 8 178 *The New England Colonies*	Lesson 1 *The Puritans Come to America*	180
		Lesson 2 *Life in New England*	186
		Lesson 3 *Challenging Authority*	191
		Lesson 4 *Trade in New England*	198
	Chapter 9 206 *The Middle Colonies*	Lesson 1 *The Land of the Middle Colonies*	208
		Lesson 2 *A Mixture of Many Cultures*	213
		Lesson 3 *Farming and Trade*	224
Unit 4 232 **The Struggle for Independence**	**Chapter 10** 234 *Crisis with Britain*	Lesson 1 *Ties to Great Britain*	236
		Lesson 2 *The Seven Years' War*	241
		Lesson 3 *A New British Policy*	247
	Chapter 11 258 *War Breaks Out*	Lesson 1 *Forming a New Government*	260
		Lesson 2 *Fighting the War*	268
		Lesson 3 *Building a New Society*	284

	Chapter 12	290	Lesson 1 *Forming a Government*	292
	Searching for Unity		Lesson 2 *The Constitution*	297
			Lesson 3 *Becoming American*	306

Unit 5 312
Life in a Growing Nation

Chapter 13	314	Lesson 1 *Launching a New Government*	316
Birth of a New Nation		Lesson 2 *Jefferson and National Unity*	320
		Lesson 3 *Economic Life of the New Nation*	324
		Lesson 4 *Everyday Life in the Young Nation*	329
Chapter 14	338	Lesson 1 *The Moving Frontier*	340
Moving West		Lesson 2 *Life on the New Frontier*	345
		Lesson 3 *The Next Frontier*	352
		Lesson 4 *The American Indians in Retreat*	360
Chapter 15	368	Lesson 1 *Texas and the Struggle with Mexico*	370
Settling the Far West		Lesson 2 *The Road to Oregon*	377
		Lesson 3 *Migrating to California and Utah*	383
		Lesson 4 *Conflicts with the American Indians*	389

Unit 6 398
A Nation in Conflict

Chapter 16	400	Lesson 1 *Plantation Society*	402
Southern Society		Lesson 2 *A Look at Slavery*	407
		Lesson 3 *Life in the Other South*	413
Chapter 17	420	Lesson 1 *Industrial Growth*	422
The Industrial North		Lesson 2 *New People, New Problems*	426
		Lesson 3 *Life in Northern Cities*	430
		Lesson 4 *Making a Better Society*	434
Chapter 18	442	Lesson 1 *Crisis and Compromise*	444
A Divided Nation		Lesson 2 *The Growing Conflict*	450
		Lesson 3 *A House Divided*	462

Unit 7 472
Toward the Modern Age

Chapter 19	474	Lesson 1 *Outbreak of the War*	476
The Civil War and Reconstruction		Lesson 2 *The Home Fronts*	483
		Lesson 3 *The End of the War*	489
		Lesson 4 *Reconstruction*	494
Chapter 20	502	Lesson 1 *Changes on the Great Plains*	504
Life in a Changing America		Lesson 2 *Entering the Modern Age*	516
		Lesson 3 *Coming to America*	522
		Lesson 4 *Into Growing Cities*	530
Conclusion	536		
A Look at the Twentieth Century			

Time/Space Databank 575

Declaration of Independence	576	Gazetteer	630
Constitution	580	Biographical Dictionary	633
Minipedia	600	Glossary	638
Atlas	614	Index	643
Glossary of Geographic Terms	628	Acknowledgments	652

Understanding Skills

Each "Understanding Skills" feature gives you the opportunity to learn and practice a skill related to the topic you are studying.

Reference Books: Using Encyclopedias	9
Latitude and Longitude: Locating Cities	48
Visuals: Comparing Art and Photos	62
Artifacts: Interpreting Information	69
Climate: Observing the Seasons	93
B.C. and A.D.: Using Timelines	99
Map Directions: Tracing Routes	123
Summaries: Combining Information	136
Line Graphs: Choosing the Right Scale	148
Symbols: Interpreting Flow Lines	174
Scale: Choosing the Right Map	202
Tables: Comparing Information	229
Critical Thinking: Interpreting Political Cartoons	254
How to Outline: Organizing What You Read	275
Critical Thinking: Identifying Fact and Opinion	304
Graphic Organizers: Using Cluster Diagrams	334
Map Making: Using Landmarks as Guides	358
Cause and Effect: Using Word Clues and Diagrams	376
Self-Expression: Interpreting History Visually	417
Group Projects: Working Together	439
Point of View: Asking Good Questions	457
Reports: Giving an Oral Report	467
Map Symbols: Making Location Decisions	521

Understanding Concepts

Each "Understanding Concepts" feature gives you more information about a concept that is important to the lesson you are reading.

Culture	18
Interdependence	40
Historical Perspective	60
Land Use	92
Expansion	114
Colonialism	146
Slavery	168
Dissent	192
Tolerance	216
Taxation	252
Equality	264
Heroism	307
Nationalism	321
The Frontier	348
Demographic Change	392
Social Class	414
Activism	437
Compromise	448
Citizenship	498
Mechanization	518

Making Decisions

Much of history is made of people's decisions. These pages take you step-by-step through fascinating problems from history and today. What will you decide?

Money for Exploration	116
Patriot or Loyalist?	266
Should I Go West with My Family?	394
Immigration: Open or Restricted?	528

Literature

Throughout history people have expressed their deepest feelings and beliefs through literature. Reading these stories, legends, and shorter passages that appear in the lessons will help you experience what life was like for people of other times and places.

Gooseberries to Oranges, by Barbara Cohen	22
"How the Turtle Beat the Rabbit," *A Cherokee Folktale*	84
What's the Big Idea, Ben Franklin? by Jean Fritz	220
Sybil Ludington's Ride, by Erick Berry	276
"Davy Crockett" by Anne Malcolmson	350
"Carrying the Running-Aways" from *The People Could Fly: American Black Folktales,* by Virginia Hamilton	458
An Orphan for Nebraska, by Charlene Joy Talbot	508

Primary Sources

Reading the exact words of the people who made and lived history is the best way to get a sense of how they saw themselves and the times in which they lived. You will find more than 50 primary sources throughout this book, including the following:

Gottlieb Mittelberger, from *Journey to Pennsylvania,* 1756	14
John Mandevelle, from *Travels,* 1356	104
Marco Polo, from *Description of the World,* 1298	106
Edward Winslow, from a letter, 1621	138
Richard Frethorne, from a letter, 1623	156
John Smith, from *A Generall Historie of Virginia,* 1624	159
Nathaniel Bacon, from a speech, 1676	166
Olaudah Equiano, from *Narrative,* 1814	172
Jonathan Edwards, from "Sinners in the Hands of an Angry God," 1741	195
Peter Kalm, from *Travels in North America,* 1770	209
William Penn, from *Concessions to the Province of Pennsylvania,* 1681	212
Andrew Burnaby, from *Travels through the Middle Settlements in North America,* 1759	213
Benjamin Franklin, from a letter, 1754	238
Patrick Henry, from a speech, 1775	253
Abigail Adams, from a letter, 1776	284
Thomas Paine, from a letter, 1796	318
Thomas Jefferson, from a message to Congress	353
Black Hawk, description of a battle	365
Sojourner Truth, from a speech, 1851	438
John Quincy Adams, from his diary, March 1, 1820	444
Abraham Lincoln, from a speech, 1858	463
Robert E. Lee, from a letter, 1861	477
Louisa May Alcott, from her journal, 1862–1863	481
Red Cloud, from a speech, 1870	504

Exploring

The story of the past is hidden all around you in the world of the present. "Exploring" pages tell you the secrets of how to find it.

The Immigrant Experience	10
Colonial Living	196
Early Photography	468

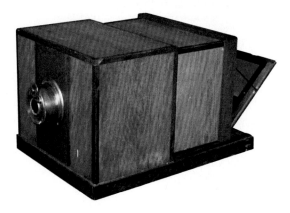

A Closer Look

Take a closer look at the objects and pictures spread out on these special pages. With the clues you see, you'll become a historical detective.

Musical Instruments	7
The Layers of a Map	38
Primary Sources	66
The Voyage of Columbus	112
Pilgrim Woodworking	141
West African Culture	170
Harvest Time	226
Boston Tea Party	251
Life at the Convention	298
New York Harbor, 1830	326
The Lewis and Clark Expedition	354
The Oregon Trail	380
Slave Culture	410
A Walking City	431
Immigrant Children	526

A Moment in Time

A person from the past is frozen at an exciting moment. You'll get to know these people by reading about where they are, what they're wearing, and the objects around them.

An Iroquois Clan Leader	96
A Puritan Girl	188
Continental Soldier	271
A Frontiersman	343
A Black Abolitionist	454
A Civil War Nurse	485

Charts, Diagrams, and Timelines

These visual presentations of information help give you a clearer picture of the people, places, and events you are studying.

Key Events in the History of New Orleans	6
Ethnic Diversity in Three Cities Today	8
Immigration to the United States Since 1820	13
Unrest in Boston, 1765–1770	61
Developments Leading to the Age of Exploration	106
Items Exchanged Between Indians and Europeans	121
Events Leading to the Settlement of the Northern Colonies	138
Beaver Trade	148
Canadian Fur Trade, 1675–1685	148
Fur Trade at Fort Albany, 1710–1780	149
French Population of Quebec, 1610–1700	151
European Settlers in Virginia, 1607–1630	158
Population of Virginia, 1610–1700	176
Life Expectancy of 20-Year-Old Males, 1650	184
The Early Colonies, 1600–1750	229
Two Middle Colonies	231
Colonial Trade with Great Britain, 1700–1770	239
The British-French Conflict, 1689–1763	242
The Effects of British Taxation, 1764–1770	249
Price Increases During the Revolutionary War, 1776–1779	285
Disputed Land Claims in the 1780s	292
Chain of Debt	295
Checks and Balances in the Constitution	301
Typical Monthly Wages, 1818	325
Religious Groups in the United States, 1820	330
Trans-Appalachian Population, 1790–1820	344
Population Growth in California, 1848–1852	386
The California Gold Rush, 1848–1853	397
Growth of Cotton and Slavery, 1800–1860	404
Southern Society, 1850	405
Immigration to the United States, 1820–1859	427
Urban Population Growth, 1800–1860	432
Congressional Representation of North and South, 1810–1850	445
Northern versus Southern Resources, 1861	476
Abolition of Slavery by State	482
The Civil War Compared to All Other Wars	491
Reconstruction Amendments	496
Immigration to the United States, 1870–1910	523
Population Changes, 1870–1910	532
School Enrollment	541
The Struggle for Women's Right to Vote	542
Money Spent on Movies	549
General Electric Stock Prices, 1928–1931	550
Impact of the Stock Market Crash	551
The Civil Rights Struggle, 1954–1965	562
Women in the Work Force	563
U.S. Troops in Vietnam	567

Maps

The events of history have been shaped by the places in which they occurred. Each map in this book tells its own story about these events and places.

North America: Physical	G1
United States: Years of Entry into the Union	G2
Central Washington, D.C.	G4
The Far West, 1848	G5
Texas: Political	G6
Some Native American Lands in the Southwest	G7
Historic Sites in Vicksburg, Mississippi	G8
Latitude, Longitude, and Hemispheres	G9
Projection: Mercator and Peters	G10
Northeastern United States: Physical	G11
The Route of Marquette and Joliet, 1673	G12
The Revolutionary War in New Jersey and Pennsylvania, 1776–1778	G13
Presidential Election of 1992	G14
The Mississippi River and New Orleans	5
Galarza's Route to the U.S.	15
Ethnic Diversity in the United States	35
Geographic Regions of the United States	36
Population Under the Age of 18	39
Equator	42
Prime Meridian	42
Latitude	43
Longitude	43
Robinson Projection	44
Mercator Projection	45
Goode's Projection	46
United States: Latitude and Longitude	48
Fall-Line Cities	51
Fault-Line Cities	51
Indian Land Lost, 1775–Today	53
First Human Settlement in the Americas	82
North American Cultures, 500 B.C.–A.D. 1500	88
The Iroquois Nation, 1550	97
Voyages of Columbus, Dias, and Da Gama	111
French, Dutch, and English Voyages of Exploration, 1497–1609	120
Magellan's Route Around the Earth	123
Verrazano's Voyage of Exploration, 1524	125
Spanish and French Exploration of America, 1519–1682	130
English Colonies, 1607–1690	133
New England Colonies, 1620–1640	139
Middle Colonies, 1650–1690	144
The Fight for Land in Virginia, about 1660	165
Where Slaves Came from in Africa	174
Where Slaves Were Sent in the New World	175
Cash Crops Exported to Great Britain	177
Settlement in New England, 1650–1750	184
The Atlantic Trade Cycle	199
New England	203
Massachusetts	203
Boston	203
The Middle Colonies	209
Population Diversity in the Middle Colonies	218
Middle Colony Trade	226
Ethnic Divisions in Colonial America	237
European Land Claims in North America, 1689 and 1763	243
Major Events of the Revolutionary War, 1775–1783	272
The Battle of Yorktown, 1781	273
United States, 1790	274
Northwest Territory, 1787	293
Support for Ratifying the Constitution	302
Presidential Election of 1800	319
The War of 1812	322
The Appalachian Frontier, 1787–1830	342
Exploring the Western Frontier	353
Indian Land Lost, 1756–1830	361
Mexico and Texas, 1821–1825	371
Lands Gained by the United States, 1848–1853	375
Indian Groups in the Western United States, 1860	390
The Cotton Kingdom, 1820 and 1860	403
Development of Canals	424
Development of Railroads	425
Immigration to the United States, 1820–1859	427
The Missouri Compromise, 1820	446
The Compromise of 1850	449
The Kansas-Nebraska Act, 1854	455
Secession of Southern States	466
The *Monitor* vs. the *Merrimack*	478
Major Battles of the Civil War	490
Presidential Election of 1876	499
Battles Fought Between the Plains Indians and the U.S. Army	507
Steel Industry in the Great Lakes Region, 1890–1920	521
Immigration to the United States, 1870–1910	523
Growth of Cities, 1880 and 1900	531
World War II	557
A Divided Vietnam, 1954–1975	566
Goods from Around the World	572
Where the Indians Lived	608
How the Indians Lived	608
The United States After the Revolutionary War	612
The Louisiana Purchase of 1803	612
Expansion in the Mid-1800s	612
World: Political	614
World: Physical	616
United States: Overview	618
United States: Political	620
United States: Physical	622
North America: Political/Physical	624
United States: Population Density, 1980	625
United States: Time Zones	625
United States: Climate	626
United States: Vegetation	626
United States: Precipitation	627
United States: Land Use and Resources	627

Starting Out

What makes this textbook so much more interesting than others you've used? In this book, the people of the past speak directly to you, through their actual words and the objects they used. You'll walk inside their houses and look inside their cooking pots. You'll follow them as they go to school, build cities, fight wars, work out settlements for peace.

When and where? The timeline at the beginning of each lesson and the lesson title tell you the time and place.

From unit to chapter to lesson— each step lets you see history in closer detail. The maps and photos show you where events happened. The art introduces you to the people.

Right from the beginning the lesson opener pulls you into the sights, the sounds, the smells of what life was like at that time, in that place. Here it is 1906 aboard a ship traveling from Russia to America.

Like a road sign, the question that always appears here tells you what to think about while you read the lesson.

Look for these key terms. They are listed here so that you can watch for them. The first time they appear in the lesson they are shown in heavy black print and defined. Key terms are also defined in the Glossary.

LESSON 3

Coming to America

THINKING FOCUS

What were the lives of immigrants like in the United States between 1870 and 1914?

Key Term
- racism
- nativism

➤ *This Italian mother and her children arrived in the United States with all their belongings in two clumsy bundles. Each of them was given a landing pass (shown below).*

Red Star Line
Landing Card
MAJESTIC No.
Manifest Sheet No.

It was not a pleasure trip, that 14-day journey aboard ship. Crammed into a dark, stuffy cabin with four other people, we spent the nights on sheetless bunks and most of the days standing in line for food that was ladled out to us as though we were cattle. Mother, Sheyna, and Zipke were seasick most of the time, but I felt well and can remember staring at the sea for hours wondering what Milwaukee would be like.

Golda Meir, who later became the prime minister of Israel, wrote these words about her journey to America in 1906. She and her mother and two sisters traveled by ship from Russia to New York. From there they continued to Milwaukee, where they joined her father.

It took courage for Meir's family to leave everything they knew and move to a new country. "Going to America then was almost like going to the moon." Meir remembered. But thousands of others dared to do what Meir's family did. Between 1860 and 1914, about 25 million immigrants made the voyage to America.

Letters, diaries, books—short passages from these primary sources let people from the past speak to you. When you see a tan background, a red initial letter, and a gray bar, you know that the quotation is a primary source.

Giving you the inside story is the purpose of two special paragraphs. Across Time & Space connects what you're reading to things that happened centuries ago or continents away. Its companion, How Do We Know?, tells you where information about the past comes from. (See page 532 for an example.)

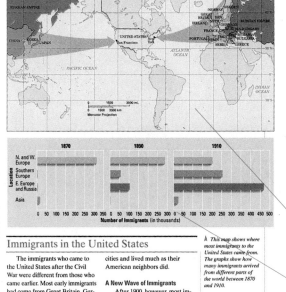

The titles outline the lesson. The red titles tell you the main topics discussed in the lesson on "Coming to America." The blue titles tell you the subtopics.

Every map tells a story. The maps in the book tell the story of where people came from and what the land was like. Here three bar graphs add to the map's story of immigration to the United States from 1870 to 1910.

Continuing On

As you get to know the people of the past, you'll want ways of understanding and remembering them better. This book gives you some tools to use in learning about people and places and remembering what you've learned.

Frozen at a moment in time, the Iroquois clan leader captures your attention. You learn all about her, through her headband, buckskin clothing, and moccasins, and the things she holds in her hands.

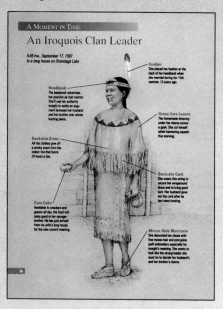

The things people make and use tell a great deal about them. In this book you'll find lots of photographs of the paintings and statues people made and the coins, tools, and weapons they used.

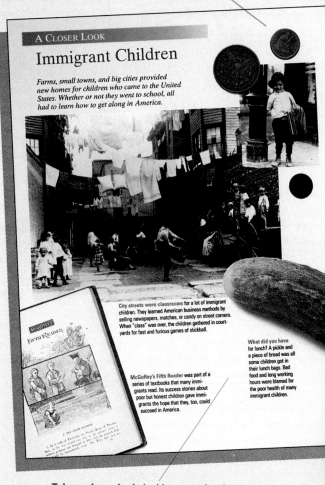

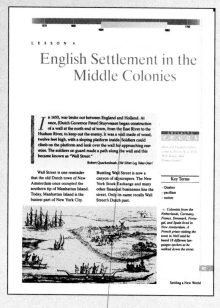

Every age has its great storytellers. Each chapter includes short examples of fine writing from or about the period. The literature is always printed on a tan background with a blue initial letter and a multicolored bar.

Take a closer look, in this case at immigrant children. Look at the games they played, the food they ate, and the schoolbooks they read.

Some tools you'll always use. The Understanding pages walk you through skills that you will use again and again, as a student and later on in life.

You're in charge of your reading. See the red square at the end of the text? Now find the red square over in the margin. If you can answer the question there, then you probably understood what you just read. If you can't, perhaps you'd better go back and read that part of the lesson again.

A special kind of Understanding page looks at concepts—the big ideas that help put all the pieces together. This section helps you understand ideas like Land Use, the Frontier, and in this case, Mechanization, or using machines to do work.

A picture is worth a thousand words. But just a few words in a caption can help you understand a picture, a photograph, a map, or in this case, a cartoon.

After you read the lesson, stop and review what you've read. The first question is the same one you started out with. The second question connects the lesson to what you've studied earlier. Other questions and an activity help you think about the lesson you've read. Chapter Review questions help you tie the lessons together. (See pages 534 and 535 for an example.)

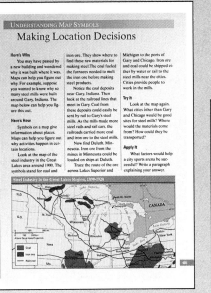

Also Featuring

Some special pages show up only once in every unit, not in every lesson in the book. These features continue the story by letting you explore an idea or activity, or read a story about another time and place. The Time/Space Databank in the back of the book brings together resources you will use again and again.

School isn't the only place where you can learn social studies. This feature gives you a chance to explore history and geography outside the classroom—at home or in your own neighborhood.

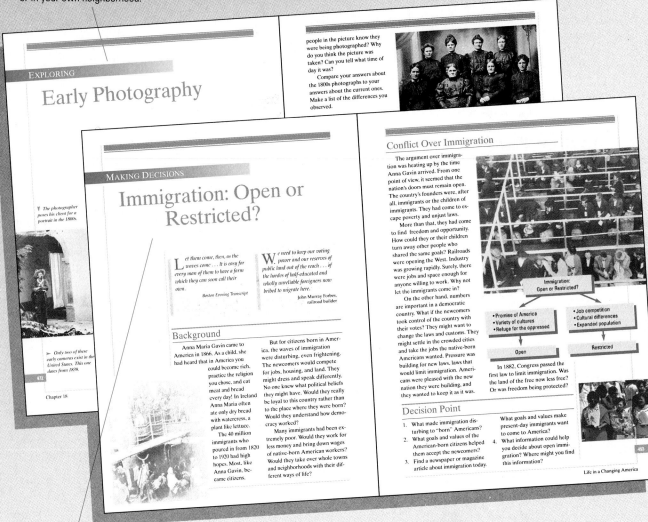

EXPLORING

Early Photography

▼ *The photographer poses his client for a portrait in the 1800s.*

➤ *Only two of these early cameras exist in the United States. This one dates from 1839.*

472

Chapter 18

people in the picture know they were being photographed? Why do you think the picture was taken? Can you tell what time of day it was?

Compare your answers about the 1800s photographs to your answers about the current ones. Make a list of the differences you observed.

MAKING DECISIONS

Immigration: Open or Restricted?

L et them come, then, as the waves come . . . It is easy for every man of them to have a farm which they can soon call their own.

Boston Evening Transcript

W e need to keep our voting power and our reserves of public land out of the reach . . . of the hordes of half-educated and wholly unreliable foreigners now bribed to migrate here.

John Murray Forbes, railroad builder

Background

Anna Maria Gavin came to America in 1866. As a child, she had heard that in America you could become rich, practice the religion you chose, and eat meat and bread every day! In Ireland Anna Maria often ate only dry bread with watercress, a plant like lettuce.

The 40 million immigrants who poured in from 1820 to 1920 had high hopes. Most, like Anna Gavin, became citizens.

But for citizens born in America, the waves of immigration were disturbing, even frightening. The newcomers would compete for jobs, housing, and land. They might dress and speak differently. No one knew what political beliefs they might have. Would they really be loyal to this country rather than to the place where they were born? Would they understand how democracy worked?

Many immigrants had been extremely poor. Would they work for less money and bring down wages of native-born American workers? Would they take over whole towns and neighborhoods with their different ways of life?

Conflict Over Immigration

The argument over immigration was heating up by the time Anna Gavin arrived. From one point of view, it seemed that the nation's doors must remain open. The country's founders were, after all, immigrants or the children of immigrants. They had come to escape poverty and unjust laws.

More than that, they had come to find freedom and opportunity. How could they or their children turn away other people who shared the same goals? Railroads were opening the West. Industry was growing rapidly. Surely, there were jobs and space enough for anyone willing to work. Why not let the immigrants come in?

On the other hand, numbers are important in a democratic country. What if the newcomers took control of the country with their votes? They might want to change the laws and customs. They might settle in the crowded cities and take the jobs the native-born Americans wanted. Pressure was building for new laws, laws that would limit immigration. Americans were pleased with the new nation they were building, and they wanted to keep it as it was.

Immigration: Open or Restricted?

- •Promise of America
- •Variety of cultures
- •Refuge for the oppressed

Open

- •Job competition
- •Cultural differences
- •Expanded population

Restricted

In 1882, Congress passed the first law to limit immigration. Was the land of the free now less free? Or was freedom being protected?

Decision Point

1. What made immigration disturbing to "born" Americans?
2. What goals and values of the American-born citizens helped them accept the newcomers?
3. Find a newspaper or magazine article about immigration today.
4. What goals and values make present-day immigrants want to come to America?
5. What information could help you decide about open immigration? Where might you find this information?

Life in a Changing America

493

What would you do? The Making Decisions pages show you an important decision from the past. Then you practice the steps that will help you to make a good choice.

Stories have always been important parts of people's lives. Each unit in the book has at least one story about the time and place you're studying. In this case, it's a story of an immigrant boy who goes to live in Nebraska.

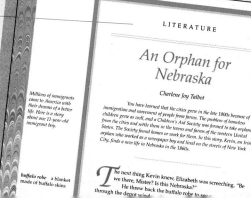

LITERATURE

An Orphan for Nebraska

Charlene Joy Talbot

Millions of immigrants came to America with their dreams of a better life. Here is a story about one 11-year-old immigrant boy.

You have learned that the cities grew in the late 1800s because of immigration and movement of people from farms. The problem of homeless children grew as well, and a Children's Aid Society was formed to take orphans from the cities and settle them in the towns and farms of the western United States. The Society found homes or work for them. In this story, Kevin, an Irish orphan who worked as a newspaper boy and lived on the streets of New York City, finds a new life in Nebraska in the 1860s.

buffalo robe a blanket made of buffalo skins

T he next thing Kevin knew, Elizabeth was screeching. "Be we there, Mister? Is this Nebraska?"

He threw back the buffalo robe to see
through the depot wind...

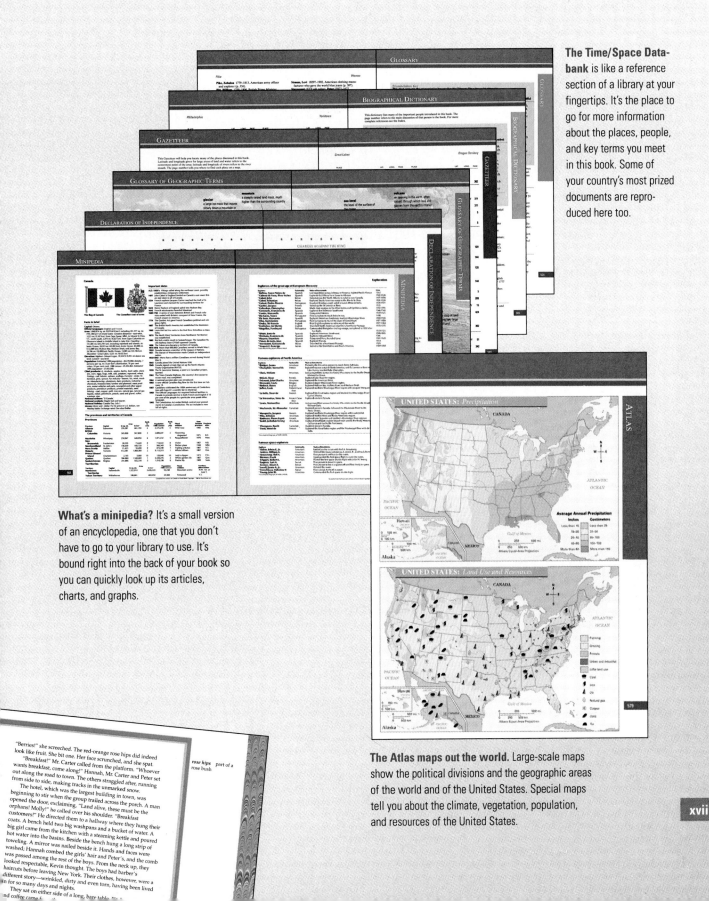

The Time/Space Data-bank is like a reference section of a library at your fingertips. It's the place to go for more information about the places, people, and key terms you meet in this book. Some of your country's most prized documents are repro-duced here too.

What's a minipedia? It's a small version of an encyclopedia, one that you don't have to go to your library to use. It's bound right into the back of your book so you can quickly look up its articles, charts, and graphs.

The Atlas maps out the world. Large-scale maps show the political divisions and the geographic areas of the world and of the United States. Special maps tell you about the climate, vegetation, population, and resources of the United States.

"Berries!" she screeched. The red-orange rose hips did indeed look like fruit. She bit one. Her face scrunched, and she spat.

"Breakfast!" Mr. Carter called from the platform. "Whoever wants breakfast, come along!" Hannah, Mr. Carter and Peter set out along the road to town. The others straggled after, running from side to side, making tracks in the unmarked snow.

The hotel, which was the largest building in town, was beginning to stir when the group trailed across the porch. A man opened the door, exclaiming. "Land alive, these must be the orphans! Molly!" he called over his shoulder. "Breakfast customers!" He directed them to a hallway where they hung their coats. A bench held two big washpans and a bucket of water. A big girl came from the kitchen with a steaming kettle and poured hot water into the basins. Beside the bench hung a long strip of toweling. A mirror was nailed beside it. Hands and faces were washed; Hannah combed the girls' hair and Peter's, and the comb was passed among the rest of the boys. From the neck up, they looked respectable, Kevin thought. Their clothes, however, were a different story—wrinkled, dirty and even torn, having been lived in for so many days and nights.

They sat on either side of a long, bare table. Tin
nd coffee came t

rose hips part of a
rose bush

Map and Globe Handbook

*Y*ou're about to begin an exciting journey—a journey using maps and globes. With some help from your imagination, you'll see the earth from far out in space. Then, you'll zero in on North America and go across the United States. The first stop will be Texas. You will visit the Far West and Washington, D.C., our nation's capital. Get ready to go back in time and join a party of French explorers. You'll also see where American soldiers fought for freedom from Britain.

Your adventure will help you learn more about maps and globes. Move on to page G1 to start your journey.

Contents

Mapping Our Planet	**G1**
Understanding a Map	**G2**
Using a Compass Rose	**G4**
Using A Map Legend	**G5**
Using A Map Scale	**G6**
Using an Inset Map	**G7**
Using a Map Grid	**G8**
Understanding Globes and Projections	
Latitude, Longitude, and Hemispheres	**G9**
Projections	**G10**
Reading Different Kinds of Maps	
A Physical Map	**G11**
A Special Purpose Map: A Route Map	**G12**
A Special Purpose Map: Mapping a War	**G13**
A Special Purpose Map: Mapping an Election	**G14**
Using Geographic References	**G15**

Mapping Our Planet

A map is an exact drawing of all or part of the earth. Look right for a view of the earth from space. Then zoom in on the closeup of North America. Like that picture, the map below it shows North America as you would see it from space. Mapmakers study such pictures to draw maps.

From space, the earth looks like a swirl of clouds, land, and water. Notice the color of the water, land, and clouds.

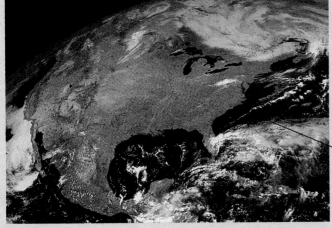

As you come closer to the earth, you see the coastline of the continent of North America.

North America: Physical

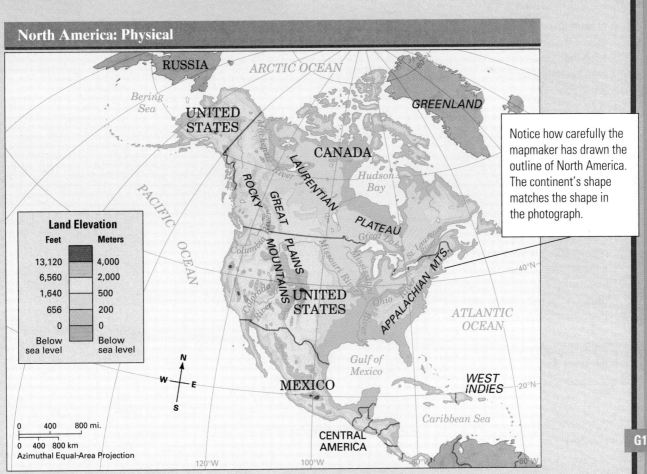

Notice how carefully the mapmaker has drawn the outline of North America. The continent's shape matches the shape in the photograph.

RUSSIA

ARCTIC OCEAN

Bering Sea

UNITED STATES

GREENLAND

CANADA

ROCKY

LAURENTIAN

Hudson Bay

PLATEAU

Mackenzie River

GREAT

PLAINS

MOUNTAINS

Great Lakes

St. Lawrence River

PACIFIC OCEAN

Columbia

Missouri River

Mississippi River

Ohio River

APPALACHIAN MTS.

ATLANTIC OCEAN

Colorado River

UNITED STATES

40°N

Land Elevation

Feet	Meters
13,120	4,000
6,560	2,000
1,640	500
656	200
0	0
Below sea level	Below sea level

Gulf of Mexico

WEST INDIES

20°N

MEXICO

Caribbean Sea

N
W E
S

0   400   800 mi.

0   400   800 km

Azimuthal Equal-Area Projection

CENTRAL AMERICA

120°W   100°W   80°W   60°W

Understanding a Map

Quickly look through the Map and Globe Handbook. Notice that the maps have different sizes and shapes and give different kinds of information. For example, the map on page G6 shows the state boundary and major cities of Texas. The map on page G12 shows the route of two early French explorers.

The **title** tells you the place shown on the map. Usually, the title also tells you what kind of map you are using.

The **grid** is made up of lines that form a pattern of squares on a map. The lines have numbers or letters to help you find a place. This map's grid is made up of lines of **latitude** and lines of **longitude**. Lines of **latitude** run east to west around the globe. Lines of **longitude** run around the globe from the North Pole to the South Pole.

An **inset** is a small map inside a larger one. The inset shows a different area or gives different information than the larger map does. On this map, Alaska and Hawaii are in insets. They are so far away from the other states that they do not fit on the larger map.

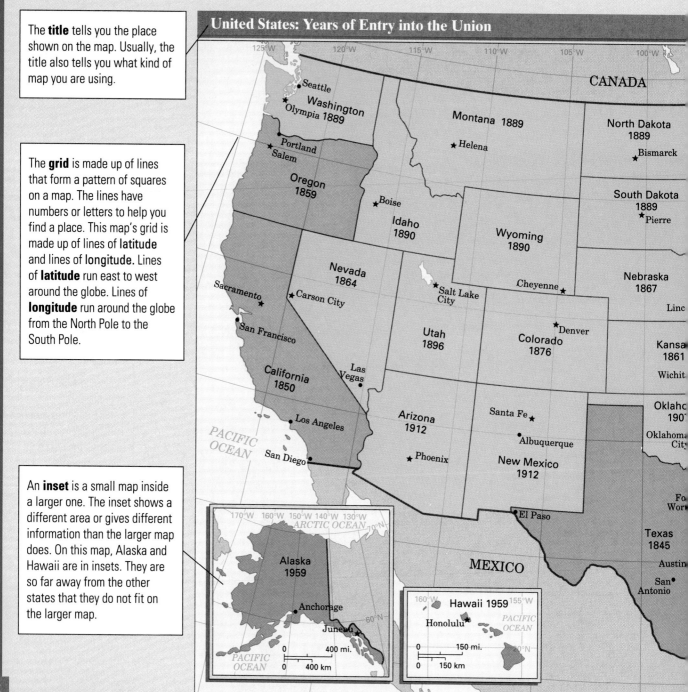

United States: Years of Entry into the Union

Though maps can be quite different, they all have certain features that are alike. Every part of a map tells you something important. You can understand maps better once you know how to use these features.

The map below is a historical map of the United States. It gives information about an earlier time in history. From this map, you'll learn when each state entered the Union. You'll also learn about some important map parts.

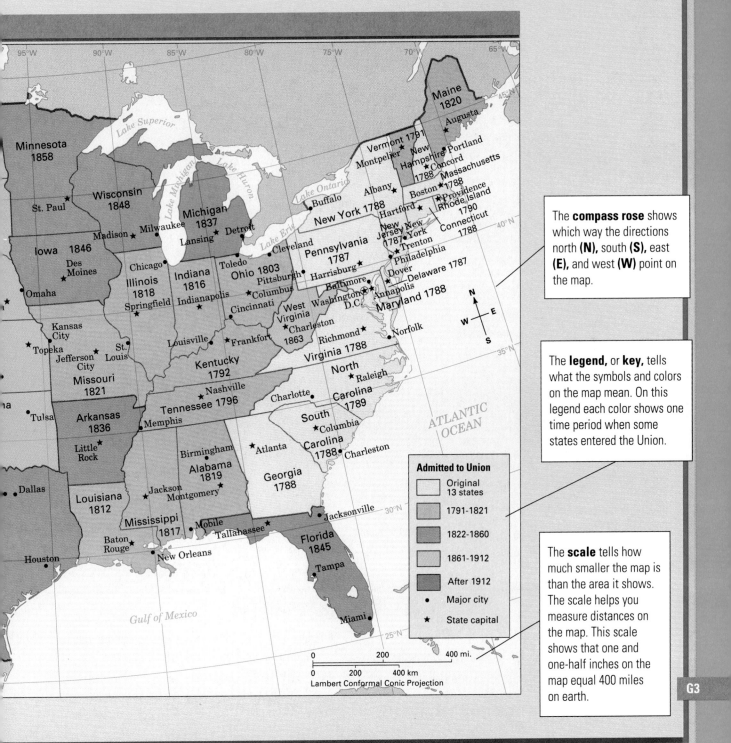

The **compass rose** shows which way the directions north **(N)**, south **(S)**, east **(E)**, and west **(W)** point on the map.

The **legend,** or **key,** tells what the symbols and colors on the map mean. On this legend each color shows one time period when some states entered the Union.

Admitted to Union

	Original 13 states
	1791-1821
	1822-1860
	1861-1912
	After 1912
•	Major city
★	State capital

The **scale** tells how much smaller the map is than the area it shows. The scale helps you measure distances on the map. This scale shows that one and one-half inches on the map equal 400 miles on earth.

0   200   400 mi.

0   200   400 km

Lambert Conformal Conic Projection

Using a Compass Rose

The closer a place is to the bottom of the map, the farther south the place is. Thus, you know that the Washington Monument is south of the White House.

Suppose you visit Washington, D.C. Picture yourself in front of the White House. You want to walk to the Washington Monument. In which direction should you walk? The compass rose on your map can show you. The tips of the compass rose point to the cardinal, or main, directions—these are north **(N)**, south **(S)**, east **(E)**, and west **(W)**.

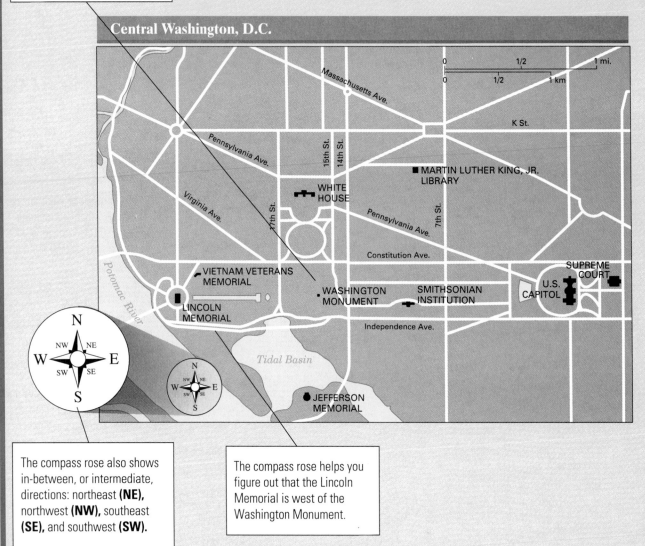

Central Washington, D.C.

The compass rose also shows in-between, or intermediate, directions: northeast **(NE)**, northwest **(NW)**, southeast **(SE)**, and southwest **(SW)**.

The compass rose helps you figure out that the Lincoln Memorial is west of the Washington Monument.

MAP SKILLS

1. **REVIEW** Is the U.S. Capitol Building located north, south, east, or west of the Washington Monument?

2. **REVIEW** Name a monument that is north of the Jefferson Memorial.

3. **THINK ABOUT IT** Look at the compass rose on the map on page 425. Is north directly at the top of the map or is it slightly at an angle? How can you tell?

4. **TRY IT** Use the compass rose on a community map to find the direction or directions you travel between home and school.

Using a Map Legend

What does a circle mean on the map below? Maps use such symbols to give important information. A symbol is a drawing, shape, or line that shows where something is on a map. A map legend, or key, shows what the symbols and colors on the map mean. Look at this map of the United States' Far West in 1848. The legend shows what the symbols used on the map mean.

This square marks the place where a trading post stood. What was its name?

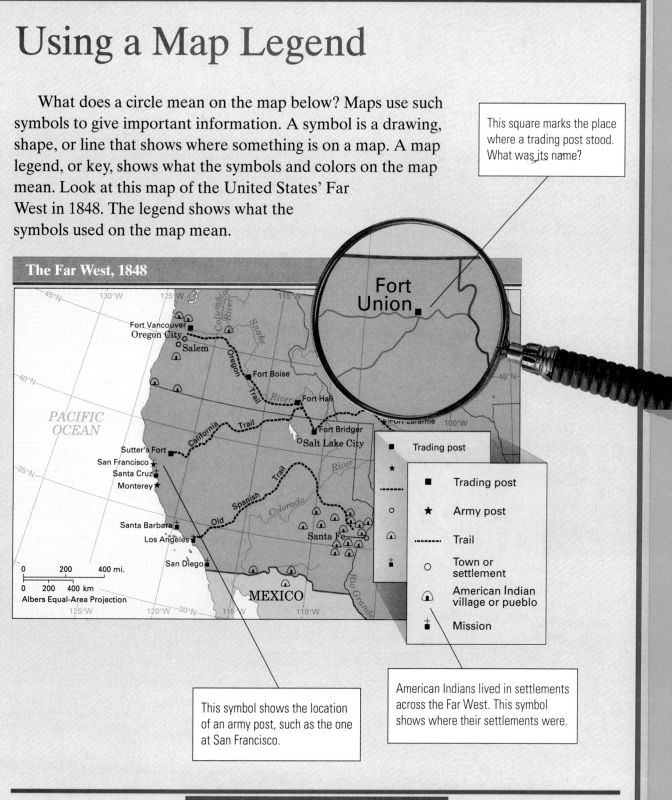

The Far West, 1848

■	Trading post
★	Army post
------	Trail
○	Town or settlement
⌂	American Indian village or pueblo
‡	Mission

This symbol shows the location of an army post, such as the one at San Francisco.

American Indians lived in settlements across the Far West. This symbol shows where their settlements were.

MAP SKILLS

1. REVIEW Name at least two missions shown on the map.

2. THINK ABOUT IT Follow the Oregon Trail from east to west. Name an army post and trading post along the way.

3. TRY IT Imagine that you are the mapmaker for your community. What symbols would you use to show playgrounds, schools, or restaurants? What symbols would you use to show houses or apartment buildings? Draw a legend with at least five symbols.

Using a Map Scale

To measure the distance between two cities, lay a piece of paper between them. Mark each city on the paper, as shown in the picture. Next, compare the distance you marked on the paper to the scale. The student in the picture is measuring the distance between Houston, Texas, and Baton Rouge, Louisiana.

How far is San Antonio from Abilene? One way to find out is by using this map's scale. The scale is the line that helps you measure the distance between places on a map.

Look at the scale line in the corner of this map. The line is one inch long. The numbers tell you that one inch on the map equals 200 miles in Texas. Now you can measure the distance from San Antonio to Abilene.

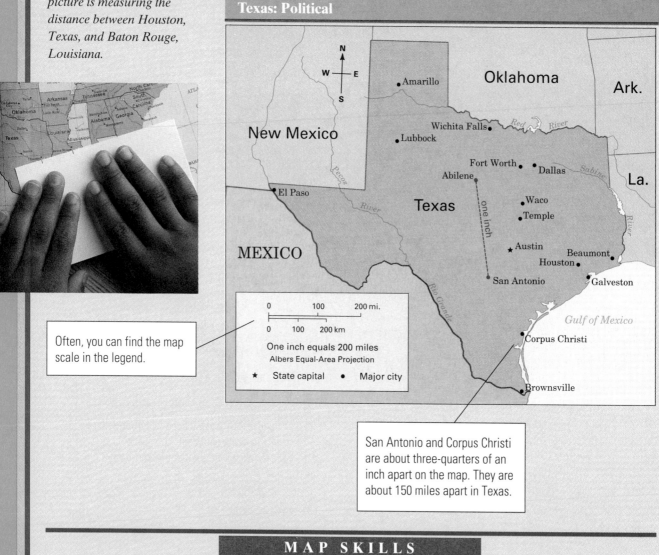

Texas: Political

Often, you can find the map scale in the legend.

0   100   200 mi.
0   100   200 km

One inch equals 200 miles
Albers Equal-Area Projection

★ State capital   ● Major city

San Antonio and Corpus Christi are about three-quarters of an inch apart on the map. They are about 150 miles apart in Texas.

MAP SKILLS

1. **REVIEW** Measure the distance between Abilene and Waco. How many miles apart are the two cities?

2. **THINK ABOUT IT** Turn to the map on page 199 of your book. About how many miles is it from London, England, to Boston, on the east coast of the U.S.?

3. **THINK ABOUT IT** Compare this map's scale with the one on page 615. What does the difference between them tell you about the areas on the two maps?

4. **TRY IT** Draw a scale map of your neighborhood. Draw the scale line on your map.

Using an Inset Map

Suppose you're planning a trip to the lands of Native Americans shown on the larger map below. How can you find these lands? To answer that question, look at the inset map. An inset map is a small map inside a larger one. The inset shows you details or gives you information about the main map. This kind of inset is called a locator inset. It helps you find, or locate, the main map's area.

▼ *The Navajo, like other Native Americans, keep traditions alive with stories, songs, and ceremonies.*

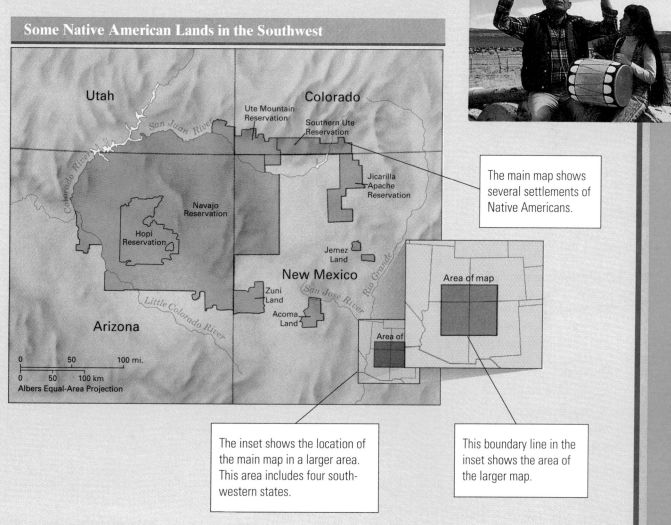

Some Native American Lands in the Southwest

The main map shows several settlements of Native Americans.

The inset shows the location of the main map in a larger area. This area includes four southwestern states.

This boundary line in the inset shows the area of the larger map.

MAP SKILLS

1. **REVIEW** The locator inset shows that the main map's area lies mostly in which two states?

2. **THINK ABOUT IT** Look at the map on page 97 of your book. This map has a locator inset. What does the main map show? What does the inset show?

3. **TRY IT** Draw a map of the United States to be used as a locator inset. You can trace one from page 531. Then shade in the four states of Utah, Colorado, Arizona, and New Mexico. Your locator inset can help someone find the four states shown on this map.

Using a Map Grid

Suppose you're visiting Vicksburg, Mississippi, the site of an important Civil War battle. You want to see the Vicksburg National Military Park. If you can use this map's grid, you can find the park.

A grid is a set of lines drawn on a map. The lines form squares. On this map of Vicksburg, numbers run across the top and bottom of the grid. Letters run along each side. Each square is named by its letter and number. The index is a list of the grid squares where important places are located on the map. For example, the Grey Oaks Mansion lies in square **D3.**

▲ *Once you find the Vicksburg National Military Park, you'll see reminders of the Civil War, such as this cannon.*

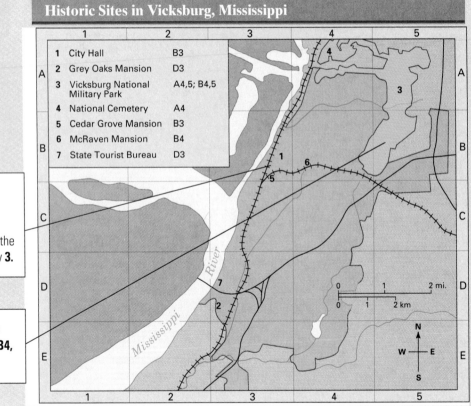

Historic Sites in Vicksburg, Mississippi

1	City Hall	B3
2	Grey Oaks Mansion	D3
3	Vicksburg National Military Park	A4,5; B4,5
4	National Cemetery	A4
5	Cedar Grove Mansion	B3
6	McRaven Mansion	B4
7	State Tourist Bureau	D3

The index shows that Vicksburg's City Hall is in square **B3**. It is labeled with the number 1. You can find it on the map where row **B** meets row **3**.

The National Military Park is located on squares **A4, A5, B4,** and **B5.**

MAP SKILLS

1. REVIEW In which square can you find the State Tourist Bureau?

2. THINK ABOUT IT How would you tell someone where the McRaven Mansion lies on this map of Vicksburg sites?

3. TRY IT Draw a simple map with a grid. Number your up-and-down rows of boxes. Put letters next to the boxes that go across your map. Make a list of the places. Write the name of the square where each place can be found. Use this list as an index for your map.

Understanding Globes and Projections

Look at the world map on pages 614–615. Next look at a globe. Notice that they both show the land and water areas of earth, but in different ways. A globe has the same shape as the earth—a sphere or ball. It is a small model of the earth.

Latitude, Longitude, and Hemispheres

Mapmakers draw lines on the globe called lines of latitude and longitude. The line of latitude that circles the earth at its center is called the equator. The lines of longitude are drawn from the North Pole to the South Pole. The equator divides the earth into hemispheres.

The prime meridian lies at 0° longitude. Halfway around the world, 180° away, is another imaginary line. These lines divide the earth into the Eastern and Western hemispheres.

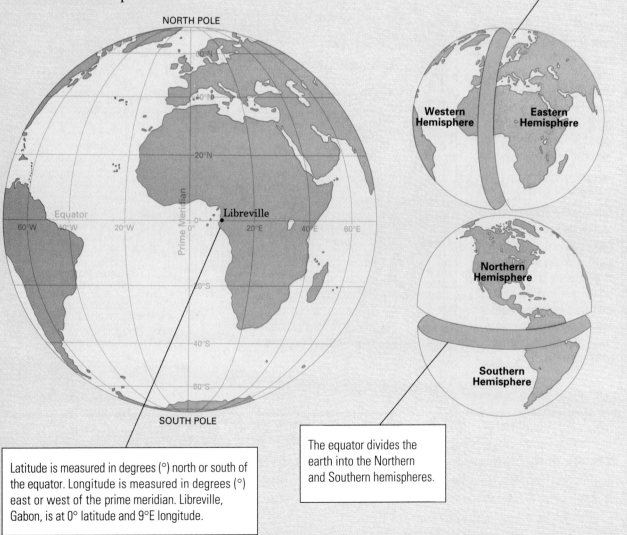

Latitude is measured in degrees (°) north or south of the equator. Longitude is measured in degrees (°) east or west of the prime meridian. Libreville, Gabon, is at 0° latitude and 9°E longitude.

The equator divides the earth into the Northern and Southern hemispheres.

Projections

A flat map cannot show how the earth curves. It stretches out some land and water areas. When a mapmaker draws the whole earth, it is a projection of the earth's surface. Different mapmakers have created different projections. Gerhardus Mercator drew the Mercator Projection in 1569. German mapmaker Arno Peters drew the Peters Projection in 1974.

A globe can show the exact shape of earth because it is a model of the planet.

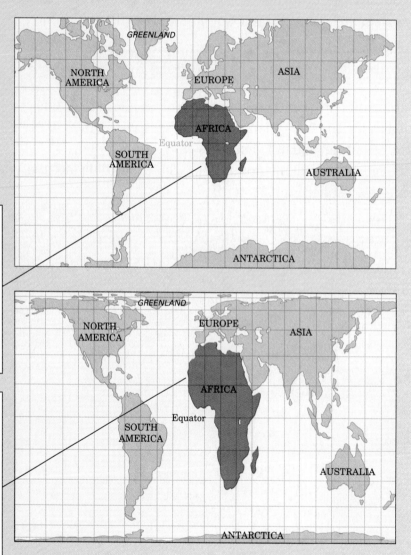

The Mercator Projection shows most of the continents as they look on a globe. However, the projection stretches out the lands near the North Pole and South Pole. Africa is highlighted in red. Compare the different size of Africa on this projection and on the one below.

Compare the shapes of the continents on this Peters Projection with those on a globe. This projection's continents are the right size but the shapes of the continents are not as they appear on a globe. Compare the shape of South America to its shape on a globe.

MAP AND GLOBE SKILLS

1. **REVIEW** In which two hemispheres is Australia? In which two hemispheres is the United States?

2. **THINK ABOUT IT** Why do you think mapmakers created different projections when they drew world maps?

3. **TRY IT** Find Greenland on the Mercator and Peters projections above. Then find Greenland on a globe. How have the projections changed Greenland's size and shape?

Reading Different Kinds of Maps

Look back at the many kinds of maps in this part of the book. Different kinds of maps give different information and answer different questions. Study the next four maps to see what you learn from each.

A Physical Map

Picture snowy mountains against a blue sky. A physical map can tell you where to find such a view. A physical map shows the elevation of the land. Elevation is the number of feet an area rises above, or falls below, sea level. On this physical map the color of an area shows its elevation.

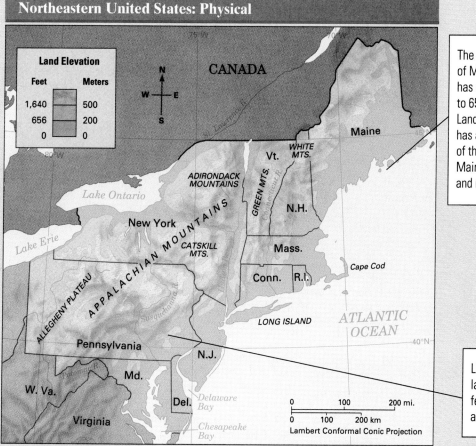

Northeastern United States: Physical

Land Elevation

Feet	Meters
1,640	500
656	200
0	0

The dark green along the coast of Maine tells you that the land has a low elevation, from 0 to 656 feet above sea level. Land colored yellow and orange has a higher elevation. Areas of these colors in western Maine probably have hills and mountains.

Light green shows land that is from 656 feet to 1,640 feet above sea level.

0   100   200 mi.
0   100   200 km
Lambert Conformal Conic Projection

A Special Purpose Map: A Route Map

Imagine yourself among a group of French explorers in 1673. You're drawing a map of the route they follow. A route map shows the movement of people or goods across an area. The map below shows the route that French explorers Jacques Marquette and Louis Joliet followed in 1673.

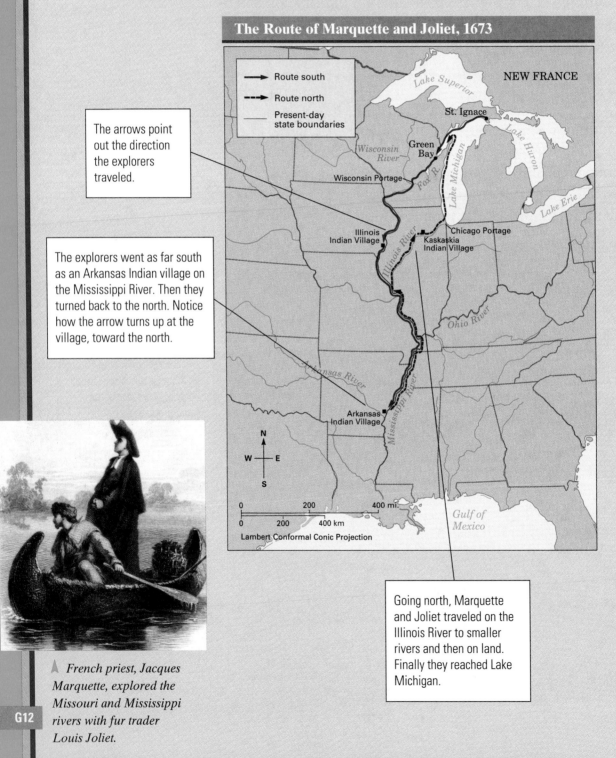

The Route of Marquette and Joliet, 1673

→ Route south

- -▸ Route north

—— Present-day state boundaries

NEW FRANCE

Lake Superior

St. Ignace

Wisconsin River

Green Bay

Wisconsin Portage

Fox R.

Lake Michigan

Lake Huron

Lake Erie

Illinois Indian Village

Chicago Portage

Kaskaskia Indian Village

Illinois River

Ohio River

Arkansas River

Arkansas Indian Village

Mississippi River

N W E S

0   200   400 mi.
0   200   400 km

Lambert Conformal Conic Projection

Gulf of Mexico

The arrows point out the direction the explorers traveled.

The explorers went as far south as an Arkansas Indian village on the Mississippi River. Then they turned back to the north. Notice how the arrow turns up at the village, toward the north.

Going north, Marquette and Joliet traveled on the Illinois River to smaller rivers and then on land. Finally they reached Lake Michigan.

French priest, Jacques Marquette, explored the Missouri and Mississippi rivers with fur trader Louis Joliet.

A Special Purpose Map: Mapping a War

A special purpose map gives one kind of information about an area. A special purpose map can give information about an area's people, animals, weather, history, or many other things. The map below shows where Revolutionary War battles were fought from 1776 to 1778. The legend explains the battle symbols you see on the map.

The Revolutionary War in New Jersey and Pennsylvania, 1776–1778

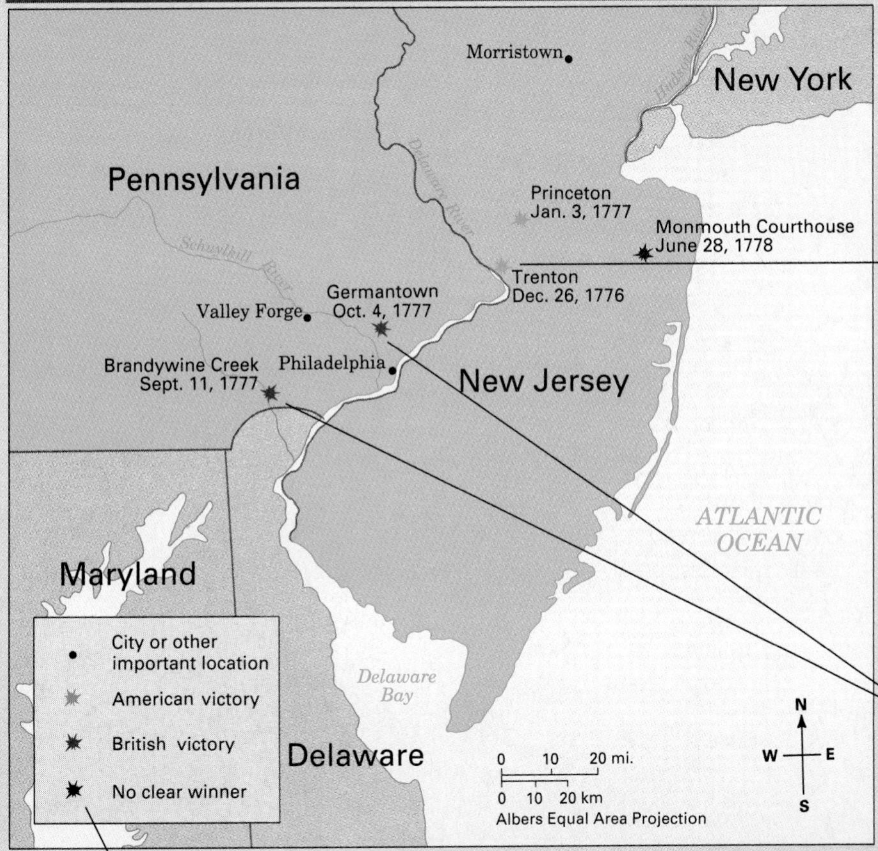

Morristown
New York
Hudson River
Pennsylvania
Delaware River
Princeton
Jan. 3, 1777
Monmouth Courthouse
June 28, 1778
Schuylkill River
Trenton
Dec. 26, 1776
Germantown
Oct. 4, 1777
Valley Forge
Brandywine Creek
Sept. 11, 1777
Philadelphia
New Jersey
ATLANTIC
OCEAN
Maryland
City or other important location
American victory
British victory
No clear winner
Delaware Bay
Delaware
0 10 20 mi.
0 10 20 km
Albers Equal Area Projection
N
W
E
S

This symbol shows that the Americans won the battle at Trenton in December of 1776.

Americans lost battles at Brandywine Creek and Germantown in September and October of 1777.

By comparing the symbol on the map at Monmouth with the symbol here you know that neither side really won the Battle of Monmouth in June of 1778.

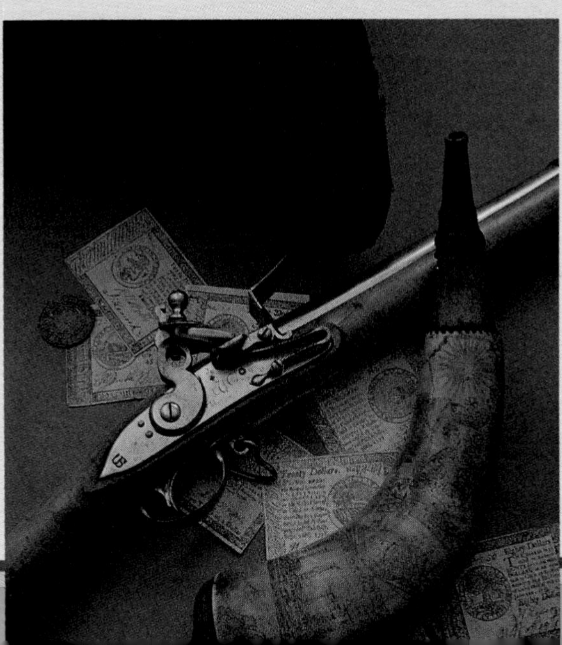

Revolutionary soldiers carried rifles, called muskets, and powder horns filled with gunpowder. Notice that the photograph also shows money issued by the new American government.

A Special Purpose Map: Mapping an Election

This 1992 election map shows which candidate for President won the most votes in each state. It also shows the number of electoral votes each state can give its winner (two electoral votes for its senators and one for each member of the House of Representatives). The map shows that Bill Clinton won. He had enough electoral votes to win the election.

In 1992, Democrat Bill Clinton ran for President against Republican George Bush. The third candidate was Ross Perot, an independent—not a Republican or a Democrat.

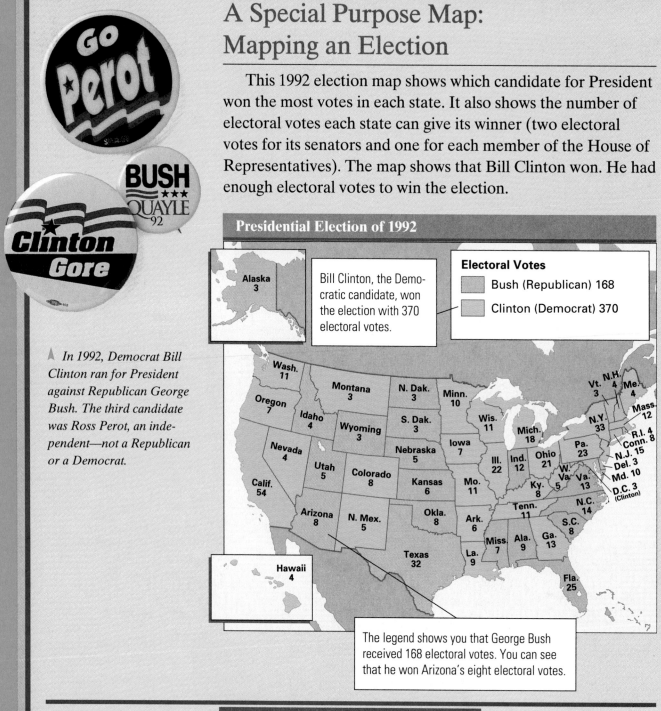

Presidential Election of 1992

Bill Clinton, the Democratic candidate, won the election with 370 electoral votes.

Electoral Votes
- Bush (Republican) 168
- Clinton (Democrat) 370

The legend shows you that George Bush received 168 electoral votes. You can see that he won Arizona's eight electoral votes.

MAP SKILLS

1. **REVIEW** Look at the map on page G11. In which two states is all land 0 to 656 feet above sea level?

2. **REVIEW** Look at the map on page 111. Toward which land did Vasco da Gama sail?

3. **REVIEW** Look at the map on page G13. When was the Battle of Trenton fought?

4. **REVIEW** Look at the map on page 319. Who were the candidates in the presidential election of 1800?

5. **THINK ABOUT IT** You have learned about many different kinds of maps. If you were going to write a report on a country you did not know much about, what kinds of maps would you look for? Why?

6. **TRY IT** Make a special purpose map that shows something interesting about your state. Make sure your legend explains what your map's symbols and colors show.

Using Geographic References

What are Alaska's major mountain ranges? Where is Savannah, Georgia? Some of the different parts of the Time/Space Databank at the end of the book will help you answer such questions. The Atlas, on pages 614–627, has world, United States, and special purpose maps. The Glossary of Geographic Terms, on pages 628–629, shows and explains some of the earth's natural features. The Gazetteer, on pages 630–632, gives the location of many places in the world. It also tells you where in the book you can find each place on a map.

This map section from page 622 of the Atlas shows Alaska mountain ranges.

PLACE	LAT.	LONG.	PAGE
Santa Fe (capital of New Mexico)	35°N	106°W	**375**
Saratoga (city in New York; site of Revolutionary War battle)	43°N	75°W	**272**
Savannah (oldest city in Georgia)	32°N	81°W	**272**
Spain (country in Europe)	40°N	5°W	**523**
St. Lawrence R. (forms part of Canada-U.S. boundary)	49°N	67°W	**274**
St. Louis (largest city in Missouri; on Mississippi R.)	39°N	90°W	**424**
Strait of Magellan (waterway from the Atlantic Ocean to			

This entry from page 632 of the Gazetteer tells you where the city of Savannah is. It tells the city's latitude and longitude and on what page you can find Savannah on a map.

This definition of a delta comes from page 629 of the Glossary of Geographic Terms. The picture helps you understand what the term means.

delta
a triangular area of land formed by deposits at the mouth of a river

REFERENCES SKILLS

1. **REVIEW** You need to find out what a plateau is. In what section of the Time/Space Databank do you look? What is a plateau?

2. **THINK ABOUT IT** You need to learn about the Hudson River. You find the river on the map on pages 622–623 of the Atlas. You want to find a more detailed map of the area through which the river flows. Where in your book can you find the information you need?

3. **TRY IT** Look at the special purpose maps on pages 626–627 of the Atlas. What kind of climate does your state have?

Unit 1

The United States: Past and Present

The story of America is a story of people and the land. From long before 2000 B.C.—when American Indians had settled throughout North America—to the present, people from all over the world have come to America. They crossed rivers, climbed mountains, and built homes from one coast to another. The people who settled this land created our nation. The people and land continue to shape the United States today.

2000 B.C.

Thomas Moran, Green River Wyoming, 1907.
Collection of The Gerald Peters Gallery, Santa Fe, New Mexico.

Today

Chapter 1

A Nation of Many Peoples

More than 200 years ago, a French settler named Michel-Guillaume Jean de Crèvecoeur asked, "What then is the American?" Crèvecoeur believed that the United States was a land where people from different places could live together. From the earliest time, America has been a land of many peoples. This rich mix of cultures has shaped every part of life in the United States today.

The Eskimo, or Inuit, people probably arrived in America about 4,000 years ago. These people remain an important part of the vast variety of cultures in America today.

Benjamin Banneker (right) was an important American astronomer, inventor, and writer in the 1700s. His ancestors came from Africa and Europe.

2000 B.C.

Before 1900, most people moving to the United States came from Europe. The photograph above shows two Swedish-Americans in the early 1900s.

Today, many people in the United States practice the customs of their homelands. Here, a group of Mexican-Americans celebrate a festival in Phoenix, Arizona.

Many different religions thrive in the United States today. This toy, called a dreidel, is used during the Jewish festival of Chanukah.

More than 300,000 Chinese came to the United States during the 1800s. The brush shown above is used to paint the characters of the Chinese language.

Today

B.C. | A.D.
2000 1500 1000 500 500 1000 1500
1718 TODAY

L E S S O N 1

A Tale of One City

THINKING FOCUS

What makes New Orleans an example of pluralism?

Key Terms

- culture
- pluralism

In the tent over here, a crowd is tapping its feet to the beat of a Dixieland band. Dixieland began among African Americans in New Orleans nearly 100 years ago. On the stage over there, a string band is playing spirited Cajun *(KAY juhn)* tunes. This kind of music can be traced to the French-Canadian settlers who came to New Orleans in the 1700s.

In another tent, a band made up of a guitar, an accordion, and a washboard is playing zydeco *(ZY dih koh)* music. This kind of music mixes French and Caribbean tunes with the blues.

As you walk around, you see brass bands like the ones that march through New Orleans during jazz funerals. You also see parades of people dressed up like the American Indians whose ancestors settled in Louisiana many centuries before Europeans arrived.

It is spring and you are among many people in the city of New Orleans, Louisiana. Together you are celebrating the history of this city at the New Orleans Jazz and Heritage Festival. For more facts about some of the musical instruments at the festival, see A Closer Look on page 7.

Now step up to one of the food stands. Try New Orleans dishes such as gumbo, jambalaya, alligator po-boy sandwiches, and stewed rabbit. All in all, this festival shows you the many people, sights,

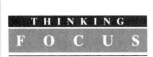

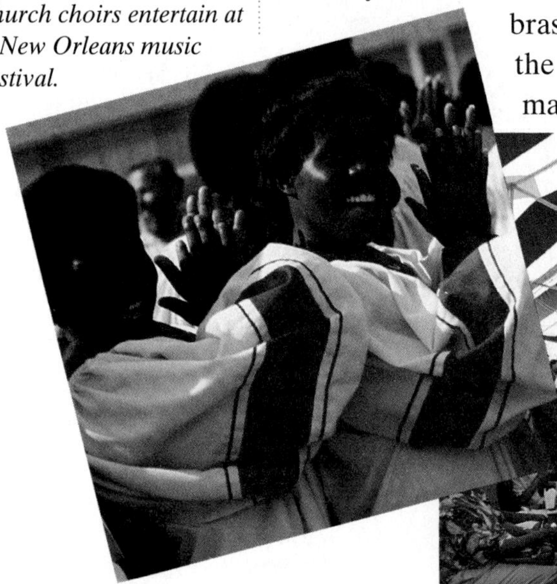

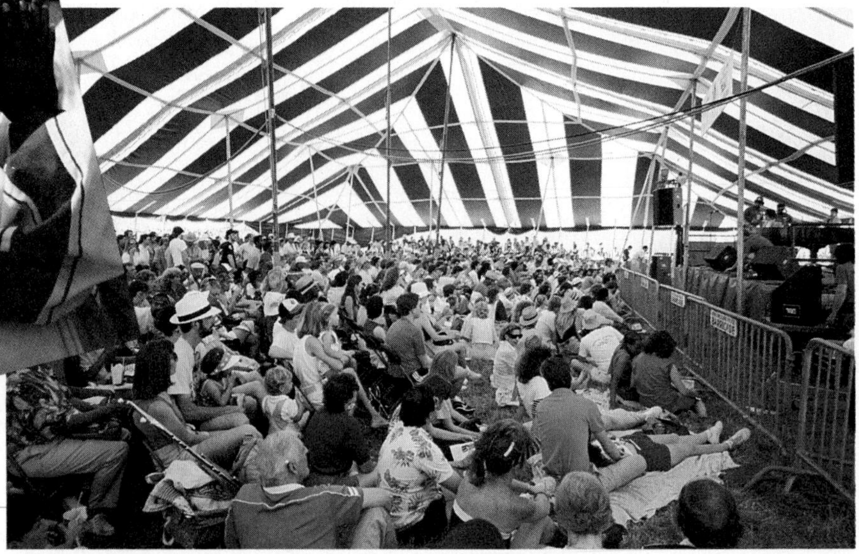

Jazz bands and church choirs entertain at a New Orleans music festival.

sounds, and tastes that make up this wonderful city. It also gives you an idea of the rich mixture of people—the ethnic diversity—that can be found all around these United States.

Where Is New Orleans?

Why does the city of New Orleans have such a rich and diverse mixture of people? Take a look at its location.

As you can see on the map below, New Orleans lies near the mouth of the Mississippi River. The Mississippi begins in Minnesota and flows south to the Gulf of Mexico. People of different backgrounds—American Indians and European explorers—came down the Mississippi from the north. From the south, people from many different countries entered the Mississippi through the Gulf of Mexico. These people all came to New Orleans.

◄ *The wide bend of the Mississippi River stretches out behind New Orleans.*

▼ *Find New Orleans on this map. Why do you think its location attracted so many different people?*

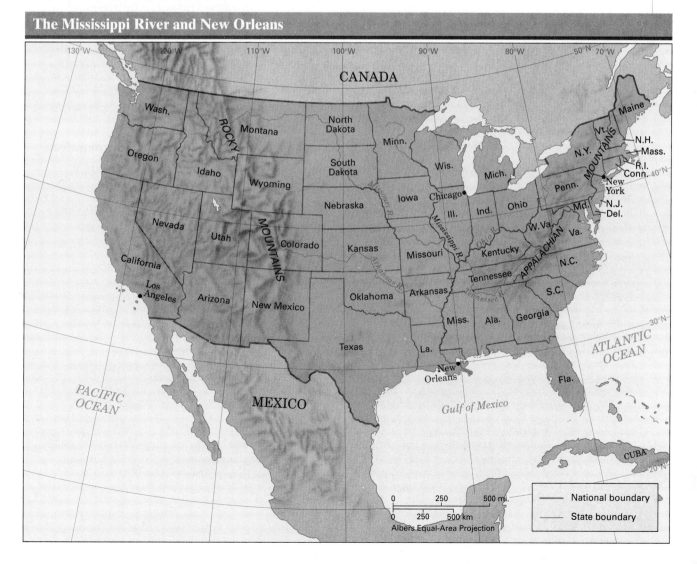

The Mississippi River and New Orleans

At different times, France and Spain governed New Orleans. During these times, French and Spanish settlers, African slaves, and frontier people of various backgrounds arrived in New Orleans.

More people came during the War of 1812 and during the Civil War. In both wars New Orleans was a key battleground. During times of peace, trade on the river made New Orleans an important seaport. ■

Who Lives in New Orleans?

Across Time & Space

Cajuns are an important ethnic group in New Orleans. The word Cajun *originally came from the word* Acadian. *Acadia was a region of Canada settled by people from France. However, the British forced the Acadians to leave Canada in the 1750s. Many of them moved to Louisiana. Today, the Cajun culture still has traces of its French-Canadian roots.*

■ *What is pluralism?*

▼ *According to this timeline, how many different ethnic groups played a part in the history of New Orleans?*

In 1835, Joseph Holt Ingraham had this to say about the people of New Orleans:

If the market at New Orleans represents that city, so truly does New Orleans represent every other city and nation upon earth. I know of none where is congregated so great a variety of the human species of every language and color.

These people gave and still give New Orleans a special **culture** or way of life. Look at the timeline on this page. Notice the many people who have left their mark on New Orleans.

One group of people—the Creoles—have a special place in New Orleans's history. Having

French or Spanish backgrounds, they form an important culture.

In many ways, Creoles show the great diversity of New Orleans. Creole food is a mix of European, Native American, and African cooking. Creoles cook with spices from Spain and the West Indies. Their meals often include long, crusty loaves of French bread. They also serve the kind of wild game—turkeys, rabbits, squirrels—that American Indians hunted. Their cooks are famous for the wonderful way they prepare many foods.

New Orleans is made up of people from many backgrounds. This kind of culture is called a pluralistic culture, or **pluralism.** In a pluralistic culture, life is exciting. People work and live together, learning to appreciate each other's differences. ■

Key Events in the History of New Orleans

Before 1682, Chickasaw, Choctaw, and Natchez live in the area

1764, Acadians begin arriving soon after France gives city to Spain.

1851, Over 50,000 immigrants, mostly German and Irish, arrive.

1867, The first Chinese immigrants arrive.

| 1700 | 1750 | 1800 | 1850 | 1900 | 1950 | 2000 |

1718, Sieur de Bienville founds New Orleans in French territory.

1800, France regains Louisiana from Spain then sells it to the United States in 1803.

1887-1914, Several thousand Italian immigrants come to New Orleans yearly.

1980s, Many Southeast Asians settle in New Orleans.

Musical Instruments

When you turn on your boom box, you're listening to history. The music you hear is made by instruments created long ago in other parts of the world.

Crash, splash, pang, swish, sizzle, and ride are names for different cymbals that drummers use today. It is believed musicians played the first cymbals more than 4,000 years ago in parts of Asia.

Out of the Congo region of Africa came conga drums. Latin American workers went to work in the Congo in the early 1900s. They created exciting dance beats to play on the congas, and brought the music and the drums back across the ocean.

Musicians kept tinkering with the Chinese mouth organ after it was brought to Europe in 1777. Eventually they turned it into something new: the accordion. German immigrants took their accordions to Louisiana. Today the accordion plays a key part in Louisiana's spicy regional music.

Arabs brought instruments called *gitterns* when they invaded Spain in A.D. 711. From gitterns, the Spaniards developed the guitar, and they took guitars with them when they colonized America. Later, American jazz musicians plugged guitars into electric amplifiers and turned them up *loud!*

How Is America Like New Orleans?

New Orleans is only one example of pluralism in the United States. In fact, you can find people from different backgrounds living together all over the nation.

Find Los Angeles on the map on page 5. People with Irish, German, English, Chinese, Japanese, African, Mexican, and other backgrounds have settled there.

A woman named Harriett Lane Levy wrote a book about growing up as a Jew in San Francisco in the late 1800s. Here Levy describes the people of many different backgrounds who lived in her neighborhood:

■ *Why do historians say that the United States is a pluralistic culture?*

▼ *According to the graph, which ethnic group is largest in New York?*

> The baker was German; the fish man, Italian; the grocer, a Jew; the butcher, Irish; the steam laundryman, a New Englander. The vegetable vendor and the regular laundryman who came to the house were Chinese.
>
> Harriett Lane Levy, *920 O'Farrell Street*, 1947

The United States is a pluralistic culture. This was true in the past, and it is true today. You will see this as you study the stories of the many people who make up the United States.

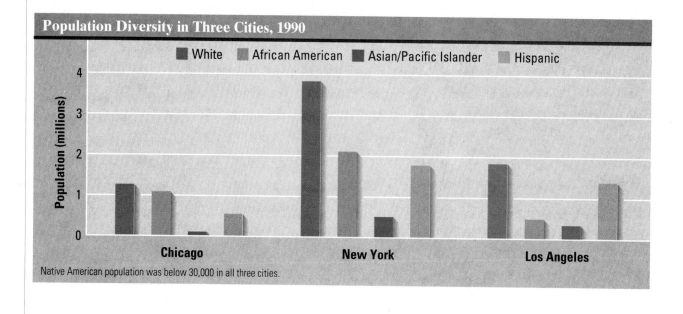

Population Diversity in Three Cities, 1990

■ White ■ African American ■ Asian/Pacific Islander ■ Hispanic

Population (millions)

Chicago   New York   Los Angeles

Native American population was below 30,000 in all three cities.

R E V I E W

1. **FOCUS** What makes New Orleans an example of pluralism?

2. **GEOGRAPHY** How did the location of New Orleans lead to its becoming a pluralistic culture?

3. **CRITICAL THINKING** Do you consider your town or city to be a pluralistic community? Explain.

4. **ACTIVITY** Find three examples of how your community has borrowed from other cultures. Examples may include the name of a town or building, holidays the community celebrates, local heroes, or popular foods. What ethnic groups contributed to your community's history?

Using Encyclopedias

Here's Why

You often need to use reference materials to get information. Encyclopedias are reference books with information about many subjects. This chapter tells about the New Orleans Jazz and Heritage Festival. Suppose you want to know more about that city. An encyclopedia can give you an overview of New Orleans.

Here's How

Articles in an encyclopedia are arranged alphabetically. A one-volume encyclopedia has an index in the back that lists all its topics or articles with their page numbers. If an encyclopedia has many volumes, its entire last volume may be an index.

The part of an index below shows N:278—volume N, page 278—as the location of the main article about New Orleans. Part of the article on page 278 is shown below. It is divided into sections to make it easier to understand. Each section has its own title or subhead.

At the end of the article, this encyclopedia tells you about articles related to your topic. It also lists additional resources.

Try It

In the back of this book is a Minipedia, reference material arranged like an encyclopedia. Find the article on Immigration on page 605.

This article includes graphs and charts. Look at the graph on immigration since 1820. How many immigrants came to the United States in 1921? In 1980? Look at the chart of major waves of immigration to find out which group came because of religious persecution.

Apply It

Use an encyclopedia to find information about your state. When did it become part of the United States? Does a natural feature or historical event make it special? What is its major crop or industry?

Heading

Pronunciations

More information in the encyclopedia

New Orleans

New Orleans, *AWR lee uhnz, awr LEENZ,* or *AWR luhnz,* is the largest city in Louisiana and one of the world's busiest ports. It is also a leading business, cultural, and industrial center of the Southern United States. New Orleans lies along the Mississippi River about 100 miles (160 kilometers) north of where the river flows into the Gulf of Mexico.

Subhead ——————— **The city**

New Orleans covers 364 square miles (943 square kilometers), including 165 square miles (427 square kilometers) of inland water. The city occupies all of Orleans parish and has the same boundaries as the parish. In Louisiana, counties are called *parishes.*

Related articles in *World Book* include:
Armstrong, Louis
Civil War (Capture of New Orleans)
Bienville, Sieur de
Louisiana Purchase

Additional resources ———— Other places to find information
Fodor's New Orleans. McKay, 1983.
Huber, Leonard V. *New Orleans: A Pictorial History.* Crown, 1982.

Index ———— Guide to the encyclopedia
New Orleans [Louisiana] **N:278**
with pictures and maps
Civil War (Capture of New Orleans)
Ci:629
Louisiana (Territorial Days) **l:502;**
picture on L:503

Adapted from The World Book Encyclopedia. © *1990 World Book, Inc. by permission.*

The Immigrant Experience

I nterviewing an immigrant to the United States will help you understand the dreams and hopes that built America. People came here from all over the world for many different reasons. Each one has a story to tell.

Get Ready

The person you interview can be a relative, friend, neighbor, fellow student, or teacher. If you don't know anyone who is an immigrant, ask your family or your teacher to help you. Be sure to have your notebook, a list of questions, a pencil or pen, and possibly a tape recorder. Ask permission to record the interview.

Find Out

The person you're interviewing may be eager to tell you an interesting story. If so, listen to the story before you go on with your questions. Remember to ask about the journey

1. Where were you born?
2. When did you come to America?
3. Who was your first American friend?

to America and the reasons for immigrating. How did the person feel? Scared? Excited? Where did he or she live? Go to school? Get his or her first job? Learn to speak English?

Move Ahead

Tape a large world map to the classroom wall. Use pins or colored pens to show where the people you interviewed came from. Mark the places in this country where they first settled. How many people came directly to your community?

Read your interview to the class. If someone else interviewed the same person, combine your information and take turns reading aloud. If you heard a very exciting story, turn it into a short play. Ask some classmates to help you act it out.

Explore Some More

After sharing your interviews, you may have more questions about the immigrant experience. Choose a particular ethnic group and find out as much as you can about it.

Learn what foods, customs, music, arts, or crafts this group brought to America. Are immigrants from this country still coming to America in large numbers?

You can arrange another interview with someone who knows a lot about the ethnic group you've chosen. Museums, cultural centers, churches, and libraries can also be sources of information as can some special programs featuring ethnic groups.

Foreign language newspapers help people keep in touch with their countries of origin.

L E S S O N   2

A Land of Immigrants

*How has immigration
made the United States a
pluralistic country?*

Key Terms

- immigrant
- descendant

> That night we shared a small room. . . . with two ladies and their
> children. There was little space for anything besides the army
> cots lined up in two rows. There were no windows in the adobe
> room and the only light came from the kitchen. . . . Our wet clothes and
> shoes were arranged near the stove to dry.
>
> In the sunny morning of the next day we walked back to the sta-
> tion. Our train was still there, the flats and the boxcars and coaches de-
> serted, Mexican and American soldiers walking back and forth. "Look, the
> American flag," my mother said. It was flying over a building near us.
> Down the street, beyond the depot, there was a Mexican flag on a staff.
> "We are in the United States. Mexico is over there."

The story you just read is by
Ernesto Galarza from his book
Barrio Boy. As a young boy in the
early 1900s, Galarza traveled with
his family from Mexico to their
new home in the United States.
They arrived late one night in the
city of Nogales, Arizona.

Ernesto Galarza begins his
story by describing his early years
in a small mountain village in Mexico. *Barrio Boy* goes on to tell how
Galarza and his family were forced
to leave their village and move to a
nearby city. Galarza's book also explains why his family finally decided to leave Mexico and come to
the United States to live. After a
difficult journey by train, the
Galarza family settled in Sacramento, California.

➤ *Ernesto Galarza
became a university
professor and an expert
on the experiences of
immigrants.*

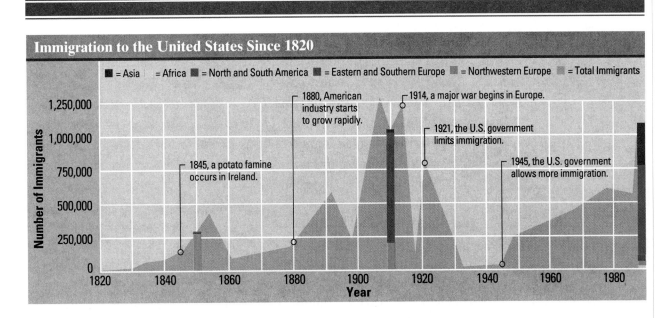

Immigration to the United States Since 1820

Legend: ■ = Asia ■ = Africa ■ = North and South America ■ = Eastern and Southern Europe ■ = Northwestern Europe ■ = Total Immigrants

1880, American industry starts to grow rapidly.

1914, a major war begins in Europe.

1921, the U.S. government limits immigration.

1845, a potato famine occurs in Ireland.

1945, the U.S. government allows more immigration.

Y-axis: Number of Immigrants — 0, 250,000, 500,000, 750,000, 1,000,000, 1,250,000

X-axis: Year — 1820, 1840, 1860, 1880, 1900, 1920, 1940, 1960, 1980

America's Many People

One reason America is so diverse is that it was settled by immigrants. An **immigrant** is a person who moves permanently from one country to live in another.

A Land of Immigrants

Everyone who lives in the United States is either an immigrant or the descendant of immigrants. **Descendants** are the children and grandchildren of earlier generations.

Even American Indians, the first people to live in America, came from Asia many thousands of years ago. Since then people from many lands have moved to this country.

All of us, somewhere in our past, have relatives who immigrated to this land. Some of us are descendants of people who came willingly to the United States in search of a new life. Others are descendants of people who came to America from Africa, most of whom were forced into slavery.

Together, immigrants and their descendants make up the people of the United States today.

People from Many Nations

Spanish, Portuguese, French, Dutch, and English people were among the first Europeans to come to North America. They first arrived during the 1500s and 1600s. Many Irish and German people came to America in the 1840s. They settled in cities like New York and Philadelphia.

In the late 1800s and early 1900s, millions of immigrants arrived from southern and eastern Europe and Asia. Italians, Russian Jews, Greeks, Poles, Chinese, and Japanese all came at that time.

Study the timeline on this page. Where did most of the immigrants come from between 1820 and 1914? Where have most come from since 1950? These people came to the United States from many different places and for many different reasons. ■

▲ *What events—in the United States or elsewhere—affected immigration? How did those events affect immigration?*

How Do We Know?

HISTORY *We know a lot about the immigrants who came to the United States from records kept at Ellis Island in New York. Ellis Island was an arrival center for immigrants from 1892 through 1943. Today it has been reopened as a museum for the immigrant experience in America.*

■ *Why do you think historians call the United States a "nation of immigrants?"*

Why People Came

Most people who came to America loved their countries and would have liked to remain there. However, conditions in immigrants' countries often did not allow people to live safely or comfortably.

In the 1600s, some English people were persecuted for their religious beliefs. In the 1840s, the Irish suffered crop failures that caused much starvation. In the 1880s, Russian Jews were persecuted because of their religion. In fear for their lives, they fled so they could live and worship in peace.

No one story can describe every immigrant's experiences. However, in telling his story, Ernesto Galarza describes feelings that were shared by other immigrants. For example, troubles at home forced Galarza's family to leave Mexico. Galarza remembered his family's poverty.

This Jewish immigrant came to New York from Russia around 1900.

■ Why did the Galarza family decide to leave Mexico and go to the United States?

A nother kind of news that Jose brought us was about the scarcity of work in the town. More peasants were coming down from the mountain villages to find a safe place for their families and to work . . . Gustavo came back one weekend from his job at the sugar mill to tell us he had been laid off.

Galarza's family was also caught in a revolution, a war between people and their government. "There was gunfire in some part of the town every night. . . . School closed and there was no sewing for my mother to do."

Like the English immigrants of the 1600s and the Irish of the 1840s, Galarza's family decided to leave their homeland. They wanted to start a new life in the United States. ■

The Trip to America

Traveling from one's homeland to a new country has often been hard. From the 1600s to the 1900s, millions of European immigrants crossed the Atlantic Ocean to America by ship. Usually the conditions on board were very uncomfortable. People were packed into dark, wet areas of the ship. Food was poor and there was often very little water.

In *Journey to Pennsylvania*, published in 1756, Gottlieb Mittelberger described a voyage made by German immigrants at that time.

An Irish man reads a poster advertising opportunities in America.

A t length, when, after a long and tedious voyage, the ships come in sight of land. . . . all creep from below on deck to see the land from afar, and they weep for joy, and pray and sing, thanking and praising God. The sight of land makes the people on board the ship, especially the sick and the half-dead, alive again . . . .

Ernesto Galarza's family traveled from Mexico to the United States by train. This journey also was difficult. Their trip was

◄ *Nearly nine million immigrants arrived in the United States between 1900 and 1910. Most came from Europe on ships like this one.*

Across Time & Space

The United States continues to accept immigrants who have left home because of political troubles and wars. These people are called refugees. In recent years the United States has accepted refugees from Cuba, Central America, the Soviet Union, and Southeast Asia.

interrupted for several weeks when Galarza became sick with measles. He stayed in a tent near the tracks with other sick children until he was well enough to travel.

When Galarza's journey began again, the train moved slowly and only during the day. At one point the tracks had been destroyed by revolutionary soldiers and had to be repaired before the train could move on.

Galarza's first memory of the United States was the sight of the American flag flying over the town of Nogales, Arizona. After 1886, the first sight of America for most European immigrants was the Statue of Liberty in New York Harbor. Whether they came by ship or by train, though, all immigrants wondered the same thing: What would their lives be like in this strange new country? ■

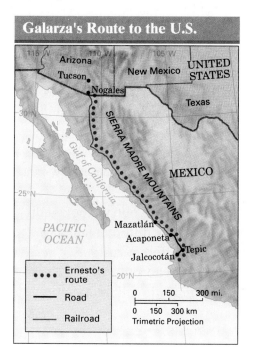

Galarza's Route to the U.S.

Key:
- •••• Ernesto's route
- —— Road
- —— Railroad

0   150   300 mi.
0   150   300 km
Trimetric Projection

◄ *In Ernesto Galarza's boyhood, there were only a few ways to go from Mexico to the United States: on a train, in a cart or wagon, or on foot.*

■ *In what ways did Galarza's trip differ from the one described by Mittelberger? In what ways was it the same?*

Life in a New Country

From Nogales, the Galarza family moved to Sacramento, California. They found life there very different from life in Mexico. The family moved to a *barrio,* a neighborhood where other Mexican people lived. But people from other countries lived there as well.

The women walked on the street in kimonos, wooden sandals, and white stockings, carrying neat black bundles on their backs and wearing their hair in puffs with long ivory needles stuck through them. When they met, they bowed.

Galarza found not only Japanese in his neighborhood, but also Filipinos, Portuguese, Italians, Poles, Koreans, and Africans. He described his neighborhood as a joyful mixture. "It was a kaleidoscope [changing pattern] of colors and languages and customs that surprised and absorbed me at every turn."

Most immigrants who arrived in America in the 1800s and 1900s shared Galarza's interest in the new country. Like Galarza, most of these people had left countries where people looked and acted in similar ways and where everyone shared a similar culture. But here in America, they found a new kind of life.

In America people looked different, spoke different languages, and had different customs. These people had become part of America's pluralistic culture. ◼

▲ *Since the late 1800s, most immigrants have begun their new lives in American cities. Sacramento, California, shown here in the 1920s, was just one of many cities where immigrants settled.*

The lower quarter [of the city] was not exclusively a Mexican barrio but a mix of nationalities. Between L and N Streets two blocks from us, the Japanese had taken over. Their homes were in the alleys behind shops.

◼ *How did Galarza's life in the United States differ from his life in Mexico?*

Galarza was fascinated by the way the Japanese women in his neighborhood dressed and acted.

R E V I E W

1. **FOCUS** How has immigration made the United States a pluralistic culture?
2. **CONNECT** Why would both New Orleans and Sacramento be considered examples of pluralism?
3. **HISTORY** What kinds of conditions might cause a person to leave his or her country and come to America?
4. **CRITICAL THINKING** When a person lives in a neighborhood with many different nationalities, what should he or she do to understand and get along well with others?
5. **ACTIVITY** After the class has had time to answer question 4, collect your classmates' ideas and make a list of helpful hints called "Living Together in a Neighborhood of Many Cultures."

LESSON 3

A Country of Many Cultures

Nine o'clock sharp the next morning, Shirley sat in the principal's office at P. S. 8. Her mother and the schoolmistress were talking. Shirley didn't understand a word. It was embarrassing. Why hadn't she, too, studied the English course on the records that Father had sent? But it was too late now. She stopped trying to understand. Suddenly, mother hissed, in Chinese. "Stop that or else!"

Shirley snapped her head down. She had been staring at the stranger. But she could not keep her eyes from rolling up again. There was something more foreign about the principal than about any other foreigner she had seen so far.

Bette Bao Lord, *In the Year of the Boar and Jackie Robinson*, 1984

THINKING
FOCUS

How does a pluralistic culture benefit America? How does it challenge America?

Key Terms

- ethnic custom
- prejudice

◀ *When this picture was taken, Bette Bao Lord was about the age of Shirley, the character in her story.*

The character in this story is an immigrant from China. She speaks little English and has a hard time making friends at school. However, she does learn to play baseball. When she learns about Jackie Robinson, the first black player to break into the major leagues, she feels "... as if she had grown as tall as the Statue of Liberty."

Benefits of Many Cultures

In a society made up of many cultures, people borrow music, foods, clothes, and other things from each other. But one of the most important things they borrow is language.

17

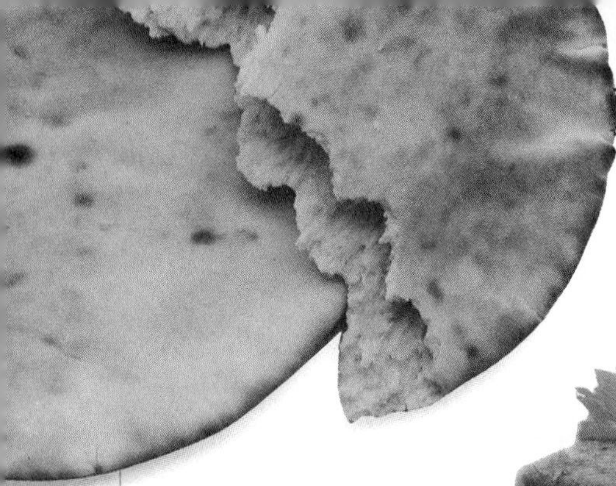

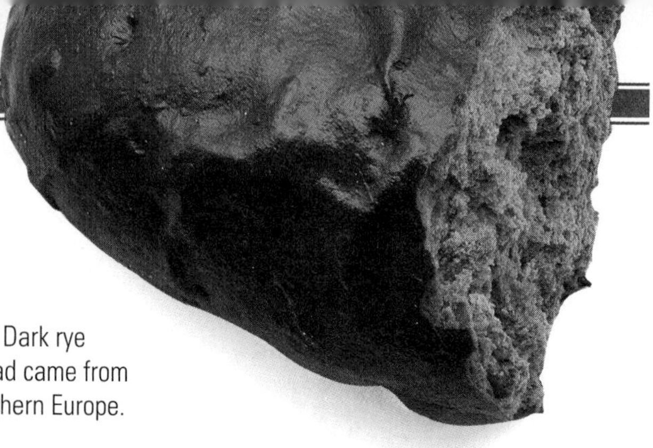

➤ Dark rye bread came from northern Europe.

▲ Greek and Syrian immigrants brought pita bread to America.

▼ American Indians baked corn bread long before Europeans arrived in America.

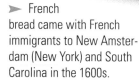

➤ French bread came with French immigrants to New Amsterdam (New York) and South Carolina in the 1600s.

You may not know that words you use every day have come from other cultures. The word *kindergarten* is German, meaning "children's garden." *Cookie* comes from Holland. *Mosquito* is Spanish. *Okra,* a type of vegetable, comes from West Africa. Early settlers in the United States learned the word from African slaves. The next time

UNDERSTANDING CULTURE

Immigrants to the United States often begin living just like other Americans. They buy the clothing, furniture, and foods used by their native-born neighbors. In this way immigrants come to feel that they share in the culture of America.

Similar Cultures

Culture is the way of life shared by a group of people. For example, many Japanese people share similar ideas about how a person should behave. These beliefs have been handed down from generation to generation. They are cultural beliefs.

A group of people who share a culture often live in the same area. However, people who live in the same area do not always have the same culture. If the people in an area do not share the same beliefs, outlooks, and values, they do not have the same culture.

Pluralistic Cultures

Pluralistic cultures are made up of many subcultures, or cultures within a culture. For example, Japanese immigrants may practice Japanese customs while still being part of American culture.

People who are part of a culture have a sense of belonging. Even in America, with its pluralism, people share many beliefs and want many of the same things in life.

18

you order a hamburger, remember that it is named after Hamburg, a city in Germany.

Like language, culture itself may slowly change over time. People who immigrated to America did not simply drop their ways of life. They kept many of their customs. A custom that is special to a group of immigrants is called an **ethnic custom.** Ethnic customs have enriched our country and given us diversity in our daily lives.

Claudia DeMonte, an artist who was raised in Astoria, an Italian neighborhood in New York, speaks fondly of her ethnic customs.

A lthough my life style today is far removed from Astoria, I am still attached to my roots, to the foods and customs. I think it is great to have lasagna for Thanksgiving and to have fish on Christmas Eve. That is a wonderful part of my life, and I hate to think that it might be lost. What makes America great is that each ethnic group still loves and eats the dishes their parents and grandparents ate. If we all dropped that and ate hamburgers . . . I think it would be tragic.

Quoted in Linda Brandi Cateura, *Growing Up Italian*, 1987

Across Time & Space

During the 1950s, teachers in many parts of the United States often forbade students to speak a foreign language in school. Today students are encouraged to express themselves in foreign languages and in English.

Ethnic customs, such as special holiday celebrations or foods like the breads you see here, help people to remember their ancestors' way of life. Bette Bao Lord, the

Jewish settlers brought matzo to New Amsterdam (New York) in 1654.

Italian bread like this may first have been made by Roman bakers almost 1,700 years ago.

Indians in Mexico and Central America first made tortillas.

Croissants have a French name, but they were first baked in Vienna, Austria, in 1683.

■ *What are some benefits of life in a pluralistic culture?*

▼ *Public places, like zoos, often put up signs that can be easily understood by everyone.*

author of the story about the Chinese immigrant Shirley, explained how she felt about keeping her Chinese customs. She said,

"I think we hyphenated [immigrant] Americans are doubly blessed. We can choose the best of both [cultures]." ■

Challenges of Many Cultures

As you have learned, pluralism has many benefits. However, pluralism also has created some challenges for America. Much of the history of the United States is the story of how America has met the challenges of pluralism.

One challenge of pluralism is the many languages spoken by people in America. You have read that Americans borrow words from other cultures. This makes our culture more rich and interesting. Sometimes, however, it is hard for Americans to understand the languages spoken by all the people they meet. You may hear different languages in your own classroom. In many places, several languages can be heard spoken in a classroom.

Many immigrants who come to America are made to feel that they must leave behind the ways of their own ethnic groups. For example, Elizabeth Wong's family came to California from China. Her parents sent Elizabeth to Chinese school after regular school, so she could learn Chinese writing and customs. Elizabeth hated Chinese school. She wanted to be an "all-American girl." Later, however, she felt sad because she had lost her Chinese customs. Here is what she says about her experience.

I thought of myself as multicultural. I preferred tacos to egg rolls; I enjoyed Cinco de Mayo [a Mexican celebration] more than Chinese New Year.

At last I was one of you; I wasn't one of them.

Sadly, I still am.

Elizabeth Wong, "The Struggle to Be an All-American Girl"

When cultures mix, people sometimes have a hard time understanding one another. Ernesto Galarza tells of an American habit he found hard to understand:

We had to get used to the Americans. They did not listen if you did not speak loudly, as they always did. In the Mexican style people would know you were enjoying their jokes tremendously if you merely smiled and shook a little, as if you were trying to swallow your mirth. In the American style there was little difference between a laugh and a roar, and until you got used to them you could hardly tell whether the boisterous Americans were roaring mad or roaring happy.

Maybe the hardest problem in a pluralistic culture is **prejudice,** disliking people without knowing anything about them. You will learn how immigrants, Native Americans, and African Americans have met with prejudice.

Pluralism is good for a nation. However, it also presents challenges. This textbook tells the story of a nation that faced those challenges as it grew. The special story of the American nation is how the people built a united country in spite of their great diversity. ■

▲ *Today, life in America is enriched by immigrant cultures. Here a group of Mexican Americans rides in a parade in Santa Fe, New Mexico.*

■ *What challenges do immigrants face in the United States?*

REVIEW

1. **FOCUS** How does pluralism benefit America? How does it challenge America?
2. **CONNECT** Do you think language was a challenge in New Orleans? Explain.
3. **CITIZENSHIP** Why is prejudice a problem in a country of many cultures?
4. **CRITICAL THINKING** Elizabeth Wong did not want to practice the customs of her parents. Why do you think young students sometimes prefer to be like their classmates rather than be seen as part of a special group?
5. **WRITING ACTIVITY** Together with a partner write a short story using at least seven words that come from languages other than English.

Gooseberries to Oranges

Barbara Cohen

A new beginning in America—this was the dream of many who came and of many who still come. America provides freedom, hope, and opportunities for education and work. Our country is woven together with the threads of many stories like this one of eight-year-old Fanny as she leaves her familiar village to join her father in New York.

As you have learned, immigrants from many nations came to America. Like Ernesto in Lesson 2, Fanny in this story gives up one life for a strange new one.

gooseberries small sour berries

mezuzah (muh ZUZ uh) a small box holding papers with words from the Bible written on them. The box is fixed to the door frame.
scroll a roll of paper with writing on it
polluted not clean
epidemic rapid spread of a disease
cholera a serious disease of the stomach and intestines

cubbyhole a small, enclosed space

L isten, darlings, and I'll tell you a story about what happened to me when I was a little girl. I lived far away, in Europe, in a village named Rohatyn. My mother was dead. My father had gone to America. I lived with Aunt Rebecca. She couldn't have loved me more if I had been her own child.

My cousin Leah loved me too. She had blue eyes and white skin, like an angel. She washed my hair. She took me for walks. In the spring we picked wild strawberries from the fields. In the summer we ate gooseberries right off the bushes. In the fall we sucked brown pears that grew on trees in front of Aunt Rebecca's little house.

But winter came, and war. We put feather pillows around the walls of the rooms so if bullets hit our house they wouldn't hurt us. Soldiers in steel helmets searched every corner, looking for boys to take away to the army. They tore the mezuzah off the door jamb because they thought gold was hidden inside. There was no gold inside the mezuzah, only a little scroll inscribed with words from the Bible.

We had nothing to eat. The well became polluted. An epidemic of cholera roared through Rohatyn. Aunt Rebecca died. Cousin Leah died. Half the village died. I was eight.

A letter arrived from Papa. "America is the golden land," he said. "Here is a ticket so that you can come to America too."

Did I want to leave my village? Did I want to leave the gooseberries and the little brown pears? But when my Aunt Elke came to get me, I went. So did Aunt Elke's children, Cousin Sylvia, Cousin Sam, Cousin Rose, and Cousin Betty.

The ship carried more people than lived in our whole village. The six of us stayed in a tiny little cubbyhole down deep inside the ship. It had no windows. There were no beds to sleep on, only hammocks, and nothing to eat except moldy bread and Swiss cheese.

Every day on the deck I saw a man studying from a book or rocking back and forth in prayer. He never spoke to me, but I liked to look at him. Papa had written that in America everyone could get an education. Everyone could be learned.

One day I saw another man holding a round, bright thing. "What kind of little ball is that?" I asked him.

"It's not a ball," the man said. "It's an orange. It's to eat." Very slowly, very carefully, he peeled away the skin. Underneath the bumpy skin were plump, juicy sections of fruit. He threw the skin over the railing and into the ocean. He pulled one section away from the others and popped it into his mouth. He chewed it slowly, and then he swallowed it. He did that with another section and another section and another section until the whole orange was gone.

A few days later I saw the orange man again. "Have you seen the man with the book?" I asked him.

"Didn't you hear?" the orange man said. "He threw himself overboard. He drowned."

"Why?" I cried. "Why did he do that?"

The orange man shrugged. "He was very sick. He was coughing blood. He knew that when he got to America they would send him back. He decided he'd rather be dead."

Every night I prayed that I wouldn't get sick, and that Aunt Elke and Sylvia, Sam, Rose, and Betty wouldn't get sick.

The ship pulled into New York harbor. We passed the Statue of Liberty. All the passengers stood on the deck and cheered.

We came to Ellis Island. Inspectors opened our bundles and examined every candlestick, every feather bed, inside and out. They screamed questions at us. We couldn't understand what they said. They grabbed us by the arms and shoulders and pushed and shoved us where they wanted us to go.

I stood in a dark corner of a huge room. A woman in a uniform took scissors and cut off my two long braids, snip, snap, snip, snap. I shoved the braids into my coat pocket. She pulled my hair this way and that way, peering at my scalp.

Then she rolled up the sleeves of my dress. She stared at my arms. They were covered with spots. I hadn't taken my dress off the whole time I was on the ship. I hadn't even known I had a rash.

Did the rash mean I was sick? I couldn't understand what anyone was saying. They pushed and shoved me to a tall brick building with a thousand windows. Inside, the rooms were very white, so white they blinded my eyes, and very clean. They were the cleanest white rooms in the universe.

For days I lay on a white bed, wearing a white gown. I cried

Ellis Island   the place in New York Harbor where immigrants entered the United States

the whole time. I was sure they were going to send me back to the old country. What would I do there all alone?

After a week the rash had disappeared from my arms and they gave me back my clothes, all wrinkled, but clean.

A man came into the long white room. He looked familiar to me, but I didn't know who he was.

He walked over to my bed. "Fanny," he said, "don't you know me? Don't you know who I am?"

"Papa?" I whispered.

"Yes, Papa," he said. He put his arms around me and hugged me. I put my arms around him and hugged him back.

Then Papa took me home. He lived on Attorney Street, in a two-room apartment with his new wife. He worked in a garment factory where he earned three dollars a week.

The street was crowded with people and shops and peddlers and cats. Voices screamed from the windows. Laundry hung from the fire escapes.

peddler   person who travels around selling goods

Papa had said America was a golden land. I had thought that meant the streets were paved with gold. They weren't. They were paved with garbage—huge barrels so stuffed with old newspapers and rotting apples and potato peels that they overflowed— and wherever I walked, I stepped on something hard or rustly or squishy.

I went to school. I learned to speak English. I learned to read it and write it too. I went to the library. They gave you books for nothing. You had to bring them back, but when you did, they let you take others.

P.S.   public school

I made a friend. Her name was Selma and she went to P.S. 174, just like me. In the summer, if it was very hot, Selma and I slept outside on the fire escape.

Next door, Mrs. Ludwig sewed sleeves into coats. One day she said to me, "Fanny, if you take this bundle of coats to the factory for me, I'll give you two nickels."

"I'll take it for you, Mrs. Ludwig," I said. "I'll take it for you anywhere."

The bundle was so big I couldn't see over it. It was heavy too. But when I got back from the factory, Mrs. Ludwig gave me two nickels, just as she had promised. I looked at the nickels for a long time. Then I went back to our flat.

Yiddish   Germanic language spoken mainly by Jews

My father was sitting at the kitchen table. I held out my hand to him. The two nickels were lying in my palm. He looked up from the Yiddish paper he was reading. He saw the nickels in my hand. "Where did you get two nickels, Fanny?" he asked me.

"Mrs. Ludwig gave them to me because I took a bundle of coats over to the factory for her," I said. "They're for you."

tsatskeleh
(TSAH tskeh leh)   my favorite

Carefully he closed my fingers over the nickels. "No, tsatskeleh," he said, "they're for you."

I took one nickel and put it under my pillow. I would use it to go with Selma to see a Charlie Chaplin movie. The other nickel I held tight in my fist.

I ran out of our flat and down five flights of steps. I ran out on the street. A fruit peddler usually stood near the curb.

Yes, she was there. I rushed over to her. "Two oranges, please," I said. I held out my nickel.

She took the nickel. "Pick out your own oranges," she said. "Pick whichever oranges you want."

I stared at the oranges for a long time. Finally I chose the two that seemed to me to be the brightest, the largest, and the roundest.

Then I ran back into our building and up the five flights of steps to our flat. I put one orange on the table in front of my father. Then I sat down next to him. I peeled the other orange very, very slowly. I pulled it apart, section by section. I sucked each section until it was dry, and then I chewed and swallowed what was left. It tasted like heaven.

If at that very moment a gate had opened, and on the other side of the gate were the wild gooseberries and little brown pears of Rohatyn, I would not have walked through that gate.

I was already home.

Further Reading

Child of the Owl. Lawrence Yep. Casey is sent to live with her grandmother in San Francisco's Chinatown. She knows nothing of her Chinese heritage and faces many puzzling situations.

Hello, My Name Is Scrambled Eggs. Jamie Gilson. Harvey's family is the sponsor of a newly arrived Vietnamese family. Harvey is determined to help the son, a boy his own age, become an instant American, but his plans get "scrambled."

Chapter Review

Reviewing Key Terms

culture (p. 6)
descendant (p. 13)
ethnic custom (p. 19)

immigrant (p. 13)
pluralism (p. 6)
prejudice (p. 21)

A. Read the sentences below. Rewrite each sentence using a key term in place of the underlined words.

1. Groups of people from many different backgrounds can make a city colorful and interesting.
2. Ernesto Galarza's family were people who moved from one country to another.
3. The people of New Orleans give the city an exciting way of life.
4. Disliking a person without knowing anything about them is a very unfair way to judge someone.

B. Each statement below describes a descendant, an ethnic custom, or a prejudice. Using information from the chapter, explain your choice.

1. A child's grandparents came to America from Russia.
2. Special foods are part of holiday celebrations for many people.
3. Brass bands sometimes march in funerals for people in New Orleans.
4. During the 1840s, many Boston businesses refused to hire Irish immigrants.
5. The way people dress and greet each other can be different from place to place.
6. The first Indians who came to America were originally from Asia.

Exploring Concepts

A. Copy the following chart on your paper. Fill in the empty columns with facts from the chapter.

Immigrant group	Why they left their homeland	Where they settled in America
French	To explore America	Louisiana
Mexican		
English		
Russian		
Irish		
African		

B. Write one or two sentences to answer each of the questions below.

1. What did New Orleans, New York City, and Sacramento have in common during the 1800s and early 1900s?
2. Why did Russian Jews come to the United States during the 1880s?
3. According to Mittelberger, how did Germans feel when they reached America?
4. What did Ernesto Galarza and Elizabeth Wong do to help themselves fit into the American culture?
5. Why do the descendants of immigrants follow their ethnic customs?
6. How has pluralism in New Orleans influenced music in that city?
7. List three challenges Americans face in a pluralistic culture.

Reviewing Skills

1. Look in the Minipedia article on Mexico on page 609. Find out what the three colors in the Mexican flag stand for, and write them down.

2. Continue studying the Minipedia article on Mexico. Then answer the following questions: What is the estimated 1993 population of Mexico? What percent of the people live in cities? What is one important national holiday? When did Mexican women win the right to vote in all elections?

3. Interview a relative or a neighbor and ask them questions about their ancestors. What country or countries did they come from? Does their family follow any special traditions or customs from that country? Ask them if they feel it is important to keep traditions.

4. Suppose you want to learn more about immigration. You are curious about the millions of immigrants who came to Ellis Island in New York City. How would you learn about it? In what kind of book would you find this information?

Using Critical Thinking

1. Martin Luther King, Jr., once said: "I have a dream that my four little children will one day live in a nation where they will not be judged by the color of their skin, but by the content of their character." What challenge to American culture was King talking about? Do you think King was referring only to his children or to all children? Explain.

2. The Sioux Indians have the following saying: "A people without history is like the wind on the buffalo grass." This means people without customs or tradition are like people without a past. Think about the saying. Do you think Elizabeth Wong and Linda Brandi Cateura would agree with the Sioux? Give reasons for your answer using information from the chapter.

3. You probably have heard people say, "Wouldn't life be boring if everyone were the same?" And likely it would be boring. Think about all the ethnic influences in your life today. Food, popular music, and clothing styles are three areas where you can see the mark of different ethnic groups. List three countries or regions of the world that you think have put their mark on our culture. Then decide how each country has given us food, music, or clothing choices that make our lives more interesting.

Preparing for Citizenship

1. **WRITING ACTIVITY** Use restaurants to measure the diversity of your town or city's culture. Find the restaurant listings in your local Yellow Pages. First, write down four types of ethnic restaurants, such as Chinese, French, or Italian. Then, list two or three restaurants under each group. Hold a discussion with four to five other students. Write down the names of some dishes served by the different restaurants.

2. **COLLABORATIVE LEARNING** Form two-person teams to look at immigrant groups in the United States today. Have each team cover a specific immigrant group, such as Mexican, Vietnamese, or Pakistani. Cut out newspaper articles and watch television programs to collect information. Research the country's flag, national holidays, or other symbols of their homeland. Write your report and display your articles.

Chapter 2
This Land of Ours

Europeans first learned about the land of America by exploring it. This map, made in 1527, shows what Europeans knew about North America after 35 years of exploration.

"From sea to shining sea . . ." The song "America the Beautiful" gives us many different pictures of our land: amber waves of grain, purple mountains, and fruited plains. Americans have explored this land, made maps of it, moved across it, and built homes on it. Each place has shaped the people who lived there and the events that happened there. In many ways the story of America is the story of its land.

Sarah Warren's needlework from the 1700s shows a garden in Boston, Massachusetts. Warren saw the America that attracted many people to move here: a land of plenty.

2000 B.C.

Today, satellite pictures give us new views of earth and the United States. Compare this image of America with the map from 1527.

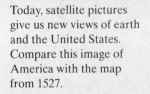

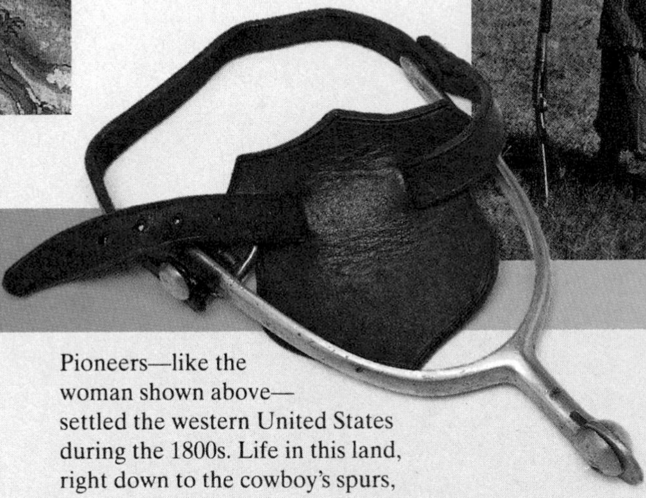

Pioneers—like the woman shown above—settled the western United States during the 1800s. Life in this land, right down to the cowboy's spurs, was shaped by the western frontier.

Today

L E S S O N   1

Understanding Geography

THINKING
F O C U S

*What types of questions
do geographers seek to
answer about a place?*

We are three-quarters of a mile in the depths of the earth, and
the great river shrinks into insignificance, as it dashes its
angry waves against the walls and cliffs, that rise to the
world above; they are but puny ripples, and we but pigmies [small peo-
ple], running up and down the sands, or lost among the boulders.

   *We have an unknown distance yet to run; an unknown river yet to
explore. What falls there are, we know not; what rocks beset the channel,
we know not; what walls rise over the river, we know not. . . . With some
eagerness, and some anxiety, and some misgiving, we enter the cañon
below, and are carried along by the swift water. . . .*

Key Term

• geography

So wrote the famous American
wilderness explorer John Wesley Powell in his diary on August 13, 1869. He

led eight men into the Grand Canyon
in Arizona. Powell and five of the
men became the first white men

➤ *The Colorado River
winds its way through the
Grand Canyon. Notice
the many layers of rock
that make up the canyon
walls.*

to travel down the Colorado River the length of the canyon.

After successful trips through the Grand Canyon, Powell became the director of the U. S. Geological Survey. In 1888, he helped found the National Geographic Society.

Studying Places and Location

John Wesley Powell was keenly interested in the geography of his native land. **Geography** is the study of the earth and the distribution of life, including people, on the earth. Geographers study the interactions of people with their environment.

Nature and People

The Grand Canyon is a place created by natural forces. It was formed over millions of years by the cutting action of the Colorado River. Many other places on the earth also have been created by nature. The Hawaiian Islands were created by volcanoes in the Pacific Ocean. Lake Michigan and the other Great Lakes were formed by melting glaciers.

Many places on the earth have been created by people. For example, the city of San Diego didn't exist until pioneers settled the area in the middle 1700s and built the Mission of San Diego de Alcalá.

Physical and Cultural Features

Every place on earth has its own special features. The physical features of a place include its climate, landforms, lakes, and rivers. The cultural features of its people include their languages, homes, food, and clothing.

Consider the Grand Canyon, which stretches for 277 miles. In some places, this deep gorge in the surface of the earth is over one mile deep and 18 miles wide. The

▲ *These storehouses for grain were made of flagstone in the Grand Canyon by Anasazi Indians between A.D. 1050 and 1150. The Anasazi were the ancestors of present-day Pueblo Indians.*

This Land of Ours

▲ *These are pieces of Indian pottery. Some designs were so widespread that they were found in both the eastern and western Anasazi area.*

■ *What features make up the physical characteristics of a place?*

canyon is made up of many tilted layers of sandstone, limestone, and shale.

The canyon has its own climate, too. The floor of the canyon can be 25° F warmer than the rim.

The Indians of the Grand Canyon also make this place special. Powell described the ruins of one Indian village he saw:

> Here, on a terrace of trap [dark rocks], we discover another group of ruins. There was evidently quite a village on this rock. Again we find mealing stones, and much broken pottery, and up in a little natural shelf in the rock, back of the ruins, we find a globular basket, that would hold perhaps a third of a bushel. It is badly broken, and, as I attempt to take it up, it falls to pieces. There are many beautiful flint chips, as if this had been the home of an old arrow maker.

Location

Geographers are also interested in the location of any place they are studying. Location is talked about in two ways. The absolute location of a place is its exact location. For example, you might say that a house is located at 945 North Hastings. The relative location of a place is where that place is in relation to other places. You might say that a house is located across the street from the fire station.

As Powell traveled through the Grand Canyon, he always checked his location. He did this with a sextant, an instrument that people use to figure out exactly where they are on the earth. Whenever Powell came upon an interesting place in the canyon, he marked its location in his journal. This way, later explorers would know exactly where to find such places in the Grand Canyon as Bright Angel Falls and Havasu Canyon. ■

Studying Movement and Interaction

In addition to the physical and cultural features of a place, geographers study the movement that takes place in and around an area. They also study interaction, the ways that people and the environment affect each other.

The Movement of People

Geographers study all kinds of movement, including the movement of consumer goods, wildlife, ideas, fads, and people. Through these studies they gain a clearer understanding of how different places are joined together and how people in these places communicate with one another.

As a geographer, John Wesley Powell was curious about the movement of Indian tribes into the Grand Canyon. He knew that some Indians had lived in the canyon for thousands of years. Others, however, had come to make their homes there just a few hundred years before Powell's trip. Why, Powell wondered, did these Indians choose to move into such a harsh environment?

It is ever a source of wonder to us why these ancient people sought such inaccessible places for their homes. . . . We know that, for a century or two after the settlement of Mexico, many expeditions were sent into the country now comprised in Arizona and New Mexico, for the purpose of bringing the town-building people under the dominion of the Spanish government. Many of their villages were destroyed, and the inhabitants fled to regions at that time unknown; and there are traditions . . . that the cañons were these unknown lands.

▲ *In this 1873 photograph, John Wesley Powell talks with Tau-Gu, Chief of the Paiutes, near the Grand Canyon. Powell had lost his right arm during the Civil War. However, he never let this injury keep him from exploring America.*

Changing the Environment

When people move to a place, they often make lasting changes there. Geographers observe these changes and study the effects they have on the geography of the land.

How do people interact with their environment? They may clear land for farms and roadways, or dam rivers to establish power plants. They might dig canals or tunnel through mountains to build railroads.

Powell observed the effects the Indians had on the Grand Canyon.

In northern Arizona, the inhabitants [people] have actually built little terraces along the face of the cliff, where a spring gushes out, and thus made their sites for gardens. It is possible that the ancient inhabitants of this place made their agricultural lands in the same way.

In this way the Indians changed the environment of the canyon when they began to farm there. ■

■ *What are some ways in which people interact with the environment?*

R E V I E W

1. **THINKING FOCUS** What types of questions do geographers seek to answer about a place?
2. **CONNECT** Why would geographers be interested in immigration and migration?
3. **GEOGRAPHY** When geographers study a place, what features do they observe?
4. **CRITICAL THINKING** Suppose one town was located on a river that led to the sea. Another town was located in the desert, near a beautiful canyon. Which town might become an important center for trade? Which town might become a place that tourists would visit? Why?
5. **ACTIVITY** Make a two-column chart titled "Places in My State." In one column, name five places created by nature. In the second column, name five places created by people. Give each column a title.

Regions of America

How do geographers define regions within the United States?

Key Terms

- cartographer
- region

➤ *Tom Sawyer and his friends floated across the United States in a hot-air balloon like the one in this engraving.*

One bright, clear, sunny day, Tom Sawyer and his two buddies, Huck Finn and Jim, set off on a grand adventure. They took to the sky in a hot-air balloon. As the trio drifted across the midsection of the United States, Huck began to worry that they weren't making much progress.

We ought to be past Illinois, oughtn't we?"

"Certainly."

"Well, we ain't."

"What's the reason we ain't?"

"I know by the color. We're right over Illinois yet. And you can see for yourself that Indiana ain't in sight."

"I wonder what's the matter with you, Huck. You know by the *color?*"

"Yes, of course I do."

"What's the color got to do with it?"

"It's got everything to do with it. Illinois is green, Indiana is pink. You show me any pink down here, if you can. No sir; it's green."

"Indiana *pink?* Why, what a lie!"

"It ain't no lie; I've seen it on the map, and it's pink."

You never see a person so aggravated and disgusted. He says:

"Well. If I was such a numskull as you, Huck Finn, I would jump over. Seen it on the map! Huck Finn, did you reckon the States was the same color out of doors as they are on the map?"

Mark Twain,
Tom Sawyer Abroad

Defining Regions

Poor Huck Finn! He kept waiting for the ground to turn pink so he would know he was over Indiana. Huck expected the land below his hot-air balloon to look just as it did on the maps he had studied in his school. He didn't realize that **cartographers**—mapmakers—often fill their maps with lines and colors to show different regions, or areas, of the world. A **region** is any area of land or water with certain characteristics that make it different from other areas.

Look at the map on the bottom of this page. This map shows land regions of the United States where different ethnic groups have settled. Notice how different regions are marked by different colors.

Regions Show Differences

To better understand the idea of regions, think of a large stadium where basketball games are held. A stadium contains many different regions, where different activities take place. For example, there is the area where the audience sits, the area where the athletes perform, and areas where merchants sell souvenirs and snacks.

These large regions are divided into smaller regions. Within the area where the audience sits, some of the seats are on the main floor, close to the action. That's one region. Other main floor seats are farther away from the court. That's a second region. Depending on which region you choose to sit in, your ticket may cost you as little as $10 or as much as $35. Each of these differences—the activities in an area, its location, and the price of a ticket—makes one region different from another.

Regions Reveal Patterns

Geographers identify regions in order to make the world easier to study. Identifying regions helps

▼ *As the colors on this map show, different ethnic groups settled in different regions of the United States.*

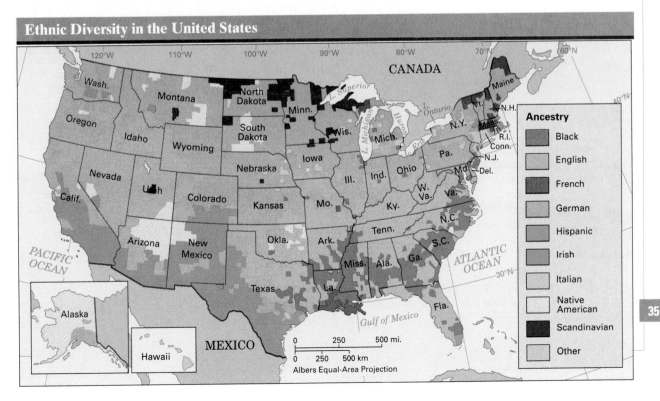

Ethnic Diversity in the United States

Ancestry
- Black
- English
- French
- German
- Hispanic
- Irish
- Italian
- Native American
- Scandinavian
- Other

35

geographers to see patterns in nature as well as patterns in human actions.

For example, geographers can divide the world into regions based on physical features such as annual rainfall or temperature. Some areas of the world always receive more moisture than other areas. Some areas are always much colder or hotter than other areas. A map that shows these regions can help you to understand more clearly the earth's climate. This, in turn, can help you to see why some areas have more people than other areas, or are better suited for growing crops.

Geographers also study regions to learn more about the people who live in those regions. For example, geographers might divide a country into regions based on the languages people speak, the kinds of work they do, or the annual incomes they earn. ■

■ *What are regions, and what do they show?*

Regions of the United States

Geographers can divide the United States into many different kinds of regions depending on what they are interested in studying. Geographers may define regions of the United States according to its types of land, its many climates, or the characteristics of its people.

▼ *The United States can be divided into regions based on its different types of land.*

Land

Look at the map at the bottom of this page. It shows the many land-form regions of the United States. Notice that the eastern and southeastern areas of the United States are made up of coastal plains, plateaus (elevated areas of flat land), and the hilly Appalachians.

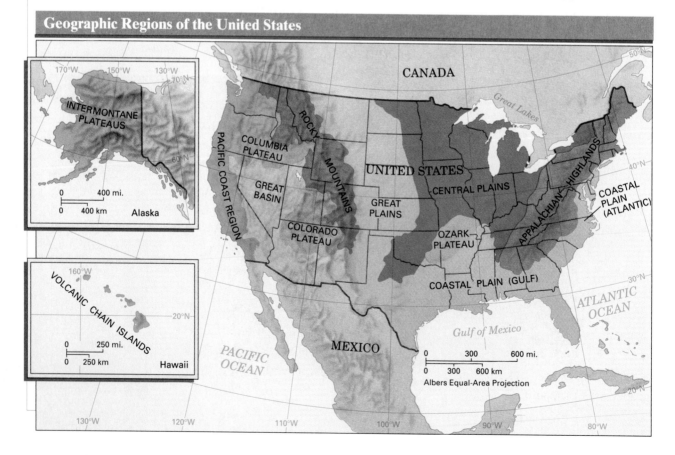

Geographic Regions of the United States

These two photographs—Vermont on the left and Hawaii on the right— were taken at the same time of year. Notice the difference in climate.

In contrast, the center of the country is mostly wide stretches of flat land called plains. This area includes the Central Plains and the Great Plains.

The West is home to several great mountain ranges, including the Rockies, the Cascades, and the Sierra Nevada. Two huge plateaus, the Columbia and the Colorado, surround a vast low-lying area called the Great Basin.

All of these landforms have different physical features. That is why they are considered different regions of the United States. To see how cartographers put together a map showing landform regions of the United States, see A Closer Look on page 38.

Climate

The United States not only includes a variety of landforms but also enjoys many different climates. For much of the year, northern Alaska is locked in ice and snow. In the southern states, the heat and humidity can be almost tropical. Hurricanes sometimes cause destruction on the East and Gulf Coasts. In the west, desert temperatures soar as high as 120° F. Actually, the United States includes every major type of climate that exists on the earth.

Look at the climate map of the United States in the Atlas on page 626. Think about the different ways that climate can affect people's lives. What can you learn about the United States by studying the country's different climate regions?

People

In order to better understand the population of the United States, geographers often divide the country into regions based on the different characteristics of its people. For example, the map on page 35 shows regions of the United States based on where different ethnic groups settled after they came to this country. Compare this map to the map on page 39, which shows how many people 18 years of age and younger live in different parts of the country.

The Layers of a Map

How is a modern map made? Just like a cake—one layer at a time. The picture below shows how the map on page 36 was assembled. Each layer of information was drawn onto see-through pieces of plastic. Then the pieces were put together to form the finished map.

To make sure each line goes exactly where it should, mapmakers use a magnifying lens.

What if a layer was missing? The information on this map would be incomplete. Mapmakers think about each layer, putting in the information that the readers will need.

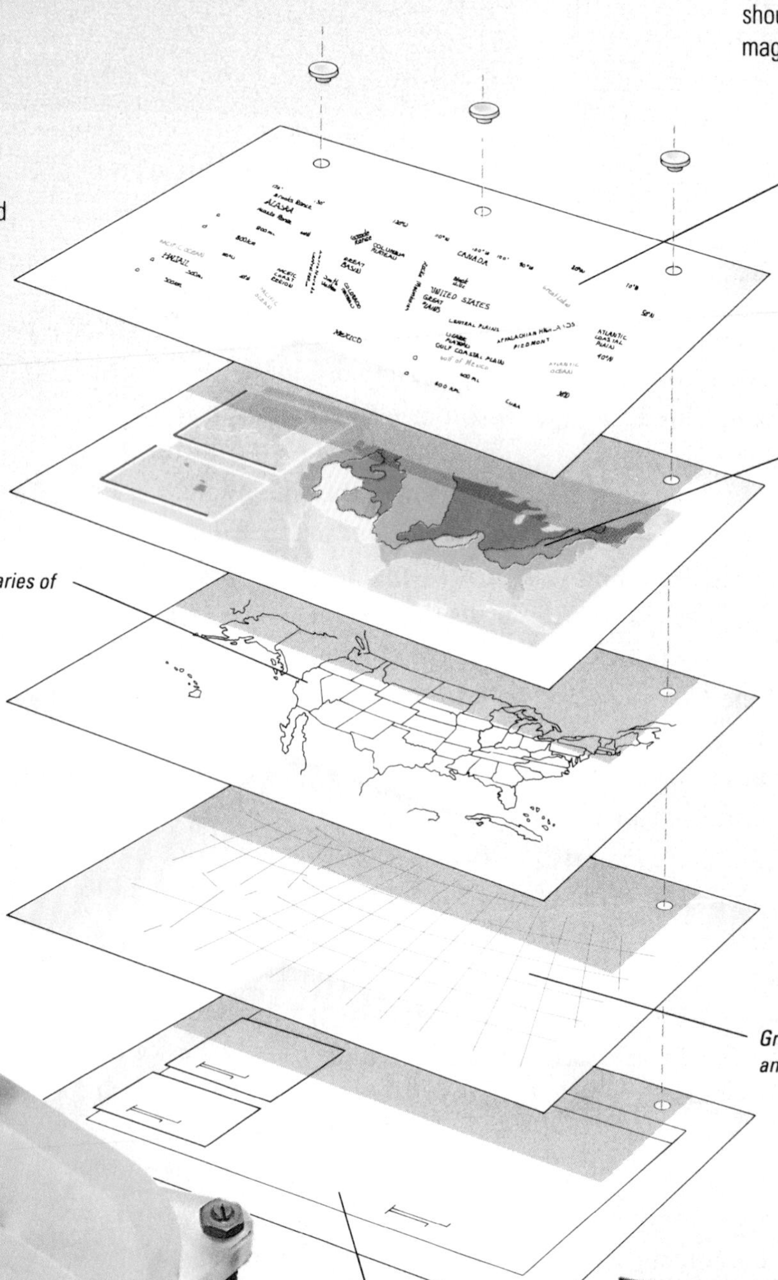

Label layer—words naming places on the map

Subject layer— colors showing special information

Political layer—boundaries of states and countries

What's my line? Longitude and latitude lines, coastlines, and state and country borders—these are just a few of the lines added to a map, layer by layer.

How is it done? With this scribing tool, mapmakers trace pencil lines, scratching them into one of the map's plastic layers.

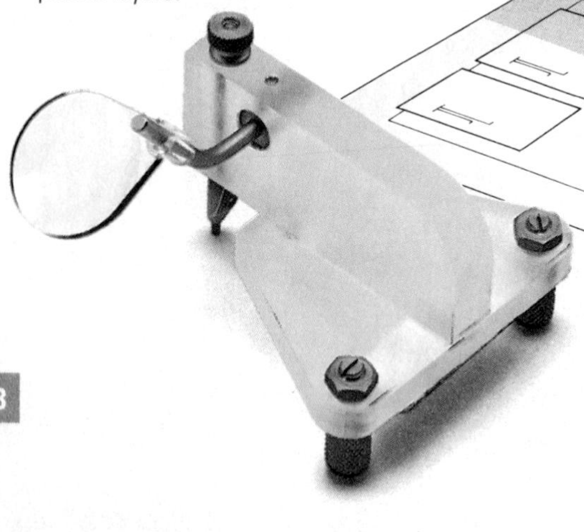

Grid layer—longitude and latitude lines

Outline layer—map boxes and scales

Who might find this information on regions based on age useful? Why?

Language is another characteristic of Americans that geographers identify and study. Nearly all Americans speak at least some English. However, not everyone speaks English the same way. Americans in different parts of the country speak English in different ways. To study these variations, geographers divide the United States into regions based on language. These regions are sometimes called dialect regions.

For instance, if you walked into a restaurant in New York and asked for a "hero," you would get a sandwich on a long roll containing meats, cheeses, and relishes. If you walked into a restaurant in Florida and asked for a "hero," you might get only blank stares. In Florida, such a sandwich is called a Cuban sandwich. In New Jersey, it's called a "hoagie"; in Iowa, a "Dagwood"; in Illinois, a "sub"; and in Rhode Island, a "grinder." In New Orleans, where the sandwich is likely to contain some seafood, it's called a "poor boy," or "po' boy." ■

◄ *Hoagie, grinder, sub, or po' boy? The sandwich remains pretty much the same, but the name changes in different parts of the country.*

■ *Name three types of regions into which the United States can be divided.*

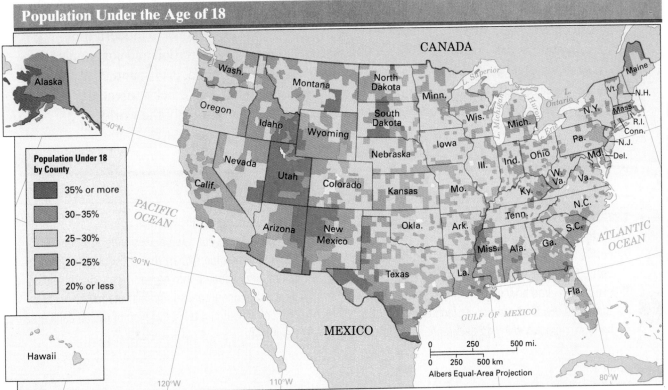

Population Under the Age of 18

CANADA

Alaska

Population Under 18 by County

- 35% or more
- 30–35%
- 25–30%
- 20–25%
- 20% or less

Hawaii

PACIFIC OCEAN

Wash.
Oregon
Montana
Idaho
Wyoming
Nevada
Utah
Calif.
Arizona
New Mexico
Colorado
North Dakota
South Dakota
Nebraska
Kansas
Okla.
Texas
Minn.
Iowa
Mo.
Ark.
La.
Wis.
Ill.
Ind.
Mich.
Ohio
Ky.
Tenn.
Miss.
Ala.
Ga.
Fla.
S.C.
N.C.
W. Va.
Va.
Pa.
N.Y.
Md.
Del.
N.J.
Conn.
R.I.
Mass.
Vt.
N.H.
Maine

L. Superior
L. Michigan
L. Huron
L. Ontario
L. Erie

MEXICO

GULF OF MEXICO

ATLANTIC OCEAN

40°N
30°N
120°W
110°W
80°W

0   250   500 mi.
0   250   500 km
Albers Equal-Area Projection

Based on Historical Atlas of the United States, National Geographic Society, 1988.

UNDERSTANDING INTERDEPENDENCE

*E*ach region of the United States makes its own special contribution to our nation. For example, farming regions produce food and other crops, while industrial regions provide manufactured goods. The people of each region both produce goods themselves and depend on other regions to provide other goods. In this way, the regions of our nation are interdependent.

Global Interdependence

Just as the regions of the United States are interdependent, the nations of the world also depend on one another to supply their needs. No nation can hope to produce all of the goods its people need to survive. Some nations lack important raw materials. Others have poor climates for growing food. And some countries have no industry for manufacturing the consumer goods they need. By trading with one another, the nations of the world have become linked in a network of global interdependence.

Other Connections

In addition to trade, our ability to communicate and move about rapidly also binds together the nations of the world. Communication satellites can beam telephone and television signals instantly to any part of the globe. Similarly, jet travel allows people to reach distant places quickly and easily. Thanks to modern transportation and communication, events and ideas today can quickly affect many parts of the world.

R E V I E W

1. **THINKING FOCUS** How do geographers define regions within the United States?
2. **CONNECT** Explain how the movement of people into a settled region can affect the area.
3. **GEOGRAPHY** Into how many regions can the United States be divided based on its landforms?
4. **CRITICAL THINKING** Why do geographers identify and study different regions within a country?
5. **ACTIVITY** Does your town have different regions? Make a two-column chart that shows how your town might be divided up into regions. One column should be a list of geographical areas of the town. The second column should tell what type of region each area belongs to.

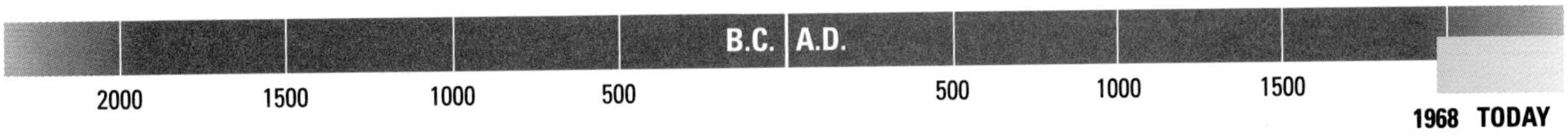

L E S S O N 3

Studying Globes and Maps

On December 21, 1968, three American astronauts rocketed into space bound for the moon. After ten orbits of the lunar surface, the crew fired the service engine of the Apollo spacecraft and headed home. As they approached the earth, astronaut Jim Lovell radioed Mission Control to describe what he saw.

In the center is South America— all the way down to Cape Horn. I can see Baja California and the Southwestern part of the U.S. It appears now that the East Coast is cloudy. I can see clouds over parts of Mexico, and parts of Central America are clear.

For colors, waters are all sort of a royal blue. Clouds, of course, are bright white. The land areas are generally a brownish, sort of dark brownish to light brown in texture.

THINKING FOCUS

How do globes and maps represent the real world?

Key Terms

- hemisphere
- parallel
- meridian
- latitude
- longitude
- projection

◄ *Astronauts returning from the moon snapped the photograph of the planet Earth (upper left), shown here with other planets in our solar system.*

41

This Land of Ours

Finding Location in the World

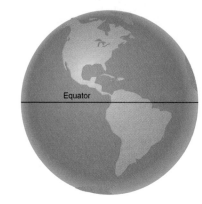

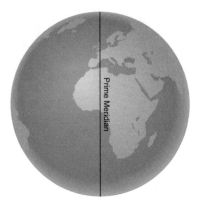

➤ *The equator, shown on the globe at near right, circles the globe. The Prime Meridian, on the globe at the far right, runs from the North Pole to the South Pole.*

Unlike Apollo astronaut Jim Lovell, you can't rocket into space to look at the earth from far away. You can, however, get much the same view that astronauts see by looking at a globe. A globe is a model of the earth that shows all of the earth's landforms and water features. Like the earth, a globe is a sphere that spins on its axis.

Water and Land

When you look at a globe, you can see that two-thirds of the earth's surface is covered with water. Oceans and seas surround large areas of land called continents. Other bodies of water, lakes and rivers, run through the continents.

Most geographers agree that there are seven continents: Africa, Antarctica, Asia, Australia, Europe, North America, and South America. Some geographers, however, prefer to think of Europe and Asia as two parts of one large continent. They call this supercontinent Eurasia. These geographers point out that Europe and Asia are not separated by any body of water. In addition, Europe and Asia are not connected by just a narrow strip of land as are North and South America.

The Poles and the Hemispheres

The earth has two geographic poles. These are the North Pole and the South Pole. Exactly halfway between these two geographic poles lies the equator. The equator is an imaginary line that circles the earth and divides it into two **hemispheres.** The word *hemisphere* comes from two Greek words, *hemi* and *sphaira. Hemi* means "half," and *sphaira* means "ball." Thus, a hemisphere is half of the earth.

The half of the earth that is north of the equator is called the Northern Hemisphere; the half that is south of the equator is called the Southern Hemisphere. Look at the maps of the Northern and

Southern hemispheres at the top of this page. Which two continents are located completely within the Southern Hemisphere?

Just as the equator divides the earth into northern and southern hemispheres, two other imaginary lines divide the earth into the Eastern Hemisphere and the Western Hemisphere. One of these lines, the prime meridian, runs from the North Pole to the South Pole, passing through the city of Greenwich, England. On the other side of the globe, a second imaginary line also runs from the North Pole to the South Pole. This line passes through the Pacific Ocean near New Zealand. This line is called the 180° meridian.

Parallels and Meridians

The lines that divide the earth into hemispheres are part of a series of lines called parallels and meridians. On a globe, these lines cross to form a grid.

It is likely the idea of a grid on the globe began with Chang Heng, a Chinese scientist and inventor who was a royal astronomer during the Han Dynasty in the A.D. 100s. Chang thought of his grid as "throwing a net over the earth."

Parallels circle the globe in an east-west direction. They are used to measure distance north and south of the equator, which is also a parallel of latitude. Like all parallel lines, parallels of latitude never meet.

▲ *The equator, the prime meridian, and the 180° meridian divide the globe into four hemispheres.*

◄ *The globe at the far left shows parallels of latitude. In what ways are they different from the meridians of longitude shown on the globe at the near left?*

Latitude

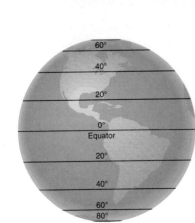

Longitude

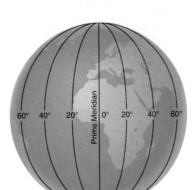

This Land of Ours

Meridians run north and south on a globe from the North Pole to the South Pole. Unlike parallels, which completely circle the globe, meridians go only halfway around it. Parallels never meet. Meridians, however, do meet—at the North and South poles.

Latitude and Longitude

Latitude is the measure of distance north or south of the equator. **Longitude** is the measure of distance east or west of the prime meridian. Geographers measure distances of latitude and longitude by degrees, which are shown by the degree symbol (°).

Latitude is measured starting at the equator, which is latitude 0°. From the equator, degrees of latitude go as far north as the North Pole, which is latitude 90° north, and as far south as the South Pole, which is latitude 90°

south. Each degree of latitude equals about 70 miles.

Distances of longitude are also measured in degrees. The Prime Meridian is longitude 0°. Any place in the world that is east of the prime meridian up to the 180° meridian has east longitude. Any place west of the prime meridian up to the 180° meridian has west longitude. East and West meet at the 180° meridian.

Because the meridians are not parallel, each degree of longitude is equal to about 70 miles only at the equator. As the meridians get closer to the North and South poles, the distance between them gets smaller and smaller, until the meridians finally meet at the poles.

Latitude and longitude are important place locators. When you know the latitude and longitude of a place, you know exactly where that place is located on a globe. ■

■ *Explain the grid system that divides the earth into hemispheres and allows places to be located exactly on a globe.*

▼ *Parallels and meridians form a grid that makes it possible to locate places on a globe precisely.*

Robinson Projection

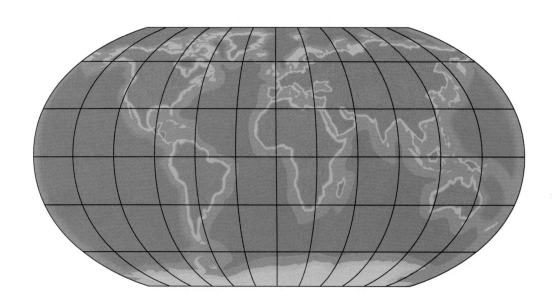

Globes to Maps

Because the earth and a globe are both spheres, a globe can show the shapes and sizes of the continents and oceans just as they are on the earth. Many times, however, a flat map is easier to use than a globe. When cartographers try to draw the curved surfaces of the earth on a flat surface, they make a **projection.**

Unfortunately, no projection can show the curved surface of the earth without changing it in some way. Arthur Robinson is a cartographer at the University of Wisconsin. He explains the problem of creating a projection by asking what would happen if a person drew a human face on an orange and then tried to remove the peel in one piece and flatten it against a table. "You'll see," Robinson says, "that in making a two-dimensional [flat] object out of a round one, something has to give." Either the face will become crooked or the

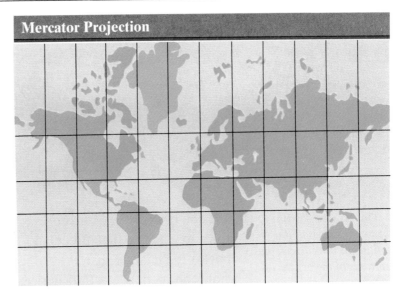

Mercator Projection

peel will break up, dividing the face into several parts.

The Mercator projection above is a good example of this problem. This projection was drawn in 1569 by Gerardus Mercator, a Flemish mathematician. Mercator's projection shows the oceans quite accurately. However, it changes the sizes of large areas of land, especially those areas near the North and South poles.

▲ Compare the size of Greenland on this Mercator projection to the size of Greenland on the Robinson projection on page 44.

Alaska appears to be in the center of the Pacific Ocean.

Europe and northwest Africa have been split. Asia appears much wider than it really is.

Antarctica has broken up into six pieces, one at the bottom of each section. It is difficult to see its real shape.

◄ When a round object like this orange (or a globe) is made into a flat, object like a map, breaks and distortions occur. Compare the way the continents appear here with the way they look on the Robinson projection on page 44.

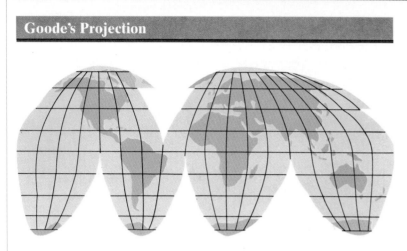

▲ *On this Goode's projection, the sizes of the continents are correct, but portions of the oceans are not shown.*

■ *Why do many projections show a false view of the earth?*

In 1988, the National Geographic Society, *which publishes* National Geographic *magazine, adopted a new world map as its standard. The society had not changed its standard world map since 1922. A panel of experts looked at more than 20 different projections before choosing the Robinson projection.*

Look back at the Mercator projection. Notice that Greenland appears to be larger than the whole continent of South America. In fact, Greenland has an area of 840,000 square miles, just a little bit larger than Mexico's 760,000 square miles. Looking at the Mercator projection, you'd never know that Greenland and Mexico are about the same size.

A projection like the Goode's projection on this page divides the world into sections. This is what Robinson was talking about when he described the orange peel breaking up. This kind of projection can show the sizes and shapes of land fairly accurately. However, some people dislike using a map with parts of the oceans cut away.

To solve these problems, Arthur Robinson made his own projection in 1963. Cartographers think the Robinson projection is a major improvement in mapmaking. It is much more accurate than other projections. ■

The Language of Maps

Every map, whether it shows the world or a plan of a shopping mall, presents a great deal of information. Some maps help you to find your way around an area. Other maps present information about the climate of an area, its population, or its points of interest. Some maps present information about important past events. In order to make full use of this information, you must first understand how to read a map.

Titles and Legends

Look at the map on page 53. What is the title of this map? The title of a map tells you its subject. Some map titles name the geographic area shown on the map. Other titles explain the purpose of the map.

Another important part of a map is the legend. The legend explains the meaning of any special lines, drawings, symbols, or colors on the map. Study the map showing ethnic settlement patterns on page 35. How many items are shown in the legend of this map? Which color does the map use to show areas where people of French origin live? Where Italian people live?

Scale

Suppose you want to know the distance between the cities of San Francisco and Bakersfield, California. You can calculate distance on a map by using a map scale. A map scale helps you to figure out distances on a map as miles or kilometers.

A map scale usually looks a little bit like a ruler. Look at the map scale on the Fault Line Cities map on page 51. The top line of the scale shows how many miles each section of the scale stands for. The bottom line of the scale shows metric measurement.

A simple way to measure distance with a scale requires using a sheet of plain, white paper. First, lay the piece of paper on the map so that the top edge runs through San Luis Obispo and Bakersfield. Then make a pencil mark on your paper at the point where San Luis Obispo is located. Make another pencil mark on the paper at the point where Bakersfield is located.

Now, put the first pencil mark at 0 on the scale, and line up the edge of the paper along the scale. Where on the scale does the second pencil mark fall? That is the distance between the two places.

If the distance you want to measure is longer than the scale itself, you will have to multiply. Move the paper along the scale as many times as you must in order to reach your pencil mark. Then multiply the largest number of miles on the scale by the number of times you moved the paper. The answer is the distance you are looking for.

Direction

When you look at a map of the world, it's fairly easy to see which direction is north, south, east, or west. You just look for the North and South geographic poles. However, on a map that shows a smaller area—just the states of Indiana and Ohio, for example—the geographic poles aren't shown. How can you find direction on a map where the poles cannot be seen?

It's easy, once you find the compass rose, a small drawing that uses one or more arrows to show the four cardinal directions: north, south, east, and west. In addition to the cardinal directions, a compass rose can also help you find intermediate, or in-between, directions: northwest, northeast, southwest, and southeast. ■

▲ This elaborate compass rose appeared on a map from 1600. The design at the top always points north.

■ What are the various devices maps use to present information?

R E V I E W

1. **THINKING FOCUS** How do globes and maps represent the real world?
2. **CONNECT** One way geographers talk about a place is to describe its location. If you wanted to describe the exact location of a place on a globe, what information would you give?
3. **GEOGRAPHY** What are parallels and meridians? How are they different?
4. **CRITICAL THINKING** If a friend told you that his town was exactly 2° due north of your town, how could you figure out the distance from your town to your friend's town?
5. **ACTIVITY** On the world map on pp. 614–615, locate the prime meridian. Then make a two-column chart. Label one column "European Countries" and the other "African Countries." In the proper columns, list the European and African countries that the prime meridian passes through.

This Land of Ours

Locating Cities

Here's Why

If you were an air-traffic controller, you would often use latitude, longitude, and altitude. With these measurements, you could describe the locations of aircraft to avoid midair collisions.

You can also use latitude and longitude to describe locations on the ground. Suppose you want to locate a city based on its latitude and longitude. How do you use that information to find the city on a map?

Here's How

Suppose you want to discover what city is located at 38°N, 98°W. Notice that the latitude markers on this map begin with 45°N. Count down the latitude lines to find 38°N latitude (between the 35° and 40° lines). Place a finger at the right of the map at 38°N latitude.

Now find the longitude 98°W. Begin at the 125° longitude line on the left, and count across by fives until you get to 100°. Longitude 98° falls between 100° and 95°. Place another finger at 98°W longitude at the top of the map. Then slide your fingers down the longitude line and across the curved latitude line to find Hutchinson, Kansas, at the intersection of 38°N and 98°W.

Try It

Look at the map of the United States and name the cities at these locations:
33°N, 85°W   *La Grange*
47°N, 123°W   *Olimpia*
43°N, 79°W   *Buffalo*
37°N, 122°W   *Santa Cruz*
30°N, 90°W   *New Orleans*

Apply It

Choose five U.S. cities from the Gazetteer starting on page 630. Write the latitude and longitude of each city on your paper.

Then work with two or three other students. Take turns naming the latitude and longitude of a city. Locate and name each person's city.

United States: Latitude and Longitude

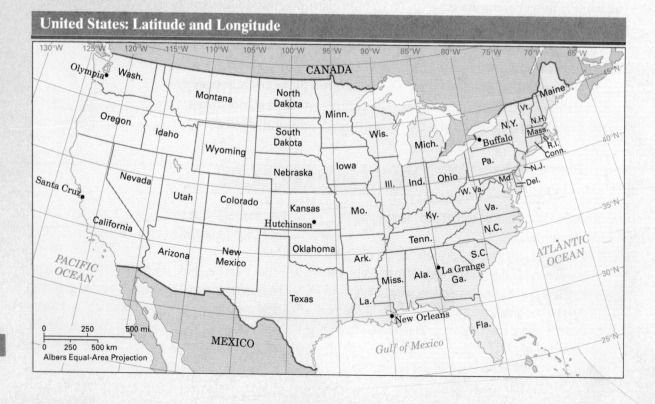

LESSON 4

Stories Maps Tell

On a sunny June afternoon in 1849, a lone eagle wheels silently in the sky above the North Platte River. Along the river's edge, 16 covered wagons roll slowly along a dry, rutted road. Trailing a small herd of dairy cattle and swaybacked pack horses, the wagon train makes its way toward Fort Kearney. It is one of the last military outposts before the Rocky Mountains. This wagon train is following the California Trail to gold country.

Seated in the back of the lead wagon, a young man studies a well-worn map. With a finger he traces the journey of the wagon train from its start in Independence, Missouri, across the Kansas River, and on toward the Continental Divide. As he looks at his map, the young man thinks about the challenges, the dangers, and the hardships ahead.

The train is in Indian country now. Scouting parties have been formed to ride ahead of the wagons and make sure the trail is clear and the people safe from attack. Ahead on the map loom the Rocky Mountains. Crossing them is probably the most difficult and dangerous part of the trip.

Despite the dangers and hardships, the young man cannot help thinking about the wagon train's

THINKING
FOCUS

What types of stories do maps tell?

Key Terms

- physical map
- fault
- historical map

◀ *Gold seekers used maps like this one to find their way to northern California.*

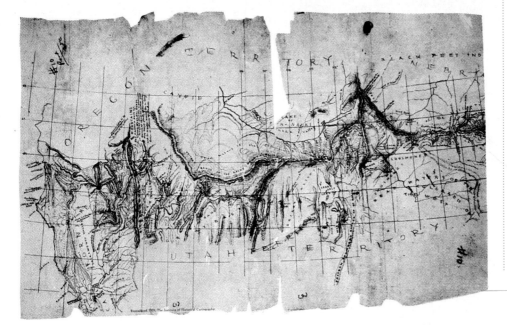

49

final destination—the Sacramento River Valley in northern California. As the wagons lumber on, the young man studies his map and dreams of gold nuggets and incredible riches. For the moment, the danger and hardship of his journey seem far away.

Stories About Places

Like the young gold miner's map of the California Trail, all maps have stories to tell. Maps tell stories about places, people, and history.

The Fall-Line Cities

The map at the top left of page 51 tells a story about the location and growth of some important cities near the East Coast of the United States. These cities include Trenton, New Jersey; Richmond, Virginia; and Augusta, Georgia.

This map is a **physical map**—one that shows land features such as mountains, rivers, and lakes. The cities are located on rivers at points where the rivers have rapids or falls. Why did cities grow up at these points?

The land along the East Coast of the United States is called the Atlantic Coastal Plain. This area is shown on the map on page 36. Where the Atlantic Coastal Plain meets the hard rock of the Piedmont Plateau, rivers and streams flowing toward the Atlantic Ocean form rapids and waterfalls. Geographers call this area the fall line. It stretches from Pennsylvania in the north all the way to Georgia in the south.

Indians paddling their canoes up the rivers along the fall line could not pass the rapids and falls. So they built villages at these points. When Europeans came to settle North America, they too found their ships blocked by the rapids and falls. Like the

These two maps tell different stories about New York City. The map on the left shows how the island of Manhattan and the other neighborhoods of New York are related to each other geographically. What is the title of the map on the right? What story does it tell?

NEW YORK CITY
and Region

Subway Map

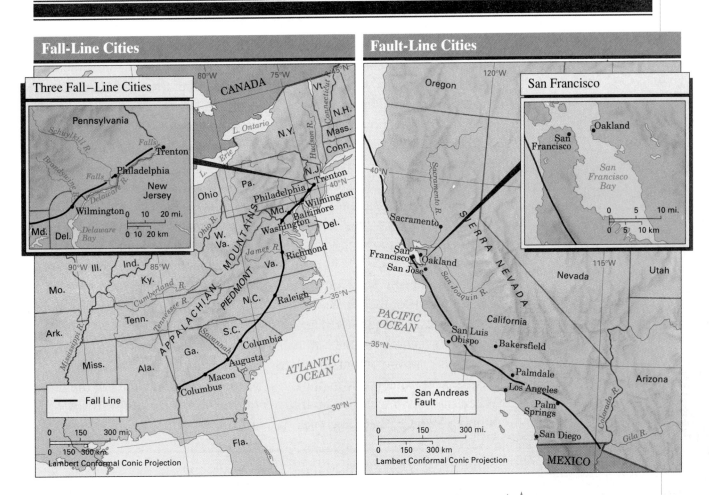

Fall-Line Cities

Three Fall-Line Cities

Fault-Line Cities

San Francisco

Indians before them, the Europeans also built towns at these sites.

The cities along the fall line could be reached easily from the sea, so many became important trading centers. Also, the cities were located near waterfalls, which were used at that time to make the power to run machinery. In this way, many of the cities built by European settlers became important manufacturing centers.

The Fault-Line Cities

The location of a city can have an important effect on its history, as the map at the top right of this page shows.

Just after 5:00 A.M., on April 18, 1906, a terrible earthquake rocked the city of San Francisco.

The quake caused stoves and gas lamps to overturn and gas lines to explode, spreading fires throughout the city that burned for days.

The quake and the fires destroyed more than 28,000 buildings. About 700 persons lost their lives. The 1906 San Francisco earthquake remains one of the worst natural disasters in the history of the United States.

Eighty-three years later, on October 17, 1989, at 5:04 P.M., another major earthquake shook the city of San Francisco. This time, the damage caused by the quake was not as bad as in 1906. Still, many buildings in the city were damaged beyond repair and had to be destroyed. A mile-long section of a double-decker freeway collapsed, as did a section of the Bay

▲ *These maps show the fall-line and fault-line cities. What river runs through the city of Philadelphia? Why are the cities along the fault-line in danger?*

51

This Land of Ours

Bridge connecting San Francisco with Oakland. Again, as in 1906, broken gas lines fed fires that destroyed homes and businesses.

Back in 1906, no one knew that San Francisco had been built directly over a fault. A **fault** is a break, or crack, in the earth's crust. Notice the line on the map that runs along the west coast of California. This line shows the San Andreas Fault.

Faults happen at places where different parts of the earth's crust, called plates, rub together. The map on page 51 shows the San Andreas Fault, where the Pacific plate meets the North American plate. When the pressure caused by the rubbing of these plates becomes

too great, the plates slip past each other slightly, causing the violent movement of the ground called an earthquake. That's what happened in San Francisco.

Earth scientists continually map the San Andreas Fault and measure the pressure building up along its edges. They predict that another major earthquake—even bigger than the one in 1989—will take place there in the near future.

Over the past 15 million years, land west of the fault has moved about 190 miles northwest. This movement has occurred in brief, violent shocks such as the 1906 earthquake, when land on the fault line moved horizontally 21 feet northwest. ■

■ *How can the location of a place affect what happens there?*

▲ *These Anasazi Indian ruins are over 800 years old. Important Indian cultures like the Anasazi flourished here long before Europeans came.*

Stories About the Past

Maps can also tell us something about the past. Each of the four maps shown on page 53 is an **historical map**—a map that gives information about an earlier time in history. These four maps tell a story about Indian lands lost between 1775 and today.

When the earliest European explorers reached North America, they found a land with an estimated one to two million native people who spoke some 300 languages. As more Europeans began settling the continent, they took over lands that had belonged to the Indian tribes for centuries.

Sometimes the settlers bought this land, as in 1626 when Peter Minuit purchased the island of Manhattan from a group of Algonquin Indians. At other times, the

Indians gave their land to settlers by signing treaties that promised the Indians other lands in return. Often, however, the Indians lost their land in bloody battles with settlers who thought the land was theirs for the taking.

The first map on page 53 shows the United States in 1775. Indians held nearly all of the land in North America. The only exceptions were the areas along the East Coast where the original 13 colonies had been established and some land along the Gulf of Mexico. By 1810, however, much of the Midwest and the South was held by the government or the settlers and their descendants.

The second map shows more Indian land disappearing, especially along the West Coast. This took

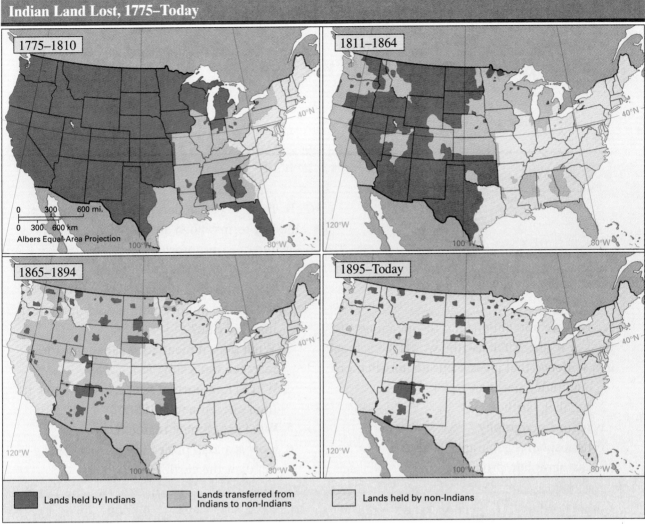

Indian Land Lost, 1775–Today

1775–1810

1811–1864

1865–1894

1895–Today

0   300   600 mi.
0   300   600 km
Albers Equal-Area Projection

Lands held by Indians

Lands transferred from
Indians to non-Indians

Lands held by non-Indians

Based on Historical Atlas of the United States, *National Geographic Society, 1988.*

place because of the California gold rush of the 1850s and the opening of the Oregon Territory. During this time, the U.S. government signed many treaties with the Indian tribes on the West Coast. The government promised the Indians new territory in exchange for their land on the coast, which was thought to hold valuable gold deposits. The promises were not kept, and the Indians were left with only small areas of land.

The third map shows that the Indians had lost most of their land by the beginning of the 1890s. And today, as the fourth map shows, nearly all of the land that makes up the United States is non-Indian land. In just over 200 years, North America's native peoples have become almost completely landless. ■

▲ *American Indians once claimed nearly the entire continent as their home. Today, Indians in the U.S. own very little land.*

■ *During which historical period was the least amount of Indian land lost?*

R E V I E W

1. **THINKING FOCUS** What types of stories can maps tell?
2. **CONNECT** What historical regions of the United States are shown on the four maps on this page?
3. **GEOGRAPHY** What is the difference between a physical map and an historical map?
4. **CRITICAL THINKING** Explain how the location of a city can influence its growth and its historical importance.
5. **WRITING ACTIVITY** Imagine you are a television news reporter. Your assignment is to deliver a three-minute broadcast about the cities in California that have a high risk of experiencing an earthquake. Write your broadcast, using the map on page 51 as a visual aid.

53

Chapter Review

Reviewing Key Terms

cartographer (p. 35) longitude (p. 44)
fault (p. 52) meridian (p. 44)
geography (p. 31) parallel (p. 43)
hemisphere (p. 42) physical map (p. 50)
historical map (p. 52) projection (p. 45)
latitude (p. 44) region (p. 35)

A. Be sure you understand the meanings of the key terms. Then use the words in each pair in a sentence that gives accurate information.
1. longitude, meridian
2. parallel, latitude
3. region, geography
4. hemisphere, geography
5. cartographer, projection

B. Be sure you understand the meanings of the key terms. Then answer each question by writing one or more sentences.
1. In what two ways are parallels and meridians different?
2. What kind of information does a physical map provide?
3. What does it mean to say that a historical map can tell a story?
4. Why is it important for people to know if their city is on a fault line?
5. What are climate regions?
6. How is a map projection like "throwing a net over the earth"?

Exploring Concepts

A. On your own paper, copy this map and compass rose. You may sketch or trace the outline of a map of the United States from the chapter or from the Atlas map on pages 620–621. Then use information from the chapter to complete the map by following the instructions in the next column.

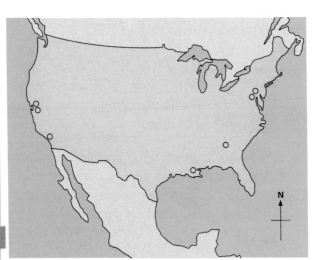

1. Color a region where little rain falls.
2. Draw and label the lines of longitude and latitude that pass through New Orleans.
3. Label the compass rose.
4. Draw and label two mountain ranges.
5. Label three fall-line cities and three fault-line cities.

B. Support each statement with facts and details from the chapter.
1. Geographical features result from natural forces.
2. Geographers study movement.
3. Regions reveal patterns.
4. The North American continent includes a wide variety of landforms.
5. Maps have many helpful features.
6. Globes and maps represent many characteristics of the real world.
7. The Mercator projection distorts the sizes of certain land masses.

Reviewing Skills

1. What does 40°N, 110°W mean? What city on the map of Utah is located near there?
2. Use the map of Utah to identify the city at each of the following locations:
   38°N, 112°W
   39°N, 110°W
   41°N, 112°W
   40°N, 112°W
3. In which cardinal direction would you go to get from 45°N, 100°W to 45°N, 110°W?
4. Use an encyclopedia to find information on the Grand Canyon National Park. What special things could you do there?
5. If you wanted to describe the exact location of Santa Fe, New Mexico, on a map, what would be the best information to give?

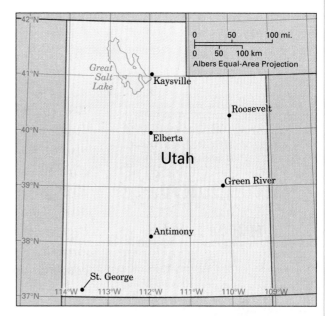

Using Critical Thinking

1. Look at the two maps on page 608 in the Minipedia. The regions on one map show different culture areas. The regions on the other show how people got food. Looking at these maps, describe how the boundaries of the regions in the two maps are similar. Then summarize the relationships you find. For example, "Most Eastern Woodlands people got food through a combination of hunting, gathering, and farming."

2. Geographers study the movements of many things, including people. Recently in the United States there has been a gradual movement of population from the Northeast to the Southwest. One result is that Los Angeles, California, has overtaken Chicago, Illinois, as the nation's second-largest city. List five questions a geographer might ask to find out causes of this type of movement.

Preparing for Citizenship

1. **ARTS ACTIVITY** Learn about the history of map-making, or cartography. Use an encyclopedia or ask a librarian for help. Look at the maps on pages 103, 105, and 127 to find out what maps from long ago look like. Notice the rich detail in their lettering and decoration. Based on your research, make a map in the style of ancient maps. You may make a map of a zoo or park, your town, or any geographical area you choose.

2. **COLLABORATIVE LEARNING** Some wild animals—including mammals, birds, fish, reptiles, and amphibians—live only in certain regions of the United States. In groups, list some of these animals. Discuss with your group how you could divide a map into wildlife regions. Name and sketch one wildlife region. Make a large class map showing all the wildlife regions the groups have found. On the map, make colorful pictures of an animal for each region.

Chapter 3
Clues to Our Past

American history is found not only in textbooks. It can be found in museums or in diaries. It may also be found in a box of photographs in your attic, or in the stories your grandparents tell. Even games and toys can help you understand how people felt and lived long ago. Almost everywhere you look you can find clues to America's past. Understanding America's past can help you understand America today.

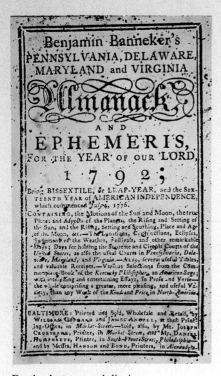

Books, letters, and diaries tell us how people in the past lived. Thousands of Americans bought this popular almanac in 1792 for its entertaining writing and scientific information.

This toy carving from the late 1700s shows how important George Washington was to Americans at that time.

2000 B.C.

Photographs give us clues about the past. This picture, taken in Oregon in 1912, tells what students wore, what their schoolrooms were like, and even what they studied.

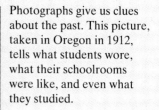

Some objects used in daily life help us understand people from different cultures. This colorful beaded saddle pouch was used by a Yakima woman while riding horseback.

The coins that colonists used in the 1600s show their close ties to England.

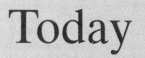

Today

What Is History?

THINKING
FOCUS

How do people learn about the events of the past?

Snow covers King Street in Boston on the morning of March 6, 1770. As you walk down the street, you notice hundreds of footprints in the dirty snow. You see a spot of red in the middle of the road. You see bullet holes in the wall of a shop across the street. You hear the excited voices of people rushing up and

down the frozen street. From their words you discover that a large crowd of people from the town fought British soldiers in King Street late last night. Several of the townspeople are dead.

Everything you have seen and heard tells you that something happened on King Street. What really happened?

Key Terms

- evidence
- history
- historian
- interpret
- chronology

➤ *John Adams's search for evidence of the Boston Massacre might have led him to these musket balls.*

Knowing What Happened

John Adams, a young Boston lawyer, asked that same question. Adams defended the British soldiers in the trials that followed the shootings of March 5, 1770. This event is known as "the Boston Massacre."

John Adams first looked for **evidence,** or proof, of what happened that night. Next, he talked to people who saw the shooting. Surely their stories would tell Adams what happened.

During the trial, however, Adams discovered that no two witnesses to the shooting told the same story. A man named Calef said that he heard the British officer tell the soldiers to fire. "I looked the officer in the face when

he gave the word and saw his mouth," Calef said.

A man named Hickling had said earlier that the officer could not have given the order to fire. "I was within a yard of him and must have heard him had he spoken it."

Even with these conflicting stories Adams was able to prove that the soldiers had not murdered the people in King Street. Adams also explained why no one had agreed on what happened. Passion and imagination, he said, "may account for variations in the testimony of honest men." He meant that many people could see the same thing, yet each could remember it differently.

The trial taught John Adams an important lesson: no one would ever know all of what happened in King Street that night. That lesson is true of all events in the past. We learn about the past through evidence and stories. Sometimes we find little evidence; sometimes we find a mountain of it. But no matter what evidence or stories exist, we can never know everything that happened. ■

■ Why isn't it possible to know everything about a past event?

Studying the Past

We cannot hope to know everything about the past. But it is important to study what we do know about the past. The study of things done and said in the past is called **history.** A person who studies the past is called a **historian.** The first thing a historian must do is look closely at the evidence of the past.

Interpretation

Historians **interpret** evidence. This means that they decide if it is important and how it should be understood. Historians ask: Will this evidence help me understand the past? Where did the evidence come from?

Knowing where evidence came from helps historians understand it. For example, look at the stories told during the trial after the Boston Massacre. If historians learn that the man named Calef hated the British soldiers in Boston, that changes their understanding of his story. Calef probably wanted to make the British soldiers look as guilty as possible.

If historians learn that the man named Hickling was the brother of a British soldier in Boston, that changes their understanding of his

▼ *Several victims of the Boston Massacre are buried in the Granary Burial Ground, shown here. A death certificate for one of them (left) is important evidence for historians.*

Clues to Our Past

➤ *Paul Revere's engraving of the massacre tells the story many Bostonians wanted to hear. People who hated the soldiers eagerly purchased this picture of the British as villains.*

story. Hickling would want to make the soldiers on King Street that night look innocent.

Knowing why somebody said or did something is important. This can be shown by looking at the color print to the right and the drawing on page 61. Both show the shooting on King Street. Both were made by Paul Revere. Yet each shows a very different version of what happened that night. As the captions explain, Paul Revere made the two pictures for different reasons. Therefore, they mean different things.

UNDERSTANDING HISTORICAL PERSPECTIVE

In 1770, the Boston Massacre was an important event. Ten years later in 1780, few Americans remembered it so clearly. Then, it was seen as just one in a series of events leading up to the American Revolution.

The Boston Massacre was seen one way by people living in 1770. It was seen in another way in 1780. These changes in the way that people see the events of the past are called changes in historical perspective.

Meanings Change

Changes in historical perspective do not change facts. The fact that five people died in the Boston Massacre does not change over time. But the meaning and importance of those facts *does* change.

You probably see the world differently than your grandparents do. In the same way, today's historians understand the past differently than the historians of 50 years ago. Today, they see new things in the past and ask new questions.

Times Change

Fifty years ago, historians studying the American West wrote about cowboys, Indians, even buffalo, but not about women. As the role of women in our society has grown, the story of women in the West has been told. This knowledge has changed our understanding of how the West was settled. Our perspective on history has changed.

So, the meaning of events may change as time passes and as we ask new questions about the past. It is important to remember that when studying the Boston Massacre—or any event of the past.

Chronology

Another way historians learn about the past is to find the order in which events happen. This is called **chronology.** Timelines show chronology and how one event leads to another. The timeline below shows fights between colonists and British soldiers and their supporters, called Tories. Here, chronology helps us to understand what happened.

Understanding History

Figuring out the order of events and interpreting evidence are basic skills used by all historians to understand the past. Those tools are also helpful to students who study history. Historians think carefully about where evidence comes from. Students should think carefully about how history is written. A student of history should know how historians do their job. ■

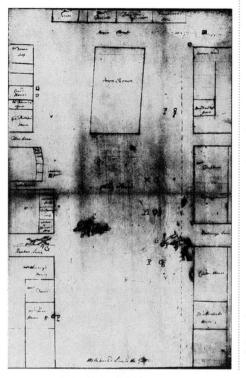

■ *Why is interpretation important to historians?*

◄ *Paul Revere drew this diagram of the shooting in King Street for the trial of the British soldiers. Here Revere tried to show where the victims of the shooting fell. He also shows the soldiers gathering on a corner on the right side of the street.*

▼ *This timeline shows the events leading up to the Boston Massacre. Here we can see the tensions between Bostonians and the British increasing from month to month.*

Unrest in Boston, 1765–1770

October 1769, About 20 colonists attack two Tories, wounding one.

October 1768, British troops arrive in Boston

March 1770, British soldiers clash with a crowd of angry colonists in King Street. The soldiers fire, killing five people and wounding six others.

| 1769 | 1770 | 1771 |

September 1769, Several colonists and soldiers start a fight in the British Coffee House.

February 1770, Over 100 colonists attack Tory businesses. In the riot, a Tory shoots and kills an 11-year-old boy.

R E V I E W

1. **FOCUS** How do people learn about the events of the past?
2. **CONNECT** Paul Revere's sketch of the Boston Massacre is really a kind of map of King Street. What does this "map" tell you about the shooting that Revere's engraving does not? What does the engraving tell you that the "map" does not?
3. **HISTORY** What is the past? What is history? How is history different from the past?
4. **CRITICAL THINKING** Look at the timeline above. How does this timeline help historians understand the Boston Massacre?
5. **WRITING ACTIVITY** Write an account of two things that happened in your classroom today. Then compare your account with those of three classmates. How and why do your stories differ?

Clues to Our Past

Comparing Art and Photos

Here's Why

It is impossible to know every detail about events from the past. Each type of historical evidence has its limitations. Each has its own advantages. Every piece of evidence is limited by the viewpoint of the person who made it. Books, newspapers, letters, and journals can reveal only what the writers of these documents know. Drawings and photographs can also reveal only the viewpoints of their creators.

You can more easily "read" the information in a drawing or in a photograph if you know how the two differ. When can you rely on a drawing or a painting? When can you rely on a photo?

Here's How

Look at the two pictures at the right. At the top is a photograph of a Pony Express rider. At the bottom is a painting of one of the first Pony Express riders around 1860. Only the painting shows the horse in motion. This is because in 1861, when the photograph was taken, cameras could not operate as fast as they can today.

Compare the two pictures. How are the two riders different? How do the horses differ? What details are different? What does each picture tell you about a Pony Express rider's life?

Try It

Look at the painting of slaves working in the field on page 442. Compare it with the photo of slaves on page 408. Use questions like those from Here's How. Write a paragraph describing what you discover.

Apply It

Study a photo. List its purpose, details that may be missing, and what was going on at the time. How would you draw the same scene? What could you express in your drawing that might be missing from the photo?

LESSON 2

What Does a Historian Do?

Samuel Argall, deputy governor of the English colony of Virginia, issued an order in 1618. He required "every man to set [plant] two acres of corn." Argall then said that anyone in the colony who did not obey the order would be made a slave.

At first glance, this order does not seem very important. It is just one of hundreds of orders issued by the deputy governor of Virginia in the 1600s. It has not been a law for more than 300 years. Most of us would not see anything meaningful or interesting in Argall's order.

But a historian studying life in colonial Virginia cannot ignore that order. To the historian, that law is a mystery waiting to be solved. Argall's order forces the historian to ask one question after

THINKING
FOCUS

How do historians study the past?

Key Terms

- primary source
- archives
- oral history
- artifact

◄ *These coins and engravings of corn and tobacco are examples of primary sources. Objects like these help historians solve the mysteries of the past.*

another: Why did the deputy governor have to order people to grow corn? Were the colonists unwilling or unable to grow corn? What was going on in the colony of Virginia in 1618?

A Trail of Questions

Historians make sense of the past by asking questions like these. The answers are often found in the records of the people who took part in past events. These records are called **primary sources.**

Many primary sources from colonial Virginia have been lost over the last 350 years. But some sources have survived. They can be found in books or in collections of records called **archives.**

A Little Corn

A historian named Edmund Morgan found enough sources to begin to make sense of Argall's order. Some sources make the order even more mysterious. Morgan read one pamphlet that said:

> *O*ne man in 48 hours may prepare as much ground and set [plant] such a quantity of corn that he may be secure for want of bread all the year following.

After reading this the historian asks: "If corn was so easy to grow, why did the deputy governor have to threaten the colonists with slavery to make them grow it?"

The answer turns up in the records of the Virginia Company of London. This company organized and paid for the settling of Virginia. Their records show that in May 1611, nothing had been planted in Virginia except for a "few seeds put into a private garden or two."

John Smith, one of the leaders of the colony, said that Argall bought 1,000 bushels of corn from the Indians. This "did greatly relieve the whole colony."

It is clear that corn was easy to grow and that it was needed to feed the colony. Yet, for some reason the colonists did not grow corn. That helps

▼ *Captain John Smith wrote about his experiences in* The Generall Historie of Virginia. *It is one of the most important sources about life in the colony.*

explain Argall's order. But if the colonists didn't plant corn, what did they do?

A Lot of Tobacco

A clue to this mystery is found in Argall's description of Jamestown, Virginia, in 1617. He said that he found "the market-place, and streets, and all other spare places planted with tobacco." Why did the colonists grow tobacco when they wouldn't raise enough corn to feed themselves?

Most people came to Virginia hoping to get rich. After they made their fortunes, they hoped to return to England. The records of the Virginia Company show that a tobacco farmer could become rich with one year's harvest.

Between 1619 and 1622, nearly 4,000 people moved from England to Virginia. Most settlers died without finding wealth in the new colony. The records of the Virginia Company show that by 1622, the colony had "lost 3,000 persons in three years." Virginia had a death rate of nearly 80 per cent.

Death was a risk for colonists everywhere in the New World. In

Raising tobacco was one of the few ways to make money in the Virginia colony. It was sold in Europe with labels like this one showing an African slave and an Indian.

the Plymouth colony of New England, almost half of the people died in the first difficult years. But 15 years after the beginning of the Virginia colony, eight out of every ten people died.

The historian looks at these facts and sources and sees a new picture of life in colonial Virginia. Virginians chose to grow tobacco rather than corn. This made the colony a deadly place for most of the people who came there. A few Virginians got rich. Most of them died. No order could change that. ■

How Do We Know?

HISTORY *In the 1930s, writers interviewed black Americans who had been slaves just before the Civil War. The stories they told had never been written down before. Today, those oral histories are some of the most important sources about slavery in the United States.*

■ *Why are primary sources important to historians?*

Other Sources, Other Questions

Official documents—laws, business records, a governor's order—tell us about the public side of history. But in order to get the whole story of the past, historians must look at these and many other sources. Study A Closer Look at Primary Sources on pages 66–67 to learn more about these sources.

Oral history is a source of history that official documents often miss or ignore. Oral history is not based on what a person has written. Instead it is based on what a person says during an interview. Oral histories preserve the experiences of people who can't write them down, such as slaves, servants, or the uneducated.

Clues to Our Past

Primary Sources

Documents, journals, photos, and objects are all primary sources of historical information. They give historians a firsthand look at the past. You may want to throw away old letters, magazines, or buttons. But, in 100 years, they could become a historian's valued primary sources.

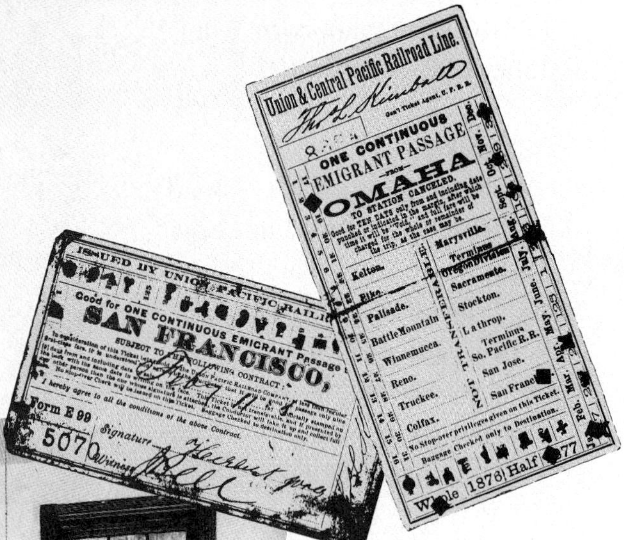

Two tickets to information is how historians would view these. Some of the towns listed here grew and faded with the railroads. How many names on the tickets do you recognize?

What do you see in this picture? Historians may look at this 1903 photo from the Tuskegee Institute in Alabama and see an equal number of men and women students. Historians might also look at the people's clothing and hair styles, or even the kind of laboratory equipment they used.

Curiosity is what this cat gives historians. Sometimes artifacts create new questions. This wooden statue of a panther was found in Florida in 1884. Archaeologists believe the carving was made by American Indians, but they're not yet sure when or why.

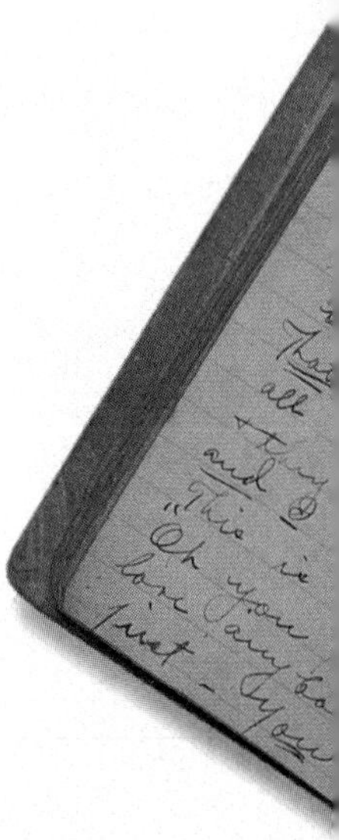

In the days before television, campaign buttons helped to tell people about a political candidate's positions. In 1896, Republicans were called "goldbugs" because they believed that the value of the U.S. dollar should be based on the value of gold.

Though his face has been worn by the play of time, this drummer was once someone's favorite toy. A historian specializing in toys could tell the soldier was made before 1850 by noting how the crank moves the soldier's arms.

What did little girls do in 1896? According to this girl's journal, they got their clothes dirty and spied on their big sisters. Journals are useful because they tell how people thought and felt about everyday matters.

> *Even the maps people drew can tell us about the past. This map was made by a man named Hondius in the 1600s. What does this map tell you about Virginia?*

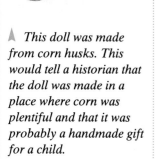

⬆ *This doll was made from corn husks. This would tell a historian that the doll was made in a place where corn was plentiful and that it was probably a handmade gift for a child.*

■ *How do literature and artifacts help historians understand the past?*

Poems, stories, myths, and novels can also tell us things about the past.

*V irginia,
Earth's only paradise,
Where nature hath in store
Fowl, venison, and fish,
And fruitfullest soil.*

This is part of a poem written by an Englishman, Michael Drayton, in 1606. He wrote it without having seen Virginia. We know that Virginia was no paradise. But Drayton's poem tells us what he expected would be there and why he might have wanted to go.

Historians can also gain information about the past by looking at the things people made. These are called **artifacts.** Paintings, tools, clothing, and furniture tell us about the people who made and used them. For example, historians have found very few chairs from Virginia in the early 1600s. In the harsh conditions of the colony, people considered chairs a luxury. They sat on backless stools or benches.

Artifacts, oral histories, poems, and documents all contain clues about the past. Like detectives, historians look for clues. Then they interpret the evidence to "solve" or make sense of the past. ■

R E V I E W

1. **FOCUS** How do historians study the past?
2. **CONNECT** Define primary source. Give two examples of primary sources used in the first lesson of this chapter.
3. **HISTORY** Why is oral history an important source of information for a historian studying slavery during the 1800s?
4. **CRITICAL THINKING** Interpret the map at the top of this page as an artifact. What do the decorations and drawings on this map tell you?
5. **WRITING ACTIVITY** Each chapter of this book has literature and primary source excerpts. Choose one and read it. Write out two questions that come to your mind after reading the source.

Chapter 3

Interpreting Information

Here's Why

Studying artifacts can help us experience history by understanding the lives of people in the past. When you visit a museum or an old building that has been restored, you often see artifacts—clothes, tools, and other objects that were used in the past. Looking at tools used during the colonial period, for example, could help you to understand more about what life was like for the people who lived in the colonies.

Here's How

Look at the objects on this page. They are used in similar ways but come from different times in history.

When you examine artifacts, ask yourself these questions:
1. What is the object used for?
2. What is the object made from?
3. How was it made?
4. What parts does it have?
5. What does it tell you about the people who used it?

The top picture shows a butter churn from the early 1900s. Churns were used to make butter from cream. This churn was made of wood, metal, and glass. The style of the churn and the cast iron parts tell you it was probably made by machine.

How did the churn work? The cream was poured into the glass container. As the wooden paddle was turned, the butter slowly thickened and had to be removed.

The way this churn works suggests an important thing about the people who used it. Making butter was a hard job that took one person a long time. Butter must have been valuable enough to people for them to spend the time needed to make it. They had to give up many hours to make a product you can quickly buy today at the grocery.

Try It

Study the picture of the food processor. Ask yourself the questions listed in Here's How.

Apply It

Borrow an object from the past such as a piece of clothing or jewelry, a tool or a piece of sports equipment. Interview the person who provides your object and find out its use and historical background. Bring the object to school and show it to your class. Have your classmates take turns trying to explain what the object is and how it was used. Then share the information you learned about the object from its owner.

Butter Churn

Food Processor

69

Clues to Our Past

L E S S O N   3

Why Study History?

How does studying history help you understand the people and events of today's world?

Key Terms

- journal
- empathy

➤ *In this painting by Karl Bodmer, Prince Maximilian meets Minnetaree chiefs at Fort Clark.*

In April 1833, the German Prince Maximilian of Wied *(veed)* set out to study the Plains Indians in the western United States. The prince left St. Louis and sailed up the Missouri River. On the boat with Maximilian were his two trained pet bears, a music box, and a thermometer to record every day's temperature in his **journal,** or daily record of his travels.

The prince also brought two helpers along with him. One of those helpers was a Swiss artist named Karl Bodmer. Bodmer's job was to draw and paint all of the sights and people that the prince wrote about. During the trip Bodmer painted wonderful landscapes, huge herds of buffalo, and Indians.

Bodmer painted many pictures of Indians. The Indians had no word for "draw." But a translator told Maximilian that the Indians thought that Bodmer could "write very correctly."

Understanding Other People

Bodmer's paintings and Maximilian's journal record the lives and habits of the Plains Indians. The explorers hoped to understand the actions, customs, and feelings of the Indians. This understanding is called **empathy.**

Different Yet Similar

It is sometimes hard to feel empathy with the people we read about in Maximilian's journal. The Plains Indians lived in a different time and place. How can we begin to understand them?

The skills of the historian can be helpful when trying to understand people from other times and other places. Looking closely at stories or pictures helps us feel empathy with others.

Look at Karl Bodmer's painting of a young Blackfoot girl on this page. At first this girl may seem somewhat different from you or your classmates. But look more closely. The expression on her face is one you might see on any of your friends' faces. Her clothes and jewelry look like clothing and jewelry worn today. Perhaps she already seems more familiar.

Other parts of the lives of the Plains Indians also seem very familiar. Maximilian wrote that one hot, summer afternoon "the Indians bathed in the river in great numbers, including women, girls, and children." They swam to a boat and jumped from it into the river, said Maximilian. "The noise from all this was very great."

Past and Present

People living in other times and places had fun the same way you do. History was made by people who felt the same things you feel.

◄ Karl Bodmer painted this Blackfoot girl in 1833. Bodmer's detailed drawings provide historians with important information about the Plains Indians.

Across Time & Space

Through old letters, interviews with family members, and other research, people today can discover their family's history. They can learn who their ancestors were, where they came from, when and why they came to the United States. This can help people understand their place in history, their families, and themselves.

▼ This leather ball and shirt were made by the Plains Indians of the 1800s. How are they like items found in your home? How are they different?

■ *How does history help you to feel empathy for other people?*

Every person you read about in this book was once the same age that you are. Many of them went to school. They all laughed, cried, slept, and ate. If you read their stories, you can begin to see why they acted as they did. In this way, understanding the past is a way of understanding yourself and the people around you. That is the first step towards understanding your world. ■

Understanding Your World

In 1781, Thomas Jefferson wrote that studying history made people good "judges of the actions and designs [plans] of men." Two hundred years later, events still need to be examined and understood. Studying the Plains Indians may help us understand the people around us. In the same way, studying yesterday's world may help us understand the world today. The skills of the historian can help us to do that.

The Skills of History

Let's look at an event that occurred not long ago. In the summer of 1988, a series of fires burned large parts of Yellowstone National Park. Thousands of primary sources on these fires exist. In September 1988, for example, *Newsweek* magazine reported:

> *Since the beginning of the summer, the worst fires in several centuries have ravaged more than 400,000 acres of Yellowstone National Park land.*

The Wall Street Journal described "flaming destruction" and "a fire-blackened ruin." *The Chicago Tribune* said that "damage to a treasured national park has been devastating." According to the *Los Angeles Times*, people complained that the park had "let the situation

▼ *The Yellowstone fires of 1988 were so large that crews of firefighters (center) could not put them out. A year later, plant life returned to burned areas of the park (right).*

get out of hand."
These people said that
the park was wrong to follow its "policy to let natural
fires burn their course."

In the autumn of 1988, the National Park Service issued a statement. Yellowstone would be "a
more interesting and educational
national park" after the fires,
according to the statement.

A newsletter called the *Greater
Yellowstone Report* said that the
fires were smaller "than reported."
Dr. Linda Wallace, a scientist,
agreed that the fires were not "a
national tragedy as some would
believe." She wrote that the fires
were part of a "natural process of
renewal."

The Uses of History

These are just a few of the
sources a future historian will use
to study the fires in Yellowstone

National Park during the
summer of 1988. That historian
will ask many questions: What
happened? Why did it happen?
What does this evidence say about
the event? Did the fires ruin Yellowstone? Or did the fires make
the park better?

Professional historians will be
asking those questions 50 or 100
years from now. You can start asking questions right now.

Just as historians will never
learn everything about the past,
you will never learn everything
about the Yellowstone fires—or
any event in the past or present.
You can, however, learn enough to
understand some of the events and
people of your world. Studying history will give you some of the skills
you need to do this. ■

*Newspapers, maga-
zines, and even T-shirts
expressed opinions about
the Yellowstone fires.*

■ *How are the skills of
the historian useful in
making sense of current
events?*

R E V I E W

1. **FOCUS** How does studying history help you to understand the people and events of today's world?
2. **CONNECT** How do the skills of the historian help you
   to feel empathy with the Plains Indians?
3. **HISTORY** Why are Bodmer's paintings and Maximilian's journals helpful to a historian studying the
   Plains Indians?
4. **CRITICAL THINKING** Several sources about the Yellowstone National Park fires are printed in this lesson.
   Which sources present the facts of the event most
   clearly? Which convey an opinion?
5. **ACTIVITY** Prepare a one-minute speech answering the
   question: "Why Study History?" Use examples from
   this lesson and the rest of the chapter.

Chapter Review

Reviewing Key Terms

archives (p. 64)
artifact (p. 68)
chronology (p. 61)
empathy (p. 71)
evidence (p. 58)
history (p. 59)

historian (p. 59)
interpret (p. 59)
journal (p. 70)
oral history (p. 65)
primary source (p. 64)

A. Decide which key term is described in each case below.

1. In a hole her dog had dug, Ann found an object that looked like a very old arrowhead.
2. Was it a real arrowhead or just a stone? If it was real, what did that mean?
3. Ann decided to look into what had been on the site of her house long ago. Who had lived there?
4. In the library she discovered a room filled with old town records and papers.
5. There were maps, diaries, contracts, and other papers from colonial times.
6. On one map she found proof that an Indian settlement had once stood on the site of her house. It seemed likely that her arrowhead was real!

B. Use each word below in a sentence that shows what the word means. Write your sentence as if it began a story.

1. journal
2. empathy
3. chronology
4. history
5. oral history
6. primary source

Exploring Concepts

A. Write one or two sentences to answer each of the following questions. Use the information in the chapter.

1. What information can artifacts like clothes or furniture give to historians?
2. What sources other than artifacts do historians use?
3. What use is it to study items like these and other parts of history?
4. What primary sources do you come into contact with from day to day?
5. Consider the clothes you wore to school today. What would they tell a visitor from the future about your life?
6. If you write letters to a friend, imagine that a historian finds them 100 years from now. How would historians find them useful?

B. Write whether you agree or disagree with each of the following statements. If you disagree, give your reasons.

1. If we have enough evidence, we can know exactly what happened in a past event.
2. Historians need to know where a piece of evidence came from.
3. It is important to determine the order in which past events occurred.
4. It is the historian's job to study the past, not to ask questions about it.
5. As historical evidence, a personal diary is as valuable as a business contract.
6. Historians usually ignore what everyday people have to say about the past.
7. Studying history helps us to understand other people.

Reviewing Skills

1. Compare the painting of a Blackfoot girl on page 71 with the photo here. The photo has a painted background. How does the girl on the right in the photo appear different from the Blackfoot girl?
2. Look at the photograph on page 383 of George Northrup, a Minnesota teacher. Use details from the photo to state what you think are Northrup's plans.
3. Look at the ball on page 71. What does it tell you about what materials were available to Plains Indians in 1870? What ball do you think has replaced it today?
4. Where would you look to find the latitude and longitude of the site where the Boston Massacre took place?
5. Imagine you discovered some tools that had been used 300 years ago but had not been touched since 1690. How would you learn about the people who had used them?

Using Critical Thinking

1. Think about your gym shoes, a T-shirt, or any other piece of clothing that says something about you. Pretend you are a historian in the future. Ask questions about this piece of clothing. What would it tell you about people in the 1990s?

2. Historical evidence can be misleading. Choose a drama, a comedy, or a game show on TV. Suppose historians living in the year A.D. 2200 saw a tape of the program. What might they misunderstand about our lives based on that program?

Preparing for Citizenship

1. **COLLECTING INFORMATION** In an encyclopedia, you can read about the money we use in the United States and how it came to look as it does. Choose a slogan or picture from an American coin or bill. Do some research and find out why that slogan or picture was used. Study money from another country. Are there any similarities between its design and that of the American money you researched? Write a paragraph summarizing what you found out.

2. **COLLABORATIVE LEARNING** In groups of four, choose a past event in your school or town—perhaps an accident, an unexpected sports victory, or a visit from a famous person. Investigate it as historians would. Assign one member of the group to research primary sources, one to interpret what happened, one to put the incidents in order, and the fourth to write the story of the event. Then the writers should meet to decide which stories will be recorded in a class History Scrapbook.

Clues to Our Past

Unit 2

Exploring and Settling America

"Men of strange appearance have come across the great water." These words describe a dream an American Indian had sometime in the 1500s. Yet for many American Indians those words tell of a real event: the arrival of Europeans in America. At first the Europeans wanted the land's riches. Later they took the land itself. Once the Europeans came, life for the American Indians was never again the same.

2000 B.C.

Unknown American Indian artist, wall painting of Spanish explorers.

A.D. 1682

Chapter 4

The First People of the Americas

In A.D. 1200, North America was home to millions of people. These people settled in every region and climate. Some lived in small hunting villages. Some grew crops. Each group worshiped its own gods and spoke its own language. In A.D. 1200, these many active peoples shared the land of North America—a place that had been their home for at least 15,000 years.

2000 B.C. Some groups of American Indians get most of their food and clothing by hunting elk (above), buffalo, deer, and other animals.

Throughout this period, American Indians invented new tools. This knife was sharper than earlier stone tools, and this bone flute shows the Indians' interest in music.

2000	1500	1000	500

2000 B.C.

A.D. 1000–1200. The Mississippians build an active and successful culture on the banks of the Mississippi River. This necklace shows a man wearing fancy jewelry—a sign of great wealth in that culture.

B.C.	A.D.		500		1000		1500

A.D. 920 The Anasazi people begin building a community called Pueblo Bonito (top) deep in the desert of present-day Arizona.

A.D. 1500

LESSON 1

People Come to the Americas

How did the changing environment affect the first Americans?

Key Terms

- glacier
- epoch
- agriculture

The hunters shiver as an icy wind blows across the empty land. It is flat and treeless here, covered only with moss and small shrubs. Far away, the hunters can see a tall range of mountains covered with ice and snow.

The hunters are closing in on a herd of musk oxen. The bravest men circle several large oxen. The frightened animals run, and the hunters throw their spears. The fight is long and bloody, but when it is over, three huge oxen lie dead.

Now the hunters can begin the feast. They eat the meat and divide the skins, which are cut into rough coats and blankets. They chip new tools out of the bones. They rest and prepare for the next hunt.

For as long as the hunters can remember, they have searched for food across this bare land. This day, however, they have done something that has never been done before. Although they do not realize it, these hunters are the first humans ever to set foot on North America.

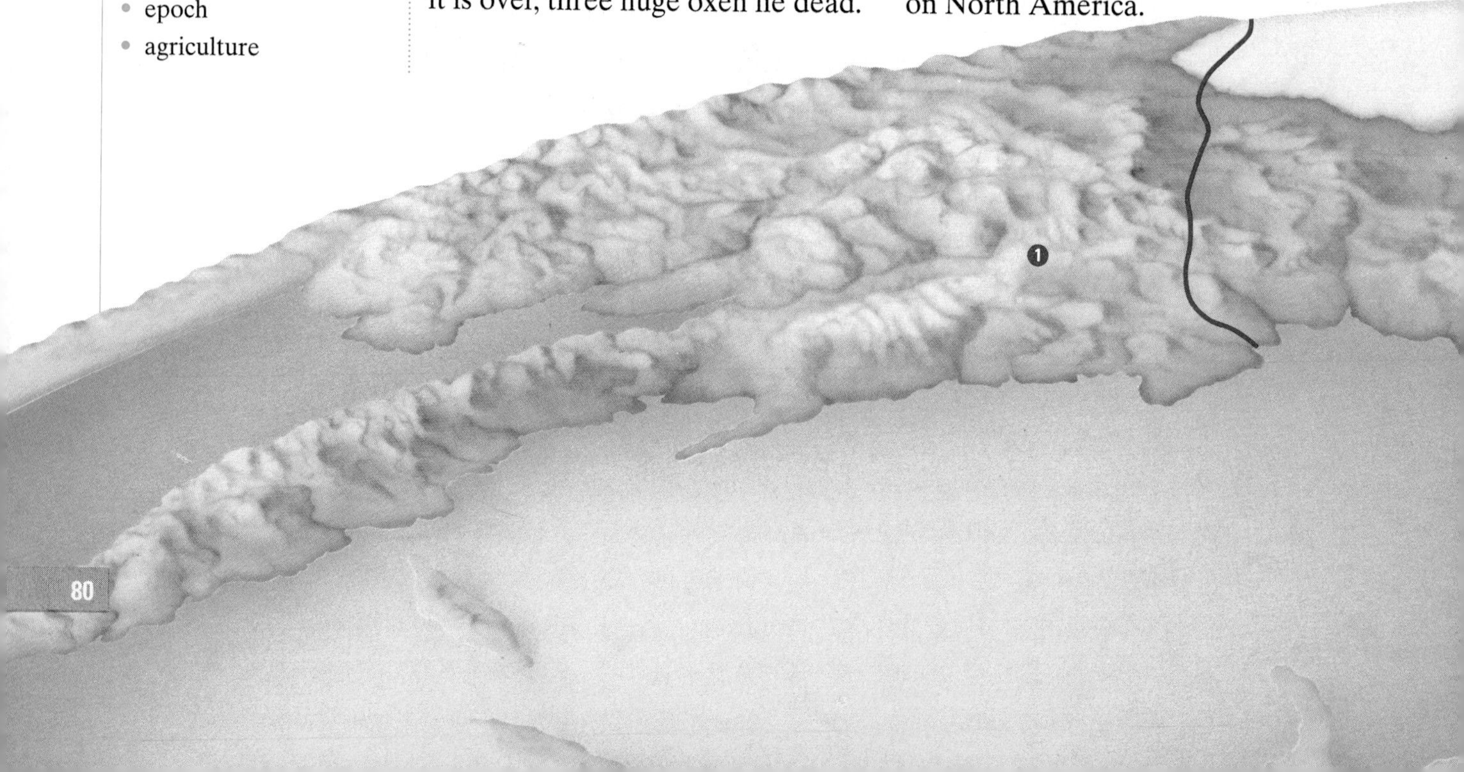

❶

From Asia to the Americas

Today, people can no longer walk from Asia to North America. The land bridge those hunters once walked across now lies beneath the icy waters of the Bering Strait. The Bering Strait is a narrow passage of water that separates the continents of Asia and North America.

No one is sure exactly when, but perhaps about 23,000 B.C., a bridge of land connected the two continents. At that time, almost one-third of the earth's surface was covered with huge sheets of ice called **glaciers.** Glaciers were sometimes up to a mile thick. They held much of the world's water in their frozen grip. As a result of these glaciers, the surface of the oceans was about 300 feet lower than today.

The highest parts of the Bering Strait were above water at that time. This dry land stretched from Asia to North America. Several different groups of humans walked across this bridge of land at different times.

The land bridge existed until about 12,000 B.C. At that time temperatures rose and caused the glaciers to melt. Over time, water from the melting glaciers covered the land bridge. People may have kept crossing the Bering Strait in boats. The time when hunters in search of food could walk from Asia to North America was over. ■

■ *How was it possible for humans to walk from Asia to the Americas?*

▼ *The photograph and the locator map show (1) Asia, (2) the Bering Strait, and (3) North America as they appear today.*

▼ *The drawing is an artist's idea of what the Bering land bridge may have looked like in 13,000 B.C. Find the land bridge that existed where the waters of the Bering Strait lie today (2). Red lines show the coastline today.*

From Hunting to Farming

How Do We Know?

HISTORY *The first Americans left no written records of their lives. Scientists have pieced together their story from spear points, bones, and other objects they left behind. By looking closely at these objects, scientists can tell how they were made, what they were used for, and how old they are.*

▼ *The progress of the first Americans from traveling hunters to settled farmers was long and slow, as this route map and timeline show. For help in using a route map, see page G12 of the* Map and Globe Handbook.

The hunters who walked across the land bridge into North America were the ancestors of the people we now call Native Americans. Their story can be divided into four **epochs,** or very important periods of history.

Hunting and Gathering

The Beringian *(bur IHN jee uhn)* epoch (13,000–9500 B.C.) began when the main group of hunters came to North America. These people found a land different from the land today. **Glaciers,** large masses of ice and snow, covered most of what is now Canada. Forests stretched across the United States. Grasslands swept south into Mexico.

North America had many of the animals that the hunters had followed from Asia—wooly mammoths were favorites. Hunters followed these animals away from the glaciers to warmer lands in the south. The paths these American Indians may have followed are shown in the map below.

Warming weather changed these lands during the Paleo-Indian epoch (9500–6000 B.C.). Some scientists believe that glaciers melted and raised the levels of oceans. The western grasslands of North America became hot deserts. As the land changed, large grass-eating animals died out for want of food.

American Indians who had hunted these animals now had to search for new sources of food. Hunters made smaller and better weapons, like the spear thrower on page 83. With weapons like these, American Indians could hunt animals that were faster.

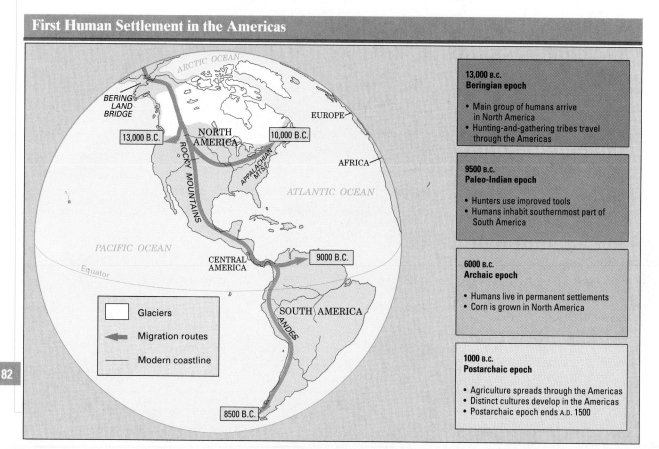

First Human Settlement in the Americas

13,000 B.C.
Beringian epoch

- Main group of humans arrive in North America
- Hunting-and-gathering tribes travel through the Americas

9500 B.C.
Paleo-Indian epoch

- Hunters use improved tools
- Humans inhabit southernmost part of South America

6000 B.C.
Archaic epoch

- Humans live in permanent settlements
- Corn is grown in North America

1000 B.C.
Postarchaic epoch

- Agriculture spreads through the Americas
- Distinct cultures develop in the Americas
- Postarchaic epoch ends A.D. 1500

Map labels: ARCTIC OCEAN; BERING LAND BRIDGE; EUROPE; NORTH AMERICA; 13,000 B.C.; 10,000 B.C.; ROCKY MOUNTAINS; APPALACHIAN MTS.; AFRICA; ATLANTIC OCEAN; PACIFIC OCEAN; Equator; CENTRAL AMERICA; 9000 B.C.; SOUTH AMERICA; ANDES; 8500 B.C.

Legend: Glaciers; Migration routes; Modern coastline

These included bison, caribou, and deer.

American Indians lived off the land during the Archaic *(ahr KAY ihk)* epoch (6000–1000 B.C.). People who lived near water, for example, built boats for fishing. Those who lived in forests gathered wild nuts and berries.

Farming and Settling

During the Archaic epoch, American Indians also learned to plant and harvest corn, beans, and other crops. After the birth of **agriculture,** as this discovery is known, they could settle in one spot and grow crops in nearby fields. These new food crops allowed American Indian groups to grow in number.

These groups developed into many different cultures during the Postarchaic epoch (1000 B.C.– A.D. 1500). By A.D. 1500, American Indians wore clothing made of everything from animal skins to cloth made from plants. Some lived in simple huts made of tree bark and mud or in wooden houses on stilts. Others lived in cities made of stone.

Some American Indians lived like the hunters who crossed the Bering land bridge. One group, called the Chipewyans *(chihp uh WY uhns)* hunted caribou across the cold, bare regions of what is now northern Canada. Other groups, like the Aztecs of Mexico, grew into powerful societies. The center of Aztec culture was the city of Tenochtitlan *(tay nawch tee TLAHN)*. In this city perhaps as many as 100,000 people lived among canals, temples, and islands. These and many other American Indian cultures lived in every region of North America around A.D. 1500. ■

Weapons like this spear thrower made hunting easier. A hunter (shown above) would (1) load the spear into the spear thrower, (2) propel the spear, and (3) release the spear. In this way, hunters could throw farther and harder than before.

■ *How did the discovery of agriculture change American Indian groups?*

REVIEW

1. **FOCUS** How did the changing environment affect the first Americans?
2. **CONNECT** How was North America different during the Beringian epoch than it is now?
3. **GEOGRAPHY** List three ways that the first Americans changed with their environment.
4. **CRITICAL THINKING** The search for food led ancient hunters throughout North and South America. How did agriculture and the development of a steady supply of food affect later American Indians?
5. **WRITING ACTIVITY** Today, scientists look for clues to how people lived long ago. Pick three objects that belong to you. In a short paragraph, describe each object. Explain why you chose it and what it would tell a scientist 3,000 years from now about how you lived.

The First People of the Americas

How the Turtle Beat the Rabbit

A Cherokee Folktale

You have learned something about American Indian society and way of life. American Indians used stories to teach what they considered proper behavior. In this familiar story of the turtle and the rabbit from "Myths of the Cherokee" by James Mooney, you see what the Cherokee thought of boastfulness. If you were a young Cherokee hearing it, how would you change your behavior?

Folktales like this one show the liveliness of Indian culture.

warrior a person who fights
boastful speaking with too much pride
dispute to discuss, argue

lodges small houses

humility free of pride

The rabbit was a great runner, and everybody knew it. No one thought the turtle anything but a slow traveler, but he was a great warrior and very boastful, and the two were always disputing about their speed. At last they agreed to decide the matter by a race. They fixed the day and the starting place and arranged to run across four mountain ridges. The one who reached the last ridge first would be the winner.

Rabbit felt so sure of victory that he said to Turtle, "You know you can't run. You can never win the race, so I'll give you a headstart to the first ridge and then you'll have only three to cross while I will have to go over four."

The turtle said that would be all right. They then both returned to their lodges for the night. Turtle, however, sent for his turtle friends and family, telling them that he needed their help.

"I know that I cannot outrun the rabbit, but I am tired of his always boasting about his great speed. It is time someone taught him a little humility. Come listen to my plan."

All his friends agreed to help out. When the day came, all the animals were there to see the race. The rabbit was at the starting point, but the turtle had already gone ahead toward the first ridge, as had been agreed to earlier. The rabbit started off with a roar from all the crowd as he sprang into action. He started off with long jumps and soon was climbing the first ridge, expecting to win the race before the turtle could get down the other side. But before he got up the mountain, he saw Turtle go over the next ridge ahead of him.

Rabbit ran on. When he reached the top he looked all around, but he

could not see the turtle because of the long grass below. He kept going down the mountain and climbed the second ridge, but when he looked up again there was Turtle just going over the top. Now he was both surprised and angry. He began making his longest leaps to catch up, but when he got to the top of the ridge, there was the turtle away in front going over the third ridge.

The rabbit was getting tired now and nearly out of breath, but he kept on down the mountain and up the other ridge until he got to the top. And he was just in time to see Turtle cross the fourth ridge and win the race!

The rabbit could not make another jump, but fell over on the ground, as the rabbit does ever since when he is too tired to run anymore. A ribbon was given to the turtle for winning the race and all the animals wondered how he could win against the rabbit. The turtle wasn't about to tell either. It was easy because all the turtle's family and friends looked just alike, and he had simply had one of them climb to each ridge before the race began. They then waited until the rabbit came in sight before hiding themselves in the long grass. That is how the turtle taught Rabbit not to be too boastful.

Further Reading

And It's Still That Way: Legends Told by Arizona Indian Children. Byrd Baylor. These are stories from several Native American tribes.

And Me, Coyote! Betty Baker. This tale, based on the creation myths of the Native Americans in California, reveals how the coyote tries to take the credit for what his brother, a World Maker, has done.

Conquista! Clyde Bulla. The story of how the Indians may have gotten their first horse is told through the experiences of Little Wolf, a young boy.

The Sound of Flutes and Other Indian Legends. Richard Erdoes collected these stories from Native American storytellers.

L E S S O N   2

Four American Indian Cultures

Key Terms

- mesa
- potlatch
- mound

Richard Wetherill squinted in the bright December light. As the winter of 1888 began, Wetherill and his brother-in-law Charles Mason looked after the family's cattle. One herd wandered across the **mesa,** one of the many steep, flat-topped mountains in that part of Colorado. Every so often, a cow strayed from the herd and got lost in the twisting canyons that separated the mesas.

Wetherill and Mason searched for one of these lost cattle in some trees near the edge of the mesa. As they reached the rim on the canyon, they saw something on the other side that made them forget about lost cattle. A village made of stone, with towers and walls, was built into the canyon wall.

When Wetherill and Mason saw that village, they saw something that had been forgotten for hundreds of years. They had found Cliff

➤ *More than 200 people lived in the village of Cliff Palace during the 1100s.*

Palace, the main village of an American Indian culture, the Anasazi *(ah nuh SAH zee)* who had lived in the Mesa Verde region.

Cliff Palace helps many people understand that a people of an age-old culture once lived in the canyons of the southwestern United States. The Anasazi were just one of the groups in North America by A.D. 1500. The story of these peoples is where the story of America begins.

In the pages that follow, you will read about four of these cultures. The map on page 88 shows where the Anasazi, the Makah *(MAHK uh)*, the Mississippians, and the Creek settled. As you read about these groups, think about where they lived. Consider also how their surroundings affected what they ate, what they lived in, and how they made sense of the world.

Anasazi: People of the Desert

The Anasazi first arrived in the deserts of the Southwest in about A.D. 100. They raised corn, beans, and later cotton near their homes on the mesas.

After about 1,000 years, the Anasazi left their settlements on the mesa tops and moved to cliff dwellings. Scholars believe that the Anasazi may have feared an enemy culture. They then moved to homes that were easier to defend from enemies. From these villages—like Cliff Palace—the Anasazi climbed up the canyon walls to tend their crops on top of the mesas.

Corn was the most important food of the Anasazi. But their corn would not survive without rain. Over time the Anasazi learned to tame the dry, desert land. They learned to "catch" rain in ditches, which carried the water to their crops.

This poem from the Tewa *(TAY wuh)* Indians, another desert people, shows how important rain was in that region.

> L ong ago in the north
> Lies the road of emergence!
> Yonder our ancestors live,
> Yonder we take our being.
>
> Yet now we come southward
> For cloud flowers blossom here
> Here the lightning flashes,
> Rain water here is falling!

▲ *The zigzag design on this Anasazi pitcher may represent lightning and rain. Without rain, the Anasazi could not have grown their multicolored corn, distant cousin of today's yellow corn (shown below).*

Rain also played an important part in Anasazi religion. The Anasazi believed that ceremonies, like exciting rain dances, would bring rain. If the rain came, their crops would grow and they would live.

Sometime in the 1200s, the rain stopped falling on the mesas. This may have caused the Anasazi to leave their homes in the cliffs.

After leaving their homes, the Anasazi moved into villages closer to water.

Today, the descendants of the Anasazi still live in the southwestern United States. But they no longer live in cliff dwellings. Those structures were occupied only when the Anasazi had enough water to grow their crops. ■

■ *How was the importance of rain shown in Anasazi culture?*

Makah: People of the Coast

The Makah lived on what is now called the Olympic Peninsula in the state of Washington. In this land of tall cedar forests, the Makah were surrounded by water —the Pacific Ocean, lakes, rivers, and streams. The fish and animals in these waters provided the Makah with food all year.

The Makah hunted and fished for these animals throughout the warm months. In summer, the Makah lived along streams and fished for salmon. In winter, the Makah moved nearer the ocean. The Makah rowed into the sea in big canoes. Armed with harpoons, they hunted whales, sea lions, and sea otters in the cold waters of the Pacific Ocean.

In winter, the Makah were able to enjoy all of the food they had gathered over the year. The Makah lived on dried salmon, other fish, and seal oil in their warm cedar houses. During the winter, they

▲ *These drawings of whales show the importance of the sea to Makah culture.*

➤ *The American Indians discussed in this lesson lived in different environments and parts of North America. For help in using latitude and longitude to identify the location of Indian cultures, see page G10 in the* Map and Globe Handbook.

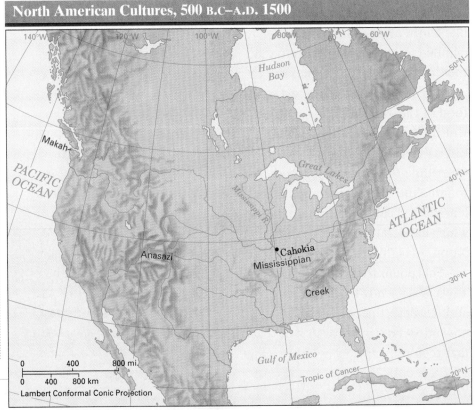

North American Cultures, 500 B.C–A.D. 1500

Hudson Bay

Makah

PACIFIC OCEAN

Great Lakes

Mississippi R.

ATLANTIC OCEAN

Anasazi

Cahokia
Mississippian

Creek

Gulf of Mexico

Tropic of Cancer

0   400   800 mi.
0 400 800 km
Lambert Conformal Conic Projection

In the mild, rainy land of the Makah, fish was an important source of food. Salmon (shown above) was the most important fish of all to the Makah.

made baskets, boxes, masks, and other objects of wood. This wood was cut from the cedar trees of the forests surrounding the Makah villages.

The Makah often had extra food and art objects. They celebrated this wealth in a **potlatch** ceremony. In this ceremony the wealthy proved their wealth and generosity by giving gifts to their guests.

The Makah were able to celebrate their wealth in potlatches most of the time. They seemed to have plenty of food. By drying and smoking salmon and other fish, they were able to store food for a long time. They were thankful for the fish that kept them from going hungry. Each year the Makah held a ceremony to honor the salmon and its return to the rivers of their land■

■ What do potlatch ceremonies tell us about the Makah?

Mississippians: People of the River

Rivers connected the Mississippians to people of other lands. The most important of these rivers was the one we call the Mississippi. Along its branches the Mississippians built a network of trade. They traded with people from the Great Lakes to the Gulf of Mexico, from the Atlantic Ocean to what is now Oklahoma.

The Mississippians traded a kind of stone used for weapons and tools to these faraway peoples. This stone is called chert. In return, the Mississippians got shells, copper, and jewelry. They brought these things back to their homes along the Mississippi River.

On the banks of the river, the Mississippians raised corn, beans, and other crops. They also built villages and towns. The largest of these towns in A.D. 1200 was Cahokia. Like other Mississippian

The First People of the Americas

■ *Why was the river an important part of Mississippian life?*

▼ *This drawing shows what Cahokia may have looked like in A.D. 1200. The mound that stood in the center of town can still be seen today near East St. Louis, Illinois (right).*

towns, Cahokia was built around a huge, steep platform called a **mound.** This mound was more than 1,000 feet long and 700 feet wide. It covered more land than the Great Pyramid of Egypt.

The mounds of Mississippian towns tell us a lot about their culture. Scholars think that it may have taken Cahokians up to 200 years to build their mound. Only a powerful class of rulers, scholars say, could lead the many workers needed to make such mounds.

Artifacts from these mounds tell us that priests were probably important among the Mississippian peoples. Headdresses, pipes, and masks have also been found in the mounds in recent centuries. These things, say historians, tell us that religion was an important part of Mississippian life.

For many years it was thought that some parts of Mississippian culture may have come from other places. Pictures of feathered snakes, winged warriors, and spiders are often found in Mississippian art. These forms also exist in the art of other American Indian societies. Some Central American societies, like the Aztec culture of Mexico, built cities around huge buildings that look like the later Mississippian mounds. But this has not been proved.

Some important parts of Mississippian life may have been brought to North America by traders. These traders may have visited the Aztecs and other groups. It is possible that parts of Mississippian culture came up the river in boats along with seashells, copper, and jewelry. ■

Creek: People of the Forest

The Creek had much in common with the Mississippians. Both cultures, for example, built mounds. Both groups lived along rivers and streams. But because they lived at different times, the Creek were different from the Mississippians in many ways.

The Creek lived in the area that is now Alabama and Georgia. There, the Creek hunted, fished, and gathered fruits and nuts. They planted corn and beans in forest clearings. Nearby, they built villages surrounded by tall wooden fences. These fences protected them from enemies.

Inside the village stood dozens of small houses. Each family had two houses. The houses were built on pieces of ground, much like the houses of today. One was a light, airy house for summer. The other was a warm, solid house for winter. The houses were arranged around a central plaza.

The town council met in this plaza. The council was made up of men who had shown their bravery or wisdom. One of these men was chosen chief. The chief and the council ruled the village together.

Creek religious ceremonies also took place in the plaza. The Green Corn Dance, for example, was a feast held after the corn harvest in mid-summer. In this ceremony, people put aside any anger with one another and vowed to live in peace. The Creek, filled with new hope, danced and then feasted on the corn. It was a festival of people living in harmony with nature. ■

■ *How did the Creek use the central plaza of their towns?*

◄ *In the forests of what is today the southeastern United States, the Creek hunted deer and gathered foods like persimmons, blackberries, raspberries, and pecans (above).*

UNDERSTANDING LAND USE

American Indian cultures respected the land. The land and its products were a part of the religions of many cultures. As you have read, the Makah honored the salmon in their ceremonies.

These feelings reflect how North American Indians used the land. They believed, for example, that the land was made for all people and that it should be shared by all people.

A Local Decision

Land use refers to how a group of people feels about the land and what they do with it. Do they build cities or live in caves? Do they grow corn in fields or do they gather berries in the forest? Do they believe that the land can be bought, sold, and owned?

American Indians did not believe that land could be owned, but other groups did. In Europe, for example, land was owned by a few powerful people. The first Europeans in North America wanted to own the land.

In this century, groups have argued about the amount of land that is to be set aside for U.S. national parks. Some people feel this land is best used to preserve forests and wildlife. Others think the land should be used for farming, mining, and building.

A Global Issue

Today, the debate over how land is used involves the entire world. We have learned that what happens on one part of the earth can affect other parts. Factories in the United States can cause pollution in Canada.

A nuclear accident can affect the entire planet. How land is used anywhere on the earth is an important matter for everyone.

How people feel land should be used is an important part of their culture. American Indians, for example, often held ceremonies connected with land use. The Creek held corn festivals after the harvest. Some cultures celebrated land use as a part of their religions. This shows they respected the land and how it was used.

R E V I E W

1. **FOCUS** How were North American Indian cultures affected by their environments?

2. **CONNECT** What do the artifacts found in mounds tell us about the Mississippians?

3. **HISTORY** How is the environment of the Anasazi people shown in their arts and religion? How is the environment of the Makah people shown in their arts and beliefs?

4. **CRITICAL THINKING** Compare and contrast Creek and Mississippian towns.

5. **ACTIVITY** Look at the article on American Indians in the Minipedia on pages 606–608. Choose an American Indian group that is not discussed in this lesson. Find the following: clothing, housing, and crafts. Look at the map on page 608 to see where this group was located.

Observing the Seasons

Here's Why

Activities change with the seasons. Thousands of years ago, American Indians based their lives on the seasons. They planted in the spring and gathered crops in the fall. They knew when the seasons changed, but they did not know why. Do you?

Here's How

Many people think seasons change because the distance between the earth and the sun changes. This is not so. What really makes the seasons change is that the angle at which the sun's rays strike the earth changes.

The diagram on this page shows the angle of the sun's rays during the year. Look at the earth on June 21 or 22 in the diagram. The Northern Hemisphere tilts toward the sun; it is summer there. The Southern Hemisphere tilts away and receives the sun's rays at an angle. It is winter there. On the diagram, a line through the center of the earth represents the earth's axis. The tilt of the axis is nearly constant.

By September 22 or 23, the earth completes one-fourth of its orbit around the sun. Northern and Southern hemispheres are both half-way between summer and winter. The sun's direct rays hit the equator. September 22 or 23 is the first day of autumn in the Northern Hemisphere and of spring in the Southern Hemisphere.

Try It

Find the part of the diagram that shows the earth when it is summer in South America. How can you tell it is summer there? What season is it in North America?

Apply It

Suppose it is summer in the United States. What kind of clothing would you need for a trip to Australia?

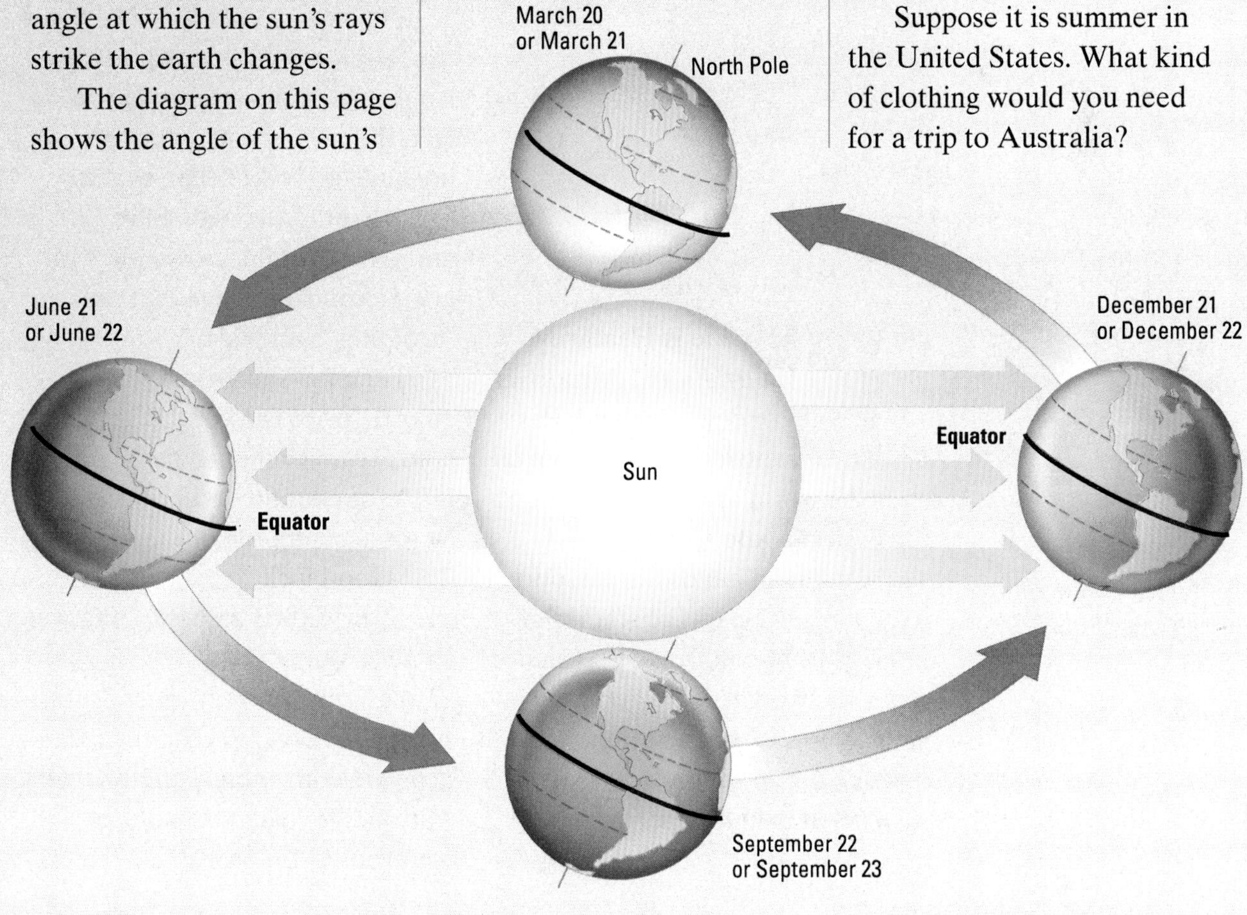

March 20 or March 21

North Pole

June 21 or June 22

Equator

Sun

December 21 or December 22

Equator

September 22 or September 23

The First People of the Americas

LESSON 3

Life in an Iroquois Village

What were the major features of Iroquois daily life?

Key Terms

- confederation
- long house

▲ *Many Iroquois still live in the United States and Canada today. This man wears his traditional Iroquois clothing only for special occasions.*

The scene is Heathrow International Airport in London, England. Passengers arriving from all over the world are passing through the customs gate.

A tall man hands his passport to a guard. It bears the stamps of more than 20 countries. In it she reads the words: *Nawyayh nenh genh awhyawk nee hoe nonh hwenth jaw gayh.*

"What country are you from?" asks the guard.

"I am from the Iroquois *(IHR uh kwoy)* Nation," he answers.

The guard looks closely at the passport. "Where is that?"

"Between the United States and Canada."

"What brings you to England?" the guard asks.

The man says that he has come to see the Iroquois team play the English team in lacrosse, an American Indian game something like hockey and soccer. The guard looks behind the man. Sure enough, several lacrosse players are wearing uniforms that say "Iroquois Nationals."

The man smiles and tells the guard, "If we can beat Team England, Team Canada, and Team USA, our country will be the lacrosse champion of the world."

"Good luck," says the guard as she returns the passport, "and welcome to our country."

"Thank you very much," answers the man. "Perhaps one day I can welcome you to the Iroquois Nation. It is one of the oldest countries in the world."

◄ *The Iroquois settled in what is today called the Finger Lakes region of New York state.*

People of the Long House

The Iroquois Nation began in the 1400s. At that time, five peoples formed a **confederation,** separate societies united for a common goal. Those peoples are shown on the map on page 97. They hoped to make peace among their members. They called themselves "People of the Long House."

The **long house** was the building where the Iroquois lived. Several family groups lived in a long house. Women were often the most important people in these groups. When an Iroquois man and woman married, for example, they lived in the long house of the woman's family. Look at the Moment in Time on page 96 to learn more about an Iroquois woman.

Work

The Iroquois who lived together in the long houses also worked together in the fields and forests outside the village. They divided their work equally between men and women.

Iroquois men cleared land around the village for farming and fished in nearby streams. They also hunted deer and other animals.

▼ *The long house was the center of life in Iroquois villages.*

An Iroquois Clan Leader

*5:45 P.M., September 17, 1597
In a long house on Onondaga Lake*

Feather
She placed her feather at the back of her headband when she married during her 15th summer, 13 years ago.

Headband
The beadwork advertises her position as clan matron. She'll use her authority tonight to settle an argument between her husband and her brother over winter hunting plans.

Green Corn Leaves
The homemade dressing under her sleeve covers a gash. She cut herself while harvesting squash this morning.

Buckskin Dress
All her clothes give off a smoky scent from the indoor fire that burns 24 hours a day.

Buckskin Cord
She wears this string to secure her wraparound dress and to bring good luck. Her husband gave her the cord after he last went hunting.

Corn Cake
Available to snackers and guests all day, the food will taste good to her younger brother. He has just arrived from his wife's long house for the clan council meeting.

Moose-Hide Moccasin
She decorated her shoes with fine moose hair and porcupine quill embroidery especially for tonight's meeting. She wants to look like the strong leader she must be to decide her husband's and her brother's claims.

The food and hides brought back by the men were shared by everyone who lived in the village. The men also fought other tribes when the Iroquois were at war.

While the men hunted, the women raised corn, beans, and squash in fields near the village. They also took charge of daily life. They made sure that everyone in the village had food, clothing, and a place to live.

Values

The Iroquois felt very close to nature as they hunted and farmed in the land around their village. They believed that every part of nature—every tree and plant, every animal—had its own spirit. They prayed to these spirits and asked for their help in hunting and farming. The Iroquois honored the land and the animals. They believed that a person should take only what was needed from nature and nothing more.

The Iroquois honored the needs of other people just as they honored the land and animals. Sometimes the harvest was small and food was scarce. Everyone in the village, however, would share their food before any one person went hungry. The Iroquois helped all the people of the village, even in the hardest times.

In every part of their lives, the Iroquois people worked together. Cooperation was an important part of the Iroquois Nation from the beginning. ■

▲ *The Iroquois raised squash as well as corn in the fields around their villages.*

■ *Find evidence to support this statement: The Iroquois valued cooperation.*

The Iroquois Nation

Without cooperation the Iroquois knew that their people could not survive. The five peoples belonging to the Iroquois Nation were often at war with one another before they united.

If a Cayuga *(kay YOO guh)* Indian killed a Seneca *(SEHN ih kuh)*, other Senecas got even by killing a Cayuga. After that, each people would keep trying to get even.

◀ *The five divisions of the Iroquois Nation were all located in the same region near Lake Ontario. The inset map shows that the Iroquois lived in what is now the northeastern part of the United States. For help in understanding an inset map, see page G7 in the* Map and Globe Handbook.

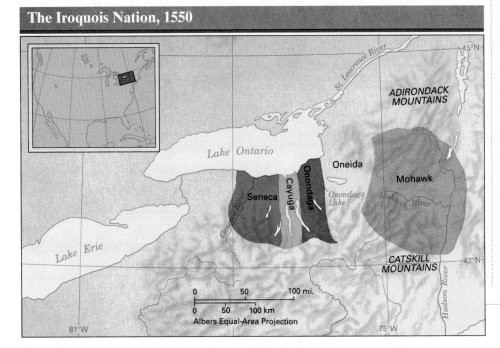

The Iroquois Nation, 1550

St. Lawrence River

45°N

ADIRONDACK MOUNTAINS

Lake Ontario

Oneida

Mohawk

Genesee River

Seneca

Cayuga

Onondaga

Onondaga Lake

Mohawk River

Lake Erie

CATSKILL MOUNTAINS

42°N

Hudson River

0   50   100 mi.

0   50   100 km

Albers Equal-Area Projection

81°W

75°W

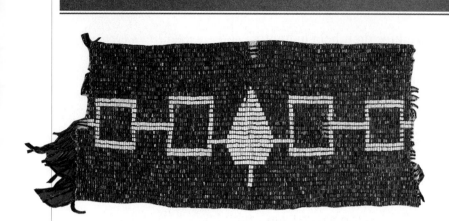

The Iroquois used wampum belts as ornaments and as a way to remember important events. The symbols on this belt show the five groups joining together into one Iroquois Nation.

Across Time & Space

Over 20,000 Iroquois live as citizens in the United States or Canada today. However, they hold Iroquois passports and call the town of Onondaga, near Syracuse, New York, their capital.

■ *Why did the five groups unite to form the Iroquois Nation?*

The Legend of Hiawatha

In Iroquois history there is a story of a Mohawk chief named Hiawatha. Tired of the endless fighting, Hiawatha longed for change. One day he met the Iroquois statesman Dekanawida *(dee kahn uh WEE duh)*, who said that the way to bring peace was to form a single Iroquois nation. Hiawatha went from one nation to another and explained Dekanawida's plan. He told the people:

> **W**e bind ourselves together by taking hold of each other's hands so firmly and forming a circle so strong that if a tree should fall upon it, it could not shake nor break it, so that our people and grandchildren shall remain in the circle in security, peace, and happiness.
>
> from an Iroquois legend

After hearing Hiawatha's words, the people formed a single Iroquois Nation in what is now the state of New York. The new nation was like an imaginary long house, with all five groups of Iroquois living together under the same roof.

Hiawatha's Legacy

Sometime in the late 1500s the Mohawk, Oneida *(oh NY duh)*, Onondaga, Cayuga, and the Seneca united. They formed a Great Council of 49 chiefs. Each group had an equal voice in the Council.

The Council brought an end to the wars and other fights among the Iroquois people. They resolved differences with words instead of blood. The Iroquois people brought many other problems before the Council. The chiefs talked about each problem until all agreed on an answer. The chiefs followed the rules laid down in the story of Hiawatha.

The story of Hiawatha was important to the Iroquois. It helped them in times of trouble. It showed how one person could make a difference in the world. Remembering the words of Hiawatha, the Iroquois worked together and built a great nation. ■

REVIEW

1. **FOCUS** What were the major features of Iroquois daily life?
2. **CONNECT** Which American Indian culture discussed in Lesson 2 is most like the Iroquois? Why?
3. **HISTORY** How did the Iroquois resolve differences between groups, villages, and individuals?
4. **CRITICAL THINKING** The Iroquois view of nature was based on sharing and cooperation. Where else is this attitude seen in Iroquois life and history?
5. **WRITING ACTIVITY** In this lesson you have learned about the Iroquois. Imagine that you live in an Iroquois village. Write an account of your day: what you eat, what you wear, what you are taught.

Using Timelines

Here's Why

Timelines can give you a sense of sequence and may suggest cause-and-effect relationships. Using a timeline also can help you to relate events that occur in different places at the same time. For example, the timeline on this page shows important events among American Indians between 1000 B.C. and A.D. 1570.

Here's How

We use the abbreviations B.C. and A.D. when we refer to years in history. Christians in Europe started this way of referring to dates. Dates B.C. are those that occur before the birth of Christ. The letters A.D. stand for the Latin phrase *Anno Domini*, which means "in the year of our Lord." Dates A.D. are those that occur after the birth of Christ.

Most dates for events that happened B.C. are not specific. The calendar as we know it had not yet been developed. People who lived then used different systems. When we do not know the precise year something happened, we give an approximate year and say, for example, *about* 500 B.C.

The timeline below shows 1000 years in the B.C. period and 1,570 years in the A.D. period. Each major division on the timeline represents a period of 500 years. Dates are written at the beginning of each time period. Each event is written on the timeline at the date when it took place. For an event that spans a period of time, you would place marks on the timeline at the beginning and end of that period and shade the line between the marks.

Try It

Copy the timeline below onto your own paper. Add the following events to it:

- About A.D. 1200, Mississippians complete mound at Cahokia.
- About 250 B.C., Eastern Plains Indians live in permanent villages.
- A.D. 1070–1130, Anasazi build apartment buildings with impressive architecture.
- About A.D. 1050, Anasazi grow cotton.

Apply It

Make a timeline that shows five to ten events in your own life. Use *about* for any dates you are unsure of.

700 B.C.–A.D. 700, Anasazi build pithouses

About 1300, Anasazi migrate from San Juan River area

About 1500, Mississippian culture at its peak

1000   500   B.C. A.D.   500   1000   1500

About 1000 B.C., Postarchaic Epoch begins

About A.D. 600, Anasazi make pottery and use bows and arrows

About 1200, Aztec culture begins

About 1500, Creek culture begins

About 1570, Hiawatha leads founding of Iroquois Great Council

The First People of the Americas

Chapter Review

Reviewing Key Terms

agriculture (p. 83)
confederation (p. 95)
epoch (p. 82)
glacier (p. 81)

long house (p. 95)
mesa (p. 86)
mound (p. 90)
potlatch (p. 89)

A. The following clues refer to key terms. Use a dictionary to help you figure out the answers. Then use each term in a sentence that shows you understand the meaning.
1. Which term comes from the Latin word *mensa*, meaning "table"?
2. Which term comes from two words— *ager* and *cultura*?
3. Which term is related to *glacé*, "having a glazed, glossy surface"?

4. Which term comes from the word *patshatl*?
5. Which term means a period of time that is "highly significant or important"?
6. Which term begins with three letters that mean "together" and has an ending that means "an action or process"?
7. Which term refers to something that covers more land than the Great Pyramid of Egypt?

B. Imagine you are visiting an Iroquois family. Write a paragraph in your diary to describe your activities. Include these terms:
1. long house
2. agriculture

Exploring Concepts

A. Write one paragraph to summarize each lesson in this chapter.
Lesson 1: Tell about changes in environment for each of the following epochs:

Beringian   Paleo-Indian
Archaic   Postarchaic

Lesson 2: Give examples of how the people of these American Indian groups used their environment:

Anasazi   Makah
Mississippians   Creek

Lesson 3: Tell about the accomplishments of the Iroquois people using these concepts:

family   work   values

B. Answer each question with information from the chapter.
1. How is the Bering Strait different today than it was about 15,000 years ago? What changes explain the difference?

2. How did the early American Indians get food to eat before they learned the skills of agriculture?
3. What was Richard Wetherill's and Charles Mason's discovery and why was it important to people?
4. What did the Anasazi do to save the precious water they needed? What happened when the water supply stopped?
5. How were the Makah and the Mississippians more fortunate than the people of the desert?
6. What did Makah ceremonies celebrate and why?
7. What three questions did each American Indian culture answer in its own way?
8. How did the Iroquois people work toward keeping peace among themselves?
9. Who were the leaders of Iroquois clans? What were some of their responsibilities?

Reviewing Skills

1. Use the diagram to answer the following questions: What season is it in the Northern Hemisphere? How can you tell this from the diagram? What season is it in the Southern Hemisphere? How is this shown in the diagram?

2. Use the diagram to explain why the seasons north and south of the equator are opposite.

3. Use the map on page 82 to make a timeline showing the following events:
   - Humans arrive in North America
   - Humans reach the tip of South America
   - Paleo-Indian epoch begins
   - Migration of hunting and gathering tribes throughout the Americas
   - Agriculture spreads throughout the Americas

4. What headings would you check in an encyclopedia to find articles about the changing seasons?

5. Suppose you are asked to tell about the technology that existed among the five American Indian cultures covered in this chapter. What type of visual evidence from the past would help you?

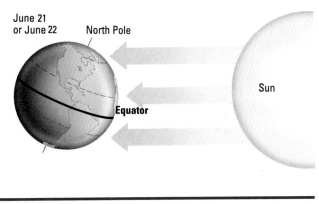

June 21 or June 22   North Pole

Sun

Equator

Using Critical Thinking

1. Imagine that you lived during the time of the American Indian cultures that you studied in this chapter. Which culture would you choose to belong to? Give reasons for your choice.

2. The Creeks and the Europeans had different ideas about how the land should be used. Compare the Creeks' ideas with those of the Europeans. Which ideas do you think are better? Explain your opinion.

3. The Iroquois nation provides passports for their people, even though they are citizens of the United States or Canada. Why do you think some Iroquois people feel strongly about this? Do you agree or disagree with their system?

Preparing for Citizenship

1. **WRITING ACTIVITY** Imagine that you are a planter who is desperate for rain. Without rain, your crops will die and you will not have food for your family. Write a poem, song, or story that tells how important the rain is to your life.

2. **ARTS ACTIVITY** Make a diorama to represent a dwelling or activity of one American Indian group. You may choose a group from the chapter or a group from pages 606 and 607 of the Minipedia.

3. **COLLABORATIVE LEARNING** Help to create a radio program called "Voices of the Past." Form small groups based on the Indian cultures you studied in this chapter. Each group will prepare a script, appoint an announcer, and choose speakers to represent members of the culture. The announcer will ask each speaker questions about the culture they were part of, when they lived, where their lands were, and something about their daily life.

The First People of the Americas

Chapter 5
The Age of Exploration

For centuries Europeans had dreamed of a faster route to the riches of Asia. In the 1400s new ships, inventions, and discoveries made that dream a reality. Soon, almost every kingdom in Europe sent explorers across the western ocean. Those earliest explorers did not find a new route to Asia. Instead, they stumbled upon lands that had been unknown to Europeans.

Throughout this period, improved instruments help explorers sail ships more accurately. The cross-staff (above) and this compass of the 1620s (below) made longer ocean voyages possible.

1300	1350	1400	1450

1356

1469 Ferdinand of Aragon and Isabella of Castile marry. The rulers, shown above holding court, grant large sums of money for exploration.

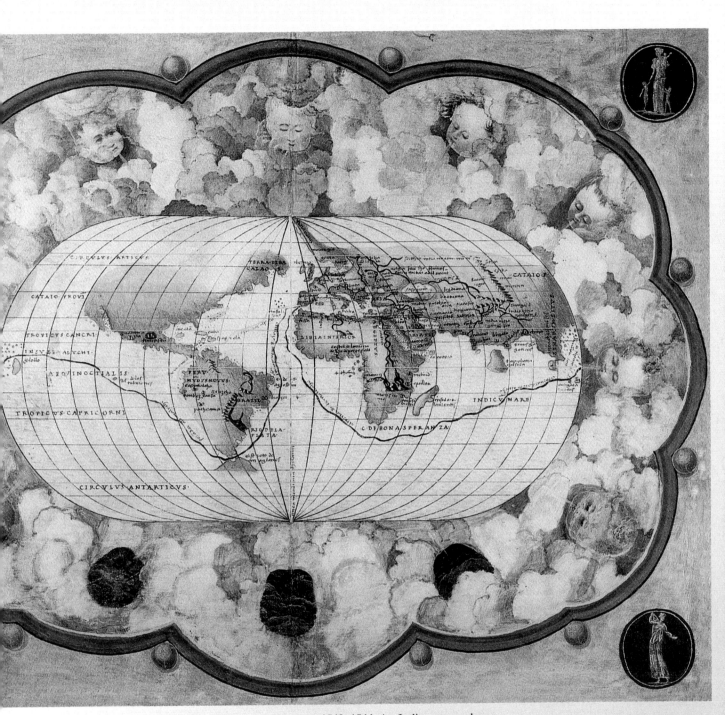

1543–1544 An Italian mapmaker named Battista Agnese makes the map above. It shows the routes Spanish ships took on the first voyage around the earth 20 years earlier.

| 1500 | 1550 | 1600 | 1650 |

1492 After a voyage of two months, Christopher Columbus reaches the New World.

1650

LESSON 1

Europe in the Age of Exploration

THINKING FOCUS

Why did Europeans look for sea routes to Asia in the 1400s?

Key Terms

* technology
* navigate

➤ *This illustration from an ancient map of the world shows a sea monster swallowing a ship.*

I magine an island where monsters 28 to 30 feet tall live. In 1356, Sir John Mandeville told of such a place in his *Travels,* a book that told stories of things supposedly seen by travelers to Asia and Africa.

And they have no clothes to wear except the skins of beasts, which they cover their bodies with. They eat no bread; but they eat raw flesh. . . . They will more readily eat human flesh than any other. Thanks to them no pilgrim dare enter this isle; for if they see a ship in the sea with men aboard, they will wade into the sea to take the men.

Strange tales also told of a snake that

lived in the Atlantic Ocean. Flames sprang from around its neck. Eyes 16 feet across glared at its enemies. Another rhinoceros-like creature was said to gobble up crabs 12 feet wide.

Most Europeans in the 1400s knew little about the world beyond their own villages. Many believed that monsters roamed over distant lands and seas. But in the 1400s, Europeans began to explore these unknown areas. Within 50 years, exploration changed the way Europeans saw the world.

How Europeans Saw the World

The map on page 105 shows the European idea of the world in the 1400s. Like most maps of the time, this one mixed real geographical knowledge with stories and guesses. People knew of only

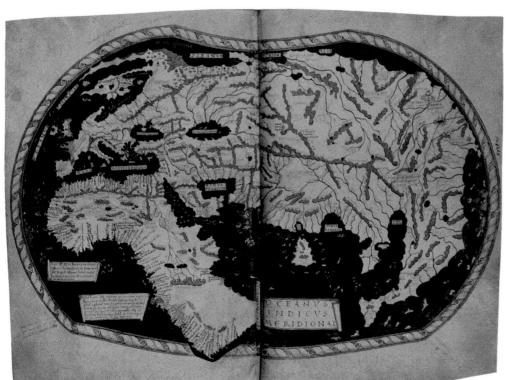

▼ *A beautiful compass rose like this often decorated early maps.*

■ *How much did Europeans in the 1400s know about the world around them?*

three continents—Europe, Africa, and Asia.

Educated people knew that the earth was round and that Asia lay across the Atlantic. Not everyone believed that monsters hid underwater or that the sea near the equator was boiling hot. But even those who did not believe the stories did not think it would be possible to sail across the ocean.

Sailors didn't have the skills needed for long voyages. Once they were out of sight of land, they could not tell how far they had gone or in what direction.

However, political events and trade awakened new interest in the outside world. Also, developments in **technology,** knowledge used for making things, let nations begin to explore the world's oceans. ■

Reasons for Exploration

The changes in European society began with a series of religious wars called the Crusades. From 1096 to about 1291, European Christians fought Muslims, people who believed in the religion of Islam. Christians fought to gain control of Jerusalem and other areas they believed were holy.

The Crusades took Europeans to the Mediterranean area, northeast Africa, and southwest Asia. There they saw Italian and Arab merchants in control of busy trade centers. These merchants traded spices, fine silks, and gems from India, China, and Japan.

Desire for Trade

Word of these riches excited Europeans, and they dreamed of trading with Asia themselves.

These fine goods would make life in Europe better. For example, before refrigeration, people could use spices like pepper and nutmeg from Asia to slow the rotting process and hide the taste of rotting meat.

Europeans also learned of the riches of Asia by reading. They read, for example, this description of an Indian king:

> The king is no more clothed than the rest, except that he has a piece of richer cloth, and is honorably distinguished by various kinds of ornaments, such as a collar set with jewels, sapphires, emeralds, and rubies, of immense value. He also wears . . . a fine silken string containing 104 large handsome pearls and rubies. . . . On each arm he wears three gold bracelets, adorned with pearls and jewels; on three different parts of the leg, golden bands ornamented in the same manner; and on the toes of his feet, as well as on his fingers, rings of great value.
>
> Marco Polo, *Description of the World*, 1298

The invention of the printing press in the 1400s made books such as Marco Polo's journals widely available to the public for the first time. Polo, an adventurer from Venice, Italy, traveled through India and China in the late 1200s. His book described the people and things he found there. Europeans dreamed of having such things for themselves.

Duty to Spread Christianity

Besides dreams of riches, Europeans had other reasons for wanting to open routes to Asia and Africa. They saw exploration as a way to spread Christianity.

The Crusades had not won Jerusalem from the Muslims. However, Europeans had not lost their crusading spirit. They were certain that Christianity was the only true religion. Therefore, they believed it was their duty to convert all non-Christians to Christianity. ■

■ *What did Europeans hope to gain from their explorations?*

▼ *As the timeline shows, events over 400 years combined to produce the age of exploration.*

Developments Leading to the Age of Exploration

About 1000 Arabic triangular sails that allow ships to sail into the wind gain widespread use among Europeans.

1190 Magnetic compass comes into use in Europe.

1000   1100   1200

1096–1291 Crusades expose Europeans to new technology and luxury goods.

About 1200 Development of rudder enables one person to steer ship.

Technological Developments

Contact between Europe and Asia did more than create the desire for trade and for spreading Christianity. It also led to important developments in shipbuilding and in the ability to **navigate,** or chart the course of a journey.

In the 1400s, even the most experienced sailors feared sailing in strange waters. An unexpected rock formation or ocean current could cause a shipwreck or take a ship off course. Also, sailors never knew when they might be in enemy territory. Before they could undertake long voyages, explorers needed the equipment to get them safely home.

Ships and Sails

For about 1,000 years, European ships moved by means of square-rigged sails. These ships could hold their own against tossing waves during short trips along the coast. However, they could sail only in the same direction as the wind. Thus they could not make long voyages without being blown off course.

In the Mediterranean area, lateen *(luh TEEN)* sails became popular because they could catch winds from the sides and from the rear of a ship. A lateen sail looked like a triangle along the length of a ship.

The development of the rudder allowed Portuguese shipbuilders in the 1400s to create a new ship called a caravel *(KAR uh vehl)*. The rudder made it possible for sailors to steer ships with lateen sails without a large crew of oarsmen. The creation of the caravel brought about a major improvement in sailing. Not only was the

How Do We Know?

HISTORY *Historians have learned about developments in shipbuilding by studying drawings, port records, and ship-for-hire agreements. They have also dug up sunken ships, such as the* Grâce Dieu, *which sank in 1418 and was brought to the surface in England in 1933. Studying this ship has told historians a great deal about the ships used in European exploration.*

About 1300 Iron guns first used aboard ships.

1479 Ferdinand and Isabella unite Spain.

About 1480 Astrolabe measures distance more accurately.

| 1300 | 1400 | 1500 |

1271 Marco Polo travels to the Orient.

1455 Gutenberg's printing press improves the spread of information.

The Age of Exploration

▲ *A sailor could find latitude by measuring the angle of the horizon in relation to the North Star. To do this he used a cross-staff. The sailor aimed the crosspiece so that it lined up with the star at its top and the horizon at its bottom. The lower the North Star in the sky, the farther south the ship.*

■ *What major technological developments made exploration possible in the 1400s?*

for use on land. Sailors could not get accurate readings on the bouncing deck of a ship. The drawing on this page shows how sailors used the more reliable cross-staff to figure latitude.

Although sailors could figure out their latitude, they had no way to measure longitude. Along the shore, landmarks allowed sailors to correct a course. But on the open sea, they could only guess longitude by figuring how long and how far they had traveled.

caravel capable of great speed, but it was much easier to control than ships had been up to this time. The development of the caravel was a key factor in launching the age of exploration.

Navigation

Exploration needed more than ships, however. Sailors had to know where they were going and how far they had come, especially when out of sight of land.

European sailors had used the compass to find direction since about 1200. They measured latitude by turning the pointer on a metal disk called an astrolabe (*AS truh layb*) toward the sun. However, astrolabes were designed

Weapons

As explorers set out on unknown seas, they depended on another kind of technology: weapons. Sailors did not know who they might have to conquer or defend themselves against. Sailors on the first overseas ships carried weapons familiar to them—swords, spears, bows, and armor. As technology improved, more powerful weapons such as guns and cannons came into use. These weapons established the method of naval warfare used until the end of wooden warships. They also made Europeans feel nearly all-powerful over the peoples they met. ■

R E V I E W

1. **FOCUS** Why did Europeans look for new sea routes to Asia in the 1400s?
2. **CONNECT** How did sailors use the cross-staff to figure their latitude?
3. **HISTORY** What influence did the writings of Marco Polo have upon Europeans?
4. **CULTURE** Why was the triangular lateen sail an improvement over the old square-rigged sail?
5. **CRITICAL THINKING** New technology was necessary for

early exploration. What exploration today depends on new technology?
6. **ACTIVITY** Make up a story such as a traveler at the time of the Crusades might have told to frighten and impress his listeners. Include some frightening monster or force of nature such as a sea serpent or boiling water at the equator. Share your story with the class.

Chapter 5

LESSON 2

Portuguese and Spanish Exploration

W hy did Prince
Henry of Portugal
choose to live in
the town of Sagres
(SAH greesh), in southwest Portugal? He had once shown promise
as a military leader. At 21, Henry
had boldly fought the North African Muslims and captured the city
of Ceuta *(SAY oot uh)* for the
Portuguese.

But in 1420, at age 26, Henry
almost never left Sagres. He liked
to stay with the mathematicians,
mapmakers, shipbuilders, and captains at what was called his "school
of navigation."

Members of the court of King
John, Henry's father, wondered
why Henry chose such a quiet,

lonely life. They did not see that
the scholars at Sagres would start
the greatest period of exploration
in history.

THINKING
FOCUS

*What were the most im-
portant results of Por-
tuguese and Spanish
explorations?*

Key Terms

* expedition
* colony

▲ *Prince Henry the
Navigator never went
on a voyage of discovery
himself. However, he de-
voted his life to studying
the coast of Africa.*

Portuguese Exploration

Henry had not forgotten the
sights he saw while fighting in
North Africa. The Muslims there
controlled a great trading center.
They sold gold and ivory from
African lands south of the Sahara,
and spices and silks from India,

China, and Japan. If only Portugal
could share in these riches, Henry
thought.

Muslims controlled the land
routes to Asia. The Portuguese
also wanted to have spices and
silks, but they didn't want to pay

109

The Age of Exploration

This drawing was made in 1502. The ship is like those used by the Portuguese explorers.

■ *How did Portuguese exploration add to Europeans' knowledge of the world?*

▼ *Columbus's coat of arms includes a castle and a lion, symbols of the kingdoms of Ferdinand and Isabella. It also has anchors to symbolize Columbus's title as Admiral of the Ocean Sea, and a drawing of the islands he explored.*

the high prices being charged in Europe. They couldn't send their own traders to Asia because they couldn't get past the armed Muslims. However, Prince Henry thought they might be able to reach Asia and East Africa by sea.

Henry ordered the experts at Sagres to find a sea route to Africa and Asia. Then he searched for sailors brave enough to lead these voyages. Henry paid for a series of **expeditions,** or organized journeys, down the west coast of Africa. His captains returned bearing gold and ivory. But Henry wanted them to go farther south. He would not be happy until one of his ships sailed all the way to the Indian Ocean.

Henry the Navigator, as he was called, died in 1460. In 1488, Bartolomeu Dias rounded the southern tip of Africa. Then, in 1497, Vasco da Gama began a voyage that would match Henry's dreams. He sailed all the way around Africa to India. The map on page 111 shows the routes Dias and da Gama took.

The journey to India and back to Portugal covered over 27,000 miles and lasted over two years. Along the way, da Gama and his crew battled disease, storms, and even attacks by rival traders. But in the end, da Gama succeeded in opening the door to Portuguese trade with Asia. ■

Early Spanish Exploration

Christopher Columbus, a captain from Genoa, Italy, had sailed aboard Portuguese trade ships. He knew that the Portuguese were trying to reach Asia by sailing around Africa. However, Columbus had studied maps of Ptolemy *(TAHL uh mee),* a Greek geographer who lived around A.D. 150. Columbus became convinced that the shortest route to Asia, or the Indies, was straight west across the Atlantic.

Voyages of Columbus

Columbus knew that such a voyage would cost a great deal of money. For eight years he tried to persuade European rulers to pay for his voyage.

Many people said his idea was too dangerous and would cost too much. Finally, in 1492, Columbus heard that King Ferdinand and Queen Isabella of Spain would give him the money he needed to sail.

The king and queen wanted to spread Spanish power. After years of war, they had driven the North African Muslims out of southern Spain. Now they wanted to win a share of the rich trade with Asia.

Columbus left Palos, Spain, on August 3, 1492, with his crew and three ships. After a stop at the Canary Islands off Africa, he set a course straight across the Atlantic.

Because he was afraid that the crew would refuse to go on, Columbus kept his own secret records

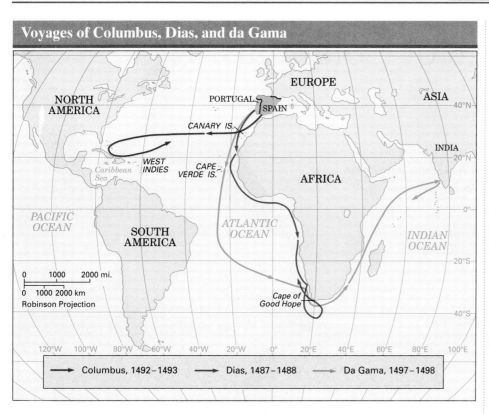

Voyages of Columbus, Dias, and da Gama

NORTH AMERICA
EUROPE
PORTUGAL
SPAIN
CANARY IS.
40°N
ASIA
WEST INDIES
Caribbean Sea
CAPE VERDE IS.
INDIA
20°N
AFRICA
PACIFIC OCEAN
ATLANTIC OCEAN
0°
SOUTH AMERICA
INDIAN OCEAN
20°S
Cape of Good Hope
40°S

0 1000 2000 mi.
0 1000 2000 km
Robinson Projection

120°W 100°W 80°W 60°W 40°W 20°W 0° 20°E 40°E 60°E 80°E 100°E

→ Columbus, 1492–1493   → Dias, 1487–1488   → Da Gama, 1497–1498

◄ *This map shows Columbus's first voyage and the voyages of Dias and da Gama. Which routes led to Asia?*

▲ *This painting of Columbus, done about 20 years after his death, was probably copied from an earlier portrait.*

of how far he believed they had sailed each day. He insisted that they sail on.

On October 12, Columbus landed on a tiny Caribbean island that is today one of the Bahama Islands. He named it "San Salvador"—Holy Savior. Believing he had reached the Indies, he called the Taino people there "Indios" (Indians). The Taino were fearful of the ships until they saw men get off them. Then they welcomed the Spanish with gifts.

In a letter he sent to Spain in 1493, Columbus wrote

Their Highnesses can see that I shall give them as much gold as they want if their Highnesses will render me a little help; besides spice and cotton, as much as their Highnesses shall command. . . .

Columbus returned to Spain in March 1493 with six Taino captives as well as plants and gold for the Spanish rulers. They were so impressed that they gave him 17 ships and 1,200 men to form a **colony,** a settlement governed by a distant country, in the Indies. For more information about Columbus's voyage, see A Closer Look on the next two pages.

On his second voyage (September 1493 to the spring of 1496), Columbus set off with a large fleet carrying more than 1,000 passengers. They founded a settlement on the island of Hispaniola, where the Dominican Republic and Haiti are today. Columbus also explored the islands of Puerto Rico, Cuba, and Jamaica. Columbus made two later voyages in 1498 and 1502.

However, he failed to find the riches of Asia. He never knew that he had found a continent new to Europeans.

Across Time & Space

Columbus was not really the first European to explore the Americas. In the late 900s, a group of Norse, or Scandinavian, explorers sailed from Iceland and Greenland. A few settled briefly in what is now Newfoundland, Canada. But few Europeans ever knew of that settlement, and it was only remembered as a legend in Scandinavia by 1400.

111

The Voyage of Columbus

On September 9, 1492, Columbus wrote in his ship's log: "This day we completely lost sight of land, and many men sighed and wept for fear they would not see it again for a long time." The log tells the story of the trip aboard the Niña, the Pinta, and the Santa María, as the expedition sailed into unknown regions of the Atlantic Ocean.

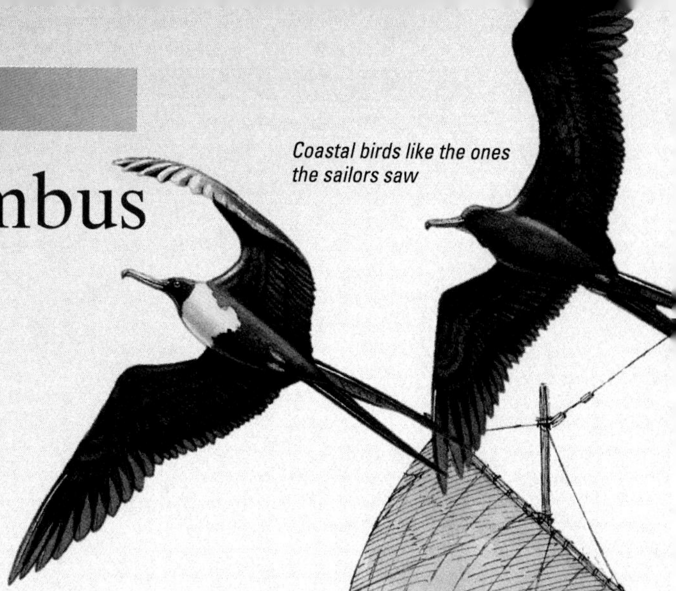

Coastal birds like the ones the sailors saw

September 20, 1492
The sailors grew afraid their ships would get stuck in thick seaweed, called sargassum.

Sargassum

Niña

September 22, 1492
"The crew is agitated, thinking that no winds blow in these parts that will return them to Spain."
The Log of Christopher Columbus

Santa María

Deck—where the men worked and slept

Pinta

September 24, 1492
"I am having serious trouble with the crew. . . . I am told by a few trusted men (and these are few in number) that if I persist in going onward, the best course of action will be to throw me into the sea some night."
The Log of Christopher Columbus

Crow's nest—for the lookout to stand in

October 12, 1492
The explorers had not seen land for 33 days. On this night, Columbus finally heard a boom from the *Pinta*'s gun—the signal that land had been sighted!

Captain's cabin— where Columbus slept, dined with his officers, and wrote in his log

October 9, 1492
All night the men could hear birds flying overhead and see them against the moon. The birds gave the men hope that they were nearing land.

Hold—where food, water, and other supplies were stored

Lead weight and marked rope for measuring depth of water so the ships wouldn't run aground

Explorers After Columbus

News that Columbus had reached land by sailing west led other European voyagers to try to claim new lands. Geographers, however, suspected that Columbus had not reached Asia. In 1507, a German mapmaker named the new continent "America" after the Italian explorer Amerigo Vespucci *(vehs POOT chee)*. Vespucci had made a voyage to the New World for Spain and another for Portugal. Later he wrote a book about them.

In 1513, Vasco Núñez de Balboa, whose crew included Africans as well as Europeans, crossed Panama on foot and arrived at the Pacific Ocean. Another ocean stood between Spain and the Indies! In 1521, the Portuguese explorer Ferdinand Magellan became the first European to sail west across the Pacific. Magellan's crew continued west from Asia, returning to Spain in 1522. The crew had completed the first known trip around the globe. ■

■ *Why did Columbus believe he had reached Asia?*

How Do We Know?

Cortés's victory over the Aztecs is one of the best-documented military campaigns in history. A Spanish soldier, Bernal Díaz, kept a journal that describes Cortés's mistakes and cruelties. Aztec written histories of the conquest also survive.

The Search for Gold

Even though America was not Asia, the Spanish kept searching for riches. In 1519, Hernan Cortés went to Mexico, which was said to have huge gold mines.

With 17 horses and an army of 600 Spaniards and some Africans, Cortés marched inland from Mexico's east coast to Tenochtitlan *(tay nawch tee TLAHN)*, the huge

UNDERSTANDING EXPANSION

The rulers of Spain sent explorers all over the world. They wanted to expand the influence of their country. Historians use the word *expansion* to describe the actions of a country that occupies or controls another country. As a country expands, people often move from that country into the new land.

Kinds of Expansion

Expansion often involves war. One country may start a war to expand into land owned by another country.

A country may buy land for expansion. In 1803, President Thomas Jefferson was able to expand the United States by buying a large part of America from France.

Today, a country might expand its influence by trading with other countries. For example, Japan now sells its products around the world. Your family may own a car or a stereo produced by a Japanese company. In this way, Japanese culture expands its influence as Japanese business expands.

Expansion and Change

Expansion often has dramatic effects. When one country occupies another, it usually changes the land it occupies.

The expansion of Spain into the Americas brought death through disease to great numbers of native peoples. The culture of Spain—Spanish language, food, and architecture—became dominant in the lands Spain occupied.

capital city of the Aztecs. Thousands of Indians defeated by the Aztecs joined this army. A messenger to Montezuma *(mahn tuh ZOO muh)*, the Aztec king, announced that light-skinned men had come on "small mountains floating on the waves of the sea."

Aztec Defeat

Montezuma waited too long to fight off the invaders, believing Cortés to be a god of Aztec legend.

In the meantime, Cortés's army had entered the city and blocked off its exits. With no way to get food, the Aztecs were trapped.

Cortés's army took the Aztecs' gold and jewels. Then they destroyed the buildings. The city lay in ruins when the last Aztecs gave up in 1521. After four months of battle, Cortés had beaten an empire of more than five million. On the ruins he built Mexico City, which became the capital of a Spanish empire.

Treasure Hunters

After Cortés's victory, other Spaniards came to take treasure from native peoples. In South America, the invaders defeated the Inca and the Chibcha *(CHIHB chuh)*, who lived in present-day Peru and Colombia, and took over their gold and silver mines.

Francisco Coronado and Hernando de Soto led expeditions made up of Spanish and African explorers into North America. Coronado searched for cities of gold and silver in what is now New Mexico. He found no rich cities, but the explorations allowed Spain to claim lands in southern North America. By the mid-1500s, Spain had become the most powerful nation in Europe. ■

Objects like this gold lizard from Peru fed the dreams of explorers who searched for cities of gold.

◄ *The painting on the left shows Indians leaving their village as the Spanish approach on horseback.*

■ *What were the consequences of the Spaniards' search for gold in the Americas?*

R E V I E W

1. **FOCUS** What were the most important results of Portuguese and Spanish explorations?
2. **CONNECT** How did Prince Henry the Navigator's experiences in North Africa influence him to look for a route to Asia?
3. **GEOGRAPHY** Find Mexico City on the map of North America on page 624 of the Atlas. Use the distance scale on the map to estimate how far Mexico City is from the east coast of Mexico, which was where Cortés landed.
4. **CRITICAL THINKING** Why do you think Columbus was considered a failure at the time of his death?
5. **ACTIVITY** Tell about a place—Antarctica, the bottom of the ocean, the moon—that you would like to explore. What dangers might there be in getting there? What would you expect to find there?

Money for Exploration

Ferdinand and Isabella provided money for Columbus's voyage. They are shown in the painting and coins below. Columbus gave coins like these to natives on his arrival in America.

> The end of Spain and the beginning of India are not far distant but close, and it is evident that this sea is navigable in a few days with a fair wind.
>
> *Imago Mundi [A World Geography], c. 1410*

> His (Columbus's) promises and offers were impossible and vain and worthy of rejection . . . (I)t was not . . . proper . . . for their royal authority to favor an affair that . . . appeared uncertain and impossible to any educated person . . . "
>
> Bartolomé de las Casas, on the report of the royal committee

Background

Christopher Columbus was sure he could sail west, circle the earth, and reach the Indies—the European name for eastern Asia. But Columbus had a hard time persuading any European rulers to fund his voyage.

In trying to persuade Ferdinand and Isabella of Spain, Columbus explained how Spain could benefit. He pointed out that a better trade route to Asia could bring Spain great wealth and power. Spanish merchants would have wonderful new metals, cloth, and spices to sell. Spanish products would find new buyers. The Spanish flag would lead the way across the "western ocean." The power of Spain would circle the globe. And along the way, the Spanish could bring Christianity to foreign places.

Ferdinand and Isabella's committee of advisors foresaw other results. They warned that the earth was far larger than Columbus thought. The "western ocean" was huge and dangerous and could not be crossed. Supporting Columbus's plan would waste Spanish lives and money. The country and its government would be laughed at for believing such nonsense.

Conflict over Exploration

Would Ferdinand and Isabella listen to their advisors or would they grant Columbus's request? The decision was a difficult one. We cannot know what line of thinking finally led them to support Columbus. However, they must have carefully considered the possible consequences of each alternative.

The safe choice would have been to reject Columbus's request. The advantages of saying no would include putting money to other uses such as strengthening the army and navy, improving roads and public buildings, and funding the arts. The main disadvantage would be giving up the possibility of gaining wealth and trading advantages.

Saying yes was the high-risk choice. If Columbus succeeded, Spain would get all of the benefits that Columbus had promised. If he failed, Spain might suffer just as the royal advisors had warned.

Ferdinand and Isabella finally decided to risk giving Columbus ships and money. Their decision had one major consequence that no one could have predicted— Columbus reached a land entirely unknown to Europeans.

The Spanish flag (below) carried a castle and a lion, symbols of Ferdinand and Isabella.

Flag from The World Book Encyclopedia. © 1993 World Book, Inc. By Permission

Should we pay for Columbus's voyage?

- Expand Spain's power
- Christianize the Indies
- Trade with the East
- Discover new lands

Pay

- Fear of failure
- Dangers of journey
- Waste of money

Don't pay

Decision Point

1. What advantages and disadvantages might King Ferdinand and Queen Isabella of Spain have considered before making their decision?

2. Why do you think Ferdinand and Isabella decided to support Columbus? Do you think you would have made the same decision? Why or why not?

3. Based on this example, do you think it is possible to predict all the consequences of a decision? Explain.

4. For more than 30 years, the United States has launched missions to explore outer space (see Minipedia p. 601). What are some advantages to continuing this exploration? What are some disadvantages?

5. Do you think that space exploration might lead to an unpredictable discovery? If so, how might that affect your decision about whether the United States should spend billions of dollars on space exploration?

Modern explorers like astronauts have used flags to mark their discoveries.

The Age of Exploration

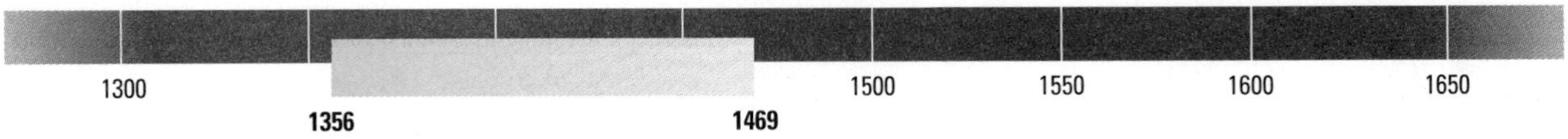

L E S S O N   3

French, Dutch, and English Voyages

THINKING
FOCUS

Why did the French, Dutch, and English decide to begin exploring in the Western Hemisphere?

Key Terms

- Northwest Passage
- contagious disease

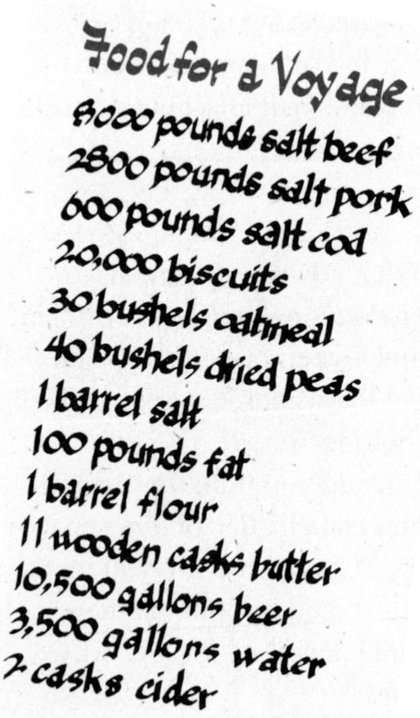

➤ *The supplies listed here were expected to feed 190 sailors for three months. How would you like eating these foods for three months?*

What's for dinner? For sailors on long sea voyages in the 1500s, the food seldom changed. Night after night, month after month, voyagers lived on a diet of salted meat, dried beans or peas, and hard biscuits. If the crew stopped on land during the journey, they might enjoy fresh fruit or meat. Only dried or heavily salted foods would keep for more than a few days. And the sailors had no way to keep rats or insects out of their food. Sailors on Columbus's ships ate after dark so as not to see the worms.

Bad food was not the only hardship sailors faced. Lack of vitamin C in the diet caused scurvy, a painful and often fatal disease. Over half the crew on Vasco da Gama's voyage to India in 1497 died of scurvy.

Barrels holding the precious supply of fresh water often sprang leaks. Frequent storms made life miserable. Yet despite such conditions, exploration grew rapidly during the 1500s.

Food for a Voyage
8000 pounds salt beef
2800 pounds salt pork
600 pounds salt cod
20,000 biscuits
30 bushels oatmeal
40 bushels dried peas
1 barrel salt
100 pounds fat
1 barrel flour
11 wooden casks butter
10,500 gallons beer
3,500 gallons water
2 casks cider

Exploration of North America

To explain why he risked crossing an unknown ocean, Spanish explorer Bernal Díaz wrote, ". . . for the service of God and His Majesty . . . and to procure wealth which all men desire." By the mid-1500s,

◄ *Compare this map made in 1526 to the one shown on page 105. How are the Indian and Atlantic oceans different on the later map? How much of the coast of North America does this map show?*

overseas travel was still dangerous but not quite so mysterious. Although Spanish and Portuguese explorers tried to keep their knowledge secret, information leaked out. Maps like the one above showed that explorers had new knowledge of the American coastline.

In addition to learning of new lands and routes, French, Dutch, and English rulers knew that exploration had made Spain and Portugal rich. Portugal controlled the eastern routes to Asia, Africa, and part of South America. Spain claimed Central America and the rest of South America. Other explorers, therefore, decided to sail to the northern part of America to seek fame and fortune.

French Voyages

The French sent out the first of several voyages in 1524. King Francis I hired an Italian, Giovanni da Verrazano *(vehr uh ZAH noh)*, to search for the **Northwest Passage,** a legendary water route to China through North America.

Verrazano landed near what is now North Carolina and mapped the coast as far north as Maine.

Jacques Cartier *(kahr TYAY)* continued the search for the Northwest Passage in 1535. Cartier sailed up the St. Lawrence River, in the hope that it might lead him to China. His route is shown on the map on page 120. The river's rapids and ice stopped his ship.

Cartier and his crew spent a winter in an Iroquois village at the place that is now Montreal. He discovered that this land, which the

◄ *This drawing from the late 1500s shows a French explorer with his Indian hosts.*

The Age of Exploration

Indians called Canada, was rich with fish, game, and furs. Indians taught the visitors how to make cornbread and how to cure scurvy by drinking tea made from bark. However, the harsh winters and the lack of gold and silks discouraged the French from settling in North America.

Dutch Voyages

The Dutch began exploring more than 100 years after Columbus's voyages. In 1595, the Dutch sent ships to take over Portuguese trade centers in Asia. To manage their growing trade, the Dutch started the East India Company in 1602. The company paid for expeditions to Australia and to islands in the South Pacific.

Managers of the Dutch East India Company thought that find-

▼ *The explorers' routes are shown on a special kind of map called a projection. To learn more about projections, see page G10 in the* Map and Globe Handbook.

ing the Northwest Passage to Asia would give them even greater control over trade. In 1609, the company hired an English sailor named Henry Hudson to lead the

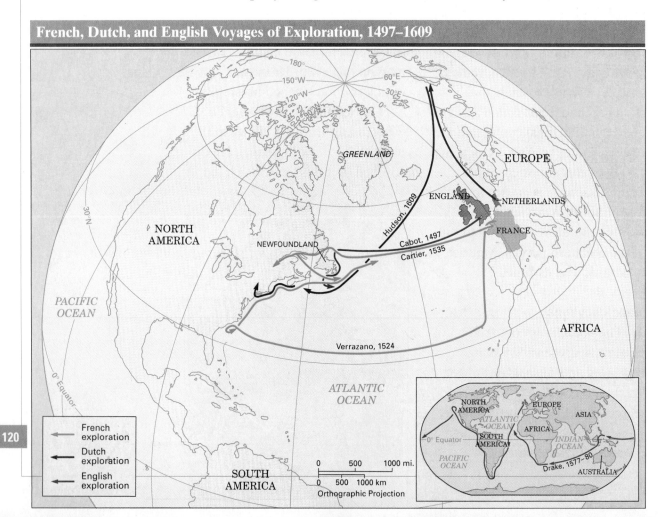

French, Dutch, and English Voyages of Exploration, 1497–1609

French exploration
Dutch exploration
English exploration

Hudson, 1609
Cabot, 1497
Cartier, 1535
Verrazano, 1524
Drake, 1577–80

Orthographic Projection

first Dutch expedition to North America. Look at the map on page 120 to see Hudson's route. Hudson explored the river, later named for him, near what is now New York City. The Indians he met were interested in fur trading.

In the early 1600s, the Dutch set up trading posts at places that are now Albany and New York City. However, this trade did not bring the Dutch as much money as trading centers in southeast Asia and west Africa.

English Voyages

Like the Dutch, the English were slow to get started on overseas exploration. In 1497, King Henry VII hired John Cabot, an Italian sea captain, to sail west to Asia. Cabot was to explore the unknown lands and establish trade.

On one voyage, Cabot landed on an island he called "New Found Land." It is now the Canadian province of Newfoundland. There he found cod and salmon but no gold or spices.

After Cabot's voyages, most English exploration stopped. Throughout the 1500s, the English were busy with problems at home and battles with other nations. England and Spain had become enemies.

In 1577, England's Queen Elizabeth sent Francis Drake, a sailor with the English navy, on a secret voyage. Drake sailed around the tip of South America and up its western coast. Along the way, he stole from Spanish ships and trading centers and loaded his own ship with treasures.

Drake sailed north along the coast of present-day California and claimed this land for England. He returned home by crossing the Pacific. Thus, he became the first Englishman to sail around the world. Like other explorers, Drake cared more about wealth and glory than about settling a new land. ■

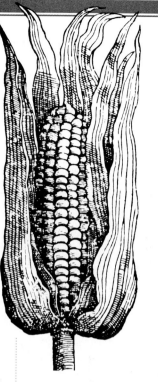

▲ *This drawing of corn shows one of the first foods brought to Europe from the Americas.*

■ *What areas did the French, Dutch, and English explore, and why?*

Impact on American Indians

The first contact between Europeans and Indians had great impact on both peoples. Some Europeans became rich from the gold, silver, furs, and fish they got from the Indians. The foods Europeans ate changed. Corn, potatoes, cocoa, and other foods such as those listed at the right were shipped to Europe.

However, contact with Europeans brought deadly diseases, slavery, and the breakup of Indian societies throughout the Americas. A **contagious disease** is a sickness

Items Exchanged Between Indians and Europeans	
From Europeans to Indians	**From Indians to Europeans**
Bananas	Chocolate
Cattle	Corn
Chickens	Peanuts
Horses	Potatoes
Pigs	Pumpkins
Sheep	Squash
Sugar cane	Sweet potatoes
Wheat	Tobacco
	Tomatoes

◄ *This chart shows some of the items that were exchanged between the Americas and Europe.*

The Age of Exploration

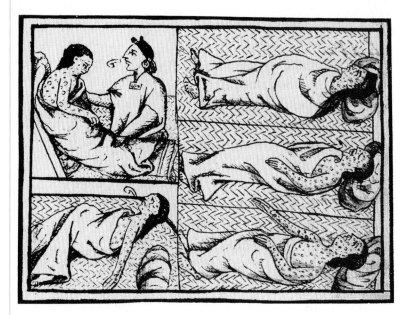

This Mexican drawing from the 1500s shows the deadly effects of smallpox. When Cortés invaded Mexico, about 25 million people lived there. Fifty years later, only about one-tenth this number lived in Mexico.

■ How did the lives of Europeans and Indians change after explorers established contact between the two groups?

that spreads from one person to another. These diseases swept through Indian communities, killing many thousands.

Smallpox was the most contagious and most deadly of these diseases. By 1650, smallpox had killed three-fourths of the Indians who once lived in North and South America.

The use of force and violence by Europeans also killed thousands of Indians. European colonists in South and Central America pushed Indians off their lands and forced them to work long hours on farms and in mines. Many died of exhaustion. For

those Indians who survived disease and forced labor, life changed greatly. Many explorers believed everyone should be Christian. They even used force to make Indians become Christians.

Some Indian groups tried to fight the Europeans, but few succeeded. Spears and arrows were no match for European guns. Also, Indians had never seen horses before. At first, horses terrified Indians and allowed Europeans to escape attack.

As more Europeans sailed to America, contact between Europeans and Indians steadily increased. Indians were especially interested in trading for the weapons, tools, and cooking utensils made by Europeans. They also began to breed horses, sheep, cows, pigs, and chickens, and to grow wheat and rice. Many of these items improved the lives of Indians, and relations between Indians and Europeans were often friendly.

However, in the 1600s, more and more Europeans settled in America. Fights and trouble grew as the Europeans claimed lands that had belonged to the Indians for thousands of years. ■

R E V I E W

1. **FOCUS** Why did the French, Dutch, and English rulers decide to begin the exploration of the Western Hemisphere?

2. **CONNECT** What did the first French, Dutch, and English explorers learn from the earlier voyages of Spanish and Portuguese explorers?

3. **HISTORY** How did the introduction of contagious diseases carried by European explorers and settlers affect American Indians?

4. **CRITICAL THINKING** Compare the results of French, Dutch, and English exploration with those of the Spanish and Portuguese.

5. **WRITING ACTIVITY** Imagine you are an Iroquois living in Canada in the 1500s. Three ships carrying European explorers arrive on the shore of your community. Write a description of the people, their ships, and the things they brought with them. Also describe your reaction to these new sights.

Tracing Routes

Here's Why

If you understand how a map shows directions, you can use a map to see and describe a route from one place to another. For example, you can describe the route of Ferdinand Magellan's crew as they sailed all the way around the earth. The map on this page shows the route they followed.

Here's How

Look for the direction arrow at the bottom center of the map. The arrow shows which direction is north, which is south, which is east, and which is west. North, south, east, and west are cardinal, or main, directions. Between cardinal directions are intermediate directions. For example, the direction between north and east is northeast. You can use intermediate directions to describe Magellan's route.

From Spain, Magellan sailed southwest across the Atlantic Ocean and along the coast of South America to its tip. Then he sailed into the Strait of Magellan.

Try It

Use cardinal and intermediate directions to finish describing Magellan's voyage. Leaving the Strait of Magellan, he sailed ___?___ across the Pacific. From the Philippines, his crew sailed ___?___ to Timor. They continued ___?___ to the Cape of Good Hope and from there ___?___ to Spain.

Apply It

Refer to the world map on pages 614 and 615, and trace an outline of continents. Then locate Miami, Florida, on the U.S. map on pages 620 and 621. Mark Miami on your outline. Draw a line to show a route from Miami to New Zealand. Then use cardinal and intermediate directions to describe the route.

Magellan's Route Around the Earth

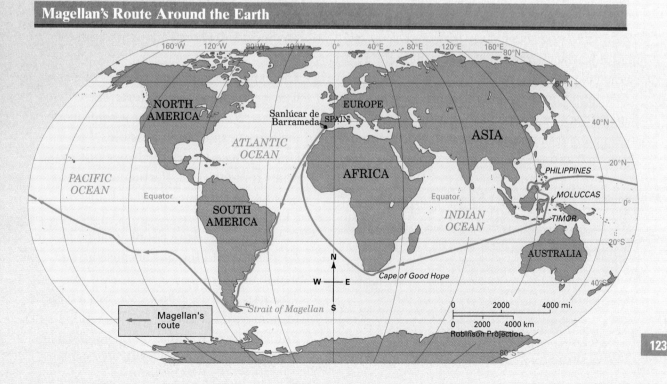

123

Chapter Review

Reviewing Key Terms

colony (p. 111)
contagious disease (p. 121)
expedition (p. 110)
navigate (p. 107)
Northwest Passage (p. 119)
technology (p. 105)

A. Imagine you are keeping a log, or journal, on a sea voyage. Five log entries that refer to key terms are started below. Add one sentence to each entry, using the key term. Be sure your sentences show you understand the meaning of the terms.

1. We heard about a possible water route to China through North America.
2. Tools that were recently invented are helping us reach these new lands.
3. Every day more sailors are becoming sick, suffering from the same terrible illness.
4. In planning our course, we knew we might face dangerous waters.
5. Our journey was organized and paid for by a wealthy prince.
6. Soon we'll form a settlement that will be governed by our native country.

B. Write a sentence for each pair of key terms. Write each sentence as if it were the beginning of a newspaper article.

1. Northwest Passage, navigate
2. technology, expedition
3. contagious disease, colony

Exploring Concepts

A. You can show important achievements of European explorers on a chart. Copy and complete the following chart on your own paper. The first row has been done for you. Use information in the chapter to help you fill in the rest of the chart.

If you wish to expand the chart, look at page 601 of the Minipedia. You will find information about famous explorers of North America as well as modern-day space explorers.

Country	Explorer's Name	Area Explored
Italy (Venice)	Marco Polo	India, China
Portugal		
Spain		
France		
Netherlands		
England		

B. Support the following statements with facts and details from the chapter.

1. Lack of knowledge and fear affected the way most Europeans thought about the world.
2. The experience of the Crusades increased European interest in exploration.
3. Important improvements for ships made the age of exploration possible.
4. Unless Prince Henry the Navigator found a water route to Asia, Portuguese traders could not get to the riches of India and China.
5. Columbus called the people that he met in the New World Indians because he had a wrong idea.
6. The arrival of the Europeans was a tragedy for American Indians.
7. Francis Drake was one of the people who demonstrated that the earth was a sphere.

Reviewing Skills

1. Look at the map of Verrazano's voyage. Use cardinal and intermediate directions to answer the following questions:
   a. In what direction did Verrazano sail from France to the Madeira Islands?
   b. What direction was he going as he sailed from the Madeira Islands to North America?
   c. What direction did he go along the coast of North America to Newfoundland?
2. Find the latitude and longitude of the Madeira Islands on the map.
3. Suppose you want to tell about European exploration. What visual device would best help you to show European voyages of exploration in chronological order?

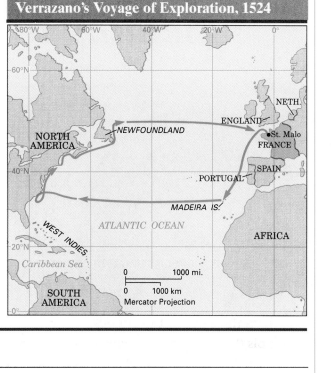

Verrazano's Voyage of Exploration, 1524

Using Critical Thinking

1. Today, many people object to reading or hearing that Christopher Columbus "discovered" America. They do not agree with the European explorers who called America a "new world." Why do you think some people feel this way? Do you agree or disagree with their objection? Be ready to explain your answers based on material from the chapter.

2. Describe European ideas of the world before the explorers began their voyages. Compare those ideas with the ideas of later Europeans after the voyages of exploration. Then predict how people's ideas about the earth, the solar system, and the universe may change as the exploration of space continues. Think about finding new planets and perhaps other forms of life.

Preparing for Citizenship

1. **ARTS ACTIVITY** Create a mural about Aztec life. The first scenes can show what life was like before the Spanish conquered the Aztec empire. The next group of scenes can show the battle between the Aztecs and Cortés's army. The last part can show what their capital city looked like after the battle. Invite other classes to see the mural.

2. **GROUP ACTIVITY** Work with a few classmates to create food items from American Indian cultures or from one of these countries: Spain, Italy, France, Holland, or England.

Check the library for recipes in cookbooks or magazines.

3. **COLLABORATIVE LEARNING** Prepare a television documentary called "You Were There." Imagine that a few reporters meet one of Columbus's ships after its return voyage. The crew members answer the reporters' questions about the "new world." Join a group to work on researching the script, writing the dialogue, and acting out the roles of Christopher Columbus, the reporters, and crew members.

The Age of Exploration

Chapter 6

Settling a New World

By 1585, the race to settle the New World had begun. In the South the Spanish had grown wealthy from gold and silver. In the North the French had become rich trading with Indians for furs. In between, the English tried to start their own colonies. Though the English were slow to settle the New World, their colonies became the most powerful in America.

1585 Sir Walter Raleigh (above) sends a group of English colonists to settle Roanoke Island in what is now North Carolina. The colony fails within five years.

1619 The Spanish build the mission of San Gerónimo in present-day New Mexico (above). The Spanish have come to America to find gold and silver and to convert Indians to Christianity.

1575

1600

1625

1585

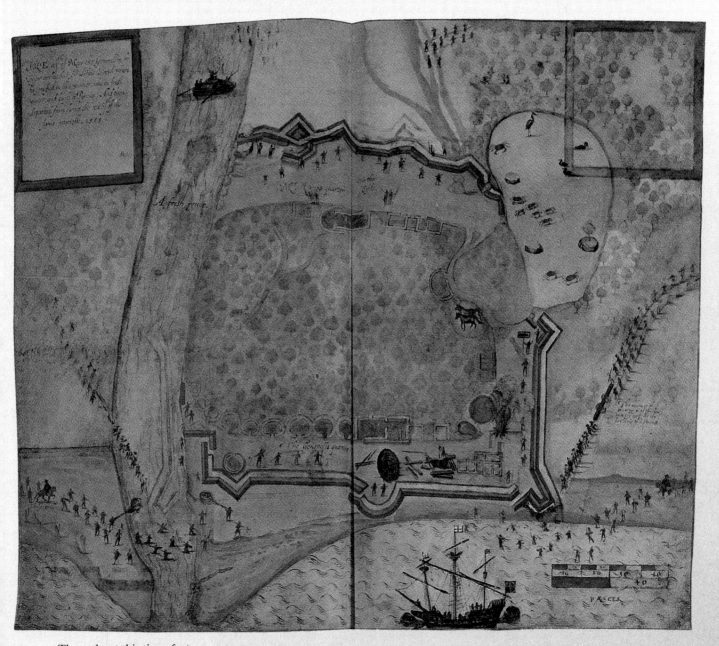

Throughout this time, forts like the one shown in this 1585 painting by John White protected European colonists from American Indians and other settlers.

1650

1675

1700

1664 The Dutch surrender their colony of New Netherland to the English, who rename it New York.

1682 French explorer Sieur de la Salle reaches the mouth of the Mississippi River. He claims the surrounding land for France and calls it Louisiana.

1682

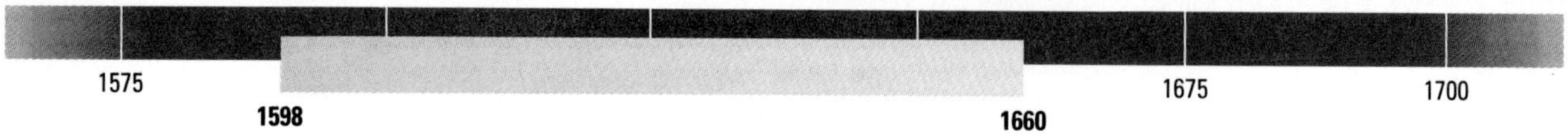

LESSON 1

Spanish and French Colonization

THINKING FOCUS

Why did the Spanish and the French establish colonies in North America?

Key Terms

- colonization
- encomienda
- mission
- tax
- fort

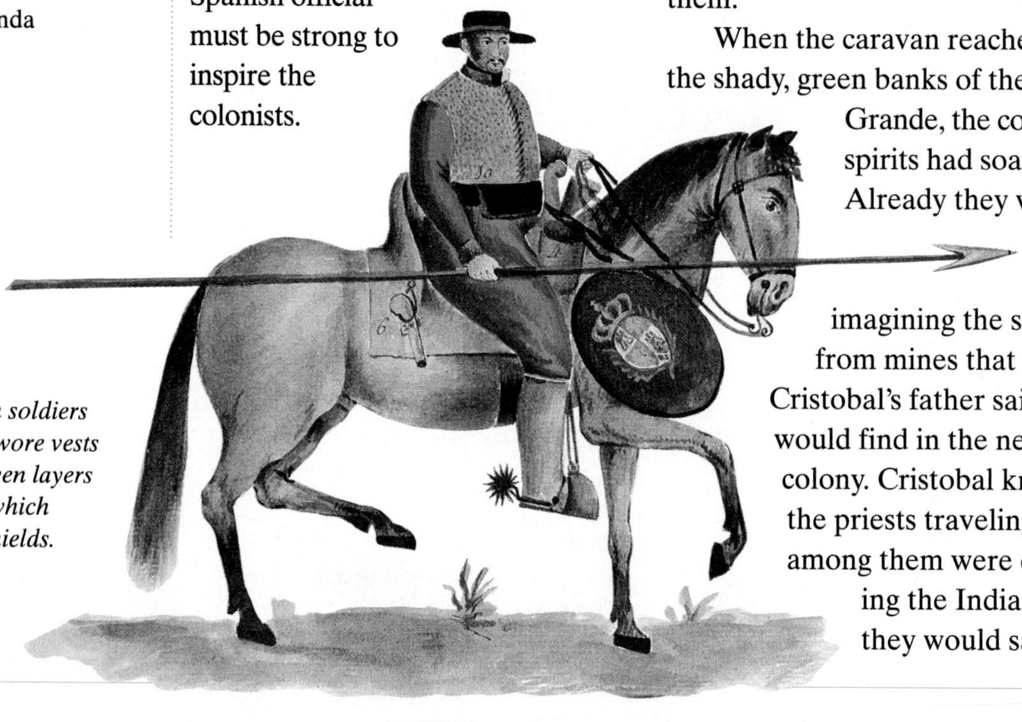

► *Spanish soldiers sometimes wore vests made of seven layers of leather, which served as shields.*

Ten-year-old Cristobal de Oñate *(aw NYAH teh)* drooped under the weight of his armor. He glanced up at his father—Juan de Oñate, governor of a new colony and captain-general in the army of Philip II, King of Spain. How proudly his father sat in his velvet saddle!

Immediately, Cristobal straightened. Hadn't his father appointed him lieutenant governor? A high Spanish official must be strong to inspire the colonists.

Cristobal turned to look at the hundreds of men, women, and children journeying north along the Rio Grande. For months this group of Europeans and a few Africans had pushed forward across the Mexican highlands and through the desert. Eighty-three creaking wagons formed a caravan carrying the colonists' household goods. Some 10,000 farm animals—cattle, horses, hogs, oxen, mules, goats, and sheep—plodded along beside them.

When the caravan reached the shady, green banks of the Rio Grande, the colonists' spirits had soared. Already they were imagining the silver from mines that Cristobal's father said they would find in the new colony. Cristobal knew the priests traveling among them were counting the Indian souls they would save.

On April 30, 1598, Juan de Oñate commanded the expedition to halt near the site of the future town of El Paso. A priest raised his cross high above the river, and Oñate formally claimed the land for Spain. Henceforth, the land north of the Rio Grande would be called New Mexico. Spain would rule this land and all its native Indians with the "power of life and death, over high and low, from the leaves of the trees to the stones and sands of the river. . . ."

Spanish Settlers in New Mexico

When he claimed New Mexico for Spain, Oñate was helping Spain colonize part of North America. In **colonization,** a country sends settlers to a distant land and rules the settlements from afar.

To govern its new territory, Spain placed wealthy Spanish settlers in charge of **encomiendas** *(ehn koh mee EHN dahs),* huge estates that often included several Indian villages. The landowners forced Indians to work on their estates while they searched for mines.

Oñate never found mines in New Mexico. He did find dozens of Indian villages that the Spanish called pueblos. The people who lived in the pueblos belonged to Indian tribes, such as the Zuni and the Hopi. They lived in flat-roofed houses made of stone and plastered with dried mud.

Before Oñate arrived in 1598, the Indians lived in peace. They worked hard tending crops of corn, beans, and squash in the dry desert climate. They also grew cotton and wove it into cloth for shirts and dresses. Much of the Indians' social life centered around religion. They worshiped spirits in nature that they believed sent rain and good harvests.

But along with the settlers, Oñate also brought priests to

Across Time & Space

New Mexico was not the first permanent Spanish settlement in what is now the United States. The Spanish established St. Augustine, Florida, in 1565. The settlers there fought off pirates who tried to capture Spanish ships carrying gold from the Gulf of Mexico to Spain. Today St. Augustine is the oldest city in the United States founded by Europeans.

◄ *The Zuni and Hopi people of New Mexico sent this document to King Philip II of Spain. It asked the king to stop the harsh treatment of Indians.*

129

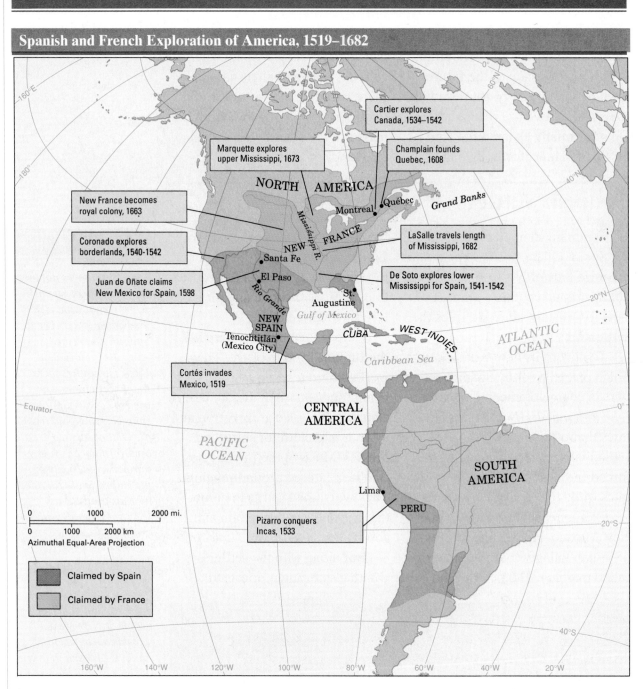

Spanish and French Exploration of America, 1519–1682

Cartier explores
Canada, 1534–1542

Marquette explores
upper Mississippi, 1673

Champlain founds
Quebec, 1608

NORTH   AMERICA

New France becomes
royal colony, 1663

Montreal · Québec   *Grand Banks*

NEW   FRANCE

Coronado explores
borderlands, 1540-1542

Santa Fe

LaSalle travels length
of Mississippi, 1682

Juan de Oñate claims
New Mexico for Spain, 1598

El Paso

De Soto explores lower
Mississippi for Spain, 1541-1542

Rio Grande

St.
Augustine
Gulf of Mexico

NEW
SPAIN

CUBA   WEST INDIES   ATLANTIC
OCEAN

Tenochtitlán·
(Mexico City)

Caribbean Sea

Cortés invades
Mexico, 1519

CENTRAL
AMERICA

Equator

*PACIFIC
OCEAN*

SOUTH
AMERICA

Lima·

PERU

0   1000   2000 mi.

0   1000   2000 km
Azimuthal Equal-Area Projection

Pizarro conquers
Incas, 1533

Claimed by Spain

Claimed by France

▲ *Trace Oñate's route
north along the Rio
Grande to El Paso. No-
tice that Oñate's claim
spread Spanish control
into what is now the
southwestern United
States.*

■ *How did the Spanish
in New Mexico meet
their needs for food
and housing?*

New Mexico. The priests set up
missions, churches and schools to
teach the Indians about the Roman Catholic faith. However,
many Indians secretly continued
to worship their own gods.

The Indians put up buildings
and tended orchards for the priests.
They also grew crops and herded
sheep and cattle for Spanish
landowners. Spanish soldiers made
sure the Indians did their work.

The Indians even paid taxes to
the government in Santa Fe, New
Mexico's capital. A **tax** is money
or property that a person must
pay to the government. The
money was used to pay the salaries
of soldiers and government officials. The Indians paid their taxes
in the form of cotton shirts and
wool blankets. Many Spanish officials grew rich by selling these
goods in Mexico. ■

French Traders in Canada

While the Spanish were colonizing the southern part of North America, the French were exploring the northern part. Like the Spanish, the French hoped to find precious metals. Instead they found other riches—fish and fur.

Fishing and Fur Trading

During John Cabot's 1497 voyage to North America, he explored the shallow waters off what is now Newfoundland. He reported that "the sea there is swarming with fish." By the early 1500s, fishing fleets from all over Europe were harvesting these rich fishing grounds, which mapmakers named the Grand Banks.

Many French fleets fished in the Grand Banks and along Canada's east coast. Often the fishermen came ashore. Indians offered to trade beaver furs for the Frenchmen's axes, knives, and other metal goods. In France, the fishermen sold the furs for as much as 200 times the cost of the axes and knives. By 1600, fur trading was France's chief interest in North America. The Indians benefited from these exchanges as well, because they got useful metal goods.

Champlain and Quebec

Other Europeans besides the French wanted a share of the fur trade. Traders gave guns and alcohol to the Indians. They hoped these gifts would win the Indians' friendship—and trade. The French decided they needed a **fort,** or military post, in North America to protect their interests. Explorer and geographer Samuel de Champlain founded Quebec in 1608 at a narrow point on the St. Lawrence River. At Quebec, the French could easily stop rival traders from bringing their furs down the river.

Champlain thought of Quebec as more than a fort and a trading post. He asked the French government to send farmers and families. About 100 French soldiers, workers, wives, and children arrived in Quebec in 1633 to start to build a settlement. By the 1660s, about 550 French people lived in Quebec. ■

This hat of wool and beaver fur was made in Europe in the early 1600s. Hats like this were so valuable they were often kept in one family for generations.

Traders used tokens in their trading practices with Indians.

■ *How did trade with the Indians lead to French settlements in North America?*

R E V I E W

1. **FOCUS** Why did the Spanish and the French establish colonies in North America?
2. **CONNECT** How did Oñate's conquest of the Hopi and Zuñi people in New Mexico differ from Cortés's conquest of the Aztec of Mexico?
3. **GEOGRAPHY** How did geography affect Samuel de Champlain's choice of a settlement?
4. **CRITICAL THINKING** Why were the Indians in Canada willing to trade beaver furs for axes and knives?
5. **ACTIVITY** Spanish settlers in the Southwest and in Florida gave Spanish names to many towns and other geographical features, such as bodies of water. They also influenced the food, language, and building styles of these regions. Study a map of these areas and list the Spanish place names you find. Also list other examples of Spanish influence.

L E S S O N   2

English Settlement in the South

THINKING
F O C U S

What were early contacts like between Indians and English colonists?

Key Terms

- investor
- profit

➤ *In the lower right corner of White's painting is an Algonquin prayer ceremony. Dancers move in a circle around wooden stakes carved at the top with men's faces. Their bodies are decorated with designs painted in bright colors.*

John White first landed on sandy Roanoke Island off the coast of present-day North Carolina in 1585. White's duty was to paint pictures of the region that would encourage future settlers. When White went back to England the following year, he took with him dozens of drawings and paintings he had made while exploring the region. They showed daily life in the small villages of the Algonquin *(al GAHNG kwihn)* people.

White's paintings, like the one on this page, show that the Algonquin lived in long houses. The curving roofs of the houses were held up by a frame of bendable young trees. This frame was covered with bark or mats of cattail stalks. The mats could be rolled up for light and air. The floors of the houses were hard-packed dirt, with raised platforms for resting and sleeping.

In the upper right corner of White's painting is a field of ripe corn. It is guarded by a watchman in a small hut. The watchman was a human scarecrow. His cries kept birds and other animals from eating the corn.

SECOTON

132

Origins of English Settlement

The Algonquin people had lived in peace for many years along the Atlantic coast. Many of the English settlers who came to America in the late 1580s hoped to use the Indians to make money. English merchants wanted to trade wool cloth and other things made in English factories for Indian products. They knew they could sell corn, furs, tobacco, and beaded necklaces for a high price in England. The English also knew that Indian slaves in Mexico had mined gold and silver for Spain. As a result, Spain had become very wealthy. The English hoped their colonies would make them rich as well.

Plans for Colonies

An English geographer named Richard Hakluyt was excited about the idea of English colonies in America. He was convinced that England could not allow Catholic Spain and France to control North America. In the 1580s, he wrote several small books that described America's riches and beauty. The books asked Protestant English settlers to move there. In America, Hakluyt wrote, "the earth bringeth fourth all things in abundance, as in the first creation, without toil or labour."

The English colonists did not want to claim land for farming, as Spanish colonists had done. Instead, the English planned at first to make their money through trade. They hoped to set up trading posts at the heads of rivers.

Indians would bring furs, corn, and tobacco to these posts to trade for European products. Only friendly Indians would be good trading partners. Therefore, Hakluyt wrote that the Indians were peaceful people who were willing to trade fairly.

Failures at Roanoke

In 1585, Hakluyt's friend Walter Raleigh arranged to send a group of English settlers to

English settlers came to North America for different reasons. The settlers who founded Jamestown wanted to make money through trade. The settlers who started Plymouth came to find religious freedom. The English took over Dutch New Amsterdam to get its fine harbor.

English Colonies, 1607–1690

New England colonies

Middle colonies

Southern colonies

America. Raleigh was a rich member of the court of England's Queen Elizabeth I. He paid for the settlers' ship and supplies. The colony they started on Roanoke, however, was not a success. The colonists returned to England the following year.

John White returned with more than 100 colonists in 1587. They built houses and traded with the Indians. A shortage of supplies, however, forced them to send White back to England for more. Due to war between England and Spain, supply ships did not reach the settlers for three years. When White arrived in 1590, he found only traces of the settlement. The colonists had mysteriously disappeared. Nobody is sure what happened to them. They may have gone to live with the Croatoan Indians. Or they may have been killed by warring Indian groups. ◼

◤ *This gold coin dates from the reign of Queen Elizabeth I (1558–1603) and carries her portrait.*

➤ *John White drew this map of Virginia in 1585. It shows the location of Roanoke Island and several Indian villages.*

◼ *Why did the English want to start colonies on the coast of North America?*

▼ *This English soldier's helmet was dug up near the site of the Jamestown settlement.*

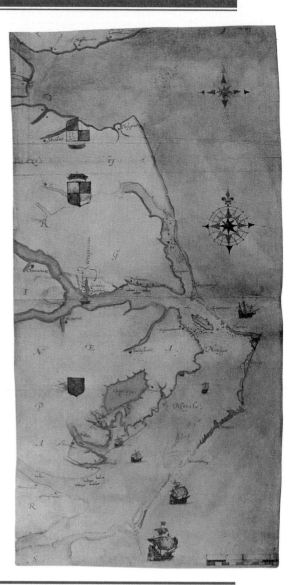

The English Arrive in Virginia

The Roanoke settlers were not able to start an English colony. But the rich land of North America soon made other colonists willing to try. In May 1607, about 105 English colonists landed near Chesapeake Bay, Virginia. They named their new settlement Jamestown, after King James I of England.

The Jamestown colony was paid for by 100 rich **investors**—people who put up money for a business. These investors formed the Virginia Company. Its purpose was to start an English settlement that would earn a **profit,** money made by a business after all expenses have been met.

At first the colonists were hopeful and excited. But by January 1608, only about 32 of the 105 settlers who started Jamestown were still alive. You will read more about what happened to the colonists in Chapter 7. However, one reason the colony almost failed was that the English hoped to repeat the success of the Spanish. The first settlers did not want to work planting crops. Instead, they searched for gold and silver. But they found neither. The Algonquin had no gold and silver treasures for the English to take. Since the English had only a few soldiers, they could not even force the Indians to work for them as the Spanish had done. The Jamestown colonists had planned a prosperous trade with the Indians. But in the early years they could only buy, borrow, or steal food from the Indians to try to stay alive. ■

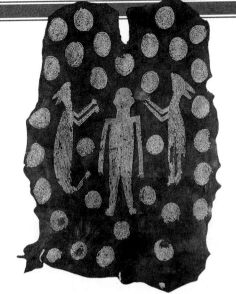

◄ *This deerskin cloak decorated with shells was brought to England from Jamestown in the 1600s. It is believed to have belonged to the powerful chief Powhatan.*

■ *In what ways was Jamestown different from Spanish colonies in the Americas?*

Maryland and the Caribbean

Another new English colony was more successful than Jamestown. In 1632, George Calvert, later called Lord Baltimore, was given land by King Charles I of England. Calvert planned to start a colony north of Chesapeake Bay. The first group of colonists arrived on the Potomac River in 1634. Many of the settlers were Catholics, as was Calvert. They wanted to leave England because Protestants there often treated Catholics cruelly. Unlike the Jamestown colonists, the first thing the Maryland settlers did was to plant gardens to grow food.

Other English colonists tried to take over islands in the Caribbean Sea. Their first efforts, on the islands of St. Lucia and Grenada, failed. Indians who lived on these islands forced the English to leave. However, in 1627 the English started a colony on Barbados, where no Indians were living. They set up plantations for growing tobacco and sugar cane. ■

■ *How were the early years at the Maryland colony different from the early years at Jamestown?*

REVIEW

1. **FOCUS** What were early contacts like between Indians and English colonists?
2. **CONNECT** How did English plans for making money in America differ from the methods used by the Spanish? Which colonists made the most money? Give reasons for your answer.
3. **HISTORY** In what ways were the reasons the Jamestown colonists came to America different from the reasons the settlers in Maryland came?
4. **CRITICAL THINKING** By 1600, people in England had heard stories about the cruelty of the Spanish colonists toward the Indians in Mexico. What effect do you think these stories had on English colonists thinking of settling in America?
5. **ACTIVITY** Make up the kind of advertisement that Hakluyt might have written to make people want to colonize Virginia. Add pictures that might have caught the eye and held the interest of settlers.

135

Settling a New World

Combining Information

Here's Why

When you do research about a topic, you often find that two books or articles include different information about the same subject. When this happens, you need to know how to summarize and combine the information from those sources.

Look at the painting on the next page. It gives you a picture of the life of Hopi Indians before the Europeans arrived. You get a clearer idea from this painting than you would from looking at a portrait of one Hopi. Just as the painter combined images into one painting, you can combine the main ideas from several written sources into one document. This gives you a more complete idea about what the life of Indians was like than you would get from reading only one source.

Suppose you wanted to learn about the lifestyle of the Hopi before they had contact with the Spanish. This chapter gives you some information. But you may wish to learn more about the Hopi from other sources. Then you will need to combine the information from your sources.

Here's How

The paragraphs on the left and right sides of this page summarize information from two different sources.

Read the paragraph on the left. It summarizes a section from a book about North American Indians. It tells about the peaceful ways of life and the farming methods of the Hopi.

Now read the paragraph on the right. It summarizes a section from a different book about North American Indians. This summary contains information about the Hopi agriculture, art, and mining.

Finally, read the paragraph in the tinted box. It summarizes and combines the information from the two sources.

To summarize information, write sentences in your own words that briefly state

Hopi means "peaceful ones." The Hopi could, and did, fight fiercely to defend their homes and freedom, but they did not begin war against others. Instead, they focused their energy on farming. They developed methods of irrigation to water their crops. They were able to grow corn, squash, beans, and cotton in the desert.

The Hopi achieved a high level of cultural development before contact with Europeans. They were especially skillful in the areas of agriculture, mining, and art. Their methods of farming allowed them to grow corn, beans, and squash in the desert. They mined and used coal for cooking their food, for preparing pigments for their art, and for firing their pottery. Their name meant "peaceful ones," and although they would fight to protect their homes, they did not start wars.

In the 300 years before Europeans came to North America, the Hopi developed skills: agriculture, mural and pottery painting, and coal mining. They grew plants with deep roots in the dry soil. They mined and used coal for cooking, heating, and firing pottery. They used earth and plant colors to paint pottery and colorful murals.

the main ideas. After writing summaries of all your sources, combine the information into one statement. Use the following steps:

1. List the main ideas from the paragraph on the left:
   a. The Hopi were willing and able to defend themselves.
   b. The Hopi did not start wars.
   c. The Hopi irrigated the desert and grew crops of corn, squash, beans, and cotton there.

2. List the main ideas from the paragraph on the right:
   a. Before the Europeans came to North America, the Hopi had developed their own advanced culture.
   b. They grew plants in the desert.
   c. They mined and used coal.
   d. They made pottery and painted with pigments.

3. Combine the main ideas of both sources. The new paragraph, in the tinted box, tells more about Hopi life than either of the summary paragraphs.

Try It

Zuñi and Hopi houses were different from those of the Algonquin. For your

source on the Algonquin, reread the paragraph on page 132 that tells about the Algonquin long houses. Write the main ideas of the paragraph.

For your source on Hopi and Zuñi dwellings, read the description in the paragraph at the top of the second column on page 129. Write the main ideas from this source.

Combine the information from your two summaries. Create a new paragraph that compares the Algonquin dwellings with the Hopi and Zuñi dwellings.

Apply It

Look at the pages on North American Indians in the Minipedia on pages 606–608. Write a summary of the information you find there about the Plains Indians.

Then look up information about the Plains Indians in an encyclopedia or book of your choice and briefly summarize the additional information you find. Finally, write a paragraph or two combining information from your two summaries.

137

L E S S O N   3

English Settlement in New England

*O*ur harvest being gotten in, our Governor sent four men on fowling [hunting for ducks, geese, and turkeys] that we might after a more special manner rejoice together, after we had gathered the fruit of our labours. They four in one day killed as much fowl as, with a little help beside, served the Company almost a week. At which time, amongst other recreations, we exercised our arms [shot off guns], many of the Indians coming amongst us, and amongst the rest their greatest king, Massasoit with some 90 men, whom for three days we entertained and feasted.

THINKING
F O C U S

Why did Puritan settlers start colonies in New England?

These words are from a letter written by Edward Winslow in the fall of 1621. Winslow and 50 other English colonists were celebrating a bountiful harvest—their first at the new Plymouth Colony.

Key Terms

- Puritan
- Separatist
- Pilgrim

Why the Pilgrims Came

Today we remember the harvest feast celebrated by the Plymouth colonists as the first Thanksgiving. In fact, one reason the settlers came to Plymouth was to start a colony where they could

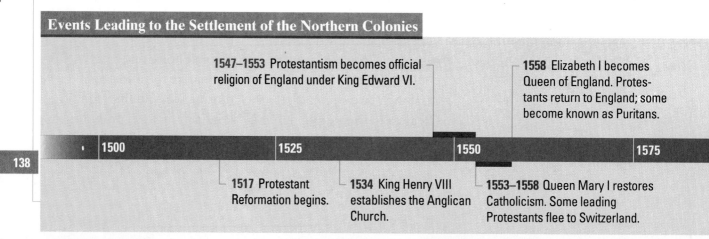

Events Leading to the Settlement of the Northern Colonies

1547–1553 Protestantism becomes official religion of England under King Edward VI.

1558 Elizabeth I becomes Queen of England. Protestants return to England; some become known as Puritans.

1500   **1525**   **1550**   **1575**

1517 Protestant Reformation begins.

1534 King Henry VIII establishes the Anglican Church.

1553–1558 Queen Mary I restores Catholicism. Some leading Protestants flee to Switzerland.

both keep English customs like the harvest feast and practice their kind of Christianity.

To understand why the colonists came to Plymouth, you need to know something about English church history. In 1534, King Henry VIII broke away from the Roman Catholic Church and started the Church of England. However, religious services in the new church didn't change a great deal. They were still very much like Catholic services.

Some English people wanted to purify the Church of England. They wanted to get rid of all re- minders of Catholic services, such as the rich clothing worn by priests. They said that Bible study and sermons were more important than beautiful ceremonies. Be- cause they wanted to purify the church, these people were known as **Puritans.**

Some Puritans formed separate churches, and so were known as **Separatists.** English law said that everyone in the country must at- tend the Church of England. Be- cause they were afraid of being put in prison, three Separatist groups left England for the Netherlands.

One Separatist group moved to Leyden in 1609. William Bradford,

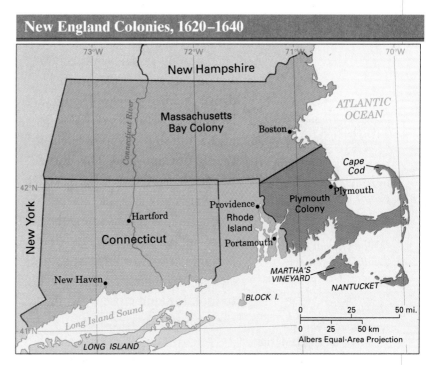

New England Colonies, 1620–1640

a leader of the group, wrote that his followers "knew they were pil- grims"—people on a holy journey. Thus, this group of Separatists be- came known as **Pilgrims.** Because they could not speak Dutch, the Pilgrims never felt at home in the Netherlands.

In 1619, the Virginia Com- pany gave the Pilgrims permis- sion to settle in Virginia. A group of London merchants, hoping to earn money from the new colony, agreed to pay expenses. When the *Mayflower* left England in Septem- ber 1620, it carried about 100 Pilgrims and hired workers. ■

Study this map of the New England Colo- nies. What present-day state includes both Ply- mouth Colony and Mas- sachusetts Bay Colony?

■ *Why did the Pilgrims leave England and, later, the Netherlands?*

▼ *Events in English church history led the Pil- grims to settle in Massachusetts.*

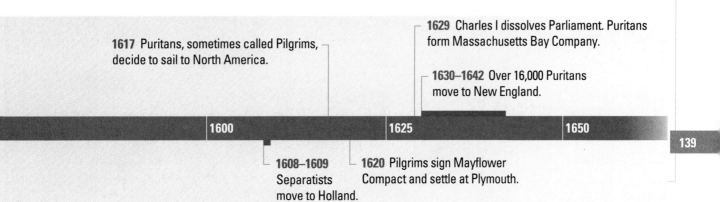

1617 Puritans, sometimes called Pilgrims, decide to sail to North America.

1629 Charles I dissolves Parliament. Puritans form Massachusetts Bay Company.

1630–1642 Over 16,000 Puritans move to New England.

1600   1625   1650

1608–1609 Separatists move to Holland.

1620 Pilgrims sign Mayflower Compact and settle at Plymouth.

The Pilgrim Experience

How Do We Know?

HISTORY *The Pilgrims were not the first English people to think that Plymouth was a good place to settle. We know this from a journal kept by English sea captain Thomas Dermer. When he sailed into Plymouth Bay in 1619, Dermer wrote that Plymouth would be an excellent site for a colony.*

The Pilgrims never reached Virginia. Strong ocean storms drove the *Mayflower* off course. In November, after nearly 10 weeks at sea, the ship dropped anchor off the tip of Cape Cod. This curved peninsula is on the Atlantic coast of what is now Massachusetts. Though the Pilgrims knew they were hundreds of miles north of Virginia, they were too tired and sick to travel farther. They decided to look for land close by to start their settlement.

Mayflower Compact

Not every passenger on the *Mayflower* was happy with the Pilgrims' decision. Some of the hired workers said that they had only agreed to settle in Virginia. To end this argument, the Pilgrims wrote an agreement called the Mayflower Compact. It said that for the general good of the colony, everyone would go along with its leaders' decisions.

Plymouth Plantation

Next, the Pilgrims sent a group of men to look for a place to settle. The men explored a small bay on the western edge of Cape Cod. Captain John Smith of Jamestown had discovered this bay in 1614. Smith had named the bay "Plymouth" and the whole region "New England." The men found a swift-running stream with clear, fresh drinking water. The area seemed ideal for a settlement. In December, the Pilgrims anchored the *Mayflower* in the bay and began building Plymouth Plantation.

The Pilgrims had to make everything they needed for their colony. Read A Closer Look to discover how they made furniture.

➤ *The Pilgrims lived aboard the* Mayflower *until they built houses. These reconstructed buildings in Plymouth, Massachusetts, show the settlement as it looked in 1627.*

Pilgrim Woodworking

The Pilgrims weren't able to bring much furniture with them on their tiny ship. Would they have to sit on the floors of their new homes? No, they wouldn't—they did bring their furniture-making tools.

How precious tools like this hammer must have been to the Pilgrims! They also brought axes, chisels, and hatchets to the timber-rich land.

The Pilgrims stored Bibles in hand-carved boxes like these. The carving on the lid of this box used to show the lion and unicorn symbol of England. Later, when America was at war with England, someone scraped off the lion.

Poles made of sturdy Massachusetts ash

Woven rush seat, added later

With only a saw to help you turn trees into furniture, you'd want the blade to last. A good cover like the one here kept the saw blade from rusting.

A small man, colonist Myles Standish sawed the legs off this chair. He probably cut the chair down so his feet could reach the floor.

Wood pieces joined without nails

141

Settling a New World

Samoset Bids Pilgrims Welcome, *a painting by Charles Hoffbauer, shows the first Indian to visit the Pilgrims. Samoset had learned to speak English from fishermen who visited the New England coast from time to time.*

■ *What were the advantages and disadvantages of the Pilgrims' choice of Plymouth as a place to settle?*

The Pilgrims had a difficult time surviving the first winter. The weather was freezing, and food supplies were low. Half the colonists died of sickness.

When spring came, many Indians visited the Pilgrims. The most important was Massasoit, chief of the Wampanoag *(wahm puh NOH ag).* Massasoit allowed a Pawtuxet Indian named Squanto to live at Plymouth. Squanto taught the Pilgrims the best places to hunt and fish. He also taught them how to plant corn by putting a fish in each hill of seeds as fertilizer. ■

By Charles Hoffbauer "Samoset Bids Pilgrims Welcome" collection: New England Mutual Life Insurance Company

An Indian is pictured on the official seal of the Massachusetts colony.

■ *Why did many Puritans move to Massachusetts in 1630?*

The Founding of Massachusetts Bay

While the Pilgrims were building their settlement at Plymouth, events in England made many other Puritans think about moving to North America.

Charles I became king in 1625. He kept up the pressure and threatened to put all Puritans in prison. Moreover, England was going through economic hard times. A large number of Puritan farmers and shopkeepers were losing money. Many Puritans liked the idea of starting a colony in North America. There they could build their own churches and, at the same time, run businesses that would earn a profit.

In 1628, the Massachusetts Bay Company got from King Charles I the right to settle north of Plymouth. The company elected John Winthrop, a Puritan landowner, governor of the Massachusetts Bay Colony. In 1630, Winthrop's ship, the *Arbella,* led a fleet of 11 ships to New England. The ships carried some 700 men, women, and children. The Puritans built settlements at Boston and Cambridge. ■

R E V I E W

1. **FOCUS** Why did Puritan settlers start colonies in New England?

2. **CONNECT** How did the Puritans' reasons for colonization differ from those of the Virginia colonists?

3. **HISTORY** In what ways did the Pilgrims and the American Indians help each other? How did each group benefit from their contact?

4. **CRITICAL THINKING** The Pilgrims at Plymouth Colony and the Puritans at Massachusetts Bay Colony came to America with strong religious beliefs. How do you think these beliefs affected the settlers' ability to survive the hardships of life in a new colony?

5. **ACTIVITY** Imagine that you are a young Wampanoag coming to the Pilgrims' harvest feast. You have never seen European people before. What questions would you would want to ask the Pilgrims?

L E S S O N   4

English Settlement in the Middle Colonies

*I*n 1653, war broke out between England and Holland. At once, [Dutch Governor Peter] Stuyvesant began construction of a wall at the north end of town, from the East River to the Hudson River, to keep out the enemy. It was a wall made of wood, twelve feet high, with a sloping platform inside. Soldiers could climb on the platform and look over the wall for approaching enemies. The soldiers on guard made a path along the wall and this became known as "Wall Street."

Robert Quackenbush, *Old Silver Leg Takes Over!*

THINKING FOCUS

How did English settlers come to live in New York, New Jersey, and Pennsylvania?

Wall Street is one reminder that the old Dutch town of New Amsterdam once occupied the southern tip of Manhattan Island. Today, Manhattan Island is the busiest part of New York City.

Bustling Wall Street is now a canyon of skyscrapers. The New York Stock Exchange and many other financial businesses line the street. Only its name recalls Wall Street's Dutch past.

Key Terms

• Quaker
• pacifism
• racism

◄ *Colonists from the Netherlands, Germany, France, Denmark, Portugal, and Spain lived in New Amsterdam. A French priest visiting the town in 1643 said he heard 18 different languages spoken as he walked down the street.*

143

Settling a New World

The Colony of New Netherland

New Amsterdam was the capital of the Dutch colony of New Netherland. The colony was started by Dutch merchants. Since the late 1500s, the Dutch had been among the most successful sailors and traders in the world.

Dutch merchants were always looking for more business. They knew that English and French sailors shipped valuable cargoes of fish and furs to Europe. To get part of this trade, the Dutch needed an American colony.

The Dutch Found New Amsterdam

In 1621, a group of Dutch merchants formed the Dutch West India Company. Three years later, the company sent about 30 families to settle along the Hudson River in what is now New York State. Because the Netherlands was a small country, the company advertised for settlers all over Europe.

By 1650, New Amsterdam was an important business center.

Merchants had a profitable trade with the Iroquois, exchanging knives and guns for furs. The city hummed with successful businesses like shipbuilding. Farmers settled on rich lands that are now part of New Jersey, Delaware, and Connecticut. There they raised cattle, corn, and wheat for trade.

The English Take Over

King Charles II of England noticed the success of New Amsterdam. Charles was eager to take the fine harbor at New Amsterdam away from the Dutch. He wanted English merchants to control its rich trade in beef, pork, wheat, tobacco, fish, and furs. Moreover, the geography of New Netherland interested the king. If England could make the Dutch leave, it could unite its American colonies. New England in the north would be connected to Virginia and Maryland in the south.

In 1664, King Charles directed his brother, the Duke of York, to send English warships to New Amsterdam. When the people of the city saw the ships' cannons aimed at their homes, they begged Peter Stuyvesant, the governor, to surrender. Besides fearing for their lives, many felt they might be better off under English rule. Stuyvesant had no choice but to give up without a fight.

The new English governor, Richard Nicolls, quickly changed the name of New Amsterdam. He called the settlement New York in honor of the Duke of York.■

■ *Why did England take control of the Dutch colony of New Netherland?*

▼ *The Dutch colony of New Netherland was sandwiched between New England to the east and Pennsylvania and New Jersey to the south and west.*

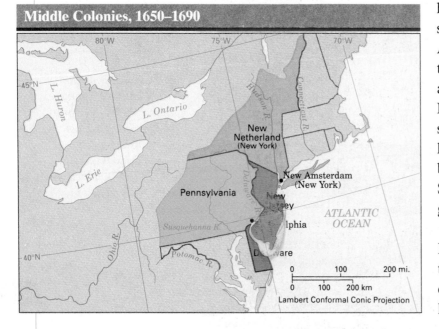

Middle Colonies, 1650–1690

80°W 75°W 70°W

45°N

L. Huron

L. Ontario

L. Erie

Hudson R.

Connecticut R.

New Netherland (New York)

New Amsterdam (New York)

Pennsylvania

Delaware R.

New Jersey

Susquehanna R.

Philadelphia

ATLANTIC OCEAN

Ohio R.

Potomac R.

Delaware

40°N

0   100   200 mi.
0   100   200 km
Lambert Conformal Conic Projection

The Founding of Pennsylvania

After the English took control of New Netherland, a few English farmers moved to the hills and valleys of what is now Pennsylvania. But this region was still mostly empty of white settlers when an Englishman named William Penn founded a colony there. Penn started this colony to make a home for another religious group that was persecuted in England.

The Quakers

The **Quakers,** or the Religious Society of Friends, were founded about 1652 by an Englishman named George Fox. Fox taught that all people were equal in God's sight and therefore should be treated with equal love and respect. Fox also believed that each person has a little bit of God inside. For this reason, he said, people do not need priests or services to get in touch with God. Quakers also thought that war was wrong. Because of this belief, called **pacifism,** Quakers would not join the army or pay taxes to support it.

Like the Puritans, the Quakers were often fined, jailed, and even killed by the English government. Between 1661 and 1680, about 15,000 of the 60,000 Quakers in England had been sent to jail for their beliefs. Once, George Fox himself was on trial. He told the judge "to tremble at the Word of the Lord." Since Fox had mentioned trembling, the judge called him a "Quaker." Soon all of Fox's followers were being called Quakers. The Quakers' simple beliefs attracted many English people. One of the best-known Quakers was a rich young man named William Penn.

▲ *Quaker women often wore bonnets like the one above. They also wore hats like those the women in the painting are wearing.*

◄ A Quaker Meeting *was painted in 1640 by Egbert van Heemskerk. At religious services like this, anyone who wanted to could speak to the congregation.*

145

William Penn

This portrait shows William Penn when he was 65 years old. Francis Place, the artist, did the portrait entirely in chalk.

William Penn was born in London in 1644. His father was an admiral in the English navy. Like many of the young Englishmen from important families, Penn went to Oxford University. But Penn had to leave Oxford because he would not go to Church of England services. Instead, he held private prayer meetings with some of his friends. When Penn was in his early twenties, he started going to Quaker meetings. He also spoke in public about Quaker beliefs. He was put in jail many times for these actions.

Penn saw that there was "no hope in England" for people who did not belong to the Church of England to lead a peaceful life. King Charles II owed a large sum of money to Penn's father. Penn asked the king to repay the debt by

UNDERSTANDING COLONIALISM

Colonies gave England more land for its people to settle. England also wanted to increase its trade by having colonies in North America. England's colonies made it possible to compete with the French, Spanish, and Dutch for trade in Indian products such as deer and beaver skins. When a country decides to settle and govern land in areas outside its borders, that policy is called colonialism.

Control of Colonies

In the Americas, colonialism took many forms. In some colonies, many of the original inhabitants were killed in war or died of disease, and the colonizing country sent new settlers. Native Americans who tried to stop the colonists from taking land were usually prevented from doing so by the colonizing country's soldiers.

Most ruling countries had to approve the laws that governed their colonies. Because the country was richer and stronger, people in the colony were forced to obey these laws. People from the ruling country often thought they were better than people in the colony.

Racism in Colonies

European people were of a different race, or skin color, than the Indians. The feeling of being better than the people of another race is called **racism**. The racism of many Europeans made them think it was their right to take away the land of the Indians. Europeans also forced the Indians to work, sometimes as slaves. Believing themselves to be superior to the Africans, the Europeans brought them as slaves to the Americas.

Colonialism Today

In the last 50 years many colonies have gained independence. The United States government, however, still has some control over such territories as Guam and the U.S. Virgin Islands.

giving him a large piece of land in North America to start a colony for English Quakers. In 1681, the king agreed. He granted Penn an area just south of New York. It became known as Pennsylvania. ■

■ *What were William Penn's reasons for founding the colony of Pennsylvania?*

Relations with the Indians

*G*od has written his law in our hearts, by which we are taught and commanded to love, and to help, and to do good to one another. Now this great God hath been pleased to make me concerned in your parts of the world; and the King of the country where I live hath given me a great province therein; but I desire to enjoy it with your love and consent, that we may always live together as neighbors and friends.

These words are from a letter written by William Penn to the Delaware Indians of Pennsylvania. Because of his belief that all people are equal in God's sight, Penn wanted to keep peace between white settlers and Indians. In 1681, Penn asked a friend in Pennsylvania to read this letter to the Delaware in their own language. He hoped his letter would show the Delaware that he intended to treat them fairly.

When Penn arrived in Pennsylvania in 1682, he worked out a treaty with the Delaware. Penn promised to pay the Indians for their land and to respect their rights. However, after Penn's death in 1718, thousands of colonists poured into Pennsylvania. Many of these new settlers did not have the same beliefs as the Quakers. These settlers did not always follow Penn's practice of treating the Indians fairly. ■

How Do We Know?

HISTORY *Mrs. Preston, an early Pennsylvania colonist, described William Penn in her letters. She told how on his first meeting with the Delaware, Penn sat on the ground and ate corn with them. She also said that the Indians held a jumping contest and that Penn won.*

■ *How did William Penn establish peaceful relations with the Indians in Pennsylvania?*

◄ *Tamanend, the chief of the Delaware people, gave Penn a beaded friendship belt. On the belt was a picture of a Quaker and an Indian clasping hands.*

R E V I E W

1. **FOCUS** How did English settlers come to live in New York, New Jersey, and Pennsylvania?
2. **CONNECT** In what ways were William Penn's reasons for founding Pennsylvania similar to John Winthrop's reasons for founding the Massachusetts Bay Colony?
3. **HISTORY** What were the main beliefs of the Quakers? How did these beliefs affect relations between the Quakers and the Delaware?
4. **CRITICAL THINKING** List some general reasons why countries establish colonies. Then tell which of these reasons best apply to the colonies of New Netherland, New York, and Pennsylvania.
5. **WRITING ACTIVITY** Write a news story for a Philadelphia newspaper in 1682. The article should describe William Penn's meeting with the Delaware to work out a treaty of friendship.

147

Settling a New World

Choosing the Right Scale

Here's Why

Statistics, which are facts using numbers, can be shown in several different ways. In this textbook and in newspapers and magazines, you have seen information presented in charts, tables, bar graphs, line graphs, and pie graphs.

Most graphs differ from charts and tables because they show visually the relationship between two sets of numbers. Line graphs are used to show changes that occur in the numbers over time. If, for example, you wanted to show how the beaver fur trade in Canada changed between 1675 and 1685, would you

know how? By learning how to make your own line graphs, you will be able to show these changes.

Here's How

First, collect your data. The table below gives the information on the beaver trade that was used to make the two line graphs on this page.

Next, create the grid for your graph. A grid is a pattern of evenly spaced horizontal and vertical lines. A well-drawn grid has squares that are exactly the same size. You can also use specially marked graph paper for this purpose.

A line graph has two base lines, or axes. The horizontal axis is the base line that goes across the bottom of the graph, from left to right. Look at the two graphs below. In both these graphs, the horizontal axis is marked in one-year sections, from 1675 to 1685.

The vertical axis is the base line that goes up the left side of the graph, from the bottom to the top. On the graph at the left, the amount of beaver fur sold each year is shown in increases of 100,000 pounds, from 0 to 700,000. On the graph on the right, the fur sold is shown in increases of 25,000 pounds,

Beaver Trade (in thousands of pounds)										
Year	1675	1676	1677	1678	1679	1680	1681	1682	1683	1684	1685
Pounds	61	70	92	80	68	69	83	90	95	49	138

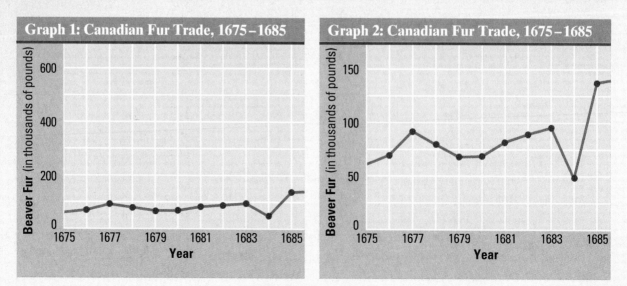

Fur Trade at Fort Albany, 1710–1780

Year	Beaver Furs Traded	Year	Beaver Furs Traded	Year	Beaver Furs Traded
1710	4	1735	32	1760	30
1715	14	1740	37	1765	28
1720	28	1745	30	1770	26
1725	27	1750	27	1775	10
1730	41	1755	25	1780	4

from 0 to 175,000. As you can see, the scale used for the vertical axis of the graph shown on the left is four times greater than the scale used for the vertical axis of the graph on the right.

These two graphs show the importance of choosing the right scale for your graph. The information presented on these two graphs is the same. To check this, use the graph on the left to find out how many pounds of fur were exported in the year 1683. To do this, move your finger up from the 1683 mark on the horizontal axis until you reach the data line. Now move your finger left across the graph to the numbers on the vertical axis. You can see that the data line is at about 95,000 pounds at the year 1683. Now try the same thing on the right-hand side of the graph. Did you get the same data? You should.

Although both graphs give you the same information, the one on the right is much easier to read. Because

the vertical scale on the left is in large increases, you can only guess at the actual amount of fur sold each year. Also, the graphs do not look the same. The graph on the left shows little change over the 10-year period. The graph on the right more clearly shows the changes. The fur trade was over twice as large in 1685 than it was in 1675.

In deciding what scale to use for a graph that you are making, think about the highest and lowest values you have to graph. Each axis should be numbered so that the complete set of points and connecting lines cover most of the graph. Use standard increases, such as 1, 5, or 10 years and 5, 10, 25, or 50,000 pounds.

Try It

Use the information from the table on this page to make a graph of fur trade at Fort Albany during the years 1710 to 1780. Notice that in this table the numbers of furs

traded at just one trading station are given. Find a horizontal axis that gives you 15 sets of information. Find a vertical axis that allows you to show the number of beaver furs traded from 0 to 40 in 8 increases.

Apply It

Follow the steps used in Here's How to make a graph showing some data that change over time. For example, show the change in your height over a period of years. Or show the change over years of the number of students in your class, or the batting average of your favorite baseball player.

Chapter Review

Reviewing Key Terms

colonization (p. 129) profit (p. 134)
encomienda (p. 129) Puritan (p. 139)
fort (p. 131) Quaker (p. 145)
investor (p. 134) racism (p.146)
mission (p. 130) Separatist (p. 139)
pacifism (p. 145) tax (p. 130)
Pilgrim (p. 139)

A. The following quotations express beliefs. Write the key term that identifies each speaker or belief.

1. "All people should be treated equally."
2. "Bible study is more important than beautiful church ceremonies."
3. "The resources in the colonies will make me rich."
4. "I would rather risk jail than belong to the Church of England."
5. "All war is wrong."
6. "We went on a holy journey to America."

B. Write an explanation of why the following items could be important to you if you were either a European settler or an Indian.

1. colonization
2. tax
3. mission
4. profit
5. fort
6. encomienda
7. racism

Exploring Concepts

A. Copy and complete the chart by writing any missing information. The first line has been completed for you.

Date	Who?	From Where?	What?
1598	Juan de Onãte	Spain	Settled New Mexico
1608			Founded Quebec
1620		England	
1624	Thirty families		
1630	Puritans		
1664		England	

B. Study the following pairs of words. Write two or three sentences that describe how the two items are connected.

1. pueblos
   long houses
2. John White
   Richard Hakluyt
3. Thanksgiving
   Squanto
4. Puritans
   Separatists
5. Charles I
   Henry VIII
6. beaver furs
   knives and axes
7. *Mayflower*
   Arbella
8. William Penn
   Peter Stuyvesant

Reviewing Skills

1. Read on pages 129 and 130 about how the Spanish treated Indians in New Mexico. Then read the two paragraphs at the top of page 142 about how the Wampanoag and the Pilgrims got along. Summarize and combine details from the two sections. Write your own paragraph, explaining how Indians treated, and were treated by, colonists.

2. Graph the population of Quebec based on the table. Put the dates one-half inch apart per 10 years on the horizontal axis. Place your population figures one-half inch apart per 1,000 people on the vertical axis.

3. To stress how quickly the population grew, which scale of your graph would you change? How would you change it?

4. What artifacts might you find in a museum of French Canadian history?

5. Where would you look to find the latitude and longitude of the Spanish colony at St. Augustine, Florida?

French Population of Quebec, 1610–1700			
Year	Population (estimated)	Year	Population (estimated)
1610	18	1663	2,500
1620	60	1673	6,705
1630	100	1680	9,719
1640	359	1686	11,130
1650	675	1700	15,000

Using Critical Thinking

1. As you know, Manhattan was once the Dutch colony of New Amsterdam. Today, it is home to the United Nations, an organization of countries from all over the world. Could you say that, in a way, the New Amsterdam of the 1600s was also home to a kind of united nations? Why was this possibly true? Give historical facts from the chapter as reasons.

2. William Penn had unusual ideas for his time about how the Indians who lived near English settlements should be treated. He believed that settlers should pay the Indians for their land, respect their rights, and be good neighbors to them. Would Penn's beliefs be more popular today? Name some ways that people's treatment of other ethnic groups has improved in 300 years.

Preparing for Citizenship

1. **WRITING ACTIVITY** Imagine that you are an explorer preparing to lead a voyage of exploration to a planet many light-years from Earth. The time is the distant future. Earlier trips have revealed life on the planet. Think about the mistakes European explorers made in their approach to the American Indians. Then create a list of guidelines for the explorers who will go with you to use in approaching the people they find on the planet. What is the most important thing they can do to be sure of a peaceful meeting?

2. **COLLABORATIVE LEARNING** Plan "An Update on European Settlements in North America." Each group of three students should choose a colony. Assign one person to research what that area is like today, one to study its history, and one to decide in what form you'll present your report. For example, if you chose New York you might write a brochure encouraging tourists to visit. In that case, you would want to emphasize cultural and recreational activities that are likely to appeal to your readers.

Unit 3

Life in the English Colonies

English colonizers who came to America in the 1600s often faced disease, hunger, and battles with Indians defending their land. But as English colonies grew, and the Indians were forced to move or were killed by diseases, life for many of the new residents became more settled. Some even became rich. New York merchant William Denning and his family are shown here.

1607

William Williams, The Dennings, 1772.
Collection of Mr. and Mrs. W. Denning Harvey.

1759

Chapter 7
The Southern Colonies

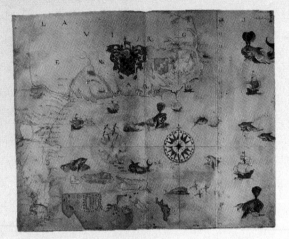

The Englishmen who landed in Virginia in 1607 expected to get rich. But instead of gold or silver, the colonists found a plant called tobacco. After a slow and difficult start, some Virginians were able to make money growing tobacco. Many planters bought African slaves and forced them to work in their fields. Using this system, a few Virginians soon became the wealthiest people in the colonies.

During this time, English colonists settled along the east coast of Virginia and the Carolinas, shown in the map above.

A TOBACCO PLANTATION

1600

1625

1650

1619 Africans arrive in the South.

1607

1614 John Rolfe sends the first shipment of Virginia tobacco to England. Tobacco (above) sells for six times the price of wheat.

Throughout this period, Jamestown was the capital of Virginia. This photograph shows all that remains of the settlement today.

1670 In Virginia, new laws decree that all imported non-Christian servants will remain servants for life.

1675 About 4,000 slaves now live in Virginia and Maryland.

1675

1700

1725

1676 Colonist Nathaniel Bacon leads a revolt against the English governor of Virginia. Bacon demands more protection from Indian attacks on the colony.

1682

L E S S O N 1

A New Settlement in Virginia

THINKING
F O C U S

In what ways were early settlers unprepared for what they found in Jamestown?

Key Terms

- life expectancy
- indentured servant
- plantation
- House of Burgesses
- representative

➤ *The Virginia Company's advertisements praised the fertile land of Virginia.*

Think of a place where the winters are "dry and fair" and the summers have "many great and sudden showers of rain." In this place, the woods and fields are filled with "rare and delectable [tasty] birds," and the rivers "abound with fish both great and small."

In 1613, this is how preacher Alexander Whitaker described Jamestown in his sermon "Good News from Virginia." The Virginia Company of London printed reports by Whitaker and other settlers. They wanted to make people wish to move to Virginia.

Richard Frethorne is one person who did sail from England to Virginia. He was a servant who wanted to start a new life. In a letter written in 1623, Frethorne said of Virginia:

I have nothing to comfort me, nor is there nothing to be gotten here but sickness and death . . . I have nothing at all—no, not a shirt to my back but two rags.

In fact, Virginia was just as beautiful as Whitaker had described. However, the land was also dangerous and unhealthy. Men like Frethorne found little "good news" there.

Dangers Hide in the Land

The Virginia Company sent men who wanted to make money to Virginia. At first, these men delighted in the land. As they sailed along the coast they enjoyed the "fair meadows." At night they camped on shore. Once they found oysters "thicke as stones." One passenger, George Percy, described the landscape and wildlife.

Mosquitos that carried malaria lived in swamps near Jamestown.

There are also great store [numbers] of Vines in bignesse of a mans thigh, running up to the tops of the Trees in great abundance. We also did see many Squirels, Conies [rabbits], Black Birds with crimson wings . . .

George Percy, *Observations*, 1607

These men stood in wonder at the beauty of Virginia. They had mixed feelings of both fear and hope.

Choosing a Place to Settle

The men decided to build their settlement on the James River. The place they chose had many advantages. First, the settlement was far enough up the river to protect the settlers from ocean attack. Second, the river would provide an easy escape route from the Indians if one was needed. Third, the river could be used to carry goods to and from the settlement. In other ways, however, the place, which the settlers called Jamestown, was a poor choice.

Illness and Hard Times

During high tide, salt water from the ocean poured into the James River. When the men drank from the river, the salty water made them sick. Also the swampland they settled on was full of mosquitos

John Smith, one of the principal founders of Jamestown, made this surprisingly accurate map of Virginia in 1606.

157

carrying germs that caused malaria, yellow fever, and other deadly diseases. The **life expectancy**—the number of years a person could expect to live—was low because of disease. Just as bad, the men had no idea how to grow crops on the swampy land.

The men thought they would find gold quickly and then return to England. However, they found no gold. When winter came, they shivered in their drafty, poorly made homes. Many wondered if they could survive the hidden dangers of this strange land. ■

■ *What were the advantages and disadvantages of Jamestown as a location for settlement?*

John Smith Leads the Settlers

By December 1607, just six months after landing at Jamestown, 73 of the original 105 settlers had

➤ *John Smith saved Jamestown from complete starvation in the winter of 1607.*

died. This first group of settlers were soldiers, gentlemen adventurers, and others who wanted to get rich and return to England. The gentlemen adventurers were not used to doing hard work such as farming and chopping wood. They did not bring their wives or children with them. So, the men did not settle down in families. They bickered and fought with one another.

Among the early settlers was an able soldier named John Smith. Because he had traveled widely and fought in many wars, John

Smith was used to making decisions. He was a short man who always stood up very straight. His beard and curled moustache gave him a stern and serious look. During the first winter in 1607, when the settlers argued and refused to work, John Smith took control. He realized that the settlers needed direction in order to survive. He was very strict with the settlers, making everyone work. He declared, "You must obay this for a law, that he that will not worke, shall not eate." If Smith heard a man swear, he poured water down his sleeve.

Smith not only directed the settlers, but also tried to bargain with

➤ *The population of Virginia went up and down, as new settlers arrived and others died of disease.*

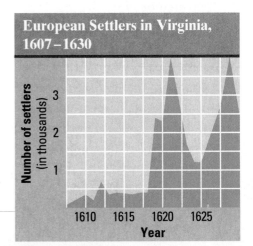

European Settlers in Virginia, 1607–1630

Number of settlers (in thousands)

3

2

1

1610   1615   1620   1625
Year

In this engraving from 1618, John Smith meets with the Indians near Jamestown. Smith traded beads, like the ones below, for corn.

the Algonquin Indians. Smith was able to trade hatchets, beads, and copper for corn and beans to feed the starving settlers. Smith was careful, though, not to give guns to Chief Powhatan. The tall chief towered above Smith. Powhatan wanted to take guns from the settlers. At one point Powhatan's men tied Smith up and almost killed him. Here is how Smith wrote about his adventure:

> Their clubs were raised, and in another moment I should have been dead, when Pocahontas, the King's dearest daughter, a child of ten years old, finding no entreaties [pleas] could prevail to save me, darted forward, and taking my head in her arms, laid her own upon it, and thus prevented my death.
>
> John Smith, *A Generall Historie of Virginia*, 1624

Who were the people who first settled in Virginia? What were their backgrounds? Why did they come to Virginia?

The Colony Changes

John Smith sailed back to England late in 1609 to heal the severe wounds he suffered in a gunpowder accident. He also returned because some officials of the Virginia Company did not like his stern ways

159

and wanted him to leave. Jamestown then suffered the worst winter yet. It was called the "starving time." People ate dogs, rats, and mice. The terrible winter is described in a novel by Scott O'Dell:

> *W*e ventured outside the fort only to bury our dead, but only at night in shallow graves, for the earth was frozen and we feared death from savage arrows. Inside the fort stalked famine and pestilence [hunger and disease]. Huts of the dead and pickets from the stockade were burned for firewood.
>
> Scott O'Dell, *The Serpent Never Sleeps*

New Ideas to Save the Colony

Hunger, disease, no gold! By 1609, Jamestown was a complete failure as far as the Virginia Company was concerned. The company knew it had to do something. Maybe if the colony had more hard-working settlers, it would do well.

In 1609, the company had begun sending **indentured servants** to Virginia. These servants signed an indenture, or agreement, promising the company five to seven years of unpaid labor. In return, the servants received free passage across the ocean. At the end of their service, the servants got 100 acres of land and their "freedom dues"—clothing, tools, and often a gun.

The need to find good workers continued. By 1616, the Virginia Company did even more to get settlers who were eager to work. The company made a promise to people: 50 acres of land, plus 50 acres for

➤ *This drawing shows how a typical Virginian settlement of the 1600s might have looked. How did settlers defend themselves from attacks?*

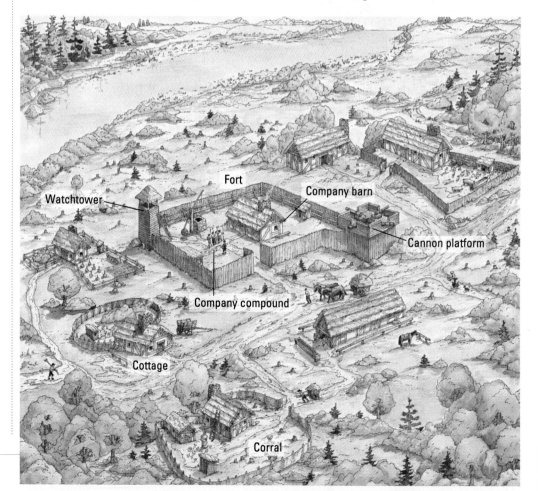

Watchtower

Fort

Company barn

Cannon platform

Company compound

Cottage

Corral

Because tobacco is an annual crop, new seeds had to be planted each spring.

Tobacco plants were carefully tended. After about 24 weeks, the plants were ready to be cut down.

Tobacco stalks were hung in the sun for a brief period to wilt the leaves.

After wilting, tobacco was hung inside barns to dry, or cure.

Cured tobacco leaves were stripped from their stalks.

Tobacco leaves were layered into barrels. A heavy weight packed the leaves down tightly. The barrels of tobacco were then shipped to warehouses to await inspection.

◄ *Planters needed many workers to grow, dry, and cure the tobacco plant. When full, tobacco barrels like the one shown here weighed about 1,000 pounds.*

every indentured servant they brought. Men came across the Atlantic Ocean with many indentured servants. They received hundreds of acres of land. The large farms they owned were called **plantations.** In time, Virginia became a colony in which a few rich planters owned most of the land by the rivers.

The Virginia Company also decided to give the people a voice in the government. In this way, settlers would have to care about the success of the colony. In 1619, the company formed a law-making body. It was called the **House of Burgesses.** A burgess was a type of **representative**—a person who spoke for the settlers and voted on laws for the colony. All free white men could vote for a representative. The House of Burgesses was the first time the English in America had a representative government.

A Profitable Crop

The settlers never found gold in Virginia. But with tobacco, Virginians did finally find a crop that would make some of them very rich. Smoking had become popular in Europe, so many people wanted to buy tobacco. In 1613, a settler named John Rolfe found a high-grade tobacco from the West Indies. This tobacco grew well in Virginia.

Across Time & Space

King James I of England thought smoking was unpleasant and dangerous. But he still welcomed the money the tobacco trade brought to his treasury. Today, we know that tobacco is a leading cause of lung cancer, responsible for about 146,000 deaths a year in the United States.

161

The Southern Colonies

![Portrait of Pocahontas]

Ætatis suæ 21. Aᵒ.1616.

Matoaks als Rebecka daughter to the mighty Prince Powhatan Emperour of Attanoughkomouck als Virginia converted and baptized in the Christian faith, and Wife to the worᵗ Mᵗ Tho: Rolff.

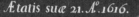

▲ *After Pocahontas married John Rolfe, she toured England. The English treated her as a princess.*

■ *How did the discovery of tobacco as a crop affect Virginia?*

John Rolfe not only found the ideal crop for Virginia, but he also found a way to improve conditions with Chief Powhatan. In 1614, he married Powhatan's daughter, Pocahontas. The settlers hoped that this marriage would bring a lasting peace in the colony. Pocahontas's marriage to John Rolfe did bring some peace to Jamestown, but not a lasting peace. Pocahontas died from smallpox only three years after her marriage. Strange as it may seem, it was John Rolfe's crop of tobacco that made things worse with the Powhatans.

The problem was land. The settlers demanded more and more Indian land for growing tobacco. The Indians feared that they would soon have no place to live. They had to protect their homeland.

Tensions between settlers and Indians increased. In 1622, the settlers killed a Powhatan war chief and religious leader named Nemattanew. In response, the Indians launched a surprise attack on farms up and down the James River. They killed 347 settlers, almost one-third of all the settlers in Virginia at that time.

The Indians wanted to drive the settlers into the Atlantic, and they almost succeeded. The settlers fought back fiercely, however. By the end of the year, the Indians were in retreat.

After this attack, the Virginia Company failed. King James blamed the company for not building enough forts. He decided to rule the colony himself. As for the settlers—they wanted to drive the Indians from Virginia. ■

R E V I E W

1. **FOCUS** In what ways were early settlers unprepared for what they found in Jamestown?
2. **CONNECT** Compare the attitude of the first settlers of Jamestown to Spanish adventurers in the New World.
3. **HISTORY** In what ways did Pocahontas help Jamestown settlers?
4. **CRITICAL THINKING** John Smith hoped that Jamestown would one day become a great city. However, the town never had more than 175 permanent residents. Why do you think this was the case?
5. **WRITING ACTIVITY** Imagine that you are hired to write a motto for Jamestown. Finish this sentence several times with your ideas. "Jamestown: the city. . ."

162

L E S S O N   2

Rebellion in Virginia

Elizabeth Bacon sat down and wrote her sister-in-law a letter to calm her nerves. She wrote about her husband:

> The country does so really love him, that they would not leave him alone anywhere; there was not anybody against him but the Governor and a few of his great men. . . . Surely if your brother's crime had been so great all the country would not have been for him.
>
> Elizabeth Bacon, letter dated 1676

What was Nathaniel Bacon's crime? Why was the governor against him? And why did "all the country" love him?

Nathaniel Bacon had stood up to the governor of Virginia, William Berkeley. Bacon was a talented leader who wanted to be allowed to organize attacks against the Susquehannock *(suhs kwuh HAN nahk)* and other Indians on the Virginia frontier. He was not happy with the way Governor Berkeley handled Indian attacks on settlers who lived far from Jamestown. Bacon was not satisfied with the government of Virginia.

THINKING FOCUS

What caused Bacon's Rebellion?

Key Terms

• council
• rebel

The Government of Virginia

William Berkeley, the king's chosen governor, kept a firm grip on the government of Virginia. He hand-picked his advisers, or the members of his **council.** He personally chose people to run the courts, lead the militia, build forts, and trade with the Indians.

No Elections

The governor also had the power to call meetings of the House of Burgesses. Berkeley did not like the idea of common people having a voice in the government. So he did not call a new election of the House from 1662 until 1676. For 14 years, the people in Virginia did not have a chance to vote for new members.

High Taxes

For a long time, Berkeley was able to get the House to do as he liked. He raised taxes. The small planters hated the taxes. They

▲ *Nathaniel Bacon stood up for frontier settlers but brutally attacked American Indians.*

163

The Southern Colonies

► *William Berkeley traded with the Indians for beaver furs. Traders dried and stretched beaver pelts like this one. The hoop is made from a tree branch.*

■ *Find examples from the text to support Nathaniel Bacon's statement, "All the power and sway is got into the hands of the rich."*

Voting Laws

Berkeley even talked the House into changing the voting laws, so that men without land could not vote. Remember that before 1670, all the free men in the colony could vote for the House of Burgesses. Berkeley did not trust poor people who did not own land. He thought they might stand up to him and cause trouble. So the House took their vote away. ■

felt that the government took their money but did not give them protection in return.

The Fight for Land

Men needed land in order to vote. However, large landholders already owned most of the good land near the rivers. Any remaining land was very expensive or hard to get. So ordinary settlers found it harder and harder to become landowners. Even indentured servants who finished their terms of work were forced deep into the frontier to claim their 50 acres of land. These parcels of land were far from water and thick with forest. Algonquin Indians still lived in these areas, too.

By 1675, land-hungry settlers outnumbered the Indians. Many thought that destroying the Indians would solve their land problems.

In the summer of 1675, frontier settlers slaughtered several Indians. The Indians fought back by killing several settlers. Planters and soldiers attacked the Indians again. Each attack led to another attack by the other side.

► *White settlers cut trees, cleared fields, and built houses on Indian land in Virginia.*

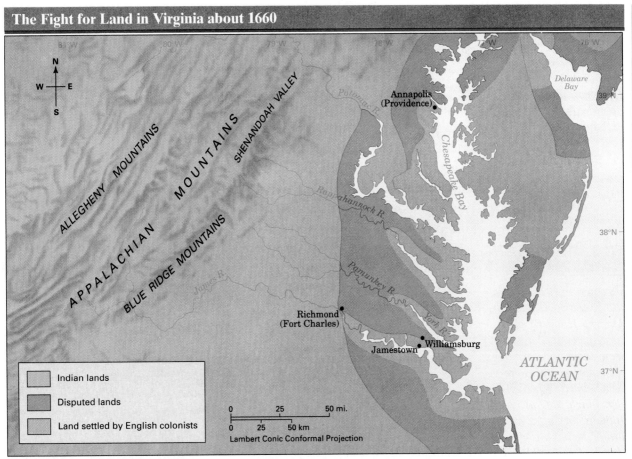

Map legend:
- Indian lands
- Disputed lands
- Land settled by English colonists

0 25 50 mi.
0 25 50 km
Lambert Conic Conformal Projection

Tempers were hot. The settlers asked Governor Berkeley to make the Indians leave the frontier. Instead, the governor ordered a string of forts built to separate the two groups.

The settlers were not happy with the governor's idea. They knew that the governor and plantation owners in eastern Virginia did not have to fear the Indians. Almost all the Indians now lived on the frontier. Frontier settlers accused the governor of building the forts so he could give jobs to his friends. Worse yet, they thought that he secretly wanted to protect the Indians. For years, people whispered that Berkeley was growing even richer as he traded for beaver skins with the Algonquin tribes. The Indian attacks continued. That's when Nathaniel Bacon took charge of the fight. ■

▲ As the number of settlers increased in the late 1600s, the Indians were pushed farther and farther west. To learn more about using the map's scale to figure out how far they had to move, see page G6 of the Map and Globe Handbook.

■ Why was land ownership so important to the Virginia settlers?

Bacon's Rebellion

Nathaniel Bacon was not a poor man. As a matter of fact, he owned a big plantation, and he sat on the Governor's council. However, as a new settler to the colony, Bacon had new ideas.

The settlers wanted Bacon to lead them against the Indians, even though they did not have the governor's orders to march. After attacking several Indian villages, Bacon and his followers returned to Jamestown. There, Governor Berkeley declared him a **rebel,** one who uses violence to fight the government. Berkeley cried, "Now I behold the greatest rebel that ever was in Virginia!"

■ *Why was Bacon's Rebellion important to the struggle of common men?*

Jamestown Burns

Bacon and Berkeley could never really come to an understanding. Bacon wanted more power to protect frontier settlements. Berkeley continued to hold back. At one point, Bacon and 500 men stormed into a council meeting in Jamestown. Berkeley boldly faced Bacon, tore open his own coat and cried out, "Here, shoot me—'fore God, fair mark!"

Bacon refused to kill him, saying:

> *S*ir, *I come not, nor intend, to hurt a hair of your honor's head . . . I come for a commission [order] against the heathen who daily inhumanly murder us and spill our brethren's blood.*

Nathaniel Bacon,
reported speech, 1676

At one point in their terrible fight, Bacon and his men burned Jamestown to the ground. They did not want the governor to control it. The flames danced in the sky and lit the river waters.

King Charles II then sent troops to control Bacon. By the time they arrived, though, Bacon had died of swamp fever. His men soon went back to their plantations.

After the Rebellion

Bacon's Rebellion showed that common men would not stand by and let the government control them. The rebellion also showed that frontier settlers could be cruel to native people.

Life in Virginia slowly settled down. More women came to the colony. The number of families grew. The colonists wanted to stay and find success in Virginia. ■

R E V I E W

1. **FOCUS** What caused Bacon's Rebellion?
2. **CONNECT** From the time of John Smith, the relation of the Indians and Virginia's settlers was filled with tension. Why did it get worse by 1675?
3. **GEOGRAPHY** Why was life on the frontier more difficult than life near a town?
4. **CRITICAL THINKING** Do you think if Nathaniel Bacon

had never come to Virginia, Governor Berkeley would never have faced a rebellion?

5. **ACTIVITY** Choose two of your classmates to role play with you the roles of Bacon, Berkeley, and a Susquehannock chief. Discuss your problems and hopes for the future.

LESSON 3

Slavery in the Southern Colonies

The slave ship "filled me with astonishment, which was soon converted into terror." A man named Olaudah Equiano wrote these words. As a young man Equiano was taken from his home in Africa and sold to a slave trader. The trader brought him across the ocean to America. There he became a slave.

Years later, Equiano described his ocean journey in a book. Once aboard the ship, he recalled, "The heat of the climate, added to the number in the ship, which was so crowded that each had scarcely room to turn himself, almost suffocated us."

Some Africans chose death over slavery. Equiano watched as two men "who were chained together, preferring death to such a life of misery, somehow made through the nettings, and jumped into the sea."

THINKING FOCUS

How did the slave trade begin and develop in the southern colonies?

Key Terms

- slavery
- export
- cash crop

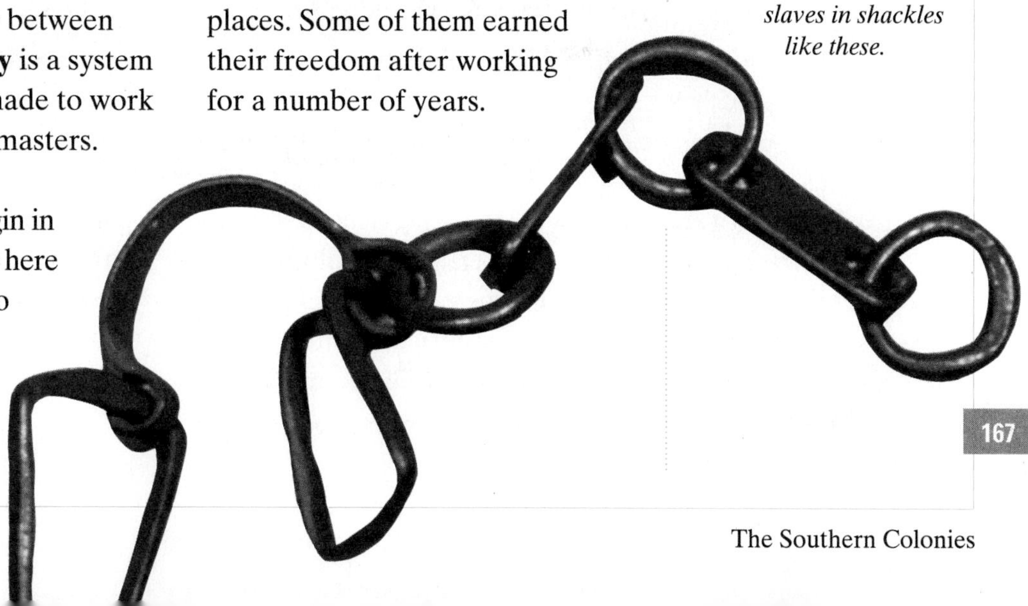

▼ *Planters often put slaves in shackles like these.*

The Beginnings of African Slavery

Olaudah Equiano was one of about 10 million Africans who were sold into slavery between 1570 and 1870. **Slavery** is a system in which people are made to work without pay for their masters. Slaves have no rights.

Slavery did not begin in the Americas, but only here were people forced into slavery because of their race. In the ancient world, prisoners taken in wars were sometimes enslaved. These slaves came from many different places. Some of them earned their freedom after working for a number of years.

167

Slaves were brought to the New World to raise sugar. Refined sugar, molasses, and rum came from the sugar cane.

1400s and early 1500s, Spain founded colonies in the West Indies, where they discovered a new form of wealth there in sugar. Sugar became an **export**—a crop sent overseas to Europe for sale. It brought so much money that it quickly became known as white gold.

The Spanish needed strong workers to do the hard work of stooping to plant and cut sugar cane. They tried to make slaves of the Indian people of the West Indies. Most of these people died of harsh treatment and disease. The Spanish then turned to using African slaves in their fields.

The Dutch, French, and English also founded colonies in the West Indies and followed the same

In the New World, however, slavery was different—and in many ways more cruel. Overwhelmingly, slaves were African, though some were Indian. Once a person became a slave that person was a slave for life. And any child of a slave mother was also a slave for life.

The Spanish and Portuguese were the first people to use African slaves in the New World. In the late

UNDERSTANDING SLAVERY

European colonists were not the first people to use slaves. Slavery, a system of forced labor in which people work without pay for their masters, had existed nearly as long as human civilization.

The first known slaves lived about 3500 B.C. in western Asia. In ancient Athens, in the 400s B.C., up to one-third of the population were slaves. Societies in China, India, and Africa also practiced slavery.

In some areas of Africa, people who became slaves

through war, debt, or theft still had some of the same legal rights as free citizens. Slavery was often a temporary condition caused by misfortune or wrongdoing. Rarely were people forced into slavery only because of their race, religion, or ethnic group.

However, the Europeans who settled in the Americas developed a cruel and inhuman system of slavery. In the Americas white people owned black and Indian laborers.

By the 1700s, many English colonies had passed laws decreeing that only Africans and Indians could be enslaved. Some colonies ruled that masters could not grant their slaves freedom.

Slavery remained legal in the southern United States until 1865, after the Civil War. Today, all but a few societies throughout the world have outlawed slavery.

path. At first, the English used indentured servants to grow sugar. But few of these people would put up with the hard work in the hot and wet West Indies. They preferred to work in North America. Eventually, the English followed the example of other European colonials and began trading for African slaves. ■

▲ *Planters bought African slaves to do backbreaking work on sugar plantations.*

■ *How did the colonization of the West Indies lead to the European slave trade?*

The Slave Trade

The European traders bought slaves on the west coast of Africa, where leaders of African kingdoms had captured prisoners during battles with their enemies.

T he village was surrounded by enemies, who attacked us with clubs, long spears, and bows and arrows. After fighting for more than an hour, those who were not fortunate enough to run away were made prisoners.

Charles Ball, *Slavery in the United States: A Narrative of the Life and Adventures of Charles Ball*, 1837

The slave traders exchanged guns, cotton cloth, and other items for the African prisoners.

People Sold for Goods

The African prisoners were marched to trading forts along the coast. Prisoners from several African cultures were held at the forts. A Closer Look at West African Culture on the next two pages tells of some of these cultures.

Passage to America

The traders then herded the slaves aboard their ships for the voyage across the Atlantic Ocean.

169

The Southern Colonies

West African Culture

Through the centuries, several great West African kingdoms rose, prospered, and fell. During this period, agriculture, art, and trade all flourished. Many of these kingdoms, including those of the Akan and Yoruba peoples, continued to thrive until the 1800s, well after the introduction of the Atlantic slave trade.

The Asante Kingdom was established on trading skills, including the trade of gold. In addition to trading gold, the Akan people crafted beautiful objects like these.

Ibo women wore these beautiful brass anklets to show off family wealth. The Ibo ruled themselves democratically in small groups.

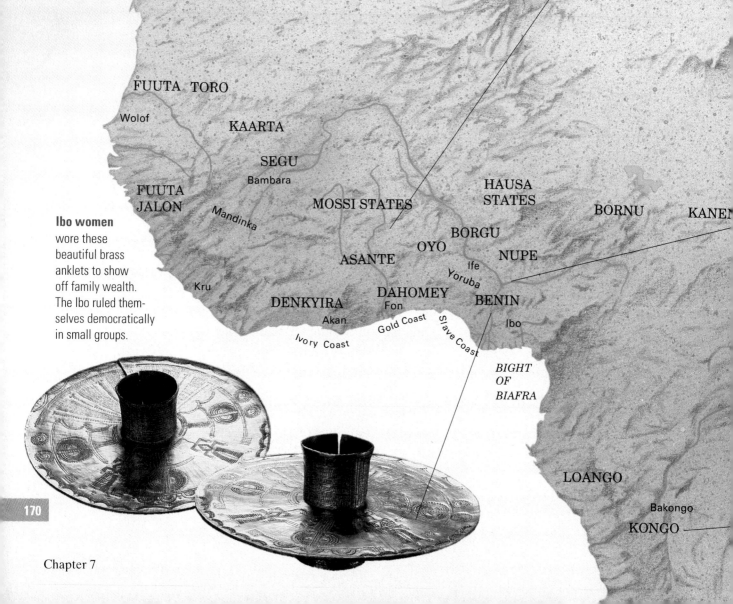

FUUTA TORO

Wolof

KAARTA

SEGU

Bambara

FUUTA JALON

Mandinka

MOSSI STATES

HAUSA STATES

BORNU

KANEM

Ibo women

BORGU

OYO

NUPE

Kru

ASANTE

Ife

Yoruba

DENKYIRA

DAHOMEY

Fon

BENIN

Akan

Ibo

Gold Coast

Ivory Coast

Slave Coast

BIGHT OF BIAFRA

LOANGO

Bakongo

KONGO

The Asantehene (Asante king) had his gold-decorated stool. The stool was very important because it stood for the soul of the Akan people. Not even the king could sit on it.

The ancient city of Benin astonished early European visitors with its wide streets and roomy houses. Benin's artists crafted many bronze images of their kings. This one shows the ideal Benin king, calm and watchful.

Carved in the Kongo Kingdom, this tortoise played a part in the ceremony marking a boy's entrance into manhood. African art, such as this wood carving, often celebrated important moments like birth, marriage, or death.

171

The Southern Colonies

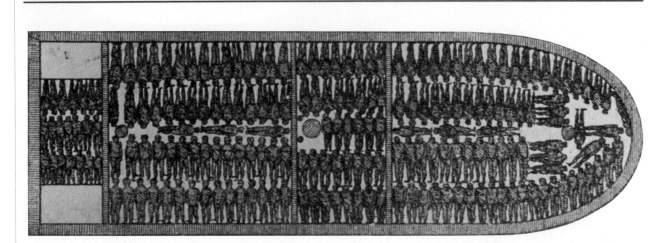

▲ *Slaves were chained together and tightly stacked in the ships. Overcrowding allowed diseases to spread throughout the slave cargo.*

■ *Describe the treatment of slaves as they were taken from Africa to North America.*

This voyage, known as the middle passage, was one of horror. In the dark holds of the ships, slaves were packed so tightly they could barely move and chained so they could not escape by jumping overboard.

Olaudah Equiano, a West African slave who was later freed, wrote about his experience on a slave ship. He described the horrible smell, the filth, the sickness, and the fear—the shouts and groans of the dying. Before being forced into slavery, Equiano had never seen a white person or heard English. He thought he had "got into a world of bad spirits."

Africans who survived the long sea voyage faced another terror in an American port: the slave auction. Equiano wrote:

> On a signal given, such as the beat of a drum, the buyers rush at once into the yard where the slaves are confined, and make choice of that parcel they like best.
>
> Olaudah Equiano, *Narrative*, published in 1814

Slavery in the Southern Colonies

Not all the blacks who came to North America in the 1600s were slaves. Among the first Africans to arrive in Virginia in 1619, many may have come as indentured servants. In the first years some who were brought over as slaves could later buy their freedom.

A Free Black

Anthony Johnson arrived in Virginia in 1621 and worked as a servant on the Richard Bennett plantation for 20 years. In the 1640s, Johnson and his wife Mary gained their freedom. They probably earned money for their freedom by selling vegetables they grew. Once free, Johnson became a successful planter. He received 200 acres and a herd of cattle. He even had servants.

By the late 1650s, though, Johnson saw that life for black people in the Virginia colony was changing. Between 1660 and 1682, the colony passed a series of strict laws regarding slavery. Johnson feared increasing trouble for all blacks.

In 1664, Johnson decided to move. He sold most of his property and moved his family to Maryland where they rented land. He gave 50 acres in Virginia to his son, Richard. But Richard Johnson never got the land. A white jury in Virginia decided that because Anthony was black, his land could be taken from him and given to a local white planter.

Strict Slave Laws

Why did the laws in Virginia about slavery get stronger? For one thing, slaves were becoming more valuable. Fewer indentured servants were coming to Virginia in the 1660s because life in England had improved.

From the illustration on page 161, you can see that planters needed a lot of workers to grow, harvest, and dry tobacco. Tobacco farmers grew tobacco as a **cash crop**—a product grown for sale rather than for the planter's own use. Eager for profits, white plantation owners supported laws that would give them full power over black tobacco workers.

Slaves and Southern Wealth

Africans were valuable workers, not only on the tobacco plantations of Virginia. They also labored on the rice plantations in the Carolina colony, founded in 1663. Some of the slaves sent to Carolina had been able rice farmers in Africa. They used their farming skills to grow rice in Carolina as well. Rice plantation owners became some of the richest men in the English colonies. Slaves, however, were given only small amounts of clothing and food. The majority of Africans were slaves, and they did not share in the wealth they helped create. ■

▲ *Africans were able to grow rice more effectively than the English settlers had.*

◄ *On this tobacco label, you can see slaves working and owners enjoying their wealth.*

■ *What events took place that led Virginia colonists to adopt slavery?*

LONDON'S VIRGINIA.

R E V I E W

1. **FOCUS** How did the slave trade begin and develop in the southern colonies?
2. **CONNECT** Contrast and compare the white settlers' attitude toward the Powhatan Indians to their attitude toward African slaves.
3. **ECONOMICS** How did tobacco farmers benefit from slavery?
4. **CRITICAL THINKING** Slavery laws were passed in Virginia to prevent slaves from rebelling against their owners. How might these laws have affected the actions of slave owners?
5. **ACTIVITY** Construct a timeline that traces the history of the slave trade. If necessary, do additional research at the library.

The Southern Colonies

Interpreting Flow Lines

Here's Why

Mapmakers often use arrows to show movement. When the thickness is varied to show the quantity of what is being moved, the arrows are called graduated flow lines. Graduated means the size gets larger or smaller. Flow lines show that something is flowing or moving.

Graduated flow lines on a map give you a lot of information very quickly. They show you where something comes from, where it is going, and how the quantity is divided. Graduated flow lines are not very precise ways of indicating quantity.

To find exact amounts, you might want to consult a table.

Suppose you want to find out how many slaves were sent across the Atlantic Ocean and what parts of Africa they came from. You can do this by looking at a map with graduated flow lines.

Here's How

The maps at the bottom of this page and page 175 show the slave trade between Africa and the Western Hemisphere, 1701–1810. The graduated flow lines show how many African people were taken from their homelands in different parts of

Africa and sent to colonies in North and South America. Use a ruler or mark a piece of paper to measure the width of the arrow. Compare the ruler or paper to the legend. This tells you that the total number of slaves was more than 6 million for the period.

Look at the tail of the arrow on the map on this page. It shows the places from which the slaves originally came. See how the tail is broken into two sections. Each section shows about how many people came from West Africa and Central and Southeast Africa.

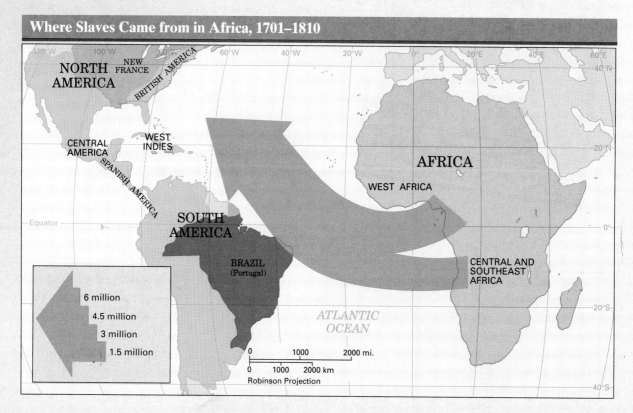

Where Slaves Came from in Africa, 1701–1810

NORTH AMERICA • NEW FRANCE • BRITISH AMERICA • CENTRAL AMERICA • WEST INDIES • SPANISH AMERICA • SOUTH AMERICA • BRAZIL (Portugal) • AFRICA • WEST AFRICA • CENTRAL AND SOUTHEAST AFRICA • ATLANTIC OCEAN • Equator

6 million
4.5 million
3 million
1.5 million

0   1000   2000 mi.
0 1000 2000 km
Robinson Projection

You can see that the flow line coming from West Africa is the thickest. This means that the largest number of slaves—just over 3.2 million—came from West Africa.

The flow line from Central and Southeast Africa is thicker than the "1.5 million" section of the legend and thinner than the "3 million" section. It stands for slightly more than 2 million slaves.

Now compare the width of the line flowing from West Africa to the arrowhead in the legend. You can see that the number of slaves from West Africa is more than 3 million.

Try It

Look at the map below. Compare the graduated flow line on this map with the one on the first map. You can see that this time the head, rather than the tail, of the arrow is broken into sections. This map focuses on where the slaves were sent rather than where they came from.

Which place in the Western Hemisphere received the most slaves from Africa? Which place received the fewest? How does the graduated flow line show you this information?

Were more African people sent as slaves to British North America or to the Portuguese colony of Brazil? About how many slaves were sent to the West Indies?

Apply It

Draw a map with a graduated flow line to show where the people in your family go during the week. The tail of the arrow will be at your home. Divide the head to show each person's destination, such as work, day care, or school. If some family members stay at home, draw an arrow pointing back to your house.

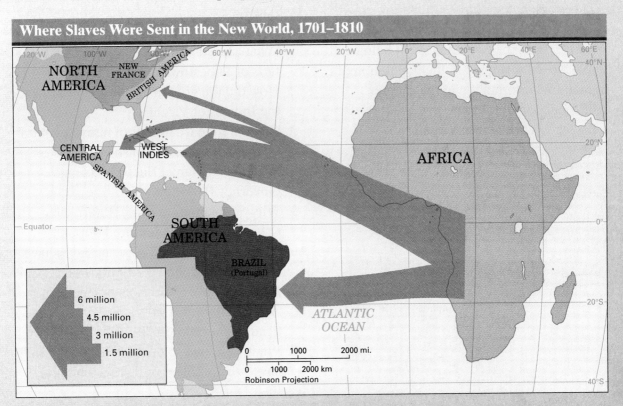

Where Slaves Were Sent in the New World, 1701–1810

NORTH AMERICA
NEW FRANCE
BRITISH AMERICA
CENTRAL AMERICA
WEST INDIES
SPANISH AMERICA
SOUTH AMERICA
BRAZIL (Portugal)
Equator
AFRICA
ATLANTIC OCEAN

6 million
4.5 million
3 million
1.5 million

0   1000   2000 mi.
0   1000   2000 km
Robinson Projection

175

Chapter Review

Reviewing Key Terms

cash crop (p. 173)
council (p. 163)
export (p.168)
House of Burgesses
(p. 161)
indentured servant (p. 160)

life expectancy (p. 158)
plantation (p. 161)
rebel (p. 165)
representative (p. 161)
slavery (p. 167)

A. Each phrase below is a clue to a key term. Write a sentence giving the key term for each clue and explaining the reasons for your choice.
1. first elected government in North America
2. grown to sell for profit
3. someone elected to a lawmaking body
4. worked in return for passage to America and the promise of land.

B. Each statement below is untrue because a key term has been used incorrectly. Using information from the chapter, rewrite each sentence correctly using the key term.
1. Life expectancy describes the tobacco plant's ability to grow in wet soil.
2. Slavery was a labor system in which slaves traded work for land.
3. Governor Berkeley made people who didn't pay their taxes work in councils.
4. Rebels defended Governor Berkeley.
5. Each Indian family had a plantation on which they raised a variety of crops.
6. Exports were tools used to grow tobacco.

Exploring Concepts

A. The graph below shows population growth in Virginia during the 1600s until 1700. On your own paper, describe how each event below might have led to a jump in the population of Virginia. Use information in the chapter.
1. introduction of tobacco
2. first slaves brought to Virginia

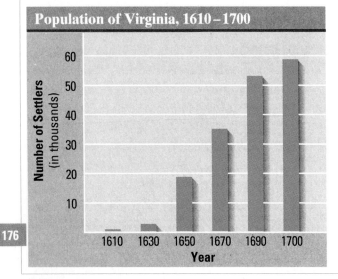

Population of Virginia, 1610–1700

Number of Settlers (in thousands)

Year: 1610 1630 1650 1670 1690 1700

B. Answer each question with information from the chapter.
1. What caused sickness among the first settlers of Jamestown?
2. How did the growth of plantations affect the Indians of Virginia?
3. Compare the treatment of native peoples by the British and Spanish in America.
4. Why did Nathaniel Bacon challenge Governor Berkeley?
5. Why did plantation owners start using slaves instead of indentured servants?
6. What knowledge did African slaves have that made Carolina plantations successful?
7. How was slavery as it was practiced in Africa different from the way it was practiced by the colonists?
8. What were two solutions tried by the Indians to the problem of the British taking their land?

Reviewing Skills

1. Look at the map on this page of cash crops exported to Great Britain from the American colonies. The graduated flow lines show how much these crops were worth in pounds sterling, the British form of money.
   a. What was the most valuable crop exported to Great Britain?
   b. What was the next most valuable?
   c. Approximately how much was the total value of all three crops in pounds sterling?
   d. What does the tail of the arrow tell you? What does the head of the arrow tell you?

2. Review the sections The Government of Virginia and The Fight for Land on pages 163 to 165. Summarize each section and combine the information in one paragraph. Who most benefited from Governor Berkeley's policies? How did his policies affect indentured servants?

3. If you wanted to show visually how quickly the number of acres of land used for raising tobacco increased in Virginia from 1612 until 1700, what would you make?

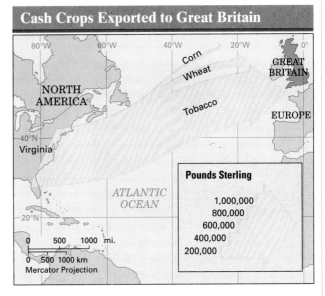

Cash Crops Exported to Great Britain

Pounds Sterling
1,000,000
800,000
600,000
400,000
200,000

Using Critical Thinking

1. When indentured servants became free, they were given 50 acres of land. This land was often in Indian territory. How would you describe the events that followed from the Indians' point of view?

2. The text says, "The majority of Africans were slaves, and they did not share in the wealth they helped create." How is wealth created? How is it shared? Write a paragraph explaining your answers.

Preparing for Citizenship

1. **WRITING ACTIVITY** Suppose you are a geographer and that time travel is possible. Write a story in which you travel in space and time to the first Jamestown settlement. Once there, you give the settlers advice based on what you know about Virginia's geography. Imagine that they listen to your advice. Then describe what they do and what the effects are.

2. **COLLABORATIVE LEARNING** Working in groups of three to four people each, plan and stage a television news interview show. Focus on one of the following topics: (1) John Smith's first encounter with Powhatan and Pocahontas, (2) John Rolfe's marriage to Pocahontas, or (3) Nathaniel Bacon's confrontation with Governor Berkeley in the House of Burgesses.

   Divide tasks among members of the group. Report the story. Give the background on the story. That is, what led to this event? Present the point of view of each person involved in the event. As a group, describe an event that could happen today that would be like the event you have chosen for your interview.

Chapter 8

The New England Colonies

"We shall be like a city upon a hill; the eyes of all people are on us." Puritan leader John Winthrop said what many settlers in New England felt in 1630. They wanted others to see them as a strong community built on Christian beliefs. Strict Puritan values shaped almost every part of life in New England. As a result the New England colonies were different from all others in America.

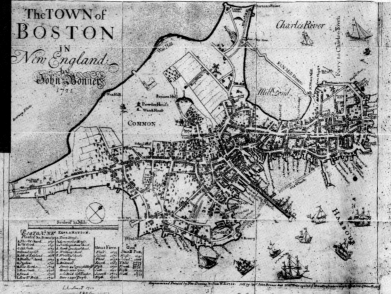

1630 The town of Boston is started by about 500 Puritans, including nine-year-old Anne Pollard. When her painting (above) was done in 1721, she was 100 years old. By the time the map (above right) was published in 1722, Boston was New England's largest city.

1663 First complete Bible printed in North America was John Eliot's translation into Algonquin.

1625	1650	1675

1630

During this period shoes like these were worn by farmers in New England. They show how simply New Englanders lived.

Religion was very important to the people of early New England. This quilt, made later, shows how churches were usually built at the center of New England villages.

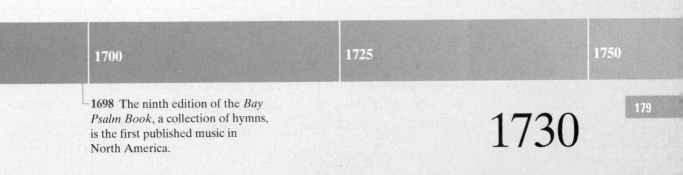

1700　　　　　　1725　　　　　　1750

1698 The ninth edition of the *Bay Psalm Book*, a collection of hymns, is the first published music in North America.

1730

L E S S O N   1

The Puritans Come to America

How did the religious beliefs of the New England settlers affect their way of life?

Key Terms

- covenant
- meetinghouse
- common

➤ *John Winthrop became the first governor of the Massachusetts Bay Colony in 1629. He served as governor 12 times until his death in 1649.*

The *Arbella* pitched and rolled on the dark waves. On board, some 100 weary, seasick passengers gathered to pray. Before their ship left England in 1630, the settlers had named John Winthrop their leader. On the long ocean voyage to their new land, Winthrop reminded them of their Christian duty to one another:

> We must love one another with a pure heart. We must bear one another's burdens, we must not look only on our own things, but also on the things of our brethren.
>
> We must delight in each other, make others' conditions our own, rejoice together, mourn together, labor and suffer together: always having before our eyes our . . . community as members of the same body.

Puritan Beliefs

The passengers on the *Arbella* were Puritans, people who wanted to reform the Church of England. They were called Puritans because they wanted to purify, or rid, their religion of Catholic influences.

The Puritans objected to grand ceremonies and statues in church. They also believed that good Christians should follow the teachings of the Bible and very strictly observe the Sabbath. In England,

The church on the left was built in Vermont in 1763. The church below, Saint Paul's in London, was completed in 1710. In which church would a Puritan be more comfortable? Why?

This letter and ink pot belonged to John Winthrop. The letter is addressed "To my very Loving Husband John . . ."at a house in London. It contains news about Winthrop's family.

many preferred to dance or play cards rather than worship on the Sabbath. Such behavior shocked the Puritans.

The Puritans also believed that the Church of England was wrong to insist that Puritan ministers obey the rulings of the bishops. According to the Puritans, the worshipers in each church, or congregation, should be able to choose its own minister and run its own affairs. This belief is called Congregationalism.

The Puritans hoped that God would enter into a **covenant,** or agreement, with them, as He had with people in the Bible. If the Puritan colony grew and was successful, the Puritans would conclude that God did indeed favor them as a chosen people. Their first concern in life would be to do God's will and lead model Christian lives. Over time, the Puritans believed, their community would be copied by people throughout the New England Colonies. If they broke their covenant with God by disobeying Him, Puritans feared that God would severely punish or even destroy the whole community. ■

■ *What disagreements did Puritans have with the Church of England?*

181

The New England Colonies

The Puritan Community

John Winthrop and about 500 other people came to Massachusetts in 1630. They were the first of thousands of Puritans to settle in the Massachusetts Bay Colony. For 11 years, small ships like the *Arbella* sailed from England bringing hopeful settlers to the New England shores.

Settling the Land

When the ships were unloaded, the Puritans would set up camp in temporary shelters, similar to those the local Indians used. The new arrivals would camp out while their leaders arranged for a permanent settlement.

The leaders of the group would apply for a charter from colonial officials to start a new town. They would also draw up a covenant that outlined how the people would live together.

The newcomers hoped to find fertile land near pure, running water. Harbors were good locations. Each family head would be given several hundred acres of farmland outside the center of town. This would be enough land for each family to farm with plenty left over to pass on to grown sons.

Building Towns

Even though they farmed, the Puritans still lived together in towns so that they could help one another. In this way, the Puritans built strong communities and kept their covenant with God.

In most Puritan towns, the settlers built a **meetinghouse,** the town's largest and most important

The homes in this Puritan village were built fairly close together. Fences kept the animals out of the fields.

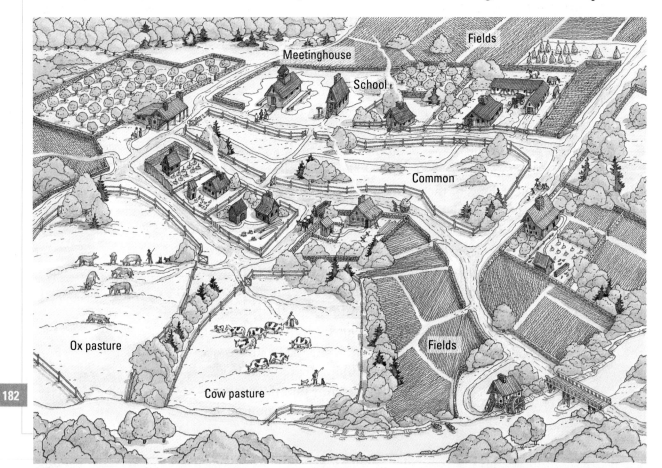

Fields

Meetinghouse

School

Common

Fields

Ox pasture

Cow pasture

building. The meetinghouse was a gathering place for religious services, celebrations, and news.

In front of the meetinghouse in a Massachusetts town was a large open pasture called a **common,** which belonged to everyone. Here the townspeople could bring their livestock to graze.

Puritan families built their homes around the common on plots of land provided by the town. Most plots were large enough to include a house, a barn, and a small vegetable garden. Nearly every family also owned some land at the edge of town where they raised corn, wheat, or oats. ■

■ *Why did the Puritans live together in towns?*

Puritans and the Land

In New England the Puritan settlers were sure they had found a land that showed their special favor with God. The evergreen and hardwood forests were full of wildlife—deer, squirrels, rabbits, and other animals. Rivers, streams, and the ocean were filled with fish and other seafood.

The Puritans believed that the difficult parts of their lives were also signs from God. The cold winters and rocky soil of New England meant to them that God wanted them to work hard together to show thanks for God's gift of salvation.

The Puritans Prosper

The Puritans were lucky to have moved to a healthy place. They had clean water from many fast-moving streams. The population in Massachusetts boomed. Soon the colony had more people than any other in English America.

Despite the healthy environment, most New Englanders did not become wealthy from farming, as the Virginia tobacco planters did. The Puritans managed to grow enough food to feed themselves, but the soil was too thin and rocky for large-scale farming.

Some settlers turned to crafts and trading to make a living. Every town had some craftspeople—men and women who made tools, home furnishings, and other equipment. Although families made their clothes, tools, soap, candles, and other everyday goods at home, it was easier to buy some goods. Blacksmiths made both horseshoes and ox-shoes. Whitesmiths made tin candleholders and tinderboxes. Joiners

▲ *Harsh but often beautiful landscapes faced the Puritans in New England winters.*

◄ *The Puritans used this cranberry rake to gather ripe berries.*

183

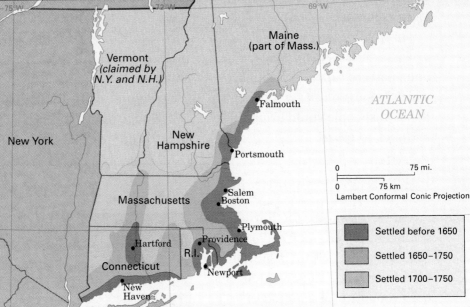

Settlement in New England, 1650–1750

Maine
(part of Mass.)

Vermont
(claimed by
N.Y. and N.H.)

New York

New
Hampshire

Falmouth

Portsmouth

ATLANTIC
OCEAN

0   75 mi.
0   75 km
Lambert Conformal Conic Projection

Massachusetts

Salem
Boston

Plymouth

Hartford

Providence

R.I.

Connecticut

Newport

New
Haven

Settled before 1650

Settled 1650–1750

Settled 1700–1750

➤ *This map's legend will help you discover how Puritan settlements grew along the East Coast of what is now the United States. To understand more about map legends, see page G5 in the* Map and Globe Handbook.

How Do We Know?

HISTORY *Ships' records reveal that the Puritans brought animals and supplies with them when they sailed to Massachusetts. They also brought military equipment, including armor and swords. They thought that they might have to defend their new homes from Indians whose lands they were invading.*

➤ *Life in the New England colonies could be harsh. Still, New Englanders enjoyed a much longer life expectancy than did the people in the southern colonies or Great Britain.*

fashioned furniture from wood. Cobblers repaired shoes. Cobblers who were good at their craft became cordwainers, or shoemakers.

Some settlers turned to fishing, shipbuilding, or trading to make a living. By 1664, Boston's population depended on shipping, fishing, and trading—not farming—for their livelihood.

Two Views of Nature

To the Puritans, the forests and rocky land of New England were wild and filled with temptation. They felt their duty was to tame nature. They cleared land,

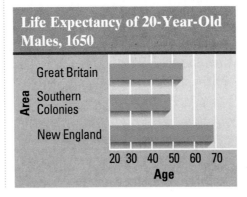

Life Expectancy of 20-Year-Old Males, 1650

Great Britain

Southern
Colonies

New England

Area

20 30 40 50 60 70
Age

planted crops, and put up fences. They also caught, killed, and traded wild animals.

The Puritan attitude toward the land was different from that of the Algonquin Indians. The Algonquins were comfortable with nature just as it was. They survived by fishing, farming, and hunting. They moved around the land in harmony with the seasons. In the summer they lived near the fields that the women had planted. Come winter, they set up temporary shelters in a protected location. When spring arrived, they camped near a river, so they could fish. After about 10 years in one place, the Algonquins would move on to more fertile land where wood was again plentiful.

Because they moved often and did not have horses or wagons, the Algonquins owned very little property. All they carried with them were bows, spears, planting sticks, and animal skins. The Algonquins

184

October–March

March–October

Migration

Migration

did not have a strong sense of personal property or individual ownership of the land.

The Puritans misunderstood the Algonquin way of life. They thought that the Algonquins were lazy. They had not "settled" the land and, thus, did not own it. Because the two groups lived differently on the land, they did not get along well together. For example, Puritans would let their pigs and cattle roam freely to find food. The Puritans did not have to worry about these animals ruining their crops or those of their neighbors, because the Puritans fenced in their crop land. The pigs and cows did ruin Algonquin crops, however. The Algonquins did not believe in fencing their land. Tensions grew worse as Puritans took over Algonquin land. Eventually war broke out between the two groups. ◾

As you can see in this illustration, the Algonquin Indians lived in harmony with the land.

◾ *How did the Puritans and the Algonquins view nature?*

R E V I E W

1. **FOCUS** How did the religious beliefs of the New England settlers affect their way of life?

2. **CONNECT** Why did many of Virginia's farmers become wealthier than farmers in New England?

3. **BELIEF SYSTEMS** Summarize the basic religious beliefs of the Puritans.

4. **SOCIAL SYSTEMS** Describe the Puritan communities. Why did they form their communities as they did?

5. **CRITICAL THINKING** Think about the ways the Puritans and the Algonquins lived. Why did their different ways of life lead to tensions between the two groups?

6. **ACTIVITY** Make a two-column chart comparing the attitudes of the Puritans and the attitudes of the Algonquin Indians about the land.

1625 | 1630 | 1690 | 1700 | 1725 | 1750

LESSON 2

Life in New England

THINKING FOCUS

What was everyday life like for the New England colonists?

Key Term

- apprentice

> Work in that household never ceased, . . . The pewter mugs had to be scoured with reeds and fine sand. There was a great kettle of soap boiling over a fire just behind the house, and all day long Judith and her mother took turns stirring it with a long stick. Judith set Kit to tend the stirring while she readied the soap barrel. Kit tried to keep a gingerly distance from the kettle. The strong fumes of lye [from the kettle] stung her eyelids and stirring the heavy mass tired her arms and shoulders. Her stirring became more and more halfhearted till Judith snatched the stick in exasperation. "It will lump on you," she scolded, "and you can just blame yourself if we have to use lumpy soap all summer."
>
> Elizabeth George Speare,
> *The Witch of Blackbird Pond*

Like Judith and Kit in Elizabeth Speare's story, Puritan children in the Massachusetts Bay Colony worked as hard as their parents. After age six, they even dressed like adults, as you can see in the painting on page 187. In fact, Puritan society looked upon its children as serious and responsible persons. Puritan children were treated rather like miniature adults.

Children in the Puritan Family

Puritan parents were warm and loving. However, they were always concerned that their children grow up in godly ways. Parents believed that any sinful ways in their children had to be disciplined.

According to Puritan beliefs, children were born "full of sin, as full as a toad is of poison." So parents took their duties seriously and sometimes were quite strict. Puritan parents might spank their children for laziness or disrespect or for running and jumping on the Sabbath. They believed that a child is "better whipped, than damned" by the devil.

For their part, Puritan children were expected to honor their parents. In 1715, a Puritan named

◄ The Mason children—David, Joanna, and Abigail—posed for this oil portrait in 1670. They are dressed in typical Puritan children's clothing.

Eleazar Moody wrote a book called *The School of Good Manners.* In his book, Moody set down some rules describing good behavior for Puritan children:

A pproach near thy parents at no time without a bow.

Dispute not, nor delay to obey thy parents commands.

Go not out of doors without thy parents leave, and return within the time by them limited.

Quarrel not nor contend with thy brethren or sisters, but live in love, peace, and unity.

Beware thou utter not any thing hard to be believed.

Let thy words be modest about those things which only concern thee.

Even though Puritan parents were strict, they tried hard to be good parents. They felt that they had to guard against spoiling their children. For this reason, they often sent their children away by age 14 to live with relatives or friends. The children spent several years as **apprentices,** learning skills such as weaving or perhaps carpentry.

Most Puritans were educated people, more so than other groups of people who came to America. Many knew how to read and write and taught their children to do so as well. See the Moment in Time on the next page to learn more about Puritan children.

▼ This hornbook wasn't really a book at all. The alphabet is written on parchment, which is attached to a wooden paddle. A thin, transparent sheet of horn protects the parchment so the "book," which was used to teach reading, would last a long time.

A·B·C·D
E·F·G·H
I·K·L·M
N·O·P·Q
R·S·T·V
W·X·Y·Z
a·e·i·o·u

187

Puritan Girl

10:19 A.M., September 23, 1647
Dorchester, Massachusetts

Hat
She almost forgot it when she ran out to collect bayberries this morning. Her mother scolded her by quoting a Bible passage that says a woman must be modest in her dress.

Apron
Made of Dutch linen, her apron is a smaller version of the ones grown women wear.

Dress
Just like her mother's, her dress fastens down the front with hooks and eyes. She would dearly love a dress with buttons, but her father says buttons are too fancy.

Collar
Like her hat, it's worn only when she goes outdoors.

Bayberries
The sweet–smelling fruit grows on a low bush, down the hill from her house. She'll collect several baskets for scented candles.

Doll
She talks softly to the corncob doll she sneaked into her basket. Her mother talks the same way to her newest brother, who is two months old.

Ash Smudge
Her apron hides a new smudge on the knee of her dress. Each day it's her job to clean the fireplace and collect ashes for soapmaking.

These pages are from The New England Primer, a reader for young children. It was published in Boston in 1727.

A In *Adam's* Fall We Sinned all.
B Thy Life to Mend This *Book* Attend.
C The *Cat* doth play And after slay.
D A *Dog* will bite A *Thief* at night.
E An *Eagles* flight Is out of sight.
F The *Idle Fool* Is whipt at School.

G As runs the *Glass* Mans life doth pass.
H My *Book* and *Heart* Shall never part.
J *Job* feels the Rod Yet blesses GOD.
K Our *KING* the good No man of blood.
L The *Lion* bold The *Lamb* doth hold.
M The *Moon* gives light In time of night.

N *Nightingales* sing In Time of Spring.
O The *Royal Oak* it was the Tree That sav'd His Royal Majestie.
P *Peter* denies His Lord and cries
Q *Queen Esther* comes in Royal State To Save the JEWS from dismal Fate.
R *Rachel* doth mourn For her first born.
S *Samuel* anoints Whom God appoints.

T *Time* cuts down all Both great and small.
U *Uriah's* beauteous Wife Made *David* seek his Life.
W *Whales* in the Sea God's Voice obey.
X *Xerxes* the great did die, And so must you & I.
Y *Youth* forward slips Death soonest nips.
Z *Zacheus* he Did climb the Tree His Lord to see.

The Puritans thought of reading as a religious skill, because studying the Bible was so important. Not learning to read was "one chief project of that old deluder [deceiver], Satan, to keep men from the knowledge of the Scriptures."

Some children learned their lessons at home. Some went to school. There they studied the Lord's Prayer and learned the alphabet from hornbooks. Boys who were going to be ministers always attended school. In 1636, the Puritans founded Harvard, the first college in America, for training Puritan ministers. ■

■ *How did Puritan parents raise their children?*

Puritan Family Life

The Puritans felt that God wanted everyone to live in a family, and almost all Puritans did. Families were large. Some had as many as 15 children.

The Family Home

Most Puritan families lived in small, two-story houses made of wood. Each had a large downstairs room called the hall or keeping room. This was the only room in the house where the fireplace was kept going all the time. Families gathered in this room to eat, do chores, and study. In winter, they slept there.

If you were to visit a family in their hall, you would see a few pieces of simple furniture. The furniture would include a wicker cradle, a few ladder-back chairs, and an oak table. There would also be a stool, a spinning wheel, and a chest with a hinged lid. You might see a kettle and a bean pot near the fireplace. The fire would warm and light the room. In the summer, candles provided light.

Family Closeness

Puritan families lived and worked closely together. They passed on their way of life from

Across Time & Space

The public school system in the United States today can trace its beginnings to Massachusetts. In 1647, the Massachusetts Bay Colony set up a public school system supported by taxes.

189

> *The fireplace in the great hall of this recon- structed Puritan house both warmed the room and served as a cooking area.*

▼ *This oak footwarmer helped the Puritans to stay warm during the cold New England win- ters. Hot coals were placed inside and the heat came up through a grating on the top, where one's feet rested. This footwarmer has a handle on it so it could be car- ried to church.*

■ *Why did Puritan families live so closely together?*

one generation to the next. Boys learned from their fathers how to cultivate oats, corn, and other crops. They also learned how to care for livestock. Girls learned from their moth- ers how to make candles and soap and also how to cook, sew, and care for children.

When a young man reached his mid-20s, he would ask his parents for permission to marry. When a son married, his father would give him a piece of the family's land. As the years passed, each family di- vided its land among several sons. After three or four generations, the land had been divided many times. The plots often were too small to farm.

With no land to work, sons began to move away from their towns in the countryside to find jobs in the cities or at sea. Some- times they looked for land to farm farther north or west. In the late 1600s, the people of New England began to wonder whether Puri- tanism could survive if children continued to move away from their families and their home towns. ■

R E V I E W

1. **FOCUS** Describe daily life for New England colonists.
2. **CONNECT** How did life in a Puritan town compare to that on a southern plantation? In what ways was it similar? How was it different?
3. **HISTORY** In Puritan families, land passed from fathers to sons. How did this practice eventually cause some Puritan families to move apart?
4. **CRITICAL THINKING** Look again at Eleazar Moody's rules for Puritan children on page 187. In what ways are these rules similar to the ones children are ex- pected to follow today?
5. **ACTIVITY** Make a chart comparing and contrasting everyday Puritan family life with modern-day family life.

LESSON 3

Challenging Authority

A nne was delighted at this unexpected visit by her Reverend Cotton. He said he had come to ask her about the weekly meetings she was holding with many of the women in the colony. Just what did they find to talk about?

She answered willingly. It was mainly the sermons of the preceding Sunday, the way the men did when they got together. . . . What else did Mistress Hutchinson and her women discuss?

Why, said Anne, that each of them had the Holy Spirit within herself, and when hard-pressed, they had but to open their Bibles and God might speak to them directly through His Word.

Cotton could hardly believe his ears. He said she must not preach such things anymore. It was the purpose of the ministers to interpret the Word.

Deborah Crawford, *Four Women in a Violent Time*, 1970

THINKING FOCUS

What conflicts erupted in Puritan society?

Key Terms

- democracy
- dissenter
- civil disobedience
- Great Awakening

The meeting between Anne Hutchinson and Reverend Cotton told about in this story actually took place. Anne Hutchinson was the wife of a merchant and the mother of fourteen children. She questioned the teachings of the ministers of the Massachusetts Bay Colony. In spite of its careful organization, the colony was soon torn by disagreement and religious conflict.

Religion and the Government

Many problems in Puritan society had to do with the relationship between the people's religion and their government. Government was to be separate from the church. Ministers, for example, could not hold political office. Even so, religion played a big role in government.

Puritan leaders did not believe in **democracy,** or rule by the will of the majority. Governor John Winthrop called democracy "the worst of all forms of Government." Winthrop believed that some men were more godly than others, and these men should have more power.

▼ *This title page is from an 1862 reprint of a book of psalms first printed in the Massachusetts Bay Colony.*

A
LITERAL REPRINT
OF THE
BAY PSALM BOOK
BEING THE
EARLIEST NEW ENGLAND VERSION
OF THE
PSALMS

In Puritan society, all the people in the colony did not vote. Only male church members could vote. Church membership was open only to those who had been admitted by other members. In this way, the colony was ruled by men who governed according to the Bible and Puritan beliefs.

Also, the Puritans did not allow any form of religious freedom. They believed that all religions other than their own were wrong and sinful in the eyes of God. For this reason, Puritans punished and banished, or sent away, people such as Quakers who did not live their lives according to Puritan beliefs. ■

➤ *Religion was an important part of Puritan life. Here Puritan families are on their way to worship.*

■ *Why did the Puritans not believe in freedom of religion?*

UNDERSTANDING DISSENT

Roger Williams and Anne Hutchinson were not the only dissenters in America's past. Dissent has occurred throughout our country's history.

Dissent and Protest

Dissent is disagreement with established policies and speaking out about that disagreement. Anne Hutchinson disagreed with Puritan religious beliefs, and she made her views known.

When dissent is especially strong, it may take the form of protest. Protest is action meant to change established policies.

Dissent Changes History

Dr. Martin Luther King, Jr., was a Baptist minister from the South who, during the 1950s and 1960s, disagreed with many established policies toward black Americans. For example, many blacks were not allowed to vote, even though the Constitution gave them that right. In some states, blacks were not allowed to eat at the same lunch counters as whites.

Dr. King made his views on these policies known. Because his disagreement was so strong, he urged his followers to protest. They tried to register to vote. They sat down at "whites-only" lunch counters.

Because of these protests, official government policies were changed. Congress passed the Civil Rights Acts of 1964 and 1968. Because of his dissent, Dr. King, like Roger Williams and Anne Hutchinson before him, helped to change history.

Dissent in Puritan Society

Persons who could not vote or did not want to worship the same way as everyone else suffered in Puritan towns. Some **dissenters**—people who disagreed with the Puritans—spoke out.

Roger Williams

Roger Williams, a young minister, did not believe the government should support one religion over another. Williams said that requiring people to attend a particular church "stinks in God's nostrils." All people should be free to worship as they choose, he claimed. He even thought that nonchurch members should be allowed to vote and that Puritan officials should be more respectful to the Algonquin Indians.

Williams's beliefs made the colonial government nervous, so they asked him to change his views. He refused. In 1635, the government decided to ship Roger Williams back to England. Massasoit, chief of the Wampanoag, helped Williams hide in the wilderness.

The following year, Williams established a new colony in what is now Rhode Island, where religion and government were separate and people could worship freely.

Anne Hutchinson

Anne Hutchinson also challenged the authority of the male Puritan government. She believed in a personal relationship with God. Such a belief greatly reduced the power of the ministers. When the colony officials ordered her to stop preaching her beliefs, Hutchinson practiced **civil disobedience**—that is, she refused to obey those colonial laws she thought were unjust.

The ministers were especially upset that a woman would dare to disobey them. They believed that women should follow the advice of men and keep quiet. Massachusetts officials made Anne Hutchinson stand trial and then banished her from the

◄ *This statue of Anne Hutchinson stands in the city of Boston, Massachusetts.*

◄ *Roger Williams was a friend to American Indians. In this book, published around 1643, he tried to translate Indian languages. He also wrote about their customs and the way they lived.*

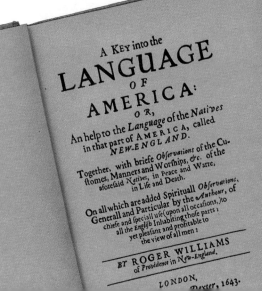

A KEY into the
LANGUAGE
OF
AMERICA:
OR,
An help to the Language of the Natives in that part of AMERICA, called NEW-ENGLAND.

Together, with briefe Observations of the Customes, Manners and Worships, &c. of the aforesaid Natives, in Peace and Warre, in Life and Death.

On all which are added Spirituall Observations, Generall and Particular by the Authour, of chiefe and speciall use (upon all occasions,) to all the English Inhabiting those parts; yet pleasant and profitable to the view of all men:

BY ROGER WILLIAMS
of Providence in New-England.

LONDON,
Dexter, 1643.

Massachusetts Bay Colony. Like Roger Williams, she fled to Rhode Island. Later, she settled in Portsmouth with her followers and continued to preach her beliefs.

Hutchinson's friend, Mary Dyer, suffered a tragic end. Puritan officials in Boston hanged her for expressing Quaker beliefs in the Puritan colony. As years went by, more and more dissenters challenged the iron-fisted control of Puritan ministers and officials. The Puritans found that punishing some dissenters did not stop others from speaking out. ■

■ *Why were Roger Williams and Anne Hutchinson banished from the Bay Colony?*

Witchcraft in Salem

The tension in the Massachusetts Bay Colony reached a high point in 1692. Two young Puritan girls, Elizabeth and Abigail, began acting strangely. They both would scream and fall to the floor as if they were unable to control themselves. They said they saw rats and other creatures swarming around them. A colonial doctor decided that Elizabeth and Abigail were victims of witchcraft.

Many people in Salem got caught up in the witch craze. First children and then older people were calling their unpopular neighbors "witches." When a person was accused, a trial would be held in the town. Within a year, 19 people, mostly old women, were found guilty of witchcraft and hanged.

Historians are not sure why the people of Salem became so hysterical about witchcraft. Some historians believe that poor farmers accused rich merchants of being witches out of jealousy. Other historians think that Puritan officials used the popular belief about witches to get rid of outspoken older women who challenged their authority. There is even a possibility that moldy grain was the cause. Such grain might have brought on an illness in people that made them seem to be possessed by devils.

After about a year, the witchcraft craze in the New England colonies died down. During that time, however, many people suffered and died because of the Puritans' fear of the devil and their beliefs about witchcraft. ■

➤ *Cotton Mather, a Puritan minister, tried to explain witchcraft in his book* The Wonders of the Invisible World, *published in 1693.*

■ *Keeping in mind their belief in community, why do you think the Puritans killed suspected witches?*

The Wonders of the Invisible World:

Being an Account of the

TRYALS
OF
Several Witches,

Lately Excuted in
NEW-ENGLAND:
And of several remarkable Curiosities therein Occurring.

Together with,
I. Observations upon the Nature, the Number, and the Operations of the Devils.
II. A short Narrative of a late outrage committed by a knot of Witches in Swede-Land, very much resembling, and so far explaining, that under which New-England has laboured.
III. Some Councels directing a due Improvement of the Terrible things lately done by the unusual and amazing Range of Evil-Spirits in New-England.
IV. A brief Discourse upon those Temptations which are the more ordinary Devices of Satan.

By COTTON MATHER.

Published by the Special Command of his EXCELLENCY the Governeur of the Province of the Massachusetts-Bay in New-England.

Printed first, at Boston in New-England; and Reprinted at London, for John Dunton, at the Raven in the Pultrey. 1693.

The Great Awakening

By the early 1700s, life in Puritan New England had changed. Dissenters such as Roger Williams and Anne Hutchinson had weakened the authority of ministers. Almost all of the original Puritan settlers were dead. Many younger Puritans preferred to live prosperous rather than religious lives. As one fish trader said, "My father came here for religion, but I came for fish."

Conservative Puritans, however, looked back fondly to the old days. Soon, new ministers caught their attention. The ministers spoke of sin in a very dramatic and emotional style and awakened the religious spirit in many people. For this reason, their religious revival is called the **Great Awakening.**

During the Great Awakening, new churches with new ideas popped up in Puritan towns. Everyone was encouraged to preach: women, servants, and even children. The sermons of ministers George Whitefield and Jonathan Edwards were more fiery than those of the old-time ministers.

The following is from Jonathan Edwards's famous sermon, "Sinners in the Hands of an Angry God," preached in 1741.

This portrait of the Reverend George Whitefield was painted around 1740. Reverend Whitefield was an important minister during the Great Awakening.

Thus it is that natural men are held in the hand of God, over the pit of hell; they have deserved the fiery pit, and are already sentenced to it. . . . [T]he devil is waiting for them, hell is gaping for them, the flames gather and flash about them.

Edwards wasn't the only minister whose words struck fear in the hearts of his church members. One listener described the sermons of Whitefield as "sharper than a two-edged sword. The [listeners'] bitter cries and groans were enough to pierce the hardest heart." ■

■ *Why is the religious revival of the mid-1700s called the Great Awakening?*

R E V I E W

1. **FOCUS** What conflicts erupted in Puritan society?

2. **CONNECT** Think about the way Puritan children were raised. Why would Puritan officials have believed that Elizabeth and Abigail were telling the truth about witchcraft in Salem?

3. **HISTORY** Were the governments of Puritan towns democracies? Why or why not?

4. **CRITICAL THINKING** Anne Hutchinson believed that people could speak directly to God. Why was her belief so threatening to Puritan ministers?

5. **ACTIVITY** Imagine you live in Puritan New England and are being persecuted for your belief in religious freedom. Create a poster that explains why you believe all people should be able to worship freely.

Colonial Living

*A*fter dark, American colonists used candles to light their homes. Like soap, cloth, medicine, and butter, candles and other necessities were homemade.

Get Ready

You would need special tools to do many of the colonists' chores, tools that would be hard to find today. Some of the work they did was dangerous or very difficult. For a taste of Early American living, though, you can either make butter from cream or design a quilt.

To make butter you need heavy cream, a small deep bowl, and a wooden spoon or an eggbeater.

For a quilt design, you'll need graph paper and colored pencils.

Find Out

To make butter, pour the cream into the bowl and beat it energetically until it thickens into butter. Write down how long this takes.

Your quilt should tell something about you. The squares can be plain patches of your favorite

Imagine this butter churn filled with cream to be turned into butter.

Colonial women made candles using the fragrant wax of bayberries.

When the wax was heated, candlewicks were dipped into it, then lifted out to dry.

colors or your school colors. If you want to make the design more personal, use your initials, numbers such as your age or address, or a clue to your hobbies. A musical note says you sing or play an instrument. A cake or a spoon says you like to cook. A football or a bat suggests your favorite sport. Remember to keep your designs simple, so that they could easily be embroidered onto the quilt squares.

Move Ahead

How long did it take you to make butter from cream? Add everyone's time and find the average. Now look at the butter churn pictured here. Imagine it filled with cream. How much time and energy do you think it would take to turn all that into butter? Compare the taste of your homemade butter with the taste of the butter or margarine you usually eat.

Display your quilt designs. Can class members identify the person who designed each square? Discuss the pattern for a "class quilt." When you decide what you want to include, ask a group to draw the squares. Hang the finished design on the bulletin board.

Explore Some More

Make a list of things you use every day, things that colonists had to make for themselves. Find out how colonists cleaned their teeth, treated fevers, or preserved food.

This silk and velvet quilt dates from about 1704.

Colonists mixed animal fat with wood ash to make soap. It was usually done outside, because the boiling mixture smelled so bad.

The New England Colonies

LESSON 4

Trade in New England

THINKING FOCUS

What effect did trade have on New England life?

Key Terms

- merchant
- Parliament
- duty
- smuggle

Andrew Belcher, a wealthy New Englander, was a clever man. He knew that he could make money selling wheat in Boston. He also knew that people in Europe would pay twice as much money for his wheat as people in Boston. Why should he care if Bostonians didn't have enough wheat to make all the bread they needed?

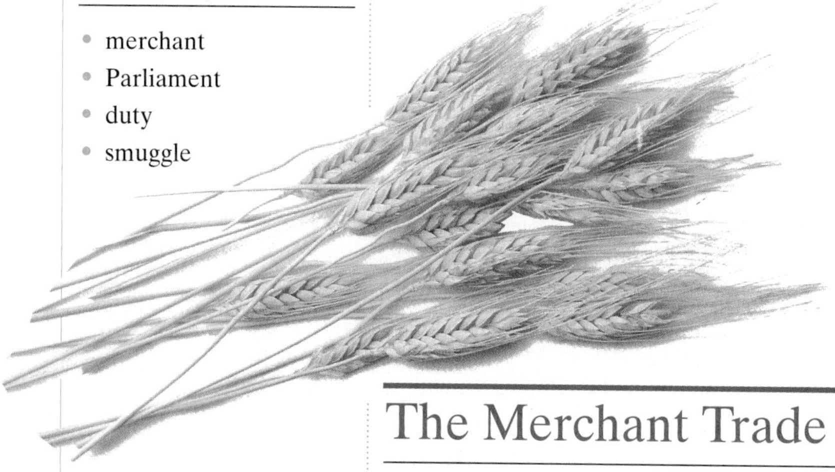

Belcher bought wheat from local farmers and loaded it onto one of his ships in Boston harbor. The hungry people of Boston heard rumors of his plan to ship wheat to Europe. Furious, the people took action. One night in April 1710, a group sawed through the rudder of Belcher's ship. Two days later people tried to run Belcher's ship aground. Belcher was outraged and demanded an indictment.

A group of citizens was accused of taking the law into their own hands. The case went to the grand jury, which dismissed it. The men on the grand jury were as wealthy and important as Belcher. But they had not forgotten the Puritan belief that people should help one another, not just themselves.

The Merchant Trade

Andrew Belcher was a **merchant,** someone who buys, transports, and sells goods. New England farmers couldn't produce cash crops like tobacco or sugar because of New England's rocky soil and cold climate. They needed a cash crop in order to buy manufactured goods from England.

The New England merchants established a trading system that allowed them to trade for these goods. They loaded their ships with fish and lumber from New England and tobacco and rice from the southern colonies. From Boston, the ships sailed to Europe or the Caribbean, where the merchants

▲ Wheat grown by New England farmers helped to feed the northern colonists. It was also an important trade item.

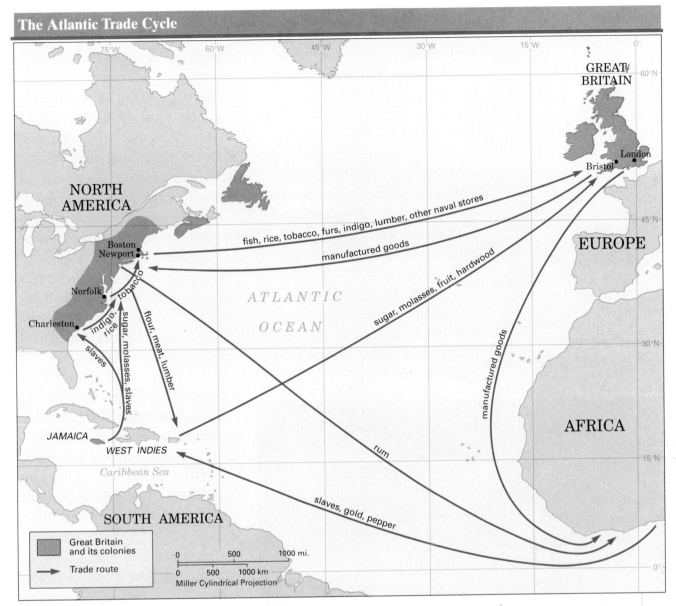

This map shows the New England merchants' trading triangle, including the usual trade routes and the goods that were bought and sold at each port.

merchants sold their cargoes for high profits. With these profits, the merchants bought manufactured goods like tools and glassware from England and wine, spices, coffee, and tea from other parts of the world.

Often, ships would sail between three different ports before returning to New England, as you can see on the map. A merchant might ship slaves from Africa to the Caribbean. There, he would sell the slaves and use the money he had earned to buy molasses. Next, he would ship the molasses back to New England, where distillers used it to make rum. Finally, the merchant would ship a cargo of rum to Africa and sell it. With that money, he would buy more slaves and start the cycle again. ■

■ How did the trading triangle benefit New England merchants?

Parliament and Colonial Trade

As New England merchants became successful, the English government worried that French and Dutch merchants would begin taking some of their profit. So from 1651 to 1696, the English

The New England Colonies

Parliament, or lawmaking body, passed a series of laws to control colonial trade.

The Navigation and Trade Acts

The Navigation Acts let England earn profits in three ways. First, the colonists had to ship their goods on English or colonial ships. No Dutch or French ship could earn money by carrying the colonies' goods.

Second, if a colonial trader wanted to buy products from any European country other than England, he had to ship the goods to England first. There the trader provided a list of the ship's cargo and paid a tax if customs officials found errors in the list. If all was in order, the trader could ship the goods to America. The trader had to do the same thing when certain colonial goods, such as rice and cotton, were shipped to Europe.

Later, England demanded that the colonists pay a tax, called a **duty,** on such items as sugar or molasses they bought in non-English colonies like the French and Dutch West Indies. These duties, which were part of the Trade Acts, discouraged the colonists from buying molasses.

Smuggling Molasses

The merchants desperately needed molasses, the main ingredient in rum. Without rum, merchants would have a hard time trading for slaves. If molasses became too expensive, the merchants would lose money.

The merchants preferred buying molasses from the French or Dutch West Indies, because it was cheaper than from the English West Indies. Rather than pay the high tax, many traders decided to **smuggle,** or sneak, the molasses into the colonies. Some traded secretly with the French and Dutch, avoiding the English tax. ■

■ *How did the Navigation and Trade Acts affect the merchant trade?*

▼ *In this detail of a painting by the American artist John Greenwood, New England sea captains enjoy themselves at an inn in Surinam, on the northeast coast of South America.*

Merchants, Sailors, and Craftspeople

The richest citizens of New England were the merchants. They rode around the port cities of Massachusetts and Rhode Island in coaches pulled by fine horses. On formal occasions, they wore embroidered vests over ruffled shirts and had their hair curled and powdered. Their wives dressed in imported satins and carried silk umbrellas when they went walking.

As these merchants gained wealth they also became more powerful. By the middle 1700s,

This miniature dining room, an exact replica of the same room in the Turner-Ingersoll House, Salem, Massachusetts, 1720, shows how wealthy New Englanders lived. The elaborate porcelain bowl below was brought back from Germany as part of the merchant trade.

merchants had replaced ministers as the most powerful people in New England society.

There would have been no rich merchants, however, without the talents of craftspeople and sailors. These people made the lifestyle of the merchants possible.

The craftspeople who supported the merchant trade included shipbuilders, sailmakers, and rope-makers. Because nearly everything was shipped in barrels, barrelmakers, or coopers, were also vital to trade. Blacksmiths forged the iron fittings for the merchants' sailing vessels.

In addition to craftspeople, sailors were needed to pilot the trading ships across the oceans. Navigators and other seafarers combined their skills to carry valuable cargoes safely to and from America's port cities. Although sailors and craftspeople rarely enjoyed the wealth and luxuries of the merchants, their work was vital to the success of the traders. ■

■ *How did sailors and craftspeople support the merchant trade?*

R E V I E W

1. **FOCUS** What effect did trade have on New England life?

2. **CONNECT** Compare and contrast these three ways of life: New England merchants, New England farmers, and Virginia farmers.

3. **ECONOMICS** Why was molasses an important trade item for the New England merchants?

4. **CRITICAL THINKING** Why might the colonists think the Navigation Acts were unfair?

5. **ACTIVITY** Should the wealthy New England merchant, Andrew Belcher, have sold wheat to Europe when people in his native Boston were suffering from wheat shortages? Should the people of Boston have damaged Belcher's ship by trying to run it aground? Hold a debate in class. Some students should defend Belcher and other students should support the angry Bostonians.

The New England Colonies

Choosing the Right Map

Here's Why

A map uses a small space, usually on paper, to show a much larger physical area. A small-scale map gives general information about a big area. A large-scale map gives a larger picture of a small area and can show more details. Suppose you wanted to understand how a place or an event in the American Revolution related to the larger picture of the war. You could examine several maps, each drawn to a different scale. Do you know how to read different scales?

Here's How

All maps are drawn to scale. The scale can change from map to map, but it will not change within the same map. An inch on the scale might stand for 2 miles on one map, 20 miles on another map, and 200 miles on another. A large-scale map on which an inch stands for only 2 miles shows those 2 miles in much greater detail than a small-scale map on which an inch stands for 200 miles.

The picture in the bottom left corner shows the Old State House. It was rebuilt in 1748 after a fire destroyed almost all of the original 1713 building. It stands in Boston today, surrounded by modern buildings and streets.

Look at the maps on page 203. Each tells you something about cities in New England. Each map shows the city of Boston. Compare the map scales.

The map of Boston has the largest scale (approximately 1 inch = 1/2 mile) and gives the greatest detail. You can find the Charles River, street names, and even certain buildings in the historic district. The Old State House is one of these. You would use this kind of map to find your way in a city.

Compare the map of Boston with the map of Massachusetts (1 inch = 50 miles). The box on the map of Massachusetts outlines the area that was shown in detail in the map of Boston. The map also tells you other things. You can find other towns in Massachusetts and see how far away they are. You can also see what states border Massachusetts. You would use this kind of map to help you find cities and towns in a region.

Now look at the map of New England (1 inch = 150 miles). The box outlines the area shown in the map of Massachusetts. The scale of this map is smaller than the scale of the map of Massachusetts. For this reason, you get an even broader view of the area in which Boston is located. It shows Boston and Massachusetts in relation to all of New England and the border of Canada. It also shows important things such as the Hudson River and Lake Ontario. You would use this kind of map to find your way from one state to another.

Each map has things that are not shown in the other two. Maps of different scales can help you understand an area and the events that happened there.

Try It

Which of the three maps on this page would you use to compare the size of Massachusetts with the size of New York? Which map would help you decide if you could live in Worcester and work in Boston? Which map would you use to visit the Old State House while walking around historic Boston? Which map would you use to figure the distance for a bicycle trip from the town of Cambridge to the Paul Revere house? Explain why each map would be best for the purpose you chose it.

Apply It

Look at the maps on page 120 in your book. The larger of the two maps shows the routes of French, Dutch, and English explorers. The smaller map shows the route of the English explorer Sir Francis Drake. Which map includes more of the world? Which map contains more detailed information? Which map concentrates on only part of the world? Which map has the larger scale? Explain how you can tell.

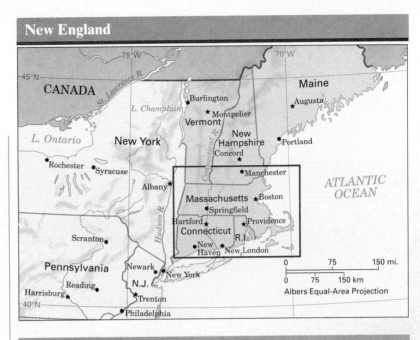

New England

Massachusetts

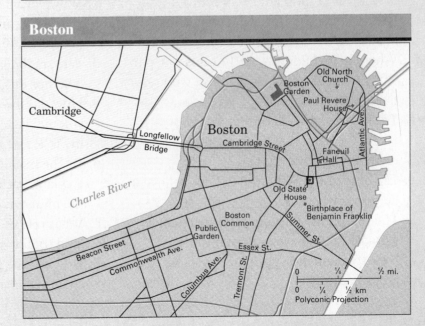

Boston

Chapter Review

Reviewing Key Terms

apprentice (p. 187)
civil disobedience (p. 193)
common (p. 183)
covenant (p. 181)
democracy (p. 191)
dissenter (p. 193)

duty (p. 200)
Great Awakening (p. 195)
meetinghouse (p. 182)
merchant (p. 198)
Parliament (p. 200)
smuggle (p. 200)

A. Write a sentence telling what role each of the following terms played in colonial New England.

1. apprentice
2. civil disobedience
3. common
4. covenant
5. democracy
6. duty
7. Great Awakening
8. meetinghouse
9. merchant
10. smuggle

B. Write a sentence to answer each question. Each sentence you write should include at least one of the key terms.

1. Who learned a craft while practicing it?
2. What did Anne Hutchinson do when Puritan officials ordered her not to preach?
3. How did Parliament discourage colonists from buying sugar in countries outside the British empire?
4. What was the religious revival in New England during the 1700s called?
5. Who passed the Navigation Acts?
6. Who bought and sold goods for profit?
7. Who disagreed with Puritan officials?

Exploring Concepts

A. On your own paper, complete the following statements using information from the chapter.

1. The passengers on the *Arbella* were called Puritans because_____.
2. Each family head was given several hundred acres of farm land in order to_____.
3. Even though they farmed, Puritans still lived together in towns because_____.
4. When their children were 14 years old, parents often sent them away to live with relatives or friends because_____.
5. The reason individual church members could not claim that God might speak directly to them was that_____.
6. Governor John Winthrop did not believe in democracy because_____.
7. The reason the Puritans punished people who did not believe in Puritanism was____.
8. New England didn't produce valuable cash crops because_____.

B. Answer each question with information from the chapter.

1. How did the arrangement of the early Puritan towns allow the Puritans to help one another?
2. Why were there problems between the Puritan settlers and their neighbors, the Algonquin Indians?
3. Why, in the late 1600s, did Puritans wonder whether Puritanism would survive?
4. How did the Puritans make sure that their colonial government would be run according to Puritan beliefs?
5. By the mid-1700s, what changes in New England society led some people to turn to the ministers of the Great Awakening?
6. What role did slaves play in the New England trading system?
7. How did the power of the Puritan merchants change by the middle 1700s?

Reviewing Skills

1. Why is a city easy to show on a large-scale map, such as a road map, but hard to show in a small-scale atlas?

2. Look at the map of Boston on page 178. Suppose you were going to walk from one part of Boston to another. What scale map would you choose? What advantages does that scale have?

3. Make a timeline of these events in the history of the Massachusetts Bay Colony.
   - In 1635, the Puritan government decides to ship the dissenter, Roger Williams, back to England.
   - A Quaker, Mary Dyer, is hanged in 1660 for expressing her religious beliefs.
   - Harvard, the first American college, is founded in 1636 to train Puritan ministers.
   - In 1651, Parliament passes the first of the Navigation Acts.
   - In 1637, Anne Hutchinson is banished from the Puritan colony for preaching her religious beliefs.
   - In 1630, the *Arbella* brings Puritans from England.
   - Roger Williams establishes a community with religious freedom in 1636.

4. If you wanted to tell someone only the most important information in this chapter, what skill would you use?

Using Critical Thinking

1. Today many people find the help of family and friends necessary in reaching difficult goals. For example, parents may help children with their homework if the children are having difficulty in school. How is this kind of help similar to the way the early Puritans tried to help each other?

2. The Puritans punished people who did not share their religious beliefs. Today religious freedom is guaranteed by the First Amendment of the United States Constitution. Why is this protection necessary?

3. Read the entries from *The School of Good Manners* on page 187. Write down what you think each rule means. Then put a check after the rules you think are still important to parents today. Explain why you think each of the checked rules is still important.

Preparing for Citizenship

1. COLLECTING INFORMATION Read a library book about Puritan New England, such as *The Witch of Blackbird Pond* by Elizabeth George Speare. Make notes about the things you find most interesting. Use your notes to tell the class what you learned.

2. GROUP ACTIVITY Show how New England trading systems worked. Get a wall map of the world and make small, cut-out ships that look like the ones used in the 1600s and 1700s. Show where the merchants traded and tell what products they bought and sold.

3. COLLABORATIVE LEARNING Put on skits about different aspects of Puritan life. Form groups of three or four to decide what aspect each group will act out. Plan to have each member play a part in the skit and write his or her own lines. First meet in your group to plan how to work. For example, different members may look up information, write an outline for the skit, and make props, costumes, and scenery. Get back together as a group to share information and write your lines. Present the skit for the class.

Chapter 9

The Middle Colonies

When William Penn, a Quaker, founded Pennsylvania in 1682, he promised settlers they could worship in any way they wished. People from all over Europe—Dutch, Germans, Swedes, and others—flocked to Pennsylvania because of the offer of religious liberty. This mix of people helped Pennsylvania and other Middle Colonies grow and prosper.

During this period William Penn promised to deal fairly with American Indians living in Pennsylvania. This medal shows Penn offering a symbol of peace to an Indian chief.

1650	1675	1700

1681

1688 Several Pennsylvania Quakers declare that they oppose slavery. Many Quakers continue to hold and trade slaves until the eve of the American Revolution. Their statement is one of the first protests against slavery in America.

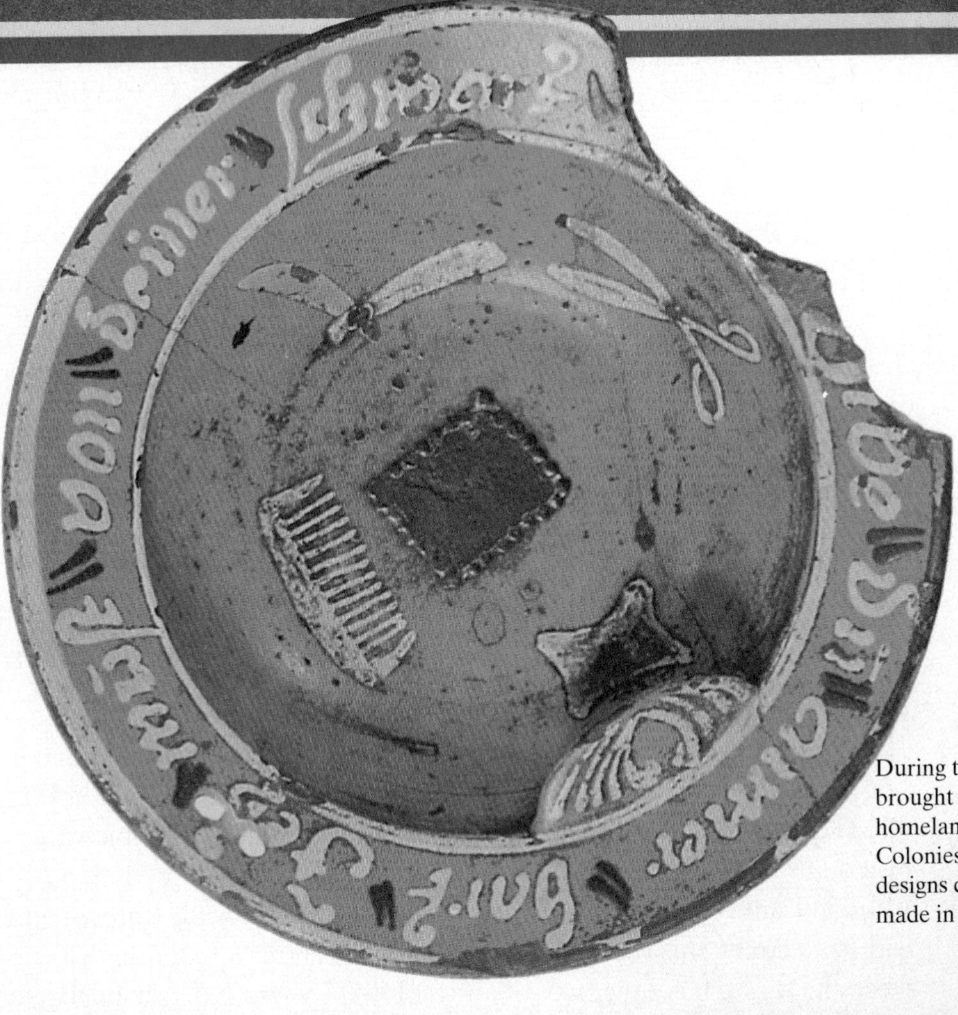

During this time immigrants brought the customs of their homelands to the Middle Colonies. German sayings and designs cover this shaving dish made in Pennsylvania in 1750.

1735 Martin Van Bergen, a Dutch settler in New York, hangs this painting of his farm. It shows the wealth many families enjoyed in the Middle Colonies.

1725

1750

1775

1730 Jewish colonists in New York City build a synagogue.

1759

L E S S O N   1

The Land of the Middle Colonies

THINKING FOCUS

How did the geography of the Middle Colonies affect the lives of the people?

Key Terms

- navigable
- treaty

The Dutch trader walked quietly from the forest, following the smell of squirrel meat roasting over a low fire in a clearing. The Iroquois traders had to be nearby; without a doubt, this was the camp where he was to meet them.

The trader stroked his thick beard. He smiled to himself, remembering the idea most people had of fur traders: wild, dishonest. With his dark beard, dirty fingernails, and torn clothing, he thought he probably looked the part.

After a little while, three Iroquois men appeared from out of the forest on the other side of camp. They were carrying heavy loads of beaver skins. As the men spread the skins before him, the trader checked them, running the back of his hand over the thick, smooth fur. The trader knew the skins were worth a lot of money. Because of heavy fur trading, only a few beavers were left in the colony. The Iroquois probably got these from tribes much farther west. In exchange for six furs, the trader gave the men rum and a few lengths of English wool.

Before it got too dark, the trader left the Indian camp. He traveled by canoe down the Mohawk River to the Hudson River. Then he paddled down the Hudson to a fur trading company in a big cabin in Albany. There he traded the furs for cash.

The Geography of the Middle Colonies

It was the fur trade on the Hudson River that first drew many Europeans to the Middle Colonies in the 1680s. The traders noticed that plants and trees grew well in the rich soil. Soon, other Europeans came not to trade fur, but to settle down and farm. Farming was a prosperous activity in the fertile Hudson and Delaware river valleys. Peter Kalm, a Swedish naturalist and traveler to the area, described the orchards on Middle Colony farms in 1748.

208

*N*ear almost every farm was a spacious orchard full of peaches and apple trees, and in some of them the fruit was fallen from the trees in such quantities as to cover nearly the whole surface. Part of it they left to rot, since they could not take it all in and consume it.

Before they picked the fruit of such orchards, though, colonists had to find and settle their land. When they first arrived in the Middle Colonies, settlers sailed up the Hudson and Delaware rivers to find good farm land. Fortunately, both the Hudson and the Delaware were **navigable**—deep and wide enough for ships to pass. The Hudson was navigable for more than 100 miles upstream. Find the Delaware and Hudson rivers on the map below. Notice that these and other rivers flow through large parts of New York and Pennsylvania. Why would these rivers be important for settlement?

▲ *Rich, fertile soil helps crops grow very well in Pennsylvania.*

▼ *From this map, identify four Middle Colonies.*

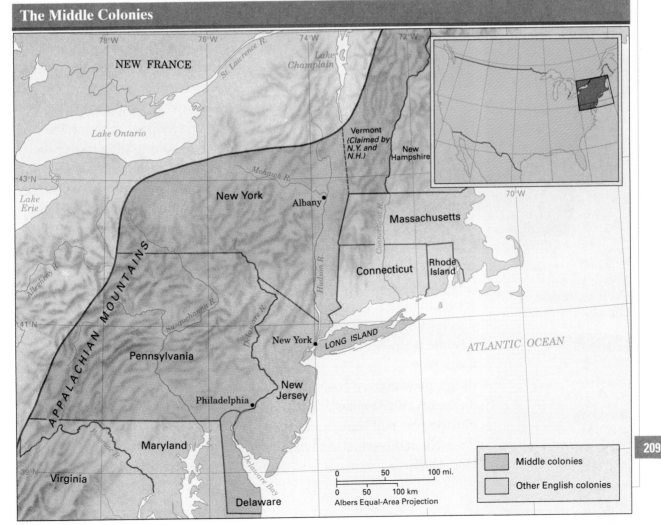

The Middle Colonies

NEW FRANCE

St. Lawrence R.

Lake Champlain

Lake Ontario

Vermont (Claimed by N.Y. and N.H.)

New Hampshire

Mohawk R.

New York

Albany

Massachusetts

Lake Erie

Connecticut R.

Hudson R.

Connecticut

Rhode Island

APPALACHIAN MOUNTAINS

Allegheny R.

Susquehanna R.

Delaware R.

New York

LONG ISLAND

ATLANTIC OCEAN

Pennsylvania

New Jersey

Philadelphia

Maryland

Potomac R.

Delaware Bay

Virginia

Delaware

0   50   100 mi.
0   50   100 km
Albers Equal-Area Projection

Middle colonies

Other English colonies

209

Before settlers could begin to plant, they had to clear huge oaks, cedars, and other trees from the hilly land. Clearing land was slow, hard work because settlers had only axes and other simple hand tools to use. Even so, farmers of the Middle Colonies were lucky compared to farmers in New England. Their soil was much more fertile than rocky New England soil.

The fertile soil and a good climate with warm, rainy summers meant good crops. Besides the apples and peaches that Kalm mentioned, farmers also grew vegetables: squash, pumpkins, beans, onions, cabbage, turnips, and others. They made jams, and pickled fruits and vegetables for their own use. They sold to traders what was left over. The geography of the river valleys favored farming so much that farmers could raise some crops just to sell. The main cash crop in Pennsylvania was wheat. In New York, it was corn.

Farmers used rivers to move their cash crops to markets in Philadelphia and New York City. Peter Kalm described the busy Hudson River.

Farmers grew many types of fruits and vegetables in the Middle Colonies.

■ *Why did geography make the Middle Colonies a good place to settle?*

D*uring eight months of the year this river is full of yachts, and other greater and lesser vessels, either going to New York or returning from thence, laden with either inland or foreign goods.*

Kalm often wrote about the usefulness of the rivers and the richness of the land. Some writers, though, were more moved by its beauty.

W*hoever has made a voyage up the Hudson must remember the Kaatskill Mountains. They are a dis-membered branch of the great Appalachian family, and are seen away to the west of the river, swelling up to a noble height, and lording it over the surrounding country. Every change of season, every change of weather, indeed, every hour of the day produces some change in the magical hues and shapes of these mountains; and they are regarded by all the good wives, far and near, as perfect barometers [a way to predict weather].*

Washington Irving,
"Rip Van Winkle"

This opening scene from the story "Rip Van Winkle" praises the Hudson River Valley. ■

Peaceful Relations with the Indians

Settlers in the Middle Colonies did well because of the fertile land and convenient rivers. However, they also prospered because they lived on good terms with native peoples.

When William Penn arrived in Pennsylvania, he encountered the Delaware, or Lenni Lenape people as they called themselves. The Delaware promised to live "in love" with the settlers: "as long as the creeks and rivers run and while the sun, moon, and stars endure." Peaceful relations with the Delaware did not last as long as "the sun, moon, and stars endure." However, they did last almost 70 years—a longer time than in the South or New England. A pleased Penn later wrote, "I have led the greatest colony into America. . . ."

Indian Relations in Pennsylvania

William Penn strongly supported the Quaker belief that all people should be treated with respect. He wanted to treat the Delaware Indians and other Indians fairly. To make sure the Delaware felt fairly treated, Penn paid them for the land King Charles II gave to him. According to legend, Penn also made a **treaty,** or agreement, of friendship with the Delaware chiefs in 1682. The painting below shows the treaty ceremony near Philadelphia.

▼ *Edward Hicks was a wandering Quaker minister. He painted* Penn's Treaty with the Indians *about 1830.*

In Pennsylvania, both Indians and settlers had to be treated equally and fairly in legal matters. Penn wrote about the treatment of Indians in *Concessions to the Province of Pennsylvania* in 1681:

That no man shall, by any-ways or means, in word, or deed, affront, or wrong any Indian, *but he shall incur the same penalty of the law, as if he had committed it against his fellow planter, and if any* Indian *shall abuse, in word, or deed, any planter of this province, that he shall not be his own judge upon the* Indian, *but he shall make his complaint to the governor of the province. . . . That the* Indians *shall have liberty to do all things relating to improvement of their ground, and providing sustenance [food] for their families, that any of the planters shall enjoy.*

Indian Relations in New York

During the time of peace in Pennsylvania, Indian wars did erupt in New York. However, the powerful Iroquois assured some stability in the colony of New York. Before the Europeans arrived, five different Iroquois nations had joined to form an organized government. The Iroquois had always made a living by hunting, farming, and fishing. After the Dutch arrived, the European demand for animal furs made fur trading a rich business for the Iroquois. They got guns from the Dutch and beat their enemies. Soon the Iroquois controlled the fur trade in a large area: from Maine to Michigan; from the St. Lawrence River in the north to as far south as Virginia.

Settlers and fur traders stood in awe of the Iroquois. For a time, no one dared challenge their control. The Iroquois kept control by playing the English against the French in order to avoid being taken over by either.

For a time, the English in New York were glad to have Iroquois protection from the French on the northern border of the colony. Governor Thomas Dongan praised them in 1687: "Those Five nations are very brave & the awe & Dread of all ye Indyans." Remember, too, the Dutch and English fur traders made money on the furs the Iroquois passed along to them. So they tried to stay on peaceful terms. ■

How Do We Know?

HISTORY *How do we know what William Penn looked like? The famous painting of the treaty ceremony shows him as older and heavier than he actually was at the time. He was 38 years old when he signed the treaty with the Delaware in 1682. We have learned that he was handsome and athletic from descriptions written by people who knew him.*

■ *How did settlers of the Middle Colonies avoid war with the Indians?*

REVIEW

1. **FOCUS** How did the geography of the Middle Colonies affect the lives of the people?
2. **CONNECT** Contrast farming in the Middle Colonies to farming in New England.
3. **HISTORY** Contrast the relations between European-Americans and the native people in New York and Pennsylvania.
4. **CRITICAL THINKING** How would farming life in the Middle Colonies have been different if the colonies had not been located in river valleys?
5. **WRITING ACTIVITY** Imagine that you and your parents have just come to the colony of Pennsylvania from England in order to farm. You decide to keep a diary of your experiences in Pennsylvania. Write the first five entries of your diary. Include descriptions of the people you meet and the places you see.

L E S S O N   2

A Mixture of Many Cultures

The Reverend Andrew Burnaby of Greenwich, England, toured the Middle Colonies in 1759. He noted in his "pocket-book" every "circumstance" that impressed him. The notes in his "pocket-book" or notebook, show that he was not hopeful for peace in the colonies. He thought that the mix of many cultures meant trouble.

They [the Middle Colonies] are composed of people of different nations, different manners, different religions, and different languages. They have a mutual jealousy of each other . . . Religious zeal, too, like a smothered fire, is secretly burning in the[ir] hearts . . .

But not all visitors to the Middle Colonies felt the same way

Why did the Middle Colonies have so many cultural groups?

Key Terms

- diversity
- tolerance

 *German fraktur is beautiful lettering used to record important events, such as weddings or baptisms.*

213

The Middle Colonies

➤ Fancy needlework was popular with the English. The sampler on the right was done with silk thread on linen.

Burnaby did about the **diversity,** or cultural and religious variety there. Peter Kalm, for example, delighted in counting all the places of worship he saw on his journey. In 1748, he noted 12 in Philadelphia alone. Though world travelers did not agree on whether or not diversity was a good thing, all agreed that it was something new.

The mixture of cultures that we enjoy in the United States today got a good start in the Middle Colonies. You can see from the everyday objects on this page that each group brought its own special traditions and skills to the Middle Colonies.

▼ Tulips and birds, like the ones on this coffeepot and plate, were a common decoration on Pennsylvania Dutch furniture and cookware.

Quaker Ideals and the "Holy Experiment"

William Penn called Pennsylvania a "holy experiment" because the colony was based on a religious belief in **tolerance**—a respect for differences. As you know, experiments do not always succeed. No one knew for sure whether or not the many different peoples who settled in the Middle Colonies could live together in peace.

When William Penn set out to plan his colony, he was inspired by the ideals of his Quaker religion. He remembered that English officials had put Quakers in jail in England. William Penn wanted to make sure that people of all religions would be able to worship freely in Pennsylvania.

Quakers truly respected differences. They believed in the spiritual equality of all people. Their strong belief in equality led them to dress and act differently from most people. They wore plain clothes without jewelry. They thought fancy dress showed special privileges. They didn't take off their hats to greet important people. Because of this, people in 17th-century England felt that Quakers had bad manners.

Quakers called everyone by the words "thee" and "thou," instead of using "thee" and "thou" for servants and children, as was the custom. They believed that all people were equal and that no one should receive special treatment. William Penn even called King Charles II "friend Charles" instead of "Your Majesty."

Not everyone who came to settle in Pennsylvania agreed with Quaker beliefs. However, people of many different religions and nationalities believed that they would be treated fairly in the Quaker colony. Pennsylvania would not be a place only for English Quakers but for everyone who wanted to live in peace.

Penn's government gave citizens more power than in any of the other colonies. Most free white males could vote for the Assembly, which made new laws. However, the king of England did have some say in the affairs of the colony. And laws did have to be approved by Penn or his appointed governor.

Although Penn's ideas and policies were very fair, democracy and tolerance in Pennsylvania were not perfect. Women, who often spoke forcefully at Quaker meetings, could not vote for Assembly members. Slavery existed in Pennsylvania. Even William Penn had a few slaves. So everything was not fair or just. However, Penn's holy experiment proved to be a step forward for American democracy. ■

■ *How did the beliefs of the Quakers affect life in Pennsylvania?*

▼ *Many paintings by Edward Hicks illustrate peaceful Quaker farm life.*

THE RESIDENCE OF DAVID TWINING 1787.

Immigration to the Middle Colonies

▶ *Travelers distributed William Penn's pamphlets all over Europe, so that many different kinds of people would know of the opportunities in Pennsylvania.*

William Penn was eager to spread the word about the benefits of his colony and attract more settlers. So he advertised Pennsylvania in several pamphlets such as the one on this page. He described Philadelphia in this way:

> The town is well-furnished with convenient mills; and what with their garden plats (the least half an acre), the fish of the river, and their labour to the countryman who begins to pay with the provisions of his own growth, they live comfortably.

Other settlers also spread the good news about Pennsylvania.

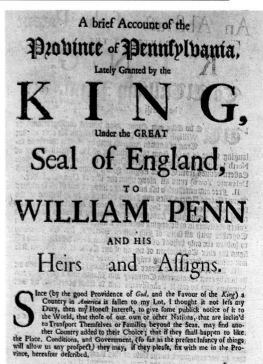

UNDERSTANDING TOLERANCE

In 1750, a German traveler to Pennsylvania wrote, "That colony possesses great liberties above all other English colonies, inasmuch as all religious sects are tolerated there." Indeed, Pennsylvania's tolerance attracted settlers from many different religious and ethnic groups.

Respecting Differences

Tolerance means respecting another's beliefs and practices even though they are different from yours. It doesn't mean agreeing with someone's beliefs or even necessarily understanding them. As Voltaire *(vohl TAIR)*, a famous French philosopher, said, "I disapprove of what you say but I will defend to the death your right to say it."

Benefits of Tolerance

The United States has been called a great melting pot, meaning that our country is a mixture of people from many different backgrounds. The United States is probably much more like a smorgasbord. This is a Swedish feast with many separate, wonderful kinds of food.

Practicing tolerance can keep peace and lead to prosperity. Today, for example, tolerance of different ways of life gives us lively cities filled with many types of music, food, and cultural events. In the colony of Pennsylvania, settlers enjoyed peace with the Indians because Quakers believed in tolerance and went out of their way to be fair to all groups.

Settlers often wrote letters home, urging friends and relatives to come. Here is what one Irish settler wrote to his sister Mary Valentine:

> *Land is of all prices . . . & Grows dearer every year by Reason of Vast Quantities of People that come here yearly from several Parts of the world, therefore thee & thy family or any that I wish well I wod [would] desire to make what Speed you can to come here the Sooner the better. We have traveled over a Pretty deal of this country . . . yet my father being curious & somewhat hard to Please Did not buy any Land until the Second day of 10th mo: Last and then he bought a Tract of Land consisting of five hundred Acres for which he gave 350 pounds. It is excellent good land.*
>
> Robert Parke, letter dated 1725

Letters, pamphlets, and even poems attracted Lutherans, Jews, Baptists, Amish, and other religious groups to Pennsylvania.

They came to be farmers or to work as indentured servants. By 1707, the colony numbered 20,000 settlers.

Immigrants from many nations sailed to the colony of New York, too. When it was still the Dutch colony of New Netherlands, a variety of people besides the Dutch settled the land: French Huguenots (HYOO guh nahts), Walloons from what is now Belgium, Swedes, Portuguese, Finns, English, and Africans. Early English and Dutch visitors to New York often wrote poems and letters home praising the colony. One poem written by Jacob Steendam, called "The Praise of New Netherland," compared New York to the Garden of Eden. Letters encouraged friends and relatives to move to New York. One Englishman wrote, "The Country itself sends forth such a fragrant smell that it may be perceived [noticed] at Sea." ■

Across Time & Space

The state advertising slogan of Pennsylvania is "You've Got a Friend in Pennsylvania." "Friends" is another word for Quakers. The slogan also means that Pennsylvania has always thought of itself as a place that welcomes many kinds of people. Its biggest city, Philadelphia, is known as the City of Brotherly Love.

■ *What caused people to settle in the Middle Colonies?*

◄ *Amish people arrived in Pennsylvania in the 1720s from Switzerland and Germany. Like the children in these modern photographs, they wore plain clothes with no decorations.*

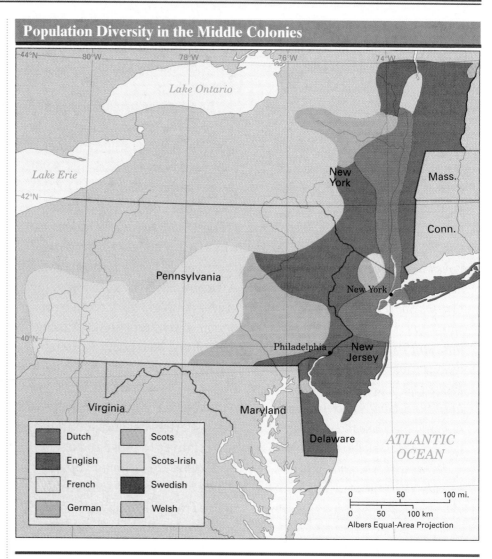

Population Diversity in the Middle Colonies

Legend:
- Dutch
- English
- French
- German
- Scots
- Scots-Irish
- Swedish
- Welsh

➤ *Use the map to locate settlements of eight different ethnic groups.*

Problems Among Different Groups

Although many ethnic groups lived in the Middle Colonies and tried to get along, they didn't always succeed. Also, they often didn't live near or get to know one another. They lived separately, in part, because of the way William Penn sold the land.

When William Penn advertised his land in Europe, he often promised each group a certain section of land where they could settle together and run their own community. For example, Quakers from Wales settled along the Schuylkill (*SKOOL kihl*) River. And one German group settled north of the Schuylkill. Look at the map showing where different groups settled. Identify the locations of various ethnic groups.

Sometimes ethnic groups got angry with each other. For example, German settlers, who became very numerous, tended to stick together and to speak only their own language. The Germans demanded more representatives in the Assembly. The Quakers did not like the growing power of the Germans. Such tensions among European settlers and between settlers and Indians disappointed William Penn.

After Penn died, settlers pushed the Delaware and other tribes farther and farther west. In 1748, Peter Kalm noted in his journal that "it is very possible for a person to have been at Philadelphia . . . for half a year together without so much as seeing an Indian. . . ."

New settlers, especially those on the frontier, did not share Penn's ideals and were eager to get new land. They took over Delaware and Iroquois lands in unfair ways. In 1742, the chief Canassateego *(kuh nas uh TEE go)* spoke against this unfair treatment:

> W*e know our lands are now become more valuable. The white people think we do not know their value; but we are sensible that the land is everlasting, and the few goods we receive for it are soon worn out and gone.*

In addition to being driven west, many Indians died from smallpox and measles—diseases the settlers brought with them. At the time of the first European settlement, there were about 15,000 Indians in Pennsylvania. By 1790, only about 1,300 remained.

In New York, as in Pennsylvania, ethnic problems flared up. The two largest groups, English and Dutch, often argued. When the English gained control, they let the Dutch keep speaking their own language and attending the Dutch Reformed Church. The English practiced tolerance by allowing these freedoms. However, since the two groups lived separately, they sometimes didn't understand each other.

Also, the poor people and the rich often clashed. A few rich Dutch owned most of the land. The English allowed these important landowners to keep their land. They even lowered their taxes. Many Dutch landowners became even richer. As a result, the poor Dutch often hated the rich Dutch as well as the English. ■

▲ *This anti-Quaker cartoon criticizes the Quakers for not considering the Bible holier than other books. The cartoon was an illustration for a poem written against Quakers in 1675.*

■ *Why didn't settlers always get along together in the Middle Colonies?*

REVIEW

1. **FOCUS** Why did the Middle Colonies have so many cultural groups?
2. **CONNECT** Compare and contrast tolerance in the Middle and Southern Colonies and New England.
3. **HISTORY** What conditions in Pennsylvania and New York led to ethnic tensions?
4. **CRITICAL THINKING** Some people believe that ethnic tension in Pennsylvania proved that Penn's experiment had failed. Analyze this opinion and then form your own.
5. **ACTIVITY** Draw a map like the one on page 218, showing the ethnic variety in your town, county, or state.

What's the Big Idea, Ben Franklin?

Jean Fritz

Benjamin Franklin is known for his many contributions to American life and history. This story tells how Franklin developed some of his inventions and ideas. As you read, see if you can describe how Franklin was able to find work he liked. What did his father do to help him get work? Do you think Franklin's life was anything like the lives of people you know?

You have read about life in the Middle Colonies in this chapter. Now read about Ben Franklin, who lived and worked there.

Leather Apron   a person who works with his hands
Latin School   a private school, teaching Latin and Greek
pulpit   a raised platform for a preacher

Benjamin was Mr. Franklin's 10th and last son. He was the youngest son of a youngest son of a youngest son of a youngest son—right back to his great-great grandfather. This made him special, Mr. Franklin thought. Besides, Benjamin was smart. Maybe he shouldn't be just another Leather Apron when he grew up.

No, Mr. Franklin decided, he shouldn't. Benjamin would be a preacher. He'd go to Latin School, then he'd go to college, then he'd climb up into a pulpit and make his father proud. So when he was 7 years old, off he went to Latin School. At the end of the year Benjamin was at the head of his class.

But he was only 8 years old. Mr. Franklin thought of all the years it would take to make Benjamin a preacher. And all the money! Besides, Mr. Franklin had been taking notice of preachers lately, especially young preachers in small churches. They had a hard time. Some went around with holes in their shoes. Now Mr. Franklin wasn't going to wait all those years and spend all that money just to have Benjamin climb up into a pulpit with holes in his shoes.

So he took Benjamin out of Latin School and put him into an ordinary writing and arithmetic school for 2 years. When Benjamin was 10, Mr. Franklin took him out of school altogether. He was old enough now to run errands, to deliver soap, to dip candles. When he was 12 years old, they'd decide what kind of a Leather Apron man he would be. Then he'd become an apprentice and learn the trade.

Benjamin didn't mind becoming a Leather Apron, but he did

dip candles   to make candles
apprentice   a person learning a trade from a skilled craftsman

mind becoming an apprentice. And no wonder. An apprentice had to sign a paper saying he would obey his master until he was 21 years old; he would keep his master's secrets; he would be on duty as his master demanded both day and night. In other words, an apprentice lost 9 good years of freedom to learn a trade that Benjamin thought he could learn in far less time. And if there was one thing that Benjamin liked, it was his freedom.

So when he was 12 years old, Benjamin told his father that he might go to sea.

His father didn't care for that idea. Look what happened to his brother Josiah when he went to sea, Mr. Franklin said. If Benjamin didn't want to be an apprentice, he should stay home and go into the soap and candle business.

But Benjamin didn't care for soap and candles. Besides, look what happened to his brother Ebenezer in the soapsuds.

Of course Benjamin knew his father had a good business. His candles sold well. Even the night watchmen in Boston carried Mr. Franklin's candles on their rounds. And his soap sold well. Barbers said it made the best lather for shaving. Housewives said it was so mild that it could be used on scarlet cloth.

There was, however, one thing wrong with the business. It smelled. The hot stale grease that was used to make candles had a disgusting smell. The boiling lye that was used to make soap had a sharp, nasty smell and it stung a person's nose. Benjamin was determined he was not going to spend his life smelling those smells.

So Mr. Franklin took Benjamin to different shops to show him how hatters made hats, how cutlers made knives, how coopers made barrels. All these trades seemed interesting to Benjamin, but to learn any of them he'd have to become an apprentice. And Benjamin said no.

In the end, after much arguing, Mr. Franklin talked Benjamin into becoming an apprentice to his brother James, a printer. It worked out just as Benjamin thought it would. He learned the printing business quickly. And there he was. Stuck until he was 21. Being an apprentice to his brother was no easier than being an apprentice to anyone else. James thought Benjamin was vain (which was probably true) and argumentative (which was undoubtedly true), and he treated Benjamin as strictly, if not more strictly, than the other apprentices.

Benjamin could not bear to think of all those years going to waste. So he decided to use every spare moment to learn all he could about everything he could. He would read. He would write. He would observe. He would try out new ideas.

As a starter, he tried writing a poem. It was a long poem about the capture of Blackbeard the Pirate. He showed it to his father. Mr. Franklin thought it was a terrible poem. "Forget poetry," his

Josiah ran away from home and drowned at sea

Ebenezer drowned in a tub of his father's soapsuds, when he was 16 months old

scarlet bright reddish-orange color

lye a liquid made from wood ashes, important to making soap

vain excessively proud
argumentative full of arguments

prose writing that is
not poetry

father said. "Stick to prose."

To improve his prose style, Benjamin would read an essay, turn it into poetry, wait a few weeks, then turn the poetry back into his own prose. He found this increased his vocabulary. Later he would write letters to James' newspaper, signing them Silence Dogood so James wouldn't know he had written them.

vegetarianism a diet
of vegetables and
grains

Benjamin read a book on vegetarianism and decided to quit eating meat. He asked James to give him in cash half of what he had formerly paid for his meals. James agreed. Now Benjamin could not only eat by himself and read while he was eating, he could save some of his eating money and buy books. Many times a meal was only a biscuit, a handful of raisins, and a glass of water.

Once, Benjamin read a book about swimming that described unusual tricks and strokes. Benjamin was already an expert swimmer, but now he became even more expert.

strokes movements

He learned to swim on his belly while holding both hands still, to carry his left leg in his right hand, to show both his feet out of the water, to swim with his legs tied together, to sit in the water, to cut his toenails in the water, to show 4 parts of his body out of the water at the same time, to swim while holding up one leg, to put on his boots in the water, and to leap like a goat.

In order to swim faster he tried out an idea of his own. He made wooden paddles for his hands and feet. He went faster, but the paddles were so heavy that he didn't get far.

Then he tried lying on his back, holding a kite string, and letting the kite act as a sail and pull him across the pond. This was a great success. There was only one trouble. In those days boys went swimming naked. And if Benjamin didn't want to go home naked, he had to get a friend to carry his clothes to the other side of the pond. (It had to be a good friend because the pond was a mile wide.)

Benjamin studied arithmetic, which he had failed in his last year at school. He enjoyed it so much that in later years he made a hobby of constructing what he called magic squares. Each row of 8 numbers when added up and down or across equals 260. Each of the 4 bent rows also adds up to 260. The 4 corner numbers plus the 4 middle numbers add up to 260.

contradict disagree
opponent a person
who disagrees with you

Benjamin also read a book on how to argue. The author said that a person should not flatly contradict another person. Instead he should be polite and ask questions until at last he had brought his opponent around to contradicting himself. Benjamin tried this and found that it worked.

eels long, snakelike
fish

He read a book by an Englishman with all kinds of advice. It told, among other things, how to catch eels, how to cure deafness, and how to keep horses from having nightmares.

Benjamin loved books that told you how to do things. He

liked to figure out how a person could make work easier, life more comfortable, and at the same time get ahead in the world. He even read a book on how to be good and decided that being good was probably a practical idea.

Later he would make up a list of rules for good behavior: (1) Don't eat or drink too much, (2) Don't joke or talk too much, (3) Keep your things neat, (4) Do what you set out to do, (5) Don't spend too much money, (6) Don't waste time, (7) Be sincere, (8) Be fair, (9) Don't go to extremes, (10) Keep clean, (11) Keep calm, (12) Don't fool around with girls, (13) Don't show off. He kept a notebook in his pocket so he could mark down how he was doing. He didn't expect to be perfect. Each week he concentrated on one rule.

But Benjamin liked a good time and he seldom let his rules interfere. Once he spent 6 pennies to see the first lion ever brought to America. This was a lot of money, he said, but it was worth it.

interfere to stand in the way

Still, no matter what he was doing, Benjamin was always an apprentice. He couldn't forget it and he couldn't learn to like it. When he was 17, he could stand it no longer. He ran away. He boarded a boat and on one Sunday morning in October, 1723, he landed in Philadelphia, Pennsylvania.

He was free! He found a job with a printer and began earning his own money. When he had saved enough, he bought a new suit of clothes and a watch with a long gold watch chain. When he had saved some more, he went to Boston to visit his family. He dropped in at the printshop to see James. He didn't come to apologize for running away; he came, in spite of his rules, to show off. He swaggered into the shop, letting James and his apprentices see what a grand thing it was to be your own master in a new suit of clothes. He twirled his watchchain. He jingled the money in his pockets and offered to treat everyone to a drink. (James was so angry that it took years for the brothers to make up.)

swaggered walked around showing off

Further Reading

Ben and Me. Robert Lawson. Amos, a mouse who lives in Franklin's old fur cap, tells the story of Franklin's life. Amos takes credit for most of Franklin's accomplishments.

Penn. Elizabeth Gray Vining. The continuing quarrel between William Penn and his father is the basis for this story, set in the mid-1600s. It is about some of the younger Penn's ideas after he became a Quaker.

Poor Richard's Almanac. Benjamin Franklin. This is a collection of Franklin's wise sayings.

L E S S O N   3

Farming and Trade

How were farming and trade related to each other in the Middle Colonies?

Key Terms

- patroon system
- tenant farmer
- landlord

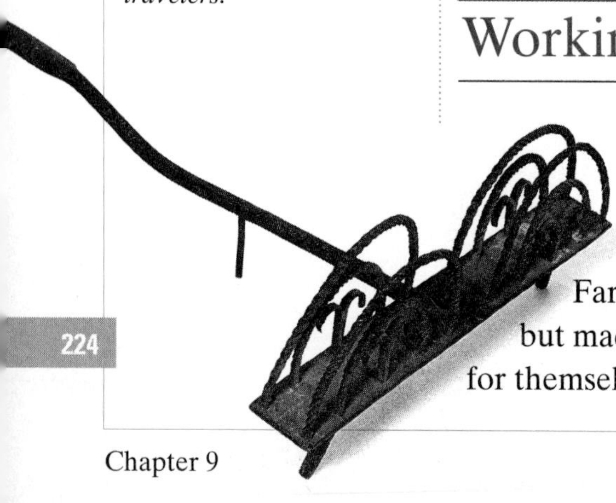

▼ *Innkeepers used wrought iron toasters and other cooking utensils to prepare breakfasts for travelers.*

A ll of a sudden the inn seemed to come alive. There was the sound of heavy boots in the hall. Horses snorted and whinnied in the courtyard. Voices called back and forth. There were the deep, throaty voices of the Germans. There were the burring voices of the Scotch-Irish. But Papa's stately voice boomed above them all as he gave out duties:

"Samuel, this be the day to sow the marshland with grass seed.

"John, thee will brand the new bullocks today.

"Thee, Thomas, will yoke the hogs so they will not stray.

"Joseph, thee and Benjamin can pry up stones to build a fence along the upland pasture."

But Benjamin was not listening. He was sniffing the air as noisily as Papa's hound dogs. The most tantalizing smells were seeping in under the door—ham and scrapple and eggs frying, pippin apples and cinnamon buns baking, and the steaming fragrance of herb tea.

Marguerite Henry and Wesley Dennis, from *Benjamin West and His Cat Grimalkin*

Benjamin in this story was a real person: Benjamin West. He grew up to paint pictures of Pennsylvania's history and is called the father of American painting. As a young boy, though, he worked long hours in his family's inn and on their farm.

Working on Family Farms

Every family member on Middle Colony farms in the 1700s was expected to work. Farmers not only farmed but made many different items for themselves and to sell. Women and girls, for example, churned butter and stamped it with designs from molds that the men or boys had made. Farmers often made their own furniture and tools. To earn extra income,

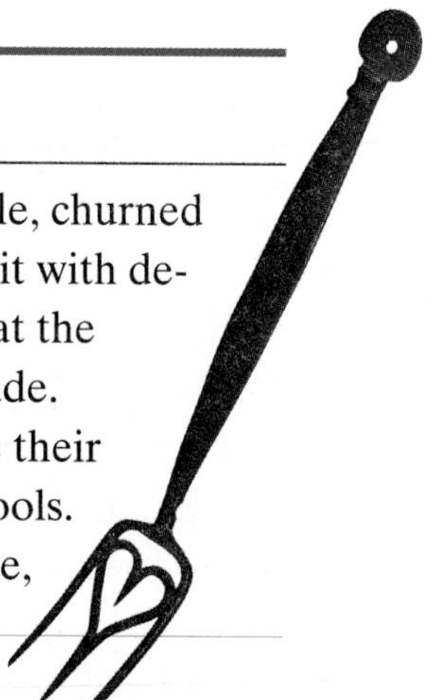

This early drawing shows farm women straining and separating milk. They were preparing to make butter and cheese.

some farm families looked for an additional trade. For example, Benjamin West's family both farmed and operated the busy Door-Latch Inn near Springfield, Pennsylvania.

Farms were usually about 200 acres, and work was heavy, as you can see in A Closer Look at Harvest Time on page 226. Farmers often had to hire or buy servants to help them. A traveler through Pennsylvania in the 1750s was a German named Gottlieb Mittelberger. He described how some terribly poor German immigrants arriving on a ship sold their children as servants to pay for their passage from Europe. "Many parents must sell and trade away their children like so many head of cattle."

Farmers needed so much help because they grew crops for people in many parts of the world. Look at the map on page 226 and notice the many places the crops went. Why might people in the West Indies and Europe need food from the Middle Colonies? ■

Men made butter stamps like this one. The beautiful designs they carved were stamped on blocks of butter. Stamped butter brought a higher price at market than did plain butter.

■ Why were Middle Colony farmers able to grow enough food for themselves and people far away?

Farming and the Standard of Living

The hard work of Middle Colony farmers often paid off. They lived well, compared to small farmers in Britain. Robert Parke, an Irish Quaker in Delaware County, Pennsylvania, wrote a letter to his sister in Ireland. Describing the good life in Pennsylvania of 1725, he wrote, "[N]ot one of the family, but what likes this country very well & wod [would] If we were in Ireland again come here . . ." He

225

The Middle Colonies

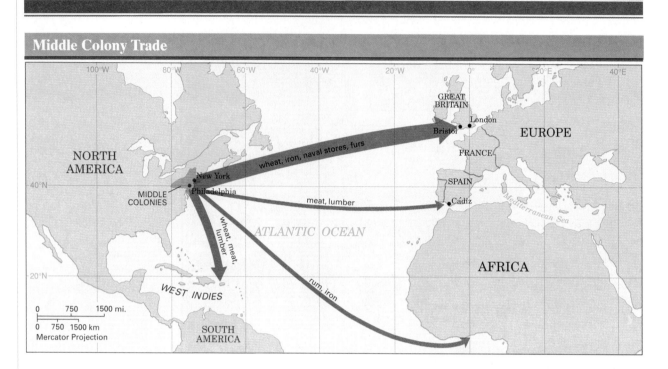

Use this map to find out where farmers in the Middle Colonies sent their products.

went on to explain that wages for working men were not high, but fair. Not many people became rich in Pennsylvania. The cash crops of the

Middle Colonies did not bring in as much wealth as tobacco in the South, for example. But the economy of the Middle Colonies was

A CLOSER LOOK

Harvest Time

It's a hot Pennsylvania July, time to harvest the rye crop. The whole family pitches in. Whatever the family doesn't use will be sold in the nearest city or even across the ocean.

The scythe's three-foot blade and long handle let you cut grain close to the ground without having to bend over.

Harvest looks easy, doesn't it?
This needlepoint scene shows a harvest in process. In real life, it took many more people to get the crop in, and harvesting was hard, sweaty work.

varied, and so many people, not just a few, enjoyed a good living. Pennsylvania became called "the best poor man's country" in the world.

Farmers in New York enjoyed this good living, even though many of them rented their farms rather than owning them. The **patroon system**—in which a few rich people owned large pieces of land—was left over from the time the Dutch colonized New York. The patroon, or owner of the land, employed **tenant farmers**—farmers who used some of the owner's land and paid him with part of their crop or with cash.

The owner they rented from—the **landlord**—gave his renters a house, tools, seeds, and supplies for free. He would also pay them if they improved the land by building a fence, adding to a house, or digging a well. For some poor farmers, renting land was a good way to start life in the Middle Colonies. ■

■ *Contrast farming in New York to farming in Pennsylvania.*

Growth of Urban Centers

As farms in the Middle Colonies were successful, farmers needed more and more help from tradesmen. For example, many farmers did not grind their own wheat. They brought the wheat to mills to be ground. The farmers, then, took the flour to market to

Grab a pitchfork and help load the cut rye onto the wagon. Even though girls and women use pitchforks to help with the harvest, they also have to do their regular dairy work. Women spend the money they earn selling milk and cheese to buy things to make their other chores easier, pins, needles, and cooking pots.

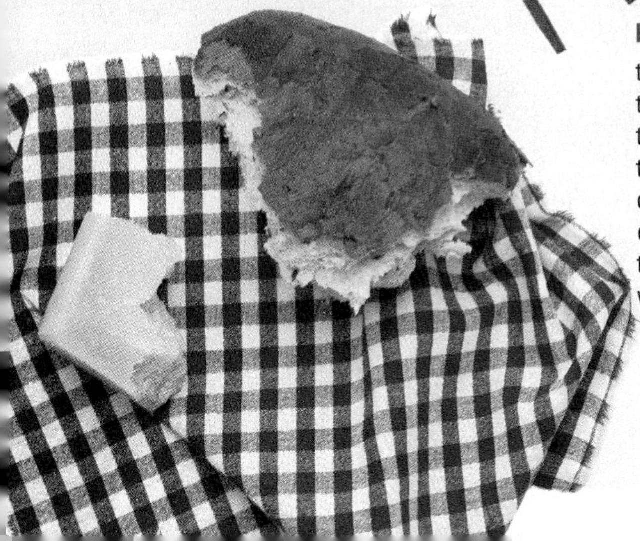

It's lunchtime! Rye bread, of course, with a hunk of homemade cheese makes a good midday meal for the harvesters. The youngest children bring lunch to the fields.

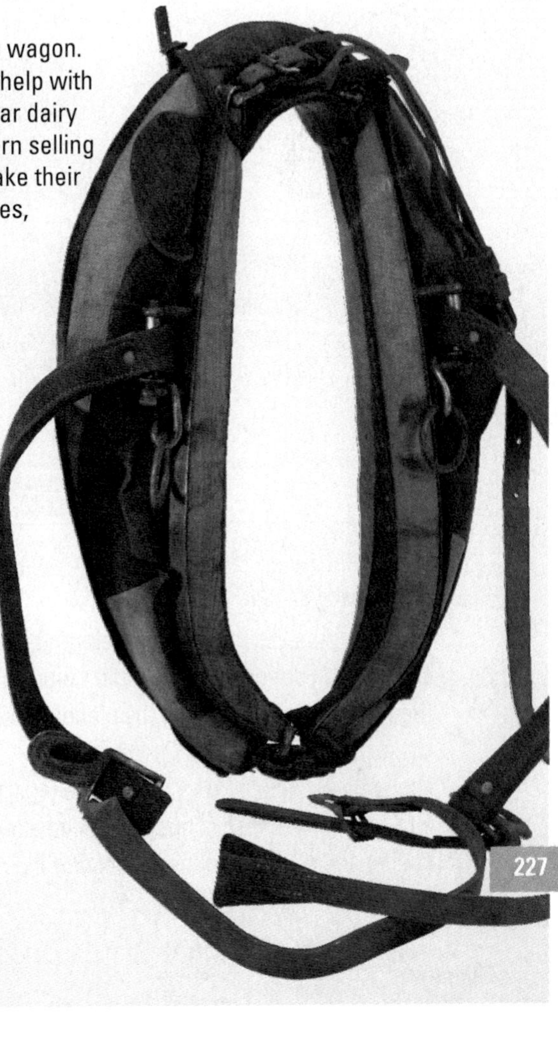

How do you get the horsepower out of the horse? The last task of the harvest is to throw the bundles of rye onto a wagon. A collar like this enables the horse to pull the wagon.

sell. Farmers traveled by boat and on land to markets in Philadelphia and New York. Since the journey was long, they might need to stop overnight at an inn, such as the Door-Latch Inn near Springfield. Keeping an inn, then, became a good business for some people, as it did for Benjamin West's mother and father.

Once the farmers got to Philadelphia or New York, they sold their goods in a town market. Then tradesmen would prepare the goods for shipping. For example, in New York, bakers took some of the farmers' flour and baked biscuits and breads to be sent overseas. Near shipyards, coopers made barrels for packing flour and salted meat. Lumberjacks cut huge oak and cedar trees for shipbuilding—an active industry in both New York and Philadelphia.

Because farmers depended on markets and shipping, the port cities of Philadelphia and New York were busy. By the middle of the 1700s, these cities were cultural as well as trade centers. Publishers printed books and newspapers. Artists painted, sculpted, and made jewelry and decorative furniture. Educated people, such as Benjamin Franklin, made scientific experiments and discussed new political ideas. In such a creative setting, thoughts about the American Revolution began to take shape. ■

▼ *This drawing,* An East Prospect of Philadelphia *(1754) by George Heap, shows the largest of all colonial cities: Philadelphia. It became a center for trade and cultural activity.*

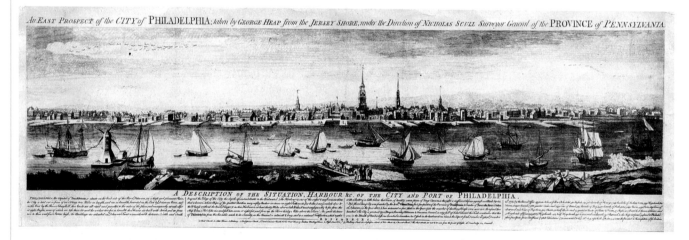

REVIEW

1. **FOCUS** How were farming and trade related to each other in the Middle Colonies?

2. **CONNECT** Analyze the reasons behind the following statement: Farmers in the Middle Colonies were neither rich nor poor. Contrast the standard of living of these farmers with those in the South.

3. **ECONOMICS** Explain how many of the jobs in the cities, such as baker, cooper, shipbuilder, and innkeeper, were related either directly or indirectly to farm life.

4. **CRITICAL THINKING** The Middle Colonies have been called the "breadbasket" of the British colonies. Why is a breadbasket a good image for the Middle Colonies?

5. **WRITING ACTIVITY** Many products were made on Middle Colony farms: candles, soap, cloth, quilts, molds, tools, furniture, and others. Choose one and research how it was made. Write a brief report to present to the class.

Comparing Information

Here's Why

A table can provide a quick overview of information. It can help you see similarities and differences in information easily. A table can also help you remember information. For example, a table may help you understand and remember what you have learned about the American colonies.

Here's How

Look at the table below. Pay special attention to the headings. The choice of headings in a table is very important in organizing the information.

Notice that the headings on the left have something in common. They tell you which group of colonies the information in each row describes. The colors also help you as you read across the rows.

Now look at the headings at the top of the table. Each heading tells what kind of information about the colonies is provided in the column directly below it.

Look at the heading at the top of the left column. It tells you that in this column you will find information about who came to the colonies. Now read the heading for the second column. Suppose you wanted to know where New England colonists came from. To find the answer, see where the second column meets the "New England Colonies" row.

A table helps you find information quickly. For example, suppose you wanted to find out where colonists lived who earned a living by fishing. Quickly read down the third column until you come to the word *fishing*. Since *fishing* is in the New England

row, you know that New England is the answer.

Try It

Copy the table onto your own paper. Then add a row to the bottom of the table with the heading "Middle Colonies." Skim through the chapter to find the information needed for the Middle Colonies. Add the information to your table. Write short entries. Be sure that the entry in each box fits both the column heading and the row heading. What did you learn about the Middle Colonies?

Apply It

Make a table that shows how you spend your spare time. Choose a title. Use the days of the week as your column headings. Times of day—such as morning, afternoon, and evening—could be row headings.

The Early Colonies, 1600–1750				
	Who came?	Where did they come from?	How did they earn a living?	Who did the work?
Southern Colonies	Men and boys Indentured servants Slaves	England Africa	Tobacco farming Rice farming	Slaves Indentured servants
New England Colonies	Families	England	Trading (general) Shipbuilding Fishing	Adults and children

Chapter Review

Reviewing Key Terms

diversity (p. 214)
landlord (p. 227)
navigable (p. 209)
patroon system (p. 227)

tenant farmer (p. 227)
tolerance (p. 214)
treaty (p. 211)

Some of the following statements are true. The rest are false. On your own paper, write *True* or *False* for each statement. Then rewrite the false statements to make them true.

1. A section of a river with waterfalls and rapids is quite likely to be navigable.
2. According to legend, William Penn made a treaty with the Delaware that led to 70 years of peace.
3. One thing the Middle Colonies lacked was cultural diversity, because the settlers spoke so many different languages.
4. William Penn based his colony on tolerance because he looked down upon people with different ways of life.
5. The patroon system helped new immigrants by enabling them to rent farmland they couldn't afford to buy.
6. Tenant farmers collected rent from landlords, who actually did the farming.
7. The Quaker ideal of tolerance helped bring diversity to the Middle Colonies.
8. Navigable rivers helped make Philadelphia and New York City major trade centers.

Exploring Concepts

A. Copy and complete the following outline using information from the chapter.

The Middle Colonies
  I. The Land of the Middle Colonies
    A. Geography of the Middle Colonies
      1. _____
      2. _____
    B. Peaceful relations with the Indians
 II. Mixture of Many Cultures
    A. Quaker ideals and the "Holy Experiment"
    B. Immigration to the Middle Colonies
    C. Problems among different groups
      1. _____
      2. _____
III. Farming and Trade
    A. _____
    B. _____
    C. _____

B. Answer each question with information from the chapter.

1. What characteristics of the geography of the Middle Colonies made it possible for many colonists to make a good living?
2. Why was tolerance an important ideal for the Middle Colonies?
3. How were the Quakers' ideals reflected in their relationships with native peoples?
4. How did Penn's "Holy Experiment" help bring prosperity to Pennsylvania?
5. Why did tensions arise among ethnic groups in the Middle Colonies?
6. How did prosperity in the Middle Colonies differ from that of the South?
7. What was the relationship between trade and farming in the Middle Colonies?
8. In what ways did farmers and city workers in the Middle Colonies depend on each other?

Reviewing Skills

1. Copy the table shown on this page onto your own sheet of paper. Complete the table using information from the chapter. Then use the table to answer the following questions.
   a. In what ways was the land of these two Middle Colonies the same?
   b. How did New York and Pennsylvania differ in their ways of farming?
   c. What major industry was important to both New York and Pennsylvania?
   d. What major exports did New York and Pennsylvania have in common?
2. Suppose you wanted to make a line graph to show the dramatic population growth in the American colonies between 1650 and 1760. Your data are as follows. The population was 50,000 in 1650. In 1700, the population had grown to 250,000. By 1760, 1,600,000 people lived in the colonies.

Make a graph using this information. How would you describe the shape of this graph?

3. Suppose you knew that the Hudson River was navigable for at least 100 miles upstream from New York City. Find a map of New York State. What part of the map will help you locate a city on the river that could ship farm products directly to New York City?

Two Middle Colonies		
	New York	**Pennsylvania**
Major city		
Major river		
Farm size and ownership		
Major crop		
Major industries		

Using Critical Thinking

1. In New York City and Philadelphia today, there are dozens of different ethnic groups speaking many different languages. Write a paragraph explaining how such ethnic diversity had its beginnings in the Middle Colonies.

2. Based on what you know and on information in the chapter, what seems to cause conflict among ethnic groups? Write a paragraph defining the problem. In a second paragraph, suggest two or three ways to reduce such conflicts.

Preparing for Citizenship

1. COLLECTING INFORMATION Find out in detail how one craft or trade would have been practiced in the Middle Colonies. Examples of crafts and trades in the chapter are milling (making flour), baking, keeping an inn, and managing a farm. Use an encyclopedia or contact a historical society to find the information. Write a descriptive report.

2. COLLABORATIVE LEARNING Make a class mural that pictures the economic life of the Middle Colonies. Divide the mural into four sections: farming, crafts, cities, and trade. Divide into four groups. Each group will be responsible for a different section of the mural. Make the mural go from west on the left to east on the right. To the left in the mural, there would be farms. To the right would be a city such as New York or Philadelphia. When the mural has been completed, list similarities and differences between the economic life of the area in colonial times and today.

231

Unit 4

The Struggle for Independence

To many people in the 1770s America was "a world turned upside down." Colonists who had once been loyal British subjects began to talk about independence. British soldiers who once had protected the colonists now threatened— even killed —some of them. While these events amazed people in America and Britain, the changes had just begun.

1720

Amos Doolittle, *A View of the Town of Concord, 1775,*
Engraving, Library of Congress.

1828

Chapter 10

Crisis with Britain

In 1754, Benjamin Franklin bragged that the "people in the colonies are as loyal . . . as any subjects" of the British Empire. Only 21 years later, Patrick Henry said he was ready to die for American independence. In those 21 years many things happened that changed American minds: taxes, riots, shootings. By 1775, the once-loyal colonists knew they wanted to rule themselves and would die to do so.

During this time, Americans became outraged by British laws. Someone even made a teapot protesting the law known as the Stamp Act in 1765 (above).

| 1710 | 1720 | 1730 | 1740 |

1720

1722–1775 Writer, printer, and inventor, Benjamin Franklin (above) is one of the best-known people in America. During this time, Franklin begins to call for the colonies to unite.

1754–1763 France and Britain fight over lands in North America in the Seven Years' War. Many colonists gain military experience in this war.

1775 In a fiery speech calling for American independence, Patrick Henry cries, "Give me liberty or give me death." Henry first won fame as a brilliant speaker in a 1763 court case, shown above.

1772 Phillis Wheatley, the first important poet of African descent in North America, writes a poem comparing America's desire for freedom to her own.

1750

1760

1770

1780

1775

L E S S O N   1

Ties to Great Britain

THINKING
F O C U S

*Why were the colonists
more loyal to Great
Britain than they were to
each other in the 1750s?*

Key Terms

- salutary neglect
- assembly
- veto

Benjamin Franklin and other Philadelphia leaders worked quickly. They were preparing to defend their city from attack in early 1764. The danger did not come from the French or any Indian tribes. Rather, the danger to the British colonists in Philadelphia came from another group of British subjects: the Paxton Boys.

The Paxton Boys were a group of 57 frontier settlers from western Pennsylvania. They were angry because Indians were attacking their farms time after time. The Indians hoped to end English settlement on their lands.

By the time the Paxton Boys marched on Philadelphia, they were 600 strong. Armed and angry, they wanted to force the colonial government to send soldiers to stop the Indian attacks.

Philadelphians had reason to be afraid of this mob. In December 1763, the Paxton Boys had raided a village of peaceful Indians at Conestoga, killing six of them. About two weeks later, they broke into the workhouse at Lancaster and killed 14 more Indian men, women, and children from Conestoga who had gone there for protection. People wondered if the Paxton Boys would attack Philadelphians next.

► *This 1764 engraving
by Henry Dawkins shows
Philadelphians lining up
in battle formation and
preparing their cannons
to face the approaching
Paxton Boys.*

236

In February 1764, the Paxton Boys reached the edge of the city. Franklin and other government officials met with their leaders. Two long days of meetings finally produced a settlement. The colonial government agreed to pay for 1,000 troops to help defend the western settlements. The crisis ended. The Paxton Boys went home, and the people of the city of Philadelphia felt safe again.

However, tensions remained. Why were British colonists, all of whom were loyal to the empire, so divided from each other?

Divisions Among the Colonists

In the 1750s, no "Americans" lived in the British colonies. People called themselves "Virginians," "New Yorkers," or some other name based on the colony they lived in. They did not think of themselves as "Americans" because they did not feel any special ties with other colonies.

However, colonists did feel strongly about troops and taxes. As in Pennsylvania, western settlers in several colonies feared attacks. They wanted the government to send troops to protect them. Many people in cities, though, did not agree. They felt that settlers should take care of their own problems. Conflicts between farmers and people in cities caused violent battles in Massachusetts, Virginia, North Carolina, and South Carolina.

Differences in language also separated colonists. Some English-speaking colonists were angry at the Germans, Dutch, French, and Swedish. Instead of speaking English, many of these colonists spoke their own language. For example, Benjamin Franklin's family came from England. He wondered why settlers from Germany should be allowed "to swarm into our settlements, and . . . establish their language and manners to the exclusion of ours." According to the map below, which colonies had large German settlements?

This map shows where the largest groups of Europeans were living in the colonies by 1750. The lines of latitude and longitude on the map can be used to identify the location of each group's settlements. To learn more about latitude and longitude, see page G9 in the Map and Globe Handbook.

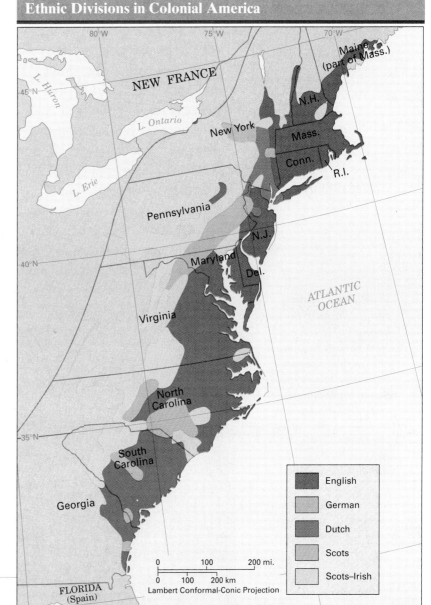

Ethnic Divisions in Colonial America

Legend:
- English
- German
- Dutch
- Scots
- Scots–Irish

NEW FRANCE

Maine (part of Mass.)

N.H.
Mass.
Conn.
R.I.
New York
Pennsylvania
N.J.
Maryland
Del.
Virginia
North Carolina
South Carolina
Georgia
FLORIDA (Spain)

ATLANTIC OCEAN

L. Huron
L. Ontario
L. Erie

0   100   200 mi.
0 100 200 km
Lambert Conformal-Conic Projection

Colonists were also divided by religion. Many Europeans fled to the colonies to escape religious conflicts. However, they brought many of these conflicts with them to America.

Visitors noted differences among the colonists. Writing of his travels through the colonies in the 1760s, Andrew Burnaby of England said, "In short, such is the difference of character, of manners, of religion, of interest, of the different colonies, that I think . . . were they left to themselves, there would soon be a civil war, from one end of the continent to the other." ■

■ *Why were the colonists divided from each other?*

Benefits and Costs of Empire

The colonists were divided from one another. However, they were united in another way. Every colony supported Britain. In a letter to a British official in 1754, Franklin wrote:

T*he people in the colonies are as loyal, and as firmly attached to the present constitution, and reigning family, as any subjects in the king's dominions [empire].*

The Benefits of Empire

The need the Paxton boys felt for protection helps explain why the colonists were so loyal to Great Britain. The British army and navy were among the most powerful in the world. The army protected the colonists from the Indians and from French troops in the Ohio Valley. The navy protected colonial ships at sea.

Colonists also liked to trade with Britain. For example, British merchants bought large amounts of tobacco, fish, and grain from their American colonies. Colonists made money selling these goods to Britain.

Many colonists had another reason to be loyal. Almost half of the colonists were from England or were descended from English settlers. Most still had family living in England.

➤ *Richard Byron painted the busy Boston harbor in 1764. By then New York and Philadelphia were starting to challenge Boston's position as the leading colonial port for trade with Britain.*

For the colonists, then, being part of the empire brought great benefits but cost little. Before 1763, Great Britain followed a policy that historians now call **salutary neglect.** The British government neglected, or paid little attention to, its North American colonies. The colonies, after all, were only a small part of a large empire.

This lack of attention was salutary, or helpful, for the American colonies. The British government did not even tax the colonists to raise money to support the British government. Colonists had to pay only local taxes. They only had to pay for the government in their own colony.

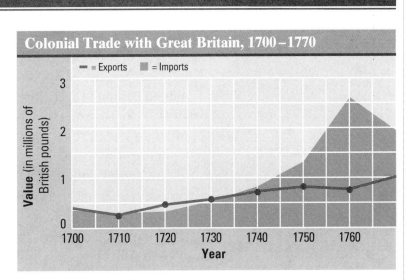

Colonial Trade with Great Britain, 1700–1770

= Exports ■ = Imports

Value (in millions of British pounds)

Year

The Costs of Empire

Even though Britain did not govern the colonies tightly, some colonists did not like British rule. Some merchants were against laws known as the Navigation Acts.

▲ *How do the changes in colonial trade with Great Britain between 1700 and 1750 help explain why colonists were loyal to Great Britain? What happened after 1750?*

◄ *The British influenced colonial life in many ways. The painting, by John Singleton Copley, portrays colonists Mary and Elizabeth Royall wearing British-style dress. The image of George II, Britain's king from 1727 to 1760, was stamped on colonial coins.*

Crisis with Britain

The family crest of the British kings in the 1700s was added to the Virginia governor's house in 1753. The crest has been rebuilt since then.

State governments today are similar to the colonial governments of the 1700s. Most states have a governor who can veto laws passed by the assembly. Today, however, governors are elected rather than appointed.

■ *How did colonists benefit from British rule?*

These acts said that tobacco, sugar, and certain other colonial goods could be shipped only to Britain or its colonies. Colonists could not sell these items to another country.

Other acts said that colonists could only buy from other countries under certain conditions. Products, except for fresh fruit and wine, were first sent to England and then shipped to the colonies. Under the acts, colonists were not permitted to trade with Asia.

Parliament also tried to control the colonists through duties. These are taxes on goods bought from other countries. The Molasses Act of 1733 made colonists pay six pence on each gallon of molasses bought from French or Dutch colonies in the West Indies. But the British did not make colonists obey the law. Merchants smuggled in molasses to avoid paying the duty.

Some colonists were also upset about British power over colonial governments. In each colony, the citizens elected an **assembly,** a group of citizens who made laws and set taxes. But, in most colonies, the king chose a governor. The governor could **veto,** or reject, colonial laws. And if the governor vetoed an act the assembly passed, it did not become a law.

Some governors did not rule their colonies wisely. In Franklin's letter to a British official, he explained how the people of the colonies viewed the governors:

They will say . . . that governors often come to the colonies merely to make fortunes, with which they intend to return to Britain; are not always men of the best abilities and integrity [honesty]; have no estates [land] here, nor any natural connections with us, that should make them heartily concerned for our welfare.

Franklin may have been right. Many governors did not rule their colonies well. But many barely ruled their colonies at all. Many colonists felt little British control over their lives. So, few disliked British rule in the 1750s. But Britain would soon have to change its policy of salutary neglect. Colonists would then think again about their ties to Britain—and to each other. ■

REVIEW

1. **FOCUS** Why were the colonists more loyal to Great Britain than they were to each other in the 1750s?

2. **CONNECT** Which colonies probably had the smallest percentage of people with relatives in England?

3. **HISTORY** How did the colonies benefit from the military strength of the British Empire?

4. **POLITICAL SYSTEMS** Explain the British policy of salutary neglect.

5. **CRITICAL THINKING** Consider how salutary neglect affected the colonists. Predict what would happen to the number of colonists who opposed British rule if Britain ended salutary neglect.

6. **WRITING ACTIVITY** Imagine you are a farmer in Pennsylvania during the 1750s. Write a letter to your cousin in Ireland explaining why you are glad your colony is part of the British Empire.

LESSON 2

The Seven Years' War

> **W**e got behind trees, logs and stumps, and covered ourselves as we could from the enemy's fire. The ground was strewed [covered] with the dead and dying. It happened that I got behind a white-oak stump, which was so small that I had to lay on my side, and stretch myself; the balls striking the ground within a hand's breadth of me every moment, and I could hear the men screaming, and see them dying all around me.
>
> David Perry, *Recollections of an Old Soldier*, 1822

David Perry was 78 years old when he remembered the deadly battle he fought in at age 17. The battle took place near Ticonderoga, New York, in 1758. It was just one conflict in a long fight

THINKING FOCUS

What were the main results of the Seven Years' War?

Key Terms

- import
- politics

◄ *This painting of the battle at Ticonderoga shows members of the Black Watch, a unit of British soldiers from Scotland. Over half of the members of the Black Watch were killed or wounded in the fighting.*

241

Crisis with Britain

between Great Britain and France for the control of most of North America. As a British colonist, Perry fought alongside soldiers in the British army.

The French won the battle at Ticonderoga. Almost 500 British and colonial soldiers died in the fighting. Those who died most likely thought they were protecting the British Empire in North America. They did not know that the war would help bring an end to the empire. As they defended the empire, Perry and the other soldiers also helped destroy it.

Rivalry Between Britain and France

The Battle of Ticonderoga was one battle in a series of four wars between Britain and France. These two countries battled for power around the world. Between 1689 and 1763, the two powers fought in Europe, in India, in the Caribbean, and in North America. Study the timeline on this page. How many years were Britain and France at war from 1689 to 1763?

In North America, Britain and France fought to control the land and its wealth. Each hoped to bring into their country more of the valuable furs and fish from North America. Each of these items was an **import,** a product brought into a country. The first three wars did not settle the conflict. The fourth war began in 1754 when French soldiers attacked British colonists. These colonists had settled on land claimed by France near the Ohio River.

Fighting in America went on until 1763, a total of nine years. However, the war is called the Seven Years' War, because Britain and France fought in Europe between 1756 and 1763. The war is also called the French and Indian War. In the war, the French joined with several Indian tribes to fight the British.

The Life of Soldiers

When the Seven Years' War began, colonists rushed to join the army. Most British colonists were Protestants. They disliked the French, who were Catholics.

▼ *Great Britain and France fought four separate wars between 1689 and 1763. In North America, all four wars were fought for control of land and resources.*

The British–French Conflict, 1689–1763

1689–1697, King William's War. England and France fight for control of land and the fur trade in North America. Fighting stops. Neither side wins any territory.

1744–1748, King George's War. British colonists capture the French fort at Louisbourg, Canada. However, the fort is returned to France at the end of the war. Neither side gains any territory.

1700	1725	1750	1775

1702–1713, Queen Anne's War. Britain wins a small victory. The British gain valuable fur-trading land near Hudson Bay, fishing villages in Nova Scotia, and a sugar-producing island in the Caribbean Sea.

1756–1763, The Seven Years' War (also called the French and Indian War). Britain wins control of lands claimed by France in eastern North America.

Also, the French had forts in Canada and along the Ohio River. These forts stopped British colonists from moving westward. Study the map below. What lands did Britain and France claim in 1689?

The colonists were ready to fight. Yet few had military experience. They looked up to the British troops because many had fought before. A Connecticut man, Gideon Hawley, said, "One of the regulars is worth five of our men."

However, the colonists soon saw that even for the tough British soldiers, war was hard. Troops often had only salt pork and biscuits to eat. And sometimes the meat was spoiled by the time it reached the troops.

The poor food made soldiers more likely to get sick. And the camps they stayed in were often very crowded, so diseases like typhoid fever spread quickly from one soldier to another. In fact, during the Seven Years' War, more soldiers died from disease than from fighting.

The Role of Indian Tribes

Colonists and Europeans were not the only ones involved in fighting. Indian tribes in northeastern North America also fought in the war. Among other groups of Indians, the Huron and the Seneca

▼ The carving on this powder horn shows the key battles fought in New York during the Seven Years' War.

▼ In 1707, England joined with Scotland and Wales to form the country called Great Britain. The English claims on the 1689 map, then, became the British claims after 1707.

European Land Claims in North America, 1689 and 1763

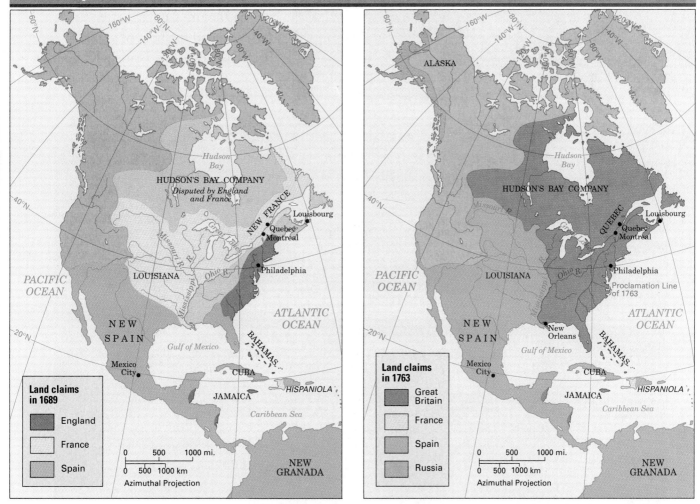

In the picture at the bottom of the page, you can see the British attacking Quebec. The engraving above it shows the death of the British general, James Wolfe, who was wounded three times in the fighting.

joined the French to fight the British.

The Seneca were part of the Iroquois Nation, a confederation of Indian groups. Some of the Iroquois tried to stay out of the war when it began. The Iroquois carefully studied **politics,** the way governments act. Sometimes the Iroquois supported the British, and sometimes the Iroquois supported the French. The Iroquois did not

want either country to win and become stronger in North America.

Early in the war, the French, the Huron, the Seneca, and other Indians joined together to win several major battles. But in 1757, William Pitt became the leader of the British government. Pitt decided that Britain should send more troops to North America. He also sent better food and more guns to aid the British troops.

The Iroquois who had stayed out of the war saw the change in the British army. They began to feel that the British might win the war. To protect their trade with Britain and its colonies, they joined the British to fight the French.

The Battle of Quebec

With more troops, better supplies, and the help of several Iroquois tribes, the British army began to win more battles. In 1759, British troops, led by 32-year-old

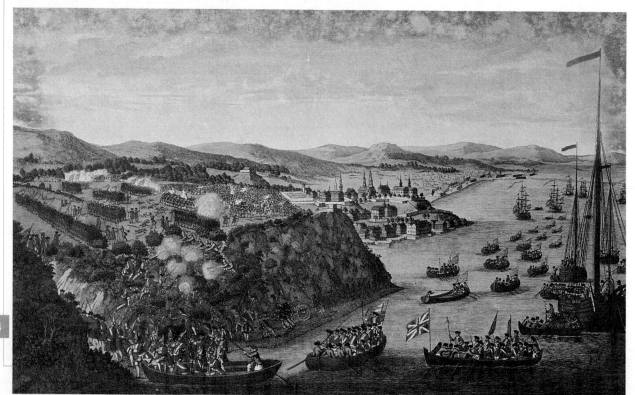

James Wolfe, got ready to attack the city of Quebec, the French capital in Canada. Quebec sat atop a cliff about 180 feet high and was defended by some 14,000 French troops. Attacking the fort would be very dangerous for the British.

However, during the night of September 12, 1759, Wolfe's British troops secretly climbed a narrow path up the steep cliff. When the French troops got up in the morning, they saw that about 4,500 British troops were in position to fight them.

Fighting soon began. The inexperienced French troops fired wildly as they moved toward the British. The well-trained British troops waited until the French got within 40 yards. Then the British opened fire with deadly aim. In 15 to 30 minutes, the British had won the battle. And they had won the key to power over most of North America. ■

■ *What was the main goal of Britain and France in the North American wars they fought between 1689 and 1763?*

Results of the War

Britain and France ended the war with the signing of the Treaty of Paris in 1763. Britain wanted all of the French lands in North America. But the French did not want the British to become too powerful. So, the treaty gave all French land west of the Mississippi River to Spain. Britain agreed to this treaty, even though Spain had helped France during the war. According to the treaty, Britain took over the French lands east of the Mississippi River.

The Proclamation of 1763

With the French defeat, many colonists eagerly prepared to move across the Appalachian Mountains. However, the British were worried. They knew that new settlements would anger the Iroquois, Delaware, Shawnee, and other Indian tribes who already lived there. To prevent fighting, the British issued the Proclamation of 1763. This act saved all land west of the Appalachians for Indians. Colonists could not settle there.

▲ *This engraving by Henry Dawkins shows leaders of an Indian tribe negotiating with the British near the end of the Seven Years' War.*

The Proclamation upset many colonists. Earlier, the French had blocked new settlements. The French had been defeated. Now, though, the British also stopped people from moving west. Many colonists wondered why they had fought the war.

The Cost of Victory

Colonial anger at Britain's Proclamation of 1763 was just one

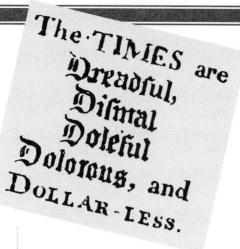

This notice appeared in the Pennsylvania Journal two years after the Seven Years' War. It expressed the colonists' feelings about the terrible effects of the war and the general lack of money.

The·TIMES are
Dreadful,
Dismal
Doleful
Dolorous, and
DOLLAR-LESS.

hardship the war caused. The British, the Indians, and the colonists each faced new troubles.

In Britain, the war had caused the government to borrow money. Between 1754 and 1763, the money Britain owed doubled. The country needed money to pay back its many loans.

Britain also had to pay the 10,000 soldiers it sent to North America. These troops were needed to protect the large new British empire. Britain now had to spend three times as much to defend its American empire as it did before the war.

For many Indian tribes, the war brought a loss of power. They could no longer use the French to help them against the British. And even 10,000 British soldiers could

not stop settlers from moving onto Indian lands.

In the colonies, the war caused great suffering. Boston, a city of about 2,200 families, lost 700 men during the war. These deaths left many widows and orphans who needed help just to buy food.

The Effect on Attitudes

The war also changed the way colonists viewed Britain. Colonists no longer needed British help to fight the French. Therefore, the colonists felt less closely tied to Britain.

Also, many colonists had become skilled soldiers in the war. They had learned that they could defend themselves. One colonist who had fought for the first time was a Virginian, George Washington. After one battle, Washington wrote to his mother that the "Virginia troops showed a good deal of bravery." Yet the British troops, he said, ran from the French like "sheep pursued by dogs."

The war taught Washington something. Colonists could fight as well as British soldiers. In a few years, the whole world would know what Washington knew. ■

■ *Name two ways the colonists benefited from the Seven Years' War.*

R E V I E W

1. **FOCUS** What were the main results of the Seven Years' War?

2. **CONNECT** In 1754, why were most British colonists content to be part of the British empire?

3. **GEOGRAPHY** How did geography make Britain's attack on Quebec difficult?

4. **HISTORY** Why did the Proclamation of 1763 fail?

5. **CRITICAL THINKING** Compare the comments about the colonial soldiers at the beginning of the Seven Years'

War with the comments about the French soldiers who attacked Wolfe's troops at Quebec. How were the two groups similar?

6. **WRITING ACTIVITY** Make two columns on your paper. In the left column, list benefits of the Seven Years' War for the colonists. In the right column, list costs of the war for the colonists. Compare the items in the two columns and explain why you think that the war helped or hurt the colonists overall.

LESSON 3

A New British Policy

In Boston, on January 25, 1774, a little boy stood quietly behind a sled he had been pushing. A man stood over him, "cursing, damning, threatening and shaking a very large cane . . . over his head."

George Robert Twelves Hewes, a shoemaker, hurried over. "Mr. Malcolm, I hope you are not going to strike this boy with that stick."

John Malcolm turned quickly. He stared angrily at Hewes.

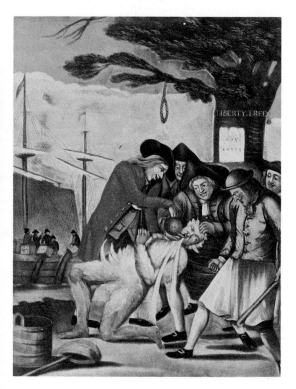

Malcolm was a colonial official. He worked for the British government, managing colonial trade. Hewes was a poor working man. Malcolm shouted that Hewes should mind his own business.

Hewes reminded Malcolm of what happened two months earlier. An angry crowd in Maine had punished Malcolm for being an informer. The crowd had poured hot tar over him, and covered him with feathers.

At this comment by Hewes, Malcolm swung his cane. The blow left Hewes lying on the ground with a bloody cut in his head. Two days later, a group of angry Bostonians took Malcolm from his home and he was tarred and feathered a second time.

Yet the colonists' anger was also directed at the British government. That anger had been building for 11 years. Before the Seven Years' War, Parliament had used duties to regulate colonial trade. Yet it had never tried to raise money from the colonists. Because of the war, though, Britain needed money. So Parliament decided to do something it had never done. It decided to tax the colonists.

THINKING FOCUS

What caused increased conflicts between the colonies and Britain after 1763?

Key Terms

- repeal
- boycott
- propaganda

◄ *This cartoon showing the tarring and feathering of a British official in the colonies may have been based on the treatment of John Malcolm.*

247

Crisis with Britain

Britain Taxes the Colonies

➤ *Why do you think the colonists used a skull to symbolize the Stamp Act?*

In 1764, Parliament first tried to tax colonists. It changed the 1733 Molasses Act into a new law called the Sugar Act. This law increased the number of customs agents. It also increased the penalties for smuggling, though it lowered the duty on molasses. By catching more smugglers, Britain hoped to make merchants pay the duty.

Eight colonial assemblies called on Parliament to **repeal,** or do away with, the Sugar Act. They said that Parliament had no right to tax the colonists because the colonists had no representatives in Parliament. Parliament did not agree. The law remained.

The Stamp Act

In March 1765, Parliament tried again to raise money from the colonists. In Britain people had to pay a stamp tax. This was an extra charge on newspapers and other items written on paper that had to have a government stamp on them. Parliament decided that colonists should also pay a stamp tax. They expected the tax would upset a few colonists. But they were not ready for what happened.

The colonists exploded in anger. They charged that the stamp tax—or any tax—was unfair. Anger came not only from merchants, but also from large groups of citizens, such as shoemakers and tailors. Colonial men formed groups called the Sons of Liberty. Colonial women formed the Daughters of Liberty. These groups held public meetings to speak out against the Stamp Act.

In some places crowds did more than protest. In Boston, Andrew Oliver had been chosen to pass out stamps. However, a crowd

of angry citizens tore down a new building Oliver owned. Then they broke into his large home and destroyed his furniture. Oliver decided to quit. Fear of attacks caused other officials to quit as well. Soon Parliament had no one to pass out the stamped paper. Parliament had to repeal the new Stamp Act, which had only been in effect a little over four months.

The Townshend Duties

In 1767, Parliament tried a third time to tax the colonists. Parliament passed duties on paper, lead, painters' colors, and tea. The duties were named after Charles Townshend. He was the British official in charge of handling money for the government.

🔺 *The British issued this stamp in 1765 for use in the colonies.*

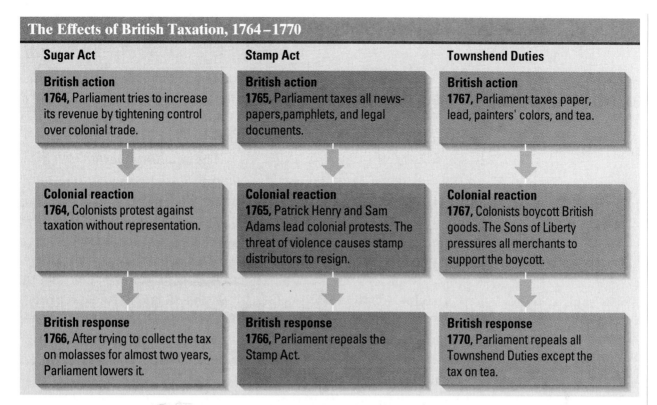

The Effects of British Taxation, 1764–1770

Sugar Act

British action
1764, Parliament tries to increase its revenue by tightening control over colonial trade.

Colonial reaction
1764, Colonists protest against taxation without representation.

British response
1766, After trying to collect the tax on molasses for almost two years, Parliament lowers it.

Stamp Act

British action
1765, Parliament taxes all newspapers, pamphlets, and legal documents.

Colonial reaction
1765, Patrick Henry and Sam Adams lead colonial protests. The threat of violence causes stamp distributors to resign.

British response
1766, Parliament repeals the Stamp Act.

Townshend Duties

British action
1767, Parliament taxes paper, lead, painters' colors, and tea.

Colonial reaction
1767, Colonists boycott British goods. The Sons of Liberty pressures all merchants to support the boycott.

British response
1770, Parliament repeals all Townshend Duties except the tax on tea.

Again the colonists cried, "No taxation without representation!" To cause the British to repeal the duties, colonial merchants agreed to **boycott,** or not buy, anything from Britain. The boycott, they thought, would cause British businesses to lose money. British merchants would then ask Parliament to repeal the duties.

Women played an important part in the boycott of British goods. Britain had a large and profitable cloth trade in the colonies. To help the boycott of British cloth, colonial women made their own. Many held spinning contests to advertise the boycott.

The boycott worked. In 1770, Parliament decided to end all of the taxes but one. Only the tax on tea remained.

The Boston Massacre

In 1768, during the argument over the Townshend duties, Parliament got worried. They feared that the colonial protests were out of control. They sent soldiers to Boston. Some colonists welcomed the soldiers. They believed the soldiers might help keep order. Other colonists were angry. They charged that the soldiers were a danger to the rights of colonists.

Anger finally exploded in violence. On March 5, 1770, between 50 and 100 Bostonians moved toward the soldiers guarding the customs house. One of the Bostonians' leaders was a black man named Crispus Attucks. The crowd yelled, then threw sticks and snowballs. Fearing for their safety, the soldiers opened fire. They killed Attucks and four other colonists.

Colonial newspapers called the action the "Boston Massacre." Through **propaganda,** or telling one side of a story to win support for a cause, the newspapers stirred up anger at the British.

Not all colonists blamed the British soldiers for the five deaths.

In the chart, notice the British reaction to colonial protests against taxation. How successful were the colonists?

Crisis with Britain

How Do We Know?

HISTORY *The memories of George Robert Twelves Hewes were written down in the 1830s by historians Benjamin Bussey Thatcher and James Hawkes. They interviewed Hewes shortly before he died. He was nearly 100 at his death.*

■ *Why did the colonists oppose paying taxes to the British?*

▼ *The arrival of tea in colonial ports was considered, as this flyer said, an "alarming crisis."*

Lawyer John Adams of Boston defended the soldiers in court. The court punished only two of the soldiers.

John Adams' cousin, Samuel Adams, was a leader in spreading the propaganda. As a boy, Sam had learned from his father about how people had defended their rights in the past. Now he urged the Boston town meeting to set up a committee. This committee would tell other colonies of British actions. Soon the other colonies started their own groups, called Committees of Correspondence. Anger at Britain was causing people in the colonies to work more closely together.

The Tea Act

Parliament still was not getting money from the colonists. And Parliament faced another problem. The British East India Company was going broke. The company sold tea and other goods from Asia. To help the company,

Parliament let it sell tea directly to colonial merchants. The merchants then sold the tea to colonists. Even with the tax, tea from the company cost less than smuggled tea.

The colonists knew that Parliament was still taxing them without their approval. In November 1773, three ships carrying East India Company tea reached Boston harbor. For almost three weeks, crowds of colonists stopped anyone from taking the hated tea off the ships. Then, in December 1773, dozens of colonists dressed up as Indians. One of these was George Robert Twelves Hewes. They silently boarded the ships. Sixty years later, Hewes described the action now known as the Boston Tea Party:

> We then were ordered by our commander to open the hatches and take out all the chests of tea and throw them overboard, and we immediately proceeded to execute his orders; first cutting and splitting the chests with our tomahawks, so as thoroughly to expose them to the effects of the water. In about three hours from the time we went on board, we had thus broken and thrown overboard every tea chest to be found in the ship; while those in the other ships were disposing of the tea in the same way, at the same time.

The Boston Tea Party was a brave move by the colonists. You can learn more about it in A Closer Look on page 251. ■

Monday Morning, December 27, 1773.
THE TEA-SHIP being arrived, every Inhabitant, who wishes to preferve the Liberty of America, is defired to meet at the STATE-HOUSE, This Morning, precifely at TEN o'Clock, to advife what is beft to be done on this alarming Crifis.

Boston Tea Party

It took three hours for American patriots to dump 90,000 pounds of tea into Boston harbor. An English woman living in Boston wrote that the event was "too shocking for me to describe." But the tea was the only thing the colonists damaged—except for one padlock, which they replaced the next day.

To mask their faces, patriots rubbed on charcoal, soot, and burnt cork.

"Shaped into dunes, the tea lay upon the water...," one person said. The Tea Party took place after low tide, when the water is very shallow. So the tea stacked up like piles of hay. Some piles were so high the tea fell back onto the ships.

Without speaking, the colonists broke open the tea chests with hatchets. When they were finished, they swept the decks clean.

Colonists Begin to Unite

The Boston Tea Party enraged the British. To punish Boston, Parliament passed what colonists called the "Intolerable Acts." These acts ended town meetings. They took away some of the power of the Massachusetts assembly. They also closed Boston harbor to almost all shipping, except for some food and fuel. The city could not import or export most goods until it paid for the tea.

Boston was a city built on trade. Closing its harbor could be terrible for its people. What would happen to Boston's many sailors, dock workers, and merchants?

Parliament hoped that closing the Boston harbor would cause the city to pay for the tea. Instead, closing the harbor caused the other colonies to help Boston. Food and supplies poured in from the other colonies.

On September 5, 1774, delegates from every colony except Georgia met in Philadelphia to talk about the British actions. This group is now known as the First Continental Congress. They voted to stop all trade with Britain.

Most colonists expected the crisis to end peacefully. They hoped Britain would return to its policy of salutary neglect. Only a few were rebels, people who were ready to overthrow the government and set up a new one.

UNDERSTANDING TAXATION

After 1763, Britain needed money to pay for the Seven Years' War. Parliament tried to raise money as most governments do: through taxation. What is taxation? What is its goal?

Types of Taxes

Governments often pass laws that require people to pay money to them. This way of raising money is called taxation.

One type of tax is the sales tax. When you buy a notebook, you may pay a small amount for sales tax. The store sends the government the extra money.

Another tax, the income tax, is based on the money a person earns. The more money a worker earns, the more tax that person must pay.

The Use of Taxes

The government then uses money from taxation to pay for goods and services that everyone needs. For example, taxes pay for operating schools, hiring police and firefighters, and building roads. Tax money also pays the salaries of the people elected to government, such as the president and members of Congress.

In the 1700s, Britain used taxes to defend its empire. The government of Boston used tax money to support widows and orphans. Today, governments still use taxes to pay the military and to help the needy.

Yet how colonists viewed one another had changed in only 20 years. In 1754, before the Seven Years' War, colonists were divided from each other. By 1774, however, colonists were joining together for protection. During the First Continental Congress, Virginia delegate Patrick Henry said something that no one would have said 20 years earlier. "The distinctions between Virginians, Pennsylvanians, New Yorkers, and New Englanders are no more. I am not a Virginian, but an American."

And something else was different since 1754. Colonists' view of Britain had changed. Then, most colonists thought Britain protected them. Now, more and more colonists thought Britain was a danger to their liberties. Patrick Henry also stated this new view of Britain. In a speech in Richmond, Virginia, in March 1775, Henry boldly declared:

A British cartoon made fun of the Boston colonists. They felt caged in when Britain closed their port.

O ur chains are forged. Their clanking may be heard on the plains of Boston! The war is inevitable—and let it come! I repeat it, sir, let it come! . . . Is life so dear, or peace so sweet, as to be purchased at the price of chains and slavery? Forbid it, Almighty God! I know not what course others may take; but as for me, give me liberty, or give me death!

In less than one month, Henry's prediction came true. The war began. ■

■ Why did the colonists begin to work with each other against the British government?

REVIEW

1. **FOCUS** What caused increased conflicts between the colonies and Great Britain after 1763?

2. **CONNECT** Why were colonists more confident of their ability to defend themselves in the 1770s than they had been in the 1750s?

3. **HISTORY** How was the reaction to the Stamp Act different from the protests against the Sugar Act?

4. **HISTORY** What was the British reaction to the Boston Tea Party?

5. **CRITICAL THINKING** Write one sentence summarizing the change in the relationship between the colonies and Great Britain between 1754 and 1775.

6. **WRITING ACTIVITY** With a group of three other students, prepare a skit about the Boston Tea Party.

Crisis with Britain

Interpreting Political Cartoons

Here's Why

Political cartoons use pictures, and often humor, to make a point about public affairs. They are fun and informative, and they can help you understand what people of the time were concerned about. For example, political cartoons from the time of the American Revolution can help you understand what was important to Americans of that time.

Here's How

Look at the cartoon on the opposite page. It was published in London, in 1776, ten months after the Battle of Lexington and Concord. The cartoon suggests that King George was greedy in trying to get more and more taxes from the American colonists. It also suggests that the king's actions caused the revolt of the colonies.

In creating cartoons, all cartoonists first depend on readers having a certain level of background knowledge. The meaning of the cartoon on the opposite page would have been clear to people who saw it in 1776.

Today, we have trouble identifying the characters in Revolutionary War cartoons, just as people 200 years from

now will have difficulty interpreting our political cartoons. In 1776, the problems between England and the colonies were known to everyone. The cartoonist could depend on the fact that people would recognize the noblemen in the picture as King George and his cabinet. Today we are not even sure who the man killing the goose is. Readers at the time would have known who that man and all the others in the picture were.

The man wearing a sash and leaning over the goose is shown on this page to give you a closer look at him. We think that he is either King George III or the British minister Lord Frederick North.

Second, cartoonists make comparisons. Here, the car-

toonist compares the American colonies to the goose that laid the golden egg in the story of "The Wise Men of Gotham and their Goose." The basket of golden eggs, shown in the upper left corner, is a symbol of the wealth England gained from the colonies.

King George III and his cabinet represent the not-so-wise men who decided to kill the goose to get more than one golden egg in a day.

Third, cartoonists sometimes use labels to identify parts of the cartoon that the reader may not understand. Find the labels "North America" and "taxes." These are parts of the cartoon that the cartoonist does not want the reader to miss.

Finally, cartoons may include written clues. Notice that the cartoonist included the story of "The Wise Men of Gotham and their Goose."

Try It

Find the cartoon on page 253. Read the caption and study the cartoon. Who are the people in the cartoon? Explain what background knowledge you need to have in order to understand the cartoon. Point out the main comparison in the cartoon.

THE WISE MEN of GOTHAM and their GOOSE

Review the Colonists Begin to Unite section of Lesson 3 if you need help. Explain the cartoon's message.

Apply It

Most newspapers print a political cartoon every day. Write a paragraph that explains a political cartoon from your newspaper. Share your cartoon and explanations with classmates.

Chapter Review

Reviewing Key Terms

assembly (p. 240)   propaganda (p. 249)
boycott (p. 249)   repeal (p. 248)
import (p. 242)   salutary neglect (p. 239)
politics (p. 244)   veto (p. 240)

A. Write a sentence to answer each question. Each sentence you write should include at least one key term.

1. Why were certain laws in the colonies not strictly enforced?
2. How could a governor stop a law from taking effect?
3. What group was chosen by the people in a colony to make its laws and set taxes?
4. How did Parliament stop the Sugar Act from taking effect?
5. How could Britain and France get furs from North America?
6. How could newspapers stir up anger among the American colonists?
7. What happened when Americans refused to buy British goods?

B. Use a dictionary to find the origins of the following words. On your own paper, write one or two sentences explaining how the word can be used to describe colonial times.

1. boycott
2. propaganda
3. politics

Exploring Concepts

A. Following the Seven Years' War, important changes took place in the colonies. These changes included the colonists' attitude toward Britain and toward each other, Britain's wealth, Britain's taxation of colonists, and the Indians' power. Copy and complete the chart below using information from the chapter.

Issue	Before War	After War
1. Colonists' attitude toward Britain	Saw Britain as protector	Saw Britain as threat
2. Colonists' attitude toward each other		
3. Britain's wealth		
4. Britain's taxation of colonists		
5. Indians' power		

B. Answer each question with information from the chapter.

1. Did all the colonial governors follow the policy of salutary neglect?
2. Why were there often violent clashes among the colonists?
3. Why did very few colonists want to revolt against the British in the 1750s?
4. What effect did colonists fighting in the Seven Years' War have on their relationship with Britain later on?
5. What part did members of the Iroquois Nation play in the Seven Years' War?
6. What was the Proclamation of 1763 and what were its effects?
7. How did the British government try to raise money from the American colonists after the costly Seven Years' War?
8. What did the colonists mean by saying "No taxation without representation"?

Reviewing Skills

1. The illustration on this page is thought to be America's first political cartoon. Benjamin Franklin drew it in 1754 to support the idea of united colonies. The cartoon was based on the superstition that a cut up snake could be put back together if its pieces were joined by sunset. The cartoon reappeared in colonial newspapers in 1765 and 1774. What did the pieces of the snake mean? What written clue did Franklin add to help explain this?

2. What did people of Franklin's time need to know in order to understand his cartoon? Why do we need background information when we discuss his cartoon?

3. The graph on page 239 shows colonial trade with Britain. This graph is based on information from a table. What headings might the table have used? Why is it more helpful to show this information on a graph than on a table?

4. What special kind of map symbol could you use to show the number of immigrants that came from Europe to each colony?

JOIN, or DIE.

Using Critical Thinking

1. Some colonists boycotted British goods for several years. What effects might the boycott have had on their everyday lives?

2. In 1770, colonists threw sticks and snowballs at British soldiers, who opened fire. Explain how newspaper reports stirred up anger against the British.

3. In the Seven Years' War, more soldiers died from diseases than from battles. Could this happen today? Why or why not?

4. After the Seven Years' War was over in America in 1763, this country was very different. Think about what life in the colonies would have been like if the war had never happened. How might the country have been different? What changes were caused by the war? Would those changes have happened anyway?

Preparing for Citizenship

1. **COLLECTING INFORMATION** Think about how colonial newspapers reported the Boston Massacre. Then find three letters to the editor in your newspaper that have strong, clear opinions on one or more of these topics: the environment; state or local government; candidates running for office. After each letter, briefly tell the writer's opinion. Then paste the articles and your explanations in a booklet. Share your information in class.

2. **COLLABORATIVE LEARNING** With a group of classmates, write and perform dramatic scenes that show how the colonists' relationship with Britain changed. The first scene should take place in the early 1750s in a colonial shop that sells British cloth. The second scene should take place in the same shop 20 years later. In both scenes, have the same characters talk about their attitudes toward the British.

Chapter 11

War Breaks Out

When the first shots of the Revolution were fired, America consisted of 13 very different and separate colonies. But when America faced the well-trained British army, the differences between the colonies did not seem so important. People throughout the nation—generals, farmers, politicians, and women at home—did their part to win the war.

During the war, many women took charge of farms and businesses while the men fought. Abigail Adams (above) ran her family's farm while her husband, John Adams, represented the United States in Britain.

1775 American Minutemen fight British troops at the bridge at Concord, Massachusetts (right). Three British soldiers and two Americans are killed.

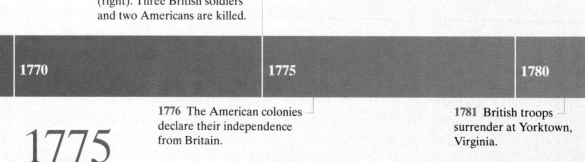

1770	1775	1780

1776 The American colonies declare their independence from Britain.

1775

1781 British troops surrender at Yorktown, Virginia.

Throughout the war, George Washington led the Continental Army through many battles. Above, Washington leads his troops across the Delaware River on Christmas night, 1776, to attack the British at Trenton.

1785

1790

1783 Britain and the United States sign a treaty ending the war. The picture above shows the American signers; the British refused to pose for the painting.

1792

L E S S O N   1

Forming a New Government

How did the colonies organize a government to lead their fight for independence?

Key Terms

- militia
- delegate
- independence
- equality

Just after midnight on April 19, 1775, the alarm bells in Lexington, Massachusetts, started to clang. Jonas Parker jumped out of bed, grabbed his musket, and ran to the common, a meadow in the center of the village. "The Redcoats are coming," he heard voices shouting.

Within minutes, Parker and 130 other farmers and shopkeepers had gathered on the common. All were clutching guns. They talked in excited whispers and stamped their feet to stay warm in the chill night air.

By 1:30 A.M., no British troops had appeared, so Captain John Parker dismissed the men. He told them to return to the green the minute they heard the beating of the drum. Men who lived nearby went home. The rest went to Monroe and Buckman taverns to keep warm and wait.

Three hours later, a scout named Thaddeus Brown galloped into town to report that the British were less than a half mile away. Immediately, 16-year-old William Diamond beat the drum, and 77 townsmen rushed to the green. There they formed two uneven lines and waited nervously. As the sun rose, a line of more than 300 British soldiers marched into view.

The colonists weren't sure what to do. No one had told them to stop the British. So they stood in their ranks, silently protesting the British force.

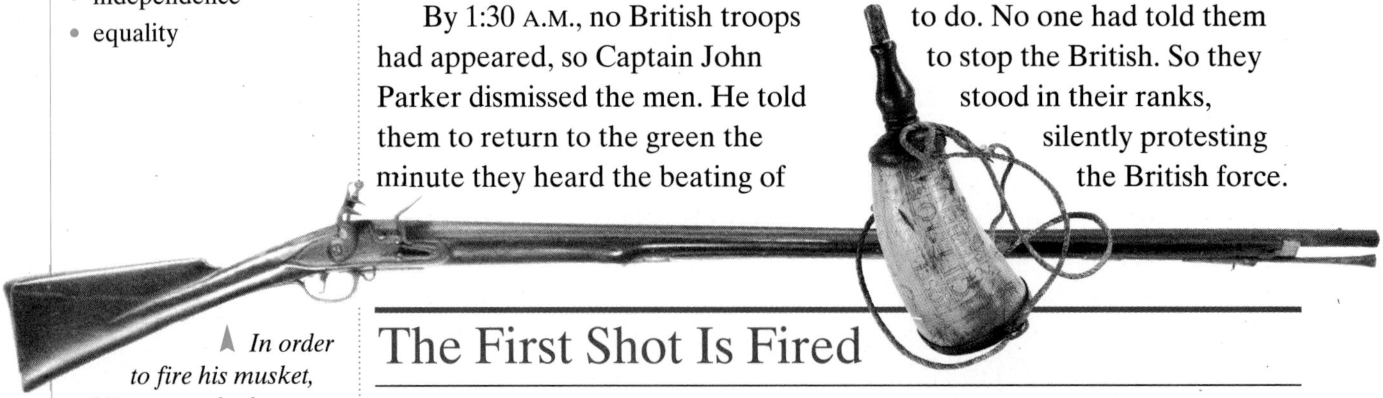

▲ *In order to fire his musket, a Minuteman had to pour gunpowder from his powder horn, shown on the right, into the barrel of the gun.*

The First Shot Is Fired

The farmers and shopkeepers who gathered on the green that morning were members of the **militia,** citizens who served as part-time soldiers. They were also called Minutemen because they were ready to fight any enemy at a minute's notice.

The British soldiers were a secret raiding party from Boston looking for hidden colonial weapons. They surprised no one, however. Paul Revere and William Dawes had ridden all night from Boston to warn the local militias. Near Concord, they got help from Samuel Prescott.

The Conflict Begins

When Major John Pitcairn, the British officer in charge, spotted the Minutemen on the green, he ordered his men into battle lines. Then he urged his horse forward, shouting at the colonists "Lay down your arms!"

Suddenly a shot rang out. The British troops charged forward. Eyewitnesses disagree on whether the British or the colonists fired first. In any case, the battle was over in minutes. Ten colonists were wounded and eight were killed, including Jonas Parker. One British soldier was hurt.

Pitcairn then marched his troops six miles to Concord. At 9:30 A.M., a group of militiamen clashed with the British at North Bridge and drove them off. Two colonists and three British soldiers were killed.

Retreat to Boston

After their losses at North Bridge, the British began their retreat to Boston. However, more than 1,000 angry militiamen from other villages gathered and fired at the Redcoats from behind trees and stone walls. Before the British reached the safety of Boston later that night, the Americans had 93 dead and wounded, the British 273. The American Revolution had begun. ■

Farmers and towns-people took up arms to defend their homes in Lexington and Concord.

■ *Why was the militia of Lexington and Concord ready to oppose the British raiding party?*

261

The Continental Congress Meets

Months earlier, in September 1774, representatives from 12 of the 13 colonies had gathered at the First Continental Congress. These representatives, or **delegates,** promised to meet again in May 1775 if the problems with Britain continued. Now blood had been shed and tensions were high. The need to meet was clear. Leaders from 12 colonies gathered in Philadelphia on May 10, 1775, for the Second Continental Congress. They had big decisions to make.

Preparing for War

Many Americans wanted the colonies and Great Britain to settle their differences. The members of Congress were prepared to try that solution. But they also knew that they had to prepare for the worst —a war for **independence,** which would free them from control by Britain.

Congress quickly began acting like an independent government.

By a small majority, they voted to organize the New England militia into an army of 22,000 "for the defense of American liberty." They named George Washington, a Virginian, to lead the forces.

Congress also agreed to issue paper money to buy gunpowder and weapons. Since they feared the British would turn the Indian tribes against them, they set up a commission to keep peace with the Indians. They also began seeking support from other European countries.

Seeking Peace

To try to avoid war, Congress sent a written request to King George III. The message stated the colonists' loyalty to the king. It blamed Parliament for trying to enslave the colonies. It also asked the king to help restore peace by ending the unfair laws he had imposed. This message was called the Olive Branch Petition.

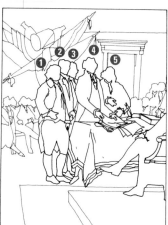

➤ *Delegates from 12 of the 13 colonies gathered in Philadelphia at the Second Continental Congress. In this painting of their meeting by John Trumbull, you can see five leaders of the new nation: 1. John Adams; 2. Roger Sherman; 3. Robert R. Livingston; 4. Thomas Jefferson; and 5. Benjamin Franklin.*

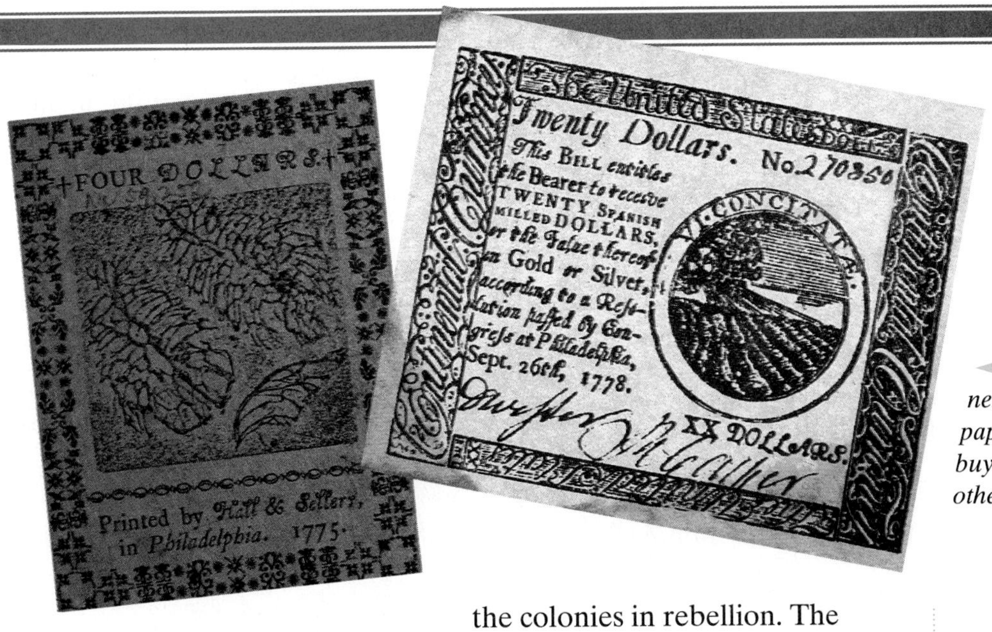

◀ *The Second Continental Congress issued paper money like this to buy gunpowder and other war supplies.*

It took a month for a ship to carry the message to King George. It took only two days for the king to reject the request and declare the colonies in rebellion. The British government outlawed trade with the colonies and sent 20,000 more troops to America. The war was under way. ■

■ *Why did the colonies need a government after Lexington and Concord, and what actions did the new government take?*

The Colonists Declare Independence

Fighting between the colonists and the British increased during the fall and winter of 1775. Militiamen placed cannons on Dorchester Heights near Boston and drove the British from the city. On January 1, 1776, ships of the British navy shelled Norfolk, Virginia, and caused a great fire that burned the town. But Americans were gaining confidence, and the idea of independence was gathering force.

Common Sense

In January 1776, Thomas Paine, an Englishman who had settled in Pennsylvania, published a bold call to revolution. His work, called *Common Sense,* asked the colonists to consider all the reasons to fight for independence.

Paine pointed out that it was not logical for a small island like Britain to rule a large continent like America. He argued strongly that the colonists should not feel loyal to a king who was ruling them harshly. He urged the colonists to separate from England. "A government of our own is our natural right," he wrote.

By April 1776, three months after it was printed, more than 120,000 copies of *Common Sense* were sold in all of the colonies. Paine's writing was simple but strong. All Americans could understand and discuss his ideas. This small pamphlet helped persuade many Americans to fight for independence.

The Declaration of Independence

As the idea of independence spread throughout the colonies, many colonies began to set up their own governments. Soon, some of the colonies began to

263

press Congress to officially declare independence from Great Britain.

On June 7, 1776, Richard Henry Lee of Virginia made a motion to the Congress that "these united colonies are, and of right ought to be, free and independent states." After much debate, Congress met on July 2, 1776, to vote on a resolution for independence. A committee of five was formed to write a Declaration of Independence, including Benjamin Franklin and John Adams. But it was Thomas Jefferson, a 33-year-old delegate from Virginia, who wrote it.

Jefferson began the Declaration with a short introduction. This paragraph promised that the Declaration would spell out the reasons the colonies had to separate from Britain.

Then, in three sections, Jefferson made the case for independence.

Thomas Jefferson penned the rough draft of the Declaration of Independence shown at the bottom of the page.

UNDERSTANDING EQUALITY

Probably the most famous words in the Declaration of Independence are the following: "We hold these truths to be self-evident, that all men are created equal." But what did Thomas Jefferson and the other signers of the Declaration mean by equal? And what does equality mean today?

Jefferson's Equality

Equality means that all people have the same rights and privileges, such as the right to vote. Equality does not mean that everyone is the same. Obviously, some people are stronger, or more artistic, or more athletic than others. People differ also in their sex, race, religion, and country of birth. In 1776, when the Declaration of Independence was written, differences like these determined a person's rights. At that time, only white men could be citizens. When Jefferson wrote that "all men" were equal, he really meant "all citizens." Women and blacks were not included.

Equality Today

Over the years, new laws have extended the rights of citizenship to all Americans equally. After the Civil War, Congress acted to give black Americans the right to vote. In 1920, women finally received this same right.

Today, equality means that the laws of the United States apply to everyone in exactly the same way. By law, all Americans have an equal opportunity to be hired for a job. Every American also has an equal right to use public buses and subways. Though the law grants these rights to everyone, African Americans and other ethnic groups have had to struggle to make sure that these laws are applied fairly.

 *Angry colonists pulled down a statue of King George. The colonists melted down the statue and made musket balls from the metal.*

In the first section, he stated a bold idea—that each citizen has natural rights that governments cannot give or take away. These included rights to "life, liberty, and the pursuit of happiness." The purpose of government was to make sure all people could enjoy these rights.

The second section was an accusation. It listed 27 ways in which King George III had misused his power. It accused him of taxing the colonists without their consent and cutting off their trade. It also said the king forced colonists to house and supply British soldiers.

The third section was a brave statement of independence. It stated that the colonies had asked the king many times to end his unfair treatment and he had refused. "We therefore declare," the Declaration then concludes, "that these united colonies are, and of right ought to be, free and independent states." You can read a copy of the Declaration of Independence on pages 576–579 of the Time/Space Databank.

Two days later, Congress voted to accept the Declaration. The date was July 4, 1776. ∎

How Do We Know?

HISTORY *Jefferson refused at first to write the Declaration. We know this because 40 years after the Declaration was signed, Adams and Jefferson wrote an account of the meetings of their committee. In the end, Jefferson agreed. "If you are decided," he told Adams, "I will do as well as I can."*

■ *What specific reasons does the Declaration of Independence give for declaring independence?*

REVIEW

1. **FOCUS** How did the colonies organize a government to lead their fight for independence?
2. **CONNECT** In what ways did King George rule the colonists harshly and unfairly before the start of the Revolutionary War?
3. **CITIZENSHIP** In the Declaration, Jefferson wrote that each citizen has natural rights. What are these natural rights, and what should government do about them?
4. **CRITICAL THINKING** Compare what Thomas Jefferson meant by equality and what this word means to Americans today. Give some examples of equality as it applies to students at your school.
5. **ACTIVITY** With other students, act out the events of the Battle of Lexington. You might start with the clanging of the alarm bell at midnight and end with the fight at dawn on the Lexington green.

Patriot or Loyalist?

> A republican form of government [elected representatives] will never suit the genius of the people or the extent of the country. The Americans are properly Britons.
>
> Elias Boudinot of New Jersey,
> to the Continental Congress,
> June, 1776

> Our Cause is the Cause of all Mankind, and we are fighting for their Liberty in defending our own.
>
> Benjamin Franklin

Background

▼ *Soldiers used tinder boxes like these to start their campfires.*

The American colonists were not all alike. Some were poor, others rich, many were somewhere in the middle. Most were from England, but many had come to America from Holland or Germany or France. Some were very well educated, while others were skilled at a trade, such as carpentry, candle making, or wheel making. Still others had come to the colonies hoping to learn a trade or buy a small farm. Colonists also differed in their religious beliefs and in their politics. How did all these people ever agree to break away from England? They didn't.

Some colonists felt very "English." They missed the relatives they'd left behind. Many of them hoped to return to England some day. Others in the colonies had become "American." This was their country, not England. Some, like Thomas Paine, no longer accepted the idea of kings. They did not want to be forced to obey distant royalty. They believed people could and should govern themselves. Others still believed that kings were meant to rule nations.

Once it was clear that there would be war with England, families and individuals had to make a difficult choice: Would they be patriot, or would they be loyalist?

Musket balls

Musket ball mold

266

Chapter 11

Conflict Over the Revolution

In this war the colonies were fighting the most powerful country in the world. If the colonies lost the war, England might demand even higher taxes and impose even stricter laws. Maybe it would be best to remain loyal to the king. When the war ended, surely this loyalty would be rewarded. Besides, the king was the rightful ruler of the British empire, and the American colonies were part of that empire.

On the other hand, there was much to be said in favor of the rebellion. The taxes were unfair, and peaceful action had brought no change. The mood of the colonies was one of great excitement. Those who were against the war would be uncomfortable at best. At worst, they could be suspected of spying or accused of treason.

England's army was strong, but the soldiers were not used to fighting as the colonists fought. Also, the English soldiers were not fighting on their own land and protecting their own homes and families. The colonial leaders also knew how harshly they could be treated if they lost the war. They intended to win.

Finally, there remained the bold idea behind the rebellion: Could people, should people, govern themselves?

Loyalist or Patriot

Loyalty to England
Fear of punishment
Family in England

→ Loyalist

Self-government
Tax relief
Create a new nation

→ Patriot

Decision Point

1. Suppose you are a colonist who wants independence, but you are opposed to war. How would you achieve your goal? What could persuade you to fight?
2. What goals and values could make a colonist decide to remain loyal to the king?
3. The colonists were fighting for certain freedoms, including the freedom to share ideas. Do you think they would allow loyalists to write and speak freely during the war? Why?
4. The colonists valued freedom of speech. They wanted to be free to criticize their government and its officials. Today we value this same freedom, but there are some limits to free speech. Can you think of at least one example? Do these limits conflict with the goals and values of free speech as the colonists saw it?

A captain in George Washington's bodyguard wore this helmet.

LESSON 2

Fighting the War

THINKING
FOCUS

How did poorly equipped American soldiers defeat Britain's armies and win independence for the colonies?

Key Terms

- republic
- revolution
- Loyalist

▼ *Continental Army drummers beat colorful drums to signal soldiers.*

General Thomas Gage, commander of all British soldiers in North America, was angry and discouraged. On this day in June 1775, he sat at his desk in Boston writing a letter to his superiors in London. He was trying to explain what had happened.

Only days before, a ragtag army of 1,600 Massachusetts volunteers held off 2,400 British on Bunker Hill and Breed's Hill north of Boston. The Redcoats charged up the hill three times. Twice the volunteers threw them back with blasts of musket fire.

His army had won in the end, Gage reminded himself. But they lost so many—1,054 British soldiers, wounded or dead!

"You will receive an account of some success against the rebels, but attended with a long list of killed or wounded on our side," Gage wrote in his letter of explanation, "so many of the latter that the hospital has hardly hands sufficient to take care of them." In describing the American soldiers, Gage wrote, "These people are now spirited up by a rage and enthusiasm, as great as ever people were possessed of."

The Soldiers Who Fought the War

The American soldiers were so "spirited up" because they believed in their cause. They were fighting to replace the British king with a **republic,** a government in which citizens elect their leaders. To them, the war was a **revolution,** a change of government by force.

Many kinds of soldiers took part in the Revolu-

tion. On the American side were militia companies who defended Bunker Hill. Militiamen enlisted for a particular battle or a few months. Since many were farmers, militiamen often went home during harvest and planting times.

In contrast, young men without families joined the Continental Army, which Congress had formed. You can learn more about Continental soldiers in A Moment in Time on page 271.

268

◄ In this painting by William Renney, a black soldier helps American forces win an important victory in South Carolina in January 1781.

▼ Deborah Sampson was so eager to fight in the war that she dressed as a man and joined the Massachusetts militia.

Many men enlisted because Congress promised to give them 100 acres of land and 20 dollars in cash if they served in the army for three years. About 5,000 free blacks also joined the Continental Army. Some were slaves who were freed as a reward for enlisting.

Some American women also went into battle. Margaret Corbin accompanied the troop of her husband, John. Like many other women of the time, Corbin did chores for the troops such as cooking and washing. But John Corbin was killed at his wife's side in a battle at Fort Washington, near New York City. Margaret Corbin took over her husband's post and fought until she herself was wounded. Deborah Sampson disguised herself as a man and served in the Massachusetts militia from 1782 to 1783.

On the British side, Britain's soldiers were full-time and well trained. This was their profession. They were well supplied with uniforms and weapons. Britain also hired German soldiers to fight in America. Some Americans who were still loyal to the king also fought for Britain. These **Loyalists** were called Tories, after a group of politicians in England who supported the king. The British army also recruited thousands of American slaves by promising them freedom. ■

■ Name a significant difference between the British and American soldiers who fought in the Revolutionary War.

War Rages in the North

In the first real battles of the war, the British army captured New York City. After that, they attacked Philadelphia. Washington's inexperienced soldiers fought off the British advance. However, the British took control of the city by September 1777. Thomas Paine later said, "These are the times that try men's souls."

Washington led his defeated troops to a camp at Valley Forge, 18 miles northwest of Philadelphia. The general and his weary soldiers spent the icy winter of 1777–1778 in the valley's harsh conditions. Since Valley Forge had no buildings, the soldiers fought the chilling cold to build simple huts.

Their worn-out shoes and clothing were little help against the cold. Worst of all, they had hardly any food. They survived on little but firecake, a thin bread of flour and water. Hundreds died—of starvation, frost-bite, or smallpox. As one soldier complained, "Here all [is] confusion —smoke and cold— hunger and filthiness."

Conditions were truly terrible, yet Washington's strength and determination held his army together. He was a stern leader, but Washington still had the trust and admiration of his men. See page 613 in the Time/Space Databank for more information about Washington.

Indian Strategies

Early in the Revolution, the Indians had tried not to take sides. But in 1777, General John Burgoyne and other British agents met with the leaders of the Iroquois nation. Many Iroquois were angry at American settlers who had taken their land. The Seneca, Cayuga, Mohawk, and Onondaga agreed to help the British.

Though Indian attacks hurt the colonies, Americans learned a valuable lesson from the Indians. During battle, the Indians fought differently from the British. Instead of standing in rows to shoot, they attacked by surprise from behind rocks and trees, then vanished.

Washington had seen the Indians fight during the Seven Years' War. He decided to adopt their hit-and-run strategy. It helped his soldiers stand up to the experienced British army.

British Plans

Iroquois fighters also joined an army in Canada under General Burgoyne. Burgoyne convinced King George that an attack from Canada was certain to end the Revolution. Two other British armies were supposed to meet Burgoyne at Albany, New York. The British hoped to weaken New England by cutting it off from the other colonies.

Because firecakes were cooked over a wood fire, they were often covered with ashes.

Burgoyne told the Iroquois that the rebellious colonists were like bad children who were arguing with their father, King George.

A Continental Soldier

5:56 P.M., September 9, 1781
At the edge of a field, half a mile
from Williamsburg, Virginia

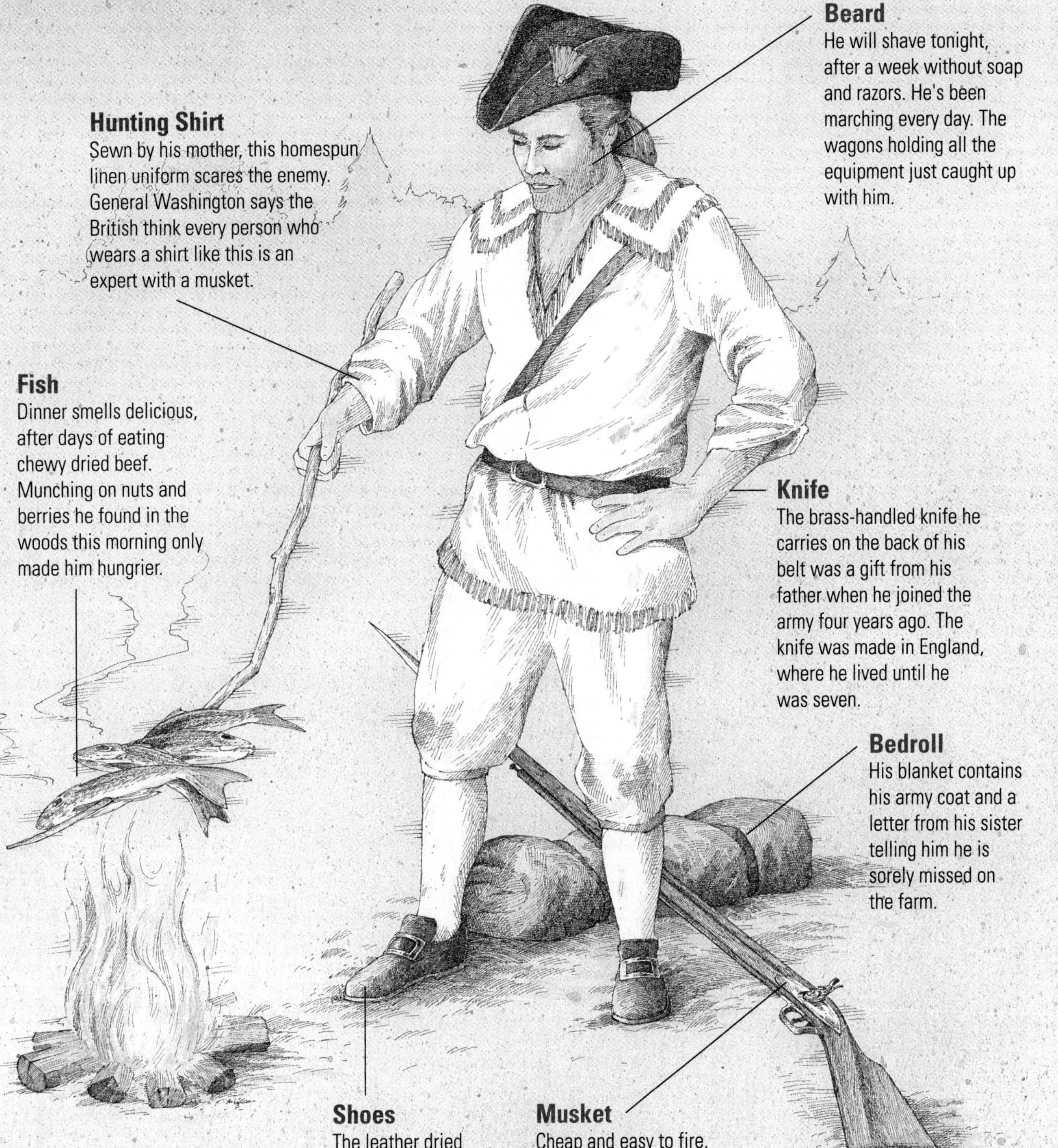

Beard
He will shave tonight, after a week without soap and razors. He's been marching every day. The wagons holding all the equipment just caught up with him.

Hunting Shirt
Sewn by his mother, this homespun linen uniform scares the enemy. General Washington says the British think every person who wears a shirt like this is an expert with a musket.

Fish
Dinner smells delicious, after days of eating chewy dried beef. Munching on nuts and berries he found in the woods this morning only made him hungrier.

Knife
The brass-handled knife he carries on the back of his belt was a gift from his father when he joined the army four years ago. The knife was made in England, where he lived until he was seven.

Bedroll
His blanket contains his army coat and a letter from his sister telling him he is sorely missed on the farm.

Shoes
The leather dried stiff and tight after several days of slogging through the rain.

Musket
Cheap and easy to fire, his musket is fitted with a bayonet for stabbing.

271

Burgoyne's army marched through a wilderness. As the British advanced, New York militiamen shot at them from behind rocks and trees. Near Saratoga, New York, Burgoyne's army clashed with 6,000 American soldiers, led by General Horatio Gates. Burgoyne hoped for help, but the two other British armies never came. After days of fighting, Burgoyne surrendered to Gates in October 1777.

The victory at Saratoga brought the Americans an important ally. The French were still angry that Britain had beaten them in the Seven Years' War. Now the French hoped to weaken Britain by helping its American colonies win their freedom. Saratoga convinced the French that America could win the war. In a February 1778 treaty, the French agreed to send soldiers and ships to fight beside the Americans. ■

■ *What made it possible for the weaker American army to fight successfully against the British?*

▼ *Though the Revolutionary War began in the New England colonies, battles took place in every part of colonial America.*

The War Moves South

After Burgoyne's defeat in the North, the British generals turned south. The British knew that the southern colonies had fewer soldiers than the North. Southern planters were not willing to leave their farms to fight because they were afraid their slaves would revolt. In fact, slaves did join the British. In Virginia, Britain formed an army unit of 600 black men. Britain also received help from the many Loyalists who lived in North Carolina and South Carolina.

As a first step in conquering the South, the British invaded Georgia with 3,500 men. They chose Georgia because of its weak army and large number of Loyalists. The 850 American defenders were outnumbered. In a battle near Savannah in December 1778, the British won control of Georgia.

However, the greatest prize in the South was Charleston, South Carolina. British forces under Sir Henry Clinton surrounded the city with 14,000 troops and 14 warships. They slowly closed in. On May 12, 1780, the more than 5,000 Americans defending the city were forced to surrender. It

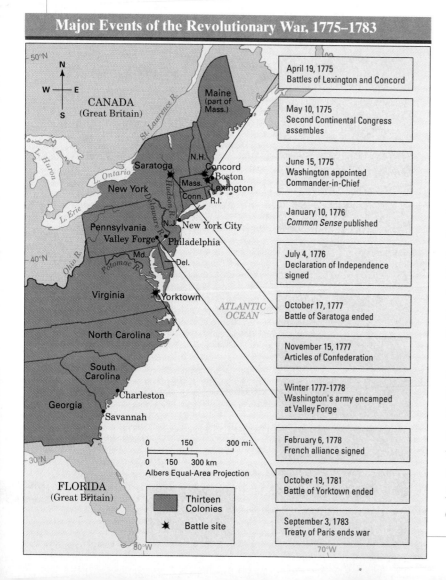

Major Events of the Revolutionary War, 1775–1783

April 19, 1775
Battles of Lexington and Concord

May 10, 1775
Second Continental Congress assembles

June 15, 1775
Washington appointed Commander-in-Chief

January 10, 1776
Common Sense published

July 4, 1776
Declaration of Independence signed

October 17, 1777
Battle of Saratoga ended

November 15, 1777
Articles of Confederation

Winter 1777–1778
Washington's army encamped at Valley Forge

February 6, 1778
French alliance signed

October 19, 1781
Battle of Yorktown ended

September 3, 1783
Treaty of Paris ends war

Thirteen Colonies

★ Battle site

0   150   300 mi.
0 150 300 km
Albers Equal-Area Projection

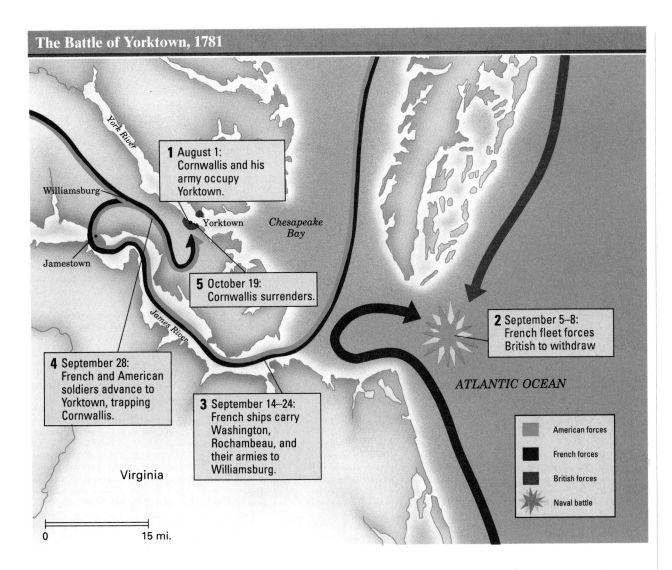

1 August 1: Cornwallis and his army occupy Yorktown.

5 October 19: Cornwallis surrenders.

4 September 28: French and American soldiers advance to Yorktown, trapping Cornwallis.

3 September 14–24: French ships carry Washington, Rochambeau, and their armies to Williamsburg.

2 September 5–8: French fleet forces British to withdraw

York River
Williamsburg
Yorktown
Chesapeake Bay
Jamestown
James River
Virginia
ATLANTIC OCEAN

American forces
French forces
British forces
Naval battle

0   15 mi.

was the worst American defeat of the war.

The Battle of Yorktown

The victory at Charleston convinced the British commander Lord Cornwallis that he could win in the South. In August 1781, Cornwallis moved his 7,000 soldiers into position at Yorktown, Virginia.

George Washington and the French generals had a brilliant plan to defeat Cornwallis at Yorktown. In August 1781, both Washington and French General Rochambeau (roh sham BOH) moved their armies swiftly south from New York. They trapped Cornwallis on the peninsula between the York and James rivers.

Cornwallis looked for help from the British navy. But he could not escape Yorktown by sea because British ships had lost control of the coast. On September 5, French Admiral DeGrasse with a fleet of 28 warships began a fierce naval battle against 19 British ships. For four days, the big cannons on the ships of both navies thundered and boomed in the heavy seas off the coast of Virginia. When a second French naval force arrived, Admiral Graves' British fleet withdrew to New York.

On the morning of September 28, the French and American armies attacked Yorktown. Outnumbered about two and a half to one on land and cut off from the

The geography of Yorktown helped the American and French forces trap and defeat Cornwallis. Compare this battle map with "The Revolutionary War in New Jersey and Pennsylvania, 1776–1778" on page G13 in the Map and Globe Handbook.

273

War Breaks Out

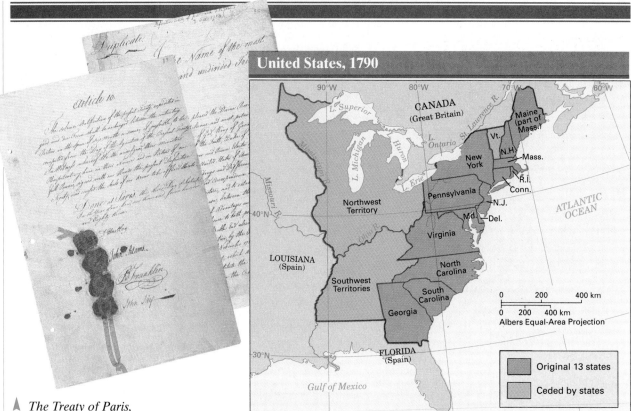

United States, 1790

CANADA (Great Britain)

Maine (part of Mass.)

Vt.

N.H.

New York

Mass.

R.I.

Conn.

N.J.

Pennsylvania

Md.

Del.

Northwest Territory

Virginia

LOUISIANA (Spain)

Southwest Territories

North Carolina

South Carolina

Georgia

FLORIDA (Spain)

Gulf of Mexico

ATLANTIC OCEAN

0   200   400 km

0   200   400 km

Albers Equal-Area Projection

Original 13 states

Ceded by states

The Treaty of Paris, shown above, ended the American struggle for independence from Britain. The map to the right shows the United States after the war. The new states ceded their old colonial land claims to the new government.

■ *Why did the British concentrate their war efforts in the southern colonies after 1778?*

sea, Cornwallis could see that his position was hopeless. On October 19, 1781, he surrendered his army to General Washington.

The Treaty of Paris

The victory at Yorktown won the war for the Americans. In April 1782, Congress sent three Americans—Benjamin Franklin, John Adams, and John Jay—to Paris. There they met with the British and worked out a treaty, or formal agreement of peace. The Treaty of Paris took effect in early 1783 after the American Congress ratified, or approved, it.

Under the treaty, the colonies were given complete independence. The treaty also gave them a great deal of land. Trace the boundaries of the United States after the Revolutionary War on the map above. What natural geographic feature formed the western boundary of the new United States? ■

REVIEW

1. **FOCUS** How did poorly equipped American soldiers defeat Britain's army and win independence for the colonies?

2. **CONNECT** How did George Washington's experiences in the Seven Years' War prepare him to lead America's fight for independence?

3. **GEOGRAPHY** How did George Washington and his French allies use the geography of Yorktown, Virginia, to help them defeat Lord Cornwallis?

4. **CRITICAL THINKING** Why did many African Americans and American Indians choose to fight on the side of the British during the Revolutionary War? In what ways were their reasons similar?

5. **ACTIVITY** Imagine that you are a junior member of General Burgoyne's staff. Your job is to persuade the Iroquois to join the British army. What will you say to the Iroquois?

Organizing What You Read

Here's Why

Learning how to outline helps you to understand and remember what you read. When you outline a lesson, you arrange the facts and ideas from the lesson under main topics and subtopics. Then by reviewing and reading over the outline, you can quickly and easily see the important points of the lesson.

Here's How

The outline on this page shows the main points of Lesson 1. Roman numerals set off the main ideas. A capital letter sets off each subtopic, which is an important point supporting the main idea. Arabic numerals set off the details that support subtopics.

■ main head
■ subtopic
■ detail

Before you begin an outline, look over the material to get an overview. Find the main ideas, important points, and supporting details. In this textbook, the headings and subheadings will help you. Sometimes, though, there aren't a lot of headings in a lesson. To make an outline in such cases, you may need to add your own subtopics based on the content.

Notice how the outline below is arranged. At least two subtopics appear under each main head. If details are listed under a subtopic, there are at least two details.

Try It

Copy the outline onto a sheet of paper. Use Lesson 2 to finish the outline.

I. The first shot is fired
  A. The conflict begins
    1. The battle of Lexington
    2. The battle of Concord
  B. Retreat to Boston
    1. Militiamen fire on Redcoats
    2. Injuries and deaths are many
II. The Continental Congress meets
  A. Preparing for war
    1. Army organized
    2. George Washington named commander-in-chief
    3. Paper money printed to buy weapons and gunpowder
    4. Peace commission formed for the Indians
    5. European support sought
  B. Seeking peace
    1. The Olive Branch Petition
    2. Trade with colonies outlawed
III. The colonists declare independence
  A. Common Sense
  B. The Declaration of Independence
    1. Introduction (Preamble)
    2. Statement of human rights
    3. Accusations against the king
    4. Statement of independence

I. The soldiers who fought the war
  A. The American side
    1. Local militia
    2. _____
  B. _____
    1. _____
    2. Hired German soldiers
    3. _____

Apply It

Outline another lesson from this textbook. Use the sample outline as a guide.

Sybil Ludington's Ride

Erick Berry

Sybil Ludington was a real person and a real hero of the Revolutionary War. Like the militiamen in Lesson 2, she was ready to fight the British.

The American Revolution was fought by famous soldiers like George Washington and ordinary people whose names we don't remember. As you have learned, many of these unknown soldiers were part-time fighters—militiamen—who had to be called together to fight a battle. How were these soldiers notified that they were needed when there was no telephone, radio, or television? Who brought the message to them? Ride with one of those ordinary people in April 1777, as 16-year-old Sybil Ludington makes a nearly 40-mile journey on horseback to deliver the message that "the British are coming."

The pitch-black night closed down like a shutter. There followed a slight struggle. For Star didn't approve of the cold wet night and wanted to return to the comfort of his stable; at least that was what Sybil hoped. But in the darkness it was quite possible she was trying to ride him through the thick trunk of the butternut tree, and to that he quite naturally objected.

No, there was a deeper dark against the black, the tree trunk. And a moment after, Star stumbled into the deep ruts of the road. Left or right? Left of course; the horse protesting only because he felt that any road was the wrong road on a night like this.

The roar of the millstream came clear above the drumming of the rain, and there on the right bulked the shape of the mill.

Jake Hunter's there on the right, she was sure of it. And here was the turn-in. There was a light too, in the kitchen. But had she really come so short a distance? For this wasn't Jake's after all, it was only the Gillettes'.

She rode Star up to the window—it was no matter that he tramped Mrs. Gillette's yarbs—and hammered noisily on the shutter with her fist. The window swung open.

"Father sent me to carry warning," she began politely, as though she were inviting the woman to supper at the Ludingtons'.

"You, gal, at this time of night!" said Mrs. Gillette. "Is aught wrong? Hitch, and come right in."

Sybil took a deep breath and tried again, this time in a firmer tone. "The British are burning Danbury. Tell Mr. Gillette that the troops are to muster immediately. Women and children to bundle

yarbs garden herbs

aught anything
hitch to tie a horse's bridle to a post
muster gather together

up their valuables and be ready to drive off livestock, if the redcoats come this way. And please spread word to your neighbors." That was her full message. She wheeled Star and headed him down the road. She hoped the woman would believe her and take warning.

Only a short ride—Star more willing now—to the Hunters'. The house was dark; could she afford time to waken them? Oh, she must, for he was a corporal in the militia and mighty dependable. But she would remember that the message she brought was military. She reined up, hammered lustily at the shutter, and shouted, "Rouse! Rouse! The British are burning Danbury!" There would be no need here to explain what that meant, what it meant to the whole countryside.

A head came out of a window, and Jake's voice said almost placidly, "That'll mean a mustering."

"And please to tell your neighbors."

She was off again, with growing sense of relief. Jake would know what to do. And she wouldn't have to stop at the next house, a half-mile farther on. Star broke into a canter, and she urged him faster, with the realization of how long it was going to take to deliver each message; even, in the darkness, to find each house. Thank goodness she had changed to trousers; by now her skirts would have been a cold, sodden mass; as it was, the shawl over her head slapped in a wet lump against her chest, carried water like a gutter along her leg; and when in passing it caught on a hanging branch she jerked away, letting it go. Hopeless to hunt for it in the dark, and anyway it was no longer protection. She could scarcely be wetter.

Two more households were wakened without difficulty, and one even remembered to thank her. Then she encountered what threatened to be a failure. Susannah Oppenshore utterly refused to waken her deaf husband.

"There's been a sight too many musterin's," she snapped at Sybil through the half-open window. "And a man's got his duty by his wife and farm. Likely enough it's a false alarm, like all the others."

277

Disgusted, furious with the woman's selfishness, scarce able to believe anyone could be so shortsighted, Sybil tried again.

"But this time the British are at Danbury. We need every soldier—"

"Let the Danbury folk fight them, then," snapped the woman. "And you go right home and quit pesterin' folks."

Sybil, glancing anxiously along the road, desperate to be off again, noted how much clearer the bare trees showed against the sky. What was that glow? Surely not moonrise, with all this rain. She turned to the woman, about to close her window.

"If you don't believe me, ma'am," she said, "look out at the sky there. 'Tis Danbury burning. You can see the glare of it on the clouds. Like enough the redcoats are marching this way even now."

"The redcoats comin' this way?" The woman's anger changed suddenly to fear. She turned to shout back into the house, "Timothy! You there, Timothy! D'you want us all to be burned in our beds? . . ."

Sybil missed the rest of it.

At Carmel settlement she paused to summon only three; one offered to ride on with her. The thought of having a human companion on the lonely dark road was tempting, so tempting. But she told him the route she was taking, the road to the lake, and begged him to spread the alarm east along the highroad. Before she was out of the settlement she heard the raucous clamor of the village bell; it bore her reassuring company for nigh a mile.

Then came a long and cheerless stretch. The yearling's first burst of energy and her own excitement were fading into a dull, dogged purpose. She tried to sing against the pelting rain. Star pricked up his ears and seemed to move more cheerfully.

She patted his neck. "Good boy!" she told him. "I don't know what we'd have done without you. Between us we've roused at least a dozen homes, and each household is spreading the alarm to others. 'Tisn't every yearling, or even full-grown horse, can put fifty or more armed men in the field to fight the enemy." And true it was.

Was the rain really easing? Hard to tell, both she and Star were so wet. But through the dark she could hear the chime of the peepers in the swamp, and once an owl floated past her face, silent as a blown feather. Here, so far from home, she was less familiar with the countryside, and it was fortunate the sky was less dark. As it was, she couldn't spare time to halt at every clearing and search for a house. But those whom she roused promised to carry on the news.

She had by now carried the alarm over eight miles or more of countryside, but that was less than a quarter of the distance she must go. Shivering, she was, with cold and weariness. But how

raucous harsh, rough sounding
nigh almost
yearling one-year-old horse

278

about Star? He was willing enough, but could a yearling, who hadn't yet come to his full growth and strength, stay the whole course?

With almost a shock she realized that she was no longer afraid of him. Not a single trick he had tried to play on the whole ride. It was as though the urgency of her errand was understood by him, as though he knew how much and how many depended on him. On, on, he swept through the night, splashing through deep rain-filled wheel ruts, fording small streams, sure-footed in the darkness. And as she talked to him, "Good fellow. Oh, Star, that was splendid. Careful now, that branch almost swept me off. Here's a bit that's bad . . ." there had grown up between them, young rider and young mount, a sympathy, a comradeship, each understanding the other, each relying on each.

At the next clearing a light already showed in the barn. She splashed up to it, and her voice, hoarse now, delivered her urgent message.

"Danbury, is it?" said the man. "I saw the light and thought as 'twas a house in Carmel burning." He finished saddling up and set down the two buckets he had tied over his shoulder. "I won't be needing these now. Reckon a musket'll be more good against the redcoats' kind of fire."

And on again, the lake glimmering on her right through its thick fringe of trees. And after the lake, someone had told her, she must look for a sharp turn right. She found it, or hoped she had. She should be turning north here, and could judge her direction by the glow in the sky. This was the least settled, most terrifying stretch of the whole route. Here were no big clearings, no farms, no mills or well-built houses. Just a few squatters, trappers, and such living with their families in small ill-built cabins among the thick untimbered forest. And in between, for a mile at a time, the road was no more than a pitch-black tunnel, with trees close-arched above her head. Once Star shied right across the track and nearly brushed her off against a tree trunk. It might be no more than a raccoon or a wandering porcupine; but there had been wolves here, even in recent years, and in wartime when men kept their powder and ball to shoot each other such critters might easily return in force.

With murmurings and a gentling hand she steadied Star to a safer pace, though her instinct urged her to escape at full gallop. "We're important, Star. So much depends on us. If you break a leg or I get swept off and stunned by a bough, the British may catch these people helpless in their beds."

In front of her, for mile after dark mile, lay a sleeping, defenseless countryside. Behind her, kindled by her message, lights had sprung up, hearthfires had been raked to a blaze, lanterns carried at a run to barns, to neighbors lying off the route. Voices called to

squatters persons illegally living on vacant land

279

voices, people were dressing, women packing in haste, men shouting for their arms, for musket and powder horn and bullet bag, and saddling or hasting away on foot. Children, bundled still sleeping from their cots, or the older ones sent on errands, given tasks; this one to help grandmother, that one to catch up the hens in readiness for flight, another to bury the *pewter* in the garden— she could imagine a hundred such happenings.

But before her, nothing but darkness, sleep, unreadiness. No, for there was a glow ahead, more than a houselight. A glow of a firelight through the trees. Soldiers, mustering, perhaps, to march to the Ludingtons', had kindled a small blaze? But it seemed unlikely.

Whoever they were they must be told. She turned Star off the road, headed him in the direction of the bonfire, and left it to him to thread his way between the rocks and undergrowth.

She could see six men or thereabouts. And horses. And, yes, firearms were propped beside the seated men as they warmed themselves at the blaze.

But no man with farming to do would be awake and camped out in the open at this time of night, and the British could scarcely have reached here as yet. But all the same it was relief to see that the men wore no colored uniform. Which made it likely they were militia.

She was near enough now to shout. And was just about to, when a stone turned under Star's hoof and went rattling down a short slope. A man sprang up from the fireside and grabbed his musket.

Sybil jerked tight the rein. The appetizing odor of roast mutton had reached her. And there, slowly turning on a greenwood spit beside the fire, was the best part of a stolen sheep.

Not British, not militia, these men. They were thieves and robbers, *cowboys or skinners*.

Desperately she turned the yearling; and, eyes blinded by the firelight, headed him back into the darkness.

A chorus of shouts. The *cutthroats* were after her.

There was no knowing what these outlaws would do if they caught her. And if they captured her, who would spread the alarm? Her safety, Star's safety, was nothing beside the safety of the whole countryside.

She had a hundred paces' start. Add a few moments while the cutthroats were catching and saddling their horses. If only she could gallop, gallop, lose herself in the darkness.

But here under the thick trees there was no chance even of picking her direction. And at every panic attempt to make for the road, boulders, a stream bed, giant tree trunks, headed her off. Star stumbled and slipped at a scrambling walk. She was lost, but in a moment she was glad of it.

pewter fine metal dishes used in colonial times

cowboys or skinners guerrillas, or independent fighters

cutthroats murderers

For from eastward in the probable direction of the road came the wrathful shout of voices. "Headed south, I cal'late."

"No, north. Or I'd have seen him. You might ha' let him past."

So they had taken her for a man? That was somehow encouraging.

But how lucky that she hadn't got down to the road and been caught between the two lots of skinners. When it served their turn these outlaws murdered as freely as they robbed, and they wouldn't think twice of putting a musket ball into an unlucky witness who had caught them roasting that stolen sheep.

She pulled up Star and waited a moment, listening. The glow of the campfire was out of sight, or perhaps they had quenched it. No sound but the creak of the saddle to Star's wearied breathing; and he, the darling, was listening too, head up, ears pricked. Then she caught a sound, a man's footfall; faint though it was, she was sure of it. Not that she could hear each step. But a stone rolled, a sodden twig snapped. It came no nearer, seemed to retreat.

In the tenseness of her waiting, moments seemed hours; as long as she was silent she was safe. But someone must carry the call to arms; she couldn't wait here till daylight, when the skinners would have moved off. And which way were they going? North or south? If she only knew.

For lack of a better plan she decided to strike east, far enough east to get behind their camp, then head north, and at a safe distance circle, to cut back west to the road. But ten minutes' slow floundering as the yearling heaved himself up one slippery rock, slithered down another, convinced her that she had lost all sense of direction; and the rise of the ground to one side had blotted out any glow from Danbury. Oh, why had she been such a fool as to turn off for that campfire? Even [her sister] Ricky, reckless as she was, would have more sense than that; Ricky, safely at home, tucked in snug and warm under the covers. Sybil almost envied her.

Twice the yearling nearly fell and all but pitched her off in his efforts to recover balance. She dismounted and tried to lead him; that might be easier for Star, but it was harder, a heap harder, for Sybil. Slipping and sliding over wet leaves, wedging a foot between rocks, blundering into tree trunks, she could have cried with sheer fatigue and vexation. And every moment of delay might be bringing the enemy closer, closer; while militiamen, badly needed, slumbered in their homes.

Suddenly, from nearby, came a man's voice. "Who's that?"

One of the cattle stealers, no doubt, thinking he had come across a comrade. She could see the darker shadow in the dimness, and he must be able to see her, for the summons came again.

And more sharply this time. "Who's there?"

She stretched out an arm, as though with a pistol. "Stand, or I fire!"

wrathful angry
cal'late calculate, figure
ha' have

quenched put out

281

cuttin' cross-lots
taking a short cut

gallantly   bravely

"Holy Moses!" in tones of surprise. "That ain't you, Sybil Ludington? It's me, Zeke Cowper, that you roused a while since. I'm cuttin' cross-lots to the other road, to pass on your warning. But cripes above, this is no place for you to be ridin'."

Sybil could have burst into tears with sheer relief. But fearful that his loud, cheerful voice might betray them, she begged him to be quiet and whispered her news of the skinners' camp.

"Once the war's won we'll hang 'em all, skinners and cowboys alike," he rumbled angrily. "But you let me lead your horse and you follow. It's only a step across here to the next road."

Zeke's idea of a "step" was a giant's stride, but they did reach the road at last, a road that lay east of the one she had been following. "Just head north, for Ben Hasbrouck's place," he advised her as he helped her back into the saddle. "Then turn east for Stormville; Ben'll show you." And promised, if he arrived first, to tell her father that, so far, all was well.

Frightened she was now, and she would admit as much, after that meeting with the skinners. It called for all the courage she could lay hand on to ride in off the road and rouse the next farm. At Ben Hasbrouck's, at the turn of the road, they set her on her new direction, and surprised her by telling her it was no later than midnight, when she had thought the dawn itself must be close. But more than half her ride was over; Star, who had gone lame for a while, had only caught a stone in his hoof, and once she had that out, he was striding out as gallantly as before. Never, as long as she lived, would she forget how brave, how helpful he was. If ever there was a good patriot, it was Star this night. Heavens, how tired she was! Every muscle ached, and legs and even arms were bruised from floundering around among those rocks. But strangely enough she had never been happier in her life, though she didn't know it herself till she found herself singing.

A mile or so later and with a good hour's ride still ahead of her, her troubles were already over; someone riding from the opposite direction had already spread the alarm. First there were lighted houses; then there were armed men, in twos and threes, striding on grimly to muster for defense, to fight for freedom. They gave her a shout and some gave her a cheer as Star, spurred on by excitement, galloped past. Soon she was traveling among a little group of horsemen, men who had come from farther west. The group included a woman riding with her husband so she could lead back the much needed team after he joined his regiment.

The procession grew till there must have been a score or more, pounding the road like a troop of cavalry. Inspired by the other horses, excited perhaps by the two or three lanterns, Star threw up his head proudly and stretched his pace. South through Stormville, where a blacksmith's apprentice was still loudly pounding on a wagon tire to spread the alarm, southeast down a road that grew more and more familiar, they swung.

Into the Ludington lane, down past the mill, which had been flung open to shelter those who couldn't squeeze into either house or barn. Constant scurrying to and fro, the rumble of men's voices, the sharp bark of orders from officers: Sybil had seen and heard it all before, but this time she was a part of it. She had received her orders and carried them out like a soldier.

At the gate someone took Star and offered to stable him. Reluctantly she surrendered him. 'Twas like giving up part of herself. "Best rub him down," said Sybil. "He's done a long ride." The gathering at the house door made way for her.

"Here she is, Colonel. Here's your aide, sir." And Father himself threw down his quill and, in full regimentals, rose from the table to greet her and hear her report, just as he would for a soldier. This surely was the proudest moment of her life.

regiment large military troop
score twenty

quill feather with sharpened tip used as a pen
full regimentals military uniform

Further Reading

Johnny Tremain. Esther Forbes. Johnny, a silversmith's apprentice, is caught up in the turbulent and exciting times of Revolutionary War Boston as he mingles with Paul Revere and other heroes.

I'm Deborah Sampson: A Soldier in the War of the Revolution. Patricia Clapp. Deborah Sampson disguised herself as a man and fought for over a year as a soldier in the revolutionary army.

My Brother Sam Is Dead. James Lincoln Collier and Christopher Collier. Tragedy strikes the Meeker family when one son joins the American rebels while the rest of the family tries to remain neutral in a Tory town.

"Paul Revere's Ride." Henry Wadsworth Longfellow. "One if by land; two if by sea"—the midnight ride of Paul Revere is told in an exciting story poem.

L E S S O N   3

Building a New Society

What effect did the Revolution have on Americans who did not fight in the American army?

I long to hear that you have declared an independency. And, by the way, in the new code of laws which I suppose it will be necessary for you to make, I desire you would remember the ladies and be more generous and favorable to them than your ancestors. Do not put such unlimited power into the hands of the husbands. Remember, all men would be tyrants if they could. If particular care and attention is not paid to the ladies, we are determined to foment [stir up] a rebellion, and will not hold ourselves bound by any laws in which we have no voice or representation.

Abigail Adams in a letter to her husband

Key Terms

- civilian
- constitution

When she wrote this letter on March 31, 1776, Abigail Adams was at home in Braintree, Massachusetts. She was busy managing the family farm. Her husband, John, was away at Congress in Philadelphia, arguing in favor of independence.

Abigail Adams was only half-joking when she warned that women would stir up their own revolution if the new government

➤ *Some colonial women ran shops like this one, in which tin pots, pans, and plates were made and repaired.*

did not remember their needs. Although colonial women could hire workers or sell land, they could not own the farms they managed. Women also could not vote.

The Revolution won representation for colonial men. Women's rights were not considered, even though women's efforts helped win the Revolution.

The Home Front

Like Abigail Adams, many colonial women took on new responsibilities during the war. While men were fighting on the battlefront, **civilians**—the people left at home—were struggling with new jobs and with money problems.

A New Role for Women

Many colonial women managed their households alone while their husbands were away fighting in the war. These women still did their traditional work, such as spinning cloth, making clothes, tending the garden and the dairy, and caring for the children and the house. But they also took over many jobs normally done by men. Some women rose at dawn and rode out on horseback to tell farm workers what to do. Others ran businesses, such as flour mills or tailor shops. At first, many men wrote letters home telling their wives what crops to plant and what bills to pay. But as time went on, husbands came to depend more and more on their wives' judgment.

For their part, women got used to making decisions for their families. Like Abigail Adams, they had no wish to return to the time when husbands and fathers had complete authority over their wives and children.

Money Problems

Among the decisions women had to make was how to manage the family's money. This grew more difficult as the war went on. The army bought tons of meat and flour to feed the soldiers. They

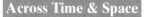
Across Time & Space

In July 1848, Elizabeth Cady Stanton and other women held a meeting at Seneca Falls, New York. Using words similar to those in the Declaration of Independence, the women declared that "woman is man's equal." Like Abigail Adams, Stanton believed that men and women should have the same political rights.

◄ *When the war began, most Americans could afford to buy brown bread at about $1.50 a loaf. After three years of war, a loaf of bread cost $9.50. At that price, few Americans could afford it.*

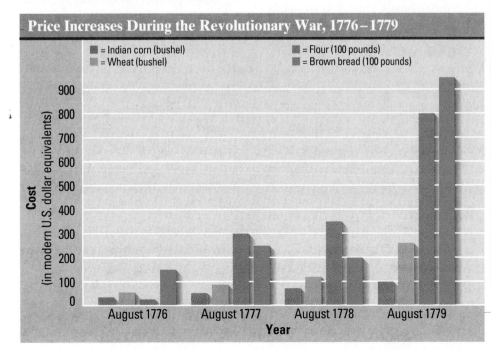

Price Increases During the Revolutionary War, 1776–1779

■ = Indian corn (bushel)   ■ = Flour (100 pounds)
■ = Wheat (bushel)   ■ = Brown bread (100 pounds)

Cost (in modern U.S. dollar equivalents)
August 1776   August 1777   August 1778   August 1779
Year

War Breaks Out

How did the war change the lives of colonial women, and what specific problems did women face?

also purchased large quantities of shoes and clothing. The army's large purchases created shortages of many essential items at home. Women and other civilians had a hard time finding such things as

coffee, tea, and grain to buy. The little that was available was very expensive, and prices rose higher every year. The chart on page 285 shows how quickly and steeply prices went up. ■

The Effects of the War

Women were not the only Americans whose lives were changed by the war. White Americans loyal to the king and African Americans who had fought for the British to gain their freedom often had to begin new lives after the war. Many Indians also lost everything they had as a result of the war.

Loyalists

Not all Americans supported the Revolution. About 500,000 Americans remained loyal to Britain. Some Loyalists were rich officials of the British government. Others had recently arrived in America. Some people who lived in towns the British controlled during the war found it wise to be Loyalists as well. They could buy food more easily if they supported the British.

Many Loyalists were treated badly by supporters of the Revolution. Congress urged the states to take away the property of Loyalists. Some Loyalists went to jail. In Pennsylvania, a person found guilty of persuading someone to join the British army could be fined, imprisoned, or even put to death.

After the war, nearly 100,000 Loyalists left their homes and moved to Great Britain, Canada, and the West Indies. The British

government gave about $20 million to Loyalists to make up for property they left behind in the United States. But most Loyalists were paid less than half of what their property was worth. Many Loyalists did not leave the new United States. They had to learn to live at peace with their neighbors.

Black and Indian Americans

About 14,000 blacks also left the United States after the war. Few got money or other help from

➤ *Some Loyalists were beaten by hotheaded supporters of the Revolution. Others were covered with pine tar and goose feathers and paraded through the streets. The unfortunate supporter of the king, shown in the cartoon on the right, is being insulted by a crowd, which has hung him from a pole.*

the British government. British officials told them that freedom from slavery was payment enough for their service. Some blacks found jobs in England, Canada, and the West Indies. Others joined the British navy. A few returned to Africa. A British company offered transportation to Sierra Leone, a country on the west coast of Africa, and 20 acres of land to any black who would settle there. In 1792, about 1,200 former slaves sailed from Nova Scotia, Canada, to Africa to begin new lives.

Indians who helped the British also had to find new homes after the war. The Iroquois faced an especially hard task. To punish the Iroquois for raids against white settlements, in which they stole horses and cattle and killed settlers, American soldiers burned Iroquois houses. They also chopped down orchards and set fire to fields of ripe corn. By spring 1780, all but two of the Iroquois villages in New York state had been destroyed.

In 1784, the Americans negotiated the Treaty of Fort Stanwix with the Iroquois. The treaty gave the United States all Iroquois land west of New York and Pennsylvania and kept the Iroquois in a small area. ■

■ *In what ways were the effects of the Revolution similar for blacks, Loyalists, and Indians?*

The Pennsylvania Constitution

Now that the war was over, the task of building a new American society could begin. The Revolution won for Americans the right to form their own national government. But what form should the new government take? For guidance, Americans could look to the governments of the 13 new states. Between 1776 and 1780, most states adopted a **constitution,** or formal plan of government.

Pennsylvania's state constitution of 1776 contained many new ideas. It gave the right to vote to all white male taxpayers, not just to men who owned property, as was common in other states. The Pennsylvania constitution also called for annual elections for members of the state legislature. This meant that each year voters could choose representatives who reflected their views and opinions. These ideas show the enthusiasm for a new kind of government—a republic, in which voters had a great deal of power. ■

■ *Name an important new idea in the Pennsylvania constitution.*

R E V I E W

1. **FOCUS** What effect did the Revolution have on Americans who did not fight in the American army?

2. **CONNECT** Abigail Adams warned that women would not be bound by laws that they could not vote to approve. How is her argument similar to the one men made against the British government?

3. **ECONOMICS** How did the war affect the price of flour? Why was this change a problem for women?

4. **CRITICAL THINKING** The Pennsylvania constitution was adopted in 1776, the same year as the publication of Thomas Paine's *Common Sense* and the signing of the Declaration of Independence. What ideas do these three documents share?

5. **WRITING ACTIVITY** Imagine that your father is away fighting. Write a letter to a friend describing how the war has affected life in your family.

Chapter Review

Reviewing Key Terms

civilian (p. 285)   Loyalist (p. 269)
constitution (p. 287)   militia (p. 260)
delegate (p. 262)   republic (p. 268)
equality (p. 264)   revolution (p. 268)
independence (p. 262)

A. Use each pair of key terms in a sentence. Your sentences should show that you understand the meanings of the terms.

1. revolution, equality
2. civilian, independence
3. delegate, constitution
4. Loyalist, republic
5. militia, civilian
6. independence, Loyalist

B. Each newspaper headline contains a key term. Write the headlines on your own paper. Then write one or two sentences that could begin a newspaper article.

1. Revolution Picks Up Speed
2. Join the Militia Today
3. Our Battle for Independence Has Just Begun
4. Citizens Demand a Republic
5. Read About Pennsylvania's Constitution
6. Delegates Gather for Second Continental Congress
7. Civilians Face Problems Keeping the Home Front Going

Exploring Concepts

A. Copy and complete the following cause-and-effect chart on your own paper. The first answer has been done for you.

Cause	Effect
Colonists were tired of heavy taxes and unfair treatment.	The colonists sent a petition to King George III of England.
	Thomas Paine wrote and published a pamphlet called *Common Sense*.
	The French signed an agreement to help the colonists fight the British army.
	Hundreds of Washington's soldiers died at Valley Forge.
	Prices of goods were high and there were shortages of essential items.

B. Answer each of the following questions. Use information from the chapter.

1. What were the differences in how the militia and the Continental Army joined the fight for independence?
2. In what ways did George Washington prove that he was probably the best person to lead the Continental forces?
3. How did the women of revolutionary times show they were able to handle many added responsibilities?
4. By 1775, which side seemed to be winning the war? By 1780, another side seemed to be winning. Explain what happened.
5. What losses did the Iroquois people suffer because of the war?
6. What were some important terms of the Treaty of Paris?
7. After the war, what happened to many Americans who had been loyal to Britain?

Reviewing Skills

1. Read Lesson 3 again. Then complete the following outline on your own paper.

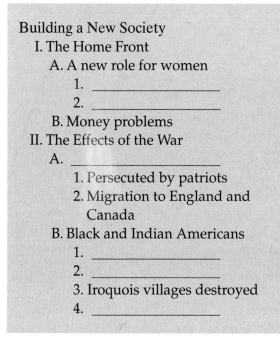

Building a New Society
I. The Home Front
   A. A new role for women
      1. _____
      2. _____
   B. Money problems
II. The Effects of the War
   A. _____
      1. Persecuted by patriots
      2. Migration to England and Canada
   B. Black and Indian Americans
      1. _____
      2. _____
      3. Iroquois villages destroyed
      4. _____

2. Using an organized approach to making an outline helps to organize your thinking. List the suggested steps for making an outline in the correct order.

3. Look at the map on page 273. Is this a large scale or a small scale map? Could you use this map as a general guide in traveling from Valley Forge, Pennsylvania to Yorktown, Virginia? Could you use it to find a particular place in Yorktown? Would you need a map with a larger scale or a smaller scale?

4. Suppose that you need to study for a test covering the battles of the American Revolution. You have to know the date of each battle, where it was fought, the names of the American and British leaders, and what the results were. Your notes include all of this information, but they are not organized. What device could you create to organize the information about the battles?

Using Critical Thinking

1. After the American victory at Saratoga in October 1777, a British leader offered to end the war. He sent a message to Benjamin Franklin saying that Britain would meet most of the American demands. His offer was refused by American leaders. If it had been accepted, what events of the Revolution would not have taken place?

2. The Second Continental Congress set up a commission to maintain peace with the Indians. Yet many Indians joined forces with the Loyalists. Why do you think this happened?

3. Review the ways that France helped the colonists on land and sea. Then tell why you agree or disagree with the statement: "If not for France, we might still be owned by England."

Preparing for Citizenship

1. **ARTS ACTIVITY** Pictures of American flags appear on pages 602 and 603 of your Minipedia. Several of the flags are from the time period you are studying in this chapter. Draw at least two of the flags. Then point out the similarities and differences.

2. **COLLABORATIVE LEARNING** Work to produce a newspaper, *The Revolutionary Times*. Form groups to include writers of news, ads, and columns representing blacks and Indians. Other groups can write Letters to the Editor or draw political cartoons. A managing editor can set deadlines. "Printers" can use typewriters or word processors and then paste up the art. Ask the school office or a copying store for help in making copies.

Chapter 12

Searching for Unity

On July 4, 1776, the American colonies declared their independence, then threw off British rule. After the Revolution, independence became America's biggest problem. The 13 British colonies had become 13 "free and independent states." But they had not become one united nation. In 1783, Americans shared little more than a name and a flag. Many people wondered: Could the states that had defeated the most powerful country in the world unite?

Throughout this time, George Washington was known as the father of the country. First as a general, then as President, Washington was an important leader in the young nation.

We the People

1760	1770	1780	1790

1775

1787 The U.S. Constitution is written. The first words of the document—"We the People"—express the idea that citizens have the power to create a government.

During this period, the eagle became the symbol of America. In 1782, Congress made the eagle the central figure on the Great Seal of the United States.

FIRST in WAR,
FIRST in PEACE,
&
FIRST in the HEARTS
OF HIS
COUNTRYMEN.

1775–1829 Americans become proud of their new nation. This painting, done between 1800 and 1810, shows some symbols of the United States: The flag, the eagle, and George Washington.

1800	1810	1820	1830

1800 The capital of the United States moves from Philadelphia to Washington, D.C.

1828

1760	1770	1775	1787	1790	1800	1810	1820	1830

LESSON 1

Forming a Government

THINKING FOCUS

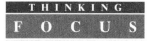

What caused Americans to want a stronger central government after the Revolutionary War?

Key Terms

- federal
- ratify
- township
- legislature

Rachel Budd, her husband, Benjamin, and their eight children moved from Connecticut to the Susquehanna River Valley in 1775 to start a farm. Their story is told in *Sketches of Eighteenth Century Life* by Michel Jean de Crèvecoeur *(krehv KUR)*. In the 1770s, Crèvecoeur traveled the Susquehanna, talking with settlers. Later he wrote about their experiences in his book.

Today, the Susquehanna Valley is part of the state of Pennsylvania. Then, both Connecticut and Pennsylvania claimed the valley as their territory. Pennsylvania sent soldiers to force out the settlers from Connecticut. Rachel explains what happened.

> *My husband, though a most peaceable man, fell victim to these disputes and was carried away prisoner to Philadelphia. We lost all our horses and cows, for in these petty wars these movables are always driven off. I was ready to starve, and ashamed to become troublesome to my neighbors.*

The neighbors' help saved Rachel and the children for eight months, until Benjamin was let go as a part of a deal between the two states. The family then began their farm again. However, as Rachel wrote, "We had no government but what the people chose to follow from day to day." And they never knew when their lives might be disrupted again.

As the chart shows, several states claimed the same areas of land during the 1780s.

Disputed Land Claims in the 1780s

States That Claimed Area	Name of Area Today
Connecticut, Pennsylvania	Northern Pennsylvania
New York, Connecticut, Virginia	Eastern Ohio
New York, Massachusetts, Virginia	Southern Michigan
Connecticut, Virginia	Northern Illinois
New York, North Carolina	Tennessee
Georgia, South Carolina	Mississippi
Georgia, South Carolina	Alabama

The Articles of Confederation

States frequently fought over land or money during and after the Revolution. The Second Continental Congress had no power to settle such fights. Congress knew that it would need national laws to govern effectively. In June 1776, a congressional committee began to draw up a plan.

A National Plan

The plan was called the Articles of Confederation. It required the states to give up some powers to a **federal** government, which had power over all the states.

The states feared an overly strong federal government. So they refused to give up two important powers: collecting taxes and making foreign trade agreements. The federal government had to get its money from the states. Often the states refused to pay.

The Articles of the Confederation gave Congress its own powers. It could declare war, deliver the mail, and sign treaties with American Indians living outside state boundaries. Congress could also settle boundary disputes between states. However, it could not force states to obey its decisions.

Before the Articles of Confederation could become law, each state had to **ratify,** or approve, them. By 1779, all but Maryland had voted approval. Maryland refused to ratify the Articles unless Congress solved a western lands dispute. Colonial charters gave seven states land west of the Appalachian Mountains. Six states,

including Maryland, had no western land. The states were in conflict over the western lands. Maryland wanted them turned over to the federal government. The states that claimed western lands agreed, but only in order to get Maryland's approval. Maryland voted for the Articles on February 27, 1781. The United States had its first official government.

The Northwest Territory

Congress could not raise money with taxes. So it sold some of the land north of the Ohio River and west of Pennsylvania. This land was called the Northwest Territory.

In 1785, Congress divided the Territory into square **townships**

▼ *This historical map indicates in red the names of states formed from the Northwest Territory. You can learn the date each state entered the Union on pages G2–G3 in the* Map and Globe Handbook.

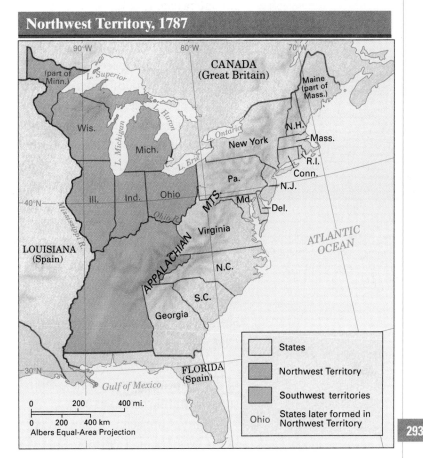

Northwest Territory, 1787

CANADA (Great Britain)

(part of Minn.)
L. Superior
Wis.
L. Michigan
Mich.
Huron
L. Erie
Ontario
New York
N.H.
Maine (part of Mass.)
Mass.
R.I.
Conn.
Pa.
N.J.
Ill.
Ind.
Ohio
Md.
Del.
MTS.
Ohio R.
Virginia
ATLANTIC OCEAN
LOUISIANA (Spain)
Mississippi R.
APPALACHIAN
N.C.
S.C.
Georgia
FLORIDA (Spain)
Gulf of Mexico

90°W   80°W   70°W
40°N
30°N

0   200   400 mi.
0   200   400 km
Albers Equal-Area Projection

Legend:
- States
- Northwest Territory
- Southwest territories
- Ohio — States later formed in Northwest Territory

Searching for Unity

> The Ohio Company bought land under the ordinance of 1785 and laid out plans for cities. The land shown in the northern part of this map was allotted to Wyandot and Delaware Indians.

▼ This photograph of present-day midwestern farmland was taken from a plane. In it you can see roads and fields that still lie along the square lines of sections that were laid out over 200 years ago.

■ In what ways were the states more powerful than the federal government under the Articles of Confederation?

that measured six miles on a side. Each township was divided into 36 sections. Each section measured one square mile, or 640 acres. Organizing the land into townships and sections helped Congress keep track of land sales and ownership in the Northwest. The federal government then sold off the sections for at least $1 an acre.

Few frontier families could afford to spend $640 to buy a whole section of land. Instead land companies often bought many sections of land in a township. Then they sold small plots to individual farmers who moved their families across the Appalachian Mountains. Congress decided that the income from the sale of land in one section of each township should be used to support public schools.

Many American Indians lived in the Northwest Territory. So

Congress passed a law that told settlers to treat Indians with "good faith," and not to try to settle on Indian lands. Another part of the law said no one could bring slaves into the Northwest Territory. Some members of Congress from southern states agreed to this law only because they believed Congress would allow slavery in new lands south of the Ohio River.

Future States

Congress had to decide how to govern its new lands. In 1784, a committee headed by Thomas Jefferson drew up a plan. With some changes, this plan became a law in 1787.

The committee decided that the United States should never have colonies. Instead the committee divided the Northwest Territory into areas that could become new states. A governor and three judges chosen by Congress would govern each area until the number of people reached 5,000 free adult men. Then the men in the region could vote for a **legislature,** a group of people elected to make laws. When the number of people grew to 60,000 free inhabitants, the region could become a state. It had to write a constitution approved by Congress. Look at the Northwest Territory map on page 293. How many states were formed from this land? ■

Money Problems

The sale of land in the Northwest Territory provided some money for Congress, but not enough to pay the government's large debts. By 1789, the nation had a foreign debt of nearly $12 million. Congress had borrowed the money to buy guns, ammunition, and other supplies during the Revolutionary War. Soldiers who had fought in the war had not always been paid. They were now demanding their back pay.

To pay these debts, Congress and many state governments printed paper money during the war. However, as more money was printed, the paper money in use became less valuable. To add to the confusion, many people did not trust paper money and insisted on being paid in gold and silver coins.

A Chain of Borrowing

By the end of the Revolutionary War, the shortage of money troubled everyone. Farmers needed cash more than anyone. State taxes were high, and farmers often had large personal debts as well. Because they had little money, farmers had to buy seed and household supplies on credit. The shopkeepers in turn borrowed from rich merchants to buy more goods to sell. Then, the American merchants borrowed from English merchants. The illustration on this page shows this chain of borrowing. What happened to American farmers in 1785 when a money crisis hit Great Britain?

Shays's Rebellion

Farmers in the western part of Massachusetts had an especially hard time paying their bills. Massachusetts farmers owed about one-third of their income for state taxes, and the Massachusetts legislature refused to issue paper money as other states had done. Those farmers who could not pay their taxes had their farms taken away by state courts. Court officials then auctioned off the farms and used the money from the sale to pay the taxes. Farmers who could not pay their personal debts were often put into prison.

A chain of borrowing linked farmers in Massachusetts to bankers in London.

Chain of Debt

1 The farmer borrows money from a merchant to buy land and supplies.

2 The merchant borrows money from a London banker to lend to the farmer.

3 A financial crisis hits London.

4 The banker demands that the merchant repay the loans quickly.

5 The merchant demands that the farmer repay the loans quickly.

6 The farmer must sell land to raise money.

> ➤ *Soldiers turn back a group of angry farmers led by Daniel Shays in a battle in Springfield, Massachusetts.*

The farmers asked the Massachusetts legislature to lower taxes and let them pay taxes and other debts with farm produce. They begged the legislature to stop jailing people who could not pay their debts. Instead the legislature listened to merchants and bankers to whom the farmers owed money. It refused to pass laws to help the farmers.

Because they could not get help through legal means, a group of farmers decided they had no choice but to rebel. Their leader was Daniel Shays, former Revolutionary War captain. In the fall of 1786, Shays led armed farmers in marches outside county courthouses in Springfield, Northampton, and other towns in western Massachusetts. The purpose was to keep the courts from meeting. If the courts did not meet, bankers and others to whom farmers owed money could not take away their farms.

In January 1787, Shays's men attacked a Springfield building where the government stored guns. The governor of Massachusetts sent soldiers paid for by wealthy Boston merchants to fight the rebels. The soldiers shot and killed four, and soon the rest of Shays's followers fled. Several rebel leaders were caught. These men were brought to trial, found guilty, and sentenced to death. Later the court set them all free, including Shays.

Shays's Rebellion failed. But it made many Americans think a stronger central government was needed to prevent such rebellions in the future. ◼

■ *Why were both the federal government and farmers in Massachusetts in debt after the Revolutionary War?*

R E V I E W

1. **FOCUS** What caused Americans to want a stronger central government after the Revolutionary War?
2. **CONNECT** How did the way Congress planned to govern the Northwest Territory differ from the way Spain and other European countries governed their American territories?
3. **ECONOMICS** What part of the Articles of Confederation made it especially difficult for Congress to pay its debts after the Revolutionary War?
4. **CRITICAL THINKING** Thomas Jefferson defended the farmers who took part in Shays's Rebellion by saying: "A little rebellion from time to time is a good thing." What does this statement mean? Do you agree with Jefferson? Give reasons for your answer.
5. **WRITING ACTIVITY** Imagine it is 1786. Your family may lose its farm in western Massachusetts because of unpaid bills. Write a letter to the Massachusetts legislature to explain why your family is in debt and ask for help.

LESSON 2

The Constitution

Benjamin Franklin had a startling idea. In 1751, 25 years before the Declaration of Independence was written, he suggested that the American colonies band together for defense. No one listened to his idea. Alexander Hamilton also had a similar plan. In 1780, he wrote a friend in Congress from the Revolutionary Army base at Liberty Pole, New Jersey. He begged Congress to call "immediately a convention of all the states" to plan a strong new government. Congress turned down Hamilton's plea that year and again in 1783.

In 1786, Virginia asked the states to send people to meet at Annapolis, Maryland, to talk about the trade problems of all the states. Only 12 men from 5 states came. And they agreed only to ask Congress to call another meeting. Even the 1787 Constitutional Convention in Philadelphia got off to a bad start. Most delegates arrived several days late. Nineteen never showed up at all.

THINKING FOCUS

How did the writers of the Constitution create a strong federal government while protecting the rights of states and individuals?

Key Terms

- compromise
- checks and balances
- separation of powers
- amendment

"The Grand Convention"

Americans had put their trust mostly in local and state governments. But by 1787 many believed that the nation needed a stronger federal government. After saying no to the idea many times, Congress voted for a convention in Philadelphia to change the Articles of Confederation. Newspapers called the meeting "the Grand Convention," but others were not so sure. Of 74 delegates named to the convention by the states, only 55 came to Philadelphia. Rhode Island refused to send anyone.

The delegates who met on May 25, 1787, were mostly rich, well-educated young men. Like Alexander Hamilton of New York, many were lawyers. Like James Madison of Virginia, many had served in Congress. The delegates elected George Washington to lead their meetings. They also voted to keep the meetings secret. This way they could speak freely, without being criticized in public for their views. For more about the convention, see A Closer Look on the next two pages.

Life at the Convention

Fifty-five delegates spent the hot summer of 1787 in Philadelphia drafting a plan to govern their new nation. On September 17, the finished Constitution was read aloud for the first time.

It was hot and sticky in the convention hall. The delegates had to keep the windows and doors closed so no one could hear their discussions. The windows kept in the heat but also kept out big bluebottle flies that were swarming through Philadelphia.

Was the sun rising or setting? During the convention, Benjamin Franklin said he wasn't sure if the sun on the back of George Washington's chair was coming up or going down. "But now at length I have the happiness to know that it is a rising and not a setting sun," Franklin said as he signed the Constitution.

Pennsylvania delegate
Gouverneur Morris wrote most of the Constitution's final wording. He was also the loudest critic of slavery at the convention.

Benjamin Franklin's voice was often too weak to be heard, so he had to write out his speeches. James Wilson, a Pennsylvania lawyer with a thick Scottish accent, read Franklin's words.

A workhorse of the convention, John Rutledge of South Carolina served on five committees. But he was so bossy the other delegates gave him the nickname Dictator John.

At 81, Benjamin Franklin was the oldest delegate at the convention and he was an important and honored figure. Franklin was one of the few delegates who was sad to see the convention end.

Searching for Unity

HISTORY *Although meetings of the Philadelphia convention were secret, we know a lot about what happened there thanks to a diary kept by James Madison of Virginia. In his own system of shorthand, he took notes on everything the delegates said and did each day. Each night he went back to his room and put his notes in final form.*

▼ *This painting by American artist Junius B. Stearns shows George Washington addressing the Constitutional Convention.*

Divided Delegates

The delegates were divided by the different interests of their home states. On May 29, Edmund Randolph of Virginia presented a plan of government that pleased the delegates from large states. Called the Virginia Plan, it outlined a whole new government with three branches, or parts. These were an executive branch headed by a president, a judicial branch with a Supreme Court and Federal courts, and a legislative branch, or Congress. The number of representatives each state could send to Congress would depend on the population of the state. States with large populations supported the Virginia Plan.

On June 15, William Paterson from the small state of New Jersey said every state should have an equal number of representatives in Congress. His idea was known as the New Jersey Plan. States with small populations backed this plan.

The Great Compromise

In June and July of 1787, the delegates argued the Virginia and New Jersey plans. Roger Sherman of Connecticut proposed a **compromise,** an agreement in which each side gets something it wants while giving up something else. Congress should have two houses, Sherman said. To please large states, representation in the House of Representatives should be based on population. To please small states, each state should have equal votes in the Senate. On July 16, the convention agreed.

Another set of compromises ended a conflict between the North and the South. The North agreed that Southern states could include three-fifths of their slaves in population counts to give them

more representatives. The South also agreed to count three-fifths of the slaves in adding up the taxes they would owe. The South agreed that the slave trade would eventually come to an end. In return, the North agreed that Congress would not outlaw the slave trade until after 1808. ■

■ *What argument divided delegates from large states and small states, and how was it resolved?*

Checks and Balances

The Great Compromise had settled how Congress would be organized. Next, the delegates worked to balance the powers of the three parts of government. They wanted to make the legislative, executive, and judicial branches equally powerful. And they wanted to protect each branch from control by the others. To accomplish this, the delegates created a system of **checks and balances.** These were ways each branch could stop, or check, the others. The delegates hoped that this system would keep any part of the government from becoming so strong it could threaten the liberty of citizens.

Look at the chart on this page. Notice how each branch can check the powers of the others. When Congress passes a law, it must be signed by the President. Only then can it can take effect. In this way, the President can check the power of Congress. How can Congress check the power of the President in return?

The delegates also balanced the government by giving each branch

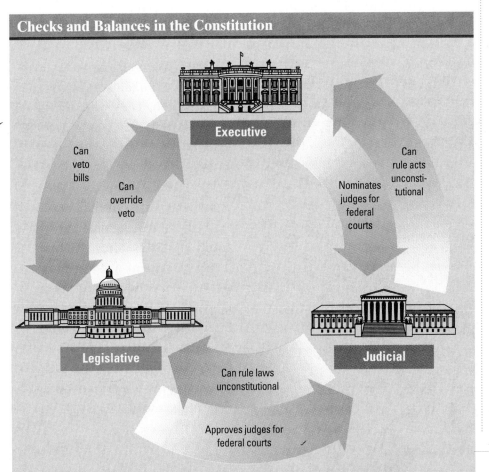

Checks and Balances in the Constitution

Executive

Can veto bills

Can override veto

Can rule acts unconstitutional

Nominates judges for federal courts

Legislative

Judicial

Can rule laws unconstitutional

Approves judges for federal courts

◄ *How does the judicial branch check the actions of the President and the Congress?*

a different job. They called this the **separation of powers.** The legislative branch would make laws that every state had to follow. The executive branch would see that the laws were obeyed. The judicial branch would rule on cases when federal laws were broken.

But who would head the executive branch? Some delegates objected to placing one person in charge. Edmund J. Randolph of

Virginia said one president might be like a king. He suggested three presidents, one from each part of the country. James Wilson of Pennsylvania argued that only a single president could be an effective leader. After much debate, the delegates voted to have one president. After all, they said, George Washington would probably be chosen first. They could trust him to use his power wisely. ■

■ *What are checks and balances, and why did the delegates include them in the Constitution?*

▼ *The first states to ratify the Constitution were Delaware, Pennsylvania, New Jersey, Georgia, Connecticut, and Massachusetts.*

Ratification of the Constitution

Finally, all the debates had been settled. Then, the delegates approved a final draft of the Constitution. Now the governments and people of the states had their turn to argue about the plan. Newspapers printed the whole Constitution. And almost everyone had something to say about its good and bad points. Each state held elections to choose representatives to attend conventions. Nine state conventions had to ratify, or accept, the Constitution for it to become law.

Many farmers and other poor citizens were against ratifying the Constitution. They were afraid that only rich men would become leaders in the new government. They feared that such leaders would ignore the needs of the many who were not rich.

Others were against the Constitution because they feared the new government would be too strong. A too-powerful government might take away people's freedoms. These people wanted the Constitution to have a bill of rights—a list of liberties and freedoms that the government could never take away.

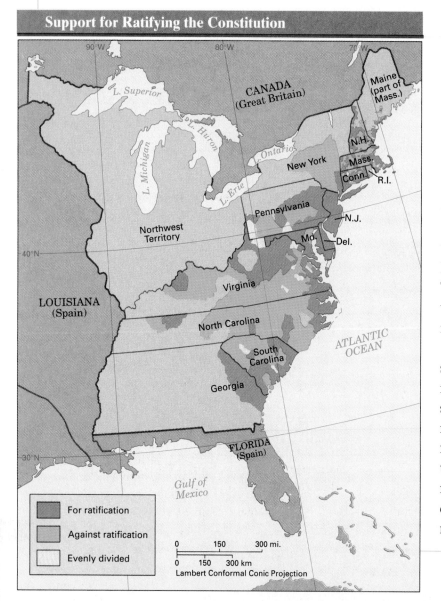

Support for Ratifying the Constitution

CANADA (Great Britain)

L. Superior

L. Michigan

L. Huron

L. Erie

Ontario

Maine (part of Mass.)

N.H.

Mass.

New York

Conn.

R.I.

Pennsylvania

N.J.

Northwest Territory

Md.

Del.

Virginia

LOUISIANA (Spain)

North Carolina

ATLANTIC OCEAN

South Carolina

Georgia

FLORIDA (Spain)

Gulf of Mexico

For ratification

Against ratification

Evenly divided

0   150   300 mi.

0   150   300 km
Lambert Conformal Conic Projection

Another group, including many merchants and wealthy farmers, favored the Constitution. They believed a strong, stable government would pass laws that would benefit their businesses. ■

■ *What arguments did citizens raise for and against the ratification of the Constitution?*

The Bill of Rights

The battle to ratify the Constitution was waged in the conventions held in each of the 13 states. Delegates to these conventions debated many of the same points raised in arguments between ordinary citizens. Six states approved the Constitution quickly. However, other states refused to go along until the Constitution included a bill of rights. James Madison of Virginia, who had worked so hard on the Constitution, was now a leader in the fight for ratification. In 1788, Madison promised that if the Constitution was ratified, he would ask Congress to add a bill of rights. Even with this promise, it took nearly two years for all 13 states to approve the Constitution.

The first Congress under the new Constitution met in March 1789. James Madison was now a representative from Virginia in the House of Representatives. On June 8, he introduced a bill of rights as one of the first items of business. By 1791, all the states had ratified it. The Bill of Rights had become part of the Constitution.

The Bill of Rights is made up of ten **amendments,** statements added to change the Constitution or to make its intentions clearer. Here is the First Amendment:

> Congress shall make no law respecting an establishment of religion, or prohibiting the free exercise thereof; or abridging the freedom of speech, or of the press; or the right of the people peaceably to assemble, and to petition the government for a redress of grievances.

Note that this amendment protects important personal liberties—freedom of religion, freedom of speech, and freedom of the press. Other parts of the Bill of Rights guarantee that people cannot be arrested without good reason and that they have the right to a trial by jury. These liberties are basic to the American way of life. ■

Across Time & Space

The Constitution has been amended only 27 times since it was written 200 years ago. The first ten amendments are the Bill of Rights. Later amendments made slavery illegal and gave black Americans, women, and people over 18 the right to vote.

■ *How did the Bill of Rights satisfy the objections of some citizens to ratifying the Constitution?*

REVIEW

1. **FOCUS** How did the writers of the Constitution create a strong federal government while protecting the rights of states and individuals?

2. **CONNECT** In what ways was the federal government created by the Constitution stronger than the federal government created by the Articles of Confederation?

3. **HISTORY** What issues divided delegates from northern and southern states? How were these differences finally resolved by the delegates?

4. **CRITICAL THINKING** Some delegates objected to having a president because a president was too much like a king. What events in their recent history may have led delegates to make this argument?

5. **ACTIVITY** Imagine you work for a newspaper in 1788. Draw a political cartoon for your paper which illustrates why the Constitution should be approved.

303

Identifying Fact and Opinion

Here's Why

Every day, you must think carefully about the things you hear and read. So knowing how to evaluate, or judge, written and spoken words is an important skill. One way you can do this is by recognizing the difference between a statement of fact and a statement of opinion.

Suppose you were reading a short biographical sketch about James Madison. Being able to distinguish between fact and opinion would help you to evaluate it.

Here's How

A fact is something that has happened or that can be observed. A fact is a statement that can be proven to be true. Proof can come from many sources—direct observation, articles or books, or artifacts dug up by archaeologists.

Read the piece about James Madison and the Constitution. Identify which statements are facts and which are opinions.

The statement highlighted in blue is a fact. Records of Virginia would show that Madison was born there in 1751. Consider this statement: "In fact, he studied so hard that he finished the regular program at the College of New Jersey (now Princeton University) in only two years." This is also a fact, because it can be proven.

An opinion tells what a person feels or believes

College records would indicate when he entered and graduated.

James Madison and the Constitution

James Madison was born on March 16, 1751, at Port Conway, Virginia. He was the oldest of 12 children. As a young man, Madison was an eager student. In fact, he studied so hard that he finished the regular program at the College of New Jersey (now Princeton University) in only two years.

During his college years, Madison developed a keen interest in politics. In 1776, he served in Virginia's first legislative assembly. It was there that he met Thomas Jefferson, who became his lifelong friend. In December 1779, Madison was elected to the Continental Congress. Later, he returned to Virginia, serving in the Virginia Assembly.

James Madison was probably the most important person at the Constitutional Convention. In fact, he is often called "The Father of the Constitution." It was Madison who planned the system of checks and balances. And it was Madison who drafted the Virginia Plan presented by Edmund Randolph. Madison's role as a mediator (MEE dee ay tur), or person who helps to solve conflicts, was equally important. In addition, Madison's *Notes on the Federal Convention* give us a record of the debates that helped to shape the Constitution.

Later, Madison served in Congress. He was Secretary of State under Thomas Jefferson. In 1808, he was elected President of the United States. His wife, Dolley Payne Madison, was well suited for the job of first lady. The writer Washington Irving found her to be charming. He remembered her as having "a smile and pleasant word for everybody."

about something. Opinions cannot be proven. The statement highlighted in green is an opinion. It is true that Madison played a major role at the Constitutional Convention. But the idea that Madison was "probably the most important person there" is an opinion. The statement cannot be proven true or false. Instead, it tells how the author felt about the delegates to the convention. The clue words *probably* and *most important* help you to recognize the sentence as an opinion.

Although opinions can't be proven, they can still be valuable. Learning about the opinions of people from the past helps us to understand why they acted as they did. For example, the strong opinions of many colonists made them willing to fight in the Revolutionary War. It is also important to note that two people, faced with the same set of facts, may form very different opinions. Both opinions can be valuable.

A statement about the opinions of others can be a fact. Look at the last two sentences, about Washington Irving. These statements are facts. You can prove this by reading Washington Irving's

writing in which he refers to Dolley Madison as having "a smile and a pleasant word for everybody."

Try It

Reread the piece about James Madison. Write down the sentences that are facts. Next, tell which sentences express opinions. For each statement of fact, suggest where to look for proof. For each opinion, tell how you know it is an opinion. Be

sure to list any clue words that tell you a statement is an opinion.

Apply It

Find an editorial in your local newspaper. You might want to look for an editorial on a topic that you find interesting. Highlight the facts in one color and the opinions in another color. Circle any clue words that indicate opinions. Did you find more facts or opinions?

LESSON 3

Becoming American

THINKING FOCUS

How did artists, writers, and government leaders help the people of the United States start thinking of themselves as Americans?

Key Terms

- hero
- patriotism

Shortly after George Washington died, Parson Mason Weems published a book about Washington's life. In his book, Weems wrote that when George was just six years old, he chopped down one of his father's cherry trees. When his father sternly asked George if he knew what had happened to the tree, the future first President of the United States replied, "I cannot tell a lie. I did it with my hatchet." Because George bravely told the truth, Weems wrote, his father was willing to forgive him.

Weems's book became quite popular. Soon everyone knew the story of George Washington and the cherry tree. Over the years, many writers and other artists repeated the story. The painting on this page, by the American artist Grant Wood, is one such example.

The cherry tree story and many other incidents in Weems's book never actually happened. Weems added made-up events to the real story of George Washington's life to make Washington seem even more of a hero to the American people than he already was.

➤ *The man drawing back the curtain in this 1939 painting by Grant Wood is Parson Weems. He is pointing to the central character in the story he made up about George Washington.*

New American Heroes

A **hero** is a person who shows great strength, courage, or noble purpose. In the early days of the United States, artists and writers helped to make heroes of people who played important roles in the founding of this country. When these people were featured in stories, paintings, and sculptures, they were portrayed as brave, honest, wise, and smart.

Look at the illustration on this page. It shows a woman known today as Molly Pitcher, although her real name may have been Mary Ludwig. The painting shows Molly taking her fallen husband's place in battle during the Revolutionary War. The story of her heroism was told often and celebrated in American art and literature.

Molly Pitcher was just one of many new American heroes. Some of these celebrated Americans, like Molly, Paul Revere, and George Washington, had acted bravely during the Revolutionary

▲ *Molly Pitcher carried water to the troops during the Battle of Monmouth in 1778. When her husband fell from heat stroke, she took his place.*

UNDERSTANDING HEROISM

George Washington and Molly Pitcher were heroes of the Revolutionary War. Americans have long admired their bravery and courage.

How a Hero Acts

Heroes are people who act bravely in dangerous or difficult situations. Sometimes, but not always, their brave actions take place in war time. During the Civil War, Clara Barton was a battlefield nurse. She continued taking care of the wounded even as cannonballs exploded around her. Clara Barton later founded the American Red Cross.

In this century, Rosa Parks, a black woman from Alabama, became a hero in the struggle for civil rights. She refused to obey the Alabama law that said black people had to sit in the back of the bus. Her refusal eventually led to a change in the law.

Why We Have Heroes

Heroes are an important part of a nation's tradition. They are people we can look up to, people whose brave actions display the best part of the human spirit. Heroes like Clara Barton and Rosa Parks serve as models for all Americans. Their acts of heroism are goals for all of us.

1776, Liberty Bell is rung to celebrate the Declaration of Independence.

1782, Great Seal is adopted

1800, the White House is completed

| 1780 | 1790 | 1800 |

These events and symbols helped create our American identity.

■ *How did the creation of new heroes help people think of themselves as Americans?*

War. Others were political leaders, like John Adams, Benjamin Franklin, and Thomas Jefferson. They had acted bravely by speaking up for American independence from Great Britain.

Poems, stories, illustrations, and statues of famous people like these helped create a strong and positive image of the new Americans. These heroes had been born in America, not England. They helped Americans build new ideas of themselves. Their actions made people proud to be citizens of this new country called the United States of America. ■

An American Way of Life

Everything Americans did—from the way they talked to the holidays they celebrated—was especially their own.

An American Dictionary

Schoolmaster Noah Webster wanted Americans to have spelling books and dictionaries that listed words used by Americans. So he published *The American Spelling-Book* in 1783. It simplified spelling by leaving out the *u* in words like *colour* and spelling *wagon* with one *g*. Then in 1828 he published *An American Dictionary of the English Language.* Words in the dictionary included the names of items found only in this country. Some of these names were American Indian words, such as *wigwam, moccasin,* and *raccoon.* Other words came out of the lives of the American

Webster's dictionary included 12,000 words and 40,000 definitions that had never before been in a dictionary.

1827, John James Audubon publishes *The Birds of America* and shows Americans the beauty of their land.

| 1810 | 1820 | 1830 |

pioneers. These words included *prairie, log cabin,* and *popcorn.*

Webster's dictionary showed Americans that they shared a common and special language. Now they could discover the meanings of unfamiliar words that didn't exist in any other English-language dictionaries. In this way Webster helped Americans to write and talk to each other more easily and clearly.

Holidays and Symbols

The government of the United States helped to bring together the citizens of the new country by choosing national symbols and creating national holidays. In 1777, Congress approved a national flag.

In 1782, Congress chose another national symbol—the Great Seal of the United States. The seal is used on important government documents.

Holidays were also considered important in helping people to feel part of the new nation. In all the states, the Fourth of July was celebrated as Independence Day, recognizing approval of the Declaration of Independence on that day in 1776.

The creation of these symbols and holidays helped to establish a feeling of **patriotism,** or love of country. The American flag and the Great Seal of the United States reminded Americans that they were part of a proud new nation. Americans now all shared a common bond as citizens of a new nation. ■

■ What events or ideas caused a feeling of patriotism to grow in Americans after the Revolutionary War?

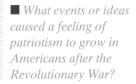

R E V I E W

1. **FOCUS** How did artists, writers, and government leaders help the people of the United States start thinking of themselves as Americans?

2. **CONNECT** What brave deeds or wise political actions were Molly Pitcher and George Washington noted for? What other men and women who took part in the Revolutionary War have become American heroes?

3. **HISTORY** In what ways did Noah Webster's *Dictionary* help unify Americans?

4. **CRITICAL THINKING** George Washington and other early national heroes made Americans feel proud of their country. Think of some national heroes that Americans admire today. What qualities do these heroes share?

5. **WRITING ACTIVITY** Choose a man or woman you think of as an American hero. Write a brief paragraph or two that tells in your own words what you admire about the person you have chosen.

Chapter Review

Reviewing Key Terms

amendment (p. 303)
checks and balances
 (p. 301)
compromise (p. 300)
federal (p. 293)
hero (p. 307)
legislature (p. 294)
patriotism (p. 309)
ratify (p. 293)
separation of powers
 (p. 302)
township (p. 293)

A. Use the following terms in a paragraph about the Constitution.
1. amendment
2. federal
3. compromise
4. checks and balances
5. separation of powers

B. Write *True* or *False* for each statement. Rewrite the false statements to make them true.
1. A legislature tries criminals.
2. A township was one mile on a side.
3. Heroes' brave actions often are inspired by patriotism.
4. The Philadelphia Convention could ratify the Constitution.

Exploring Concepts

A. Fill in the missing information about the Articles of Confederation and the Constitution.

Articles of Confederation
Powers of the States
  1. Collect taxes
  2. _____
Powers of the Federal Government
  1. _____
  2. _____
The Constitution
The Three Branches
  1. Executive
  2. _____
  3. _____
The System of Checks and Balances
  1. President can veto bills
  2. _____
  3. _____
  4. _____
  5. _____
  6. _____

B. Answer each question with information from the chapter.
1. Why couldn't the Second Continental Congress govern effectively?
2. What were the states afraid would happen under the Articles of Confederation?
3. What did Shays's Rebellion accomplish?
4. What were the important points of the Virginia Plan? How was the New Jersey Plan different from the Virginia Plan?
5. What terms of the Great Compromise settled the debate between the Virginia Plan and the New Jersey Plan?
6. How does the separation of powers create a fair government?
7. What were some qualities that people admired in the first American heroes?
8. What were some words that only Americans needed in their dictionaries?
9. How did symbols and national holidays help patriotism grow among the American people?

Reviewing Skills

1. Read the following sentences. On a separate sheet of paper, tell which of the sentences express facts and which ones express opinions.
   a. The New Jersey Plan would have been better for all of the states than the Virginia Plan.
   b. Roger Sherman said that Congress should have two houses.
   c. Of the 74 delegates that were named by the states to attend the convention, only 55 actually arrived in Philadelphia for the event.
   d. By 1787, many people believed that the nation needed a stronger government.
   e. George Washington was the most important person in the colonies.
   f. The land that is now the state of Tennessee was once claimed as territory by both New York and North Carolina.
2. Every one of the delegates to the Constitutional Convention was sure that most of the people really wanted them to change the way the government was organized. Is this statement a fact or an opinion? Explain your answer.
3. Read the paragraph at the top of page 302 about the Constitutional Convention's debate about a head for the executive branch. What opinion did Edmund J. Randolph have about the subject of executive leadership? What opinion did James Wilson express? With which opinion did most of the delegates eventually agree?
4. The Constitutional Convention met in May of 1787 in Philadelphia, Pennsylvania. It was summer in Philadelphia during the convention. What season was it in the Southern Hemisphere at that time? How do you know?
5. If you were asked to explain in a few sentences the main points of a lesson from this chapter, what steps would you follow to do that?

Using Critical Thinking

1. Imagine that the Philadelphia Convention passed the Virginia Plan instead of the Sherman compromise. Which house of Congress would not exist today? How do you think your state's voice in Congress would change? Support your answer with both facts from the chapter and your own ideas.
2. Study the First Amendment to the United States Constitution on page 303. Think about all the rights that the First Amendment gives us. List the ways our lives would change if we didn't have these rights. Add any rights you think may be missing from the First Amendment.

Preparing for Citizenship

1. **COLLECTING INFORMATION** Look through newspapers for articles about the mayor of your city or town. Cut out the articles that show the mayor using the powers of his or her office. Paste them onto sheets of paper. Below each article, tell what official powers the mayor is using. Bind the sheets into your own book entitled, *Our Living Government.*
2. **COLLABORATIVE LEARNING** Plan and present a skit on the argument over whether the United States should have one or three presidents. Work in committees that do these jobs: write the script for supporting one president; write the script for supporting three presidents; perform the speaking parts; make the props.

311

Unit 5

Life in a
Growing Nation

When George Washington became president in 1789 an exciting time in American life began. The people of the young nation were learning to use a new form of government. They were also building cities and exploring western lands. Many Americans set out to turn the rich land into farms. Farm life could be hard, but often it had its rewards. Barn raising parties and fall harvest fairs, like the one shown here, helped Americans celebrate the success of their growing nation.

1763

Artist unknown, Pennsylvania Dutch Harvest Festival, 1853. Courtesy of owner (John Knight).

1860

Chapter 13

Birth of a New Nation

The years following the birth of the new nation were full of new beginnings. Everything was happening for the first time: electing the first president, starting the first political parties, coining the first U.S. money. Slowly the new nation took form. Sometimes people disagreed. Sometimes they even wondered if they would succeed.

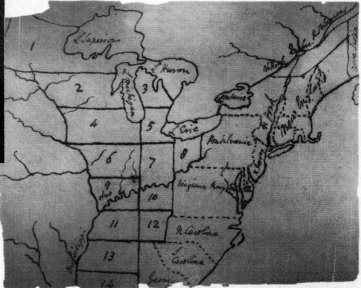

1801–1808 The nation grows during Thomas Jefferson's presidency. Earlier he had proposed a plan for 14 new states (above): 2 was called Michigania and 5 was Metropotamia.

1789 George Washington is sworn in as the first President of the United States.

1780

1790

1800

1788

1793–1795 George Washington does not want his portrait on U.S. coins. Congress uses the goddess of liberty instead.

Throughout this period one-room schoolhouses sprang up as the nation built a system of public schools.

1810

1820

1830

1807 Robert Fulton makes the first successful steamboat voyage.

1824

LESSON 1

Launching a New Government

THINKING FOCUS

How did Jefferson's view of the future of the United States differ from Hamilton's view?

Key Terms

- precedent
- Cabinet
- political party
- Federalist
- Republican

► *People sewed special buttons on their clothes to honor Washington on the day he became president in 1789. Two of these buttons are shown above.*

George Washington became our first president on April 30, 1789 in New York City. Members of Congress discussed what to call him. Your Excellency? His High Mightiness? His Highness, the President of the United States of America, and Protector of Their Liberties?

But Americans had just fought against Britain's king. They did not want their new leader thinking he was like a king. People knew that what they called Washington would set a **precedent,** a model to follow in years to come. Congress finally chose a plain, simple form of address: "Mr. President." It has been used ever since.

Setting Goals at Home

Washington's closest advisers were the men he chose to run the departments of the government. These advisers later became known as the **Cabinet.** One Cabinet leader was Alexander Hamilton, the Secretary of the Treasury. Hamilton was a lawyer from New York. He hoped that the United States would become a land of strong businesses and growing cities. He feared that a weak national government could not keep order.

The Secretary of State, Thomas Jefferson, did not agree with Hamilton. As a farmer, Jefferson thought farmers were "the chosen people of God." He dreamed of a country of farms and small towns. He feared that a strong national government could hurt liberty.

The different views of America caused conflicts between Jefferson and Hamilton. Hamilton wanted a strong national government to help businesses grow. To do this, he thought that the government should set up a national bank. The bank could help businesses grow by lending money to them. Jefferson did not want the bank. Small farmers had little need for it.

Washington asked each adviser to write his thoughts about the bank. Jefferson wrote that the national government should do only what the U.S. Constitution clearly allowed. The Constitution did not speak about a national bank. Thus, Jefferson said, no bank should be set up.

Hamilton took an entire week to prepare his answer. Under the Constitution, he noted, Congress could make all laws that were "necessary and proper" for the United States. He said that a bank was "proper" because it would help the nation grow richer.

Washington finally agreed with Hamilton. The bank opened. Washington thus set a precedent for understanding the "necessary and proper" clause broadly. This allowed the national government to grow more powerful. ■

How did Jefferson and Hamilton interpret the Constitution differently?

Shaping Foreign Policy

Thomas Jefferson and Alexander Hamilton had another important difference. They did not agree on how the United States should act in the world.

In 1789, the French people began a sweeping revolution that led to the overthrow of their king, Louis XVI. France's European neighbors feared that their own people might also revolt. France's neighbors then went to war to defeat the revolutionaries. By 1793, France was fighting several countries, including Britain.

Jefferson thought the United States should help France. The two nations had an agreement of friendship. Also, Jefferson believed that the United States should help the common people of France, who had overthrown an unfair government led by a king.

Secretary of the Treasury Hamilton did not want to help France. He said that the United States could lose its rich trade with

Great Britain if it helped France. Also, the revolution in France was the kind of fighting by common

▼ *This etching of the first Cabinet shows, from left, Henry Knox, Thomas Jefferson, Edmund Randolph, Alexander Hamilton, and George Washington.*

➤ *How do you know that the print showing the French Revolution was done by someone critical of the revolution?*

■ *How did Americans view France's revolution?*

citizens that worried Hamilton. Revolutionaries had killed many people who were against reforms. Among those killed were the king and queen of France.

At first many Americans agreed with Jefferson. They supported the revolution in France. People remembered how France had helped them win independence. They thought it was America's turn to help France. Also, the enemy was Great Britain again. Many Americans still did not like Britain.

Washington, though, agreed with Hamilton. He felt that the young nation was too weak to fight Britain. The United States did not help France. This decision set another precedent. The United States would stay out of wars in Europe. ■

Forming Political Parties

▼ *Campaign posters and political cartoons are tools that people use to sway opinion about an issue or perhaps a person. The campaign poster of 1804 on the right is favorable toward Thomas Jefferson. The political cartoon of 1807 on the left compares him unfavorably with George Washington.*

Washington won a second term in 1792. He feared that political fighting was destroying the nation. Yet by 1796, the nation was even more sharply divided. Washington's belief in Hamilton had turned many of his old friends into bitter enemies. In a letter printed in a newspaper, Thomas Paine attacked Washington.

A s to you sir . . . the world will be puzzled to decide . . . whether you have abandoned [given up] good principles, or whether you ever had any.

Washington decided not to run again. The race for president became a contest between people with different goals for the United States. Like Jefferson, most small farmers and workers

LOOK ON THIS PICTURE, AND ON THIS

HERE IS

THIS WA?

REPUBLICANS
Turn out, turn out and save your Country from ruin !

From an *Emperor*—from a *King*—from the iron grasp of a *British Tory Faction*—an unprincipled banditti of British speculators. The hireling tools and emissaries of his majesty king George the 3d have thronged our city and diffused the poison of principles among us.
DOWN WITH THE TORIES, DOWN WITH THE BRITISH FACTION,
Before they have it in their power to enslave you, and reduce your families to distress by heavy taxation. Republicans want no Tribute-liars—they want no ship Ocean-liars—they want no Rufus King's for Lords —they want no Varick to lord it over them—they want no Jones for senator, who fought with the British against the Americans in time of the war.—But they want in their places such men as
Jefferson & Clinton,
who fought their Country's Battles in the year '76

wanted a weak national government. They wanted common citizens to take part in government.

Like Hamilton, most merchants and rich landowners wanted a strong national government. They believed it would keep order and help business to grow.

Federalists and Republicans

People set up groups, now called **political parties,** to support their favorite candidates. Hamilton's friends formed the **Federalist** party and helped John Adams run for president.

Jefferson's friends formed the **Republican** party and helped Jefferson run for president. This party is not the same Republican party as today. Rather, Jefferson's party later became what is now the Democratic party.

The Sedition Act

Adams defeated Jefferson in the 1796 election. In 1798, Congress tried to stop the Republicans from attacking Federalist policies. They passed the Sedition Act, which punished people who spoke against the government. Benjamin Franklin's grandson was one of those thrown into prison by Federalist actions.

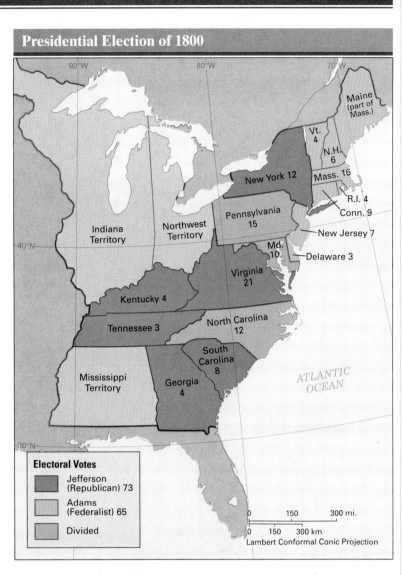

Presidential Election of 1800

Electoral Votes

- Jefferson (Republican) 73
- Adams (Federalist) 65
- Divided

Lambert Conformal Conic Projection

He died in prison. But the Sedition Act did not unite the country. The United States still had two parties for the next presidential election. In 1800, though, Jefferson won. Could he bring the people together? ■

▲ *Which regions of the country voted for Thomas Jefferson?*

■ *How did Federalists and Republicans differ?*

R E V I E W

1. **FOCUS** How did Jefferson's view of the future of the United States differ from Hamilton's view?
2. **CONNECT** Compare the Sedition Act and the First Amendment.
3. **POLITICAL SYSTEMS** What did Jefferson think the phrase "necessary and proper" meant?
4. **HISTORY** Explain whether Washington acted more like a Federalist or a Republican.
5. **CRITICAL THINKING** Today, the federal government helps farmers by lending them money at a lower cost than banks do. How do you think Hamilton and Jefferson would view this program?
6. **WRITING ACTIVITY** Pretend you are either a Federalist or a Republican candidate for Congress in 1800. Write a one-minute campaign speech. Explain why people should vote for your party's candidates.

319

L E S S O N   2

Jefferson and National Unity

THINKING FOCUS

How did the people of the United States become more strongly united in the early 1800s?

Key Terms

- nationalism
- impressment
- War Hawk
- Monroe Doctrine

➤ *Jefferson was the first president to begin his term in Washington, D.C. The unfinished capital city symbolized just how new and undeveloped the entire nation was in 1800.*

N o guards, no coach, not even a horse waited at the door for Thomas Jefferson as he left his rented room in Washington, D.C. He wore no powdered wig and carried no sword. His clothes were simple. He looked like any other citizen out for a walk.

The tall, red-haired Virginian tried to keep his shoes clean as he strolled up muddy New Jersey Avenue. A few friends walked with him. Some soldiers from Maryland pulled a cannon down the street— the only sign that Jefferson was on important business.

When Jefferson reached the north wing of the unfinished Capitol, he entered. There he promised to serve honestly and well as the third president of the United States.

A New Party Takes Power

Jefferson's simple taking of office matched his Republican view of government. Jefferson favored the common citizen and would govern in a simpler manner than Washington and Adams. He would select advisers for their support of his ideas. Federalists worried. Under Jefferson, they warned, the country would be governed by "the worthless" and "the dishonest."

The Federalists did not need to worry. Jefferson did not throw out what the Federalists had done. He tried to bring the country together. "We are all republicans," he said as he took office. "We are all federalists." During Jefferson's two terms as president, people in the United States began to feel a growing sense of **nationalism,** of belonging to a certain country.

Peace across the seas was harder to achieve than peace at home. In 1803, Britain and France went to war again. Each country wanted to stop the United States from trading with its enemy.

UNDERSTANDING NATIONALISM

In the early 1800s, people in the United States began to feel that their country had become a nation. They came to recognize that they belonged to a common culture and shared certain interests. The feeling of being part of a nation is called nationalism.

Some people confuse nationalism with patriotism—a very positive feeling about a country. Patriots often feel that their country is the best one in the world.

Nationalism and Nations

Nationalists often feel that everyone who shares the same language, customs, and values should live under one government. In the late 1700s, the region where the Poles lived was divided into areas controlled by German, Russian, and Austrian rulers. In 1918, the Polish areas were combined to form the nation of Poland.

At other times two groups that have very different cultures may live in one country. For example, the country of Pakistan was formed in 1947. It joined the Muslims who had lived in the extreme east and west of British India. The people of East and West Pakistan shared the same religion, but they differed in many other ways. They spoke different languages and had many different customs and traditions. In 1971, the eastern part of Pakistan broke away and formed the nation of Bangladesh.

Nationalism and Heroes

Heroes help build nationalism. They remind people that they share many values. George Washington and Thomas Jefferson are two of America's most popular heroes. They helped lead the 13 colonies to declare their independence in 1776. People called the new country the United States. But only later, when nationalism developed, were the states truly united.

■ *What trade problems did the United States have under Jefferson?*

Britain and France each caught hundreds of American merchant ships and stole their goods. In bold acts called **impressment,** the British carried off thousands of American sailors and made them work in the British navy.

These British and French acts made Americans angry. In 1807, Jefferson stopped U.S. trade with all countries. He hoped to make Britain and France respect the rights of U.S. ships.

Yet this act hurt the United States more than it hurt Britain or France. Buildings filled up with goods that could not be sold. James Madison, elected president in 1808, opened trade again with all countries by 1810. ■

A Second War with Britain

Madison, like Jefferson, was a Republican from Virginia. And like Jefferson, he did not want war. But British attacks went on. Also, Britain was giving guns to the Shawnee Indians. The Shawnee were attacking U.S. settlements on Shawnee land in the territories of Indiana and Michigan. On June 18, 1812, Congress, led by a group called the **War Hawks,** declared war on Britain. Study the map on this page. Can you tell where the major battles happened?

For two years, the war was evenly fought. Then, on August 24, 1814, British soldiers stormed into Washington, D.C. They set fire to the Capitol and the White House. In just hours, the buildings were wrapped "in one sheet of fire." Fear swept the city. Madison, his wife Dolley, and the people of Washington fled into the country.

▲ *Dolley Madison took key government papers as she fled the burning White House in 1814.*

➤ *The large map shows all major battles in the War of 1812. The small map shows the Great Lakes battles.*

Across Time & Space

Two weeks after the treaty ending the War of 1812 was signed in Europe, U.S. troops under Andrew Jackson defeated the British at New Orleans. Because travel across the ocean was slow, troops had not heard about the treaty. Today, our news crosses oceans in seconds.

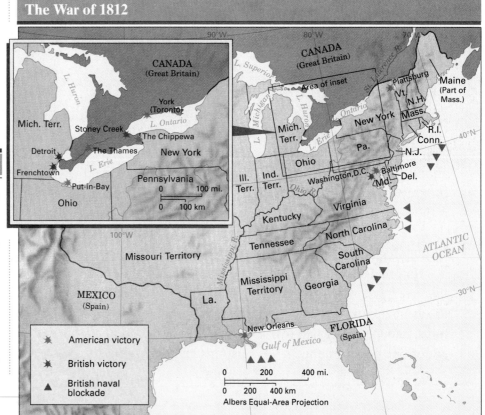

The War of 1812

American victory
British victory
British naval blockade

Albers Equal-Area Projection

In six months, the Americans drove the British off the Atlantic coast. With no victory in sight for either the British or the Americans, a peace treaty was signed in December 1814. A final battle at New Orleans in January 1815 ended the War of 1812. ■

■ *Why did the United States go to war against Great Britain?*

A Rise in Nationalism

At first, the War of 1812 split the United States. Many New England Federalists did not want the war. Some even said that New England should leave the country.

Yet fighting together helped to unite the country. The war reminded Americans that they shared many values. After the war political battles died down. The Federalist party almost died out. In the 1816 presidential election, Republican James Monroe won easily. One newspaper even claimed that the election began an "Era of Good Feelings."

While nationalism grew in the United States, the Spanish holdings in the Americas were falling apart. Between 1791 and 1822, most Spanish lands in the Americas became free. Monroe feared that Spain, or France, might take over these new nations. He did not want Europeans to hold land in America.

In 1823, James Monroe warned European countries to stay out of the Americas, or risk war with the United States. In return, the United States would stay out of European business. This statement, now called the **Monroe Doctrine,** showed the growing strength of the United States. ■

▲ *This flag flew over Fort McHenry, Baltimore, in the War of 1812. It inspired Francis Scott Key to write the "The Star Spangled Banner."*

■ *What was the Era of Good Feelings?*

◄ *How does this carving show national pride?*

U. S. Custom House, 1805.

R E V I E W

1. **FOCUS** How did the people of the United States become more strongly united in the early 1800s?
2. **CONNECT** How was Jefferson's action on trade similar to the British action on Boston trade just before the Revolutionary War?
3. **CITIZENSHIP** Define and give examples of the idea of nationalism.
4. **GEOGRAPHY** Why would merchants in New England be less likely to support a war against Britain than would people in other regions?
5. **CRITICAL THINKING** Explain whether or not you think the United States had a right to issue the Monroe Doctrine.
6. **WRITING ACTIVITY** Write a newspaper story from a Federalist viewpoint describing Jefferson's inauguration in 1801.

L E S S O N 3

Economic Life of the New Nation

THINKING FOCUS

How was the economy of the United States changing between 1788 and 1824?

Key Terms

- surplus
- textile

The farmer's wife, and a young woman who looked like her sister, were spinning, and three little children were playing about. The woman told me that they spun and wove all the cotton and woollen garments of the family, and knit all the stockings; her husband, though not a shoe-maker by trade, made all the shoes. She manufactured all the soap and candles they used, and prepared her sugar from the sugar-trees on their farm. All she wanted with money, she said, was to buy coffee [and]tea. . . .

These words, telling of an early Ohio farm, were written by Frances Trollope, an English woman who lived in the United States in the 1820s. Trollope was interested in how farm families grew or made most of what they needed. The farmer's wife "seemed . . . proud of her independence." But she told Trollope sadly:

Tis strange to us to see company: I expect the sun may rise and set a hundred times before I shall see another human that does not belong to the family.

Agriculture and Trade

The Ohio family made most of what it needed. What they did not make, they got by trading with neighbors. Many frontier families lived on such farms.

Changes in Agriculture

Farming across the United States was changing, however. More and more farmers produced a **surplus.** That is, they raised more than they needed for themselves. Farmers usually loaded their extra flour, pork, or other goods on wagons and took them to nearby towns to sell. Soon, however, some farmers began to grow fewer crops. Instead of growing everything they needed, these farmers raised only one or two crops. They grew crops they could sell for cash. They began to depend on the money they received.

An Increase in Trade

Farm families had made most things they used. With more money, however, they could afford to buy more goods. As they bought things, they made work for shoe-makers and other skilled workers. They created a need for factory-made goods like **textiles**—cloth made from cotton or wool.

Farmers in each part of the country grew different crops. In the south more and more farmers raised cotton, especially after 1820. In the middle states such as Ohio, Indiana, and Illinois, more farmers only grew corn and raised hogs. So much pork was shipped through Cincinnati that people called it "Porkopolis." On a walk through Cincinnati one day, Frances Trollope came across a brook that she described as "red with the stream from a pig slaughter-house."

Growth of Port Cities

By 1820, farmers were selling more of what they grew. As sales went up, port cities such as New York and New Orleans became busier.

Cotton, wheat, flour, beef, and pork were the main goods farmers were able to sell.

New inventions made trade easier. Before 1807, shipping goods down the rivers was easy. However, boats going up the rivers, against the current, moved slowly. In 1807, Robert Fulton developed the first steam-powered boat that worked well. Steamboats went upriver much faster. Fulton's new steam-powered boat went about five miles per hour.

The steamboat made it possible for trade on the river to increase. This helped a number of port cities grow more rapidly. A Closer Look on the next page tells you more about port cities. ■

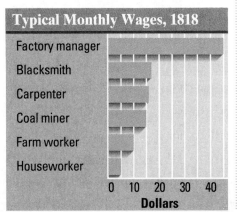

Typical Monthly Wages, 1818

Factory manager	
Blacksmith	
Carpenter	
Coal miner	
Farm worker	
Houseworker	

0 10 20 30 40
Dollars

■ *How was farming changing in the early 1800s?*

◄ *As the chart shows, monthly wages in 1818 were low compared to today, but so were prices. Some everyday items are shown below. Bread flour was 3 cents per pound; nails, 9 cents per pound; candles, 15 cents each; and coffee beans 16 cents per pound. Most cloth sold for about 16 cents a yard.*

New York Harbor, 1830

By 1830, the nation's busiest port was a forest of ship masts. Dock workers busily loaded ships with American farm products and unloaded cargo from as far away as China. Auctioneers stood on sugar barrels, shouting at the merchants who crowded the docks.

Forty cents of every dollar earned on cotton fell into the hands of New York's merchants. In 1830, they made almost $12 million! Captains stowed America's number-one export wherever they could, sometimes even using a bundle or two as a table.

Apples, cheese, and grain from the U.S. heartland made their way to Europe from northeastern ports like New York.

Belgian lace was just one of the luxury items merchants eagerly awaited on the docks. The next ship might be carrying silk and tea from China, sharp knives from Britain, or fine wine from France.

Southern tobacco, America's number-two export, left New York for European markets. Ships returning from Europe carried manufactured goods like tools and clothes. Some ships carried people, too—tourists who enjoyed every shipboard luxury, and immigrants crammed into the ship's smelly hold.

South Street, New York, on the East River

Clothes for cloves: that was the swap between the United States and the East African island of Zanzibar. Trading spicy cloves for American cloth was so successful the African term *merikani* (American) came to mean cotton goods or blankets.

327

Birth of a New Nation

Wealth and Inequality

The changes in farming caused other changes in the economy. Though most people still lived on farms, the number of people in business was growing. And as trade grew, so did the number of very wealthy people in the nation.

One of the richest merchants in America in the 1790s was the first person in the United States to own $1 million worth of property.

In the early 1800s, workers used wooden plates while wealthy people could afford beautiful plates imported from China.

■ Why did economic differences among Americans increase in the early 1800s?

Elias Derby. He lived in the booming port city of Salem, Massachusetts. His three-story mansion had 15 rooms. It was filled with French carpets, satin-covered furniture, and marble tables. Derby was

The Growth of Poverty

As trade grew, people moved to cities looking for work. As cities grew, the prices of food and housing went up. Workers with little money suffered. The number of poor people in cities grew.

The South also had many very rich and very poor people. Though most people in the South were small farmers who owned no slaves, a few whites owned large plantations. These rich families lived in large homes and owned hundreds of slaves.

A New Problem for America

The growth of trade caused a problem for the United States. As merchants and plantation owners got richer, many workers, both free and slave, got poorer. Was the United States still a land of equality, as promised in the Declaration of Independence? The people had to decide what kind of country they wanted to become. ■

REVIEW

1. **FOCUS** How was the economy in the United States changing between 1788 and 1824?

2. **CONNECT** Explain why Alexander Hamilton would support the changes occurring in the United States between 1788 and 1824.

3. **CITIZENSHIP** How did the growth of trade challenge one traditional idea about citizenship?

4. **ECONOMICS** Why would the middle states have greater equality than would port cities or the South?

5. **CRITICAL THINKING** Think about how the economic changes discussed in this lesson would influence the relationships among people. Explain whether these changes would make people in the United States more or less closely united with each other.

6. **WRITING ACTIVITY** Imagine you were an English citizen reading Frances Trollope's book just after it was written. Make a list of five questions you would like to have her answer about life in the United States.

LESSON 4

Everyday Life in the Young Nation

"Y ou will never have a correct idea of what a wilderness is till you come to visit me," wrote Elias Pym Fordham from Cincinnati, Ohio, in 1818. He went on, saying:

T o be at an unknown distance from the dwellings of man . . . and then to lie at night in a blanket, with your feet to a fire, with your rifle hugged in your arms, listening to the howling wolves, and starting at the shriek of the terrible panther: This it is to be in a wilderness alone.

The nation had thriving cities as well as rugged frontier areas. Many people liked the cities best.

Anne Royall visited Philadelphia in the 1820s. In telling about her trip, she wrote:

T he profusion [large amount] of merchandize which lines the streets and windows is incredible. Dry goods are strewed [spread out] along the side-walks, near the store doors; flannels, cloths, muslins, silks. . . . But it is at night that the wealth and splendor of Philadelphia appears to the best advantage; the windows being lighted with numerous lamps and gas-lights, which, with the lamps in the streets, and the luster [light] of the glittering wares in the windows, present a scene of astonishing beauty.

THINKING FOCUS

How did daily life in the young republic change from 1789 to 1824?

Key Terms

- camp meeting
- common school

Changes in Religion

As the United States grew, people developed different ways of life. The differences between the frontier and the city were just one kind of difference. The nation also had people of many religious

groups. Most immigrants were Christians from Europe. However, they brought several different beliefs to the United States.

Most settlers from Britain were Congregationalists, Quakers,

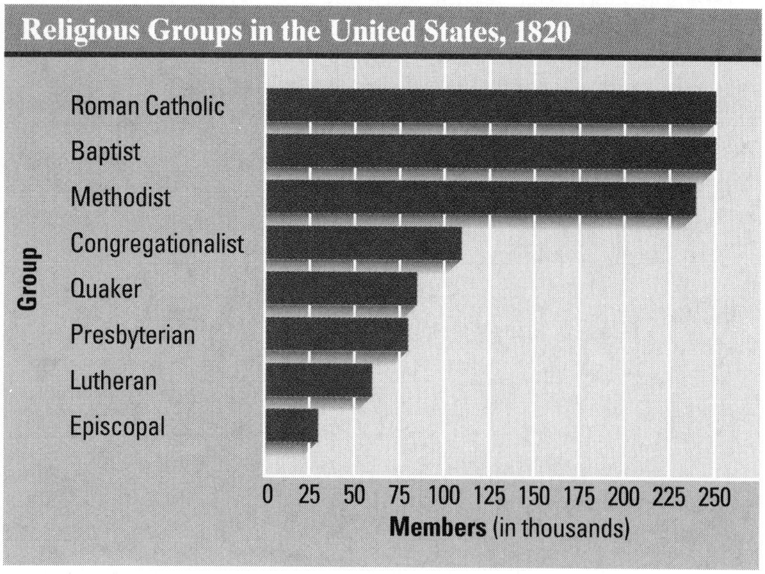

Religious Groups in the United States, 1820
Group
Roman Catholic
Baptist
Methodist
Congregationalist
Quaker
Presbyterian
Lutheran
Episcopal
0 25 50 75 100 125 150 175 200 225 250
Members (in thousands)

This chart shows some of the largest religious groups in the United States. Dozens of smaller groups also existed.

or members of the Church of England. Shortly after the Revolutionary War, members of the Church of England in the United States decided to break away from the English church. They formed the Episcopal Church.

Many settlers from Scotland were Presbyterians. They followed the teachings of John Knox, a Scottish religious leader in the 1500s.

Many people from Sweden and northern Germany were Lutherans. This group got its name from Martin Luther, a German religious leader of the 1500s. Most settlers from southern Germany and from Ireland were Roman Catholics.

In the United States, people worshiped in different ways in the early 1800s. In cities and towns, most people attended churches. In many small villages and in fields on the edges of towns, though, men and women held huge prayer meetings, or **camp meetings.** These were more like rallies than quiet church services. Preachers gave thunderous sermons. People shouted and sang hymns. Many rolled around on the ground in excitement.

Baptists or Methodists led many of these camp meetings. The Baptists had a long history in America. One of the first Baptists in America was Roger Williams. Williams founded the colony of Rhode Island in the 1630s.

The Methodists got started 100 years later. They followed the teaching of John Wesley, an English clergyman who had preached in Georgia in the 1730s. ■

■ *Why was religious diversity growing in the United States in the early 1800s?*

Growth of the Free Black Community

Most American settlers had come from Europe. But the new nation also had many people who traced their roots to Africa.

How Blacks Became Free

In 1820, about one-eighth of all blacks in the United States were free. Some had won freedom by serving in the army during the Revolutionary War or the War of 1812. A few owners let their slaves work for money and then buy their freedom. Many saved enough to free their whole family.

Some slaves were freed by their owners. George Washington gave his slaves their freedom in his will. Other slaves escaped and moved north, but they lived in daily fear of being discovered.

How Blacks Lived and Worked

Several thousand free blacks lived in northern cities. In these cities they were not as likely to be

Paul Cuffe became a wealthy merchant in the early 1800s.

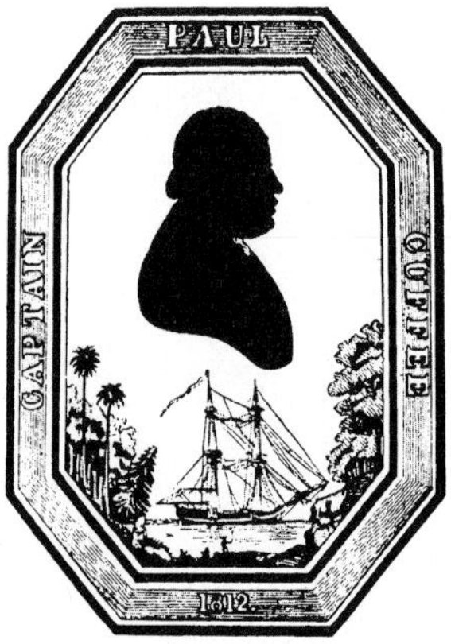

PAUL
CAPTAIN
CUFFEE
1812

kidnapped into slavery. But, free blacks faced hardships in the north and in the south.

In the north, blacks suffered from unfair treatment by whites. Few blacks were hired for high-paying jobs. But some free blacks became skilled workers, such as shoemakers and mechanics. Black women often worked as house servants. Some made a living by sewing. Black men often worked as laborers, hotel porters, waiters, and sailors.

Benjamin Banneker was one of the most successful free blacks. He was born near Baltimore in 1731. Although mostly self-taught, for a short time he attended a small private school for both black students and white students. In 1791, he helped to survey the city of Washington, D.C. Banneker was a skilled astronomer. He also printed his weather predictions in an annual book.

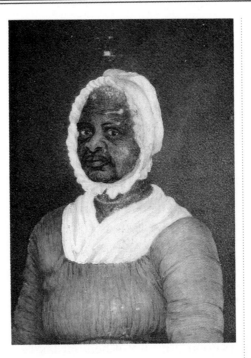

◄ Elizabeth Freeman was a slave in Massachusetts. But after she was beaten, she left the family and won her freedom in a court case.

Black Churches

Blacks wanted to worship in their own ways and resented sitting in separate pews in white churches. In the 1790s, they began to form their own churches, which helped the sick and needy and taught reading. Church music was influenced by their African heritage. ■

■ *How were the lives of most free black Americans different from those of white Americans?*

◄ Lemuel Haynes was the minister of a mostly white Congregational church in Vermont.

331

Changes in the Family

Family life in the new republic also was changing. Since colonial times, women had been responsible for raising large families–only one of their many responsibilities. During the Revolutionary War, many women took over the family farm or other businesses while their husbands were away fighting.

Raising Children

After the war, women were also expected to raise their children as good citizens. "When our land is filled with virtuous and patriotic mothers," wrote clergyman John Abbott, "then will it be filled with virtuous and patriotic men." As patriotic mothers, women were expected to teach their children the values of hard work and pride in their country.

The mother's role in the family became more important in cities and towns. The needs of trade and business often took men to jobs away from the home. As men worked outside the home, they spent less time with their children.

Earning Money

Even life on the farm was changing. Farmers made less of what they needed and more of what they could sell. Money became more important on the farm. To bring in money, daughters in farm families sometimes worked as servants in other people's homes. Other women made money sewing clothes or making brooms, hats, or other items for sale.

Women had time for such things, as families became smaller. In one town, the common family of the mid-1700s had nine children. By the early 1800s, the town's average family had six children. The same change happened in many towns. Farm families, though, stayed large. ■

▲ *Toy animals such as this sheep were popular with children in the early 1800s.*

■ *How did the lives of farm women in the United States change as commerce developed?*

HISTORY *One source of information about how women ran farms is the set of long letters between John Adams and his wife. John was away on government business most of the time between 1778 and 1800. Abigail successfully ran the farm and raised the children.*

➤ *This painting was done around 1800. How does it show the different roles of men and women in the family?*

Growth of Public Schools

For children, life was also changing in other ways. Public schools were one-room buildings called **common schools.** Students of all ages and abilities studied in the same room:

> The boys in the writing class were scratching away busily in their copy-books. In the corner by the fireplace Jonathan's big brother, Andrew, was working over his arithmetic, setting down his figures on a large piece of birch bark. And the smallest children were standing in a straight row before the new schoolmaster, saying their spelling lesson.
>
> Enid LaMonte Meadowcroft,
> *By Wagon and Flatboat*

Not all children attended common schools. Children from rich families often went to private schools. And many children who lived on farms had to work rather than go to school. Farm families needed all hands in the fields during harvest season.

The first common schools were started by settlers in New England. They opened schools soon after arriving in America. Then, in 1787, the Northwest Ordinance set up a way to pay for schools in all the territories. As the settlers moved to the west, they set up new schools. Public schools soon gave people great pride in their nation.

People hoped that schools would do more than teach students how to read, write, and do math. They wanted schools to make young people into good citizens. ■

▲ How is this spelling book from the early 1800s different from the books you use in school today?

■ What were schools like in the United States in the early 1800s?

R E V I E W

1. **FOCUS** How did daily life in the young republic change from 1789 to 1824?

2. **CONNECT** Study the picture of Washington's cabinet shown on page 317. How were the people in the president's cabinet unlike the people of the United States as a whole in 1788?

3. **CITIZENSHIP** Think about the differences between the North and the South. Why did thousands of free blacks live in northern cities?

4. **ECONOMICS** How did changes in the economy influence the role of men and women as parents?

5. **CRITICAL THINKING** Why do you think the followers of the Church of England became Episcopalians shortly after the Revolutionary War?

6. **WRITING ACTIVITY** Write a letter to send to an imaginary student living in the United States in 1800. Describe your own school today and explain some ways that it differs from the schools of the past.

Using Cluster Diagrams

Here's Why

Diagramming is a good way to organize and remember information. One kind of diagram is called a cluster diagram. A cluster diagram looks something like a wheel. The main idea of the diagram is in the middle. Details are placed around the main idea like the spokes of the wheel. Cluster diagrams are very helpful because they center your attention and make summarizing easier.

In Lesson 1 you read about how Alexander Hamilton and Thomas Jefferson tried to help George Washington build a new nation. You also learned that Hamilton and Jefferson strongly disagreed about many government policies. One way to arrange and summarize their political views is to build two cluster diagrams, one for Hamilton and one for Jefferson.

Here's How

In the cluster diagram below, pieces of information are connected to the figure in the middle. What can you learn at a glance from this cluster diagram?

The first step is to note the subject of the cluster diagram. The center identifies the person or main subject of the diagram. What is the subject of this diagram?

Next, note the different categories. The categories in this diagram state Alexander Hamilton's political party and his positions on the French Revolution, government, and economics. Look at page 316, paragraph 5. Find information that explains why the phrase "large, strong federal" was given as a detail under Government. Then find the material on pages 316 and 317 that explains placing the phrase "Manufacturing and trade; national bank" in the economy category.

Now copy the cluster diagram below on a separate sheet of paper. Finish the first category in the diagram by finding the name of Hamilton's political party on page 319. Finish the second category by turning to pages 317 and 318 and finding a description of Hamilton's ideas on the French Revolution.

Alexander Hamilton

1 — Political party

2 — French Revolution

Government — Large, strong, federal

Economy — Manufacturing and trade; national bank

Thomas Jefferson

(Handwritten labels on the diagram circles: "Republic" on circle 1; "Hep gham" on circle 2; "Small limited government" on circle 3; "Farming" on circle 4.)

What other categories might be added to the cluster diagram about Hamilton?

The diagram can help you to arrange and remember information about Hamilton. Without looking at it, try to see the diagram in your mind. Then tell what you know about Hamilton.

Try It

Look at the cluster diagram above. Thomas Jefferson is the subject.

Copy the cluster diagram onto a sheet of paper. If you are comparing Jefferson's views to those of Hamilton, what should the four categories used in this cluster diagram be?

Write one category on each line. Then look through the material on pages 316, 317, and 319. Find the information to finish each of the categories. Try adding new categories to the diagram to increase the amount of information it contains.

After you have finished your cluster diagram, take a good look at it. Then turn your paper over. Try to picture your diagram. Without looking at your diagram, tell a classmate what you know about Thomas Jefferson.

Look at the cluster diagram about Hamilton and the diagram about Jefferson. How do the ideas of these two great men compare? What is one example of a subject on which they do not agree? Explain how comparing the two diagrams gives you a clearer idea of how Hamilton and Jefferson thought.

Now make your own cluster diagrams about other leaders mentioned in Chapter 13. Select George Washington, James Madison, or James Monroe.

Apply It

Cluster diagrams can help you arrange information about people who are living today. Pick a favorite political candidate or movie star. Maybe a candidate for student council would make a good subject for a cluster diagram. Think about what makes that person special and what things and ideas represent him or her. Build a cluster diagram that shows these important points.

If you choose a student council candidate, try using his or her stated beliefs about the office as the categories. Be sure to include his or her ideas about the duties involved with the office. Then find out about the other candidates running for the same office. Make a cluster diagram for each candidate. Use his or her stated beliefs in the same way as you did on the first diagram. Share your cluster diagrams with your classmates. Ask them to explain what they can tell about the candidates for student council from your cluster diagrams.

Chapter Review

Reviewing Key Terms

Cabinet (p. 316)
camp meeting (p. 330)
common school (p. 333)
Federalist (p. 319)
impressment (p. 322)
Monroe Doctrine (p. 323)
nationalism (p. 321)

political party (p. 319)
precedent (p. 316)
Republican (p. 319)
surplus (p. 324)
textile (p. 325)
War Hawk (p. 322)

A. Each of the following words is related in some way to one of the key terms. Write the correct key term next to the words on the list below.
1. unified
2. sailor
3. extra
4. religion
5. weave
6. advise
7. pattern

B. Some of the following statements are true. The rest are false. Write True or False for each statement. Then rewrite the false statements to make them true.
1. Most Federalists were workers and common citizens.
2. A War Hawk favored declaring war on Britain in 1812.
3. A common school had only one classroom for all its students.
4. Republicans wanted a weak national government.
5. The Monroe Doctrine helped schools.
6. As farmers became more efficient, they produced a surplus of crops.
7. Each political party supported a candidate in the 1796 election.

Exploring Concepts

A. Write one or two sentences to answer each of the questions below.
1. Did the growth of nationalism reduce the influence of one political party? If so, which one and why?
2. What groups of people benefited from the growth in commerce? Which groups were harmed by it?
3. Who did the Northwest Ordinance help to educate, and how?
4. What feeling brings together people who share the same culture?
5. Which two men in particular debated the course of America's future?
6. What groups of people outside the United States were affected by the Monroe Doctrine?

B. Write whether you agree or disagree with each of the following statements. If you disagree, give your reasons.
1. The early settlers in the wilderness felt safe in their new land.
2. Immigrants brought many different religious beliefs to the United States.
3. The only role of women in colonial America was to cook and care for children.
4. Some blacks served in the army and thus earned their freedom.
5. Benjamin Banneker was one of many well-known, successful blacks in 1790.
6. With the growth of commerce, the fathers' role in families began to change.
7. Camp meetings were a quiet time for Americans to think about religion.

Reviewing Skills

1. Use the cluster diagram on this page to answer this question: Why was Cincinnati called "Porkopolis" in the 1820s? Then think of an "-opolis" name for your hometown. Make a cluster diagram that illustrates why the name you created is a good one for your town.

2. Reread pages 324–333. Make one cluster diagram with "wilderness" in the center and another with "city." Make your webs compare everyday life in those two places.

3. Choose one of the groups of immigrants referred to in Lesson 4. Then find information about the history of this group in America by looking in an encyclopedia. List the name of the encyclopedia and the volume number. Write down the title of the article you found. Then write two facts from the article.

4. Imagine that you lived in the United States in the 1800s. How would you organize and present facts about the changing American economy in order to explain it to someone from another country?

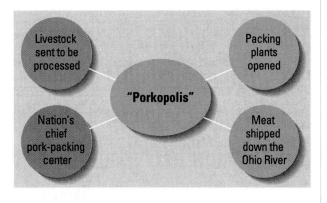

Using Critical Thinking

1. Alexander Hamilton wanted America to become a nation of merchants. Thomas Jefferson thought it should stay a nation of farms and small towns. What do you think your life would be like today if America had not become an industrial country?

2. Thomas Jefferson stated, "Difference of opinion is advantageous in religion." Many present-day immigrants bring different religions to the United States. What are the advantages of this to the communities where the immigrants live?

3. Nationalism developed in the United States after the War of 1812. Fighting in a war often strengthens people's sense of nationalism. Why do you think this happens?

Preparing for Citizenship

1. **INTERVIEWING** Interview the principal of your school. Ask him or her how the local government helps pay for the school's expenses. Present the results of the interview to the class.

2. **GROUP ACTIVITY** Meet with a small group of classmates. Discuss why a Boston newspaper claimed that the presidential election of 1816 started an "Era of Good Feelings." Do you think our country is living in an era of good feeling today? Present your main points to the class.

3. **COLLABORATIVE LEARNING** Each group of four students should choose a popular TV program about a family. The group will write and perform a scene using the characters from that show but placing them in the United States of the early 1800s. Work together to write a scene that will take four or five minutes to perform. Assign one person to play each character. Show how the family members of 200 years ago behaved differently from those on the present-day program.

Chapter 14
Moving West

Throughout this period, tens of thousands of people poured through the Cumberland Gap in the Appalachian Mountains.

Even before America won its independence, settlers were pushing west of the Appalachian Mountains. Americans found adventure and opportunity in these new lands. Many dreamed of building a better life by starting over in places like Kentucky and Tennessee. One minister even declared: "Heaven is a Kentucky of a place!"

1803 The United States buys the Louisiana Territory from France for $15 million. The new land, shown in the map above, doubles the size of the young country.

1750	1775	1800

1763

1804–1806 Meriwether Lewis and William Clark explore the land west of the Mississippi River. Lewis is shown above with a page from a book about their trip.

1800–1832 Most settlers travel to new homes on the frontier in sturdy covered wagons.

1825

1850

1875

1832

L E S S O N   1

The Moving Frontier

THINKING FOCUS

Why did pioneers move to settlements across the Appalachian Mountains?

Key Terms

- pioneer
- ordinance

➤ *Daniel Boone started the movement west by building the Wilderness Road through the rugged Cumberland Gap. This statue of Boone shows him as a young man wearing an animal skin hat. It is generally believed that Boone never wore a coonskin cap.*

When the men gathered around the campfire, Daniel Boone always had an exciting story for them. He might tell about the time he was trapped by stampeding buffalo. He couldn't outrun the herd, so he aimed his rifle at the lead buffalo. He killed it with a single shot. Then he used the body as a shelter as the herd thundered past.

Or he might tell about the day a band of Shawnee closed in on him with tomahawks raised. He was on the edge of a cliff. The only way to escape was to jump, so he did. Luckily, he landed in the branches of a tree.

The Shawnee admired Daniel Boone. So did the men around the campfire. They were quite proud to ride with the greatest woodsman on the frontier.

In 1775, Boone led about 30 frontiersmen into the Appalachian Mountains. They went to build the

Wilderness Road, a narrow trail winding through dense forests and steep mountain passes. The road opened the lands west of the Appalachians to settlers. It led to a region known as "Kentucky," a Cherokee word meaning land of tomorrow. During the next 20 years, thousands of settlers would travel this road to reach the frontier and start a new life.

To the men and women who followed him west, Daniel Boone stood for boldness, courage, and the restless spirit of adventure. Some Americans feel the same way about him today.

> *W*hen Daniel Boone goes by, at night,
> The phantom deer arise
> And all lost, wild America
> Is burning in their eyes.
>
> Rosemary and Stephen Benét,
> *A Book of Americans*, 1933

The Appalachian Frontier

Daniel Boone first reached Kentucky in 1769. During the next few years, Boone led several groups of **pioneers,** or early settlers, to Kentucky. He later bragged that his wife Rebecca and their daughters were "the first white women that ever stood on the banks of the Kentucky River."

The region Boone explored was part of a huge territory. It stretched from the Great Lakes in the north to the Gulf of Mexico in the south, from the Appalachians in the east to the Mississippi River in the west. Trace the outline of this territory on the map on page 342. What present-day states were part of this area?

France claimed most of this land before 1763. The French were only interested in the furs they could take from the region. French hunters and trappers roamed the forests and paddled up rivers in search of beaver, deer, bear, and other animals.

Control passed to the British after the Seven Years' War. The British knew that white settlers wanted to move west. They also knew that the Indians would resist any white settlers who tried to live on their land.

In an effort to keep the peace, the British passed a law called the Proclamation of 1763. It said that the lands west of the Appalachians belonged to the Shawnee, Cherokee, and other Indian peoples who were already living there. The Proclamation ordered colonists to keep out of these specified lands. ■

How Do We Know?

HISTORY *Daniel Boone became a legend in his own time. In 1784, a pioneer named John Filson wrote a book called* The Discovery and Settlement of Kentucky. *The book contained exciting accounts of Boone's adventures.*

■ *Who owned the lands west of the Appalachians in the 1700s?*

Early Pioneers

The Proclamation of 1763 did not stop frontiersmen like Daniel Boone. It didn't stop the pioneers who followed, either. People crossed the Appalachians for many reasons. Some wanted cheap land for farming. Others were running away from bills that they couldn't pay. Some were running away from the law. All hoped the frontier would be the answer to their dreams. "Heaven is a Kentucky of a place!" one minister told his church members.

Look at the map at the bottom of the page. Trace the path of the Wilderness Road that Daniel Boone built in 1775. During the late 1700s and early 1800s, thousands of pioneers moved west along this road. The Wilderness Road was not a smooth, wide highway. It was a narrow, rocky trail. The trail was barely wide enough for a horse. To learn more about the special skills of frontiersmen like Daniel Boone, see A Moment in Time on the next page.

Across Time & Space

Some of the early pioneer roads later became highways for automobiles. The route Boone took up Moccasin Gap and across the Clinch River in Virginia is now U.S. 58. In Kentucky, Boone's men cut through thickets and blazed what is now Interstate 75.

➤ How many states were carved out of the Old Northwest? How many were carved out of the Old Southwest? The map's compass rose helps you to see how these territories were named. To learn more about directions on a map, see page G4 in the Map and Globe Handbook.

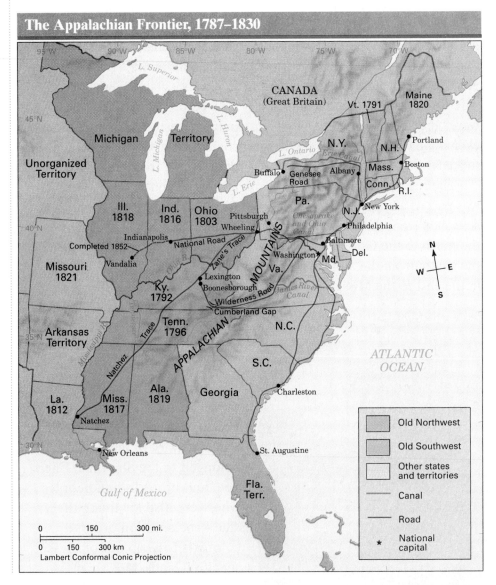

The Appalachian Frontier, 1787–1830

Old Northwest
Old Southwest
Other states and territories
Canal
Road
★ National capital

0   150   300 mi.
0   150   300 km
Lambert Conformal Conic Projection

A Frontiersman

5:48 p.m., October 21, 1785
Overlooking the Auglaize River, between the
present-day cities of Dayton and Toledo, Ohio.

Shirt
The roomy chest pocket of his shirt holds a bit of deer jerky. It tastes good with the dried squash his wife packed when he began his 200-mile journey 18 days ago.

Eyes
Sharp-eyed from years of hunting, he spies a tree with a twisted branch. This "road sign" lets him know he's just a three-day canoe ride from the Shawnee village he seeks.

Buckskin Jacket
His sturdy coat protects him from thorny branches along the densely wooded trail.

Shot Pouch
When he's ready for supper, he'll reach into his pouch to get shot for his rifle. He's learned to be careful not to cut his finger on the needle he uses to repair his moccasins.

Leather Bag
Inside is the compass that led him due west into Indian territory. The bag also holds a gift of salt the Indians will prize and a bone wedge he'll use to strip bark for a canoe.

Leather Rifle Case
The Indians he trades furs with gave him this treasured gift. He thanked them in the Shawnee language he learned as a child in Pennsylvania.

Rifle
With this weapon, he'll "bark" a squirrel for supper tonight. When he shoots the part of the tree right next to the squirrel, the impact will kill the animal without tearing up its body.

Moccasins
He stuffed his homemade shoes with dry leaves against the morning chill.

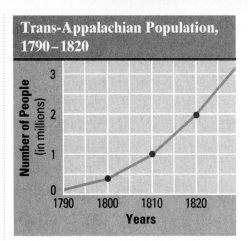

Trans-Appalachian Population, 1790–1820

Number of People (in millions)

Years

A trip over the Wilderness Road could be hard. The pioneers packed pots and pans, bedding, seed, and tools. They had to walk, but nothing could stop them. In 1775, there were only 150 pioneers living on the frontier west of the Appalachians. By 1810, the population of that same frontier area had reached a million.

As settlers moved to the frontier, Indians saw their land and their culture under constant attack. They lost more and more land each year. They tried to work out treaties with the settlers, but the treaties never lasted very long. The settlers were willing to buy land, but they would take it if they could not buy it. The situation got worse. As settlers poured in, Indians were forced to move farther west. ■

The Northwest Ordinance

As settlers moved west, the U.S. government had to decide how to organize the territory west of the Appalachians. Kentucky became the nation's 15th state in 1792. Tennessee became the 16th state in 1796.

The lands north of the Ohio River needed some kind of government. In 1787, Congress passed the Northwest Ordinance. An **ordinance** is a law. The Northwest Ordinance established a way that territories could be created. Each territory could become a state once the white population reached 60,000. The ordinance guaranteed freedom of religion for the area, and it outlawed slavery. In addition, it promised to use "the utmost good faith" in protecting the rights of the Indians.

The days of the hunter and trapper in the area were drawing to a close. The frontier was moving west once again. ■

R E V I E W

1. **FOCUS** Why did pioneers move to settlements across the Appalachian Mountains?

2. **CONNECT** As settlers moved west, the U.S. government had to govern a faraway territory. In what ways was this task similar to the problem facing the British government as it tried to rule its American colonies in the 1770s? What methods did each government use?

3. **ECONOMICS** How did the needs of new settlers conflict with the needs of Indian tribes already living in the territory west of the Appalachians?

4. **CRITICAL THINKING** As more settlers crossed the Appalachians, the Indians were forced to move to hunting grounds farther west. What do you think happened as settlers also moved farther west?

5. **WRITING ACTIVITY** Suppose you were a pioneer traveling with your family along the Wilderness Road to Kentucky. Write a letter to a relative back East telling about your adventures.

LESSON 2

Life on the New Frontier

Rain was falling when the Fowlers left Pittsburgh, but Amy Fowler didn't mind. She was excited. She, her parents, and her seven brothers and sisters were bound for a new life.

The Fowlers' flatboat was one of a dozen going west that rainy April morning in 1788. The other boats belonged to Amy's aunts and uncles. They had come from central Pennsylvania to Pittsburgh, where they bought the flatboats. Now they were drifting down the Ohio River, headed for Kentucky.

Everything the Fowlers owned was on the deck of the 40-foot boat: clothes, a wagon, a horse, even a cow. The Fowlers had stretched cloth above the deck to provide shelter from storms.

Amy was only 10 years old, but she had to help her mother with the cooking and laundry. All the work was done on the boat, because the family feared unfriendly Indians and wild animals on shore. It was a risky two-week journey down the river. But the Fowlers braved the dangers to begin a new life.

THINKING FOCUS

What was life on the new frontier like for settlers in the early 1800s?

Key Terms

* tributary
* canal

◄ *In 1788, the Fowlers traveled down the Ohio River on a flatboat similar to this. Over 500 boats went down the river that year. They carried about 20,000 pioneers, 8,000 horses, 2,400 head of cattle, 1,000 sheep, and 700 wagons.*

345

Moving West

River Routes and Trails West

■ *What were the two main ways of travel for pioneers heading west?*

The Fowlers were just one family out of thousands who floated down the Ohio River to the frontier between 1780 and 1820. Rivers were major routes for people moving west.

Many pioneers chose to travel on the Ohio River or one of its tributaries. A **tributary** is a small river that flows into a larger one. Pioneers who wanted to go to Tennessee, for example, could take the Cumberland, a major tributary of the Ohio River.

In the 1820s and 1830s, workers dug a number of **canals,** or waterways, to connect rivers and lakes. The Erie Canal, for example, was finished in 1825. It joined the Hudson River to the Great Lakes. The canals encouraged even more pioneer movement.

Other pioneers traveled west by land. Many walked Daniel Boone's Wilderness Road to Kentucky and Tennessee. Others took Zane's Trace from what is now Wheeling, West Virginia, to Maysville, Kentucky. Later others took the National Road. It ran through Ohio and Indiana to Vandalia, Illinois.

Travel over these routes was hard and often dangerous. The roads cut through dense forests and across roaring streams. They were cold and muddy in the springtime, hot and dusty in the summer. One young woman wrote to a friend in 1810: "The reason so few are willing to return from the Western country is not that the country is so good but because the journey is so bad." ■

Pioneers on the Frontier

▼ *Pioneers moved west as families. The photo shows a pioneer family in Wisconsin. They even brought the family cat.*

The pioneers of the late 1700s were the first group of settlers to move into western lands. The pioneers braved rough roads and dangerous rivers, the heat of summer and the cold of winter—all for the chance to start a new life.

A traveler on the Wilderness Road in 1796 described what he saw this way:

> Women and children in the month of December traveling a wilderness through ice and snow, passing large rivers and creeks without shoe or stocking and barely as many rags as covers their nakedness, without money or provisions except what the wilderness affords (provides).

He asked some of the pioneers what they wanted in Kentucky. The answer was "land." They had never seen Kentucky, but they knew about the land. The soil was rich, and the land was cheap.

When pioneers like the Fowlers reached a spot that looked promising, they often built a small fort known as a frontier station. First they cleared the trees off a square piece of land near the river. Then they built two-story log houses at each corner of the square. They connected the buildings with high wooden walls.

At first, everyone lived inside the walls of the frontier station. Later, the settlers built log houses outside the walls. The houses were still close enough so that families could rush to the safety of the station in time of danger.

The new settlers helped each other whenever they could. They cleared land and built houses and barns. They planted crops and started fruit orchards. They grew enough food for their families, plus some extra to sell or trade.

Many of the first settlers on the Appalachian frontier were people like Daniel Boone. They got "the itching foot" when too many farmers moved to an area. When this happened, the first settlers pushed farther west.

This is the way the west was settled. Year after year, pioneers

The photos show a reconstructed frontier station at Boonesborough, Kentucky. Daniel Boone moved to Boonesborough with his wife Rebecca and their daughter in September 1775. They were among the first pioneer families to settle west of the Mississippi.

Moving West

pushed on from one frontier to another. After the War of 1812, they settled the rich lands of the Michigan Territory. By the 1830s, they had reached the banks of the Mississippi River. There were settlements in Illinois, Wisconsin, and Missouri. ■

Life in Early Settlements

As the frontier stations became towns, more settlers arrived to start businesses. Amy Fowler saw her Kentucky station grow into a real town as she grew up.

A year after her father started his farm, a blacksmith arrived to shoe horses. He could also make tools and other metal products. Later, a carpenter arrived to make furniture and other wooden goods.

Next, a miller constructed a gristmill for grinding grain. A gristmill was always built on a swift-running stream. The miller needed water power to turn the millstone. At harvest time Amy's family brought wagonloads of wheat and corn to the gristmill to be ground into flour.

Amy's family was happy to see a storekeeper set up shop. The store sold goods like sugar and tea, needles and thread, hammers and saws. It also sold simple machines like butter churns and spinning wheels.

UNDERSTANDING THE FRONTIER

Pioneers like the Fowlers knew that life on the frontier would be challenging. They were willing to accept the danger and hardship, however. For them, the frontier represented a chance for a better life.

The Changing Frontier

In Daniel Boone's time, the frontier was seen as a dividing line separating white and Indian settlement. As pioneers moved west, the frontier moved, too. It was always a step ahead of them.

A frontier doesn't always have to divide people. It can also be an area where people from different cultures meet.

The Frontier Spirit

The frontier experience shaped America's thinking. After settling the West, Americans developed a new spirit. They were confident they could take on any challenge.

In 1960, presidential candidate John Kennedy called on America to face "the new frontier."

He meant that America should attack its problems today in the same spirit it had once settled the frontier.

The New Frontier

Today, the new frontier includes learning to care for the environment, ending poverty and hunger—any problem we want to solve. Attacking our problems with courage will lead to a better life for all.

The frontier black-smith (left) is making a horseshoe. Blacksmiths also made hinges, hooks —anything made of metal. The leather worker (right) is cleaning a hide. Leather workers made harnesses, saddles, and the like.

The leather pouch is from this period. It was used for carrying personal items.

Every few weeks, a frontier doctor arrived at the settlement on horseback. The doctor was welcome. Dangerous diseases such as pneumonia, measles, and tuberculosis spread easily in small, crowded cabins. Even a simple sore throat or ear infection could turn into a serious illness.

Larger towns like Lexington, Kentucky, soon had churches and schools. But the Fowlers did not live near a school. Amy's mother taught the children to read and write.

The frontier settlements brought settlers into close contact with Indians living in the area. Some Indians became friendly with the settlers. They traded fur for the settlers' tools and clothing. Often, they even helped farmers raise their crops. Other Indians tried to stop settlers from moving onto lands belonging to Indian peoples. ■

■ *What were some of the signs that a frontier station was becoming a town?*

R E V I E W

1. **FOCUS** What was life on the new frontier like for settlers in the early 1800s?

2. **CONNECT** How was life on the frontier similar to life in the early colonies?

3. **ECONOMICS** Why did people want to make the dangerous and uncomfortable trip to settle in western lands?

4. **GEOGRAPHY** How did people in the early 1800s move from place to place? Why was travel difficult?

5. **CRITICAL THINKING** Compare Amy Fowler's trip in 1788 with a trip you might take today from Pittsburgh, Pennsylvania, to Lexington, Kentucky. Study the maps on pages 620–623 to get an idea of the mountains and rivers along the way.

6. **ACTIVITY** Draw a picture of a flatboat loaded with a family's possessions. You may refer to the painting on page 345.

349

Moving West

Davy Crockett

Anne Malcolmson

Like Daniel Boone, Davy Crockett loved the wilderness. Here is a tall tale about this real frontiersman.

Life on the American frontier was not easy as you have learned. For entertainment the settlers told stories. Many of these were tall tales about real and imaginary people. Davy Crockett was a favorite subject.

When Davy Crockett went to Congress, he didn't waste his time making dull speeches. He told stories. He had a great many stories to tell, too—stories of his life as a hunter, a backwoodsman, and an Indian fighter. Sometimes he was carried away by his stories. People began to expect almost anything from him.

His fame spread far and wide. During his second term in Washington, it was feared that the world was coming to an end. Halley's Comet shone in the sky. This was a particularly bright comet with a long tail. It came fearfully close to the earth. Bits of burning metal flew off and showered fields and forests. The sky was streaked with shooting stars.

This comet had appeared before. Whenever it came close to our planet something dreadful happened. People feared it meant disaster again. But with Davy in Congress they thought they might be safe. They sent a committee to him, just as people send committees to Washington today. They asked him to help them. At last he agreed. If the comet came any closer, said he, he would climb to the top of the Appalachian Mountains. There he would stand until he could catch the old comet and wring off its tail. This made the committee feel better and they went home satisfied.

Davy Crockett was born in the Tennessee hills. As a tiny baby, he was cradled in the shell of a snapping turtle. His crib cover was a panther's skin. A crocodile curled itself up into a ball for his pillow. From the very beginning he was a remarkable person.

As a young man he fought in the Indian Wars. All over the Tennessee and Arkansas country he hunted coon and bear. He even tried his hand at farming. Everything he saw and did gave him a new story to tell.

Throughout the Shakes, as his part of Tennessee was called, Davy was famous for his grin. It spread from ear to ear. No one could look at it without smiling back. People thought that it had

backwoodsman
a person from the wilderness

comet a ball of dust and ice that circles the sun
Halley's Comet
a comet seen every 76 years named for Edmund Halley
shooting star a stone or metal that travels toward Earth from outer space at a great speed

coon raccoon

strange powers, and told how Davy had once grinned a coon out of a tree.

On the top branch of a pine sat the fat little coon, grinning like a Cheshire cat. Davy needed a new cap. He liked the markings on the little creature's tail. But he had left Betsey, his long rifle, at home. All he could do was to stand there and grin. He stretched his lips as far as they could go and fixed his snapping eyes on the coon. After an hour the animal gave up. The glare from Crockett's smile was too much. Down fell the raccoon. He had been out-grinned by the hunter.

On another occasion in the Shakes, Davy saw another coon. This time he decided to grin him down for the fun of it. Davy grinned and grinned, but nothing happened. He stood there all night long, grinning. Rattler, his hunting dog, who usually went wild with excitement when his master hunted a coon, acted very strangely. He paid no attention, but curled up at the foot of the tree and slept soundly.

In the morning, Hunter Crockett saw his mistake. What he thought was a coon was only a big knot on the branch. What a fool he had been, grinning at a tree all night long! His grin had not been wasted, however. It had burned all the bark off the tree.

Beside Rattler and Betsey, Crockett had two unusual hunting companions. His favorite was his old bear, Death Hug. Davy had brought him up from a tiny cub. He had a saddle and bridle made for the old creature and often rode him around the wilderness. Death Hug saved his life on one occasion. Davy was surrounded by angry Indians, who were out for his scalp. As soon as the bear saw the danger he leapt into a tree with his master on his back. From branch to branch he swung, faster than the Indians could follow. He crossed the whole forest this way and came down in friendly country.

The second was an alligator whom he called Mississippi. Davy and Death Hug were skating on the frozen Niagara River, above the falls. It was getting on toward spring. Without any warning, their piece of ice broke off from the rest and headed for the falls. They were indeed in a pickle! But Death Hug saved the day. Davy locked his arms around Death Hug's waist. He guided the chunk of ice over the great waterfall and they landed safely at the bottom, without even a ducking.

cheshire cat the grinning cat from the book *Alice in Wonderland*

cap Davy wants a hat made from fur of raccoon, including the striped tail

knot a hard lump where a branch grows out from the tree

scalp skin and hair cut from the body of an enemy

pickle a bad situation

ducking to get wet

Further Reading

By Wagon and Flatboat. Enid L. Meadowcroft. This is the story of a family who moves west to Ohio. The Burds find their travels full of adventure.

Daniel Boone. Laurie Lawlor. Many tall tales were told about Daniel Boone. This biography, however, tells about the man behind the legend.

The Next Frontier

**THINKING
FOCUS**

*What were the main re-
sults of purchasing the
Louisiana Territory?*

Key Term

• Louisiana Purchase

➤ *The pocket watch
contains a portrait of
James Monroe, the man
who made the decision to
purchase the Louisiana
Territory.*

In 1802, American settlers were moving west into the lands beyond the Appalachians. At the same time, events were unfolding in France that would change the future development of the United States.

Napoleon Bonaparte, the ruler of France, was worried about the French colony of what is now Haiti in the West Indies. He had already sent thousands of troops there to crush a revolt of black slaves. He would need to send thousands more. In addition, Napoleon found himself on the verge of war with Great Britain. Wars cost money, and Napoleon was going to need lots of it.

President Thomas Jefferson worried about the French controlling the Louisiana Territory. He sent James Monroe to Paris to buy New Orleans from France. Owning this Mississippi River port would safeguard American trade.

When Monroe arrived in Paris, he found that Napoleon wanted to sell the entire Louisiana Territory for $15 million. Monroe thought hard. Congress had said he could spend $2 million for New Orleans. The President had given him permission to offer as much as $10 million. If Monroe spent just $5 million more, he could double the size of the United States. What should he do?

The Louisiana Purchase

Monroe decided to take the risk. On April 30, 1803, he agreed to the **Louisiana Purchase,** in which he bought 828,000 square miles of land west of the Mississippi River.

Find the Louisiana Territory on the map on the next page. The United States bought this land for less than three cents an acre. Compare it with the map on pages 620–621 in the Atlas. What present-day states make up this area?

President Jefferson was happy with Monroe's purchase, but some

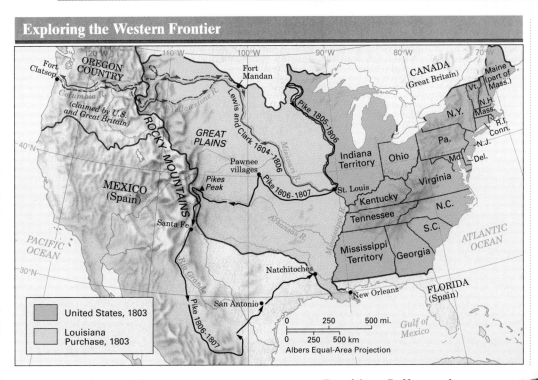

The Louisiana Purchase stretched from the Mississippi River all the way to the Rocky Mountains. Note the routes of explorers Lewis and Clark and Pike on this map.

▼ *The official seal of France (below) was attached to the Lousiana Purchase document.*

members of Congress were not. They said the Constitution did not allow the president to buy new territory without permission of Congress. Jefferson urged Congress to agree with his actions.

This treaty must of course be laid before both Houses. . . . They, I presume, will see their duty to their country in ratifying and paying for it. . . . It is the case of the guardian [adult] investing the money of his ward [child] in purchasing an important adjacent territory, and saying to him when of age, I did this for your good.

President Jefferson knew little about the new territory. New Orleans was a trade center for the frontier west of the Appalachians. Hunters and trappers brought furs to the city by traveling down rivers that fed into the Mississippi.

President Jefferson wondered if one of the rivers flowed to the Pacific Ocean. If so, it would form a trade route across the continent. To explore this territory, Jefferson chose two men. One was Meriwether Lewis, his secretary. The other was William Clark, an army officer. ■

■ *Why did people in the United States disagree about whether or not the country should buy the Louisiana Territory?*

The Lewis and Clark Expedition

President Jefferson sent Lewis and Clark on an expedition, or journey of discovery. They were to travel up the Missouri River and make their way to the Pacific. They were to map the area as they traveled, and they were to find out as much as they could about the plants and animals living there. To learn more about the Lewis and Clark expedition, see A Closer Look on the following pages.

353

The Lewis and Clark Expedition

Thomas Jefferson had been eager to know about the unexplored part of America since he was a young man. As President, he was in a position to satisfy his curiosity. He insisted that Lewis and Clark take notes on climate, rivers, mountains, plants, animals, and the peoples they encountered. Without such notes, he said, "history becomes fable instead of facts."

Sacajawea, a young Shoshone woman (shown above, standing with her arms outstretched) went with the expedition. Sacajawea helped translate and buy food and horses. Most important, when other Indians saw her and her baby, they knew that the expedition was peaceful.

Map of Columbia River, from the Lewis and Clark journals

With this pocket compass, Clark recorded the exact direction the group traveled every day. Later he could draw accurate maps of the country they went through.

This large buffalo skin was like a book for one of the Indian cultures the expedition met. The Mandan people gave Lewis and Clark the skin, which records a battle between the Mandan and their enemies.

Salmonberries often made a meal for the expedition when they ran short of other food. The cook baked the berries into cakes, which Clark thought were very tasty. The Shoshone showed the men how to dry the berries and store them for later use.

This page from the journal of Lewis and Clark shows how they carefully recorded each new animal and plant they saw. These precious journals were almost lost when one of the boats overturned in a river. Sacajawea saved them.

How Do We Know?

HISTORY *People today know what happened to Lewis and Clark, because the explorers kept very complete journals. Since the purpose of their expedition was to do research, they took thorough notes on much of what they saw.*

■ *What was the main goal of the Lewis and Clark expedition?*

Lewis and Clark chose 40 to 50 frontiersmen and hunters for the trip. The group included a black slave named York. In May 1804, the explorers set off from St. Louis in riverboats. They spent the winter with the Mandan Indian tribes in what is now North Dakota. In the spring, they continued the journey. By that time, Sacajawea *(sak uh juh WEE uh)*, a Shoshone, had joined the expedition with her husband.

When the explorers came out of the Rocky Mountains, they met the Nez Perce *(nehz purs)* Indians. They traded with the Nez Perce for fresh supplies. The explorers then built canoes and paddled down the Columbia River. They reached the Pacific in November 1805, after 18 exhausting months.

Lewis and Clark shipped their reports and maps back to President Jefferson. The reports gave Americans a better understanding of the huge territory that was now part of the United States. Lewis and Clark didn't find a river route to the Pacific, but they showed that overland travel was possible. They also laid a foundation for friendly relations with the Indians. ■

Zebulon Pike's Expedition

Lewis and Clark returned to St. Louis in September 1806. Even before that, President Jefferson sent other explorers to scout different parts of the Louisiana Territory. For example, he sent Zebulon Pike, a lieutenant in the army, to explore the Southwest. Pike set out in July 1806 with 22 men. These explorers made their way across present-day Kansas to Colorado. They reached the Rocky Mountains on November 15. Pike described the moment in his journal:

> *At two in the afternoon I could distinguish a mountain to our right. . . . When our small party arrived on the hill, they gave three cheers.*

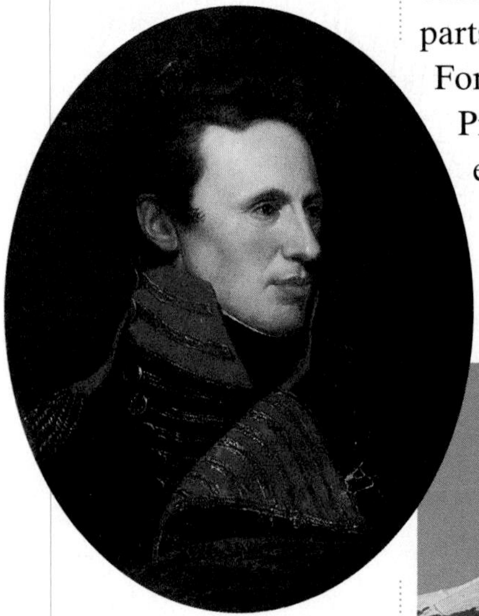

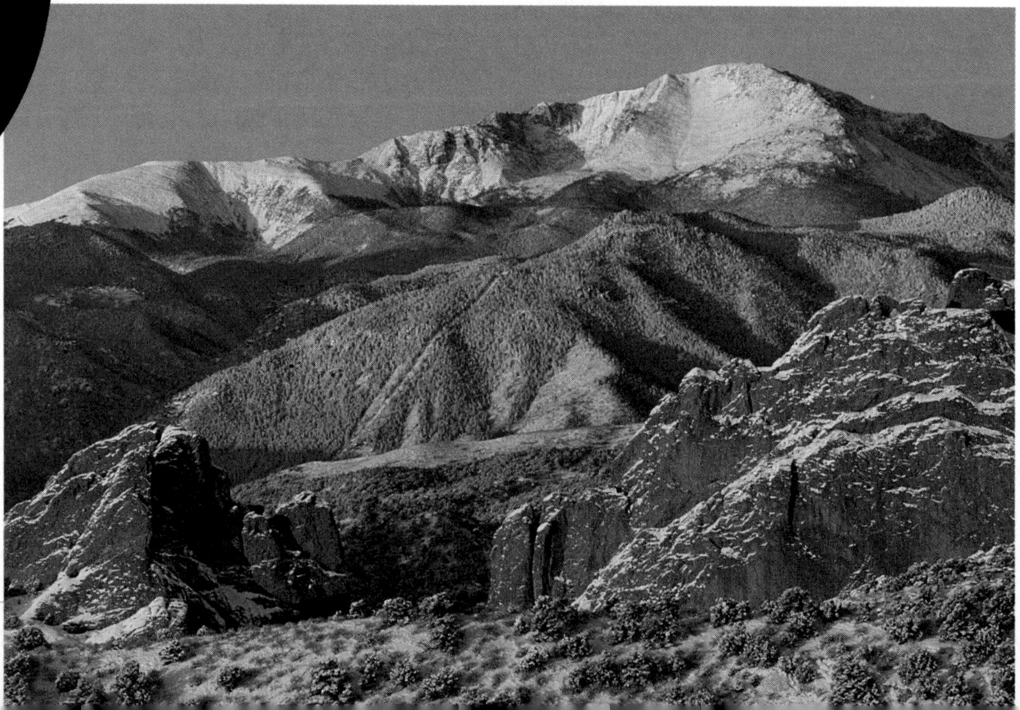

▲ *Zebulon Pike never did climb to the top of Pikes Peak. Visitors today can reach the top easily, either by road or by cog railroad.*

Pike and three of his men tried to climb the mountain, but they were unsuccessful. Today, the mountain is known as Pikes Peak.

The explorers then turned south and followed the Rio Grande down into Mexico. There, Spanish troops stopped them and made them turn back. Look back at the map on page 353. Where did Pike go next?

Explorers like Pike helped to create interest in the lands beyond the Mississippi. More and more people started thinking about moving to the next frontier. ■

■ *How did explorers like Zebulon Pike hasten the movement of settlers into the Louisiana Territory?*

The Beckoning West

In some ways, the frontier of the Louisiana Territory looked like the Northwest Territory of the late 1700s. Hunters and trappers moved in first. Later, settlers started small farms. Many of these settlers were the children of pioneers who had settled Kentucky, Ohio, and Tennessee. As in earlier times, rivers were the major routes for moving west.

One of the earliest settlers in the Louisiana Territory was the restless Daniel Boone. In 1799, even before America's purchase of the land, Boone set off for a new home west of the Mississippi. With some friends and relatives, he went west on foot, leading cattle and pack horses for more than 600 miles to what is now Missouri.

Boone and his wife Rebecca built a cabin near one of their sons. The old pioneer didn't stay long, however. Until he was nearly 80, Boone had "the itching foot." He roamed the western plains that later became Kansas and the Dakotas. Some say he even climbed the Rocky Mountains.

After Boone became too old to wander, he often sat near the banks of the Missouri River, watching the wagon trains as they headed west. Sometimes young pioneers stopped to ask Boone about his travels. Had he ever gotten lost on the frontier? The old pioneer thought for a moment. Then he answered this way: "No, can't say as ever I was lost. But I was bewildered once for three days." ■

▲ *This portrait of Daniel Boone was painted in 1820, when Boone was 85 years old.*

■ *What were the pioneers like who moved west into the Louisiana Territory?*

REVIEW

1. **FOCUS** What were the main results of the purchase of the Louisiana Territory?

2. **CONNECT** How was the pattern of settlement in the Louisiana Territory similar to the pattern in the Northwest Territory?

3. **GEOGRAPHY** Why was control of the city of New Orleans considered so important to people in the United States?

4. **CRITICAL THINKING** Why did Daniel Boone keep moving westward rather than settle down in one place?

5. **CRITICAL THINKING** Compare Jefferson's decision to send Lewis and Clark on an expedition with the decision by Ferdinand and Isabella to sponsor Columbus. What did both Jefferson and the monarchs hope the explorers would find?

6. **WRITING ACTIVITY** What do you think President Jefferson wanted to know about the Louisiana Purchase? Write a list of five questions he might have asked Lewis and Clark when they returned from their expedition.

Using Landmarks as Guides

Here's Why

The first explorers of the frontier had no maps. They had to locate places and figure out distances based on their own experience. Before long, people began to develop maps of the new territories. Those mapmaking skills are valuable today. If you can draw accurate maps, you can pass on information about places you know.

Suppose you were the first person to explore a wilderness area. If you drew a map to help others, what information would you include? How would you let travelers know what landmarks to look for?

Here's How

The painting on page 359 shows a portion of western Appalachia. The map at the bottom of these two pages shows physical features, such as mountains, rivers, and swamps that an explorer might have found in this area. Symbols for these features are included in the legend at the bottom left. The legend also includes symbols for features made by humans.

The compass rose next to the legend tells you which direction is north. The scale at the bottom left of page 359 tells you how many miles an inch on the map represents. Use the legend, compass rose, and scale to trace this route west.

From Briar Lake near the east edge, you can look north toward Trapper's Peak. Note the map's symbol for a mountain peak. About three miles downriver from the waterfall is Fort Drakes. After the river forks, cross the bridge south. You can go on south toward some cabins on the Hope River or west along Little Bird River toward a salt lick. Check the legend for the symbols for waterfall, cabin, and salt lick.

Traveling west along the Little Bird River from the salt lick brings you to another bridge. Cross the bridge north and continue west along the river. When you reach a fork in the trail, at Eagle Peak, you can go south to Sugar Lake or west to the Indian settlement. It is over two miles from Sugar Lake by river to the Indian settlement.

Around the bend in the river from the Indian settlement is Gooseneck Lake. Use the scale to measure how close the western edge

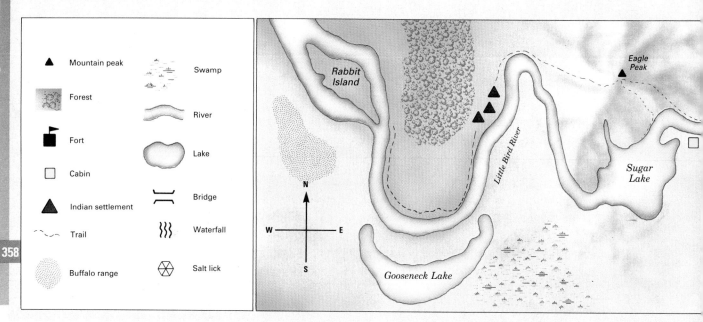

of Gooseneck Lake is to the nearest buffalo range. Finish your journey at Rabbit Island. The compass rose shows you that you will need to go north from Gooseneck Lake to get there. You can see that information from the legend, the compass rose, and the scale helped you on your journey, even in unfamiliar territory.

Try It

Trace the map on a separate sheet of paper. Imagine that as you travel through this area, you find some additional landmarks that you want to include on the map.
1. Draw a fort on the southern point of Rabbit Island.
2. Indicate a lake one mile north and one mile east of Fort Drakes.
3. Draw a canyon one-half mile south of Sugar Lake.
4. Beginning at the group of cabins that are along the Hope River, trace a five-mile-long trail northeast through the mountains.

If necessary, create new symbols to draw these new landmarks. Add any new symbols to the legend and to the map. Be sure to name your new features and label them on the map.

Apply It

Draw a map of a route that is familiar to you, such as the one from your house to your favorite restaurant. It could also be from your school to the public library, or from your school to your house.

Include a legend, compass rose, and scale by miles or by city block on the map you draw. Don't forget that others who use your map will need to recognize the symbols and landmarks that you include.

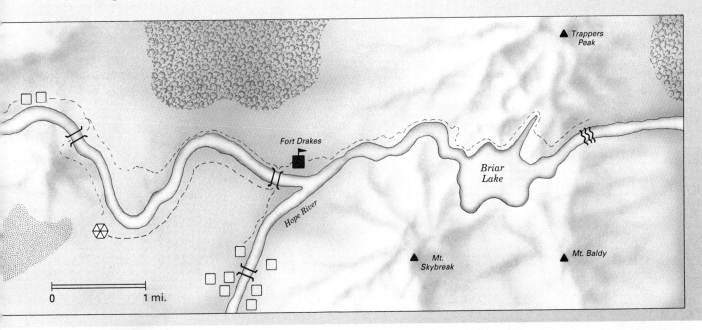

The American Indians in Retreat

THINKING FOCUS

What caused the Indians to gradually lose control of their lands?

Key Term

- Bureau of Indian Affairs

➤ *This painting originally belonged to the family of William Clark, the man who explored the Louisiana Territory. Historians think it is a portrait of Tecumseh.*

▼ *Feathers like these were worn by Shawnee warriors.*

The meeting took place in a grove of trees near the governor's house in Vincennes, Indiana. It was August 15, 1810. William Henry Harrison, governor of the Indiana Territory, was speaking. He insisted that the United States had always been fair with Indians. At these words, the Shawnee chief Tecumseh *(teh KUHM seh)* jumped to his feet. "Liar, liar!" he shouted.

Tecumseh was speaking in Shawnee. At first, Harrison did not know what Tecumseh was saying. An American army officer at the meeting did, however. He told his soldiers to cock their rifles and prepare to fire.

The Shawnee warriors stood their ground. For a moment, the soldiers and the Shawnee glared at each other. Then Harrison ordered the soldiers to lower their rifles. The tension eased, and the meeting ended.

Meetings like this were of little help in ending conflicts between Indians and settlers. Over the years Tecumseh had seen settlers take more and more land. They often cheated the Indians, paying far less than the land was worth. And it wasn't just the settlers who cheated the Indians. Harrison had bought three million acres of land for the government from Little Turtle, a chief of the Miami.

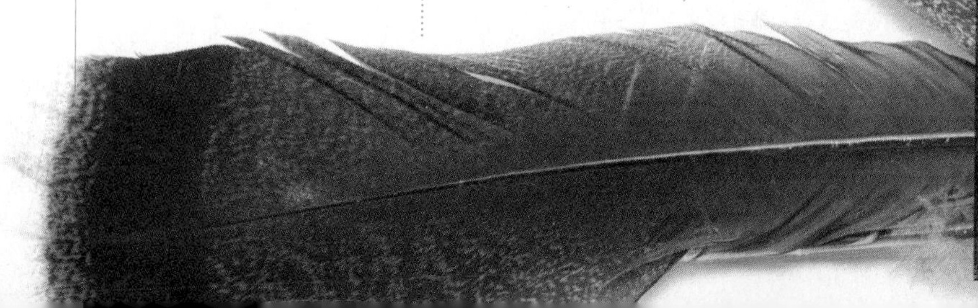

All Harrison paid was $7,000 in cash, with additional payments of $1,750 due each year.

Tecumseh felt that if the settlers were not stopped, they would soon push the Indians into the Great Lakes. The only hope was for Indians to join together and fight, no matter what their tribe.

Throughout 1808 and 1809, Tecumseh traveled around the frontier. He met with leaders of the Potawatomi, the Wyandot, and others. He wanted the tribes to put aside their differences and unite.

Unfair Treaties

A series of treaties signed during the late 1700s gave settlers the right to more and more Indian land. The map at the right shows the result. What were the only states with large Indian populations by 1830?

To Tecumseh a treaty was just a worthless piece of paper. Nobody could sell land, because nobody really "owned" it. If you could sell the land, Tecumseh said, "why not sell the air, the clouds, and the great sea . . .?"

Tecumseh knew that Indian leaders sometimes signed treaties giving away land that belonged to others. For instance, Iroquois living in New York signed a treaty at Fort Stanwix in 1784. The treaty gave settlers the right to live in western Pennsylvania. The Shawnee and other Indian tribes living in Pennsylvania had not signed the treaty. Yet it resulted in a rush of settlers onto their lands.

What the government could not win by treaty it was prepared to take by force. In July 1793,

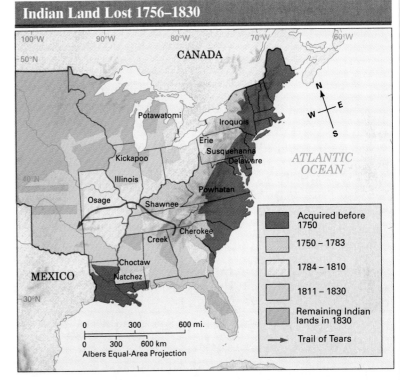

Indian Land Lost 1756–1830

CANADA

Potawatomi
Iroquois
Erie
Susquehanna
Kickapoo
Delaware
Illinois
Osage
Powhatan
Shawnee
Cherokee
Creek
Choctaw
MEXICO
Natchez

ATLANTIC OCEAN

	Acquired before 1750
	1750 – 1783
	1784 – 1810
	1811 – 1830
	Remaining Indian lands in 1830
→	Trail of Tears

0   300   600 mi.
0   300   600 km
Albers Equal-Area Projection

officials met with Indians from the Shawnee, the Kickapoo, the Miami, and other tribes at Niagara, New York. The government asked the tribes to give up land east of the Muskingum River in southwestern Ohio. In return, the government would guarantee them control over other lands in Ohio. The Shawnee said no. So did the Kickapoo and the Miami.

The government would not take no for an answer. When the Indians turned down the

Each year Indian tribes were forced to surrender more and more land. Compare this map with the Minipedia map on page 608 to see the vast lands Indians once occupied.

361

■ *Why was Tecumseh opposed to treaties?*

proposal, the government called in the army. In 1794, General Anthony Wayne defeated the Indians at the Battle of Fallen Timbers in northwestern Ohio. As a result, the Indians were forced to sign the Treaty of Greenville. They gave up rights to most of central and southern Ohio. In return, they received $20,000 in supplies and the promise of $9,500 in yearly payments. One of the Shawnee warriors who fought in the Battle of Fallen Timbers was the young Tecumseh. ■

Indian Resistance

During the next ten years, Tecumseh saw the Indians lose more and more land. Many Indians were hungry. They no longer had enough land to hunt on and to farm. When Tecumseh visited villages to urge cooperation, he found people willing to listen. They also listened to Tecumseh's younger brother, called the Shawnee Prophet. He preached that Indians had taken on too many of the white man's ways. He said that Indians must return "to the ways of our fathers."

Many young warriors joined Tecumseh and his brother. They built a new village in northwestern Indiana, along the Tippecanoe River. The village was called Prophetstown. By spring 1810, Tecumseh had an army of 1,000 warriors at Prophetstown.

The Battle of Tippecanoe

Governor Harrison worried when he saw more and more Indians joining Tecumseh and the Prophet. In 1811, Harrison

▼ *This Kurtz & Allison print shows the Battle of Tippecanoe. In losing the battle, the Indians lost their last chance to stop the advance of settlers east of the Mississippi.*

learned that Tecumseh had left Prophetstown to gather support from the Chickasaws in Tennessee and other southern Indian peoples. Harrison decided to take advantage of Tecumseh's absence. He marched an army of 1,000 men up the Wabash River to the Tippecanoe. He set up camp two miles west of Prophetstown. Harrison tried to negotiate, but the Indian leaders had made up their minds to fight. On November 7, 1811, the Indians attacked.

The Battle of Tippecanoe lasted two hours. The Prophet had told the warriors that his prayers would protect them from American bullets. It didn't work that way. About 40 Indians were killed, and the rest quickly fled. Harrison's men burned Prophetstown to the ground.

The War of 1812

When Tecumseh returned to Indiana in 1812, he tried to rebuild his forces. He made an agreement with British officials in Michigan and Canada. The British offered him guns and supplies in return for his support. The British knew that war between their country and the United States was going to start again. When it did, they wanted Tecumseh's help.

During the War of 1812, Tecumseh fought on the British side. He and his followers fought against the Americans in Canada, Ohio, and Michigan. In October 1813, Tecumseh was killed in a battle near Detroit. The general leading the American army was the Shawnee chief's old enemy, William Henry Harrison. ■

■ *How did Tecumseh hope to stop the advance of the settlers?*

Peace for a Time

After the death of Tecumseh, Indians like the Sauk *(sawk)*, the Fox, and the Kickapoo decided to leave their ancient lands. They moved across the Mississippi River to start a new life. They wanted to get as far away from the settlers as they could.

Others, including the Potawatomi, the Choctaw, and the Cherokee, wanted to stay east of the Mississippi, if possible. Between 1815 and 1830, these Indians tried to live in peace beside the Americans.

Some Indians tried to live like the settlers. Many Potawatomi in Indiana and Michigan had converted to the Catholic faith. They lived as farmers and fur traders.

Some Choctaw in Mississippi also became Christians. They sent their children to government-run schools.

In the Southeast the Cherokee took the lead in adopting the settlers' ways. Many Cherokee who stayed in their traditional lands in Alabama, Georgia, and Tennessee bought land and became farmers. Other Cherokee opened stores and mills. Wealthy Cherokee cotton farmers even bought black slaves to work on plantations. Many Cherokee also converted to Christianity.

An educated Cherokee named Sequoyah *(sih KWOY uh)* developed a written alphabet for his

▲ *During this period, the U.S. government awarded the Andrew Jackson Medal to Indian chiefs who lived peacefully with the settlers.*

363

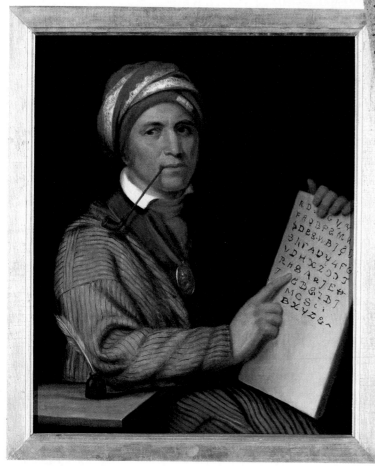

GWY CHEROKEE PHŒNIX.

NEW ECHOTA, WEDNESDAY JUNE 4, 1828.

Sequoyah developed the Cherokee alphabet over a period of 12 years.

■ *In what two ways did the Indians try to keep the peace?*

people. Another Cherokee named Elias Boudinot *(BOO dnoh)* published the *Cherokee Phoenix,* a newspaper printed in both Cherokee and English. Cherokee leaders also set up a government for their people. They wrote a constitution based on the Constitution of the United States.

During this period, the U.S. government struggled to find ways of limiting white settlement on Indian lands. In 1824, the government started the **Bureau of Indian Affairs.** This agency had the power to make treaties and control trade with the Indians.

At the same time, the government knew that the peace between the Indians and settlers could not last. People like President John Quincy Adams were urging Indians to move to the lands west of the Mississippi River. ■

Loss and Defeat

By 1830, the government was no longer asking the Indians to move away from their ancient lands. It was ordering them. Making the Indians move west was now official government policy.

The Trail of Tears

Removal treaties demanded that many Indians in the Southeast move to Indian reservations in what is now Oklahoma. States were eager to take control of Indian lands. The Choctaw, Creek, and Chickasaw moved reluctantly. The Cherokee, however, decided to stay. They fought the treaties in the courts.

One case went to the Supreme Court. It ruled that the government had no right to order the Indians off their lands. President

Andrew Jackson said this decision was ridiculous. He ignored the Supreme Court and ordered the American army to move the Cherokee by force.

Soldiers with guns marched some 18,000 Cherokee from their homes in the Southeast. Almost one-fourth of the Indians died of starvation, disease, and harsh treatment along the way. The route the Cherokee followed to Oklahoma became known as "The Trail of Tears."

Look back at the map on page 361. Trace the route of the Trail of Tears. What present-day states did the Cherokee pass through on their journey to Oklahoma?

The Black Hawk War

Many Indian tribes living in Ohio, Indiana, and Illinois were also forced to move west of the Mississippi River. The Sauk and the Fox had already moved to Iowa. Every summer some of them would cross the Mississippi to tend their old farmlands in Illinois. This upset settlers who wanted that farmland for themselves. In the summer of 1832, the settlers sent soldiers to force the Indians back to Iowa. Led by the Sauk chief Black Hawk, the Indians retreated to the west, defending themselves as they went. When they reached the Mississippi, the army attacked. Later, Black Hawk described the battle this way:

> They [the Indians] tried to give themselves up—the whites paid no attention to their entreaties—but commenced slaughtering them. In a little while the whole army arrived. Our braves, but few in number, finding that the enemy paid no regard to age or sex, and seeing that they were murdering helpless women and little children, determined to fight until they were killed.

Many women drowned as they tried to swim the Mississippi with children on their backs. Some were shot from the shore. Of 2,000 Indians who had gone into Illinois to tend their fields, only about 150 made it back to Iowa. Nothing could stop the flood of settlers determined to move west and claim the Indians' land. ■

▼ *Chief Black Hawk spent a lifetime trying to protect Indian lands from the settlers.*

■ *How did the United States government finally take over Indian lands?*

Look back at the map on page 361.

REVIEW

1. **FOCUS** What caused the Indians to gradually lose control of their lands?
2. **CONNECT** How was what happened to Indians on the Appalachian frontier similar to what happened to Indians on the eastern seaboard?
3. **CITIZENSHIP** What did Cherokee leaders do to help their tribe? What did Sequoyah and Elias Boudinot do?
4. **CRITICAL THINKING** The Supreme Court ruled that the government had no right to remove the Indians from their land, but President Andrew Jackson ordered the army to remove them anyway. What would probably happen today if the president ignored a Supreme Court decision?
5. **WRITING ACTIVITY** Write a newspaper account of the removal of 18,000 Cherokee from their homes in the Southwest to reservations in Oklahoma. Imagine that you are the first reporter to tell the American public what is happening to the Cherokee.

Chapter Review

Reviewing Key Terms

Bureau of Indian Affairs (p. 364)
ordinance (p. 344)
pioneer (p. 341)
canal (p. 346)
tributary (p. 346)
Louisiana Purchase (p. 352)

A. Be sure you understand the meanings of the key terms. Then answer each question by writing one or more sentences.

1. How are pioneers and the Louisiana Purchase related?
2. How are a tributary and a canal similar? How are they different?
3. Daniel Boone seems to stand for what it meant to be a pioneer. What qualities did he have that pioneers also had?

4. What is the Bureau of Indian Affairs? When was it established and what power did it have?
5. Ordinances were passed for the frontier. How does that show that the new frontier was being settled in an orderly way?

B. The two words in each pair are related in some way. On your own paper, write a sentence explaining how the words are related.

1. pioneer, canal
2. Bureau of Indian Affairs, ordinance
3. pioneer, ordinance

Exploring Concepts

A. Copy the cluster diagram on your paper. Then write sentences that tell something about the frontier. Begin the sentences with the terms listed. The first one is done for you.

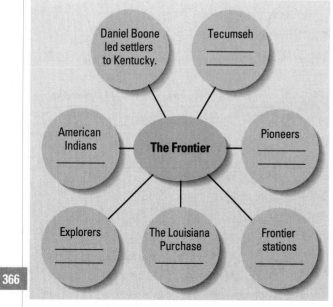

B. Answer each question with information from the chapter.

1. What were the boundaries of the Appalachian frontier?
2. How did Daniel Boone help settle the Appalachian frontier?
3. What kinds of dwellings did the settlers live in? What jobs did they do?
4. Who was sent to France to buy New Orleans? Look at the fifth entry on the chart on page 610 of the Minipedia. What happened to him in 1817?
5. What were some of the problems the American Indians faced because settlers moved into the frontier?
6. Who was Tecumseh and how did he try to help his people?
7. What did the American Indians do to live peacefully with the settlers? Did they continue to live peacefully with them? Why?

Reviewing Skills

1. Trace the map below and complete it as directed. Add new symbols to the legend.
   a. Locate a forest one-quarter mile east of Sugar Lake.
   b. Place cabins between Gooseneck Lake and the bend in the river.
   c. Mark the rapids two miles upriver from the Indian settlement.

2. Reread Lesson 3 and on your own paper, complete the outline below.

3. Suppose you wanted to see how settlers traveled from Pennsylvania to Tennessee. What might you trace or follow on a map?

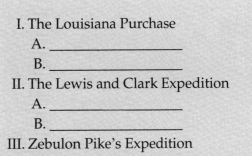

I. The Louisiana Purchase
   A. _____
   B. _____
II. The Lewis and Clark Expedition
   A. _____
   B. _____
III. Zebulon Pike's Expedition
   A. _____
   B. _____
IV. The Beckoning West
   A. _____
   B. _____

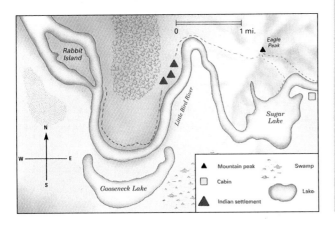

Using Critical Thinking

1. You have been reading about pioneers and frontier lands. We have no more frontier lands in our country, but are there still pioneers? Explain.

2. Imagine that you were the *first* settler in an area. Soon other settlers came and a town grew up around you. List both the advantages and disadvantages of staying in the area or moving on to new frontiers.

3. The American Indians often tried to help the settlers adapt to their new location. New families, some of them from other lands, are constantly moving into our communities. What could you and your class do to help them get settled?

Preparing for Citizenship

1. **GROUP ACTIVITY** As a class, make a map showing what changes are being made or are planned for the neighborhoods in which you live. Small groups should gather information from observation, newspapers, radio and television news, organizations, and business owners. Mark the changes on the class's map.

2. **COLLABORATIVE LEARNING** With classmates, explore a part of your school. Imagine you have never seen the area before. Working in groups of four, present the results of your expedition to the class. Each person in the group should be responsible for one of the following tasks: (1) preparing maps and drawings of the area, (2) questioning the people who work there, (3) gathering samples of things found there, and (4) organizing the information in the form of a radio newscast about a newly discovered area.

367

Chapter 15
Settling the Far West

In the 1800s, books, magazines, and newspapers all gave Americans the same message: Go west. People seeking new farms headed for Texas and Oregon. Those hoping to get rich quickly searched for gold in California. And a group seeking religious freedom, the Mormons, settled in Utah. Whatever these people dreamed about, they believed they would find it in the American West.

Throughout this period Americans headed west in covered wagons (above) and built new lives on the frontier. The woman shown at right gathers buffalo chips for fuel on the treeless prairie.

36
Independence on the Plains.   Gathering Chips.

1790	1800	1810	1820

1792

1806 Zebulon Pike explores Pikes Peak in present-day Colorado.

1843–1860 Wagon trains and stagecoaches rolling west toward California and Oregon leave deep ruts in the trails.

1830

1840

1850

1860

1849 Thousands of Americans and others catch "gold fever" and race to California. Some find gold with tools like the mining pan shown above.

1860

L E S S O N   1

Texas and the Struggle with Mexico

THINKING FOCUS

How did the United States expand its southern border to include Texas?

Key Terms

- plain
- annex

▼ *Americans headed to Texas by the thousands after reading ads like this. They were looking for rich farmland and open grassland for cattle.*

ree land in Texas! Climate so mild no house is needed!" Like magic, such advertisements lured thousands of Americans in the 1820s and 1830s.

The advertisements described rich Texas lands where wild horses, antelope, and buffalo roamed; where cherries, grapes, and plums grew wild. Best of all was the chance to buy land cheaply, or even get it free!

Many people were ready to believe the advertisements about Texas. It was a land where everyone could succeed. Some saw Texas as a place to get away from bill collectors or problems with the law. Others were poor farm families or struggling business owners hoping for a fresh start.

TEXAS FOREVER!!

Now is the time to emigrate to the Garden of America. A free passage, and all found, is offered at New Orleans to all applicants. Every settler receives a location of EIGHT HUNDRED ACRES OF LAND.

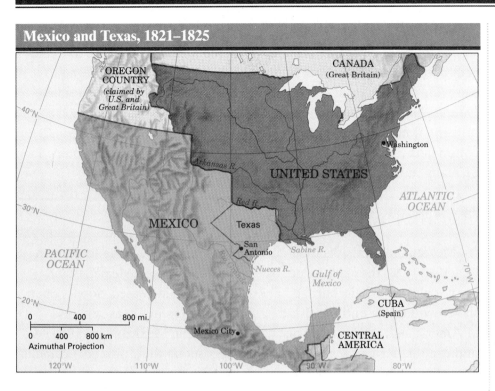

The Settlement of Texas

The settlers moved to lands that had once been part of the Spanish colony of Mexico. In 1821, Mexico won its independence from Spain. The new nation included a region called Texas, with rich farmlands and grassy **plains**—huge, flat areas without trees.

The map above shows the Mexican territory of Texas. The map on pages 620–621 in the Atlas shows the state of Texas. What present-day states were once part of Mexico?

In the early years of Mexican independence, Texas was hard to govern. Settlements were far apart and as much as 1,000 miles from the capital of Mexico City. Mexican leaders tried to strengthen their country by building the population of Texas. They hoped that by encouraging American settle-ment, they would also build strong ties of friendship and trade with the United States.

In 1823, Mexico offered large land grants to anyone bringing settlers to Texas. These people could give away farm-sized plots to the settlers. In return, the settlers had to promise to become Mexican citizens and join the Catholic Church.

One American pioneer, Stephen F. Austin, had established a colony of American families a year earlier. They settled in the rich lands along the Brazos River.

One settler, Anna Maria Campbell Reynolds, recalled that the "first night's camp on the prairies was horrible to me. . . . There was no sound to greet my ears but the howling of wolves. . . . I was frightfully blue."

371

While pioneers like Reynolds settled in, more and more Americans poured into the region. Many were Southerners from states like Georgia and Louisiana. They brought along slaves to help grow cotton in the warm Texas climate. So many settlers came to Texas that by 1835, Americans outnumbered Mexicans by close to ten to one. Mexican officials began to wonder if allowing Americans to settle in Texas had been such a good idea. They began to wonder if it was going to create trouble in the future. ■

Conflict with Mexico

Mexican officials decided to act. In 1830, they outlawed further slavery to discourage slave-owning. To end the flood of Americans, the Mexicans also outlawed American settlement altogether.

American settlers already living in Texas were upset. Many believed that they could no longer live under a Mexican government, which had become too strict. Conditions grew worse in 1834, when General Antonio López de Santa Anna became dictator of Mexico.

After Santa Anna took over, trouble between Mexicans and Americans increased. Soon, American settlers in Texas rebelled against the Mexican government. They set up their own government in 1835.

Bloodshed in Texas

In response to the settlers, Santa Anna sent several thousand soldiers to the Alamo, an old mission in San Antonio. About 200 Americans, including Davy Crockett and Jim Bowie, were holding the Alamo.

➤ *The illustration shows the Alamo during the final attack. Santa Anna sent one column of troops against the south wall and another against the east as a diversion. The main attack came at the north wall. The photo shows an Alamo flag that Santa Anna's troops captured.*

North wall

East wall

South wall

The Battle of the Alamo began on February 23, 1836. Mexican cannon pounded the Alamo walls for days. Each night the guns moved closer. By March 5, they were 200 yards away.

Early in the morning on March 6, Santa Anna directed the final attack. The Texans fought fearlessly. They threw back first one attack, then another. The Mexican troops kept coming, however, and they finally succeeded. They stormed the wall, opened the gates, and overran the Alamo's defenders. They killed almost everyone, including Bowie, Crockett, and the commander, William Travis.

The Texans' Victory

The defeat at the Alamo aroused the feelings of the American settlers. "Remember the Alamo!" became a battle cry. The Texas army, growing stronger every day, never stopped hoping for revenge.

Their chance came on April 21, 1836. Under the command of Sam Houston, the Texas army surprised Santa Anna near the San Jacinto *(san yuh SIHN toh)* River. After a fierce afternoon battle lasting only 20 minutes, they captured Santa Anna and ended the war.

In the meantime, leading American settlers met at the Texas town of Washington-on-the-Brazos to declare Texas independent. The new government moved quickly to ask the U.S. government to **annex** Texas—that is, to make it part of the United States. ■

◄ *Texas is known as the Lone Star State. This early Texas flag shows why.*

■ *Why did conflict arise between the American settlers in Texas and the Mexican government?*

The Mexican War

Most American settlers in Texas wanted to join the United States. The U.S. government, however, was in no hurry.

Statehood for Texas

One problem was that some people in Texas owned slaves. The United States contained 13 free states and 13 slave states at this time. Making Texas a state would upset the balance. Another problem was Mexico. Some U.S. government officials believed that annexing Texas would awaken old feelings and lead to another war. In 1845, however,

▼ *Once the Mexican War started, the army asked for volunteers. Men signed up by the thousands.*

EXAMINER

Extra.

MILITARY ORDERS.
GENERAL ORDERS, NO. 1

HEAD Quarters 14th Div. P. M. Washington, Pa. May 28, 184...
...igh, Commanding 14th Div. P. M., having received official information from H...
Commander-in-Chief of the militia of the Commonwealth of Pennsylvani...
the United States and the Republic of Mexico---announces to t...
...rizing the counties of Washington and Greene, the i...
Regiments of Volunteers tendering their ser...
United States and to preserve the ri...
...ited States has m...
...from Pen...

the political scene changed under new president James K. Polk. The United States did annex Texas and make it a state.

As expected, Mexico reacted angrily to the news of statehood for Texas. In November 1845, President Polk sent an ambassador to Mexico City to try to negotiate. Mexican officials, however, refused to talk.

War with Mexico

Next, President Polk, in order to start a war, commanded American forces in Texas to move down to the Rio Grande. They were now in territory that the Mexican government said was theirs. In April 1846, Mexican troops fought with an American scouting party, leaving 16 dead or wounded. The United States and Mexico were now at war.

American generals Winfield Scott and Zachary Taylor believed they needed to invade Mexico to win. They attacked from two directions. General Taylor invaded Mexico from the north, crossed the Rio Grande, won a few quick victories, and took some important Mexican towns.

General Scott sailed south to Veracruz, a port on the eastern coast of Mexico. His troops won a number of battles against the badly equipped and poorly led Mexican forces. Then General Scott marched his troops over the mountains and captured Mexico City in September 1847. The Mexican government agreed to sign a peace treaty.

These hats belonged to a U.S. soldier (left) and a Mexican cavalry officer (right). The U.S. soldiers in the painting (below) are advancing on Mexico City in 1847.

Lands Gained by the United States, 1848–1853

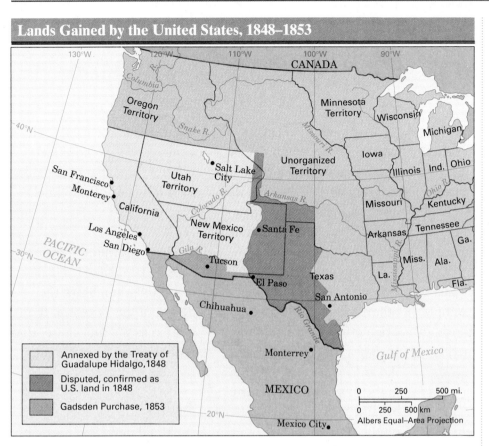

◀ *How many states or parts of states were carved out of the land that the United States received from Mexico?*

The Treaty of Guadalupe Hidalgo *(gwa duh LOO pay ee DAHL goh)* was signed on February 2, 1848. The map at the top of the page shows the result. Mexico gave up all claims to lands in Texas. What other lands did the United States receive?

The United States paid Mexico $15 million for all the land it received after the Mexican War. Five years later, the United States bought more land along Mexico's northern border. This time it paid Mexico $10 million. The purchase was arranged by James Gadsden, U.S. minister to Mexico. The United States wanted this land, known as the Gadsden Purchase, to build a railroad along a southern route to California. The southern border of the United States was now set. ■

■ *What actions showed that the U.S. government was ready for a war with Mexico?*

R E V I E W

1. **FOCUS** How did the United States expand its southern border to include Texas?

2. **CONNECT** What qualities did the first American settlers in Texas have in common with the first settlers in Kentucky?

3. **CITIZENSHIP** Why did Mexico require new American settlers in Texas to become Mexican citizens?

4. **SOCIAL SYSTEMS** Why did the American settlers want to make Texas independent?

5. **CRITICAL THINKING** No one really wanted the Mexican War. Before the war, Polk sent an ambassador to Mexico City to negotiate. Mexican officials didn't start to fight until Polk had sent troops all the way to the Rio Grande. What else could Polk have done to prevent the war? What else could the Mexican officials have done?

6. **WRITING ACTIVITY** Write an eyewitness account of the battle of the Alamo.

Settling the Far West

Using Word Clues and Diagrams

Here's Why

Your everyday life is full of causes and effects. You forget your lunch. By late in the afternoon, you are hungry. Forgetting your lunch was the *cause*, and becoming hungry was the *effect*.

History is full of causes and effects, too. For example, suppose you wanted to understand what happened in the 1820s and 1830s.

Here's How

Word clues can help you to identify causes and effects. When you read, look for such phrases as *led to, therefore, as a result of, since, brought about*, and *because*. These words suggest cause-and-effect relationships.

You can use diagrams to summarize cause-and-effect relationships. Study the diagram below. The first diagram shows how the single cause on the left resulted in the effect on the right.

Sometimes a single event sets off a "chain reaction" of other events. Look at the chain effect diagram below. It shows how the cause on the left resulted in the effect in the middle. This, in turn, became a cause for the effect on the right.

Suppose an event has more than one cause. In this case, you would use a diagram like the last one below. Note that several causes on the left resulted in the single effect on the right. Diagrams like this one are used to show complex cause-and-effect relationships that take place over long periods of time.

Try It

Use information from Lesson 1 to make a chain effect diagram. Show the defeat of the Texans at the Alamo as the first cause. End with the new government's request to annex Texas.

Apply It

Read newspaper articles to find cause-and-effect relationships. Write summaries that briefly describe each cause or effect. Make one of each of the three types of cause-and-effect diagrams based on articles you find.

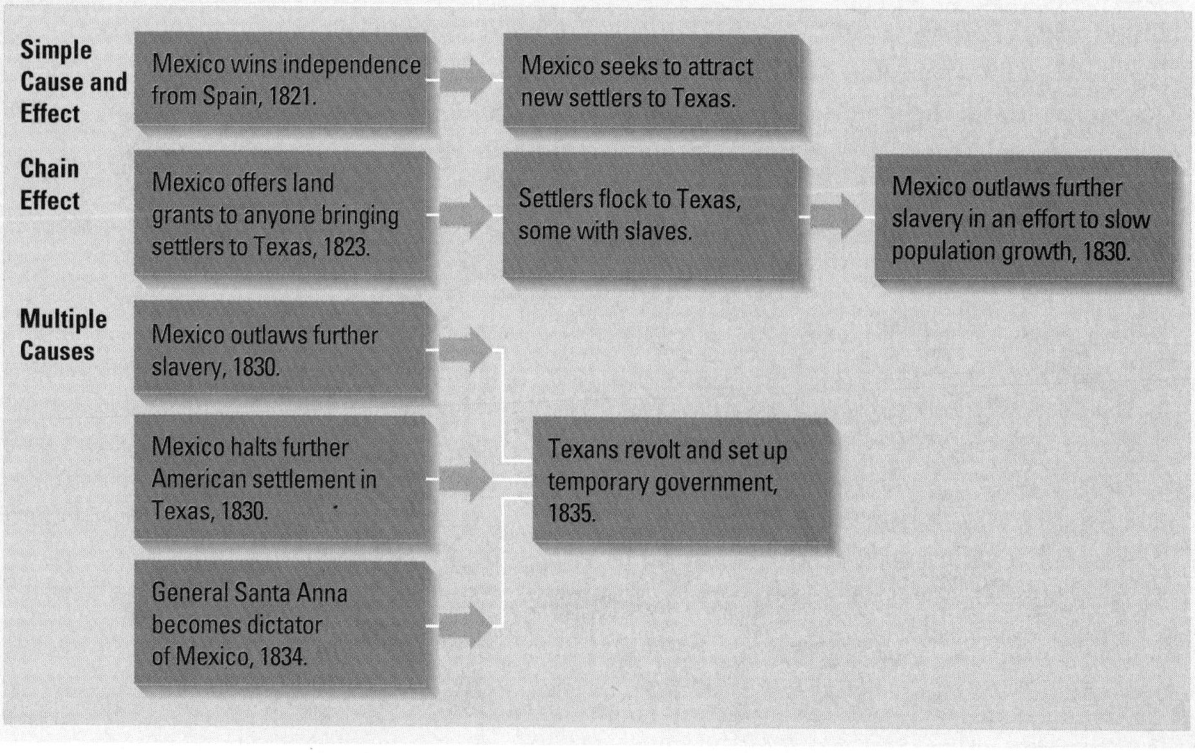

Simple Cause and Effect

Mexico wins independence from Spain, 1821. → Mexico seeks to attract new settlers to Texas.

Chain Effect

Mexico offers land grants to anyone bringing settlers to Texas, 1823. → Settlers flock to Texas, some with slaves. → Mexico outlaws further slavery in an effort to slow population growth, 1830.

Multiple Causes

Mexico outlaws further slavery, 1830. →

Mexico halts further American settlement in Texas, 1830. → Texans revolt and set up temporary government, 1835.

General Santa Anna becomes dictator of Mexico, 1834. →

LESSON 2

The Road to Oregon

Wednesday, April 20th *Cloudy. We are creeping along slowly, one wagon after another, the same old gait [pace]; and the same thing over, out of one mud hole and into another all day. Crossed a branch where the water run into the wagons. No corn to be had within 75 miles. Came 18 miles and camp.*

Wednesday, June 1st It has been raining all day long. . . . The men and boys are all soaking wet and look sad and comfortless. (The little ones and myself are shut up in the wagons from the rain. Still it will find its way in and many things are wet; and take us all together, we are a poor looking set, and all this for Oregon. . . .)

Amelia Stewart Knight, an Iowa farm wife, wrote these notes in her diary in 1853, as her covered wagon moved across what is now western Nebraska. Knight was traveling to Oregon with her husband and their seven children. The Knights were only one family among thousands who made the long trip west during the 1840s and 1850s. These people had read newspaper stories about a

THINKING FOCUS

Why were so many settlers willing to make the long and difficult journey to Oregon?

Key Terms

- migrate
- claim

◄ *The move to Oregon was a family affair, with everyone pitching in to help with the chores. In later life, most children would look back on the journey west as a great adventure.*

377

Settling the Far West

wonderful land in the Northwest called Oregon. Many writers praised Oregon's mild weather and rich soil. One writer said that beets grew up to "three feet in diameter, while turnips were five feet around." From stories like these, many people caught "Oregon fever"—a strong desire to move west and start a new life.

Oregon Fever

American interest in Oregon dated back to 1792, when an American named Robert Gray explored the mouth of a huge river. He named the river the Columbia after his sailing ship. The Columbia River flowed through the land that became known as the Oregon Territory. Lewis and Clark reached the area in 1805. The explorations of Gray and Lewis and Clark led to American claims to Oregon Territory.

American missionaries visited Oregon in the 1830s. They hoped to bring Christianity to the Indians. The missionaries liked the region, and they sent letters back east telling of its beauty. Other travelers and explorers who visited Oregon wrote glowing descriptions that appeared in newspapers and books.

It wasn't long before people like the Knights began to think that Oregon was a place where they could get a new start in life. Thousands of families decided to **migrate**—that is, to sell their homes, pack up their belongings, and settle in the new area. ■

■ *What was "Oregon fever" and how did people "catch" it?*

The Oregon Trail

Travelers to Oregon soon found that getting there was not easy. A voyage by ship was costly and took six to eight months. It was much cheaper to travel overland by covered wagon.

Most pioneers took the Oregon Trail. It stretched northwestward from Missouri for 2,000 miles over prairies, rivers, and mountains. The trip took about six months. Pioneers began the journey in the spring. That gave them just enough time to cross the western mountains before winter snows closed the mountain passes.

Preparations for the Trip

To begin the journey, families needed $600 for supplies. Many families raised the money by selling their farms. Next, they loaded their wagons and set out for Independence, Missouri, where the Oregon Trail began.

In Independence, families had to buy food for six months of travel. They stocked up on corn and beans, sugar and flour, coffee and tea, dried fruit and dried meat. When fully loaded, the wagon weighed 1,500 to 2,000 pounds.

▼ *Guidebooks like* The National Wagon Road Guide *provided pioneers with maps and practical travel tips.*

THE NATIONAL Wagon Road Guide.

In the Land of the Buffalo, followed first the Indian, then the White Man

SAN FRANCISCO; PUBLISHED BY WHITTON, TOWNE & CO

Families usually bought one or two teams of oxen. They were better than horses for pulling heavy loads. Families also bought weapons—usually shotguns and rifles—for hunting along the way and for protection.

After several days of preparation, the family loaded the wagon and set off. Rebecca West, who went to Oregon in 1853, wrote about her feelings of wonder in her diary: "The prairie, oh, the broad, the beautiful, the bounding, rolling prairie!"

Travel Along the Trail

Feelings of excitement soon gave way to the hardships of the journey. Pioneers traveled from dawn to dusk, in a wagon train of 50 or more wagons. The wagon train crawled along, averaging about 15 miles a day. At night, the pioneers pulled the wagons into a circle for safety. They often told stories, sang, or danced to help them forget the hardships of the day's travel.

The pioneers faced all kinds of problems along the trail. Bad weather, unsafe water, sickness, a broken axle—all could stop the wagon train for days. Death was always present, as one pioneer noted in her diary:

> Monday, July 28 . . . *Came past a camp of thirty-six wagons who have been camped for some time here in the mountains. They have had their cattle stampeded four or five times. There was a woman died in this train yesterday. She left six children, one of them only two days old. Poor little thing, it had better have died with its mother. They made a good picket fence around the grave.*
>
> Jane Gould Tourtillott, 1862

To learn more about the Oregon Trail, see A Closer Look on the following pages. Trace the Oregon Trail from Missouri to Oregon. Which part of the trail do you think would present the most difficulty for the pioneers?

Across Time & Space

If your family has ever taken a car trip across the United States, you may have followed part of the Oregon Trail or another famous trail. A number of today's highways follow paths taken by the great old trails that stretched west from the Missouri River. The present Interstate Highway 80 comes close to the Oregon Trail in western Nebraska and through Wyoming.

◄ *Friends and neighbors often presented departing pioneers with a memento quilt. Many were sad at the parting, feeling that they would never see each other again.*

379

Settling the Far West

The Oregon Trail

The Oregon Trail was a long, long road to a better life. Between 1840 and 1870, more than 350,000 people packed their belongings into covered wagons and headed west. Survivors endured 2,000 miles and six months of desert heat and mountain cold. For some, it led to tragedy. For others, it was a great adventure.

Death was a part of life on the trail. This steer may have died from exhaustion, starvation, or from drinking bad water. People died on the trail, too— usually from disease or accidents.

Going about two miles an hour, the oxen inched the wagons westward. When the oxen got tired, the men—in boots like these—got off the wagon and walked. As the oxen got weaker, the women and children often had to walk, too.

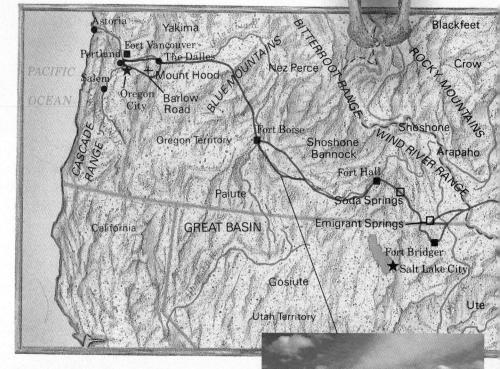

Like tracks from ghosts, these ruts carved by thousands of wagon wheels still scar the land along the Oregon Trail. Although most of them have been plowed over, hundreds of miles of trails like these remain intact.

Chapter 15

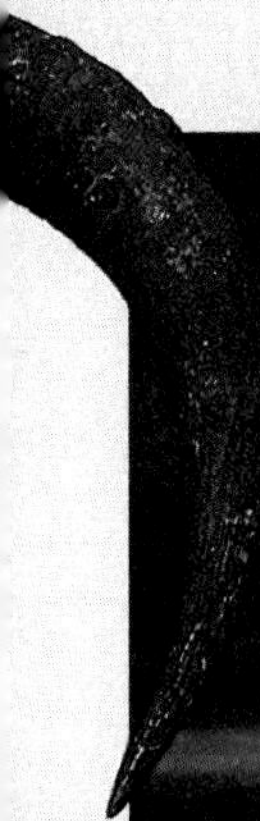

Mile after boring mile, settlers rolled across the plains of the Platte River Valley. When they saw Chimney Rock in western Nebraska, settlers knew the mountains were near. The road was about to get tougher.

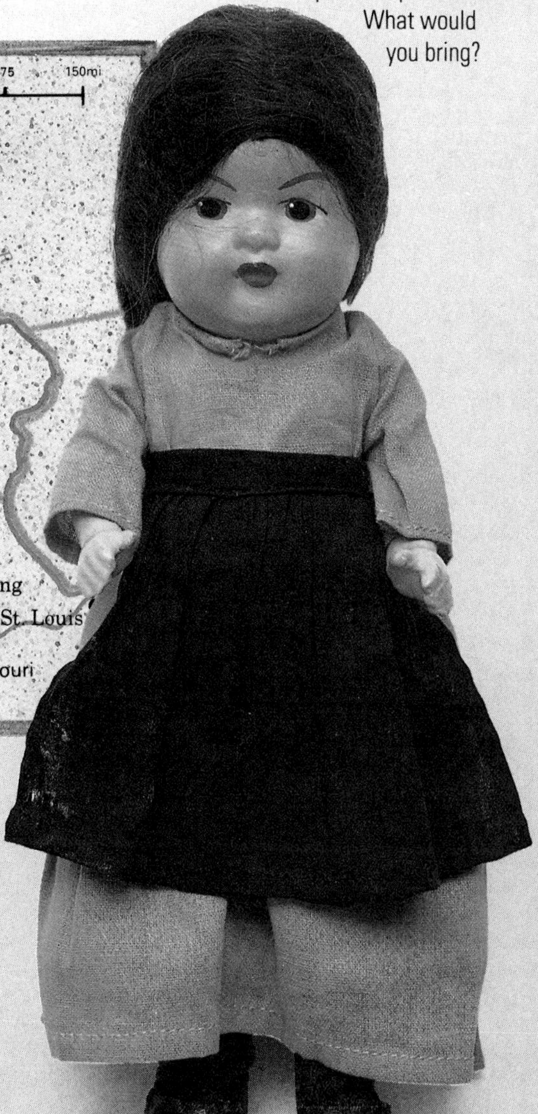

There was time to play on the trail, but little room for toys in the wagon. Children were usually allowed to bring just one. A doll like this one would have been a girl's most precious possession. What would you bring?

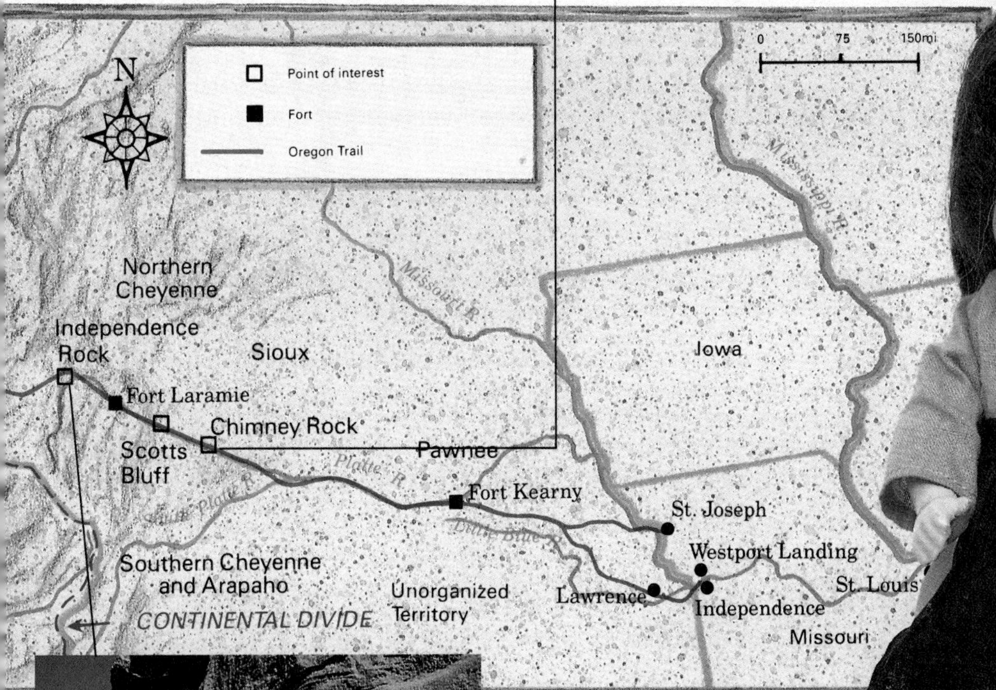

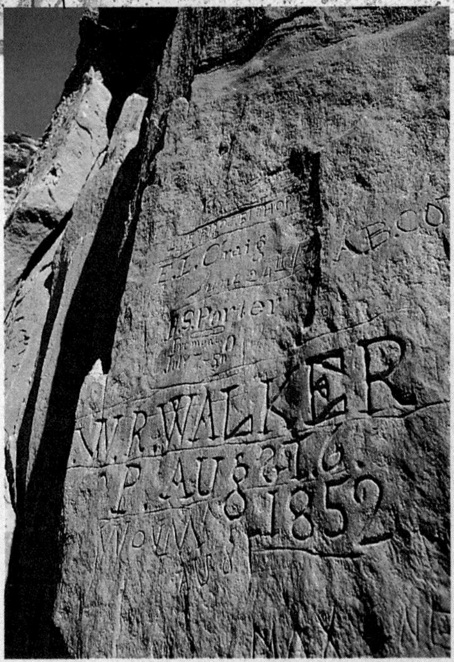

Point of interest
Fort
Oregon Trail

0   75   150mi

Northern Cheyenne

Independence Rock

Fort Laramie

Chimney Rock

Scotts Bluff

Pawnee

Sioux

Missouri R.

Iowa

St. Joseph

Westport Landing

St. Louis

Fort Kearny

Southern Cheyenne and Arapaho

CONTINENTAL DIVIDE

Unorganized Territory

Lawrence

Independence

Missouri

Platte R.

It was a good sign if settlers reached Independence Rock, Wyoming, before July 4, Independence Day. That meant they should get through the mountains before heavy snows came. Some settlers even signed their names and left messages on the rock.

381

The pioneers lost no time establishing stable communities once they reached Oregon. This schoolhouse dates from 1858.

■ *What did a pioneer family need for a trip along the Oregon Trail?*

The End of the Trail

The pioneers faced new challenges once they reached Oregon. They had to file a **claim,** a request to own a tract of land. Each family could get one square mile of land—640 acres. To keep the land, the family had to build a cabin within six months.

Building the cabin was back-breaking work. All family members who were old enough helped chop down trees and prepare the logs. The family lived in the covered wagon until the cabin was ready.

While some built the cabin, others prepared the newly cleared fields for planting. After the cabin was finished, they built furniture. It took the pioneers about six months to get settled and to feel at home in Oregon.

A New State

As the number of settlers in Oregon grew, they demanded that a government be established. Most American settlers wanted Oregon to become part of the United States, but Great Britain also claimed it.

The question of who owned Oregon was settled once and for all in 1846. James K. Polk had won the 1844 presidential election. He had promised to make Oregon a state. The British protested, but they didn't want to go to war. The two countries talked over the problem. In 1846 they agreed to a border along the 49th parallel. That is the border between the United States and Canada today.

Two years later Oregon became a territory of the United States. In February 1859 Oregon joined the Union as the 33rd state. ■

R E V I E W

1. **FOCUS** Why were so many settlers willing to make the long and difficult journey to Oregon?
2. **CONNECT** How did the United States and Great Britain handle the dispute over Oregon? How does this compare with the way the United States and Mexico handled the dispute over Texas?
3. **SOCIAL SYSTEMS** What did pioneer families have to do once they reached Oregon?
4. **GEOGRAPHY** Why did it take a wagon train six months

to make the trip between Missouri and Oregon?
5. **CRITICAL THINKING** Suppose you are living on a farm in Iowa back in 1843. Your family is beginning to think about moving to Oregon. What are some of the questions the family should discuss before making the decision?
6. **WRITING ACTIVITY** Imagine you are about to set out on the Oregon Trail. Write a diary entry telling how you feel.

L E S S O N   3

Migrating to California and Utah

"GOLD MINE FOUND!" proclaimed the newspaper headline from the tiny California settlement of San Francisco on March 15, 1848. The newspaper story went on: "In the newly made raceway [wooden channel for water] of the saw mill recently erected by Captain Sutter . . . gold has been found in considerable quantities."

It took a while for news of the gold strike to spread. By May 1848, for example, only a few hundred gold seekers had come to the lands along the American River near Sutter's mill. By the end of the year, they numbered in the thousands. Before long, people had flocked to California from cities and towns throughout the United States and from countries around the world.

Gold seekers swarmed into the foothills of the Sierra Nevada Mountains. Boom towns grew up overnight. Before it was over, the gold rush would bring more than 300,000 people into California.

THINKING FOCUS

What were the goals of the people who went to California and Utah?

Key Terms

- forty-niner
- Mormon

◄ *George W. Northrup, a Minnesota schoolteacher, had his picture taken in 1849 as he prepared to "strike it rich" in California. Unfortunately, he was killed by Indians before he got out of Minnesota.*

383

Settling the Far West

Early California

California had been part of Spanish Mexico since the 1500s. It had been largely ignored for more than 200 years. Spain finally began to encourage settlement there when it learned that Russian and British fur traders had moved into the area.

Spanish priests began building a chain of missions up and down the coast in 1769. The first settlers from Mexico, called Californios, arrived shortly thereafter. By 1821, the year Mexico won its independence from Spain, there were about 3,000 Californios and 200,000 Indians living in California.

During the next 20 years, most Californios lived and worked on great ranches with thousands and thousands of acres. The ranches raised cattle, not for beef but for the leather hides.

The first settlers from the United States made their way to California at this time. Most were traders who sold hides and furs in China. They became friends with the Californios, married into Californio families, and became Mexican citizens.

More settlers from the United States began arriving in the 1840s. They came overland in covered wagons, just like the settlers who went to Oregon. These new settlers were farmers, not traders. They did not want to become Mexican citizens. In fact, they wanted to make California part of the United States.

When the Mexican War broke out in 1846, some of these American settlers rebelled against the Mexican government. They wanted to make California an independent republic—the Bear Flag Republic. The U.S. government encouraged them. It sent troops and warships to attack Mexican strongholds.

The Mexican forces in California surrendered in 1847, just months before the Mexican War ended. Under the Treaty of Guadalupe Hidalgo, the United States gained a huge territory that included California. ■

The Gold Rush

Nine days before the Treaty of Guadalupe Hidalgo was signed, gold was discovered at Sutter's mill. John Sutter owned a large ranch in the Sacramento Valley.

Sutter had hired a carpenter named James Marshall to build a sawmill and raceway on his property, about 40 miles northeast of present-day Sacramento.

On January 24, 1848, Marshall noticed some shiny bits of metal mixed with the sand, mud, and gravel in the raceway. He picked up the glittering fragments, wrapped them in a rag, and rushed to Sutter.

Making sure that they were alone, Marshall showed Sutter what he had found. The largest pieces were no bigger than a pea. The smallest were the size of a speck. Marshall said he thought the shiny fragments were gold. At first, Sutter didn't believe it, but Marshall was right. He surely had found gold.

Dreams of Striking It Rich

News of the gold strike soon brought thousands of people to California. Farmers left their plows in the field and soldiers ran away from the army, all for gold. In faraway lands like Europe and China, gold seekers boarded ships and came to California. One observer wrote that a gold miner could earn "in one day more than double a soldier's pay for a month."

The gold seekers were called **forty-niners,** for the year 1849 when the gold rush madness was at its peak. Once they reached California, the forty-niners headed straight for the gold fields. All they could think about was striking it rich. All they dreamed about was going back home with a fortune.

Not everyone who moved to California at this time wanted to work in the gold fields. Many men and women came to start a business. Some sold clothing to the miners. Others sold food or mining equipment. Some cooked and did laundry. Others ran hotels.

HISTORY *People heading to California had many questions. Numerous guidebooks helped. For example,* The Emigrants' Guide to California *advised: "After the upper Platte Ford, for over fifty miles, the water is . . . poisonous. . . . If you would avoid sickness, abandon its use."*

▼ *Teachers, farmers, mechanics—people from all walks of life were caught up in the excitement of the gold rush. In this photograph miners use pans and wooden troughs to sift gravel for gold.*

▲ *In 1840, San Francisco was a sleepy little town of 200. By 1850, it was a bustling city of 50,000. Growth was so fast that some people had to live in tents.*

All came to California in the hope of making a profit, as this gold rush tune suggests:

> Oh, California,
>   Thou land of glittering dreams
> Where the yellow dust and diamonds, boys
> Are found in all thy streams!

The wild rush for gold lasted just four years. It peaked in 1852, when forty-niners mined gold worth more than $80 million. Prospecting continued after 1853, but the remaining gold lay deep in the ground. Miners would need costly machines to get at it.

Violence and Injustice

California gold-mining towns usually consisted of a collection of run-down buildings—stores, restaurants, boarding houses, and the like.

There were few laws in these towns, and fewer law officers. As the gold fields filled up, tempers grew short. Arguments often led to fights. Fights often led to shootings.

Prejudice also became a serious problem at this time, especially after 1852 when the gold started to give out. Mexicans, blacks, and Indians working in the gold fields all suffered from prejudice. So did forty-niners who came to California from Europe and China.

Chinese immigrants, Mexican residents, and American Indians experienced harsh injustice. As the number of Chinese immigrants grew, discrimination against them increased. Many Chinese would later be injured or killed helping to build the transcontinental railroad. Now they faced harsh discriminatory laws, such as the Foreign Miners' Tax. Also, California's Indian population was being wiped out by hunger, violence, and disease. Indians living on land purchased by a white settler became slaves by law.

Effects of the Gold Rush

A few forty-niners struck it rich, but most were not so lucky. For example, John Sutter did not become rich from the gold discovered on his property. Forty-niners looking for gold overran his land and ruined his sawmill. Sutter lost all his money and died poor.

The most lasting result of the gold rush was the effect it had on California. The gold rush changed California from a sleepy outpost to an important western land. Many businesses came to the area, and California farmers found more and more buyers for their crops.

The great increase in population made San Francisco a major city almost overnight. It helped make California ready for statehood in 1850. ■

Not everyone came to California to work in the gold fields. Levi Strauss made a fortune by selling denim pants to miners.

■ *How did the gold rush change California?*

A "Kingdom" in Utah

Another group went west in the mid-1800s, but not to find gold. These settlers were **Mormons,** members of the Church of Jesus Christ of Latter-day Saints. They are called Mormons after their sacred scripture, the Book of Mormon. Mormons placed great emphasis on the family. The Mormons went west to worship God and raise their families in their own way.

Early History of the Mormons

Joseph Smith founded the Mormon church in New York in 1830. The Mormons went through difficult times during their early years. They had to move from place to place in order to practice their religion freely. They lived in Ohio for a time, but they left after Smith was tarred and feathered. They moved to Missouri, but left after Smith was jailed. They settled in Illinois, but in 1844, Smith was jailed again. On June 27, a mob stormed the jail and murdered Smith and one of his brothers.

Brigham Young now became leader of the Mormons. He decided to carry out Smith's plan to move to the Great Basin in the Rocky Mountains. Once there, the Mormons could build "the kingdom of God on earth."

The Mormon Migration

Young planned the migration carefully. He would lead the first group of settlers. The rest would wait until he sent word to follow. They set out on the long trail west in April 1847.

▲ *Like many other settlers, Mormons were usually ready to lend their neighbors a helping hand. A barn raising was a community effort.*

After months of travel, Young and his followers entered the Great Salt Lake valley, a dry, treeless land where only sagebrush grew. "This is the place," Young said. Two hours later, the Mormons were hard at work building a new life. Young returned east to bring back the Mormons waiting in Iowa and Nebraska.

The Mormon settlement of Salt Lake City grew. Soon Young and his followers needed more people to help with the work. During the 1850s, thousands of Mormons from as far away as Europe made the difficult trip to Salt Lake City. Mark Twain described a wagon train of Mormons that he saw on his own travels west: "They were dusty and uncombed . . . and ragged, and they did look so tired!"

Mexico owned the Great Salt Lake valley when the Mormons settled there in 1847. It became U.S. land in the Treaty of Guadalupe Hidalgo the following year. The Mormons applied for statehood for Utah in 1849, but Congress made the area a territory instead. Utah did not become a state until 1896. ■

*I*n the vast, endless, rippling prairie land the column of wagons wound slowly westward, crawling over the rise and fall of the land. A thin thread of life under the hot June sun. White canvas gave off a blinding glare; the river glittered like a sheet of brown glass, this shallow, muddy Platte, all tangled in its willows and islands.

Hot, hard going. The dust made a grit in the mouth.

Annabel and Edgar Johnson, 1962
Wilderness Bride

■ *What does the story of the Mormons tell you about their beliefs?*

REVIEW

1. **FOCUS** What were the goals of the people who went to California and Utah?
2. **CONNECT** What happened after settlers from the United States flooded into Texas in the 1820s and 1830s? How was this similar to what happened in California?
3. **HISTORY** What was the most lasting effect of the gold rush?
4. **BELIEF SYSTEMS** Why did the Mormons have to move from place to place during their early years?
5. **CRITICAL THINKING** Two groups of settlers moved to California before the gold rush. How were these groups different?
6. **WRITING ACTIVITY** Imagine that you are a Texan who went to California in 1849 hoping to strike it rich. Write a letter to your parents telling about your adventures.

Chapter 15

L E S S O N 4

Conflicts with the American Indians

The Duwamish, an Indian group living in the Northwest in 1851, were forced to sell most of their ancient lands to white settlers. By the 1850s, the U.S. government was demanding more.

Seattle, a Duwamish chief, had been friendly with the settlers. Now he was troubled. In 1854, Chief Seattle responded to the government. His speech tells a great deal about the American Indians' special feelings for the land:

How did the migration of white settlers change the lives of Indians?

Key Term

- nomad

▼ *Chief Seattle's name was given to the city of Seattle, Washington, which was founded in 1853.*

The great . . . White Chief sends us word that he wants to buy our land. . . .We will consider your offer. When we have decided, we will let you know. Should we accept, I here and now make this condition: we will never be denied the right to visit, at any time, the graves of our fathers and our friends.

Every part of this earth is sacred to my people. Every hillside, every valley, every clearing and wood, is holy in the memory and experience of my people. Even those un-speaking stones along the shore are loud with events and memories in the life of my people. The ground beneath your feet responds more lovingly to our steps than yours, because it is the ashes of our grandfathers. . . . The earth is rich with the lives of our kin.

The young men, the mothers, and girls, the little children who once lived and were happy here, still love these lonely places. And at evening the forests are dark with the presence of the dead. When the last red man has vanished from this earth, and his memory is only a story among the whites, these shores will still swarm with the invisible dead of my people.

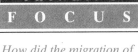

Indian Ways of Life

Across Time & Space

A number of states and cities have Indian names. The name Wyoming, for example, is an Indian word meaning "on the great plain." Its capital city of Cheyenne gets its name from the Cheyenne Indians.

▼ *Compare this map with the one on page 608 of the Minipedia. How did the western Indians live?*

As settlers on their way to Oregon and California crossed the Great Plains, they paid little attention to the American Indians. They knew little about the Indians' beliefs, their way of life, and their feelings about the land. They saw the Indians as just another obstacle on the difficult trip west.

Many different Indian peoples were living west of the Mississippi at this time. Look at the map on this page. Find the names of various Indian peoples who lived on the Great Plains.

The Plains Indians were alike in one way. They all shared a strong belief in the importance of nature and the land. The Plains Indians had a great reverence for the land. They believed it is nature's greatest gift. The land supplied everything they needed. It had to be cared for and protected.

In other respects, the Plains Indians were quite different. Each had its own territory, its own traditions, and its own language. Some Plains Indians were peaceful farmers who raised corn and other crops. Other Indians were **nomads**—people who followed the annual route of migrating animals, especially the buffalo.

Some Plains Indians, like the Sioux and Cheyenne, were great warriors who fought mainly for glory. Others, like some Blackfeet, survived by stealing food and horses from their neighbors.

Indian Groups in the Western United States, 1860

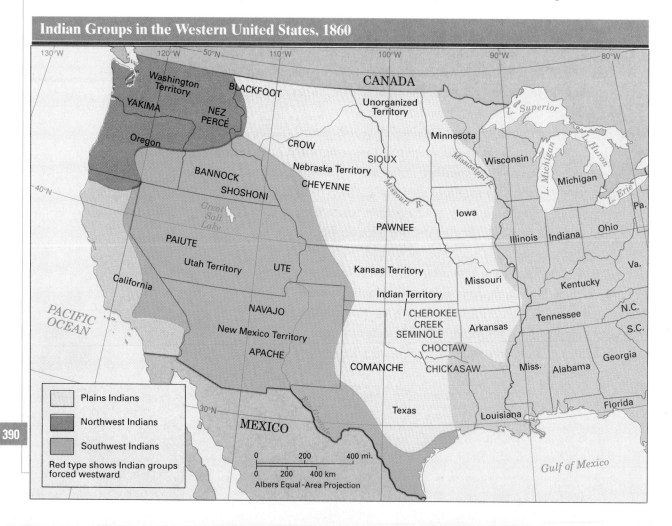

Legend:
- Plains Indians
- Northwest Indians
- Southwest Indians

Red type shows Indian groups forced westward

Many Plains Indians depended on the horse for their way of life. With horses, they could hunt buffalo. They could also strike quickly at their enemies.

Life on the plains was not always peaceful. Indians had fought with one another long before the coming of the settlers. But now the situation got worse. As settlers pushed farther and farther west, they gradually pushed one Indian people onto the land of another. Then the two groups would fight over territory, water, and hunting grounds. As one chief of the Sauk stated, "Let the Sioux keep from our lands, and there will be peace."

Little by little, the Plains Indians were beginning to understand that they all faced a common problem. More and more wagon trains were traveling across Indian land on the way to Oregon and California. How long would it be before settlers started moving onto Indian land in the Great Plains and staying there? ■

▲ *The Plains Indians often communicated by sign language. From left to right these signs mean "trade," "friend," and "white man."*

■ *How did the Indians of the Great Plains differ from each other? How were they alike?*

The Indians and the Settlers

In the early 1800s, the U.S. government made many treaties with the Indians. Time and again, however, settlers moved onto Indian land and the treaties were forgotten.

In 1824, the government tried to improve relations by starting the Bureau of Indian Affairs. Six years later, however, the government ordered thousands of Indians in the Southeast to move to Indian reservations in what is now Oklahoma. Then in 1838–1839 the Cherokee were forced to make their long march west along the Trail of Tears.

Settlers who crossed the Oregon Trail in the late 1840s had mostly peaceful contacts with the Plains Indians. As the migration

◄ *These portraits show how Indian dress was affected by contact with traders. The father, at the far left, is dressed in traditional garb—a deerskin shirt with a buffalo robe. His son is wearing a colorful blanket and glass beads bought from a trader.*

➤ *The two horsemen on the shield represent the growing conflict between Indians and settlers.*

■ *Why did the arrival of white settlers cause conflict among Indian groups?*

increased in the 1850s, however, the settlers began to upset the Indians' way of life.

For example, the settlers' horses and oxen ate grass along the trail. The Indians depended upon the grass for their own horses. In addition, settlers began killing more and more buffalo for food. This caused further trouble. The buffalo was an important food source for the Indians.

Settlers also brought diseases like smallpox and cholera to the Plains. In 1837, a smallpox epidemic swept through one tribe of 1,600. It left only 31 survivors. Forty-niners on their way to California spread cholera. Said one Cheyenne warrior, ill with cholera: "If I could see this thing, if I knew where it was, I would go there and kill it!" ■

UNDERSTANDING DEMOGRAPHIC CHANGE

In the 1830s, the U.S. government expelled thousands of Indians from tribal lands east of the Mississippi. American settlers soon occupied the vacant land.

As a result, the population in these areas changed rapidly. Before the 1830s, it was mainly American Indian. Afterwards, it became mainly white American. Historians refer to this kind of change as a demographic change.

Changes in Population

Not all changes in population are demographic changes. For example, the population of the United States increased dramatically between the years 1789 and 1840. This was not a demographic change, however, because the makeup of the population did not change.

Demographic change always involves new people coming into an area—new people with different languages, different customs, and different values.

A demographic change occurred in California during the 1840s. American settlers moving into the area were very different from the Spanish-speaking Californios already living there. A similar change occurred in the 1980s, with the arrival of thousands of immigrants from the continent of Asia.

Results of the Changes

The results of demographic change are usually positive. People discover new foods, new customs, new ideas, and everyone benefits.

This is not always the case, however. Westward expansion of the United States resulted in changes that disrupted the lives of American Indians down to the present day.

392

Government Intervention

The Indians complained about the settlers. They demanded that the government pay for damage done to Indian lands. Settlers began to fear the Plains Indians, who now began to harass wagon trains. The settlers asked the government to step in.

In 1851, the government called a meeting of nine western tribes at Fort Laramie, in what is now Wyoming. About 10,000 Indians attended. The government had two purposes for the meeting. It wanted to make travel safe for wagon trains, and it wanted to set boundaries for Indian hunting areas.

The government and the Indians signed an agreement at the Fort Laramie meeting. The Indians promised to stop harassing the wagon trains. They accepted boundaries for their territories. They also agreed to let the government build roads and forts on Indian land. In return, the federal government promised to pay each tribe $50,000 a year in food and supplies.

Not surprisingly, the agreement soon broke down. For example,

the government reduced the amount of food and supplies promised by the treaty. The government and the Plains Indians would make other agreements in the future. These would break down, too. Neither side at the Fort Laramie meeting knew that one day settlers would flood into the Great Plains to stay. Neither side knew that one day settlers would drive the Plains Indians from their beloved land. ■

▲ *After years of treaty violations on both sides, the Sioux came to Fort Laramie in 1867 to settle differences with the settlers.*

■ *How did the government respond to the problems among Indian nations and between Indians and settlers?*

R E V I E W

1. **FOCUS** How did the migration of white settlers change the lives of Indians?
2. **CONNECT** What trends have American settlers followed in their dealings with Indians since the first colonial settlement at Jamestown?
3. **SOCIAL SYSTEMS** Name some of the Indian peoples that lived on the Great Plains. How were they alike? How were they different?
4. **CRITICAL THINKING** How did the Plains Indians feel about land? How did settlers feel?
5. **WRITING ACTIVITY** Imagine you are a Plains Indian heading out on a buffalo hunt. One day you see a wagon train of settlers and their families passing through your hunting grounds. Write a short paragraph telling how you might feel.
6. **ACTIVITY** Get together with two or three friends. Make a mural showing a daily scene in a Sioux village. The Minipedia on page 606 shows Sioux clothing, tipis, crafts, and weapons.

Should I Go West with My Family?

> A portion of the emigrants of 1846 . . . lost most of their property, barely getting here with their lives. A better way (than the old road) may be found, but it is best for men with wagons and families not to try this experiment.
>
> George Abernethy, Governor of the Oregon Territory, 1847

> W hoo ha! Go it boys! We're in a perfect Oregon fever. . . . From present evidence, we suppose that no less than two or three thousand people are congregating at this point (Independence, Missouri) previous to their start upon the broad prairie.
>
> Independence Expositor, May 3, 1845

Background

In the mid-1800s, the American West represented both an opportunity and a challenge. It gave a second chance to many people, including thousands of African Americans. European immigrants were pouring into the eastern cities, competing for scarce jobs and housing.

Many people moved west to get out of the cities. In the Midwest, most good land had already been claimed by farmers. If a family found no success in Ohio or Missouri, why not follow the Oregon Trail?

The U.S. government supported western settlement even if it was at the expense of Indians such as the Nez Perce. If Americans didn't claim the land, it was feared, other nations might move in.

What did Easterners really know about the West? Very little. They heard that the land was fertile, though fresh water was often hard to find. They had read letters from early settlers, which described their encounters with dangerous animals and angry Indians whose land the settlers were taking.

What Lies Ahead?

Oregon offered free land and jobs for skilled workers and farmhands. A family could earn a good living. Oregon was a way out of overcrowded cities, an escape from unpaid bills and unhappy memories. Nearly all who were willing to work hard could succeed if they got there alive. For most of this early period, however, slaves and free blacks were excluded from, or prevented from moving to, Oregon.

The trail was lined with the graves of those who died during the journey. People froze or starved to death in blizzards. They fell, wagons and all, into deep mountain passes. They died of fevers caused by drinking unclean water.

Leaving bills and unemployment might also mean leaving friends and family or aging parents. Settlers also left schools and churches, doctors, and the familiar buildings of a town or neighborhood.

Travel to Oregon was extremely difficult and slow. Some of the settlers who took the Oregon Trail would turn back eventually. Others would persuade family and friends to move west. But as they left Missouri, they left the world they knew behind.

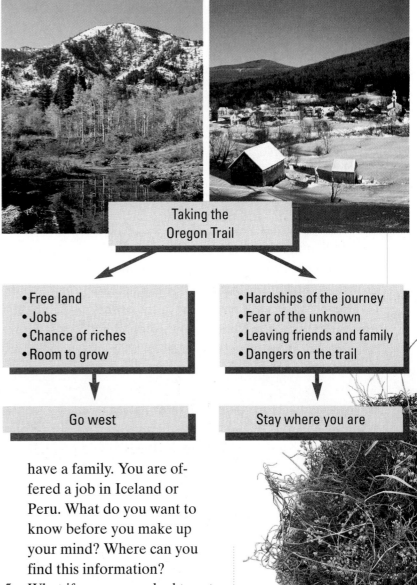

Taking the Oregon Trail

- Free land
- Jobs
- Chance of riches
- Room to grow

Go west

- Hardships of the journey
- Fear of the unknown
- Leaving friends and family
- Dangers on the trail

Stay where you are

Decision Point

1. Half your family wants to go to Oregon; half wants to stay put. What do you know that would help you decide what to do?
2. What would you want to know about Oregon? How could you get this information?
3. How do you think the western Indians felt about the increased numbers of settlers moving into Indian land?
4. Suppose you are grown and have a family. You are offered a job in Iceland or Peru. What do you want to know before you make up your mind? Where can you find this information?
5. What if you were asked to settle on another planet? What would be good reasons for going? For staying here?

Chapter Review

Reviewing Key Terms

annex (p. 373)
claim (p. 382)
forty-niner (p. 385)
migrate (p. 378)

Mormon (p. 387)
nomad (p. 390)
plain (p. 371)

A. The two words in each pair are related in some way. The first word is always a key term. On your own paper, write a sentence explaining how the words are related.

1. annex, add
2. claim, right
3. forty-niner, prospector
4. migrate, move
5. plain, flat
6. nomad, traveler
7. Mormon, religion

B. On your own paper, use each key term in a sentence that shows what the word means. Write each sentence as if you were a settler writing a letter to a friend back home.

1. claim
2. forty-niner
3. migrate
4. Mormons
5. plains
6. nomads

Exploring Concepts

A. Look at the timeline below. You will see dates for important historical events in the growth of the United States. Copy the timeline on a separate sheet of paper. Fill in the events for the years shown. Notice that the completed timeline will show two events each for the years 1846 and 1848.

B. Answer each question with information from the chapter.

1. Why did Americans migrate to Texas?
2. What were the events leading up to the Mexican War?

3. What effect did the Treaty of Guadalupe Hidalgo have on the southern border of the United States?
4. Why was the journey to Oregon so hard?
5. How were the goals of the people who migrated to California and Utah alike? How were they different?
6. During this time, the United States had conflicts with Mexico and with Great Britain. How were the conflicts similar? How were they different?
7. What were reasons for the friction between the settlers and the American Indians?

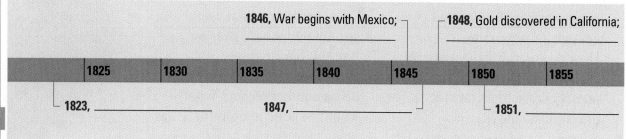

1846, War begins with Mexico;

1848, Gold discovered in California;

1825   1830   1835   1840   1845   1850   1855

1823, _____   1847, _____   1851, _____

Reviewing Skills

1. Study the diagram on this page. Was the discovery of gold a cause or an effect? Which entry is both a cause and an effect?
2. Look again at Lesson 2. Make a chain-effect diagram that explains the events that led to demands for a regional government in Oregon.
3. The map on page 390 shows the location of American Indian groups in the western United States during the 1840s and 1850s. Study the map, then copy the following paragraph onto your own paper. Complete the paragraph using cardinal and intermediate directions.

   We traveled west from Texas into the land inhabited by the Apache. From there, we journeyed _____ into Navajo country. We then traveled _____ to reach the land of the Paiute.
4. Suppose you were a settler interested in bringing more people to Texas and you had decided to create an advertisement. Would you use an illustration or a photograph of Texas in your ad? Why?

The California Gold Rush 1848–1853

Gold discovered in California, 1848. → 250,000 people from around the world arrive in California seeking gold, 1848–1853. → Increased population leads to California becoming a state, 1850.

Using Critical Thinking

1. Many people moved to Texas because they believed the advertisements about Texas. Are people as influenced by advertisements today? Explain.
2. In the 1800s, people caught "Oregon fever," an intense desire to move west and start a new life. Do you think people in the 2000s will ever be infected with "planet fever"? Why?
3. The Plains Indians had a great reverence for the land. They believed it was nature's greatest gift and had to be cared for and protected. Do you think Americans today share this belief? Explain.

Preparing for Citizenship

1. **GROUP ACTIVITY** Advertisements persuaded thousands of Americans to settle in Texas during the 1820s and 1830s. Write an advertisement that would attract people to move to your state. Include the main advantages of living in your state.
2. **ARTS ACTIVITY** Look at the Alamo Flag on page 372 and other flags in American history on pages 602–603 of the Minipedia. Choose one of the groups discussed in this chapter and design a flag for that group.
3. **COLLABORATIVE LEARNING** As a class project, paint a mural of one family's trek west on the Oregon Trail. First, as a class, decide which scenes to show. Then, working in groups of four, choose one of the scenes to paint. Each person in a group should be in charge of researching and drawing one of the following: (1) the landscape, (2) the equipment, (3) the people, and (4) the animals. Paint your scene on a large sheet of paper. Join the scenes to form the mural.

Unit 6
A Nation in Conflict

During the 1800s, the United States enjoyed booming success. Yet the nation seemed like two different places. The North was a land of bustling cities and busy factories. Southern life was shaped by the work of slaves, such as those shown here. As the North and South began to argue about slavery, Americans wondered which direction the nation would take.

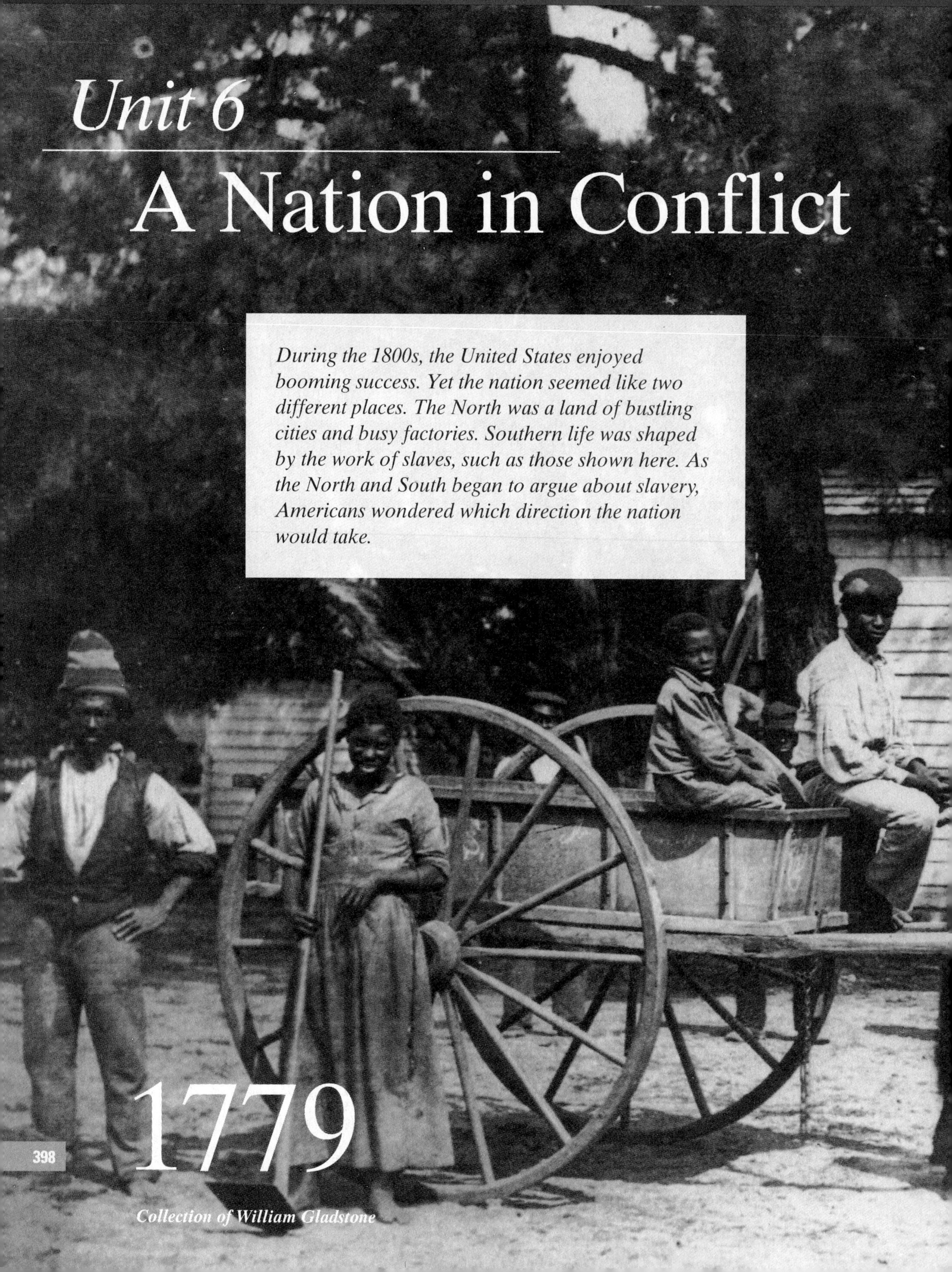

1779

Collection of William Gladstone

1861

Southern Society

Just as tobacco changed the South in the 1600s, cotton changed the South in the 1800s. Huge profits from the crop allowed a few plantation owners to live in great luxury. For poorer farmers who wanted the wealth and power of the planters, cotton was the best way to get rich. For the slaves who worked in the fields and mansions of the plantations, the cotton boom simply meant more hard work.

During this time, a few rich plantation families dominate southern society. Mary Theodosia Ford appears to be the ideal southern belle: wealthy and proper.

1793 Eli Whitney invents the cotton gin. The gin, shown in the drawing to the left, helps make cotton a profitable crop. It also leads to a huge increase in the number of slaves living in the South (above).

1750	1775	1800

1808 Congress bans the import of slaves from Africa.

1779

1820 The southern states become the world's largest producers of cotton. The South grows most of its cotton on large plantations, like the one shown above.

1860 More than three-quarters of white southerners own no slaves. Most of these people run small farms with their families, often using crude tools like this plow.

1825

1850

1875

1850 More than 3 million slaves now live in the United States.

401

1860

LESSON 1

Plantation Society

Key Terms

- cotton gin
- abolitionist

A biel Abbot, a minister from Massachusetts, often traveled to the warm South for his health. In 1818, he visited the Elms, a South Carolina rice plantation. Abbot had seen grand southern estates before and had even attended fancy parties at several plantation houses. Still, the wealth Abiel Abbot saw at the Elms greatly impressed him.

In his journal, Abbot described a fine mansion staffed by "perfect servants" who polished his shoes and straightened his clothes. One of the daughters of the family entertained him by playing the harp, and Abbot said, "the effect was magical." He and the master of the plantation "partook of a plentiful repast of tea, hominy, John Cake, & meats." His host spoke "with much knowledge of the world and books."

Abbot's account of life at the Elms differed little from a description written 34 years later by Mrs. Henry Schoolcraft, the wife of a South Carolina planter. She wrote

➤ *Drayton Hall is the name of both this South Carolina mansion, and the plantation on which it was built. Completed in 1742, Drayton Hall is the oldest plantation house still standing in the South.*

of White Hall, another South Carolina plantation: "The entrance to White Hall from the land side was a long avenue of live oaks and a hedge of evergreen." Mrs. Schoolcraft went on to describe the splendor of the house: "The house contained 21 rooms, each thirty feet square. The imposingly large architecture, set off with wings, gave the building quite the appearance of a palace."

At a wedding in the garden, tables were "groaning" from the weight of "fish, flesh, and fowl, pies, cakes, and puddings, fruits and bouquets, nuts and wines." The wedding guests danced late into the evening, and slaves attended their every need.

A South Carolina planter and investor, the Reverend John G. Drayton grew rice, cotton, and other crops on his family plantation.

King Cotton

Tobacco, rice, wheat, and indigo were important crops on plantations like the ones Abiel Abbot and Mrs. Schoolcraft visited. But cotton was king in the South. Cotton was the crop that fueled the southern economy and made the plantation owners rich.

One drawback to growing cotton was the time it took to process the crop after harvesting. Inside the fluffy bolls, or tufts, of cotton were sticky seeds. Slaves had to remove each seed by hand.

In 1793, a Massachusetts native named Eli Whitney solved the problem by inventing the **cotton gin.** Whitney's invention was a small, boxy machine that removed the seeds from cotton. Here's how it worked.

A worker fed a boll of cotton into the gin and turned a crank. Metal teeth grabbed the cotton and pulled it

The Cotton Kingdom, 1820 and 1860

The invention of the cotton gin led to a great increase in cotton production in the South. Which states gave over half of their land to cotton by 1860?

Land cultivated in cotton by 1820

Land cultivated in cotton by 1860

Southern Society

1 Metal teeth pull raw cotton through the grate.

2 Seeds, which cannot pass through the grate, are collected here.

3 Brushes sweep cotton out of the gin.

Growth of Cotton and Slavery, 1800–1860

	= 100,000 bales of cotton
	= 200,000 slaves

1800

1820

1840

1860

▲ *Eli Whitney's cotton gin made quick work of cotton seeding. The result, as the graph shows, was an increase in cotton production.*

■ *How did the invention of the cotton gin increase the need for slaves in the South?*

through narrow slits. The cotton passed through the slits easily, but the seeds could not and were left behind. Brushes swept the cleaned cotton out of the machine. One cotton gin could clean as much cotton in a day as 50 people working by hand.

The textile mills in New England and Europe bought all the cotton the South could produce. So plantation owners planted more and more cotton, using slaves to pick it and the cotton gin to clean it. The more cotton they grew, the more slaves they demanded. Thus, Eli Whitney's time- and labor-saving invention actually increased the need for slave labor. ■

The Plantation Owners

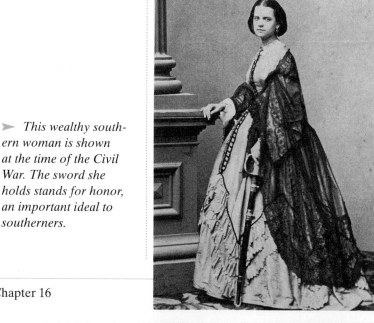

➤ *This wealthy southern woman is shown at the time of the Civil War. The sword she holds stands for honor, an important ideal to southerners.*

The huge profits some southern slave owners earned from cotton, tobacco, and other crops allowed them to live a life of wealth and leisure. This made them feel that white people were superior to other races. The diaries and letters of plantation owners provide examples of their values.

William Byrd was a planter in the South before the Revolutionary War. Byrd owned Westover, a large tobacco plantation in Virginia. In his diary, he described what he felt was his role as a southern planter and slave owner:

> I must take care to keep all my people to their Duty, to set all the Springs in motion and to make every one draw his equal Share to carry the Machine [plantation life] forward.

William Byrd thought of himself as a wise master, like a father who takes care of his family. This idea of the slave owner as a father appears often in the writings of some white people. They argued that owning slaves, like being a parent, was their duty.

White southerners also felt bound to protect their honor. A gentleman might challenge another man to a duel if he felt insulted in some way.

Planters thought it was their duty to become educated and cultured—to read, listen to music, and entertain. Abbot often made mention in his journal of the well-kept plantation libraries he saw during his many travels. ■

■ *How did the wealthy southern planters live, and what were some of their beliefs?*

The Defense of Slavery

Very few white southerners became rich enough to enjoy a wealthy style of life. In fact, less than one-third of all white southerners owned slaves. Still, nearly all white southerners defended their right to hold black slaves, in part because African slavery raised the status of all whites.

Revolt!

One bloody August night in 1831, this "right" was challenged by an angry Virginia slave named Nat Turner. Turner, a forceful preacher who said he had visions from God, believed that God wanted him to free the slaves.

On the night of August 21, Turner and seven slaves murdered Turner's owner, Joseph Travis, and his family. During the next two days, about 75 slaves joined Turner's cause, killing over 50 white people.

A force of 3,000 whites put down the revolt. Nine to ten weeks later, Turner was captured. He told

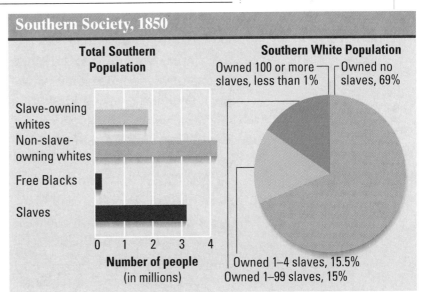

Southern Society, 1850

Total Southern Population

- Slave-owning whites
- Non-slave-owning whites
- Free Blacks
- Slaves

Number of people (in millions)
0 1 2 3 4

Southern White Population

- Owned 100 or more slaves, less than 1%
- Owned no slaves, 69%
- Owned 1–4 slaves, 15.5%
- Owned 1–99 slaves, 15%

authorities, "It was my object to carry terror and devastation wherever we went."

Although Turner was convicted and hanged, white southerners became afraid. After 1831, tensions between whites and blacks increased, especially in the South.

Attacks from the North

Slavery also was being attacked by some people in the northern

▲ *These two graphs show the distribution of people in southern society. The graph on the right shows how few southern whites owned slaves.*

Southern Society

➤ *Nat Turner, an educated slave shown preaching in this 19th-century engraving, led the most infamous slave rebellion in U.S. history. The Virginia militia captured and hanged Turner and about 20 of his fellow rebels.*

states. These people were called **abolitionists,** because they believed that slavery was wrong and should be abolished, or ended. One northern abolitionist, William Lloyd Garrison, wrote in his antislavery newspaper, *The Liberator:*

I will be as harsh as truth and as uncompromising as justice. On this subject [slavery], I do not wish to think, or speak, or write, with moderation. No! No!

■ *In what two ways was slavery challenged during the first half of the 19th century?*

Such attacks made whites in the South angry. Before Turner's revolt, a few planters had been apologetic about keeping slaves. But now they were prepared to defend slavery. They argued that slaves were better off than northerners who worked in dark, dirty factories. In defense of their investment in slaves, planters argued that blacks were an inferior race. One of their strongest arguments noted that the Constitution let states make their own laws about slavery. ■

R E V I E W

1. **FOCUS** How did cotton and slavery allow cotton planters to live a privileged life?
2. **CONNECT** How were the lives of the wealthy southern planters different from the lives of prosperous farmers in the northern states? What were some reasons for these differences?
3. **ECONOMICS** Describe how the cotton gin works and how it affected the southern economy.
4. **CRITICAL THINKING** William Byrd of Virginia said, "I must take care to keep all my people to their Duty."

Who were his people? What was their duty? How does this quote show that Byrd saw himself like a father?

5. **CRITICAL THINKING** How might life in the South have been different if Eli Whitney had not invented the cotton gin?
6. **ACTIVITY** Imagine you are a slave being urged to join Nat Turner's revolt. Will you join the revolt or not? Why? In a brief speech to your classmates, explain your decision and your reasons.

406

Chapter 16

LESSON 2

A Look at Slavery

The Reverend Josiah Henson was a former slave who escaped to Canada. In his autobiography, Reverend Henson recalled the horror of being sold at a 1795 slave auction in Maryland:

M y brothers and sisters were bid off first, and one by one, while my mother, paralyzed with grief, held me by the hand. Her turn came and she was bought by Isaac Riley of Montgomery County. Then I was

offered. . . . My mother, half distracted with the thought of parting forever from all her children, pushed though the crowd while the bidding for me was going on, to the spot where Riley was standing. She fell at his feet, and clung to his knees, entreating [begging] him in tones that a mother only could command, to buy her baby as well as herself, and spare to her one, at least, of her little ones.

Isaac Riley was unmoved by the mother's pleas. He kicked her nearly senseless. Josiah, just five years old, was bought by another man.

THINKING
FOCUS

How did slaves survive both physically and spiritually?

Key Terms

- overseer
- spiritual

◀ *Not unlike livestock, slaves were sold at public auctions like the one announced on this wall poster (far left). Slaves were forced to wear tags (left) that indicated the type of work for which they were thought to be best suited.*

VALUABLE GANG OF YOUNG NEGROES
By JOS. A. BEARD.
Will be sold at Auction,
ON WEDNESDAY, 25TH INST.
At 12 o'clock, at Banks' Arcade,
17 Valuable Young Negroes, Men and Women, Field Hands. Sold for no fault; with the best city guarantees.
Sale Positive and without reserve!
☞ TERMS CASH.
New Orleans, March 24, 1840.

The Hard Life of a Slave

All slaves lived without freedom, but not all slaves lived under the same conditions. The daily lives of slaves depended on the size of the plantation they worked, the kind of work assigned to them, and the treatment they received.

Only a few plantations had more than 100 slaves; most had fewer than 10. On the smaller plantations, white owners often worked side by side with black slaves. However, this closeness did not mean that the life of a slave was less harsh. The treatment a slave received depended on the owner's character and not on the size of the plantation.

Life Under the Overseer

The owners of large plantations in the South did not work with their slaves. They hired a white or black **overseer,** or boss, to watch over the workers while they were in the fields. When the overseer became angry or impatient, he often punished the slaves with his whip or by other means. Solomon Northup, a slave, remembered that 25 lashes was "a mere brush." Northup explained that "50 is ordinary. . . . One hundred is called severe."

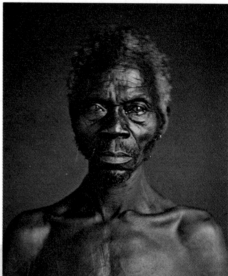

Young and old field slaves, like those below and on the right, usually worked from dawn until dusk

The overseer organized field slaves into work crews, or gangs, of 20 to 25 men, women, and children. During an average day on a cotton plantation, the field slaves worked 14 hours. Adult slaves picked nearly 200 pounds of cotton.

After he gained his freedom, Solomon Northup described the slaves' tiring schedule. He noted that the slaves were up before dawn, and that "they are not permitted to be a moment idle until it is too dark to see, and when the moon is full, they often times labor till the middle of the night."

Women were not given much time to care for their children. Sometimes, the women strapped the babies on their backs and carried them into the fields.

Harsh Treatment

Most slaves lived in drafty, one-room cabins with dirt floors. Many times, two or more families would live together in one cabin. They often slept on the ground on mattresses filled with cornhusks. Northup described his bed as "a plank 12 inches wide and 10 feet

long." His pillow was a stick. Slaves wore shabby cotton or wool clothing, and they ate the poorest food: pork fat, molasses, and cornmeal. Sometimes they could raise vegetables. But often the food did not have important nutrients.

Most slaves worked in the fields, but a few had other jobs. House slaves cleaned, cooked, washed, sewed, and took care of children in the "big house," or plantation mansion. Their jobs were sometimes easier than working in the fields, but many house slaves suffered constant criticism from their watchful owners.

Some slaves were skilled craft workers. These slaves worked as blacksmiths, carpenters, weavers, and ironworkers. Some urban slaves worked in factories or on the docks in cities such as Charleston and Savannah. These slaves sometimes felt lucky because their work was not as hard as the work of field slaves. ■

▲ These slave quarters on the Evergreen Plantation in Louisiana have been restored to their original condition. How do these cabins compare with Drayton Hall on page 402?

◄ Female house slaves, like the woman at left, often became second mothers to the children of the plantation owners.

■ How did most overseers control the slaves on large plantations?

Surviving Slavery

Slaves developed a culture that helped them survive their hard lives. Although Congress had outlawed the slave trade from Africa after 1808, an illegal slave trade lasted for 50 more years. Still, by the 1850s most slaves in the United States had been born here. These slaves mixed their African traditions with the culture of their slavemasters and American Indians to form an African-American culture.

The Influence of Religion

Religion was an important part of African American culture. The religion that most white southerners practiced promised a free and joyful life in heaven. The slaves heard the story of Moses, who led his people out of Egypt and slavery, and dreamed of the day they would be led to freedom. The slaves made their masters' religion their own. They held secret services during which they expressed their African heritage. The time and place of these meetings was communicated by code.

The Importance of Music

Christianity inspired the slaves to compose **spirituals,** religious songs expressing strong desire for a better life. One included these lines: "There's a better day a-coming, Go sound the jubilee."

The slaves also wrote songs about their daily experiences—their work, loves, and sorrows.

A CLOSER LOOK

Slave Culture

Uprooted from their African homes, American slaves developed a culture that mixed African elements and American features. Food, fabric, music—all clearly showed the influence of cultures lost but not forgotten.

The earliest banjos were hollow gourds covered with animal skin, just like West African stringed instruments. Thomas Jefferson noticed his slaves playing "the Banjer, which they brought hither from Africa." He enjoyed the pleasing music they made.

*R*abbit in the briar patch,
Squirrel in the tree,
Wish I could go hunting
But I ain't free.

The big bee flies high,
The little bee makes the honey
The black folks make the
    cotton
And the white folks get the
    money.

We raise the wheat,
They give us the corn;
We bake the bread,
They give us the crust;
We sift the meal,
They give us the skin,
And that's the way
They take us in.

The pictures on these pages show how music influenced and enriched the lives of slaves. They expressed their feelings and creativity by singing, playing instruments, and dancing.

In the book *To Be a Slave*, a slave named Betty Jones told how the slaves would gather at night to dance and have fun. "Saturday nights we'd slip out the quarters and go to the woods," Jones recalled. "Was an ol' cabin 'bout five miles away from the house and us would raise all the ruckus there we wanted to." As Betty Jones remembered, music was an important part of these gatherings. "Every gal with her beau and such music! Had two fiddles, two tambourines, two banjos and two sets of bones." ■

■ *How did the spirituals help blacks survive slavery?*

The taste of Africa lingered in foods slaves grew in the New World—peanuts, yams, radishes, greens, and rice. American "soul food" began with West African-style cooking.

Look at the way this quilt is sewn in uneven, brightly colored strips. This method is also used in African cloth patterns. Though slaves learned how to quilt in America, their quilts had creative, African-style patterns.

Resisting Slavery

■ *How did some slaves resist slavery?*

Many slaves learned to survive the suffering and shame of being treated as property; however, none was happy. They never stopped preparing for the day when they would finally be free.

Slaves often resisted in simple ways. They pretended to be sick, or they broke farm tools needed to work the fields. House slaves often took food and liquor from their masters. One slave, Charles Ball, said he had never met a slave "who believed that he violated any rule of morality by appropriating [taking] to himself anything that belonged to his master."

Sometimes acts of resistance were quite daring. Many slaves tried to escape to freedom in the North or to another state. Trying to escape was a brave but risky act, because any slave who was caught would be severely beaten. Sometimes, a recaptured slave was put to death as an example to other slaves.

Some slaves attacked their masters or organized slave revolts like the one led by Nat Turner. But these revolts had little chance of succeeding. The slaves were usually outnumbered and owners were always on the lookout for signs of rebellion. Slave owners would be sure to kill any slaves they caught planning a revolt.

Slave owners convinced themselves that slaves worked happily, but slave resistance proved them wrong. Solomon Northup predicted a "terrible day of vengeance," a feeling shared by all slaves who resisted their suffering at the hands of cruel slave masters. ■

▼ *As this poster makes clear, large amounts of money were offered to anyone who returned a runaway slave. Notice that the reward got bigger the further away the slave was caught.*

$150 REWARD

RANAWAY from the subscriber, on the night of the 2d instant, a negro man, who calls himself *Henry May*, about 22 years old, 5 feet 6 or 8 inches high, ordinary color, rather chunky built, bushy head, and has it divided mostly on one side, and keeps it very nicely combed; has been raised in the house, and is a first rate dining-room servant, and was in a tavern in Louisville for 18 months. I expect he is now in Louisville trying to make his escape to a free state, (in all probability to Cincinnati, Ohio.) Perhaps he may try to get employment on a steamboat. He is a good cook, and is handy in any capacity as a house servant. Had on when he left, a dark cassinett coatee, and dark striped cassinett pantaloons, new—he had other clothing. I will give $50 reward if taken in Louisville; 100 dollars if taken one hundred miles from Louisville in this State, and 150 dollars if taken out of this State, and delivered to me, or secured in any jail so that I can get him again.
WILLIAM BURKE.
Bardstown, Ky., September 3d, 1838.

REVIEW

1. **FOCUS** How were slaves able to survive both physically and spiritually?

2. **CONNECT** Recall how William Byrd described his duty as a slave owner. How do you think Byrd would have reacted if he had heard his slaves singing "Rabbit in the briar patch"?

3. **CULTURE** How did the slaves' family life and religious beliefs help them to live through their cruel treatment?

4. **CRITICAL THINKING** Charles Ball said that he had never met a slave who thought it was wrong to take things from a slave master. Why did slaves feel this way?

5. **WRITING ACTIVITY** Abiel Abbot and Mrs. Schoolcraft wrote descriptions of southern life. What type of description of southern life do you suppose a slave would have written? Imagine you are a slave like Josiah Henson or Charles Ball. Write a description of life in the South as you see it.

LESSON 3

Life in the Other South

In the American Revolution, a southern teenager named Andrew Jackson and his two brothers fought against the British. One of the brothers was killed. Andrew and his other brother were captured by the British and put in prison in 1781. There, the boys caught smallpox, and Andrew's remaining brother died. Not long after his mother won his release from prison, she also died. Andrew was an orphan at the age of 14.

He had grown up in the kind of poverty that was typical in the South. His family had shared a log cabin in the woods. Nevertheless, Andrew grew to be an adventurous and educated young man. He raced horses in Charleston, taught school in his home settlement, and started a successful law practice in Tennessee. In the War of 1812, he led American troops to victory.

Before long, the young man had achieved the dream of many poor southerners. He bought a great deal of land, established a large plantation, and purchased many slaves to work it. Many years later, in 1828, this poor boy of the South was elected the seventh President of the United States.

THINKING FOCUS

Why did people who owned no slaves defend slavery?

Key Term

- sharecropper

◄ *Very few southern whites lived on plantations in big houses. For most southerners, like the family pictured here, home was a one-room log cabin in the woods.*

413

Southern Society

The People of the Other South

Across Time & Space

Before the Civil War, nearly all sharecroppers were poor white southerners. After the war, however, most sharecroppers were black. During the 1930s, black sharecroppers formed a labor union to fight for better living and working conditions.

Many white southerners shared Jackson's dream of wealth and a life of privilege. They made up the "other South"—white southerners who neither owned slaves nor lived on plantations. Three-fourths of all white southerners belonged to this other South. A few traded cotton or manufactured goods. Most lived as Andrew Jackson had, in simple cabins on small farms in the mountains or foothills.

These farmers grew a little wheat, corn, and other vegetables and owned a cow or two. If they grew any cotton at all, it was just enough for their own needs. They had no money to buy slaves, so they worked the land themselves. These southern farmers were quite poor, and their lives were hard.

Some white southerners were so poor they couldn't even afford to own their own land. Usually they rented a small area to farm and gave part of everything they grew to the land's owners. These farmers were called **sharecroppers.** Sharecroppers grew barely enough food to survive. Their lives were very different from those of the rich, independent plantation owners.

Other farmers lived on good farmland near large cotton, rice, or indigo plantations. These farmers

UNDERSTANDING SOCIAL CLASS

On plantations of the South, rich planters lived in luxury and leisure. In contrast, many farmers had only poverty and hard work. Planters and poor southern farmers belonged to different social classes.

A Way of Living

A social class is a group of people who have a similar economic position and way of life in their society. People in the planters' social class had the money and free time to travel, read, and entertain their friends. People in the farmers' social class had to work from morning until night to take care of their needs and to earn the little money they had.

People in a social class often think alike about important issues. Most planters supported slavery, because it had made them rich. Poor southern farmers supported slavery because with slaves around, farmers didn't feel that they were the lowest social class.

Social Class Today

Social classes exist today just as they did in the mid-1800s. In the United States, the amount of money people have usually influences their social class. The rich enjoy a way of life that the poor cannot afford. The jobs and the education people have also reflect their social class.

Like southern planters, people in a social class today may feel so strongly about an issue that they will fight for it. Poor people hold protest marches to demand better places to live and better jobs.

earned a living by raising hogs and selling bacon and pork to local slaveowners. Most of these farmers were not poor, but the rich planters still looked down on them as just hog herders. ■

■ *How did southern whites who did not own slaves make a living?*

Life on Small Farms

Few free southerners were sharecroppers or hog herders. Most were small, independent farmers—frontiersmen, like Andrew Jackson, seeking a better life. Their land was not fertile enough to raise cotton, but they could grow corn and other vegetables. Other food came from the animals they hunted in the forest. In 1853, a traveler from the North named Frederick Law Olmsted described their houses: "The large majority of the dwellings were of logs, and even those of the white people were often without glass windows."

Religion gave some comfort to these poor southern farmers. Once a year they traveled to camp meetings, where thousands gathered in tents or sheds for a week of religious services. For those farmers who lived far from one another, the camp meeting became an important social occasion as well as a religious event.

Getting together at camp meetings was a special time because small farmers often moved in search of better land and more opportunity. At each new spot, their lives began again. They had to build new cabins and clear new land for their crops. They had to depend on just themselves, because they had lost touch with old friends and neighbors. Moving around made the farmers strong and independent, and they were proud of this spirit. ■

These books of Southern Methodist hymns were published in 1855.

■ *Why was an independent spirit so important to small southern farmers?*

◄ *This painting shows a quilting party, a chance for southern families to get together and socialize.*

Unity in Defense of Slavery

Although most small southern farmers never owned slaves, they defended the system of slavery. The success of Andrew Jackson helps to explain why poor whites were willing to stand up for the lifestyles of the rich southern slavemasters.

The poor knew that Jackson had once been one of them. The wealth and privilege he had achieved gave them hope, even as they worked their poor farmlands and lived in their log cabins. Perhaps one day they, too, would become rich, live on a large plantation, and own slaves.

Small farmers also defended slavery because it made them feel more important and richer than they were. In the "other South," the poorest whites lived in shacks no better than slaves' cabins, but they still thought they were better than black slaves.

In Mark Twain's novel *The Adventures of Huckleberry Finn,* Huck's father thinks that he is superior to blacks, even though he himself could not read and didn't have a job. In the speech that follows, you can sense that Huck's father feels threatened by a black man who has gained his freedom:

*T*hey said he was a p'fessor in a college, and could talk all kinds of languages, and knowed everything. And that ain't the wust. They said he could *vote,* when he was at home. Well, that let me out. Thinks I, what is the country a'coming to?

Rich plantation owners got the support of small farmers in defending slavery because both groups hated outside interference. They especially disliked criticism from the northern states. When northerners spoke against slavery, all southern whites, rich and poor alike, felt stung by the attack. They deeply disliked what they considered the interference of the North in southern affairs. By 1861, this resentment had grown quite strong. Many southern states were now in open rebellion against the federal government. Some had even left the Union. The terrible Civil War was just a cannon shot away. ■

■ *How did the system of slavery make poor southern whites feel important?*

R E V I E W

1. **FOCUS** Why did people who owned no slaves defend slavery?

2. **CONNECT** During the California gold rush, gold seekers dreamed of riches and power. Very few, however, realized their dreams. How was the situation of poor southern whites similar to that of the gold seekers?

3. **CULTURE** What is a camp meeting? Why were camp meetings important to southern farmers?

4. **CRITICAL THINKING** How might the South have been different if the small farmers hadn't shared the ideals of the cotton planters so closely?

5. **WRITING ACTIVITY** Imagine the year is 1840, and you are a northerner who has come to the South to visit your cousin. Your cousin's family is part of the other South described in this chapter. Write a paragraph that describes what your cousin's life is like.

Interpreting History Visually

Here's Why

Imagining what it was like to grow up during a particular historical period can give you an understanding of the people and the times. Suppose you had been the child of a plantation owner in the South before the Civil War. What if you had lived on a small farm without slaves? What would it have been like to live as a slave?

Just as you can write a report to inform others what you have learned about a topic, you also can draw a picture. In the picture you can express what you know and also what you feel.

Here's How

Paintings and works of art can help you understand how people lived in the past. They can tell you how artists feel about their subjects.

Study the details of the painting to the right. Black artist Henry Ossawa Tanner made this painting, *The Banjo Lesson*, in 1893. The father is teaching his son to play the banjo. The bare floor and mostly bare walls tell you that the family is poor. The food on the table makes you think the lesson is taking place after dinner. Note the expressions on the faces of the father and son. How do they seem to feel about the lesson and about each other?

Try It

Plan a drawing to express some aspect of life in the South in the 1840s. Imagine being the child of a plantation owner, a slave, or a farmer. Think carefully about what colors, figures, and actions you will use to convey your ideas. Draw a sketch.

Apply It

Work with pencil or color markers. Convey how you feel about a special moment such as when you first learned to do something.

417

Chapter Review

Reviewing Key Terms

abolitionist (p. 406)
cotton gin (p. 403)
overseer (p. 408)
sharecropper (p. 414)
spiritual (p. 410)

A. The following quotations express the beliefs of certain people. Write the key term that identifies each speaker.

1. "I don't own this land, I just farm it. When I sell my crops, I give some of the profits to the land owner."
2. "I'm in charge of 20 men and women. I often keep them working 14 hours a day. If they cause trouble, they better keep away from me!"
3. "No arguments will change my mind. I think slavery is absolutely wrong!"

B. Answer the questions with one or two sentences. Your answers should show that you understand the meanings of the key terms.

1. What did the sharecroppers have to share?
2. How are spirituals related to people's feelings about religion?
3. What does the cotton gin do?
4. Why did slaves probably dislike their overseers?
5. Were abolitionists upset about the treatment of plantation slaves?

Exploring Concepts

A. Copy and complete the following chart on your own paper. Compare the lifestyles of slaves, small farmers, and plantation owners. Use information from the lessons in this chapter. The first row has been done for you.

Comparing Southern Lifestyles			
	Slaves	**Small Farmers**	**Plantation Owners**
Homes	One-room cabins with dirt floors	Log cabins, often with no windows	Huge mansions with many rooms
Food			
Kinds of work			
Social life and religion			

B. The statements below are the answers to certain questions. Write the question that will make sense for each answer.

1. in palace-like houses with plenty of food
2. textile mills in New England
3. about one-fourth of free southerners
4. Nat Turner's slave revolt
5. poorly built, one-room houses; two or more families in each
6. field slaves, house slaves, craft workers, factory workers, dock workers
7. by combining a unique mixture of African, Indian, and European traditions
8. in religious songs about their sorrow
9. because slaves who tried to escape were beaten severely
10. Andrew Jackson
11. comforted both slaves and poor white farmers who lived harsh lives

Reviewing Skills

1. Imagine that you are Mrs. Schoolcraft, Josiah Henson, or Andrew Jackson. Use a form of art to express something about the life of the person you have chosen.
2. Write two short journal entries. In the first entry, write about an experience in your everyday life as a young person of today. You could describe the clothes you wear for school or how you buy groceries or prepare food.

    In the second journal entry, write about a similar experience from the viewpoint of a young person who lived in the early 1800s. This person can be from either the South or the North, free or slave, wealthy or poor. Make an illustration for one of your journal entries.
3. Illustrate the differences in lifestyle on a plantation by drawing a plantation owner's house and a slave's house.
4. List five clue words or phrases that tell you when something you are reading is opinion rather than fact.
5. Suppose you want to tell about situations or events and explain what caused them to happen. You also want to tell what the result, or effect, was. For example, what changes took place in the lives of southerners because of the invention of the cotton gin? Or, what effect did Nat Turner's revolt have on slave-owners who had always trusted their slaves? Tell the device you would use to clearly show what caused a situation and what was the effect.

Using Critical Thinking

1. Some slave owners argued that slaves were better off than factory workers in the North. Imagine you are an abolitionist visiting a plantation in the South. You are talking to a wealthy planter about slavery and he gives you this argument. How would you try to convince the planter that slaves are really much worse off than northern factory workers?
2. Plantation owners grew rich selling crops. They paid little or no wages and had plenty of demand for their products. Today's business owners seldom have those advantages. Think of a business, such as a store or factory. List some problems, such as other stores selling for less or high costs for workers. Tell some ways the owner can solve the problems.

Preparing for Citizenship

1. **WRITING ACTIVITY** Write a slave narrative—a personal story by someone who lived as a slave. Imagine that your family was split up in a slave auction. Tell how you feel about being separated from your family. Describe the work you must do, either in the plantation owner's mansion or out in the cotton or rice fields. Tell about how you and other slaves live. At the end of your narrative, tell how you imagine freedom will feel someday.
2. **COLLABORATIVE LEARNING** Present an oral report with something visual as part of a project, "From Plant to Product." In groups of two or three, choose one step in cotton growing, manufacturing, or selling. Take notes and create a poster or display. Choose from one of these topics or another one: growing cotton, ginning and baling, kinds of cotton, fiber products, cottonseed products, products from cotton linters, how cotton is made into cloth, the cotton exchange.

419

Chapter 17

The Industrial North

As the frontier stretched to the West and plantations grew in the South, northern life also changed. In large cities new factories and businesses created new jobs. These jobs attracted people from around the nation and all over the world. This growth sometimes created problems. But the new people, businesses, and experiences also made northern cities exciting places to live.

Throughout this time, many new businesses and factories started in northern cities. The picture above shows a meat-packing plant in Cincinnati in the 1850s.

1750	1775	1800

1789

1793 Using machines like the spinning frame (above), Samuel Slater opens the first successful textile mill in the United States.

During this period, trade and travel along canals helped many businesses grow and prosper. This painting shows the Union Glass Works at Kensington, Delaware, in 1827.

1831 A steam locomotive called the DeWitt Clinton (right) travels from Albany to Schenectady in New York in under one hour.

1825

1850

1875

1842 Massachusetts passes a law stating that children under 12 years of age cannot work more than 10 hours a day.

1860

L E S S O N   1

Industrial Growth

THINKING
FOCUS

How did inventions of the late 18th and early 19th centuries change the way goods were produced and transported?

Key Terms

- Industrial Revolution
- factory

➤ *The John Bull, a locomotive built for the Camden and Amboy Railroad in New Jersey, operated between 1831 and 1866. It is now in the Smithsonian Institution.*

> T*he horse was perhaps a quarter of a mile ahead when the safety valve of the engine lifted . . . The blower whistled, the steam blew off in vapory clouds, the pace increased, the passengers shouted, the engine gained on the horse, soon it lapped him . . . The race was neck and neck, nose and nose—then the engine passed the horse, and a great hurrah hailed the victory . . . But just at this time . . . the safety valve ceased to scream, and the engine for want of breath began to wheeze and pant . . . The horse gained on the machine, and passed it.*
>
> John Latrobe, *The Baltimore and Ohio Railroad, Personal Recollections*

John Latrobe wrote this description of an event that occurred in 1830. During that summer, a man named Peter Cooper had invented a steam-powered locomotive. To show people that his invention worked, Cooper bragged that his locomotive could win a race against a horse. Cooper's locomotive lost. But his remarkable invention amazed America. In a few years,

steam-powered locomotives would become fast enough to replace the horse-drawn cart as the quickest way to move goods over land.

Inventions for Industry

Between 1770 and 1840, many inventions, like the locomotive, changed the way people made and shipped goods. This period is called the **Industrial Revolution.**

Before 1770, most goods—such as clothing and shoes—were made by hand. At that time, most Americans lived on farms. A family member might need a shirt, for example.

So someone in the family would spin wool into thread, weave it into cloth, and sew the shirt.

Americans did not make all their own goods, however. Some things—such as glass, tools, and some cloth—were made in Britain and imported. During the mid-1700s, British inventors looked for ways to make these goods more cheaply and thus increase their sales. These inventors built many of the most important machines of the Industrial Revolution.

Some of these inventions involved new ways to make cloth. In the 1760s, James Hargreaves, an Englishman, invented the "spinning jenny," a machine that could spin many threads from wool at one time. Another Englishman, John Kay, invented the "flying shuttle." This device could help weave cloth much faster than one person working by hand.

The British also developed the **factory,** a large building or group of buildings where a particular product is made. Factories had enough space to house the new machines in one location. Factories and new inventions made Great Britain one of the wealthiest and most powerful countries in the world. ■

Before the Industrial Revolution, goods like shoes were made by hand. This handmade shoe is over 250 years old.

■ *How did inventions change the way people made and shipped goods?*

Industry in the United States

The British tried to keep their inventions a secret. They did not allow workers, inventors, or business people to leave Britain. In 1789, however, an Englishman named Samuel Slater memorized the plans for building a textile factory. Then, disguised as a boy, he sailed to America, and in 1793 built the first American factory, in Pawtucket, Rhode Island.

Water from streams provided the power to run textile factories, or mills, like Slater's. The streams would turn a water wheel, which was connected to a number of belts and wheels. These belts and wheels would drive the machines. Because they needed waterpower, many of the first factories were built in New England, which has many fast rivers. In these factories workers spun thread from southern cotton and wove it into cloth. This cloth

was used to make clothing for people throughout the country.

Some of the larger New England textile mills were built in Lowell, Massachusetts, in the 1820s. The workers in these factories were mostly unmarried young women who had been born and raised on New England farms. The chance to leave the farm and earn money excited these young women. However, working in the mill wasn't

Slater's Mill in Pawtucket, Rhode Island, contained machinery for spinning cotton into thread. All the workers were children, ranging in age from 7 to 12.

➤ *In the early New England mills, women used a bobbin and shuttle like the ones pictured below when weaving on a loom. In the picture at right, the women are working on a carding machine.*

■ *How did the coming of the factory system change the way young women in New England lived?*

▼ *The tremendous boom in canals changed the way goods were moved in the United States. By 1860, over 4,000 miles of canals crisscrossed the East.*

easy. For a daily wage of 30 or 35 cents, New England mill girls worked 13 hours a day.

They got only two 35- minute breaks for meals. Lucy Larcom, who had worked at Lowell as a young girl in the 1830s, remem-

bered: "In the sweet June weather I would lean far out of the window, and try not to hear the unceasing [never ending] clash of sound inside. Looking away to the hills, my whole stifled being would cry out 'Oh, that I had wings!' " ■

Changes in Transportation

By the 1820s, businessmen were building more and more factories. Farmers were growing their crops on lands that were farther and farther west. Roads were often rough and muddy. The poor roads made shipping goods by wagon slow and costly. Businessmen and farmers both needed new forms of transportation to take their products to market.

Building Canals

Americans had shipped goods on rivers throughout colonial times. However, most American rivers do not extend very far west. So people in the 19th century built canals— deep ditches filled with water and wide enough for boats. Horses walked alongside canals and pulled the boats.

The most important canal was the Erie Canal. From 1817 to 1825, workers carved the canal through 363 miles of wilderness between Albany and Buffalo, New York. The canal was 40 feet wide and 4 feet deep. After the Erie Canal was

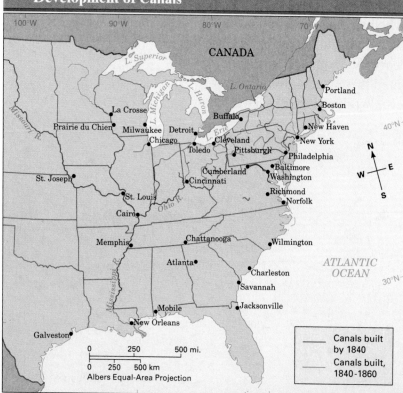

Development of Canals

Canals built by 1840

Canals built, 1840-1860

completed, boats could travel from New York City through the Great Lakes and on to the West.

Canals greatly lowered the cost of shipping. Goods that once cost $100 a ton to move between Buffalo and New York now cost only about $5 a ton. As a result of the Erie Canal, New York City grew rapidly and became the largest center of trade in the country.

Building Railroads

Many cities rushed to build new forms of transportation so they could compete with New York. These cities knew that they needed a link with the West if they were to grow and prosper. Some cities, such as Baltimore, tried to build canals. However, their canals were not as successful as the Erie Canal. Instead, these cities built railroads. The map at the right shows the boom in rail building in this period.

Railroads offered a number of advantages. First, trains could travel much faster than horse-drawn canal boats. Second, railroad routes were often more direct than waterways. Third, trains could travel all year, while rivers and

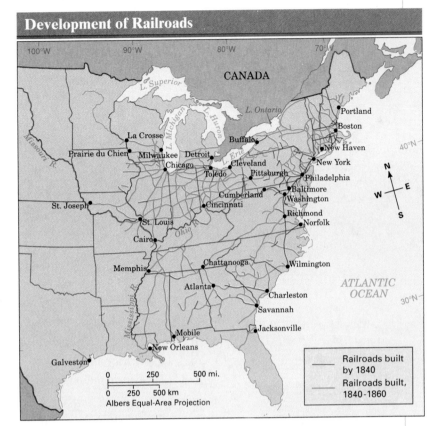

Development of Railroads

Railroads built by 1840

Railroads built, 1840-1860

canals often froze in the winter. By 1860, railroads had replaced canals as the largest carrier of goods.

The growth of transportation brought vast changes to the United States. Railroads and canals helped connect the different parts of the country. In 1800, for example, a trip from New York City to Pittsburgh took one week. By 1857, railroads and canals had shortened the same trip to one day. ■

"Rivers run only where nature pleases; railroads run wherever man pleases" stated a St. Louis newspaper in 1867. By 1860, railroads had 30,000 miles of track, up from 23 miles in 1830.

■ *How did the development of railroads and canals change the way goods were transported across the United States?*

R E V I E W

1. **FOCUS** How did inventions of the late 18th and early 19th centuries change the way goods were produced and transported?

2. **CONNECT** Why might some New England mill owners have cooperated with southern slave owners?

3. **ECONOMICS** Why did canals save money on shipping costs?

4. **CRITICAL THINKING** How would a mill girl's life differ from life on the farm?

5. **CRITICAL THINKING** In 1830, transportation along rivers was more important than overland transportation. Today, the opposite is true. Why do you think such a change occurred?

6. **ACTIVITY** Look at the map of canals on page 424 and the map of railroads on this page. Then list the ways goods could be transported from New York City to New Orleans.

The Industrial North

1750 1775 1800 1820 1860 1875

L E S S O N 2

New People, New Problems

THINKING FOCUS

What was life like for immigrants to the United States?

Key Term

- tenement

The crossing was terrible. Three days after we had left land, we had a frightful storm, and during the night we lost the mainmast and the foremast. . . . Many of the berths on the lower deck collapsed, and water poured down through the hatchways so that coffers, trunks, sacks, and all kinds of loose objects floated around in the water and were in a great part broken against the sides of the ship because of the terribly heavy sea. That many provisions were spoilt and clothes and the like damaged by the water is easy to understand. This storm lasted two days and two nights, and during this time we had to go both hungry and thirsty, since we could not manage to prepare anything . . . [and] could not get fresh water either.

Theodore C. Blegen, *Land of Their Choice*

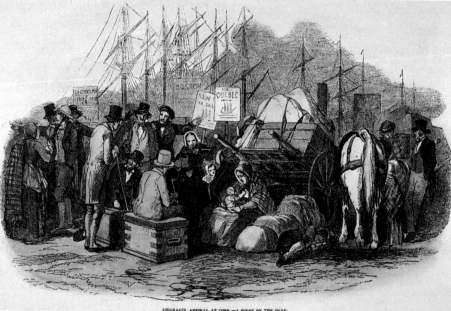

BOSTON
QUEBEC
EMIGRANTS ARRIVAL AT CORK.—A SCENE ON THE QUAY.

➤ *During the first half of the 19th century, millions of immigrants left Europe. The Irish immigrants pictured here prepare for their difficult journey from their homeland.*

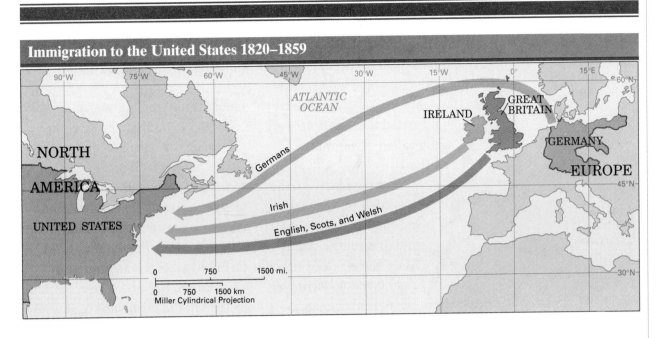

Immigration to the United States 1820–1859

The man who wrote this letter in 1853 was an immigrant—a person who has left his or her native land and come to another country. We don't know this man's name, yet we do know that, like most other immigrants, he left his homeland and came to America to start a new life. His Atlantic crossing was probably the first of many hardships he would find as he began his life in a new country.

Immigration to the United States

From 1830 to 1850, more than 2.3 million immigrants came to America. Thousands came from England, Norway, Scotland, Sweden, and Wales. But most came from Ireland and Germany.

Irish and German immigrants came to America for different reasons. The Irish came to escape starvation. Most Germans came because they believed they could lead a better life in America than in Germany.

Immigration from Ireland

Ireland lies just west of Great Britain. Because of poor soil and harsh weather, Ireland is a hard place to farm. In the early 1800s, the Irish were particularly poor.

Most families lived almost entirely on potatoes.

In the 1840s, however, a disease attacked Ireland's potato crops. From 1847 to 1854, around 750,000 Irish starved to death. At the time, a Roman Catholic priest called the Irish "the poorest and most wretched population that can be found in the world."

Without money or food, the Irish had little choice but to leave their homes. Between 1830 and 1860, nearly two million Irish people made the difficult trip to America.

Aboard ship, the immigrants faced many horrors. Because they often could afford only the cheapest

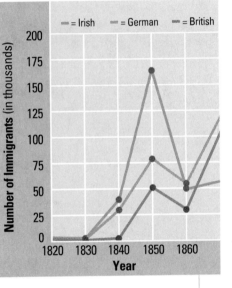

The map above shows that from 1820 to 1859, most immigrants to the United States came from Ireland, Great Britain, and Germany. As the graph shows, few Irish emigrated in the early 1800s. Why did many more Irish leave home by 1850?

427

■ *How did the immigrant experience of the Irish and the Germans differ in the period 1820 to 1860?*

tickets, immigrants filled the lowest, dampest part of the ship. Many Irish immigrants died while crossing the Atlantic Ocean. The ships that carried these people were often called "swimming coffins."

After they arrived, the Irish settled first in New York, Boston, Cincinnati, and other large cities. Most had no skills other than farming. However, many Irish immigrants began to find unskilled jobs in factories. Irish women and children worked in the textile factories of New England. Some Irishmen did hard labor digging the Erie Canal and building roads and railroads.

Immigration from Germany

Unlike the Irish, most of the Germans who came to the United States before 1860 were not poor. Many had owned small farms in Germany. Because land in America was plentiful, they immigrated in hopes of starting larger, richer farms. Most German immigrants avoided the big cities. They settled instead in the farmlands of Illinois, Ohio, Pennsylvania, and Wisconsin. From 1830 to 1860, over 1.5 million Germans immigrated to America. ■

The Move to Cities

Before 1830, immigrants who came to the United States often settled in the countryside or in small towns to work on farms or in textile mills. However, after 1830, many of the newly arrived immigrants began to settle in large cities like New York, Boston, Philadelphia, and Cincinnati.

These new immigrants settled in neighborhoods with others from their homeland. Everyone shared the same customs and traditions and spoke the same language. One such neighborhood in New York City was called "Little Germany."

■ *Why did people move to the cities, and who moved there after 1830?*

Life in [Little Germany] is almost the same as in the Old Country. Butchers, bakers, druggists—are all Germans . . . The shoe-makers, tailors, barbers, physicians, grocers, and innkeepers are Germans. The residents of [Little Germany] need not even know English in order to make a living.

Albert Robbins, *Coming to America*

Many such immigrant neighborhoods were to spring up in eastern cities in the years to come. ■

Treatment of Immigrants

By the late 1700s, only five cities had more than 8,000 people. By 1860, more than 800,000 people lived in New York City alone, partly as a result of the Erie Canal.

With such huge rises in population, cities changed dramatically. Many became overcrowded. In many ways, however, they were exciting places in which to live.

One observer wrote that New York City was the "busiest community that any man could desire to live in. In all the streets all is hurry and bustle. . . ."

Overcrowding soon became a serious problem, however. In New York, as many as four families might live in a small basement room with no heat, light, or running water.

Some landlords took advantage of people who could not afford good housing. They built **tenements,** apartment buildings with few windows and often no heat or plumbing.

In addition to poor living conditions, immigrant workers earned wages so low that they could barely rise above their poverty. Many had been very poor in their homeland. So they were willing to work for low wages in America. This angered many native-born Americans, who feared that their own wages would be cut.

To make matters worse, native-born Americans often unfairly distrusted the new immigrants simply because their ways were different. In particular, most Americans were Protestants, many of whom distrusted Catholics. Most of the new Irish immigrants and many of the German immigrants were Catholics. Protestants were afraid that they would lose political power to these Catholic immigrants. Between 1834 and 1860, anti-Irish riots broke out in many cities. In a few places, angry rioters burned Catholic churches and schools.

Many immigrants came to the United States in search of better lives. However, once they arrived, immigrants often faced problems that neither they nor native-born Americans could solve. ■

RESTRICT ALL **IMMIGRATION!**

PROTECT YOURSELF AND YOUR CHILDREN

AGAINST

Ruinous Labor and Business Competition

THROUGH

UNRESTRICTED IMMIGRATION.

▲ *As this pamphlet shows, many native-born Americans feared that immigrant labor might ruin American workers.*

◄ *Cities like New York, Boston, and Philadelphia all had slum districts in the mid-1800s.* Cliff Dwellers, *a painting by George Bellows, shows how crowded conditions had become by the late 1800s.*

■ *What three conditions did immigrants face in the United States that made their lives difficult?*

1. **FOCUS** What was life like for immigrants to the United States?
2. **CONNECT** Compare and contrast the arrival of the immigrants with that of the African slaves.
3. **CRITICAL THINKING** If you could have helped Irish immigrants in 1840, what would you have done?
4. **WRITING ACTIVITY** Write a diary entry describing your first day at school as an immigrant in a big city.

LESSON 3

Life in Northern Cities

THINKING
F O C U S

How did cities in the North change between 1830 and 1860?

Key Terms

- walking city
- slum

You must button your coat tight about you, see that your shoes are secure at the heels, settle your hat firmly on your head, look up street and down street, at the self-same moment, to see what carts and carriages are upon you, and then run for your life.

These words were written in 1837 by Dr. Asa Greene. Dr. Greene was explaining how to cross a street in New York City, which had become a crowded, noisy place. A few years before, New York and other cities had been quiet places where people could walk and talk at their leisure. But all of that had changed.

A Typical American City

Let's imagine ourselves in Cincinnati, Ohio—a typical city in 1830. Cincinnati is small enough that we can walk across the whole city in one afternoon. Cincinnati in 1830 is a **walking city,** a city with no public transportation where everyone walks to work, to the store, and to visit friends.

The 25,000 people who live here are proud of their bustling downtown. On the main streets, we must step lively, for the horse-drawn carriages move quickly. The streets have no stoplights or police officers to direct traffic. As we stand on the street, we have to watch out for the mud and dust. Most streets are unpaved. No one cleans the streets, so litter lines the

roads. In addition, hogs are everywhere. A visitor to Cincinnati in the 1830s wrote:

I am sure I should have liked Cincinnati much better if the people had not dealt so very largely in hogs . . . if determined upon a walk up Main-street, the chances were five hundred to one against my reaching the shady side without brushing by a [hog] snout fresh dripping from the kennel.

Frances Trollope,
Domestic Manners of the Americans

Study A Closer Look at the Walking City to see what it was like to live in a city in 1830. ■

A Walking City

In Cincinnati during the 1830s, you'd find everything within walking distance. Strolling around town, you'd hear steam whistles from the paddle-wheel boats on the Ohio River. You'd look in the shops where they make pigskin leather or hog-bristle brushes. Every few minutes you'd be saying hello to someone you know.

More buildings go up every day, and stand proudly in their fresh paint. But look at how low they are. Passenger elevators didn't exist yet, and nobody wanted to climb more than four flights of stairs.

Fences and walls are papered with advertisements, and ads fill the newspaper. More jobs mean more money to spend. Cincinnati is booming!

Strudel

Walk to the German neighborhood called Over the Rhine. Newcomers arrive each day, bringing their skills and customs. Can you smell the German strudel baking?

The city is growing—and all the streets need names! Here, as everywhere, streets are being named after local pioneers and national heroes. People here call one street Sausage Row.

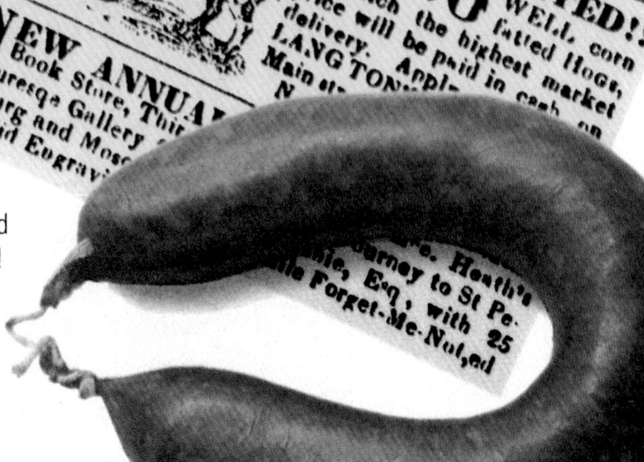

The Changing City

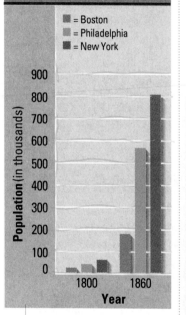

▼ Broadway and Spring Street, *a painting by Hyppolite Sebron, shows a bustling New York City in 1855. New York was the largest city in the country by far. Study the graph. What was the population of New York in 1860?*

Urban Population Growth, 1800–1860

■ = Boston
■ = Philadelphia
■ = New York

Population (in thousands)

900
800
700
600
500
400
300
200
100
0

1800   1860

Year

■ *Name several problems resulting from sudden population growth in cities.*

If we were to have visited Cincinnati 30 years later, in 1860, we would find it greatly changed. Immigrants have flooded into the city to work in the newly built factories. The population has increased more than six times to over 160,000 people. Cincinnati is now the seventh largest city in the United States. It covers more than 20 square miles.

One of the changes we would notice is the public transportation. Horse-drawn omnibuses—known today as buses—and horse-drawn railroad cars carry people throughout the downtown area. For 10 cents, a person can ride across town.

Along with improvements have come problems. Cincinnati now has **slums,** places where living conditions are poor. Sewers do not work well. Slum dwellers must dump their waste from bathrooms and kitchens onto the streets. Crimes, especially riots and drunken brawls, have become common.

The problems Cincinnati faced after 1830 were typical of cities in the North. To make cities good places to live, city leaders decided to improve the services they offered their residents. ■

New Cities, New Services

Before the 1840s, cities operated with few controls. Governments paid little attention to providing clean streets, a fresh water supply, and protection from crime and fire.

By the 1840s, however, many people understood that dirty conditions spread diseases through cities. To clean up the streets, cities built new sewer systems that carried away waste in underground

tunnels. In 1849, New York City had 70 miles of underground sewers. By 1857, 158 miles of underground sewers crisscrossed the city. Even so, over three-fourths of the city still lacked good sewers.

Fresh drinking water was scarce in most big cities. Philadelphia was among the first cities to build a water system to bring in clean water. In 1842, New York City built a system that carried in water from over 40 miles away.

Many cities suffered from high crime rates. In 1844, New York City created the nation's first paid police force, with over 800 officers.

Cities also began to protect citizens against fire. Cincinnati started a paid fire department in 1853.

Cities acted to help the poor. By 1835, four eastern cities had over 10,000 poor people. More than half were immigrants. By 1860, about 50 percent of the very poor in the United States were immigrants. To help the poor, New Yorkers started the Association for Improving the Condition of the Poor. This group, founded in 1843, gave shelter and food. It urged governments to change housing laws. New laws and services began to improve living conditions in the changing American city. ■

Across Time & Space

In the 1980s, the government of New York City began to worry that their water supply would be inadequate for the 21st century. Since only two old tunnels carried water into the city, officials decided to build a new one.

■ *Describe three ways people in cities tried to combat problems.*

REVIEW

1. **FOCUS** How did cities in the North change between 1830 and 1860?

2. **CONNECT** How was life in the North and Northeast generally different from life in the South?

3. **HISTORY** What steps did big cities take to fight crime in the 1840s and 1850s?

4. **CRITICAL THINKING** What problems in the cities of the 1840s are still problems in cities today?

5. **ACTIVITY** Draw two pictures contrasting an American city around 1820 and again around 1850. Think about how the city would have changed and how it would look different.

L E S S O N   4

Making a Better Society

How did reform movements change American society?

Key Terms

- Second Great Awakening
- utopian community
- Shaker
- reform

▼ *The Cane Ridge Meeting House was the site of an early religious revival in Kentucky.*

I saw two families including six or eight children burrowing in one cellar under a stable—a prey to famine [shortage of food] on the one hand and to vermin [insects] . . . on the other, with sickness adding its horrors to those of a polluted [dirty] atmosphere and a wintry [cold] temperature.

Horace Greeley, *Recollections of a Busy Life*, 1868

In the 1830s, Horace Greeley, an American newspaperman, visited the poor in New York City. He later wrote the description at left. America's cities during the 1830s were in a state of confusion, marked by crime, filth, and overcrowding. Angry and upset, people wondered where they could turn.

Some people looked to religion. Others retreated to "perfect" communities to escape the confusion. Still others tried to improve conditions throughout the country.

Awakening Religious Feelings

In the years from 1830 to 1860, America underwent massive changes. Many Americans found these changes upsetting and turned to religion for support and comfort.

In the early 1800s, thousands of Americans were influenced by a powerful religious movement known as the **Second Great Awakening.** During the Awakening, ministers urged people to think about sinfulness and salvation. Many attended "camp meetings," huge religious services often held in a tent. Thousands of people might travel for days to attend. There they would sit spellbound, day after day, to hear fiery sermons about good and evil. One man who attended a camp meeting described it in his autobiography.

The noise was like the roar of Niagara. The vast sea of human beings seemed to be agitated as if by a storm. I counted seven ministers, all preaching at one time, some on stumps, others on wagons. . . . Some of the people were singing, others praying, some crying for mercy. A peculiarly strange sensation came over me. My heart beat tumultuously, my knees trembled, my lips quivered, and I felt as though I must fall to the ground.

Autobiography of James B. Finley, 1801

The traveling preachers who were part of the Awakening belonged to different Protestant churches. Yet all of them spoke of a personal struggle against sin. You could improve yourself, they argued, and you could change the world, too.

Women worked actively in the religious revival. During this time they were responsible for their family's religious life. Slowly, women brought their husbands and children into the movement.

Many religious groups formed at this time. Groups like the Bible Society urged Americans to read the Bible. All hoped to improve the country's spiritual life. ∎

▲ Camp meetings such as this one from 1830 were religious revivals held outdoors. They were often attended by thousands of people.

■ What was the Second Great Awakening, and when did it occur?

Building "Perfect" Communities

During the Second Great Awakening, some people with strong religious ideas wanted to form separate communities. They believed it was possible to form a **utopian community**—a perfect village where people would live together in harmony, free from crime and poverty.

One important utopian community was formed by the United Society of Believers. This society became known as **Shakers** because many of them trembled and shook during their intense worship

services. The American Shakers were founded in the 1770s by Ann Lee, an Englishwoman. Her followers called her Mother Ann. The Shakers are remembered today for their simple but beautiful furniture and other household goods. Shakers lived simple lives and believed that all people should work for the common

▼ This Shaker water dipper is made entirely of wood. It shows the careful attention to detail typical of all Shaker products.

435

How Do We Know?

HISTORY *Because they did not believe in having children, very few Shakers are alive in America today. Those remaining are quite old. The last two Shaker colonies are at Sabbathday Lake in Maine, and in Canterbury, New Hampshire. Historians have talked to Shakers and have tape-recorded their stories.*

■ *What are utopian communities, and why did people want to form them?*

good. They lived in groups in dwellings called family houses. Men and women lived separately in different parts of the house. Shakers never married because they did not believe in having children.

More utopian communities formed in other parts of the United States. New Harmony was founded in Indiana in the 1820s. Its members tried to trade goods and services instead of paying for them with money. At Brook Farm in Massachusetts, most of the people were writers and thinkers. They believed that Americans thought too much about money and getting ahead and not enough about friendship and cooperation. ■

Changing Americans' Beliefs

For many, building a utopian community was a way of avoiding America's problems. Others wanted to **reform,** or improve, the world, not hide from it.

The Antislavery Movement

Many people believed that slavery was America's worst problem. Slavery went against America's ideal of freedom. For this reason it had to end. Abolitionists, people who wanted to end slavery, spoke and wrote of its evils. One famous abolitionist, Frederick Douglass, was born into

slavery. Douglass was tall and handsome, a powerful speaker and a brilliant writer. He told people

➤ *Frederick Douglass was born into slavery in 1817. After escaping to the North in 1838, Douglass became a leading black abolitionist.*

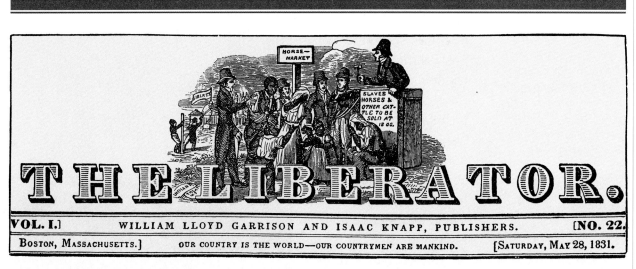

THE LIBERATOR.

VOL. I.]   WILLIAM LLOYD GARRISON AND ISAAC KNAPP, PUBLISHERS.   [NO. 22.

BOSTON, MASSACHUSETTS.]   OUR COUNTRY IS THE WORLD—OUR COUNTRYMEN ARE MANKIND.   [SATURDAY, MAY 28, 1831.

that a belief in slavery "brands your Christianity as a lie."

Like others who had been influenced by the Second Great Awakening, William Lloyd Garrison believed that he should work to reform the world. Garrison started *The Liberator,* a powerful antislavery newspaper, in 1831. Garrison demanded an immediate end to slavery in the United States.

Both Douglass and Garrison helped to make slavery a controversial issue in the early 19th century.

Women Fight for Their Rights

Many women took part in the abolitionist movement. Like other abolitionists, these women believed in the importance of liberty and human rights. They quickly learned, however, that most male

William Lloyd Garrison used The Liberator *to demand that slavery be ended at once. Note how Garrison portrayed slavery in the picture over the paper's title.*

UNITY IS STRENGTH
ORGANIZE NOW!

UNDERSTANDING ACTIVISM

Frederick Douglass and William Lloyd Garrison believed that slavery had to be destroyed. To reach their goal, both became activists, or people who take direct action to change society.

What Activists Do

Membership in a political party or in any group is not activism unless the member takes strong action in support of a cause. The person who works to make lasting changes in society is an activist.

At times activists have been mistreated. For example, Garrison was once dragged through the streets of Boston by a mob.

Activists have worked hard for change throughout American history. For example, during the 1960s, civil rights activists struggled to win equal rights for blacks. Activists traveled through the South by bus on what were called "Freedom Rides." They struggled to overturn unfair laws that denied equality to African Americans.

Importance of Activism

Activists have always helped draw America's attention to problems. Activists in the early 1800s saw few results. Yet their actions eventually brought important changes to American society.

437

➤ *During the early 1800s, women could not attend most colleges. Later in the century, the work of women's rights activists allowed women to go to schools like the one shown here.*

abolitionists would not give political rights to women. As Elizabeth Cady Stanton, whose husband was an abolitionist, said, "Many a man who advocated equality most eloquently for a Southern plantation would not tolerate it at his own fireside."

In 1830, white women had few rights. They could not vote. Married women could not own property. They were not allowed to attend most colleges or hold most jobs. When one woman applied to Harvard Medical School, students of the all-male school objected. They wrote that "no woman of true delicacy" could attend lectures about the human body in the presence of men.

To fight this prejudice, Stanton and Lucretia Mott organized a meeting of women in 1848 at Seneca Falls, New York. There they wrote a declaration of independence stating that "men and women are created equal." They also demanded that women receive their rights—to go to school, to vote, to be treated equally before the law.

Sojourner Truth was born into slavery in New York in 1797. She gained her freedom when New York banned slavery on July 4, 1827. For the rest of her life, she fought for rights for both blacks and women.

■ *Name two important reform movements of the 1800s.*

Another reformer was Sojourner Truth, who worked to reform both slavery and women's inequality. In 1851, she spoke out against people who thought women were weaker than men:

> Nobody ever helps me into carriages or over mud puddles or gives me any best place, and ain't I a woman? . . . Look at my arm. I have ploughed and planted and gathered . . . and ain't I a woman?

Reformers worked hard to change American society. Many did not gain immediate success. But future generations would see the results of their work. ■

R E V I E W

1. **FOCUS** How did reform movements change American society?

2. **CONNECT** How were America's reform movements related to its big cities?

3. **BELIEF SYSTEMS** How did the beliefs of the Second Great Awakening contribute to the growth of reform movements and utopian communities?

4. **CRITICAL THINKING** Most utopian communities of the 1800s failed within a few years after they formed. Why do you think this happened? If a utopian community formed today, do you think it would survive?

5. **ACTIVITY** What kinds of reformers are active today? Think of people in the news. Make a chart, listing people's names and their causes.

Working Together

Here's Why

Many projects are too big for one person to do and are better completed by people working together. If a group project is to succeed, members of the group must agree on their goals and the tasks that each member should do.

Group cooperation was important to the antislavery reformers. People's lives depended on being able to trust group members. Your projects may require much less risk, but they will be easier to complete if you know how to work in a group.

Here's How

Suppose your group decides to hold a rally in favor of women's rights, like the one where Sojourner Truth made her "Ain't I A Woman?" speech. Here are some things your group would need to do:

1. **Select a moderator.** The moderator's job is to make sure that everyone talks about the things that must be done.

2. **Select a scribe.** This person writes down the group's ideas and decisions.

3. **Select a timekeeper.** One person limits how long people speak, in order to keep any person or idea from taking up the whole meeting.

4. **Brainstorm.** Think of all the things that must be done to prepare for, hold, and clean up after the rally. Create a list of tasks and plan to discuss the ideas later.

5. **Agree on a plan.** Group members must agree on what needs to be done, so everyone will cooperate. When members of a group agree, that is called consensus.

By the end of the second meeting, each member should have a job. Progress reports and problems can be discussed at future meetings.

Try It

Apply steps 1–4 to another class project. What if your group were making a presentation to other classes about immigration? How would you plan it?

Apply It

Think of a project that would help your school or community. You might organize a tutoring program to help students in lower grades or a campaign to clean up litter. Then form a group and make a list of things to be done to complete the project.

439

Chapter Review

Reviewing Key Terms

factory (p. 423)
Industrial Revolution
   (p. 422)
reform (p. 436)
Second Great Awakening
   (p. 434)

Shaker (p. 435)
slum (p. 432)
tenement (p. 429)
utopian community (p. 435)
walking city (p. 430)

The key terms appear in the following letters between a sister and brother. The key terms are underlined. Copy the letters on your own paper and fill in the missing meanings where you see a space. The first one is done for you.

Dear Grace,

Here I am in a utopian community, *a perfect village away from city problems.* I miss you but my city block became a slum, an area that _____. Do our parents still hope to reform, or _____, the world? Does Father work in the factory, the _____? I'm sure Mother would like to live in a walking city where _____.

Your brother, Roger

Dear Roger,

We still live in the _____ that the papers call a tenement. Our neighbors often discuss the Industrial Revolution, a time of _____. Our parents recall the Second Great Awakening when _____. They tell about our aunt, who was a Shaker. Her group _____.

Your sister, Grace

Exploring Concepts

A. Copy this chart on your own paper. For each historical fact, list one or more reasons.

Historical Facts	Reasons
1. An Industrial Revolution took place in the United States during the 1700s and 1800s.	Increase in population and demand for goods
2. By 1860, the population of American cities had grown dramatically.	
3. In the mid-1800s, some American cities were not pleasant places.	
4. In the 1800s, Americans showed a new interest in religion, founded utopian communities, and started reform movements.	

B. Support each statement with facts and details from the chapter.
1. The American Industrial Revolution owed a great deal to people in Great Britain.
2. Girls who worked in the mills found advantages and disadvantages there.
3. After canals were built, people did not have to pay as much for goods they purchased.
4. Irish immigrants came to America just to survive; Germans came for other reasons.
5. The problems of some immigrants did not end after the difficult ocean voyage.
6. Factories and mills of the Industrial Revolution provided jobs but not always a better way of life.
7. Organizations for helping the poor were needed in American cities of the 1800s.
8. People in utopian communities had good reasons for leaving the cities.

440

Reviewing Skills

1. Suppose you wanted to put on a play about Frederick Douglass as a class project. Explain how you would organize classmates to complete the project.
2. Explain why it is important for a group to reach consensus. What happens when members can't agree on a goal or plan?
3. As you know, a project may require many tasks. Suggest ways the moderator and scribe can work together to assign jobs and track the progress that is made.
4. Give examples of rules a timekeeper could make to help group discussions move forward and remain orderly.
5. If your group were producing a play about a historical figure, how might it use a cluster diagram to organize the details involved? Name some main topics that your cluster would contain.
6. You've probably heard the saying, "A picture is worth a thousand words." Suppose you wanted to make a point about one of the subjects in this chapter—for example, immigration, women's rights, or the advantages and disadvantages of machines. If you wanted to get people's attention and use humor at the same time, what form of expression would you use?

Using Critical Thinking

1. Explain why you agree or disagree with this statement: Some inventions of modern times have changed American society as much as the steam engine and other inventions of the 18th and 19th centuries. Refer to at least two 20th century inventions in your explanation. Discuss the changes they caused. Then predict some inventions of the future. Tell what kinds of changes might come about as a result of those inventions.
2. Suppose a group of immigrants arrives in your community. What are some important things the new arrivals will need to learn about your way of life? How would you help them? What kinds of problems might they have as they adjust to the lifestyle of your neighborhood?

Preparing for Citizenship

1. **INTERVIEWING** Conduct an interview with someone who came from another country to live in your city. The person can be a relative, friend, or neighbor. Before you begin, have a discussion with classmates about the kinds of questions you will ask. Make a list of questions such as the following:
   What country did you come from?
   Why did you leave?
   How is this country different from your old country?
   What do you like best about this country?
   What were you most worried about when you first arrived?
2. **ARTS ACTIVITY** Create a large picture showing several means of transportation during the period studied in this chapter. You might want to attach some three-dimensional figures to part of your picture.
3. **COLLABORATIVE LEARNING** Gather articles about problems in your city, such as run-down housing, factory pollution, crowded schools, or roads in need of repair. Form groups to concentrate on one particular problem. Ask a local librarian to help you find articles about ways that problems are being solved. Share your information with classmates.

Chapter 18

A Divided Nation

As America expanded westward, people asked: Should the new territories be slave or free? That question made Americans see how different the North and South were. Many Southerners said they needed slavery. Many Northerners said they hated it. Politicians argued about slavery, and settlers fought over it. Soon people began to wonder: Can the North and the South stay together?

Throughout this time, more and more Americans opposed slavery. William Whipper (above), a free black, spoke out against slavery and helped runaway slaves from his home in Pennsylvania.

| 1765 | 1785 | 1805 |

1790–1800 Slavery grows more important in the South with the start of a cotton boom. Most slaves work in plantation fields (above).

1787

Harriet Beecher Stowe (left) wrote the popular novel *Uncle Tom's Cabin*. The story was first published in 1851. It showed Americans the injustice and brutality of slavery. The novel angered many people in the South.

1861 Southern states that have seceded from the Union form the Confederacy and elect Jefferson Davis as their president. Some people wear ribbons (above) to show their support for secession.

1860 Northerner Abraham Lincoln (left) is elected President of the United States. Soon after, South Carolina becomes the first state to secede from the Union.

1825

1845

1865

1820 Congress passes the Missouri Compromise. This law allows slaves in southern territories but not in northern territories.

1861

L E S S O N   1

Crisis and Compromise

THINKING
F O C U S

How did northern and southern states resolve their differences?

Key Terms

- Union
- free state
- slave state
- secede

J ohn Quincy Adams, the Secretary of State of the United States, sat at the desk in his bedroom. He was exhausted, but he never went to bed until he had written in his diary. So, late that winter evening, Adams opened his diary in the flickering lamplight and wrote at the top of the page: *March 3, 1820.*

Earlier that day, Adams had watched President James Monroe sign a document known as the Missouri Compromise. This law allowed slavery in the new state of Missouri. Some people called it one of the most important laws ever passed by Congress, but Adams was troubled by what he had seen in the last year.

Adams had seen bitter arguments erupt in Congress. Southern congressmen wanted slavery to be allowed in Missouri. But northern congressmen said that they would never allow it in the new state. Suddenly, the issue of slavery divided the nation.

The Missouri Compromise may have stopped the fight over slavery for a time, but Adams knew that the problem had not been solved. He wrote:

> I f the Union must be dissolved, slavery is precisely the question upon which it ought to break. For the present, however, this contest is laid asleep.

➤ *Slavery was an important part of the economy in southern states. Southerners argued that slaves should be counted as part of a state's population. However, slaves did not have the rights that free men had to vote or to become citizens.*

The Balance of Power

The contest over slavery in the United States had begun at the Constitutional Convention in the spring of 1787. There, delegates debated and decided many issues. Slavery was one of them.

The First Compromise

The convention decided that a state's population would determine how many representatives that state could send to Congress. The southern delegates wanted slaves counted as a part of their states' populations. Pierce Butler of South Carolina argued:

> The labor of a slave in South Carolina is as productive and valuable as that of a free man in Massachusetts. An equal representation ought to be allowed for them.

Northern delegates represented areas where few people owned slaves. They did not want them counted at all. One northern delegate argued that the slaves of the South should not have the right of representation any more than the horses and cattle of the North.

The delegates put aside their differences, however, and finally agreed to a compromise. Three-fifths of the slaves in each state would be counted in deciding the number of representatives for the state. This compromise ensured that every state would accept the U.S. Constitution. It also ensured that slavery remained legal in all of the United States.

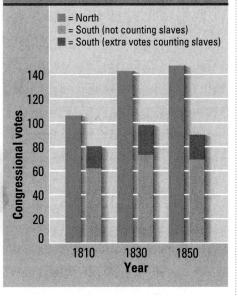

Congressional Representation of North and South, 1810–1850

- = North
- = South (not counting slaves)
- = South (extra votes counting slaves)

Congressional votes (y-axis: 0, 20, 40, 60, 80, 100, 120, 140)

Year (x-axis: 1810, 1830, 1850)

◄ *The U.S. Constitution gave slave-rich southern states 20 to 30 more votes in Congress than they would have had if they counted only free, white males.*

At that time, most Americans thought slavery would be useful only on a few large plantations in the South. There was little conflict, then, when Congress passed the Northwest Ordinance in 1787. This law made slavery illegal in the territories north of the Ohio River.

Free States and Slave States

Over the next 30 years, these lands were settled. One by one, new states joined the **Union,** as the United States was sometimes called. The new states north of the Ohio River, where slavery was not allowed, became known as **free states.** States south of the Ohio River were called **slave states.**

In the South, agriculture—and slavery—had made some planters very wealthy. Many of these wealthy planters were elected to Congress by their states. These men, therefore, wanted to preserve the freedom of planters to buy

445

A Divided Nation

land and slaves and to plant tobacco or cotton.

Farming was also important in free states. But the North was becoming a place of growing cities and booming industries. Merchants and manufacturers of the North produced cloth, shoes, guns, tools, and other goods. Northern Congressmen tried to pass laws that protected northern businesses and slave-free farms.

Because the North and South were different, each side worried that the other would get more votes in Congress and pass laws harmful to its interests. It was important, therefore, to keep a balance of northern and southern votes in Congress. ■

■ *How were Southern and Northern states different in the 1800s?*

Conflict over the Territories

In 1819, the number of slave states and free states was equal. Southerners, however, saw signs that the balance was changing. Even with the addition of new slave states, the South was losing power in Congress. The only thing that would erase southerners' fears of being outnumbered was the addition of a new slave state.

Southerners expected to get that state when Missouri applied for statehood in 1819. Since about one-sixth of the people living there were slaves, southerners thought that Missouri would be admitted as a slave state.

The Fight Over Missouri

When the subject of Missouri's statehood was brought before Congress, however, southerners were shocked. Congressman Rufus King of New York demanded that slavery not be allowed in Missouri. Any law that protected slavery, he

➤ *According to the Missouri Compromise, slavery was illegal in all territories north of 36° 30′ latitude—except Missouri. Slavery was allowed in territories south of that line.*

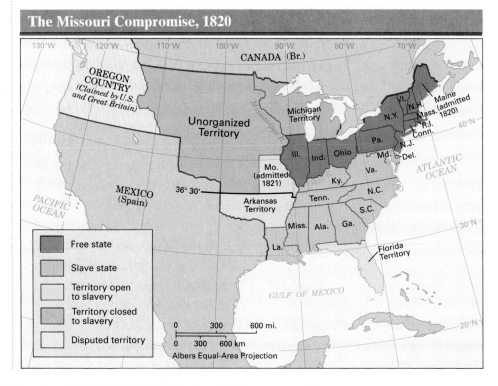

The Missouri Compromise, 1820

said, was "contrary to the law of nature, which is the law of God."

A huge uproar followed. Southerners complained that Congress had no right to prohibit slavery. Some Americans might not like slavery, they said, but it was protected by the Constitution.

Congress had never been so divided by an issue. Thomas Jefferson observed the discord and wrote: "This momentous question, like a fire-bell in the night, awakened and filled me with terror."

Clay's Solution

After months of arguments, no progress had been made on the Missouri issue. Finally, Speaker of the House Henry Clay decided to act. He knew that the conflict between North and South had to end if the nation was to survive.

Working with that goal, Clay convinced the two sides to agree to

◀ Representative Henry Clay of Kentucky owned slaves himself but often opposed other southern politicians over slavery in Congress. To Clay, nothing was more important than preserving the Union.

a "Missouri Compromise." To maintain the balance of power in the Senate, Maine was admitted as a free state and Missouri joined the Union as a slave state. Free states and slave states were again equally represented in the Senate. The map on page 446 shows how Congress solved the dispute between politicians over slavery in the territories. This compromise ended the crisis, but tensions between North and South remained. ■

■ *How did the Missouri Compromise settle the differences between free states and slave states?*

Expansion and Compromise

In the years after the Missouri Compromise, the question of extending slavery was kept out of Congress. However, other concerns occupied the nation. In the North, industries thrived and cities grew. In the South, cotton became one of the most important and profitable crops produced in the United States. And in the West, the United States and Mexico fought a war over Texas.

Texas and California

Most northerners opposed the Mexican War. They feared that the lands the United States gained from a struggle with Mexico would become slave states. Southerners supported the war for the same reason. After Texas became a slave state in 1845, they reasoned that a few more slave states carved out of Mexican land would solve their problem of a balance in Congress.

No new slave states came into the union out of those lands over the next four years, however. Northern Congressmen would not upset the balance between free states and slave states— at least, not by a slave state. Southerners were furious, then,

A Divided Nation

► *Senator John Calhoun of South Carolina was one of the most powerful politicians of his day. He supported the rights of states over those of the Union, an idea that gained support in the South in the 1850s.*

when California applied for statehood as a free state in 1849. The crisis had reached a new height.

Clay and Calhoun

Congress hoped to resolve the crisis in a series of debates in early 1850. Huge audiences crowded into the Capitol Building to watch. Massachusetts Senator Daniel Webster, a brilliant speaker, called for compromise. So did Henry Clay. He came out of retirement to re-enter the Senate. Compromise was, Clay argued, the only way to keep the nation from splitting. "I am for staying within the Union," he said.

Senator John Calhoun claimed that a state could **secede,** or leave the Union, if it didn't agree with the rest of the

UNDERSTANDING COMPROMISE

Compromise has been useful in solving problems throughout the history of the United States. It is unlikely, for example, that the Constitution would have been able to exist without it.

Compromise in the Past

At the Constitutional Convention, delegates saw that they couldn't get everything they wanted. Each delegate gave up some of what he wanted and got some of what he wanted. The delegates recognized that the Constitution was more important than their individual needs.

Compromise is not surrender. At the conclusion of the war with Mexico, the United States gained a huge territory, which included California. Mexico lost 525,000 square miles of territory. In a compromise, each side must give up something.

Compromise Today

In the United States, compromise is especially important. With so many people doing so many different things, no one can get everything he or she wants all the time. In order to live peacefully, everyone must compromise.

For example, a fire department needs a larger firehouse. The only place to build the firehouse is in a park. Families want to save the park for their children. A compromise is reached when the fire department agrees to build a small firehouse on part of the park, keeping the rest open for families.

Compromise works best when both sides are equal parts of a larger group or nation. Then, each side is willing to give something up for the good of the whole group.

But if one side feels threatened by the other, compromise doesn't work. In those cases, like the United States before 1860, compromise doesn't solve conflicts. It delays them.

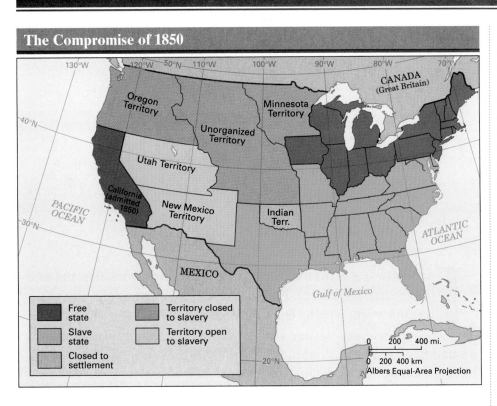

The Compromise of 1850

Legend:
- Free state
- Slave state
- Closed to settlement
- Territory closed to slavery
- Territory open to slavery

0 200 400 mi.
0 200 400 km
Albers Equal-Area Projection

◄ Under the Compromise of 1850, California was admitted to the Union as a free state, and slavery was allowed in the New Mexico and Utah territories. What part of these territories lies above the 36°30′ line of the Missouri Compromise?

nation. He asked Northern Congressmen to allow slavery in the territories. If they would not, he said, they should "let the States we both represent agree to separate and part in peace."

Clay's plea for compromise eventually won. The map on this page shows how this compromise affected the issue of slavery in the territories. The compromise also strengthened the Fugitive Slave Law of 1793.

Escaping slaves had always been a problem for slave-owners, but in the 1840s, the problem grew even worse. Northerners had begun to help slaves escape. This made it almost impossible for planters to capture slaves that had run away.

The Fugitive Slave Law required Northern citizens to help catch escaped slaves. But many Northerners hated the law as much as they hated slavery. They ignored it from the time it was passed by Congress. In this way, the Fugitive Slave Law increased the tension between Northerners and Southerners. But the Compromise of 1850 did keep the two sections of the nation together. ■

Across Time & Space

In the 1800s, speeches by politicians informed, aroused, and entertained Americans. Large crowds gathered to hear the hours-long speeches of John Calhoun and Henry Clay. Today, all many Americans hear of political speeches are 5- or 10-second excerpts on TV news.

■ How did the Compromise of 1850 increase tension between free states and slave states?

REVIEW

1. **FOCUS** How did Northern and Southern states resolve their differences?
2. **CONNECT** Why was slavery important to Southerners?
3. **POLITICAL SYSTEMS** Why was it important to keep a balance between free states and slave states?
4. **CRITICAL THINKING** Compromise can be a good way to settle a dispute. However, compromise did not resolve all of the conflicts between the North and the South in the 1800s. Why didn't it work?
5. **ACTIVITY** Henry Clay and John Calhoun tried to convince people to change their minds by making speeches. Prepare a one-minute speech on the topic of slavery in the territories. Stage a debate with your classmates.

449

A Divided Nation

LESSON 2

The Growing Conflict

How did the continuing conflict between North and South affect the United States?

Key Terms

- Underground Railroad
- popular sovereignty

➤ *John Steuart Curry's portrait* John Brown, *shown on this page, was painted between 1938 and 1940. It hangs in the State House in Topeka, Kansas.*

John Brown was tired of the politicians' arguments. He was impatient with all the speeches about slavery. He wanted to do something about it. John Brown wanted to fight slavery like a soldier fights a war.

In 1854, that fight moved into the territory of Kansas. Congress had decided to allow the people of Kansas to choose whether theirs would be a free state or a slave state. Supporters and opponents of slavery flooded across the borders in order to influence the future of the state.

Kansas, Brown thought, was the place where the battle over slavery would be fought once and for all. In 1855, Brown and five of his sons moved to Kansas to fight slavery. Tensions between proslavery and antislavery settlers were

high. Threats of violence and murder were common. This did not discourage John Brown. As time went by, he would do almost anything to end slavery.

The Attack on Slavery

Few people felt or acted the way John Brown did. However, some Americans had always believed that slavery was wrong. In the 1680s, some Pennsylvania Quakers spoke out against slavery. In the late 1700s, some leaders of

the American Revolution argued that slavery did not belong in a nation where "all men are created equal." By the 1830s, more and more Americans believed that slavery should end. These people were called abolitionists.

The *Liberator*

One of these people was William Lloyd Garrison. In 1831, he started a newspaper called the *Liberator*. In its pages, Garrison demanded an immediate and total end to slavery. There could be "no Union with slaveholders," he wrote. Such statements quickly made the *Liberator* one of the most important forces in the growing antislavery movement.

In 1833, Garrison helped start the American Anti-Slavery Society. This society tried to persuade slave owners that slavery was an evil that should be wiped out. The society did not convince many slave owners to free their slaves. However, their speeches inspired many northerners to join the struggle against slavery.

The Underground Railroad

Speeches were not enough for some abolitionists. Some people assisted slaves along the **Underground Railroad.** This was not a railroad or underground, but a series of secret escape routes from the South to free states and Canada. Many abolitionists acted as "conductors" and helped escaping slaves on the Underground Railroad. The illustration and map on pages 452–453 tell more about the Underground Railroad. The story "Carrying the Running-Aways" on pages 458–461 also tells about escaping slaves.

Frederick Douglass escaped from slavery in 1838. Once free, he began to speak

◄ *Harriet Tubman was one of the most famous conductors on the Underground Railroad. After escaping from slavery herself, Tubman returned to the South at least 19 times and helped over 300 slaves escape.*

out about his experiences. Over time, he became the best-known black abolitionist in the United States. Douglass fought slavery by giving lectures, publishing a newspaper, and writing his life story.

The stories of Douglass and other slaves made northerners realize that blacks were suffering. They were people escaping from cruelty and violence.

Uncle Tom's Cabin

Harriet Beecher Stowe did more than anyone else to make the nation see the problems of

▼ *Over 10,000 copies of* Uncle Tom's Cabin *were sold in the first few days after it was published. Few books have had such a strong impact on the United States.*

▼ *Imagine a slave named Adam as he escapes from a plantation in Ashburn, Virginia, in May 1854. Adam rests during the day and travels at night. In the darkness he walks to the north, swims across a river, and hides in forests. He meets a conductor who feeds him and leads him to a safe house.*

➤ *Adam follows a path next to a fence, and then wades across another river. After 10 days Adam reaches the town of Oxford, Pennsylvania. There, Adam is met by an abolitionist family. They feed him, give him new clothes, and arrange to send him to safety in Canada.*

slaves. In 1851, an abolitionist magazine called the *National Era* began printing chapters of Stowe's novel called *Uncle Tom's Cabin.* The scenes of violence and brutality in Stowe's novel helped people see slavery as an evil. In this one, for example, a slave describes an encounter with his owner's son.

*T*hen he turned on me, and began striking me. I held his hand, and then he screamed and kicked and ran to his father, and told him that I was fighting him. He came in a rage, and said he'd teach me who was my master; and he tied me to a tree, and cut switches for young master, and told him he might whip me till he was tired. . . . Who made this man my master?

Each week, the story of the slaves Eliza and old Uncle Tom and the cruel boss Simon Legree

unfolded. Each week, more and more people read it. Readers wept when Uncle Tom was sold from owner to owner. They cheered as Eliza escaped across the frozen Ohio River to freedom.

Uncle Tom's Cabin was published as a book in 1852. It sold over 300,000 copies in one year. By then, nearly everyone in the country had heard about it.

The South's Response

Southerners were angered by the attacks on slavery in *Uncle Tom's Cabin* and the *Liberator.* They complained loudly that the novel's description of slavery and southern life was wrong. It seemed to southerners that abolitionists would attack the South, no matter what the facts were.

These attacks only created

A lawn sculpture holding a lit lantern signals to Adam that it is safe to come into the house. Inside, Adam is hidden in a secret room behind a sliding panel.

ANTI-SLAVE-CATCHERS'
MASS
CONVENTION!

All the People of this State, who are opposed to being made SLAVES or SLAVE-CATCHERS, and to having the Free Soil of Wisconsin made the hunting-ground for *Human Kidnappers*, and all who are willing to unite in a

☞ **STATE LEAGUE,**

to defend our State Sovereignty, our State Courts, and our State and National Constitutions, against the flagrant usurpations of U. S. Judges, Commissioners, and Marshals, and their Attorneys; and to maintain inviolate those great Constitutional Safeguards of Freedom—the WRIT OF HABEAS CORPUS, and the RIGHT OF TRIAL BY JURY—as old and sacred as Constitutional Liberty itself; and all who are willing to sustain the cause of those who are prosecuted, and to be prosecuted in Wisconsin, by the agents and executors of the Kidnapping Act of 1850, for the alleged crime of rescuing a human being from the hands of kidnappers, and restoring him to himself and to Freedom, are invited to meet at

YOUNGS' HALL,
IN THIS CITY.

more tensions between the two regions. Southerners stopped sending their children to northern schools. Some northerners stopped buying cotton from slaveholding plantations. Even the Methodist and Presbyterian churches split into northern and southern sections. The entire nation seemed to be splitting in two. ∎

■ *Find evidence to support this statement: Abolitionism increased tensions between the North and the South.*

The Battle of Kansas

Senator Stephen Douglas from Illinois thought he knew how to bring the nation together again. He believed that if the people of the territories decided the issue of slavery for themselves, then the rest of the nation would not have to get involved in the problem. This idea was called **popular sovereignty** *(SAHV ur ihn tee).*

In 1854, Douglas tested this idea. He introduced a bill organizing two new states: Kansas and Nebraska. Douglas thought his Kansas-Nebraska Act would bring the nation together, just like Henry Clay's compromises in 1820 and 1850.

The Kansas-Nebraska Act became law in May 1854. The law said that the people living there could decide by popular vote whether Kansas would be a free or a slave state. The map on page 455 shows the effect of this law on slavery in the territories.

The Kansas-Nebraska Act helped to pull the nation apart. Abolitionists hated the bill. They didn't want slavery admitted into any new territory. A Moment in Time on page 454 tells how a black abolitionist fought against slavery. Southerners opposed the bill because they wanted slavery to expand freely into new lands.

Settling Kansas

Groups for and against slavery rushed into Kansas. Each side wanted to fill the state with people who would vote their way.

453

A Black Abolitionist

*11:00 P.M., December 12, 1848
In the basement of the Spring
Street African Methodist Episcopal
Zion Church in upstate New York*

Shirt
He wears with pride this warm, soft, homespun shirt his wife made. She learned to sew from her mother, who had been a house slave and seamstress.

Meeting Notice
The ink hasn't dried on the anti-slavery meeting notices he has just printed. He will post them tomorrow.

Apron
The printer's apron was a gift from the friendly Quaker who hired him as a printer's apprentice 10 years ago. He wore this apron while he learned to read, write, and run a printing press.

Bible
He is carrying a Bible that has sentences marked for study. In the morning he and his son will read the verses together. His son's school has few books and supplies. The teachers use the Bible to teach reading.

Money
Ten cents of his $3 weekly pay will go in the collection plate after the antislavery society meeting. The society uses the money to help escaping slaves.

Ripped Pants
His pants ripped when he refused to leave the whites-only section of the train. His pant leg caught on the seat as the conductor forced him off the car.

Boots
His feet are cold and wet. As the agent for an antislavery newspaper, he has walked many miles tonight to get new subscribers.

Tensions between the two groups of settlers grew throughout 1854. One proslavery paper invited southerners to bring weapons and "send the scoundrels" from the North back home. A northern minister said that rifles would be more useful than Bibles in Kansas.

Elections deciding whether Kansas would be a free state or a slave state were held in March 1855. On election day, armed men from the slave state of Missouri, called "Border Ruffians," rushed into the state and voted illegally. Every proslavery candidate in Kansas was elected with the help of "Ruffian" votes.

Bleeding Kansas

A group of antislavery settlers challenged the vote and set up a free-state government in Topeka, Kansas. The proslavery group set up a capital in Lecompton. Kansas was now split into two halves.

John Brown, the man who had come to Kansas to fight slavery, watched as violent bands from both sides burned crops. They destroyed buildings and threatened their opponents.

In May 1856, a proslavery group killed an antislavery settler. When John Brown heard about this, he organized a band of six or seven men. They traveled to a proslavery settlement near a place called Pottawatomie Creek. Brown and his men dragged five of the men out of bed in the middle of the night and murdered them.

News of John Brown's massacre spread through Kansas, and the violence increased. Fighting between free-state and slave-state bands continued through the summer of 1856.

The two groups did not agree on a constitution until 1861, when Kansas was finally admitted as a free state. Douglas thought the

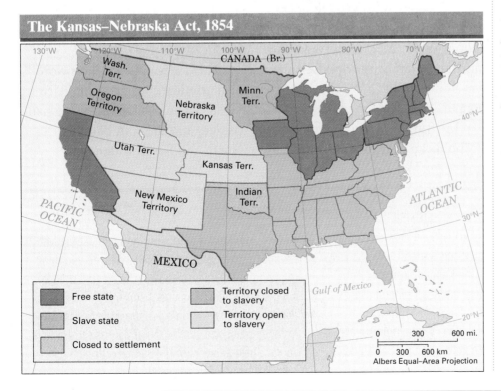

The Kansas–Nebraska Act, 1854

◀ *When Congress passed the Kansas-Nebraska Act, it meant that slavery could exist in any territory where people voted for it. This law erased the 36°30′ line of the Missouri Compromise that kept slavery out of the northern territories.*

A Divided Nation

Kansas-Nebraska Act would ease the conflicts between sections of the country. Instead, it brought civil war to the territories and created an even wider split between North and South. ■

The Geography of Politics

The Republicans' first presidential candidate was John C. Fremont. He lost the election of 1856, but won a majority of the votes in free states.

The question of slavery had split Kansas in two. It had also begun to divide American political parties into two camps.

The Democrats were successful in all parts of the country in the late 1840s and 1850s. But now slavery divided the party.

Stephen Douglas was one of the party's leaders in the 1850s. He believed that popular sovereignty was the only way to hold the nation together.

Again, Douglas was caught between two groups. Many southern Democrats turned to more radical candidates who would protect slavery. Many northern Democrats opposed slavery and wouldn't compromise any longer. They left the party.

In 1854, a new party—the Republican Party—was formed. It brought together abolitionists, other opponents of slavery, and former northern Democrats. Some Republicans wanted to forbid slavery immediately. Others did not think that the United States was ready for such a sudden change. These people were willing to allow slavery where it already existed, but wanted to keep it out of the territories. This group was led by a man named Abraham Lincoln.

The tall, awkward-looking Lincoln was from Illinois. He had served a term in Congress and had spoken out against slavery throughout his career. But it was not until Lincoln joined the Republicans that he became an important political figure. His clever and forceful speeches—on slavery and other subjects—made him a leader of the new party.

Now, sectional conflicts were also political conflicts—and vice versa. The era of compromise had passed, and the split between North and South widened. ■

■ *How did American political parties change in the 1850s?*

REVIEW

1. **FOCUS** How did the continuing conflict between North and South affect the United States?
2. **CONNECT** In what way was the Kansas-Nebraska Act like the Missouri Compromise and the Compromise of 1850?
3. **ETHICS** How do you think the ideas of abolitionism affected the actions of people in the 1830s, 1840s, and 1850s?
4. **CRITICAL THINKING** Americans had lived with slavery for a long time before the 1850s. Why do you think reading the *Liberator* and *Uncle Tom's Cabin* made people feel so strongly about slavery?
5. **WRITING ACTIVITY** Imagine you are a slave who has escaped along the Underground Railroad to Pennsylvania. Write an account of your new life and how it differs from your life as a slave.

Asking Good Questions

Here's Why

In order to understand issues and make decisions with an informed and open mind, you need to be able to ask good questions. Listening courteously to a different viewpoint or to new information does not mean you agree with that side. It means that you are giving all points of view a fair hearing.

The ability to ask good questions is a skill used by good newspaper or television reporters. When reporters write articles about current issues, they must investigate different sides of the issue. The rule for good reporting is to always ask: Who? What? When? Where? and Why? or How?

Suppose you had to vote on the Compromise of 1850. How would you become informed about this important issue?

Here's How

The chapter presents different sides of the slavery issue. On page 446 find the question, "How were the southern and northern states different in the 1800s?" This is a good question because it is neutral: it helps us study both sides. The word *different* tells you to look at both sides. Find other neutral words in the lesson that you could use in your own questions.

Here is how a reporter's five key questions could be used to compare the viewpoints of Henry Clay and John Calhoun on slavery:

Who? Henry Clay
What? He wanted states to compromise on permitting slavery in new states and territories.
When? 1850
Where? Congress
Why? He wanted the union to survive.

Who? John Calhoun
What? He wanted to allow slavery in the territories or give the states the option to leave the union.
When? 1850
Where? Congress
Why? He believed the question of slavery was up to the people of a state or territory, not Congress.

Try It

Imagine you are interviewing Henry Clay or John Calhoun just before the Compromise of 1850. Write two neutral questions that you could ask about the slavery issue. Tell how Clay or Calhoun might have answered.

Apply It

You are the host of a television talk show. The topic: Should parents limit the kind and amount of television children watch? To be fair to both sides of the issue, what two guests would you invite? Write two neutral questions to ask each guest.

who?
what?
when?
where?
why?
how?

Carrying the Running-Aways

Told by Virginia Hamilton

You have read about the Underground Railroad and the way it was used to help runaway slaves escape. This story is from a book of Black American folktales called The People Could Fly. *It is a true story first told by Arnold Gragston, a slave in Kentucky. This story stands for thousands of such tales of escape to the North and freedom. The man who helped the runaways was John Rankin, a Presbyterian minister who lived in Ripley, Ohio. From 1825 to 1865 more than 2,000 slaves were sheltered at Rankin's underground railroad station.*

Never had any idea of carryin the runnin-away slaves over the river. Even though I was right there on the plantation, right by that big river, it never got in my mind to do somethin like that. But one night the woman whose house I had gone courtin to said she knew a pretty girl wanted to cross the river and would I take her. Well, I met the girl and she was awful pretty. And soon the woman was tellin me how to get across, how to go, and when to leave.

Well, I had to think about it. But each day, that girl or the woman would come around, ask me would I row the girl across the river to a place called Ripley. Well, I finally said I would. And one night I went over to the woman's house. My owner trusted me and let me come and go as I pleased, long as I didn't try to read or write anythin. For writin and readin was forbidden to slaves.

Now, I had heard about the other side of the river from the other slaves. But I thought it was just like the side where we lived on the plantation. I thought there were slaves and masters over there, too, and overseers and rawhide whips they used on us. That's why I was so scared. I thought I'd land the girl over there and some overseer didn't know us would beat us for bein out at night. They could do that, you know.

    Well I did it. Oh, it was a long rowin time in the cold, with me worryin. But pretty soon I see a light way up high. Then I remembered the woman told me to watch for a light. Told me to row to the light, which is what I did. And when I got to it, there were two men. They reached down and grabbed the girl. Then one of the men took me by the arm. Said, "You about hungry?" And if he hadn't been holdin me, I would of fell out of that rowboat.

Well, that was my first trip. I was scared for a long time after that. But pretty soon I got over it, as other folks asked me to take them across the river. Two and three at a time, I'd take them. I got used to making three or four trips every month.

Now it was funny. I never saw my passengers after that first girl. Because I took them on the nights when the moon was not showin, it was cloudy. And I always met them in the open or in a house with no light. So I never saw them, couldn't recognize them, and couldn't describe them. But I would say to them, "What you say?" And they would say the password. Sounded like "Menare." Seemed the word came from the Bible somewhere, but I don't know. And they would have to say that word before I took them across.

Well, there in Ripley was a man named Mr. Rankins, the rest was John, I think. He had a "station" there for escaping slaves. Ohio was a free state, I found out, so once they got across, Mr. Rankins would see to them. We went at night so we could continue back for more and to be sure no slave catchers would follow us there.

Mr. Rankins had a big light about thirty feet high up and it burned all night. It meant freedom for slaves if they could get to that bright flame.

I worked hard and almost got caught. I'd been rowing fugitives for almost four years. It was in 1863 and it was a night I carried twelve runnin-aways across the river to Mr. Rankins'. I stepped out of the boat back in Kentucky and they were after me. Don't know how they found out. But the slave catchers, didn't know them, were on my trail. I ran away from the plantation and all who I knew there. I lived in the fields and in the woods. Even in caves. Sometimes I slept up in the tree branches. Or in a hay pile. I couldn't get across the river now, it was watched so closely.

Finally, I did get across. Late one night me and my wife went. I had gone back to the plantation to get her. Mr. Rankins had him a bell by this time, along with the light. We were rowin and rowin. We could see the light and hear that bell, but it seemed we weren't gettin any closer. It took forever, it seemed.

menare a made up word

station a stop on the Underground Railroad

fugitives people who have fled

That was because we were so scared and it was so dark and we knew we could get caught and never get gone.

Well, we did get there. We pulled up there and went on to freedom. It was only a few months before all the slaves was freed.

We didn't stay on at Ripley. We went on to Detroit because I wasn't taking any chances. I have children and grandchildren now. Well, you know, the bigger ones don't care so much to hear about those times. But the little ones, well, they never get tired of hearin how their grandpa brought emancipation to loads of slaves he could touch and feel in the dark but never ever see.

emancipation   to be set free

Further Reading

Brady. Jean Fritz. Brady cannot keep a secret, so his parents haven't told him they are agents for the Underground Railroad. He finds out and when his father is hurt, takes over to help with an escape.

The Drinking Gourd. Ferdinand Monjo. Tommy, sent home from church after he plays a prank, finds a runaway slave family hiding in the barn. Tommy saves the family from a search party of slave catchers.

A Gathering of Days: A New England Girl's Journal, 1830-32. Joan Blos. Catherine and her friends find a note from a fugitive slave asking for help. They leave food and a blanket where the slave will find it, thus helping someone they never meet.

To Be a Slave. Julius Lester. In the 1930s, the Federal Writers' Project interviewed ex-slaves about their experiences. Their powerful stories are presented in this stirring book.

LESSON 3

A House Divided

THINKING
FOCUS

Why did efforts to resolve the issue of slavery fail?

Key Terms

- secessionist
- Confederacy

➤ *Though he later won his freedom, Dred Scott spent most of his life as a slave—the property of another person.*

Throughout his long life as a slave, Dred Scott wanted freedom.

As a boy in Missouri, he knew slaves who ran away. Some of them found freedom in northern states. Dred Scott did not run away, but he did want to be free.

When he was about 30 years old, Dred Scott was bought by John Emerson, a doctor in the U.S. Army. Scott traveled with his new owner to the free state of Illinois and the Wisconsin Territory. They spent about four years in places that did not allow slavery. At the end of that time, Scott returned to Missouri, still a slave.

When Dr. Emerson died a few years later in 1843, Dred Scott thought he might be freed. Many slaves were freed when their owners died. Dr. Emerson, however, left everything he owned—including his slaves—to his wife. For Dred Scott, there had to be a new way to find freedom.

In 1846, with the help of some abolitionists, Dred Scott sued Mrs. Emerson for his freedom. He argued that he had lived in free states for four years. That, he said, made him a free man. The case was discussed in one court after another for 11 years without a final decision. Finally, the case was brought to the U.S. Supreme Court.

CAUTION!!
COLORED PEOPLE
OF **BOSTON**, ONE & ALL,
You are hereby respectfully CAUTIONED and advised, to avoid conversing with the
Watchmen and **Police Officers**
of **Boston**,
For since the recent ORDER OF THE MAYOR & ALDERMEN, they are empowered to act as
KIDNAPPERS
AND
Slave Catchers,
And they have already been actually employed in
KIDNAPPING, CATCHING, AND KEEPING
SLAVES. Therefore, if you value your LIBERTY,
and the Welfare of the Fugitives among you, Shun
them in every possible manner, as so many HOUNDS
on the track of the most unfortunate of your race.
Keep a Sharp Look Out for
KIDNAPPERS, and have
TOP EYE open.
APRIL 24, 1851.

The Search for a Solution

By the time the Dred Scott case came to the Supreme Court, it was no longer just a case about one man's freedom. The entire nation looked to the court to settle the issue of slavery once and for all.

On March 6, 1857, the Supreme Court declared that Dred Scott was still a slave. Chief Justice Roger Taney declared that Scott did not become free when his owner took him into a territory where Congress had forbidden slavery. Congress, in his opinion, had no power to take property away from citizens. The Missouri Compromise itself was declared unconstitutional by the Court.

In the North, reactions to the decision were strong. Frederick Douglass called the decision "a most scandalous and devilish perversion of the Constitution." Many politicians were shocked that the Court no longer allowed Congress to prohibit slavery.

Stephen Douglas agreed that Congress had been wrong in forbidding slavery. He still thought popular sovereignty was the best way to resolve the question of slavery.

Abraham Lincoln, however, thought the only way to resolve the question was to keep slaves out of the territories and let slavery die

◄ *Thousands of Illinois voters came to hear the debates between Abraham Lincoln and Stephen Douglas. The rest of the nation followed these debates in newspapers.*

out in the South. People all over the nation began to learn of Lincoln's views on slavery when he challenged Stephen Douglas in the election for senator from Illinois. When he was nominated in June 1858, Lincoln told the crowd of Republicans:

A *house divided against itself cannot stand. I believe this government cannot endure, permanently half slave and half free. I do not expect the Union to be dissolved—I do not expect the house to fall—but I do expect it will cease to be divided. It will become all one thing or all the other.*

In the Illinois campaign of 1858, voters learned about the candidates and their opinions though a series of seven public debates.

463

A Divided Nation

The candidates traveled from town to town, discussing the greatest issue of the day: slavery.

In one debate, Douglas said that he didn't mind letting slavery go on forever. Lincoln disagreed. "Republicans . . . look upon it as a moral, social, and political wrong," he said.

Illinois voters reelected Stephen Douglas as senator in November 1858. Lincoln lost the election, but his statements on slavery in the debates made him one of the leading antislavery spokesmen in the country.

After his experiences in Kansas, John Brown still wanted to fight, not debate. Brown planned to start a slave revolt in Virginia.

He would lead an army of free blacks and escaped slaves through the South and destroy slavery. In October 1859, Brown captured a federal weapons warehouse in Harpers Ferry, Virginia. For two days he and his band fought off U.S. troops. Finally, Robert E. Lee and his troops stormed the armory and captured Brown. Six weeks later he was convicted of treason and hanged.

To some people, John Brown seemed to stand for the whole conflict over slavery. To some abolitionists, Brown had sacrificed his life for the cause of freedom for slaves. To southerners, he was a dangerous man who would do anything to wipe out slavery and their way of life. ■

■ *Why didn't the Dred Scott decision end the conflict over slavery?*

The Election of 1860

Many southerners believed that the presidential election of 1860 would decide the future of slavery in the United States. The Democratic party split over the issue. Southern Democrats wanted a candidate to protect slavery. They nominated John Breckinridge of Kentucky.

Northern Democrats chose Stephen Douglas. He still believed that the people of the territories should decide the issue of slavery for themselves.

Abraham Lincoln, the Republican candidate for president, knew that the two Democratic candidates might split the proslavery vote. Lincoln knew that if he could win enough votes in northern states he had a chance to become president.

On a chilly Election Day, Lincoln waited for news about the election at the telegraph office in

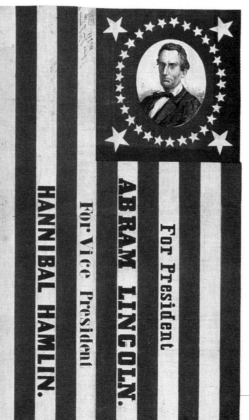

▼ *The debates with Stephen Douglas in 1858 made Abraham Lincoln famous. In 1860, Lincoln was nominated as the Republican party's candidate for president.*

HANNIBAL HAMLIN.
For Vice President
ABRAM LINCOLN.
For President

his hometown of Springfield, Illinois. Finally, the news arrived: Lincoln had won. Abraham Lincoln, the northerner who said he hated slavery, would be the 16th President of the United States. ■

■ *How did proslavery Democrats help Lincoln win the election of 1860?*

The Reaction of the South

Long before Lincoln received news of his victory, southern leaders had made plans to secede from the United States. All through the campaign, southerners thought their worst fears were coming true. They feared that Lincoln would keep slaveholders off new land. The South would lose its political power if no new slave states were admitted. They also feared that Lincoln would abolish slavery.

CHARLESTON
MERCURY
EXTRA:
Passed unanimously at 1.15 o'clock, P. M., December 20th, 1860.
AN ORDINANCE
To dissolve the Union between the State of South Carolina and other States united with her under the compact entitled "The Constitution of the United States of America."
We, the People of the State of South Carolina, in Convention assembled, do declare and ordain, and it is hereby declared and ordained,
That the Ordinance adopted by us in Convention, on the twenty-third day of May, in the year of our Lord one thousand seven hundred and eighty-eight, whereby the Constitution of the United States of America was ratified, and also, all Acts and parts of Acts of the General Assembly of this State, ratifying amendments of the said Constitution, are hereby repealed; and that the union now subsisting between South Carolina and other States, under the name of "The United States of America," is hereby dissolved.
THE
UNION
IS
DISSOLVED!

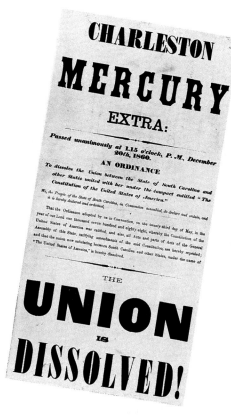

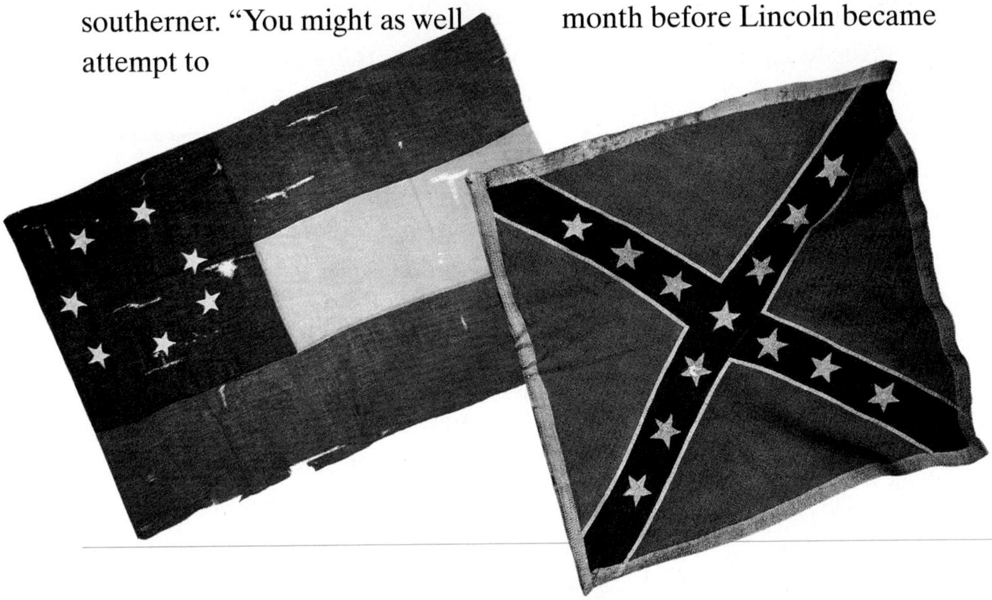

A group of secessionists in South Carolina voted to take the state out of the Union in December 1860. In the next two months, six other states followed them.

As much as some southerners hated and feared Lincoln, they cheered his election. These **secessionists,** as they were called, argued that a state had the right to leave the Union if the government of the United States acted against the state's interests. The secessionists believed that Lincoln's victory would convince other southerners to join them in forming their own independent country. They were right. "People are wild," wrote one southerner. "You might as well attempt to control a tornado as attempt to stop them."

Southern leaders didn't wait until Lincoln took office to leave the Union. By February 1861, one month before Lincoln became

By February 1861, seven southern states had elected a president and formed a government. Later they chose flags, shown on the left, for their new country.

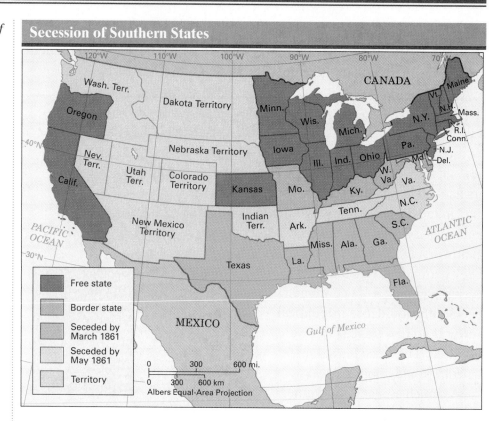

Secession of Southern States

After over 60 years of conflict and crisis, the United States split into two separate sections in 1861. Border states were divided over whether to secede or stay within the Union.

president, seven southern states had seceded. They elected a former U.S. congressman from Mississippi, Jefferson Davis, president of the Confederate States of America, or the **Confederacy,** as it was sometimes called. Look at the map above. Which states made up the Confederacy?

South Carolina demanded all U.S. military troops leave the forts in the state. But Lincoln regarded those forts as U.S. property. He refused to remove the

troops. Early in April, Union ships brought supplies to Fort Sumter in Charleston, South Carolina. On April 12, the Confederate gunners began firing on Fort Sumter. "Shot and shell went screaming over Sumter as if an army of devils were swooping around it," wrote one Union soldier.

On April 13 the Union troops surrendered the fort. Although no one had been killed in 34 hours of shelling, the war had begun. ■

■ *Why did Southerners leave the Union?*

R E V I E W

1. **FOCUS** Why did efforts to resolve the question of slavery fail?

2. **CONNECT** What politician first suggested the idea of seceding from the Union? What region of the country did he represent?

3. **HISTORY** Why did the election of Abraham Lincoln frighten southerners? Why did it also make some of them happy?

4. **CRITICAL THINKING** Speaking of slavery, Lincoln said, "It will become all one thing or all the other." Why do you think he believed that?

5. **ACTIVITY** Make a chart of the three candidates for president in the election of 1860 discussed in this lesson. Include the following for each: name, party, home state, beliefs or statements about slavery.

Giving an Oral Report

Here's Why

You will often make oral reports in your classes. If you know how to prepare and present a good report, you can enjoy and learn from these assignments. Suppose you had to prepare an oral report about Black Hawk, the Sauk chief. Would you know where to begin?

Here's How

Read through the following eight steps for preparing an oral report. Consider how you might use each step to prepare your report.

1. **Narrow the topic.** You might choose to talk about Black Hawk's views on treaties the government made with the Indians.
2. **Collect information.** Start with your textbook. Then look at encyclopedias, books, and magazine articles about the Sauk Indians.
3. **Take notes.** Make a detailed outline of all the ideas you want to include in your report.
4. **Prepare a set of note cards.** Write down the ideas from your outline that you want to present in your talk. You can refer to these note cards while presenting your report.
5. **Write an introduction and conclusion.** You might use a dramatic quote from Black Hawk's autobiography to grab your audience's attention. End by summarizing your main points.
6. **Use visual aids.** Show pictures, posters, charts, maps, or artifacts to highlight parts of your report.
7. **Practice.** Ask someone to listen to you and to time your presentation.
8. **Give the final presentation.** Be sure to look directly at your audience and speak clearly.

Try It

Follow the steps in Here's How to prepare an oral report about a person opposed to slavery. Choose someone such as William Lloyd Garrison, Frederick Douglass, Harriet Tubman, Harriet Beecher Stowe, or John Brown.

Apply It

Suppose you wanted to tell your family about uses for a home computer. How would you use the eight steps to convince your family to buy a computer?

Early Photography

A Frenchman named Joseph-Nicéphore Niépce took the first true photograph in 1826. During the Civil War, photographs became a way to preserve personal and national memories. Ever since, pictures have changed our lives and become part of them.

The photographer poses his client for a portrait in the 1800s.

Get Ready

Find a current magazine with many kinds of photographs. Keep the magazine open next to these pages in your textbook. All of the photographs below are from the 1800s. Use a notebook to write down what you observe about the historic prints and the current ones you found.

Find Out

Study both sets of photographs—the ones on these pages and the ones in your magazine. Notice the lighting, the backgrounds, and the people's poses. Make a list of questions to answer about each photograph. Did the

➤ *Only two of these early cameras exist in the United States. This one dates from 1839.*

people in the picture know they were being photographed? Why do you think the picture was taken? Can you tell what time of day it was?

Compare your answers about the 1800s photographs to your answers about the current ones. Make a list of the differences you observed.

Move Ahead

Make a combined list of questions you and your classmates answered. Did most of you agree about the differences between historic photos and current ones?

Why are the older pictures different from the current ones? Check your school or classroom reference books to find out how you would have had your picture taken in the 1840s. How long would you have had to sit still? Ask a volunteer to sit or stand for that amount of time. What position does the person choose? What happens to his or her facial expression?

Explore Some More

To learn more about current photography, study newspaper photographs for a week. Make

▲ Dorothy J. Rainey and her seven daughters pose rigidly for a group portrait.

a scrapbook of the pictures that you find that could not have been taken 150 years ago. Next to each picture, note the reason. You will find night scenes, action shots, candid photos of people caught unaware and beautiful color scenes.

If you also look at family or school pictures, you will see how we have come to depend on film to record our history.

▲ The baby's left hand is a blur of motion in this early photo of a baby girl and her nursemaid.

◄ This picture was taken outside a traveling darkroom.

Chapter Review

Reviewing Key Terms

Confederacy (p. 466)
free state (p. 445)
popular sovereignty (p. 453)
secede (p. 448)

secessionist (p. 465)
slave state (p. 445)
Underground Railroad (p. 451)
Union (p. 445)

A. The two words in each pair are related in some important way. On your own paper, write a sentence which explains how the words are related.

1. Union, Confederacy
2. free state, slave state
3. Underground Railroad, free state
4. popular sovereignty, slave state
5. secessionist, secede

B. Some of the following statements are true. The rest are false. Write *True* or *False* for each statement. Then rewrite the false statements to make them true.

1. Popular sovereignty was an election in new territories to fill public offices.
2. Thousands of slaves escaped to freedom through the secret route to the North called the Underground Railroad.
3. Secessionists cheered when Abraham Lincoln was elected President of the United States because they believed he would keep the Union together.

Exploring Concepts

A. The debate over slavery in the United States began in 1787 at the Philadelphia Convention and lasted until 1865. The U.S. government made the following important decisions regarding slavery. Copy the decisions. For each one, write an explanation of what was decided and what it meant. The first one has been done for you.

1. Three-fifths Compromise
   Three-fifths of the slaves would be counted in a state's population when representation in Congress was decided. This meant that slavery would remain legal in the United States.
2. Northwest Ordinance
3. Missouri Compromise
4. Compromise of 1850
5. Kansas-Nebraska Act
6. Dred Scott Decision

B. Answer each question with information from the chapter.

1. What three compromises did the North and the South make to keep the nation together?
2. Why did the North and the South want to avoid being outnumbered in Congress?
3. What caused John Brown to go to Kansas in 1855? How was his protest against slavery different from those before him?
4. Were Northerners pleased or angry about the Dred Scott decision? Why?
5. What stand on slavery did Abraham Lincoln take during the Lincoln-Douglas debates?
6. What was the abolitionists' goal? How do you suppose they might have felt about the outbreak of the Civil War?

470

Reviewing Skills

1. Imagine that you are a member of a state legislature considering Amendment 26 on allowing 18-year-olds to vote. What questions would you ask to decide how to vote on this question?
2. What neutral questions would you ask the following people to learn about the effects of the Dred Scott decision: Dred Scott, Abraham Lincoln, and Chief Justice Roger Taney?
3. Between 1787 and 1857, the government made several important decisions about slavery. Look back in the chapter for the dates. Make a timeline that shows the following decisions.
   a. Three-fifths Compromise
   b. Kansas-Nebraska Act
   c. Dred Scott Decision
   d. Missouri Compromise
4. Suppose you belong to a group that is assigned to make a report on two to three events leading up to the Civil War. What steps should the group take to work together to plan the report?

Using Critical Thinking

1. Making compromises kept North and South together for years. Think of a problem, one in your town, at school, or among your friends, that could be solved by each side compromising. How might the compromise work?
2. South Carolina Senator John C. Calhoun favored states rights over those of the nation. He believed that a state could secede from the Union if the state did not agree with the rest of the nation. Do you think that Senator Calhoun's policy would work in the United States today? Why or why not? Describe what you think would happen.
3. Harriet Beecher Stowe and John Brown both became heroes to many abolitionists. Compare their goals, their methods, and their successes. Do you approve or disapprove of what they did? Explain.

Preparing for Citizenship

1. **WRITING ACTIVITY** Get more information about the 1858 Lincoln-Douglas debates. Then write a newspaper article in which you report the debates. Be sure to report both sides of the issues.
2. **ARTS ACTIVITY** With a partner, plan and draw two political cartoons that capture people's reactions to President Lincoln's election. In one cartoon, show the feelings of southerners. In the other, show the reaction of northerners.
3. **GROUP ACTIVITY** *The Liberator* and abolitionist pamphlets helped to build support for the antislavery movement. Plan and write a pamphlet about a present-day issue. Inform your readers about the issue. Then arouse support for your position. Distribute your pamphlet to other classes.
4. **COLLABORATIVE LEARNING** During the 1800s, Frederick Douglass was the best-known black abolitionist in the United States. During the 1950s and 1960s, Dr. Martin Luther King, Jr., led the civil rights movement in the United States. Form groups to study each leader. Assign some members to study the leader's life and report their findings to the group. Other members use the findings to write a brief play showing what the leader achieved. The remaining members perform the play for the class.

A Divided Nation

Toward the Modern Age

The Civil War settled the issue of slavery and preserved the Union. Few African Americans, however, felt free and equal. The proud Southern states went through a difficult period called Reconstruction. Americans poured westward, filling the Great Plains and displacing the American Indians. Immigrants came to work on the land or in the factories of the nation's cities. The country offered great promise for many Americans.

1848

Frédéric Auguste Bartholdi, **Liberty Enlightening the World,** *1884. New York City Harbor, New York. Photo from Image Bank.*

1914

Chapter 19

Civil War and Reconstruction

For four years the armies of the Union and the Confederacy battled one another. The South was the battleground for most of the fighting. When the Civil War ended, Southerners found their land, economy, and way of life torn apart. During the time known as Reconstruction, the South began to rebuild. North and South finally reunited as one nation.

This soldier (left) was one of almost 200,000 African Americans who fought for the Union. A small number fought for the South, but not until the last year of the war.

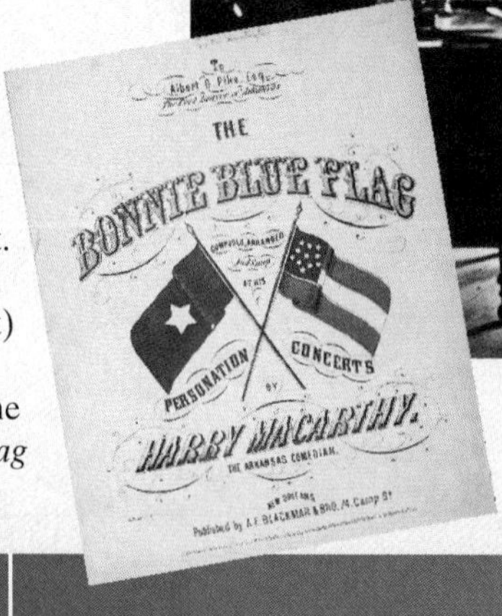

1861–1865 Volunteers on both home fronts help in the war effort. Members of the Women's Central Association of Relief (upper right) count shipments to Northern soldiers. Popular music, such as the Confederate song *Bonnie Blue Flag* (right), shows people's loyalty.

1860

1864

1868

1861

1865 War finally ends on April 9, when Confederate General Lee surrenders to Union General Grant at Appomattox Court house in Virginia.

A few days before the end of the war, Southern troops set fire to their capital, Richmond, Virginia. Thousands of citizens fled before the Union Army arrived.

1876 Rutherford B. Hayes runs for President against Samuel J. Tilden. The parties dispute the results. The inauguration of the Republican, Hayes, in 1877 is part of a compromise that ends Reconstruction.

	1872		1876		1880

1870 Hiram Revels of Mississippi becomes the first African American to be elected to the U.S. Senate. During Reconstruction, 16 African Americans are elected to Congress.

1877

LESSON 1

Outbreak of the War

THINKING
FOCUS

How did both the Union and the Confederate armies show their military power during the early battles of the Civil War?

Key Terms

- blockade
- emancipation

➤ *In May 1861, thousands of young men, like the one shown on this page, volunteered to fight. At that time, it seemed that the Union's strengths (below) ensured a quick Northern victory.*

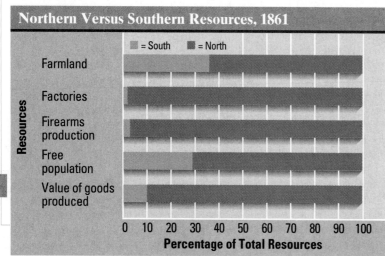

N ews of the war came to the Upson family of Indiana on a warm April day. "Father and I were husking out some corn," wrote 15-year-old Theodore Upson in his diary. A friend ran up and told them about the Confederate attack. "Rebels have fired upon and taken Fort Sumter."

They returned to the house in silence. Theodore's father looked pale. Theodore's grandmother asked what the trouble was. Mr. Upson told her war had started. "Oh, my poor children in the South!" she cried. "Oh, to think that I should have lived to see the day when brother should rise against brother."

North and South

After the fall of Fort Sumter, four more Southern states joined the seven already in the Confederacy. Virginia split, with the eastern part joining the Confederacy.

Arkansas, North Carolina, and Tennessee also seceded, or left, the Union.

Across the country, people took sides. Many in the North saw the war as a fight to save the Union. Northerners shouted, "The Union Forever!"

Most white Southerners had a different view. Some Southern families sent their husbands and sons off to war shouting, "States Rights!" Southerners felt that states should have the power to make their own laws about slavery and other issues. The Confederate

Northern Versus Southern Resources, 1861

■ = South   ■ = North

Resources
- Farmland
- Factories
- Firearms production
- Free population
- Value of goods produced

0 10 20 30 40 50 60 70 80 90 100
Percentage of Total Resources

states were those slave states that decided to secede from the Union. They were ready to fight for their independence.

The North expected to win the war quickly. President Lincoln at first asked states to send soldiers for only 90 days. He had reason to feel confident. The North greatly outnumbered the South in people, railroads, factories, natural resources, and money.

However, the South had several important strengths. The North was invading the South, so Southerners fought harder to protect their homes and property. Also, many of the best officers in the U.S. Army joined with the South. Robert E. Lee turned down

the command of the Union forces after his home state of Virginia seceded. He did not agree with secession but explained sadly, "I cannot raise my hand against my birthplace, my home, my children." Instead, Lee took command of Virginia's forces. ■

The mythical figure of Lady Liberty appeared on both a Southern flag (left) and a Northern emblem (right)

■ *What were the strengths of the North and the South at the start of the Civil War?*

Early Battles

The first battle in July 1861 began like a holiday outing. Union supporters packed picnic lunches and followed soldiers from Washington, D.C., into Virginia. Newspaper reporters also came to get the story.

Armies from the North and the South met near a stream called Bull Run, about 25 miles from Washington, D.C. At first Confederates held the Union soldiers back. Then the Confederates attacked. Fierce fighting broke out, and the Confederate army won the battle.

The Battle of Bull Run showed the North that it would not win the

▼ *In battle, some soldiers loaded their rifles by hand and fired one bullet at a time. Union troops wore blue uniforms, and gray was the official color of Confederate uniforms. In the confusion of battle, it was not always possible to tell the two sides apart.*

Civil War and Reconstruction

war easily. Congress passed laws calling for troops to serve three years. President Lincoln's generals had a plan to save the Union. The Union's "anaconda plan" was named for the snake that squeezes its prey to death. The Union planned to squeeze the strength out of the South by a **blockade,** or closing, of Southern ocean ports. Union ships would stop supplies and keep Southerners from earning money by selling cotton to other countries.

Under the anaconda plan, Union ships would take control of the Mississippi River. Confederate states would then be unable to send boats with supplies and soldiers to other Confederate states. Finally, Union forces would try to capture Richmond, the Confederate capital.

The South also had plans. One was to destroy Union ships. In 1862, the South sent its iron-sided steamship, *Merrimack,* up the James River. (The South

➤ *The* Monitor *and the* Merrimack *(right) fought the first battle ever between ironclad warships. Later, the U.S. Navy built a large fleet of ironclads like the one below, right. The map shows the location of the two ships near Chesapeake Bay.*

renamed the ship the *Virginia*.) The *Merrimack* was far stronger than the Union's wooden ships. When Union ships fired at it, the cannonballs could not pierce the ship's sides.

The next day, the Union sent its own iron ship, the *Monitor,* to attack the *Merrimack.* The two ships battled, with no clear winner.

Then, in the fall of 1862, Lee's army marched north into Maryland and headed toward Pennsylvania. Union forces in the area got unexpected help in the town of Frederick. Union soldiers found three cigars wrapped in paper. On the paper, someone had written the positions of Confederate troops.

The Union army soon met Confederate troops at Antietam Creek in Maryland. The Union won, and forced Lee's troops back.

In the first two years of the war, most of the fighting took place in Virginia. The Union army tried again and again to capture Richmond. Each time, Lee's army fiercely defended the city.

It seemed that the Union army would never capture Richmond. Many felt the North needed a strong military leader like Lee. At this time, a little known Union soldier named Ulysses S. Grant had begun to win some battles. Later, President Lincoln asked Grant to command the Union Army. ■

How Do We Know?

The Civil War was one of the first major conflicts recorded by photography. Matthew Brady was a photographer who carried a heavy camera into dangerous areas to make pictures. The thousands of images photographers produced help us to better understand the people who lived through, and died in the Civil War.

■ *How would the anaconda plan squeeze the strength out of the South?*

A Soldier's Life

In most battles, soldiers stood out in the open, shooting at one another until one side pulled back. Cannonballs hit the ground and threw large chunks of dirt and grass in the air. Rifles fired loudly for hours on end. The wounded lay on the field without medical care.

◄ *Civil War soldiers (left) faced long hours of boredom. Here, a group of Union soldiers waits for the start of a battle.*

▼ *Dinner for soldiers was usually salt pork, coffee, and a biscuit called hardtack, shown below. Soldiers sometimes stole fresh food from Southern farms near their camps.*

Some African American soldiers (top and right) received Medals of Honor (above) for their bravery during the Civil War. They fought in many battles, including Vicksburg and Petersburg.

"What a medley of sounds," wrote one soldier about a battle. "The incessant roar of the rifle, the screaming of bullets, the forest on fire, men cheering, groaning, yelling, swearing, and praying!"

When soldiers were not fighting in battles, the days were long and boring. Troops spent hours marching in step and practicing drills. The war dragged on for months, and then years. Soldiers often sang songs to pass the time.

Homesickness was a problem for most soldiers. They looked forward to any news from home. Confederate soldiers worried that their families were in danger from the invading Union army.

Troops slept in tents or in open fields, through rain and snow. Since the men couldn't wash every day, lice and disease spread among them. Soldiers also got sick from unsafe drinking water. Doctors didn't wash their hands or change their bloodstained clothes between operations. They didn't understand that they themselves were spreading disease in hospitals. More soldiers died from diseases in crowded dirty army hospitals than from bullets.

More than 186,000 African Americans served with the Union in the Civil War. Many were from the North, but some had been freed from slavery in the South. They served in all-black units, usually under white officers. Black troops did not get the same treatment as white soldiers. For example, African Americans received lower pay and rarely rose above the rank of captain. Black soldiers often did not get proper uniforms and shoes.

Women on both sides helped in the war effort. Writer Louisa May Alcott, like many other women, volunteered as a nurse at a hospital in Washington, D.C. Alcott dressed

wounds, read books to the soldiers, wrote letters for them, and gave medicine. She found the hospital ". . . cold, damp, full of vile odors from wounds, kitchens, washrooms, stables." Some Southern women became nurses when their homes were turned into army hospitals.

Women also joined the army as spies, telling their sides about enemy plans. Women could more easily sneak by officials who did not suspect them. If caught, women spies were not punished as much as men were. Men found to be spies often were hanged or shot.

Many American Indians and Hispanic Americans also joined the war effort. They were divided in their loyalties. General Ely Parker, a Seneca Indian, served on General Grant's staff. In the West, many Cherokee fought for the Confederacy. ■

(Left) Ely Samuel Parker, a Seneca, became a Union general. (Above) The illustration shows Mexican American Santos Benavides on the right, riding with his two brothers. Benavides was a Confederate colonel in the Civil War.

■ *What was the daily life of Civil War soldiers like?*

◄ *Rose O'Neal Greenhow (left, with daughter) spied for the Confederacy.*

Emancipation Proclamation

By the President of the United States of America:

A Proclamation.

Whereas, on the twenty-second day of September, in the year of our Lord one thousand eight hundred and sixty-two, a proclamation was issued by the President of the United States, containing, among other things, the following, to wit:

"That on the first day of January, in the year of our Lord one thousand eight hundred and sixty-three, all persons held as slaves within any State or designated part of a State, the people whereof shall then be in rebellion against the...

Abolition of Slavery by State

Before 1863	Maine, N.H., Vermont, Mass., Ohio, Indiana, Mich., Illinois, Wis., Iowa, Minn., Oregon, Calif., R.I., Conn., New York, Pa., N.J., Kansas, Nevada
Due to the Emancipation Proclamation	Virginia, North Carolina, South Carolina, Georgia, Florida, Alabama, Mississippi, Arkansas, Louisiana, Texas
After the Emancipation Proclamation	Delaware, Maryland, West Virginia, Tennessee, Missouri, Kentucky

Because of the Emancipation Proclamation (top), many African Americans were able to join the Union army. The chart above shows when states abolished slavery.

■ *What was the Emancipation Proclamation?*

As the war went on, African Americans, abolitionists, and members of Lincoln's Republican party asked him to end slavery. By the end of 1862, Lincoln agreed to end slavery in the Confederate states. However, he waited to tell the nation until the Union army had turned back Lee's forces at the battle of Antietam.

Soon after, on January 1, 1863, Lincoln issued the Emancipation Proclamation. It stated that all enslaved people held in "any state in rebellion against the United States, shall be then, thenceforward, and forever free."

The Emancipation Proclamation did not free enslaved people in any state that had stayed in the Union. Also, many slaves in Confederate states could not get their freedom right away. Slave owners still fought hard to keep them enslaved.

However, the Emancipation Proclamation changed the goals of the war. It showed that the North was fighting the war to save the Union and to end slavery. Lincoln's announcement led large numbers of free African Americans from the North and South to join the Union army. ■

Before the war, President Lincoln, like most Northerners, cared most about saving the Union. **Emancipation,** or freeing slaves, was not as important to them. Lincoln feared that freeing enslaved people might mean losing the support of border states, like Missouri and Kentucky, where people supported slavery.

REVIEW

1. **FOCUS** How did both the Union and the Confederate armies show their military power during the early battles of the Civil War?

2. **CONNECT** Why did President Lincoln change his mind about ending slavery?

3. **GEOGRAPHY** Why was the Mississippi River an important prize in the war in the West?

4. **CRITICAL THINKING** Why was the South in favor of states' rights?

5. **WRITING ACTIVITY** Imagine you are a young soldier in the Union or Confederate army. Write a letter home describing the worst parts of army life.

L E S S O N   2

The Home Fronts

Union troops blocked supply routes. Southerners experienced food shortages. Stores charged high prices for the little food they sold. Desperate, Southern women took matters into their own hands. The bread riots of 1863 had begun.

During the worst of these riots in Richmond, a mob of about 1,000 raided stores for food. "Bread! Bread!" they cried out. "Our children are starving while the rich roll in wealth!" Confederate president Jefferson Davis threatened to order soldiers to fire on the angry crowds. The crowd broke up, however. Soon, the Confederate government began handing out rice to the people. Stores agreed to drop food prices.

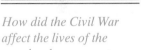

THINKING
FOCUS

How did the Civil War affect the lives of the people who were not fighting?

Hard Times in the South

Bread was just one of many items that Southerners found hard to get. People had to get along without many supplies. People used sharp needles from bushes for sewing. They used hog's hair to

Key Terms

- inflation
- draft

◄ *In this painting, a Southern woman reads a letter from the soldier in her family. Relatives and slaves from the family's plantation, listen as she reads.*

483

make paint brushes. They boiled raspberry leaves for tea.

Greedy business people added to the problem. They grabbed goods before anyone else had a chance. Then they resold them at higher prices. The problem of rising prices, or **inflation,** hurt many families. Their money didn't buy as much as it had before. At the beginning of the war, the average Southern family paid $6.65 for one month's food. By the middle of 1863, the same food cost $68 in Confederate states. In Richmond, a barrel of flour that cost $70 in the fall of 1863 cost $425 two years later, in 1865.

Some Southerners had to feed the starving Confederate army.

■ *How did inflation hurt Southern families?*

Soldiers took pigs, cows, fruit, wheat, and corn from nearby farms. When the army paid the farmers, it was with Confederate money of little value. Farmers sometimes hid their cows and pigs in the woods to keep them from the army.

When soldiers came to a farm, they often found a woman running it. Husbands, brothers, and sons were away at war. Women struggled to do all the work. Many women had to take charge of their plantations. Slaves played an important role in producing crops. When they weren't taking care of their homes and families, some women were helping the Confederate war effort. Women knitted socks, sewed shirts, and made bandages. ■

Life in the North

In the North, women held fairs to raise money. One fair raised more than $1 million for the Union. Some women worked in factories, making army supplies. Others, like the woman in the Moment in Time at right, became nurses in battlefront hospitals.

Union women, too, were often left alone to take care of farms and families. "Our hired man left to enlist [join the army] just as corn planting commenced [started]," wrote one Iowa woman, "so I shouldered my hoe and have worked out ever since."

➤ *In the North, many women helped the union by taking jobs in factories.*

A Civil W

10:00 A.M., July 5,1863
At a federal field hospital near
Gettysburg

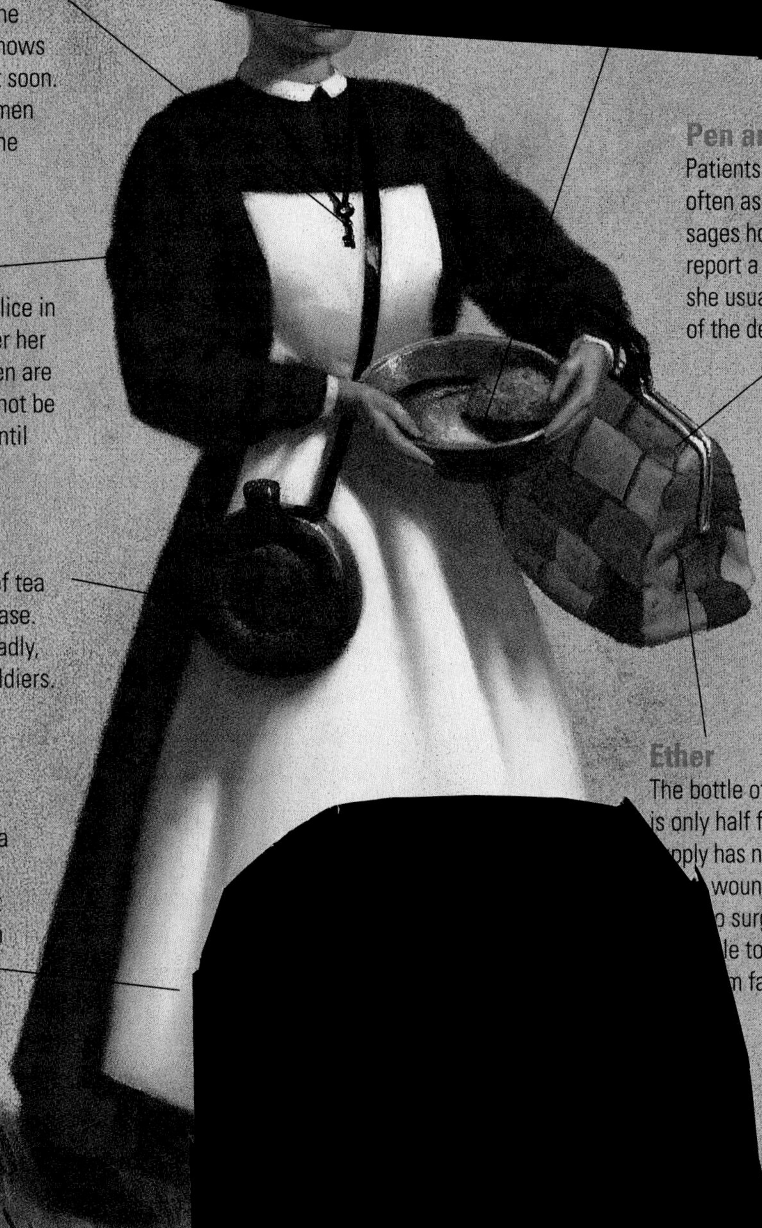

Key
A small key dangles from her neck.
It reminds her she must check the
lemons in the storeroom. She knows
she won't get another shipment soon.
Without them, she'll see more men
with bleeding gums—a sign of the
disease scurvy.

Undershirt
Last night she found three lice in
the flannel undershirt under her
dress. If more wounded men are
brought in today, she may not be
able to wash her clothes until
tomorrow.

Flask
A sip from this container of beef tea
helps the soldiers fight off disease.
Diseases in the hospital are deadly,
and affect nurses as well as soldiers.

Dress
She wears a simple apron and a
dress, without her usual wide
hoop skirt. She can move about
more easily in this dress, which
meets hospital requirements.

Pen and Paper
Patients too weak to write
often ask her to send messages home. If she has to
report a death to a family
she usually encloses a lock
of the dead soldier's hair.

Ether
The bottle of ether in her bag
is only half full. The hospital's
supply has nearly run out.
wounded soldiers
surgery, she holds
to their noses to
fall asleep.

485

onfederacy. Few Northern-
rs saw their homes or facto-
es destroyed. In some
orthern cities, business was
etter than before the war.

People were hired by factories to make guns, boots,
and tents. Railroads needed
orkers. The war also helped
northern farmers, who sold their
crops to feed the Union armies.

Because demand for food and
goods was high, prices in the North
also rose. Dishonest business people used the sudden demand for
goods to cheat the government.
They sold the government cheaply
made goods at high prices. Some
army blankets fell apart and soles
came off shoes. ◼

*▲ No longer a part of the
Union, the Confederate
government issued its own
money. Notice the name
"Confederate States of
America" on the bills.*

*◼ What hardships did
Northerners face
because of the war?*

Midwestern women sent food to
General Grant's army in the South.
One reporter joked that "a line of
vegetables connected Chicago and
Vicksburg."

The North felt the economic
sting of war much less than the

Opposition to the War

On both sides, suffering turned
people against the war that seemed
endless. Many Confederates and
Unionists felt that men belonged
at home with their families. Some
soldiers who tried to leave the
army were shot.

Anti-war feelings were strong
in mountain areas of the South.
White farmers there had few if any
slaves, and most did not want to
die to keep slavery alive. Poor men
in the Confederacy also resented
the **draft,** which forced them to
join the army. By law, white men
aged 18 to 35 had to join for three
years. However, a rich man could
pay a poor man to serve for him.
Wealthy men paid as much as
$6,000 to escape from fighting.

In 1862, a Confederate law ex-
cused men from serving who
owned at least 20 slaves. This
made the poor whites even angrier.
Many soldiers, forced to serve,
called the war "a rich man's war
and a poor man's fight."

Draft laws were also unpopular
in the Union. Many poor workers

*➤ Some South-
erners were
against the Civil
War. At right,
they are shown
in a secret
meeting, dis-
cussing their
feelings.*

were angry that rich men could pay to avoid fighting. In some places, opposition to the draft resulted in riots. The worst riot was in New York City in July, 1863. A group of mostly Irish immigrants who faced the draft feared that freed African Americans would take their jobs. For four days, they attacked African Americans. In their anger, the rioters robbed homes and stores. They burned down a black orphanage. Some 1,000 people were killed or wounded in the riots, mostly African Americans.

The Peace Democrats were another Northern group against the war. They blamed President Lincoln for rising prices. They also blamed him for the slow progress toward victory. The Peace Democrats warned about the end of slavery. Like the New York City rioters, they said the North would be flooded with freed African Americans who would take over jobs. The Peace Democrats'

THE COPPERHEAD PARTY.—IN FAVOR OF *A VIGOROUS PROSECUTION OF PEACE!*

anti-war campaign won them seats in Congress in the 1862 election.

Lincoln's party, the Republicans, spoke out against these anti-war Democrats. They compared these Democrats to a poisonous snake, a copperhead, striking at the government. Because of this, Peace Democrats became known as Copperheads. Although many people disagreed with the war, Lincoln won re-election in 1864. ■

The cartoon shows a comic view of "Copperheads," as Republicans called the anti-war Democrats.

■ *Why did the Civil War draft anger poor whites?*

New Roles for Government

The Confederate government began to feel it needed to control more industries in order to get supplies. The Confederacy wanted all troops, supplies, and weapons under government control. When the army needed men, the draft was established. Some Southern factories came under government control. At the urging of the government, farmers moved away from growing cotton and tobacco. They began growing food products. But because the railroads were not used

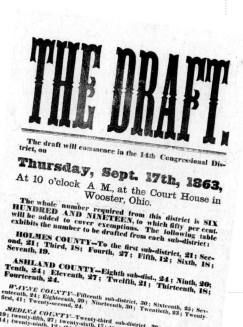

THE DRAFT.

The draft will commence in the 14th Congressional District, on
Thursday, Sept. 17th, 1863,
At 10 o'clock A. M., at the Court House in Wooster, Ohio.

The whole number required from this district is SIX HUNDRED AND NINETEEN, to which fifty per cent. will be added to cover exemptions. The following table exhibits the number to be drafted from each sub-district:

HOLMES COUNTY—To the first sub-district, 21; Second, 21; Third, 18; Fourth, 27; Fifth, 12; Sixth, 18; Seventh, 19.

ASHLAND COUNTY—Eighth sub-dist., 24; Ninth, 20; Tenth, 24; Eleventh, 27; Twelfth, 21; Thirteenth, 18; Fourteenth, 24.

WAYNE COUNTY—Fifteenth sub-district, 30; Sixteenth, 25; Seventeenth, 24; Eighteenth, 29; Nineteenth, 30; Twentieth, 23; Twenty-first, 41; Twenty-second, 24.

MEDINA COUNTY—Twenty-third sub-district, 39; twenty-fourth, 19; twenty-fifth, 27; twenty-sixth, 17; twenty-seventh, 14; twenty-ninth, 12; thirtieth, 15; thirty-first, 15.

LORAIN COUNTY—33d sub-district, 16; 33d...

The draft was one sign of the growing power of government in the North and in the South. Posters like this one called on men to sign up for the war draft.

▲ *The Union government controlled the settlement of the vast areas of the Great Plains. The government made these lands available under the Homestead Act.*

■ *How did the government begin using more power during the Civil War?*

until late in the war, the food was not getting to the troops.

In the Union, the powers of President Lincoln and Congress also grew. The government began making people pay taxes on the money they earned. Americans grew angry when Lincoln jailed without a trial Northerners who opposed the war.

Congress passed many new laws that helped the Union. Northern factories were paid to supply Union armies with clothes and guns.

By 1862, the government in Washington, D.C., was spending $2.5 million a day on the war.

Even with the war, Congress found time to pass the Homestead Act in 1862. The Homestead Act was a law that offered thousands of families free land in the West. After five years of farming, the land became theirs. The government also picked a route for the new coast-to-coast railroad. When it was built after the war, the railroad carried thousands of people west. ■

R E V I E W

1. **FOCUS** How did the Civil War affect the lives of the people who were not fighting?

2. **CONNECT** How did women aid the war effort?

3. **ECONOMICS** What caused the prices of food and other items to rise during the war?

4. **CRITICAL THINKING** Why did many Union and Confederate men find the draft laws unfair?

5. **WRITING ACTIVITY** Imagine you are against the Civil War. Write a newspaper article from the point of view of a Southern farmer describing your opposition.

Chapter 19

L E S S O N 3

The End of the War

I don't see how this charge can succeed," said Confederate General James Longstreet, "but General Lee has ordered it."

Longstreet spoke on the final day of the Battle of Gettysburg, Pennsylvania, in July 1863. Union soldiers held the hill at Cemetery Ridge. Longstreet ordered General George Pickett to take the hill.

"Forward!" rang the battle cry. The 15,000 Confederate soldiers began to march across the open field. With nothing to protect them, thousands were shot.

The Confederacy lost the bloody battle at Gettysburg. In fact, the battle proved to be a turning point in the war. The Confederate loss ended Lee's hopes of invading the Union.

Final Battles

Four months later, Lincoln went to Gettysburg. He gave a short speech and said part of the battlefield would be a cemetery for those who had died. He spoke about equality and democracy, reminding Americans of the Declaration of Independence.

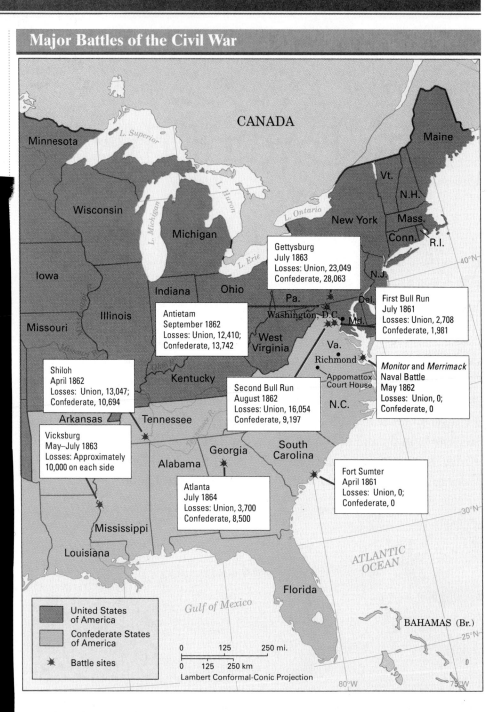

Gettysburg
July 1863
Losses: Union, 23,049
Confederate, 28,063

First Bull Run
July 1861
Losses: Union, 2,708
Confederate, 1,981

Antietam
September 1862
Losses: Union, 12,410;
Confederate, 13,742

Monitor and *Merrimack*
Naval Battle
May 1862
Losses: Union, 0;
Confederate, 0

Shiloh
April 1862
Losses: Union, 13,047;
Confederate, 10,694

Second Bull Run
August 1862
Losses: Union, 16,054
Confederate, 9,197

Vicksburg
May–July 1863
Losses: Approximately
10,000 on each side

Fort Sumter
April 1861
Losses: Union, 0;
Confederate, 0

Atlanta
July 1864
Losses: Union, 3,700
Confederate, 8,500

CANADA

ATLANTIC OCEAN

Gulf of Mexico

BAHAMAS (Br.)

United States of America

Confederate States of America

* Battle sites

0   125   250 mi.
0   125   250 km
Lambert Conformal-Conic Projection

Lincoln's Gettysburg Address began: "Four score and seven years ago our fathers brought forth on this continent, a new nation, conceived in Liberty, and dedicated to the proposition [idea] that all men are created equal."

Lincoln called the struggle for racial equality "unfinished work." It had begun with the American Revolution. Now Americans had to work for a "new birth of freedom" by ending slavery. If they did not, then the soldiers buried at Gettysburg died for nothing.

Another Union victory in July 1863 ended the war in the West. Union troops under General Ulysses Grant took Vicksburg, Mississippi, after more than a month of fighting. Inside the city Southerners survived by eating

The Civil War left large parts of the South in ruins. Rubble was all that was left of Richmond (above). Cemeteries (left) were created, and graves quickly dug, to bury the huge numbers of soldiers killed.

Americans finally had freedom. The war ended nearly 250 years of slavery. Unfortunately, many whites continued to treat African Americans unfairly. It would be many years before all African Americans would get full civil rights.

In the North, change also came after the Civil War. Industry grew between 1865 and the late 1800s. Companies produced more railroad tracks, steam engines, and farm equipment. Factories in Ohio, Illinois, and Pennsylvania began making large amounts of steel. Coal mining grew as coal became fuel for steam-run machines. ■

The country was no longer a group of separate states, each looking after its own interests. The United States was once again one country under one federal government. Though there was much healing to do, both Northern states and the former Confederate states would work together as one nation.

With the passing of the Thirteenth Amendment in 1865, African

What did the passing of the 13th Amendment mean to African Americans?

R E V I E W

1. **FOCUS** How did the final battles of the Civil War affect the United States?
2. **CONNECT** How were Sherman's goals different from the goals of generals at Bull Run or Antietam?
3. **HISTORY** Why was Gettysburg a turning point ?
4. **CRITICAL THINKING** How do you think the Civil War affected the wealth of the former Confederate states?
5. **ACTIVITY** Role play a conversation between a Union and a Confederate soldier. Have each one tell how he feels about the surrender at Appomattox.

Civil War and Reconstruction

L E S S O N   4

Reconstruction

THINKING FOCUS

What were the successes and failures of the era of Reconstruction?

Key Terms

- Reconstruction
- segregation

➤ *After the Civil War, free African American families began to build new lives for themselves.*

Katie Rowe chopped cotton hour after hour in the blazing summer sun. She and many other enslaved African Americans worked the fields of an Arkansas plantation.

One afternoon as they were working, a horn sounded. Someone told them to go up to the owner's house.

There at the house sat a white man wearing a broad black hat. As she told a writer years later, he spoke kindly to them. He told them they were free, just as he was. They were their own bosses now. Then he wished them good luck, climbed on his horse, and rode away. On that fourth day of June in 1865, Katie felt she first began to live.

New Lives

Katie, like millions of African Americans, won her freedom with the South's defeat. Freedom was guaranteed in 1865 by the Thirteenth Amendment. But the South lay in ruins, and African Americans were often unsure of where to go. Katie and many others stayed on plantations. There they worked for little pay.

Many African Americans thought they would get land for farms. Republican senator Charles Sumner had said, "The great plantations . . . must be broken up and the freedmen must have the pieces." Unfortunately, the freed slaves did not get land.

Instead, they often became sharecroppers. White landowners gave each sharecropper a cabin, land, tools, seeds, and sometimes a mule to pull the plow. In return, sharecroppers planted crops and paid the landowner part of the harvest. The owner's share was usually half the crop.

Sharecroppers earned little for their hard work because owners took advantage of them. While crops were growing, they often had to borrow money from the owner

to buy food and clothing. Repayment took their profit. Many felt enslaved all over again. ■

◄ *After emancipation, African Americans made important changes in their lives. They built small houses. They started their own communities and churches, like the first Negro Baptist Church in Savannah, Georgia (left).*

■ *What was life like for many freed African Americans in the years after the Civil War?*

Educating a New Society

Before the war, enslaved African Americans did not go to school. In most Southern states they were forbidden by law to read or write. In March 1865, Congress set up the Freedmen's Bureau, which helped African Americans get the schooling they wanted.

African Americans joined in raising money to pay teachers and buy land for black schools. African American families gave teachers rooms and meals in their homes.

Most new schools had few supplies. Classes met in churches, basements, and homes. Students used old newspapers or dictionaries to learn to read. Often, after school, children went home and taught their parents the alphabet.

African Americans also started colleges. The American Missionary Association started colleges in the South. The Freedmen's Bureau set up Howard University, Fisk University, and other schools. ■

■ *How were African Americans in the South able to get an education after winning their freedom?*

◄ *After the war, many African Americans were educated in Freedmen's Bureau schools.*

Conflict over Reuniting

Congress and the President could not agree on how to rebuild the South and bring it back into the Union. This era of rebuilding is called **Reconstruction.**

Lincoln had hoped that Reconstruction would heal the nation's wounds. He did not want to punish the South. With Lincoln's death in 1865, Vice President Andrew Johnson took over as President. Johnson, a Southerner, had his own plan for Reconstruction. His plan offered few rights and no protection for freed slaves. Later, he wanted to put former Confederate leaders back in power.

Under Johnson, some former Confederate leaders ran new state governments in the South. These leaders refused to share power with the freed slaves. They passed laws that took newly gained rights away from the freed slaves. Land-owners, for example, were allowed to whip black workers. Some Southern whites used violence and murder to frighten blacks.

Republicans in Congress opposed Johnson's plan. They wanted full rights for freed slaves. Congress began a battle with the President. Congress refused to admit the new Southern lawmakers. In 1866, Congress passed a civil rights act to assure the rights of freed slaves. The act passed despite the President's veto. That same year, Congress passed the Fourteenth Amendment. This amendment made African Americans United States citizens. It also said that former Southern leaders could not serve in government. To re-enter the Union, a Southern state had to approve the Fourteenth Amendment.

The Republicans in Congress took over power from the new state

➤ *Congress hoped to win more rights of citizenship for African Americans by passing the Thirteenth, Fourteenth, and Fifteenth Amendments. For example, the Fourteenth Amendment defined "citizens" as anyone born or naturalized in the United States. This new definition included African Americans.*

Reconstruction Amendments

13th	Passed by Congress in 1865 Abolished slavery in the United States.
14th	Passed by Congress in 1868 1. Defined United States citizenship. 2. Prohibited interference with a citizen's right to vote.
15th	Passed by Congress in 1870 Prohibited the denial of the right to vote because of race or previous enslavement.

YES   N

The End of Reconstruction

After 1869, Reconstruction began to fade. From 1869 to 1877, Ulysses S. Grant was President. In the South, white Democrats began taking over state governments again. U.S. troops failed to end the violence against African Americans. The troops began to leave.

The 1876 presidential election, in which Democrat Samuel Tilden opposed Republican Rutherford B. Hayes, helped end Reconstruction. Although Tilden won the most votes, the parties disagreed on vote counts in several Southern states. Congress settled the problem. The Southern Democrats accepted Hayes as President. In return, Northern Republicans promised to remove the remaining troops.

As Reconstruction ended, African Americans' hopes for equality faded. Southern governments forced African American children to go to all-black schools. **Segregation,** or separation of the races, became the rule in the South. Reconstruction had failed to win freedom and equality for African Americans. ■

◄ *The nation elected Rutherford B. Hayes President in 1876. The map shows that Hayes won in only three Southern states, however.*

■ *How did Reconstruction end?*

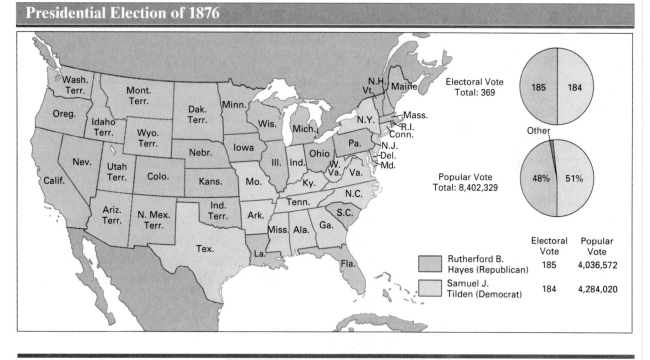

Presidential Election of 1876

Electoral Vote Total: 369
185 | 184

Popular Vote Total: 8,402,329
Other
48% | 51%

	Electoral Vote	Popular Vote
Rutherford B. Hayes (Republican)	185	4,036,572
Samuel J. Tilden (Democrat)	184	4,284,020

R E V I E W

1. **FOCUS** What were the successes and failures of the era of Reconstruction?

2. **CONNECT** How did the lives of African Americans in the South during Reconstruction compare to their lives before the war?

3. **ECONOMICS** What was sharecropping and how did it affect the lives of the former slaves?

4. **CRITICAL THINKING** Why do you think white Southerners wanted to keep blacks from voting? In what ways did some do so?

5. **WRITING ACTIVITY** Imagine you are a former enslaved African American in 1866. Write a letter to your granddaughter describing your hopes for Reconstruction.

Chapter Review

Reviewing Key Terms

assassinate (p. 492)   Gettysburg Address (p. 489)
blockade (p. 478)   inflation (p. 483)
draft (p. 486)   Reconstruction (p. 496)
emancipation (p. 482)   segregation (p. 499)

A. On your own paper, copy the sentences below. Use a key term to fill in the blank in each sentence.

1. _____ was the period of rebuilding the South after the Civil War lasting until 1876.
2. Men aged 18 to 35 had to sign up for the _____ during the Civil War.
3. _____ meant freedom for enslaved African Americans.

B. Some of the following statements are true. The rest are false. Write *True* or *False* for each statement. Then rewrite the false statements to make them true.

1. Segregation brought African Americans and whites together.
2. Many people believed that more than one person was involved in the assassination of President Lincoln.
3. In a period of inflation, prices of items go down.
4. The Union Navy's blockade of Southern ports stopped the Confederacy from exporting cotton.

Exploring Concepts

A. Complete the summary paragraph below. Use information from the chapter.
The Civil War was a bloody war between the Union and the _____. It lasted ____ years, from _____ to 1865. The state in which the most battles were fought was _____. The Battle of _____ , fought in the North, was a turning point in the war. With little hope left for a Confederate victory General Robert E. Lee surrendered to General Ulysses S. _____ at _____ . The period known as _____ was a time when the country tried to rebuild the South. It would also try to bring the former Confederate states back into the _____ .

B. Answer each question with information from the chapter.

1. How did the anaconda plan hope to squeeze the life out of the Confederacy?

2. Why did Lincoln wait until the war started to end slavery?
3. Why didn't the Union feel the sting of war as the Confederacy did?
4. Why were some groups against the draft laws during the Civil War?
5. What message did Lincoln want the Gettysburg Address to give Americans during the Civil War?
6. How did Sherman try to break the spirit of the Confederacy?
7. Why did Congress decide to impeach President Johnson?
8. In what ways did African Americans work to make their lives better after the Civil War?
9. Who were the people called carpetbaggers and scalawags?
10. Why did many sharecroppers feel enslaved again?

Reviewing Skills

1. Look at the map on page 490 showing Civil War battles. Could this map help you drive from New York to Tennessee? Explain.
2. Imagine that you are a member of the 1866 Congress trying to get other members to vote for the Fourteenth Amendment. Discuss how you would persuade fellow members of Congress to support the right of African Americans, and all other people too, to become citizens.

Using Critical Thinking

1. President Johnson and Congress did not agree on a plan for Reconstruction. Describe how the two sides could have compromised on this issue. Use a Venn diagram like the one on the right to help you. Write each side's plan in the correct circle. Write the points on which they agreed in the space where the circles meet. Then use the diagram to help you reach a compromise.
2. During the Civil War, women had to take over many jobs they had not done before. These included running plantations, working in factories, and giving medical care. Think of an example of a person today who might have to act in an emergency situation that is different from their usual task.
3. Read the final version of Lincoln's Gettysburg Address on page 604 of the Minipedia. What do you think Lincoln meant when he talked of government "of the people, by the people, and for the people"?

President Johnson's Plan
1. No protection for freed slaves.
2. ...

Agree on:

Congress's Plan
1. Protection for freed slaves.
2. ...

Preparing for Citize...

1. **WRITING ACTIVITY** The Civil War ... families left behind. Write a ... view with a Southern woma... run the family's plantation. ...
2. **COLLECTING INFORMATION** Find m... about President Andrew Joh... his personal views on slavery... Do you think his views made ... candidate for President?
3. **ARTS ACTIVITY** Create a recruiting ... nurses for either the North or t...

...nd words to convince people ...hospitals.

...ARNING When the Confederate ...d from the Union, they had to ...wn laws. Form small groups, ...up representing a seceded ...rch your state at the time of the ...rite new laws that would serve ...nterests—on crops, education, ...sues. Present your demands at ...ting of Confederate States."

501

Chapter 20
Life in a Changing America

A new America emerged after the Civil War. Railroads brought many settlers to the Great Plains. Tragically, these new settlers helped destroy the buffalo herds and the Plains Indians' way of life. Meanwhile, more and more people moved from farms and foreign countries to large cities where new factories provided plenty of jobs. As the United States entered the modern age, people worked to build better lives.

Red Cloud (above), leader of the Oglala Sioux, fought the U.S. Army to try to save hunting grounds for his people.

1860

1860

80

1890

1890 Indian wars end with the Battle of Wounded Knee.

1900 The United States now has four transcontinental railroad lines. This early map of American railroads (above) was made in 1869.

1900	1910	1920	1930

1896 Charles and J. Frank Duryea build 13 gas-powered automobiles, starting the U.S. auto industry.

1880-1920 Electric trolleys replace horse-drawn streetcars in many American cities. A model of one of these new trolleys is shown above.

1914

1860 1865 1890 1900 1910 1920 1930

LESSON 1

Changes on the Great Plains

THINKING FOCUS

How did life on the Great Plains change after the Civil War?

Key Terms

- Great Plains
- exodus

Red Cloud looked out the window of the railroad car speeding past the villages and farms of white settlers. For two years—from 1865 to 1867—the great chief of the Oglala Sioux had fought successfully to keep white men off his land. Now in 1870 the treaty had been broken, and he was traveling to Washington, D.C., to meet with the "Great Father" of the white man, President Ulysses S. Grant.

In Washington, Red Cloud was given a tour of the capital. He dined at the White House. Then Red Cloud and 15 other Oglala Sioux got down to business. At a meeting with U.S. officials, the chief spoke strongly, asking for justice for his people. Red Cloud said:

> *The white children have surrounded me and left me nothing but an island. When we first had this land we were strong. Now we are melting like snow on the hillside, while you are growing like spring grass.*

Still, Red Cloud's efforts were not enough. Most white people continued to believe that American Indians would have to change their way of life. Railroads now crossed their hunting grounds. New settlers were carving the Great Plains into ranches, farms, and towns.

Plains Indian Life

In the 1600s and 1700s, the number of American Indians living on the Great Plains increased. The **Great Plains** stretch from the Missouri River in the east, westward to the Rocky Mountains. The Plains continue into Canada in the north. Horses, brought by the Spanish in the 1600s, introduced great changes to the Plains Indians' way of life. Horses made it easier for them to follow the buffalo herds.

As more groups of American Indians moved to the Plains, fighting often broke out between them. In the 1800s, fighting also broke

1890, the buffalo herds had disappeared from the Great Plains. Settlers filled the open range with ranches and homesteads.

out between Plains Indians and white hunters. These hunters nearly wiped out the buffalo. The result was to destroy the Indian way of life because they needed the meat, hide, and bones of the buffalo to live. ■

■ *How did white hunters destroy the way of life of the Plains Indians?*

The Life of Settlers

After the Civil War, thousands of whites began to move onto the Great Plains. Many were Union soldiers. The government sent them west to work at the U.S. Army forts across the plains. Former soldiers and their families came west looking for new jobs and land.

Whites and African Americans from the South also went west after the war. The war had destroyed the economy of the South. Enslaved people were no longer forced to work Southern fields. However, violence against African Americans by the Ku Klux Klan and other anti-black groups threatened their lives. In 1879, thousands of poor black farmers took their property and moved west. It was a mass leaving, or **exodus,** by these African American farmers, who became known as "Exodusters."

Life on the plains was hard. Winters brought icy winds and snow. Inside, families huddled around fires, trying to keep warm. The region was a dry land with tall grasses. Pioneer houses had dirt floors and sod walls. Summer brought swarms of insects that destroyed crops.

◄ *African Americans went west to escape discrimination in the South. Nat Love, shown here, was a famous cowboy who drove cattle across the prairies for 20 years.*

505

Harvey Dunn's painting, Buffalo Bones Plowed Under, *shows a settler on the vast Great Plains.*

■ *Why did settlers on the Great Plains live hard lives?*

Before the Battle of the Little Big Horn, Sitting Bull warned the Sioux that taking the guns and horses of U.S. soldiers would prove a curse to the Sioux nation.

Farm families had to work hard—building fences, plowing fields, caring for their animals, and trying to stay warm and well fed.

Some new arrivals to the plains used new technology to work their farms. Windmills pumped water up from deep in the earth. Barbed wire fenced in animals. Sturdy plows dug into the hard plains soil.

Some Southern whites became cattle ranchers on the Great Plains.

During the Civil War, ranchers in south Texas had been unable to ship their cattle to the South and the Caribbean. Texas herds grew very large. After the war, ranchers hired cowboys to drive the cattle to railroads. Trains carried the cattle to Chicago's giant stockyards. There, the cattle were slaughtered for meat and hides. By the 1880s, refrigerated railroad cars carried meat from Chicago to eastern cities.

Many settlers on the Great Plains came from Europe. The railroads offered special fares for trainloads of immigrants. Farmers from Germany and Norway settled in South Dakota. A Czechoslovakian farming community grew up in Nebraska.

Immigrants from Ukraine were the first to grow winter wheat on the Great Plains. Winter wheat allowed farmers to grow two crops each year. By 1900, people around the world depended on wheat and other grains from the Great Plains. ■

Wars and Treaties

As settlers moved onto Indian lands, many Plains Indians were forced to fight to protect their homelands. To end the fighting, the U.S government signed treaties with some Indian nations. The government promised them land where they could hunt and roam freely. White settlers were to stay away from the land reserved for Indians. Unfortunately, these promises were often broken, causing bloody battles to break out.

One of the most violent clashes took place in June 1876, along the Little Big Horn River in Montana. The U.S. government wanted land that the Sioux held sacred. The Sioux and their allies fought to keep the land, led by Crazy Horse of the Oglala Sioux and Sitting Bull of the Hunkpapas. The Indians defeated U.S. Army forces led by General George Custer. Custer and all his men were killed. Less than a year later, soldiers

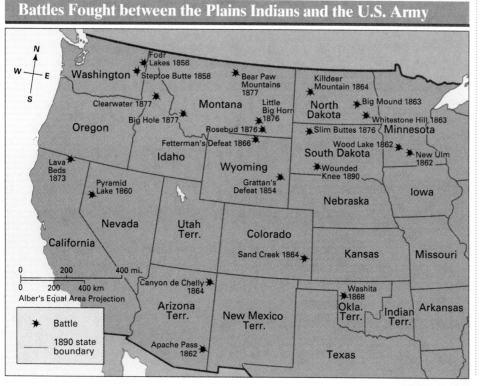

Battles Fought between the Plains Indians and the U.S. Army

Washington
Four Lakes 1858
Steptoe Butte 1858
Clearwater 1877
Oregon
Big Hole 1877
Idaho
Lava Beds 1873
Pyramid Lake 1860
Nevada
California
California
Montana
Bear Paw Mountains 1877
Little Big Horn 1876
Rosebud 1876
Fetterman's Defeat 1866
Wyoming
Grattan's Defeat 1854
Utah Terr.
Killdeer Mountain 1864
North Dakota
Big Mound 1863
Whitestone Hill 1863
Slim Buttes 1876
Minnesota
Wood Lake 1862
South Dakota
New Ulm 1862
Wounded Knee 1890
Iowa
Nebraska
Colorado
Sand Creek 1864
Kansas
Missouri

0   200   400 mi.
0   200   400 km
Alber's Equal Area Projection

★ Battle
— 1890 state boundary

Canyon de Chelly 1864
Arizona Terr.
New Mexico Terr.
Apache Pass 1862
Washita 1868
Okla. Terr.
Indian Terr.
Arkansas
Texas

◄ This map shows many of the important battles the Plains Indians fought against the U.S. Army. Next to buffalo hunting, warfare became the main activity of the Plains Indians. Indian warriors showed great bravery in battle.

▼ At age 23, George Armstrong Custer (below) became a temporary general in the Union army. He was later killed at Little Big Horn. That battle became known as "Custer's Last Stand."

defeated Crazy Horse's warriors. In 1881, Sitting Bull surrendered.

The last major battle took place at Wounded Knee, South Dakota. In December, 1890, U.S. soldiers had taken a group of Sioux to an army camp there to disarm them. These Sioux were followers of the Ghost Dance religion. This religion promised the return of the buffalo and the disappearance of white settlements. A month earlier, the U.S. government had banned the Ghost Dance. Whites feared the dance might lead to Indian uprisings.

When soldiers tried to take guns away from the Sioux, the Sioux resisted. They thought they would be protected by their special Ghost shirts. During the struggle to take a gun away from one Sioux, the gun went off. The soldiers began to fire back. They ended up slaughtering hundreds of Sioux men, women, and children. ■

■ What caused the battles at Little Big Horn and Wounded Knee?

REVIEW

1. **FOCUS** How did life on the Great Plains change after the Civil War?

2. **CONNECT** Compare Red Cloud, the chief of the Oglala Sioux, with the Shawnee chief Tecumseh, discussed in Chapter 14.

3. **HISTORY** Where did the new settlers on the Great Plains come from?

4. **CRITICAL THINKING** How did the disappearance of the buffalo affect the Plains Indians?

5. **WRITING ACTIVITY** Write a paragraph describing how you imagine the Great Plains looked before the Civil War. In a second paragraph, describe what you think the Great Plains looked like in the late 1800s after many white settlers had arrived.

Life in a Changing America

An Orphan for Nebraska

Charlene Joy Talbot

You have learned that the cities grew in the late 1800s because of immigration and movement of people from farms. The problem of homeless children grew as well, and a Children's Aid Society was formed to take orphans from the cities and settle them in the towns and farms of the western United States. The Society found homes or work for them. In this story, Kevin, an Irish orphan who worked as a newspaper boy and lived on the streets of New York City, finds a new life in Nebraska in the 1860s.

Millions of immigrants came to America with their dreams of a better life. Here is a story about one 11-year-old immigrant boy.

buffalo robe a blanket made of buffalo skins

The next thing Kevin knew, Elizabeth was screeching, "Be we there, Mister? Is this Nebraska?"

He threw back the buffalo robe to see sun streaming through the depot window. Elizabeth, George and Maggie were crowding out the door. He heard them running on the platform.

Kevin tied his shoes, fumbling in his haste. Then he, too, was flying out the door.

The countryside was so flat that the station platform felt like a hilltop. Shining steel rails cut across the prairie in both directions. Away over some fields Kevin saw a scattering of one- and two-story buildings. Everywhere else snowy wastelands spread to the horizon, except for one line of bare trees.

George was looking bewildered. "Where's Cottonwood City?"

Kevin, used to the villages of Ireland, said, "That's it."

Hiram came running at them.

"That's not a city! There's more of us than there is houses!" Which wasn't really true.

"Come on!" Kevin set off at top speed toward some clumps of tall weedstalks surrounding snow-covered piles of lumber. The three boys ran past Maggie and Elizabeth, who were galloping round and round a shock of corn in the nearest field. Maggie stopped suddenly. She picked up an ear that had fallen to the ground. Yellow corn peeked from beneath the pale, dried husk.

"Look at this!" She ran shrieking to Mr. Carter.

Elizabeth found the winter remains of a patch of prairie roses.

shock a bundle of cornstalks standing upright

"Berries!" she screeched. The red-orange rose hips did indeed look like fruit. She bit one. Her face scrunched, and she spat.

"Breakfast!" Mr. Carter called from the platform. "Whoever wants breakfast, come along!" Hannah, Mr. Carter and Peter set out along the road to town. The others straggled after, running from side to side, making tracks in the unmarked snow.

The hotel, which was the largest building in town, was beginning to stir when the group trailed across the porch. A man opened the door, exclaiming, "Land alive, these must be the orphans! Molly!" he called over his shoulder. "Breakfast customers!" He directed them to a hallway where they hung their coats. A bench held two big washpans and a bucket of water. A big girl came from the kitchen with a steaming kettle and poured hot water into the basins. Beside the bench hung a long strip of toweling. A mirror was nailed beside it. Hands and faces were washed; Hannah combed the girls' hair and Peter's, and the comb was passed among the rest of the boys. From the neck up, they looked respectable, Kevin thought. The boys had barber's haircuts before leaving New York. Their clothes, however, were a different story—wrinkled, dirty and even torn, having been lived in for so many days and nights.

They sat on either side of a long, bare table. Pitchers of milk and coffee came from the kitchen, followed by platters of buckwheat cakes and sausage, with sorghum syrup to pour over. There was a pitcher of cream for the coffee and molded hills of butter to spread on the pancakes. After all that, Molly brought out dried apple pies.

Some of the town's bachelors boarded at the hotel. One by one men drifted in, sat at the long table and stared at the children while they cut through stacks of pancakes. They were bearded and booted. Kevin wished his new shoes had been boots.

When the youngsters had eaten all they could hold, Mr. Carter inquired the way to the church, and they filed into the main street, which was wide and rutted and ran east to west like the railroad track. Whichever way Kevin looked, he could see open prairie beyond the houses.

"How can they call this a city?" he whispered to Mr. Carter.

"They're hoping lots of people will move here and make it one."

Despite the cold and the early hour, saddle horses were tied to the hitching rails along the street. Men stood gossiping in twos and threes on the board sidewalks, and families drove past in wagons.

Everyone stared. Mr. Carter led the children into the church. Everywhere they heard whispering: "There's the orphans!" "—little, ain't he? They must not have any food in New York City."

---

rose hips part of a rose bush

sorghum syrup a sweet, sticky syrup

bachelor unmarried man

hitching rails long poles for tying animals

The preacher, wearing a black suit, welcomed them. He shook hands with Mr. Carter and sent them all to the empty second row. The first row was full of small, pale-haired children who eyed them over the back of the pew. One pointed at Kevin's hair and they all giggled.

Kevin's breakfast was now a lump in his stomach as big as a washtub. Maggie had thrown hers up. Peter's bruises still showed, and Dolly looked ready to cry.

Could anybody possibly want any of us, Kevin wondered. James and Hiram were acting too smart for their britches, as if they didn't care whether anyone wanted them or not.

The children had to sit through Sunday school and then church. It passed in a blur. Everyone but Peter knew they were being inspected. The actual choosing would be that afternoon at the courthouse, which was to be opened even though it was Sunday.

After church Mr. Carter took his group back to the hotel. The owner had offered them a free meal, but no one did justice to it, partly due to the **mammoth** breakfast, but mostly to the **ordeal** ahead. The dining room seemed full of silent, staring faces. Used to loud city voices, the children found these quiet people frightening. No one had any desire to explore. They waited **docilely** for what would happen.

The courthouse was one big room. It stood in the corner of an empty square. "The building's only temporary," the preacher apologized as they trailed toward it. "We plan to build a fine stone one. Everything's booming; taxpayers, churchgoers moving in so fast a person can't keep count."

"How are the schools?" Mr. Carter asked.

The preacher beamed. "We have a fine one here in town— fifteen pupils. In the country . . . well, each **township** does the best it can. Have to educate the young, you know. They're the most important crop the prairie produces, after all." He smiled.

The youngsters stared back amazed. George's mouth actually dropped open, and Hiram nudged James. Never had any of them, except Kevin, been considered anything but a nuisance, an extra mouth to feed.

A crowd was standing about the door, so Kevin was not surprised to see that inside the room was full and men were lining the wall. If *this* many people wanted children . . . perhaps they did have a chance.

The orphans were led to two railed-off benches at the front of the room. The preacher stepped to the platform.

"Ladies and gentlemen," he began. "We are happy to see so many faces this crisp and sunny afternoon." And he began to tell them how wonderful their community was. Kevin heard **guffaws** from the back row at some of the more **extravagant** praise. When

mammoth huge
ordeal difficult situation

docilely quietly

township an area 36 miles square

guffaws hearty laughs
extravagant grand

510

he said that southern Nebraska was on the same world parallel as Italy, some wag said, "You sure you don't mean Switzerland, mister?" People chuckled, because everyone knew that Italy was warm and sunny and Switzerland was full of ice and snow. But in general his listeners seemed to enjoy being told about their wonderful choice of a home. He was loudly clapped, after which he introduced Mr. Carter.

Mr. Carter told his audience that thousands of homeless children roamed the streets of New York City. He explained that the Children's Aid Society worked to move them into the country where they could grow into useful men and women instead of beggars and criminals. "These are not young criminals or paupers," he said. "They are simply homeless, unfortunate boys and girls. They are the best material, folks, that a farmer or a master could desire to make into good workers on the farm or in the house."

"How about the little 'uns, mister?" the same voice called. "What's they good for?"

There was some good-natured laughter, but Dolly threw her head into Hannah's lap and began to cry.

Mr. Carter glanced toward her and then said with dignity, "They are good for loving. As our Saviour said, 'Even as you do it unto the least of these, you do it unto me.' I know there are warmhearted people here who will want to do just that."

He sat down beside the children on the bench, and the preacher stood up.

"Let us pray. . . ."

After the prayer he announced: "Mr. Carter and I will be here for the rest of the afternoon. Those who wish to interview a child or apply for one will please come forward."

Immediately a big, black-bearded man made his way down the aisle. He was followed by a nicely dressed woman with happy black eyes.

"This is Mr. Thayer, our blacksmith, and this is his wife." The preacher introduced them to Mr. Carter. "He also runs the livery stable."

The boys caught their breath at that. To be taking care of horses was what they all wanted.

"So you folks want a boy?" the preacher said.

Mr. Thayer's laugh rang through the room like a hammer on an anvil. He looked down at his wife and then back toward the bench where he'd been sitting. Following his glance Kevin saw a row of young men, as like to their father as a family of blackbirds.

"Ain't five boys enough? What we want is that black-haired gal." And Mrs. Thayer stepped to the railing and looked straight at Hannah. "Would you like to come to us, my dear? It's all menfolk but me, but you could have your own room."

parallel latitude
wag a smart aleck

'uns ones

blacksmith maker of iron tools and horse-shoes
livery stable boarding stable for horses

anvil an iron block on which metal is shaped

And so Hannah was the first one chosen. Hiram, George and James were speechless with envy. Except for Dolly's tears, the farewells were cheerful. Her new family bundled her away.

After that some farmers came forward. The preacher vouched for the standing of each one in the community, and the men described their farms, their horses and other livestock. Each boy was to get his schooling, his board and room, and one hundred dollars if he stayed until he was twenty-one. In that way the futures of James, Hiram, and even George were settled. The boys thanked Mr. Carter, promised to write to the society, and went away to their new lives without a backward glance.

"I have one more boy here old enough to do farm work," Mr. Carter told the gathering. But the remaining farmers shook their heads. "That lad!" one said. "There ain't enough of him to hold down a plow." "Look at that white skin," another scoffed. "One day in the sun would sizzle him like a fried tomato."

Elizabeth was picked next.

"My wife wants a girl old enough to help with the children," announced the next man. Mr. Carter suggested Elizabeth. "Kind of small for eight, ain't she?" the man said. "But if that's the oldest one left, she'll have to do. My young'uns is two and three."

"Mr. Phelps is our general storekeeper," the preacher explained. "He and his family live over the store."

Kevin was watching a young couple. The man kept looking toward Dolly or Peter. Then he would confer with his wife again. He seemed to be urging her. She was quietly crying.

The courtroom was clearing out. A bank of snowclouds had come up in the west, people reported. Kevin heard teams brought up outside, and men came stomping in to collect their families. The people who remained, sitting or standing about, were apparently townsfolk, making the most of the entertainment. Who took the children and why would be something to talk about for months.

The sad couple, as Kevin thought of them, came up and asked for Peter. "Their only child died last fall of diphtheria," the preacher said after they left.

Kevin was beginning to wonder if he and Dolly and Maggie would have to sleep at the railroad station again when there was a stir at the door. A snow-powdered figure burst through the crowd and came striding towards the platform. Kevin's heart leaped. Here was a purposeful man, just the kind he, Kevin, would like to work for. The man was small, dark and energetic, his coat was belted closely, his cap had ear flaps, and his legs were encased in leggings.

"I've got orders for two girls," he shouted when he was halfway down the aisle. "I'm a rancher up on Deer Creek. My wife wants one, and Mrs. Higgins wants the other. I'm not too

---

vouched   guaranteed

scoffed   made fun of

team   horses harnessed together

diphtheria   serious disease of the throat

leggings   leather pants

late, am I?" He looked towards the youngsters. "Those two will do fine. Snow's been following me all the way in. If I'm gonna get back, I've got to take 'em and skedaddle."

Mr. Carter looked at the preacher.

"Mr. Jacques," the preacher said quickly.

Mr. Jacques bounded to the railing. "Here's a pair of pretties!" he exclaimed. "My wife and Mrs. Higgins are just a-setting up there on Deer Creek waiting for you."

The little girls looked at him round-eyed.

Everything was quickly arranged. Mr. Carter helped bundle the girls into Mr. Jacques's sleigh, and they dashed away with a jingle of sleighbells.

Kevin shrank back on the bench and wished he could disappear. What would Mr. Carter do with him?

Mr. Carter came back into the room and made his way around the railing. He sat beside Kevin and patted his hand. Kevin caught his lower lip between his teeth. He *would* not cry. He was *not* a criminal, set off from these strangers by a railing.

"I always save my best till last," Mr. Carter said with a smile.

Another stir at the door made them both look up. The man who came in was slim and black-bearded and walked with a limp. Like the other young men, he was bundled into a worn blue army overcoat. An alertness in his manner reminded Kevin of the men who worked on Newspaper Row. He was not surprised when the preacher introduced the newcomer as "the editor of the *Cottonwood Clarion,* our lively newspaper."

The man shook hands with Mr. Carter. "Euclid Smith's my name. I expected to get back to town last night, but my horse threw a shoe. I was over at Grand Island," he explained, "picking up a load of newsprint. The editor there bought more than he could pay for." He glanced at Kevin. "Are they all gone but this one?"

The preacher nodded. "We found fine homes for all the rest," he bragged. "Not one of these children will ever regret coming to our community."

"I'm sure they won't," Mr. Carter agreed.

"I'd like the names of the families who took them," Euclid Smith said, "for next week's paper." The preacher showed him the list.

"Mr. Smith," the preacher said while the editor was copying the list, "weren't you looking for a printer's devil a while back?"

The editor glanced at Kevin. "I need an older lad, one who's had more schooling."

"This boy's eleven and reads very well," Mr. Carter said quickly. "Come here, Kevin. He's small for his age, that's all. The farmers say he'd burn to a crisp in the fields." Mr. Carter put his arm across Kevin's shoulders.

skedaddle to hurry

sleigh horse-drawn carriage with runners instead of wheels for use on snow

printer's devil errand boy in a print shop

Euclid Smith straightened from his task of copying and looked Kevin up and down. Kevin stared back, liking what he saw. He hoped suddenly, desperately, that the newspaperman would like *him*.

"I don't have time to look after a child," the editor protested. "Don't even have time to look after myself."

"He won't need looking after," Mr. Carter said. "This boy's bright and quick. It's my guess you can teach him just about anything."

Euclid Smith fingered his beard. Then he asked a surprising question. "Can you cook?"

"Some, sir." Kevin's mother had taught him to peel potatoes and make tea.

"Mr. Smith's a bachelor," the preacher explained.

"What can you read?" Euclid Smith asked.

"Newspapers, sir. . . . books."

"How about handwriting? Here—read this." He put the half-copied list into Kevin's hands.

Kevin read aloud: "Hannah Moore, ten, to Mr. and Mrs. Lije Thayer; James Albert, thirteen, to Mr. Harold Connor; Hiram Hostetter, twelve, to Mr. John Swenson—"

"All right, that's enough." He fingered his beard again. "I don't know. Think you'd like printshop work?"

Kevin was nearly speechless with yearning. His 'yes' came out in a whisper from his dry throat.

Euclid Smith looked at the other two men as though he'd been backed into a corner. "I only came to get the story. I'm not sure—I hardly make ends meet as it is."

One of the onlookers lounged up. "Go on, take him, Yuke—What are you waiting for?"

"By George, Jake, I'm waiting for you to pay for your subscription!"

The man called Jake dug in his pocket, produced two quarters, and handed them over. "There you are—four bits." He winked at Kevin.

"All right, by gum, I'll take him," Euclid Smith told Mr. Carter. "I hope you like beans and cornmeal, boy."

Kevin nodded. His throat was too full to speak. He had never thought of such a thing as working in a newspaper office. Mr. Carter was right: the best offer *had* come last.

While Euclid Smith finished copying the list, Kevin said goodbye to Mr. Carter and promised to write.

"Ready to go?" Euclid Smith asked. "We'll stop at the store and get you a tick to sleep on. You're lucky I've got some spare bedding. I suppose you haven't had supper?"

"No, Mr. Smith."

"You don't have to call me Mister," the editor said. "You

subscription   an agreement to receive issues of a publication
bit   12$\frac{1}{2}$ cents
by gum   mild swearing, no specific meaning

tick   cloth mattress cover

514

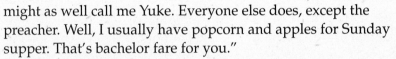

KEVIN

might as well call me Yuke. Everyone else does, except the preacher. Well, I usually have popcorn and apples for Sunday supper. That's bachelor fare for you."

Not even the promise of bread and water could have marred Kevin's happiness.

Further Reading

Call Me Ruth. Marilyn Sachs. In the early 1900s, Rifka and her mother come to the U.S. from Russia. Rifka adapts easily and even takes an American name. Her mother has a difficult time adjusting and only when she becomes involved with the unionization movement does she accept her new life.

The Great Wheel. Robert Lawson. An Irish boy seeking adventure in America comes to Chicago. He finds work on the construction of the great wheel invented by George Ferris which is a highlight of the Columbian Exposition in 1893.

The Long Winter. Laura Ingalls Wilder. Part of the "Little House on the Prairie" series, this story tells of the winter of 1880–81 in the Dakota Territory. The Ingalls have moved to town because of the harsh weather. A series of blizzards bury the town stopping all travel in and out. Shortages of food and fuel threaten the Ingalls and the townspeople.

My Prairie Year. Brett Harvey. Nine-year-old Eleanor Plaisted moves with her family from Maine to the Dakotas in 1889. This true story describes the perils and pleasures of homesteading.

LESSON 2

Entering the Modern Age

THINKING FOCUS

How did the rapid growth of industry affect the lives of working men and women in the United States?

Key Terms

- mechanization
- labor union
- strike

▼ *Railroads are the subject of this quilt made in 1884.*

Puffing and snorting, two black locomotives stood face to face at Promontory, Utah. It was a clear, cool morning in May 1869. Dozens of railroad workers stood on top of the engines. Some of them milled about on the ground. They all watched Leland Stanford get ready for the big moment.

As president of the Central Pacific Railroad, Stanford would hammer a golden spike into a special silver-banded railroad tie. That spike would complete the first railroad to stretch from the Atlantic Ocean to the Pacific Ocean.

A telegraph operator tapped out a description of the event. "Hats off! Prayer is being offered." The news traveled across telegraph wires to the rest of the nation. "We have got done praying. The spike is about to be presented."

Stanford stepped forward and drove the spike into the tie. "One, two, three—done!" tapped the telegraph operator. Across the country cannons boomed, bells rang, and parades began in celebration of the grand event.

Changes in a New Age

To many people, the driving of the golden spike was the start of a new, modern age in America. Telegraph lines carried news to and from every corner of the country. Huge factories produced materials for growing industries and cities. And, perhaps most important, railroads banded the entire nation together.

The Railroad Industry

During the 1870s and 1880s, many companies built railroads in other parts of the United States. By 1880, about 95,000 miles of track crisscrossed the country.

This rail system was one of the most costly projects ever attempted in the United States. But both private investors and the government saw how important railroads could be. People, goods, and mail would move across the nation faster than ever before on trains.

Congress gave land, and investors spent millions of dollars to build the railroads.

Once they were completed, the railroads were expensive to run. They used more machinery and employed more people than any business in America ever had. They also made more money than any American business had before. Railroads were the first big business in the United States.

The success of the railroads helped other industries to succeed as well. The steel industry, for example, was completely changed by the railroads.

The Steel Industry

The railroads needed huge amounts of steel for tracks and other equipment. This need caused the steel industry to grow as never before. Soon, steel was being made more quickly and cheaply than ever.

Steel mills were built along the railroad lines where raw materials, such as iron ore and coal, could be brought by trains. Finished steel rails were also sent by train to wherever new railroads were being built. Other steel products—wire, needles, screws, nails, pots, and pans—were shipped by train to stores throughout the country.

Carnegie's Industry

As industries grew, owners of companies looked for more profitable ways to run their businesses. Sometimes this meant having the lowest prices. Sometimes it meant paying employees the lowest wages. In the case of Andrew Carnegie, it meant controlling an entire industry.

▲ The steel industry made men like Andrew Carnegie rich. Life for the factory workers, however, was dangerous and difficult.

Life in a Changing America

*I*n the 1870s, machines were doing many jobs that people used to do. Once workers had been paid well to do skilled jobs. Suddenly, they were paid poorly to do simple, boring tasks. They experienced firsthand one of the problems connected with **mechanization**—the use of machines to do work.

Changes on the Farm

Mechanization did help some people. In the early 1800s, wheat was harvested by hand. A farmer walked up and down the rows of wheat swinging a long, curved blade to cut the wheat. In the 1830s, Cyrus H. McCormick invented a mechanical reaper.

This mechanical reaper made the farmer's job much easier. It also meant that fewer workers were required to harvest wheat.

Changes in Factories

Mechanization allowed people to produce more goods. It kept prices for goods down and it created jobs for people to produce and service the machines.

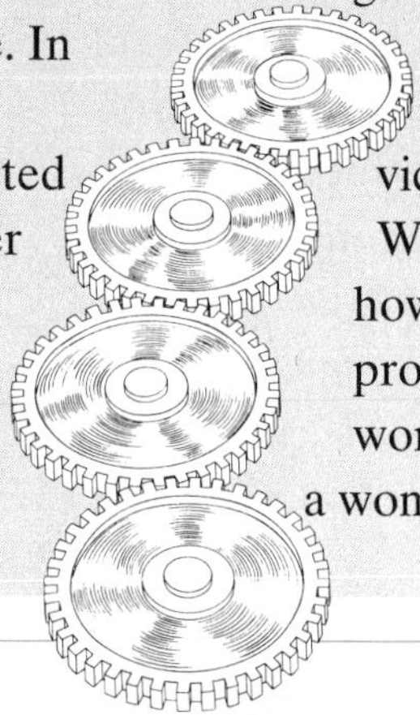

With mechanization, however, came many problems for factory workers. For example, a woman working on an assembly line repeated one simple job again and again. Workers once felt the satisfaction of creating a tool or a toy themselves. But in mechanized factories, workers came to feel like replaceable parts of a large machine.

Factory workers worked long hours. They earned low wages. They performed boring jobs in unsafe conditions. Workers who are bored and badly treated rarely do good work. They may begin to think about ways to get better wages and working conditions.

Mechanization helped workers produce more goods. But it also created problems of boredom and dissatisfaction for workers.

◄ *In the late 1800s and early 1900s, children often worked as long and hard as adults. These boys worked at a coal mine in Pennsylvania in 1911.*

Working in a New Age

The lives of factory workers were also changed by the growth of industry. But few people thought the change was for the better.

Men, women, and many children worked 10 hours a day, six days a week. They were usually paid less than $10 each week. The process of mechanization led factory owners to use machines for jobs that people had once done. This meant that most of the jobs that people did in factories were boring and dangerous. One worker said that he was treated "like any piece of machinery."

These poor conditions made factory workers angry. It seemed unfair that a few bosses had so much control over so many workers. As their anger increased, workers began to organize **labor unions.**

These organizations demanded better conditions and higher pay from a company. If the company refused, workers would **strike,** or refuse to work until they got what they wanted.

A Fight for Change

Sometimes these strikes became violent. The clash between the owner and workers of the Pullman Palace Car Company of Chicago is one of the most famous.

In 1894, the Pullman Company, which made railway cars, decided

▼ *Labor unions organized workers into groups that could stand up against powerful factory owners. This poster invited workers to a meeting in Chicago on May 4, 1886.*

> *Unions won higher wages and better working conditions for many different people—from carpenters to garment workers (right).*

■ *What did the labor unions hope to do for workers?*

to cut the wages of their workers by 25 percent. Workers protested by calling a strike.

News of the strike spread through the nation. President Grover Cleveland ordered U.S. soldiers to Chicago to end the strike. In July 1894, soldiers and armed guards hired by the Pullman Company clashed with striking workers. About a dozen people were killed and over $300,000 of railroad property was destroyed before workers finally ended the strike.

The striking workers did not get anything they had asked for. But the strike let the nation know about their problems.

A Change for the Better

Between 1881 and 1905, more than 6 million U.S. workers took part in over 36,000 strikes. Slowly, unions began to win victories for workers. By 1917, for example, every state had at least one law that prevented children under 12 from working at some types of jobs.

Labor unions remain an important force in American life. They continue to seek better conditions for workers in every state. ■

R E V I E W

1. **FOCUS** How did the rapid growth of industry affect the lives of working men and women in the United States?

2. **CONNECT** How did railroads influence the growth of industry? How did they make transportation of products easier and faster than before 1860?

3. **ECONOMICS** Why did workers in the late 1800s form labor unions and organize strikes?

4. **CRITICAL THINKING** Why do you think that some strikes became violent?

5. **WRITING ACTIVITY** Many people in the late 1800s worked 10 hours a day, six days a week, in a factory. Write two journal entries as if you were a factory worker who lived at that time.

Making Location Decisions

Here's Why

You may have passed by a new building and wondered why it was built where it was. Maps can help you figure out why. For example, suppose you wanted to know why so many steel mills were built around Gary, Indiana. The map below can help you figure this out.

Here's How

Symbols and colors on a map give information about places. Maps can help you figure out why activities happen in certain locations.

Look at the map of the steel industry in the Great Lakes area around 1900. The colored areas stand for coal and iron ore. They show where to find these raw materials for making steel. The coal fueled the furnaces needed to melt the iron ore before making steel products.

Notice the coal deposits near Gary, Indiana. Then look at the railroad lines that meet in Gary. Coal from these deposits could easily be sent by rail to Gary's steel mills. As the mills made more steel rails and rail cars, the railroads carried more coal and iron ore to the steel mills.

Now find Duluth, Minnesota. Iron ore from the mines in Minnesota could be loaded on ships at Duluth.

Trace the route of the ore across Lakes Superior and Michigan to the ports of Gary and Chicago. Iron ore and coal could be shipped either by water or rail to the steel mills near the cities. Cities provide people to work in the mills.

Try It

Look at the map again. What cities other than Gary and Chicago would be good sites for steel mills? Where would the materials come from? How could they be transported?

Apply It

What factors would help a city sports arena be successful? Write a paragraph

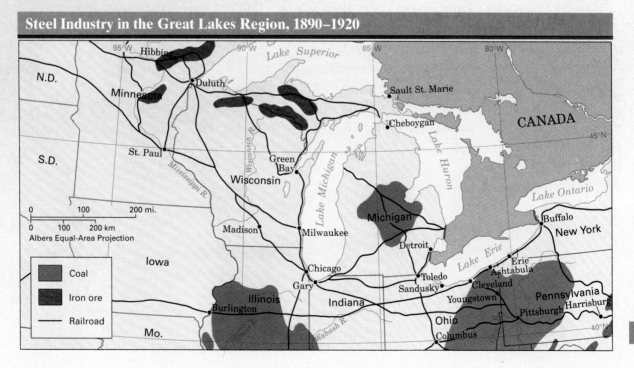

Steel Industry in the Great Lakes Region, 1890–1920

0 100 200 mi.
0 100 200 km
Albers Equal-Area Projection

Coal
Iron ore
Railroad

L E S S O N   3

Coming to America

THINKING FOCUS

What were the lives of immigrants like in the United States between 1870 and 1914?

Key Term

• racism
• nativism

➤ *This Italian mother and her children arrived in the United States with all their belongings in two clumsy bundles. Each of them was given a landing pass (shown below).*

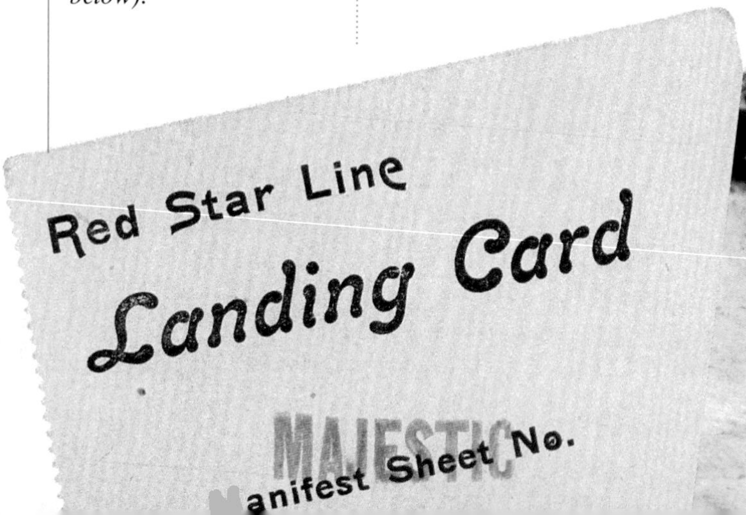

*I*t was not a pleasure trip, that 14-day journey aboard ship. Crammed into a dark, stuffy cabin with four other people, we spent the nights on sheetless bunks and most of the days standing in line for food that was ladled out to us as though we were cattle. Mother, Sheyna, and Zipke were seasick most of the time, but I felt well and can remember staring at the sea for hours wondering what Milwaukee would be like.

Golda Meir, who later became the prime minister of Israel, wrote these words about her journey to America in 1906. She and her mother and two sisters traveled by ship from Russia to New York. From there they continued to Milwaukee, where they joined her father.

It took courage for Meir's family to leave everything they knew and move to a new country. "Going to America then was almost like going to the moon," Meir remembered. But thousands of others dared to do what Meir's family did. Between 1860 and 1914, about 25 million immigrants made the voyage to America.

Red Star Line
Landing Card

MAJESTIC
Manifest Sheet No.

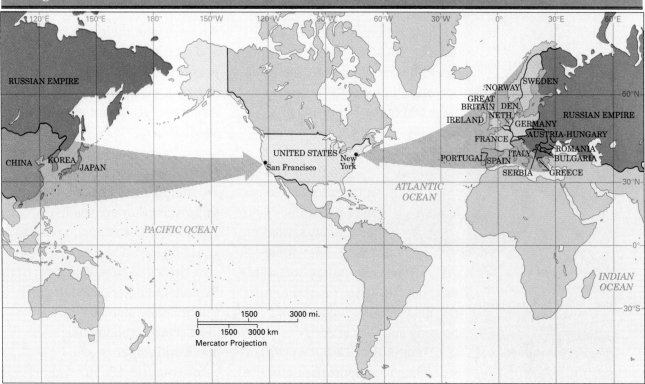

Immigration to the United States, 1870-1910

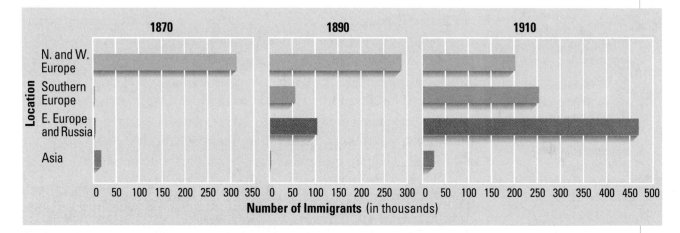

1870

Location	
N. and W. Europe	
Southern Europe	
E. Europe and Russia	
Asia	

0 50 100 150 200 250 300 350

1890

0 50 100 150 200 250 300

1910

0 50 100 150 200 250 300 350 400 450 500

Number of Immigrants (in thousands)

Immigrants in the United States

The immigrants who came to the United States after the Civil War were different from those who came earlier. Most early immigrants had come from Great Britain, Germany, and other countries of northern Europe. Some came to escape governments who treated them unfairly. Many came in search of a better life. Many of these immigrants already spoke English or learned it quickly. They settled on farms or in cities and lived much as their American neighbors did.

A New Wave of Immigrants

After 1900, however, most immigrants came from eastern and southern Europe. These people also escaped from economic hardships and political problems in their home countries. The map and graphs on this page show where these immigrants came from. Many

This map shows where most immigrants to the United States came from. The graphs show how many immigrants arrived from different parts of the world between 1870 and 1910.

523

Life in a Changing America

of these people could not speak English. Most were unskilled workers who wanted jobs in American factories. Look at the article on page 605 of the Minipedia to learn more about these new immigrants.

Some European immigrants had relatives and friends who had already settled in America. They sometimes sent money home for the boat trip. They offered to help friends from their villages find housing and jobs in America.

To unskilled European workers struggling to support their families, America promised plenty of jobs. In Eastern Europe, Jews were often persecuted for their religion. To them, America offered the promise of a place where all religions would be allowed.

With these hopes and plans, millions left their homes, families, and friends. They set off for America with their small savings and their most precious possessions—things like family portraits, an ancestor's wedding ring, and a grandmother's silver candlesticks.

A New Home for Immigrants

Immigrants faced many hardships when they arrived in America. Many were too poor to leave the crowded tenements of port cities like New York or Boston. Others traveled to cities where family members or friends lived. They settled in neighborhoods with other people from their home countries. Soon, many American cities had Jewish, Italian, Polish, and other ethnic neighborhoods.

Life in these neighborhoods gave immigrants some of the comforts of their home lands. Anna Fodorovich, a Russian immigrant, described her neighborhood in Pittsburgh.

▲ Immigrants often brought items from their homeland with them to America. These painted Easter eggs, for example, came from Russia.

Across Time & Space

A hundred years ago, most immigrants to the United States came from Europe. Today, about one-third of all immigrants come from Mexico. Like European immigrants, many Mexicans cross the border looking for better jobs and a better life. Another large group of immigrants comes from Asian countries such as China, the Philippines, Korea, and Vietnam.

➤ This photograph of a New York neighborhood is from the early 1900s. A Jewish shopkeeper advertises with signs printed in Hebrew letters.

*T*he Russian Church was in the Hill District then. So every Sunday morning my brother would take me and we would walk over the bridge to church. . . . And there were all kinds of Russian stores. So, we bought herring and black bread and we got together. That's how we met people.

Nicolette DiLucente told how her neighborhood celebrated an Italian saint's day. "All the people were from the same town," she said. "We decorated the whole street, made special foods, and we celebrated."

Immigrant neighborhoods were often run down and over-crowded. But they were also filled with familiar languages, customs, and foods of the old country. These ethnic neighborhoods helped make the immigrants' new land seem a little less strange. To learn more about the lives of immigrants look at A Closer Look at Immigrant Children on page 526. ■

◄ This shop in San Francisco's Chinatown sold such ethnic foods as Chinese cabbage, mushrooms, tea, and ginger.

■ Why did immigrants often settle in ethnic neighborhoods?

Immigrants and Politics

As immigrant neighborhoods became more crowded, they needed more city services. People needed protection from fire and crime. They needed garbage collection, street repairs and schools.

Bosses Help Immigrants

Many immigrants turned to local politicians, called bosses, to get these services. These politicians often made important improvements in the immigrant neighborhoods. In return, immigrants would vote for the boss that helped them in the next election.

Many immigrants had never before had the right to vote in Europe. Voting meant little to them at first. But as time went on, they were happy to give their votes to whoever would help them.

Bosses Help Themselves

Bosses became very powerful as a result of these immigrant votes. Some bosses took advantage of the immigrants and made themselves very rich.

The most famous of these bosses was William Tweed of New York. Tweed promised to make city improvements, just as all bosses did. But Tweed kept the money he raised. After he swindled New York out of millions of dollars, Tweed was arrested and sent to jail.

Life in a Changing America

Immigrant Children

Farms, small towns, and big cities provided new homes for children who came to the United States. Whether or not they went to school, all had to learn how to get along in America.

City streets were classrooms for a lot of immigrant children. They learned American business methods by selling newspapers, matches, or candy on street corners. When "class" was over, the children gathered in court-yards for fast and furious games of stickball.

McGuffey's Fifth Reader was part of a series of textbooks that many immigrants read. Its success stories about poor but honest children gave immigrants the hope that they, too, could succeed in America.

What did you have for lunch? A pickle and a piece of bread was all some children got in their lunch bags. Bad food and long working hours were blamed for the poor health of many immigrant children.

MᶜGUFFEY'S
FIFTH READER.

I. THE GOOD READER.

1. IT is told of Frederick the Great, King of Prussia, as he was seated one day in his private room, a ... was brought to him with the request that ... ly read. The King had just re-

(58)

Bosses were often the first experience immigrants had of politics and democracy in America. Some bosses took advantage of immigrants, but others helped them in their new homes. ■

■ *How did political bosses get immigrants to vote for them?*

Immigrants and Other Americans

Many immigrants faced problems because of the attitudes of the people already living in the United States. Some Americans feared that immigrants would steal their jobs by working for lower wages. Other Americans felt they were better than immigrants who belonged to a different race or ethnic group. Some people treated native-born Americans better than they treated immigrants. This attitude is called **nativism.**

Nativism caused pain and hardship for many immigrants. Most western states would not allow Japanese immigrants to own property. Many clubs did not accept Jewish immigrants as members. Many private schools and colleges limited their Jewish enrollment.

Nativist beliefs led Congress to pass laws keeping many immigrants from coming to the United States. In 1882, Congress passed a law that stopped Chinese immigration. In 1917, Congress voted to re-

quire immigrants to pass a reading test in English. Other laws passed in the 1920s limited the number of immigrants from southern and eastern Europe. As a result of these laws, immigration to the United States fell sharply.

Millions of immigrants came to the United States between 1860 and 1914. Their experiences, joys, and problems have been shared by the millions of immigrants who have come to the United States since that time. ■

▲ *This cartoon shows that many of the people who were most prejudiced against immigrants were the children of immigrants themselves.*

■ *Why did some labor union members fear immigrants?*

R E V I E W

1. **FOCUS** What were the lives of immigrants like in the United States between 1870 and 1914?
2. **CONNECT** How was immigration before 1900 different from immigration after 1900?
3. **CULTURE** Why did immigrants from the same country tend to live in the same neighborhood?
4. **CRITICAL THINKING** What are some of the reasons for nativism? Can you think of any groups of immigrants who meet with hostility when they arrive in the United States today? What do you think are the reasons for this?
5. **WRITING ACTIVITY** Interview someone who can tell you how they or their ancestors traveled to this country. This can be someone in your own family or in the family of a friend. Ask these questions: Why did they leave their old country? Where did they settle? What work did they do? What did they like best and least about their new home?

527

Immigration: Open or ？

Boston Evening Transcript

> W e need to keep our voting power and our reserves of public land out of the reach . . . of the hordes of half-educated and wholly unreliable foreigners now bribed to migrate here.
>
> **John Murray Forbes,**
> **railroad builder**

Background

Anna Maria Gavin came to America in 1866. As a child, she had heard that in America you could become rich, practice the religion you choose, and eat meat and bread every day! In Ireland Anna Maria often ate only dry bread with watercress, a plant like lettuce.

The nearly 34 million immigrants who poured in from 1820 to 1920 had high hopes. Many, like Anna Gavin, became citizens.

But for citizens born in America, the waves of immigration were disturbing, even frightening. The newcomers would compete for jobs, housing, and land. They might dress and speak differently. No one knew what political beliefs they might have. Would they really be loyal to this country rather than to the place where they were born? Would they understand how democracy worked?

Many immigrants had been extremely poor. Would they work for less money and bring down wages of native-born American workers? Would they take over whole towns and neighborhoods with their different ways of life?

Conflict Over Immigration

The argument over immigration was heating up by the time Anna Gavin arrived. From one point of view, it seemed that the nation's doors must remain open. The country's founders were, after all, immigrants or the children of immigrants. They had come to escape poverty and unjust laws.

More than that, they had come to find freedom and opportunity. How could they or their children turn away other people who shared the same goals? Railroads were opening the West. Industry was growing rapidly. Surely, there were jobs and space enough for anyone willing to work. Why not let the immigrants come in?

On the other hand, numbers are important in a democratic country. What if the newcomers took control of the country with their v

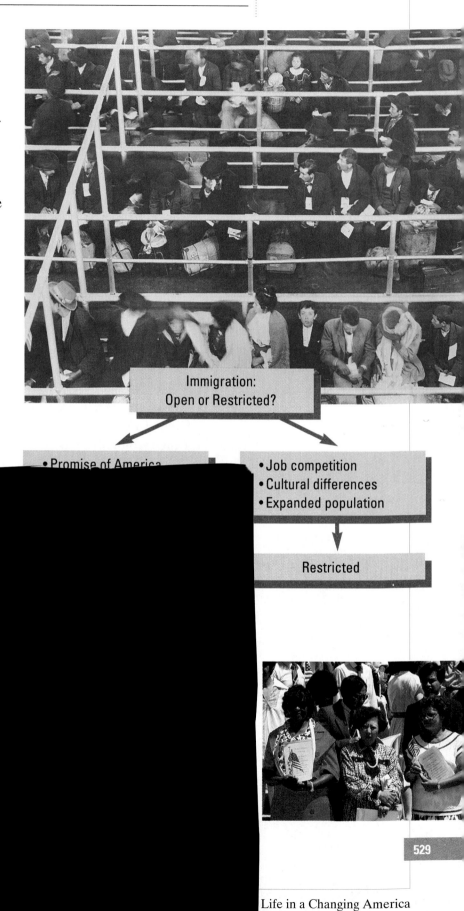

Immigration:
Open or Restricted?

• Promise of America

• Job competition
• Cultural differences
• Expanded population

Restricted

LESSON 4

Into Growing Cities

When Caroline Meeber boarded the afternoon train for Chicago, her total outfit consisted of a small trunk, a cheap imitation alligator-skin satchel, a small lunch in a paper box, and a yellow leather snap purse, containing her ticket, a scrap of paper with her sister's address in Van Buren Street, and four dollars in money. It was in August, 1889. She was eighteen years of age.

Theodore Dreiser, *Sister Carrie*, 1900

The main character in Theodore Dreiser's novel felt restless in her hometown. Carrie Meeber longed for the fashionable clothes and glamorous life that she hoped to find in the big city.

Carrie spoke English, but in many ways she was as much a

THINKING
FOCUS

How did cities grow and change in the years between 1870 and 1914?

Key Terms

- ghetto
- middle class

➤ *Good jobs and new opportunities drew people into Chicago and other growing American cities. Some things, like this beaded purse, were available only in big cities.*

foreigner in Chicago as immigrants from Russia and Italy. The city was not at all like the world she had known. She had no working skills. Still, Carrie set out to find a job in Chicago's business district. She wandered all day, looking for jobs and finding none. Finally, she found work in a factory for $4.50 a week.

Growth of Cities

To many Americans, cities promised good jobs and new opportunities. The excitement of busy city life drew many native-born Americans away from their farms and small towns. As a result, cities grew at an amazing rate. In 1860, only about 6 million people lived in U.S. cities. By 1920, more than 54 million people were city dwellers. The map to the right shows how much cities changed in the years between 1880 and 1900.

For example, by 1889 over 500,000 people already lived in Chicago. Its streets, houses, and businesses covered 75 square miles. Factories were built all around the city. Many railroads ran through Chicago. Railroad companies bought huge pieces of land in this booming city.

Leaving the Farm

In America's rural areas, well-paying jobs for farm workers were hard to find. The main reason was mechanization. Mechanical reapers and harvesters allowed farmers to produce more with fewer workers. Farms no longer needed armies of seasonal workers to prepare the land and to harvest the crops. As a result, many farm workers lost their jobs.

The farmers who could not afford new machines looked for other opportunities. They saw the city as a place to start over.

Moving North

In addition to white farmers and their families, many black Americans moved from the rural

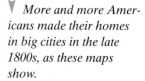
More and more Americans made their homes in big cities in the late 1800s, as these maps show.

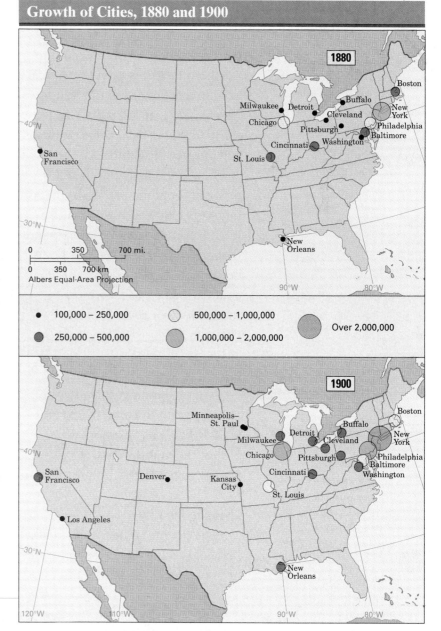

Growth of Cities, 1880 and 1900

- 100,000 – 250,000
- 250,000 – 500,000
- 500,000 – 1,000,000
- 1,000,000 – 2,000,000
- Over 2,000,000

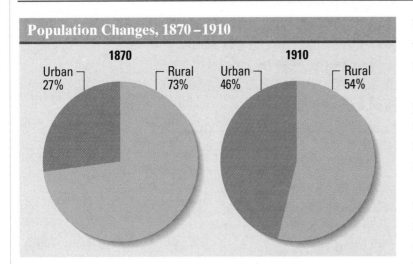

Population Changes, 1870–1910

1870
Urban 27%
Rural 73%

1910
Urban 46%
Rural 54%

▲ *These graphs show how the population shifted from rural to urban areas between 1870 and 1910.*

➤ *Many black families moved from southern farms to northern cities in the early 1900s.*

■ *How did mechanization affect farm workers?*

How Do We Know?

HISTORY *Immigrants often built churches and synagogues in the style of their native land. Many of these buildings remain. We can study the style of these buildings and discover what groups first settled a neighborhood.*

South to northern cities like New York, Chicago, and Philadelphia. Blacks moved to the cities to find better jobs, just as many other Americans had. African Americans could earn higher wages in northern factories than they could earn in any factory in the South. Nevertheless, in 1920 the vast majority (85%) of African Americans still lived in the South.

Black people experienced many of the same problems the immigrants had. But blacks, unlike most European immigrants, found it almost impossible to move into better neighborhoods when they could afford to. Most whites refused to sell or rent houses to blacks. Blacks who did move met with bitter prejudice from white neighbors.

Most black Americans lived in poor neighborhoods. The parts of a city where minority groups are forced to live because of prejudice and poverty are called **ghettos.**

Black ghettos, like all ghettos of the poor, were overcrowded and run-down. The streets were often dirty and dangerous. Still, black culture blossomed. Jazz clubs, social organizations, churches, and sports helped people cope with the difficulties of ghetto life. ■

Growth of the Middle Class

Not everyone in the city was an immigrant or came from rural areas. Many city dwellers were part of the **middle class,** people who were neither rich nor poor.

Living in the City

The people of the middle class held jobs as file clerks, secretaries, or bookkeepers in banks and business offices. Others owned their own small businesses, such as grocery or clothing stores. As cities grew and more businesses were located there, the middle class grew as well.

Gradually, more and more middle-class people saw the problems of the city. Some felt that greedy politicians hurt honest businesses. Many people feared that crime and sickness in poorer neighborhoods would spread to their homes.

Improving the City

To protect their neighborhoods and their families, some middle-class people formed civic organizations. These groups worked to improve city government. They worked to clean up city water and milk supplies, build parks and playgrounds, and improve schools.

As hard as they tried, there were some things that reformers could not change. America's cities were centers for manufacturing. Railroads cut through cities and factories grew up next to them. No one wanted to live close to a rail line or a large factory. But for a long time, it was not possible for most people to move away.

Escaping the City

In the 1860s, most workers had to walk to and from their jobs. By the 1870s and 1880s, however, public transportation systems were operating in most large cities. Cable cars and trolley cars made it possible for people to live miles away from their jobs.

In the 1880s and 1890s, trolley lines were built into the country around large cities. Developers bought land along the trolley lines and built the first suburbs. Suburbs had houses for single families, yards, and quiet tree-lined streets.

MAYWOOD 1873.

Changing the City

As middle-class families moved away, cities changed. Stores, offices, factories, and warehouses lined the inner-city streets.

But not only the cities changed in the late 1800s. Railroads connected the nation. By 1914, telephones and electric light bulbs appeared in homes. The lives of many workers and immigrants proved that not all these changes were good. But in both the good and bad changes, Americans saw that they had entered a new, modern age. ■

▲ *Some people escaped the problems of growing cities by moving to suburbs like Maywood, Illinois, outside of Chicago.*

■ *What made it possible for middle-class families to move to the suburbs?*

R E V I E W

1. **FOCUS** How did cities grow and change between the years 1870 and 1914?
2. **CONNECT** What were some reasons rural people had for moving to the city?
3. **ECONOMICS** Why did people of the middle class feel they had a stake in solving a city's problems?
4. **CRITICAL THINKING** Europeans came to America as immigrants, blacks moved north, rural people moved to cities, and middle-class people moved to the suburbs. Why were so many people doing so much moving?
5. **WRITING ACTIVITY** In the late 1800s and early 1900s, many people moved into cities. At the same time, many people were moving out of the city into suburbs. Make a chart listing reasons for moving into cities in one column and reasons for moving out of cities in another.

Life in a Changing America

Chapter Review

Reviewing Key Terms

exodus (p. 505)   mechanization (p. 518)
ghetto (p. 532)   middle class (p. 532)
Great Plains (p. 504) nativism (p. 527)
labor union (p. 519) strike (p. 519)

A. The following quotations express the feelings of various people. For each statement, identify the key term most closely associated with it.

1. "I'm not the richest person in town, but I'm not the poorest either—and I have a pretty good job in a business office."
2. "We do all the work, and the factory owners want to keep all the money. But if we stick together, we'll get what we deserve."
3. "We should stop letting so many immigrants into our country to take our jobs."
4. "It isn't fair that I have to live in the inner city, in a crumbling building that doesn't even have running water."
5. "Machines can do some kind of work twice as fast as humans can, and they cost less in the long run."
6. "Freedom has not brought me economic prosperity, so I decided to go west to make a new life for myself and my family."

B. The following sets of words are related in some way. For each set, write a short paragraph explaining how the words are related.

1. mechanization: labor union: strike
2. ghetto: nativism
3. exodus: Great Plains

Exploring Concepts

A. Copy the following cause-and-effect chart on your paper. Then write one effect for each cause. Some causes may have more than one effect.

Cause	Effect
The number of factories increased.	The demand for unskilled workers grew.
Workers wanted improved working conditions.	
Europeans sought jobs and freedom.	
Farming became mechanized.	
Middle-class people wanted better neighborhoods. Transportation improved.	

B. Support each of the following statements with facts and details from the chapter.

1. White settlers on the Great Plains changed the Indians' way of life.
2. Technology helped change the west.
3. Labor unions helped to improve the lives of workers.
4. Mechanization affected both factory workers and farm workers.
5. Immigrants moving to city neighborhoods led to the rise of political bosses.
6. Black culture developed in northern cities.
7. Cities grew quickly from 1860 to 1920.
8. By the 1870s, workers no longer had to live very close to their jobs.
9. As the suburbs grew, the nature of cities changed.

Reviewing Skills

1. What three factors should you consider when you choose a location for any purpose?
2. What would you look for on a map if you were trying to decide where to locate:
   - a. a shopping center?
   - b. a paper factory?
   - c. a wild animal park?
3. The railroads had a major effect on American society. What had an effect on the growth of railroads? Use the information from pages 516–518 in your book to draw a multiple-causes diagram that illustrates the cause for the following effect: The railroads grew quickly.
4. Suppose you wanted to understand more about the lives of people in three different economic classes—factory workers, middle-class workers, and farm workers—in the years after the Civil War. What kind of diagram might you draw to record details about the lives, work, and problems of the three groups?

Using Critical Thinking

1. Golda Meir wrote of her family's immigration to America in 1906 that the journey "was almost like going to the moon." What do you think she meant? Do you think immigrants to the United States today experience similar feelings?
2. By 1890 the U.S. Army had defeated the Plains Indians. These Indians had strived to keep their lands and way of life. . . . What do you think of the government's plan of placing the Indians on reservations? What, if any, were the advantages and disadvantages of this policy for Indian peoples?
3. Most immigrants today no longer come from southern and eastern Europe. Look in the Minipedia (p. 605) to find out where they do come from and why they leave their native lands. Why do you think the areas from which immigrants come change over time?
4. Political bosses were sometimes greedy and dishonest, but they also did some good. How were they helpful? Do you think politicians today can do a better job of serving the public?

Preparing for Citizenship

1. **WRITING ACTIVITY** Imagine you are a factory worker in the 1870s. How do you spend your time? Where do you live? How is life different from your life today? Look for descriptions and facts in an encyclopedia. Write a short story as if you were transported to the past as a factory worker.
2. **GROUP ACTIVITY** Choose a partner and debate the roles of a machine you or your family use today. Your subject might be, for example, a vacuum cleaner or a computer. One person should present the advantages of the machine and the other person should present the disadvantages. Base your views on personal experiences. Use examples to support your opinions.
3. **COLLABORATIVE LEARNING** In groups of three, survey the immigrant influences in your neighborhood. Assign one person to listen for different languages and music styles, one to list names, and one to note the style and decoration of homes and restaurants. What countries are represented? Clip photos that show ethnic influences from local newspapers. Then meet in large groups to combine them into a poster.

535

Life in a Changing America

Conclusion

A Look at the Twentieth Century

Since 1900, the United States has changed greatly. Progressives fought for laws to make life better. Technology helped win World War I and brought growth and prosperity. Poverty came with the 1930s, but victory in World War II helped end the hard times. It also made the United States a world power with a strong rival—the Soviet Union. At home, Americans fought for their rights. As the twenty-first century approaches, the United States becomes more a part of the world community.

The Progressive Era In the early 1900s, some children worked in mines ten hours or more a day. Jane Addams and other reformers, known as progressives, fought to outlaw child labor. Other progressives, including Theodore Roosevelt (right), tried to limit the power of big business.

1900	1910	1920

Section 1: **The Progressive Era**

Section 2: **The Era of World War I**

Section 3: **The Postwar Boom and Crash**

1909 Ida Wells-Barnett, (right) an African American journalist, helped to found the National Association for the Advancement of Colored People (NAACP). This organization supported racial equality.

The Era of World War I The use of poisonous gas helped make World War I deadly. The women shown at right were collecting peach pits. Seven pounds of pits were needed to make the charcoal for the filter in each gas mask.

1900

World War II and Its Results Soldiers from the United States fought in Europe, Africa, and Asia. Many adults who were not in the military worked in weapons factories. The U.S. government forced many Japanese Americans (below) into prison camps.

The Depression and the New Deal The poverty of the 1930s caused widespread concern. Under President Franklin D. Roosevelt (left), the federal government started several programs to help people. The initials of the names of some of these programs are shown in the cartoon below.

LIFE

1930

1940

1950

Section 4: **The Depression and the New Deal**

Section 5: **World War II and Its Results**

1945 The United States dropped atomic bombs on the Japanese cities of Hiroshima and Nagasaki. Japan quickly surrendered, and World War II ended.

The Postwar Boom and Crash During the prosperous 1920s, most people had jobs and lived comfortably. Many families bought their first car. During this period, a lively new form of music, jazz, became popular.

1950

1950s A new style of music, rock and roll, became popular with young people. The new music was influenced by various styles of African American music.

1969 On July 20, Neil Armstrong became the first person to walk on the moon. The Saturn V rocket (right) that launched the Apollo spacecraft with Armstrong and two other astronauts on board was over 360 feet tall.

The Cold War and Vietnam In 1963, the assassination of President John F. Kennedy (below) shocked the nation. Under Kennedy, United States involvement in a war in Vietnam had grown. By 1973, though, protests against the war helped force the United States to leave Vietnam.

1950

1960

1970

Section 6: **The Struggle for Equality**
Section 7: **The Cold War and Vietnam**

Section 8: **A Global Age**

The Struggle for Equality Throughout the 1950s and 1960s, African Americans and other groups fought to win equality in the United States. Two important African American leaders were Dr. Martin Luther King, Jr. and Malcolm X (right). An important Native American leader was Russell Means (far right).

538

1950

1980s and 1990s Many groups continued to fight for their rights. Above, a group demonstrates for day care, an important issue to the women's movement and to African Americans. Some older Americans fought for their rights through the Gray Panthers, started by Maggie Kuhn (left, in front).

A Global Age Since 1965, Americans have become more closely connected to the rest of the world. Increasing immigration and concern for the environment have linked the United States to other countries.

1980	1990	2000

1990 Antonia Novello (left), a Hispanic American, became Surgeon General of the United States.

1992 The people of the United States elected Bill Clinton as President.

Present

Presidents								Landmark: Women Win the Right to Vote
Benjamin Harrison **1889-1893**	William McKinley **1897-1901**				William H. Taft **1909-1913**			
1890	**1895**	**1900**	**1905**	**1910**	**1915**	**1920**		
	Grover Cleveland **1893-1897**	Theodore Roosevelt **1901-1909**			Woodrow Wilson **1913-1921**			

SECTION 1

The Progressive Era

THINKING FOCUS

How did the progressives work to make life better in the United States?

Key Terms

- progressive
- suffrage

➤ *Jane Addams was a progressive and social reformer. In addition to starting Hull House, she also gave lectures and wrote books on solving social problems.*

The neighborhood smelled awful. Garbage clogged the streets. Flies swarmed everywhere. Several families often crowded into small wooden houses that had no water. Men, women, and even young children worked long hours in dark, dirty factories called "sweatshops."

That's what you would have seen if you had visited Chicago's west side in the late 1800s and early 1900s. People from many countries came to city neighborhoods like the one just described. As they came, cities grew rapidly. Most of the immigrants came in search of jobs in the growing number of factories. They hoped to find a better life. Unfortunately, many new arrivals found only crowded, dirty neighborhoods and low-paying jobs.

One woman, Jane Addams, believed she could make life better in these neighborhoods. She fixed up a large old house in Chicago and named it Hull House. Hull House became a settlement house, a place where immigrants could get help in their new land. At Hull House they could learn English, get job skills, and enroll their young children in school.

Attacking Problems of the Cities

Cities grew more and more crowded. Old buildings were unsafe places to work and to live. Many people shared Jane Addams's desire to improve the cities. These reformers, who were called **progressives,** started

Conclusion

schools and health centers. They wanted the government to pass helpful laws. Progressives were concerned about unhealthy or unsafe conditions in buildings. In one factory, they found children working at dangerous machines for 16 hours a day. A New York building with only 264 toilets and no bathtubs housed 2,781 people.

Many building owners did not think the government should set rules for them. Sometimes, only a disaster changed their minds. On March 25, 1911, a fire trapped 146 workers at the Triangle Shirtwaist Company in New York. The clothing factory had only one fire escape for 850 workers. The city then passed tougher safety laws.

Another problem in the cities was dishonest political leaders. Such leaders were more concerned with making money than with solving their cities' problems. One of the most famous and powerful groups in New York City was known as Tammany Hall. These city leaders stole many millions of dollars of government money.

Controlling Big Business

Theodore Roosevelt and Woodrow Wilson were progressive U.S. presidents who worked for people's well-being. Under Roosevelt, Congress set up a department to keep watch on workers' rights. It tried to make sure businesses were run in a fair way. Roosevelt worked to limit the power of big companies. He did not want one company to control an industry like railroads, oil, or sugar. If that happened, the company could charge higher prices for its products.

Progressives also felt concerned about child labor. Under Wilson, they helped get a child labor law passed. It prevented mines from hiring workers under 16 years old. On other jobs, children between 14 and 16 could work no more than 8 hours a day and 48 hours a week.

▲ *In the early 1900s, young children often worked long hours in factories like this cotton mill.*

Issues of the Time

Changes in Education

John Dewey said science classes should appeal to students' curiosity about the world around them. He was one of the progressives working to improve schools in the early 1900s. Progressives felt that schools should offer gym, art, and music. Many progressive reforms are still in our schools today.

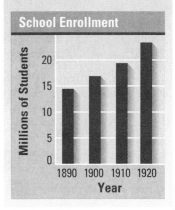

School Enrollment

541

...he first state in which women gained
... rights. Some states followed, but
...en still did not have this right.
...s such as the National Woman's
...ght for the vote. Like the woman
... page 543, many marched and spoke

...Wyoming enters the Union and becomes
...st state that allows women to vote.

| | 1900 | 1925 |

1872, Susan B. Anthony
is arrested for voting in the
Presidential election of 1872.

1918–1920, Congress approves a proposed
Constitutional amendment to give women the vote.
In 1920, the states approve the Nineteenth Amendment.

Facing Racial Problems

African Americans often faced discrimination, or unfair
treatment. Like other groups such as Asian Americans and
Native Americans, African Americans often had difficulty
getting jobs, buying homes, and entering public places. Black
leaders looked for ways to overcome discrimination. Ida
Wells-Barnett wrote newspaper stories that told of the horrible
lynching of African Americans accused of crimes. Her work

➤ *Booker T. Washington
(left) felt that African Americans
needed to learn job skills to get
ahead in life. For that reason,
he started Tuskegee Institute in
Alabama. W. E. B. Du Bois
told African Americans to fight
against unfair treatment.*

542

out. On August 26, 1920, the Nineteenth Amendment, became part of the Constitution, giving women full voting rights. All adult Americans could now participate in government by voting.

In the late 1800s and early 1900s, more women than ever before became a force in the shaping of society. They organized hospitals and began attending colleges in greater numbers. They fought for higher pay and better schools. Some women worked to make the selling of liquor against the law. Women also formed the National Consumers' League. This group asked people not to buy products from companies that used child labor. Women were an important force in the progressive movement.

helped change the laws to make sure African Americans got fair trials. Millions of African Americans admired Marcus Garvey's teachings and his "Back to Africa" movement. Booker T. Washington said that getting job skills was the best way to get ahead. His school, the Tuskegee Institute, trained African American students for jobs.

W. E. B. Du Bois felt African Americans needed more than job training. He wanted them to attend college and learn more about the world. Du Bois helped start the National Association for the Advancement of Colored People (NAACP) in 1909. The National Urban League was started in 1910. These groups still work for the civil rights of African Americans.

REVIEW

1. **FOCUS** How did the progressives work to make life better in the United States?

2. **POLITICAL SYSTEMS** What laws did Congress pass to protect people in the early 1900s?

3. **CRITICAL THINKING** How did the role of women change in the early 1900s?

4. **ACTIVITY** List four things you would change in your neighborhood to make it better.

SECTION 2

The Era of World War I

THINKING FOCUS

How did World War I change the United States?

Key Terms

- alliance
- pacifist
- communism

▼ *The writer of this headline did not yet know about the many passengers who died as the* Lusitania *went down.*

O n May 7, 1915, the British passenger ship *Lusitania* sailed near the coast of Ireland. Some passengers relaxed over coffee in the dining room. Others walked on the sunny decks. Still, the battlefields of World War I, where France and Britain were fighting against Germany, must have been on their minds.

Suddenly, at 2:10 P.M., the periscope of a German submarine appeared and a torpedo streaked across the water. When it hit the *Lusitania,* there was an explosion. A second explosion soon followed. In only 18 minutes the ship sank. Nearly 1,200 of the 2,000 passengers died, among them 128 Americans.

Newspapers called the Germans "murderers" and "pirates." Some Americans wanted their country to fight back. However, President Woodrow Wilson knew the ship had been carrying weapons to Britain. He also knew that if he sent ships or soldiers against Germany, the United States would be at war.

RACING RESULTS ★★★★★ **The Evening Telegram** BASEBALL EXTRA

LUSITANIA BLOWN UP BY GERMANS; LOSS OF LIFE REPORTED SLIGHT
EXTRA!

The Lusitania, the largest and fastest steamship in passenger service, was torpedoed by a German submarine off the coast of Ireland at two o'clock this afternoon.

An official announcement given out in London this evening says the vessel remained afloat "at least twenty minutes" after the explosion.

A despatch from London, timed twenty minutes to seven o'clock, says it is believed there was no great loss of life." The passengers numbered 1,253 and the crew about 750. Late this afternoon it was stated that about twenty of the Lusitania's boats were afloat near where the steamship sank and that a Greek steamship, several patrol boats, and two motor fishing boats were standing by the small boats. The patrol boats and the other fishing boats took the smaller craft in tow and started for Kinsale.

The Great War

In the late 1800s, European countries split into two groups. Each group formed an **alliance,** a partnership. Countries within an alliance promised to fight together in case of war. Countries were already fighting for control of seaports and colonies for the resources and profits they provided. Smaller countries battled to break away from the big countries that ruled them. It seemed that any event might set off a major war. One event finally did.

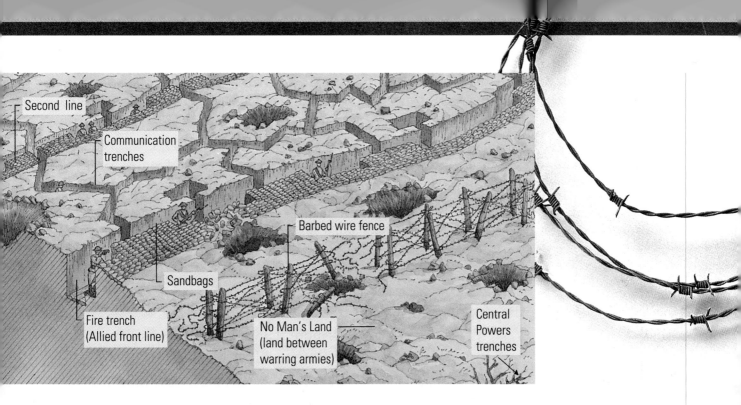

Second line

Communication trenches

Barbed wire fence

Sandbags

Fire trench (Allied front line)

No Man's Land (land between warring armies)

Central Powers trenches

On June 28, 1914, Archduke Francis Ferdinand, heir to the Austro-Hungarian throne, was shot and killed. Austria-Hungary blamed its neighbor, Serbia, and declared war. Germany joined with Austria-Hungary to form the Central Powers. Serbia joined with Britain, France, and Russia to form the Allies. Other countries were forced to join because of alliances. World War I, called The Great War, had begun.

The Central Powers and the Allies fought bitter battles. By December, the armies had dug themselves into ditches called trenches along a 400-mile front. The soldiers lived in, and fought from, the trenches. Trenches gave the men some protection from enemy fire. Trench fighting made World War I drag on. A single battle at the Somme River in France in 1916 lasted nearly five months. More than one million French, British, and German soldiers died. The Allies won the battle, but they paid a high price to advance just five miles.

◄ *American troops charge from the trenches in World War I (left). Soldiers positioned barbed wire around trenches to help protect themselves. The drawing (above, left) gives a detailed look at how the armies set up their trenches.*

Issues of the Time

Immigration

U.S. businesses needed workers to replace those fighting the war. Immigrants filled that role.

Many Mexicans moved to the United States to escape a revolution at home. Some joined African Americans and white women in holding down important jobs in factories. Other Mexican Americans worked on building projects.

545

The Home Front

News from Europe about the war divided Americans. Some immigrants supported their native countries where relatives still lived. **Pacifists,** people against war of any kind, spoke up for peace. President Wilson also wanted the United States to stay out of the war. Yet, the United States government loaned the Allies money and sold them food and weapons. Then Germany attacked American ships carrying supplies. On April 6, 1917, the United States declared war on Germany.

Americans at War

By November, 1918, more than two million Americans were part of the war effort in Europe. Many of them fought in a single battle at Meuse-Argonne *(MYOOZ ar GON),* France, that

Landmark

The Red Scare

Russia fought on the Allied side in World War I. After a revolution in 1917, Russia set up a new communist system of government. Under **communism**, the government owned all property and controlled businesses. In the United States, some people were attracted to communism. To some workers, communism seemed to promise a better life. However, while communism sounded good to some, others worried about the violence often used by communists.

The United States government began to consider certain people a threat to the country. These included American communists, labor union leaders, and even Russian immigrants. Many of these people were innocent of any crime. Still, police arrested thousands they believed to be communists. Communists were called "Reds" because the new Russian flag was red. This widespread fear of communism was known as the "Red Scare." The cartoon shows Uncle Sam sending some Reds back to Russia.

The Red Scare ended late in 1920. That year Warren G. Harding was elected President. He told Americans that there had been too much worry about communism. However, many people continued to see communism as a threat to freedom in the United States.

The Cheerful Giver--Or, Do Your Christmas Shipping Early

lasted for 47 hard days. The bloody battle helped the Allies finally win the war.

The American soldiers in World War I came from many groups. A large number of Mexican Americans served in the armed forces. One brave African American unit from Harlem in New York City fought on the front line in France for 191 days. After the war, France awarded them and three other African American regiments awards for bravery.

▲ *President Wilson (right) poses with leaders of the other Allied countries at Versailles, France.*

Results of the War

The war tore Europe apart. Millions of soldiers and civilians died. The bombing blasted cities, streets, schools, and factories. The war separated families and left many homeless. Old empires fell, and new countries arose. The old empire of Austria-Hungary became the countries of Austria, Hungary, and Czechoslovakia. The breakup of the empire also added land to Italy, Poland, Romania, and Yugoslavia. Part of the Ottoman Empire became the country of Turkey.

The war ended in 1918. Some leaders signed a peace treaty at Versailles *(ver SI),* France, on June 28, 1919. There President Wilson presented his idea for forming a "League of Nations" to settle future problems peacefully. Many Americans disagreed with Wilson. They thought the League would force the United States into more wars. The United States Senate voted against approving the Treaty of Versailles. The United States then signed a separate treaty with Germany.

The Great War helped make the United States a world power. American money and resources played a part in winning the war. After the war, the United States helped rebuild Europe.

REVIEW

1. **FOCUS** How did World War I change the United States?

2. **CITIZENSHIP** How did the war divide Americans?

3. **CRITICAL THINKING** Why did other countries see the United States as more powerful after the war?

4. **WRITING ACTIVITY** Imagine you are a Russian American living in the United States in 1920. Write in your diary your concerns and feelings about the way you are treated in the United States.

547

Woodrow Wilson **1913-1921** Calvin Coolidge **1923-1929**

Landmark:
Stock Market Crash

	1920	1921	1922	1923	1924	1925	1926	1927	1928	1929	1930

Presidents Warren G. Harding **1921-1923**

Herbert C. Hoover **1929-1933**

S E C T I O N 3

The Postwar Boom and Crash

THINKING
F O C U S

How did machines bring change to the United States in the 1920s?

Key Terms

- assembly line
- stock

➤ *Songwriters of the day told of the adventures of the popular Charles Lindbergh.*

▼ *Radios became common in the early 1920s.*

Cheering crowds lined the parade route in Washington, D.C. Adults and children waved flags as marching bands passed by. Moviemakers filmed the car carrying "Lucky Lindy." From May 20 to 21, 1927, Charles Lindbergh had flown his small plane from New York City to Paris, France. He had become the first person to fly alone across the Atlantic Ocean. Americans were welcoming their hero home.

On top of the Washington Monument, a radio reporter asked the crowd to cheer for Lindy: "Make it the greatest cheer that ever went up!" The message was the longest network broadcast up to that time. More than 25 million people listened and cheered for Lindbergh and for America.

Machines Shape New Lives

Lindbergh's flight was one of many exciting technical advances made in the United States during the 1920s. The invention of new machines changed people's lives. Farm families

548

Conclusion

tuned in on their new radios to hear news from the cities. People dialed their shiny black telephones and spoke to friends and relatives thousands of miles away. More Americans than ever owned automobiles, thanks to Henry Ford.

Henry Ford was an inventor and car maker. At first, Ford had his workers put together cars from start to finish, one at a time. Then in 1913, Ford began using an **assembly line.** In this system, cars moved from worker to worker. Each worker would perform the same task on each car that rolled by.

With the assembly line, workers could build cars faster. As a result, Ford's cars cost less. In 1908, before the assembly line, workers built a Model T Ford in about 12½ hours. The car sold for $850. In 1914, workers built a Model T in about 1½ hours and that car sold for less than $400. Thus, many more Americans could afford cars.

Other products also rolled off assembly lines. Radios, record players, vacuum cleaners, and washing machines came into many homes. Those who could afford to, threw out their old-fashioned ice boxes and bought new electric refrigerators.

With the new machines came new jobs. Companies built new factories, thus providing jobs for construction workers. Stores hired salespeople. Offices hired clerks and typists. Advertising became an important new business. American cities grew and became brighter places with jobs for many.

Langston Hughes wrote short stories and poems in the 1920s about the lives of African Americans.

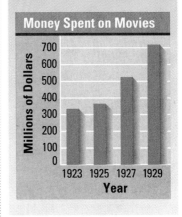

A Center of African American Life

Between 1910 and 1920, many African Americans came to the New York City neighborhood called Harlem. Harlem became the center for black art, writing, and music. People moved there from southern states, from the Caribbean Islands, and from Africa. In Harlem, they shared their common African heritage.

Important black writers like Claude McKay and Countee Cullen, and leaders like W. E. B. Du Bois and James Weldon Johnson lived in Harlem. Zora Neale Hurston's books showed her gift for story-telling. Langston Hughes was perhaps the best known black writer. His first book of poems, *The Weary Blues,* was published in

1926 when he was just 24 years old. Hughes described the joys, hardships, and hopes of African Americans in the 1920s.

African American art, books, and music spread from Harlem to other places. Radios and record players around the world played various kinds of African American music— jazz, blues, and gospel. Jazz became so popular that people often called the years after World War I "The Jazz Age."

Signs of Trouble

Although new inventions had created many jobs, there were signs that trouble was coming. Many workers lost their jobs to machines that could do the same work faster. Banks were lending people money to buy **stock**, or shares in a company. Companies were producing more goods, but there were not enough people able to buy them. Some companies began to lose money. In the 1920s, stock buyers expected American companies to keep making money. Unfortunately, they were wrong.

Landmark

The Stock Market Crash

People bought and sold stock in companies at the New York Stock Exchange. As stock prices rose, Americans bought more stock, hoping to make more money. This caused the price of the stock to rise rapidly during the summer of 1929.

Then stock prices began to fall. People rushed to sell their stocks so they wouldn't lose their money. On Tuesday, October 29, stockholders panicked and sold more than 16 million shares. With everyone selling at once, stocks became worthless. The market "crashed." Stock owners lost billions of dollars. The crash left many people and businesses as poor as the man in the photo.

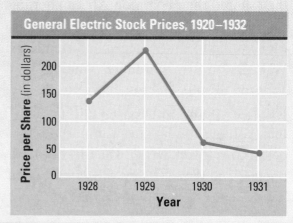

General Electric Stock Prices, 1920–1932

After the Crash

The stock market crash brought the hardest times that Americans had ever known. Companies couldn't sell their products and had to fire workers. Between 1929 and 1932, about 100,000 people lost their jobs every week. More than 4,000 banks went out of business. The banks closed their doors because they were unable to collect on loans made to customers. Because of bank closings, thousands of people lost their life savings and homes.

Families struggled to survive. One woman borrowed 50 cents from a friend and bought stale bread for about 3 cents a loaf. Along with two meals, that was all her family had to eat for eleven days. Another family bought a small amount of meat and made a stew from vegetables that had fallen from a wagon in the street. They reheated the pot of stew for several days in order to provide food for themselves.

The U.S. government had no plan ready to help the huge number of struggling and unemployed people. City and state governments ran short of money as times got worse.

◄ *One problem led to another after the stock market crashed in 1929. The result was widespread poverty and unemployment as many businesses closed.*

Impact of the Stock Market Crash

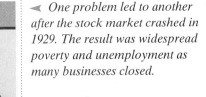

1. Stock prices decline and investors lose their savings.
2. With less savings, banks have less money to loan to businesses.
3. Businesses produce less and fire many workers.
4. Without jobs, people buy fewer goods.
5. As sales go down, many businesses close.
6. Many more workers lose their jobs.
7. People buy less and less.

REVIEW

1. **FOCUS** How did machines bring change to the United States in the 1920s?

2. **ECONOMICS** Why do you think so many more cars were sold after the start of Henry Ford's assembly line form of production?

3. **CRITICAL THINKING** Moviegoing stayed popular in the hard times of the 1930s. Why do you think this was so?

4. **ACTIVITY** Imagine that you have a job in a company that makes refrigerators. Write about your life before and after the stock market crash.

551

Herbert C. Hoover **1929-1933**

Landmark: Social Security

| **1929** | **1930** | **1931** | **1932** | **1933** | **1934** | **1935** | **1936** | **1937** | **1938** | **1939** | **1940** |

Presidents

Franklin D. Roosevelt **1933-1945**

SECTION 4

The Depression and the New Deal

THINKING
FOCUS

How did the role of the U.S. government change when hard times hit?

Key Words

- Depression
- New Deal

Homeless people slept on the streets under newspapers they called "Hoover blankets." Others built "Hooverville" towns of tents and shacks. People named these for President Herbert Hoover. By 1932, most Americans blamed the Republican President for the country's hard times. After the stock market crash, Americans struggled through the Depression. The **Depression** was a particularly severe economic period in the 1930s. Thousands of people were out of work and almost everyone suffered.

Franklin Delano Roosevelt, known as FDR, was the Democratic Party's candidate for President in the election of 1932. He sent a message of hope to Americans. Voters responded and elected FDR by about seven million votes over Hoover.

▼ *During the hard times of the Depression, FDR met with many Americans, such as these farmers.*

President Franklin D. Roosevelt

Roosevelt took office on March 4, 1933. In his first speech, he told Americans he wanted to put them back to work. He gave them hope that the country would once again be strong.

Americans liked many things about Roosevelt. They admired his bravery, for one thing. In 1921, at age 39, he came down with polio. The disease left him almost unable to walk. FDR went back to public life in a wheelchair.

Before becoming President, Roosevelt was governor of New York State. There, he started programs to aid farmers, to help older people, and to give money to those without jobs.

Although hard times went on through the 1930s, Americans elected FDR four times. He served longer than any other President in history. Americans liked his "fireside chats," the radio speeches in which he tried to give them hope for the future.

Eleanor Roosevelt, the First Lady, also cared about people. She worked to end racial discrimination and spoke out for peace around the world.

New Federal Programs

Once he became President, Roosevelt moved quickly to rebuild America. His plan, the **New Deal,** was to form government agencies to help people. One, the Works Progress Administration (WPA), put more than eight million people to work building dams, roads, post offices, playgrounds, and theaters. The WPA also gave jobs to artists, writers, actors, and musicians. A government project built dams on the Tennessee River to make electricity and control floods. Another program helped farmers buy needed equipment.

Under the New Deal, the government spent billions of dollars to create jobs for people. FDR hoped these programs would cause Americans to buy more goods. He hoped this would get businesses going again.

▼ *A New Deal agency gave Eitaro Ishigaki (left) the job of creating this wall painting. The poster (right) promotes the Civilian Conservation Corps, another New Deal agency.*

553

Social Security

The Depression was especially hard for older people. Bank closings wiped out the life savings of many people over 65. At that time, most companies did not give retired workers a pension, or retirement pay. Among the few companies who had promised a pension, some did not have the money to pay it.

Congress passed a law in 1935 to help older people when they retired. This law, the Social Security Act, set up a system for people 65 and older. They received cards (left) and read about the new program in booklets (right). Under the law, both workers and their companies paid money to a

SOCIAL SECURITY ACT
ACCOUNT NUMBER
030-16-3257
HAS BEEN   ESTABLISHED FOR
J. Harold Lamontagne
WORKER'S SIGNATURE

Not everyone liked the New Deal. Small farm owners disliked one program that controlled the amount of crops they could grow. Some companies didn't like another program that gave certain workers a minimum wage. This program also gave some workers extra pay for working more than 44 hours a week. Companies didn't like the idea of government trying to regulate the way they ran their businesses.

Effects of the New Deal

The New Deal helped many Americans. One program started under the New Deal still protects people's savings in banks today. Laws passed under the New Deal still make sure workers receive a minimum wage.

Mexican Americans felt FDR supported their rights. A farm program set up camps for migrant workers in California. American Indians also made gains under the New Deal. One program

▼ FDR appointed a group of high-level African American advisors known as the "Black Cabinet." The total number of African American government workers rose from 50,000 in 1933 to 200,000 by 1947.

government fund for workers' retirement savings. When people stopped working, they could collect Social Security payments from the fund. The first Social Security check was paid in 1940 to Ida Mae Fuller of Vermont. She received $22.54 the first month.

The 1935 law has been changed many times. Now it covers more people. These include workers hurt on their jobs and workers' families. Social Security has kept millions of older Americans from becoming poor. It is one of the programs started under the New Deal that continues to help Americans today.

gave loans to Indian businesses. Another program helped them improve their farming.

Roosevelt's government included people from groups that had been left out of decision-making before. FDR appointed many African Americans to government. These included Robert C. Weaver, Mary McLeod Bethune, and William Hastie, the first African American federal district judge. FDR was also the first President to appoint a woman, Frances Perkins, to his Cabinet.

The New Deal restored people's faith in the government. It also gave the President more power. FDR's programs helped but did not end the Depression. Recovery took a long time. Many new jobs came only at the start of another world war.

REVIEW

1. **FOCUS** How did the role of the U.S. government change when hard times hit?

2. **CITIZENSHIP** What protections have people come to expect from the government because of New Deal programs?

3. **CRITICAL THINKING** Why do you think so many business leaders opposed the New Deal? List two possible reasons for voting against it.

4. **ACTIVITY** Interview an older person who was a child during the Depression. Ask what he or she remembers about the time. Find out how the hard times affected this person's life. If you are unable to talk to someone, look for a book in the library in which people talk about the Depression. Write down the important comments. Make a report to the class as if you were that person telling your memories of those times.

SECTION 5

World War II and Its Results

THINKING
F O C U S

How did World War II affect the United States?

Key Terms

- dictator
- Holocaust
- superpower

▼ *"Remember Pearl Harbor" became a battle cry for Americans after the Japanese attack on the U.S. naval base there.*

December 7, 1941, seemed like just another Sunday morning. Admiral Husband E. Kimmel was at home, talking on the phone to an officer at the naval base in nearby Pearl Harbor, Hawaii. Suddenly, Kimmel heard shocking news. "The Japanese are attacking Pearl Harbor!" the officer exclaimed. Kimmel ran outside and saw hundreds of Japanese planes darkening the sky. The attackers bombed the ships of the U.S. Pacific Fleet. Over the next two hours, the Japanese destroyed eight large ships and nearly 200 U.S. planes, killing more than 2,000 Americans. The next day, the United States declared war on Japan.

The Causes of World War II

By December 1941, Europe had already been at war for two years. Adolf Hitler, supported by his Nazi *(NAHT see)* followers, was the dictator of Germany. A **dictator** is a leader with complete power. The nations of Europe stood by when Hitler sent his armies to take over Austria and Czechoslovakia *(chehk uh sluh VAH kee uh)* in 1938. Hitler did not stop there, though. On September 1, 1939, his troops invaded Poland. Finally, Great Britain and France could stand by no longer. They declared war on Germany. In 1941, the Soviet Union joined the war against Germany.

556

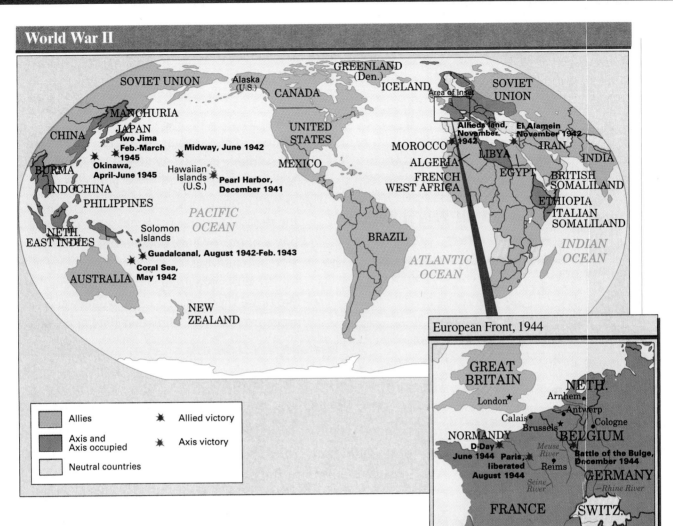

GREENLAND (Den.)

SOVIET UNION

Alaska (U.S.)

CANADA

ICELAND

Area of Inset

SOVIET UNION

MANCHURIA

CHINA

JAPAN
Iwo Jima
Feb.-March 1945

Midway, June 1942

UNITED STATES

MOROCCO

Allieds land, November 1942

El Alamein November 1942

IRAN

INDIA

BURMA

Okinawa, April-June 1945

Hawaiian Islands (U.S.)

MEXICO

ALGERIA

FRENCH WEST AFRICA

LIBYA

EGYPT

BRITISH SOMALILAND

INDOCHINA

Pearl Harbor, December 1941

ETHIOPIA
ITALIAN SOMALILAND

PHILIPPINES

PACIFIC OCEAN

NETH. EAST INDIES

Solomon Islands

BRAZIL

ATLANTIC OCEAN

INDIAN OCEAN

Guadalcanal, August 1942-Feb. 1943

AUSTRALIA

Coral Sea, May 1942

NEW ZEALAND

	Allies		Allied victory
	Axis and Axis occupied		Axis victory
	Neutral countries		

European Front, 1944

GREAT BRITAIN

London

NETH.

Arnhem

Antwerp

Calais

Brussels

Cologne

NORMANDY

BELGIUM

D-Day June 1944

Meuse River

Battle of the Bulge, December 1944

Paris liberated August 1944

Reims

GERMANY

Seine River

Rhine River

FRANCE

SWITZ.

ITALY

SPAIN

The Home Front During the War

The United States went to war against Japan, Germany, and Italy in December 1941. More than 15 million Americans served in the armed forces. African Americans and Mexican Americans enlisted in large numbers. At home, U.S. factories made tanks, planes, and guns. Millions of women took over the jobs of men who were at war.

The U.S. government feared that Japanese Americans might aid Japan. Acting out of fear and prejudice, the government sent more than 110,000 Japanese Americans to crowded prison camps. More than half were citizens of the United States. Yet no Japanese American was ever caught spying. Indeed, thousands served bravely in the armed forces.

▲ *Why do you think the war was called a world war?*

◄ *Like this drill operator, many women took on important jobs during World War II.*

557

The GI Bill

In June 1944, President Franklin Roosevelt signed the GI Bill of Rights. "GI" was a World War II nickname for U.S. soldiers. This law helped veterans, or returning soldiers, begin new lives. Under the GI Bill (shown at left), the U.S. government loaned money to soldiers who had served in the war. Now, veterans could go to college, buy a home, or have some money while they were job hunting.

The bill was a great success. Veterans, like those shown at the right, went to college in record numbers. Between 1944 and 1946,

> **Seventy-eighth Congress of the United States of America;**
>
> **At the Second Session**
>
> Begun and held at the City of Washington on Monday, the tenth day of January, one thousand nine hundred and forty-four
>
> ---
>
> **AN ACT**
>
> To provide Federal Government aid for the readjustment in civilian life of returning World War II veterans.

The War in Europe and Asia

France had fallen to the Germans in 1940. In 1942, U.S. troops joined soldiers from Britain and the Soviet Union. The three were called the Allies. Together, the Allies battled the Axis forces of Germany, Italy, and Japan.

By the spring of 1943, the Allies had driven the Axis out of North Africa. In June 1944, the Allies landed in France. From France, the Allies pushed the Germans east. At the same time, the Soviet army pushed the Germans from the other side. The Germans finally surrendered on May 7, 1945.

As the Allies marched into Germany, they freed people from prisons called concentration camps. Most of the people in these camps were Jews. The Nazis unfairly blamed the Jews for all of Germany's troubles. The Nazis had taken the Jews from

Issues of the Time

Puerto Rico

During World War II the United States fought for democracy around the world. At the same time, the country granted greater freedom to its territories. One of these was Puerto Rico. In 1948, Puerto Ricans elected their own governor. In 1952, Puerto Rico became a self-governing U.S. territory.

> ► *The Allies free prisoners after the war from Mauthausen concentration camp in Austria.*

Conclusion

the number of college students nearly doubled. Some schools became so crowded that students slept in tents. Most students were willing to put up with such hardships.

Under the GI Bill, the government loaned money to veterans who wanted to buy or build houses. Now, millions of veterans could own a home.

The government also paid job counselors to help veterans find jobs. The bill gave veterans an allowance until they did find jobs. In addition, many employers made an effort to hire veterans.

towns all across Europe. They forced them into camps, then tortured and killed them. The Nazis murdered more than six million Jews at these camps. This cruel and inhuman treatment of the Jewish people is known as the **Holocaust** *(HOHL uh kawst)*.

Even after Germany gave up, Japan kept fighting. To defeat Japan, President Harry Truman ordered a new secret weapon used. This weapon, the atomic bomb, was the most powerful bomb ever built. A U.S. plane dropped such a bomb on the city of Hiroshima *(heer oh SHEE muh)* on August 6, 1945. The blast destroyed buildings and killed or badly hurt everyone within four miles of the city. On August 9, a U.S. plane dropped another atomic bomb. This bomb hit the city of Nagasaki *(nah guh SAH kee)*. Less than a month later Japan surrendered.

By the war's end, Europe was in ruins. Japan, the major power in the Pacific, was defeated. The United States came out of the war as a world military leader, a **superpower**. Only one other superpower challenged its might—the Soviet Union.

REVIEW

1. **FOCUS** How did World War II affect the United States?
2. **CITIZENSHIP** How were Japanese Americans treated unfairly during the war?
3. **CRITICAL THINKING** How did the GI Bill help veterans after the war?

4. **WRITING ACTIVITY** Imagine you are a fifth grader during World War II writing in your diary. Your father is at war and your mother is working in a factory. Write how you feel about the war, and explain how it has changed your life.

| Harry S Truman **1945-1953** | **Landmark:** The Montgomery Bus Boycott | John F. Kennedy **1961-1963** | Richard M. Nixon **1969-1974** |

| | 1950 | 1955 | 1960 | 1965 | 1970 | 1975 |

| **Presidents** | Dwight D. Eisenhower **1953-1961** | Lyndon B. Johnson **1963-1969** | Gerald R. Ford **1974-1977** |

SECTION 6

The Struggle for Equality

Key Term

- civil rights

▼ *Thurgood Marshall (below, center) helped win the* Brown v. Board of Education of Topeka *case. Marshall later became a member of the U.S. Supreme Court.*

To reach her school in Topeka, Kansas, nine-year-old Linda Brown walked over train tracks. She walked around parked trains. Then she took a bus for nearly two miles. Only a few blocks from her house was another school. But Linda was not allowed to go to that school. It was for white students only. Linda was an African American.

In 1951, black students and white students could not go to the same school in many parts of the United States. Usually, African Americans were forced to go to schools that were not as good as those for white students. Linda Brown and her father took their case to court. Their lawyer, Thurgood Marshall, argued that schools should take children of all races. In 1954, the Supreme Court sided with the Browns.

The Fight for Equality

African Americans had long been denied their **civil rights,** the right to fair and equal treatment. The Supreme Court's ruling in *Brown* v. *Board of Education of Topeka* was one of the most important victories for the civil rights movement. The ruling encouraged many thousands of African Americans as they struggled for equality. African Americans had fought bravely for freedom in other lands during World War II. After the war, many returned to fight for their own rights at home.

The Montgomery Bus Boycott

The Montgomery, Alabama, bus boycott of 1955–1956 protested against the unfair treatment of African Americans. A boycott is the refusal to buy or use something. This year-long struggle changed the civil rights movement.

On Montgomery's buses, African Americans had to sit at the back of the bus. If all the seats for whites in front were taken, African Americans had to give up their seats. For months, African American leaders had planned a boycott of the buses to protest this unfair treatment. They finally put their plan into action after the arrest of Rosa Parks on December 1, 1955. That day, Mrs. Parks refused to give up her seat to a white man. The bus driver left the bus and summoned a police officer who arrested Mrs. Parks and took her to jail. The picture below shows police taking her fingerprints at the jail.

African American leaders met at the Dexter Avenue Baptist Church to discuss her arrest. The minister of the church was Dr. Martin Luther King, Jr. The leaders asked African Americans to show their support for Mrs. Parks by boycotting Montgomery's buses.

The African Americans of Montgomery responded. For over a year, they refused to ride buses, and instead walked to and from their jobs. Some formed car pools like those below, who are waiting for rides. The police arrested King and other boycotters, who were charged with disrupting business. King's house was even bombed. Still, African Americans refused to ride the buses.

In December 1956, the Montgomery bus company changed its unfair rules. By the end of the month, African Americans were again riding the buses—and sitting where they chose. Their boycott was an important victory in the fight for equal rights.

561

1955, Police arrest Rosa Parks in Montgomery, Alabama, for not giving up her bus seat to a white man. Her arrest sparks the Montgomery bus boycott.

1963, Martin Luther King, Jr. organizes a civil rights march in Washington, D.C. More than 60,000 marchers show their support.

1956	1960	1964	1968

1954, In *Brown versus the Board of Education* of Topeka, U.S. Supreme Court rules that segregated schools are illegal.

1964, Congress passes the Civil Rights Act of 1964.

1965, The Voting Rights Act of 1965 makes it easier for African Americans in the South to vote.

African Americans Continue to Struggle

In the 1950s and 1960s, African Americans demanded an end to segregation, the policy of keeping people of different races apart. Few people worked harder for this goal than did Martin Luther King, Jr. He taught his followers to avoid violence. Yet he also taught them not to obey unfair laws. African Americans used many methods to protest segregation. In the spring of 1963, King organized a peaceful march in Birmingham, Alabama, to protest the city's unfair treatment of African Americans. Police tried to stop the marchers with dogs, clubs, and fire hoses. Still, most protesters didn't fight back.

Another important African American leader of this time was Malcolm X. Like King, he also wanted equality for African Americans. However, Malcolm X believed in using many methods to gain equality, including forming separate African American communities.

In the summer of 1963, Dr. King helped organize a huge march and rally in Washington, D.C. He wanted a big show of support for a civil rights bill then in Congress.

▲ *Whites joined with African Americans (above) to protest unfair treatment. Martin Luther King, Jr., (right) led a march for equal rights in Washington, D.C. In the inset photo, King is shown with his wife, Coretta Scott King.*

562

Conclusion

On August 28, more than 200,000 people from all over the nation gathered near the Lincoln Memorial. It was the greatest rally for civil rights that Washington had ever seen.

There King gave his most famous speech, "I Have a Dream." He said, "I have a dream that my four little children will one day live in a nation where they will not be judged by the color of their skin but by the content of their character."

Congress did pass the act, called the Civil Rights Act of 1964. The act outlawed segregation in all public places. Employers could no longer turn someone down for a job because of race, sex, or the country they came from. A year later, Congress passed the Voting Rights Act. Under this act, whites could no longer prevent black citizens from voting.

Today, African Americans still struggle for equal rights. However, they no longer have the leadership of Martin Luther King, Jr., or Malcolm X in this fight. Both men were assassinated, or murdered, in the 1960s.

Women Fight for Their Rights

Like African Americans, women too have long protested against unfair treatment. A powerful women's movement grew during the 1960s and 1970s. Women fought to have the same rights as men. Women wanted good jobs and equal pay.

In 1972, Congress passed the Equal Rights Amendment, or the ERA. It promised women "equality of rights." However, the amendment needed to be approved by 38 states. Only 35 approved it, so the amendment did not become part of the Constitution.

Still, women have made progress. More women than ever before have been entering law school and medical school. Today women work as astronauts, firefighters, and state governors. However, the fight for equality is not over. Women continue to fight for equal wages and the right to work in whatever jobs they want.

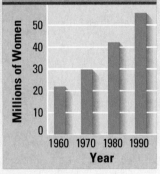

Women in the Work Force

◄ *As women demanded equal opportunites, new jobs opened up for them. These were jobs women had not held before. In the photo on the left, a woman works as a helicopter mechanic for the U.S. Army.*

563

The Wider Struggle for Rights

African Americans and women are not the only groups who have had to fight for equal rights. Many other groups have also worked for their rightful share of the American dream.

Among them were Hispanic Americans—Americans of Spanish-speaking heritage. Hispanics have fought for equality in education, in land ownership, and in many other areas. Many Hispanics are farm workers in the West. They barely make enough money to support their families. To end their poverty, César Chávez worked to form a union for farm workers. This union, the United Farm Workers of America (UFW), continues to help farm workers get better pay and working conditions.

Many Native Americans also fought against unfair treatment. Since settlers began moving west, the U.S. government had taken away Native American lands. Thousands of Native Americans were forced to live on reservations. Native Americans wanted the land returned to them. They also wanted more say about how their reservations were run.

In 1969, for only the third time, a Native American became Commissioner of Indian Affairs. In 1974, Congress passed the Indian Self-Determination and Education Assistance Act. This act gave Native Americans more control over programs on their own lands. The government also restored some land to Native Americans in Maine, New Mexico, Alaska, and Washington State.

▼ *Other groups also struggled for equality. Daniel Inouye (top photo), an Asian American, became the senator from Hawaii. Leaders like José Angel Gutierrez of Texas (left, middle photo) fought to win political power for Hispanic Americans.*

➤ *Native Americans protested unfair treatment at the Capitol in Washington, D.C.*

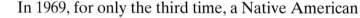

REVIEW

1. **FOCUS** What methods have Americans used to win their rights?

2. **HISTORY** What was the result of the *Brown* v. *Board of Education of Topeka* Supreme Court case? Why was this result important?

3. **CRITICAL THINKING** How did Martin Luther King, Jr., and Malcolm X differ in their fight for civil rights?

4. **WRITING ACTIVITY** Imagine you are an African American in Montgomery, Alabama, in 1955. Write an eyewitness account of the Montgomery bus boycott.

564

Conclusion

Harry S. Truman **1945-1953** ⎪ Lyndon B. Johnson **1963-1969** ⎪ James E. Carter, Jr. **1977-1981** ⎪ George H. Bush **1989-1993**

| 1945 | 1950 | 1955 | 1960 | 1965 | 1970 | 1975 | 1980 | 1985 | 1990 |

Presidents ⎪ Dwight D. Eisenhower **1953-1961** ⎪ Richard M. Nixon **1969-1974** ⎪ Ronald W. Reagan **1981-1989**

⎪ John F. Kennedy **1961-1963** ⎪ Gerald R. Ford **1974-1977**

S E C T I O N   7

The Cold War and Vietnam

I n the 1950s, the air-raid siren screamed in most schools several times a year. Writer Annie Dillard remembers that time well: "When the . . . siren sounded our teachers stopped talking and led us to the school basement. There the gym teachers . . . showed us how to lean in and fold our arms over our heads."

Many Americans feared that the Soviet Union might start a war and drop an atomic bomb on the United States. People in the Soviet Union had that same fear of the United States.

THINKING FOCUS

How did the Vietnam War affect the United States at home and abroad?

Key Terms

- Cold War
- nuclear arms
- arms race

◄ *School children of the 1950s sometimes hid beneath their desks during air-raid drills. Do you think this would have protected them from an atomic bomb explosion?*

The Superpower Rivalry

The United States and the Soviet Union came out of World War II as superpowers. The United States had powerful weapons, and factories unhurt by the war. The Soviet Union, however, had lost more than 20 million people in the war. Soviet leaders feared another attack from the West. They used their huge army to control Eastern Europe. Soviet leaders hoped to build a safe zone between their lands and the West.

565

The Soviets also hoped to spread their form of government, communism, to Eastern Europe and the world. The United States wanted to stop communism. This conflict turned into the **Cold War.** This was a war of political beliefs and the threat of military power. The Cold War never turned into actual fighting, or a "hot war," between the superpowers.

The United States became the first country to equip itself with **nuclear arms,** atomic weapons that can destroy everything for miles around. Trying to match the United States, the Soviet government began building its own nuclear arms. Thus began an **arms race.** Each side tried to build greater armies and more powerful bombs. If nations ever fought a war with these bombs, they could destroy the world.

The Fighting in Vietnam

After World War II, communists won power in several Asian countries, including China. In 1950, communists from North Korea invaded South Korea. The United States sent soldiers to stop them. Although communists did not take over South Korea, millions of people died in the fighting.

In Vietnam, communists drove out French colonial rulers in 1954. The communists won control of North Vietnam. The United States

▼ *The map below shows the division of Vietnam into North and South Vietnam. From 1964 to 1973, U.S. ground troops helped the South Vietnamese government battle the North Vietnamese and a group called the Viet Cong. The map shows major battles of the 1968 Tet Offensive. Right, a U.S. helicopter lands on rugged Vietnamese terrain.*

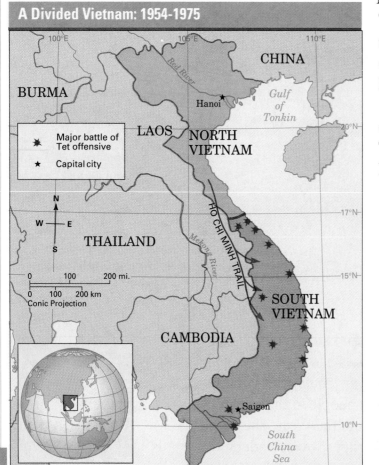

A Divided Vietnam: 1954-1975

100°E   105°E   110°E

CHINA

Red River

BURMA

Hanoi ★

Gulf of Tonkin

LAOS   NORTH VIETNAM   20°N

★ Major battle of Tet offensive

★ Capital city

N
W — E
S

THAILAND

Mekong River

HO CHI MINH TRAIL

17°N

0   100   200 mi.
0   100   200 km
Conic Projection

15°N

★ SOUTH VIETNAM

CAMBODIA

★ Saigon

10°N

South China Sea

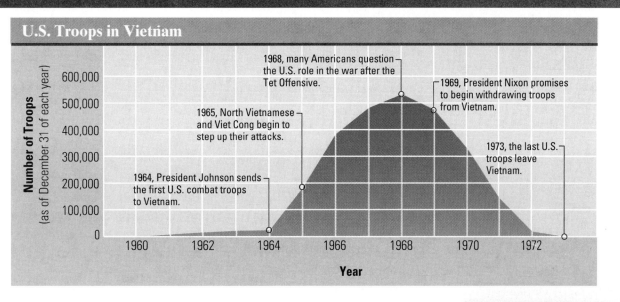

U.S. Troops in Vietnam

Number of Troops (as of December 31 of each year)

600,000
500,000
400,000
300,000
200,000
100,000
0

1968, many Americans question the U.S. role in the war after the Tet Offensive.

1969, President Nixon promises to begin withdrawing troops from Vietnam.

1965, North Vietnamese and Viet Cong begin to step up their attacks.

1973, the last U.S. troops leave Vietnam.

1964, President Johnson sends the first U.S. combat troops to Vietnam.

1960   1962   1964   1966   1968   1970   1972

Year

supported non-communist leaders in South Vietnam. The South Vietnamese leaders were unpopular, though. Many South Vietnamese also began to favor the communists.

In the 1950s the United States began to support the government of South Vietnam. Until the early 1960s the United States sent money, arms, and several hundred advisers to aid South Vietnam. Those early U.S. advisers were sent to train South Vietnam's army, not to fight.

In 1963, Lyndon Johnson became President. He did not want to lose Vietnam to the communists. A year later, Johnson told Congress that the North Vietnamese had attacked U.S. ships. Congress voted to allow Johnson to send troops to Vietnam. Over the next four years, the number of U.S. soldiers in Vietnam increased from 23,000 to 536,000.

Opposition to the War

At first, most Americans felt sure the United States would quickly win in Vietnam. The war dragged on, though. More and more U.S. soldiers died. Americans began to wonder why they were sending young men to fight in a war so far away. They knew that many South Vietnamese did not even support their own government.

Around the Vietnamese New Year, or Tet, in 1968, the fighting got worse. The North Vietnamese and the Viet Cong, the communist fighters in South Vietnam, made a number of attacks against the South. These attacks became known as the Tet Offensive. Thousands of U.S. and South Vietnamese

▲ *The graph shows the number of U.S. troops in Vietnam. President Lyndon B. Johnson (above) sent the first U.S. combat troops to Vietnam.*

567

War Protests, 1970

People in the United States disagreed bitterly over the Vietnam War. At first, mostly college students staged protests (left) and wore shirts and buttons (right) to demand an end to the war. They also wanted to end the draft, the government's way of picking men for the military. In April 1965, about 20,000 students marched in a protest in Washington, D.C.

As the war went on, people of all ages joined the protests. Many worked to elect

soldiers died during this offensive. Many Americans began to wonder if the United States could really win this war. Others argued that the United States was not trying hard enough to win.

Richard Nixon became the President in 1969. He promised to make peace in Vietnam. Soon after his election, Nixon started bringing some U.S. troops home. However, he also ordered U.S. troops into the nearby country of Cambodia to destroy North Vietnamese bases there. The fighting continued. In the spring of 1972, Nixon ordered U.S. planes to bomb Hanoi, the capital of North Vietnam. But the North Vietnamese still did not give up.

▼ *Even today, visitors leave flowers at the Vietnam Veterans Memorial in Washington, D.C.*

The Results of the War

The U.S. government finally realized that it could not win. The North Vietnamese, too, were tired of the war. In January 1973, the United States, South Vietnam, North Vietnam, and the Viet Cong signed a peace treaty in Paris.

On March 29, 1973, the last U.S. ground forces left Vietnam. South Vietnam then had to defend itself. The

anti-war candidates to Congress. Others formed groups and marched to protest against the war. Then, on May 9, 1970, in a major demonstration, 60,000 to 100,000 Americans came to Washington, D.C., to march against the Vietnam War.

Some Americans disagreed with the protesters, however. They supported the U.S. effort in the war. In fact, they wanted the United States to fight even harder.

Still, the government got the protesters' message. Their marches, letters, and pleas had an impact on the government's decision to bring the soldiers home.

fighting started again. In late 1974, North Vietnamese troops invaded South Vietnam. Less than a year later, South Vietnam gave up. To many Americans, the war seemed a failure. It had cost the United States more than $150 billion. More than 57,000 United States soldiers and more than one million South Vietnamese had died in the war.

The End of the Cold War

Although the war in Vietnam ended, the Cold War between the United States and the Soviet Union went on. Both countries continued the arms race. By the early 1990s, though, the Soviet system of government changed. Communism was abandoned and the central government ended. The Soviet Union crumbled. The Cold War was over.

REVIEW

1. **FOCUS** How did the Vietnam War affect the United States at home and abroad?

2. **HISTORY** What was the arms race? Why did many people fear it?

3. **CRITICAL THINKING** Why did some Americans oppose the Vietnam War while others supported it?

4. **WRITING ACTIVITY** Imagine you are a newspaper reporter of today writing a story on how people felt about the Vietnam War. Make a list of questions you might need to ask. Get answers from your parents or another adult who feels comfortable talking about the war. Use the answers to write your story.

SECTION 8

A Global Age

THINKING
FOCUS

In what ways is the United States now linked to the rest of the world?

Key Term

- multicultural

➤ *Moon landings (right) and supersonic jets (below) help change people's ideas of time and distance.*

On July 20, 1969, astronaut Neil Armstrong stepped from his spacecraft onto the surface of the moon. No one had ever walked on the moon before. As his foot touched the moon, he said, "That's one small step for a man, one giant leap for mankind."

Armstrong stared across space at the planet Earth. It looked beautiful and distant. From more than 220,000 miles away, Armstrong could not see any countries or borders. He saw just one world. Armstrong knew that his moon landing was a great achievement for the whole human race.

Links Around the World

When Armstrong landed on the moon, millions around the world took that first step with him. As they watched on their televisions, the moon suddenly seemed much closer.

After the moon landing, people began to think of distance in a new way. In 1620, the *Mayflower* took more than nine weeks to sail from England to Massachusetts. Today, you can fly from London to Boston, nearly the same distance, in less than seven hours. Communication has also speeded up. In the 1990s, offices around the world rely on fax (facsimile) machines. These machines send copies over phone lines. In a few minutes, a fax machine can send a copy of a letter or picture around the world.

Improved travel and communication help people around the world learn about one another. People of different countries nowadays often wear the same kinds of clothes. They play the same sports and eat the same foods. A visitor to Japan can see a baseball game and eat a hamburger. A visitor to the United States can buy a watch made in Switzerland. The same visitor can then eat in a Chinese restaurant.

The Immigration Act of 1965

In 1965, Congress passed an immigration act that produced great change in the United States. Under this law, each year the government allowed 170,000 people from countries in Africa, Asia, Australia, and Europe to come and live in the United States. Another 120,000 immigrants could come from other countries in the Americas. Before this 1965 law, U.S. immigration laws favored people coming from Northern and Western Europe. After 1965, thousands from China, India, and Korea began coming to the United States. Many immigrants, like those shown below, have become U.S. citizens.

In 1990, most immigrants who came to the United States were from Mexico. Large numbers of people also came from Asia, the Caribbean islands, Central America, and South America. With all these new immigrants, the United States has become even more **multicultural,** that is, made up of people with different ethnic backgrounds.

571

The Global Economy

Many things you own probably come from other countries. You may have a radio made in Japan. You may have sandals made in Brazil or a cotton shirt from India.

Trade links countries around the world. Nations buy food that might not be available in their own country. In turn, these nations sell machines and goods to countries whose people do not make those things. Some important items that the United States exports, or sells to other countries, are planes, cars, machine parts, and corn. Items the United States imports, or buys from other countries, include cars, computers, cameras, and televisions.

Madras fabric for making brightly colored clothing from India

Goods from Around the World

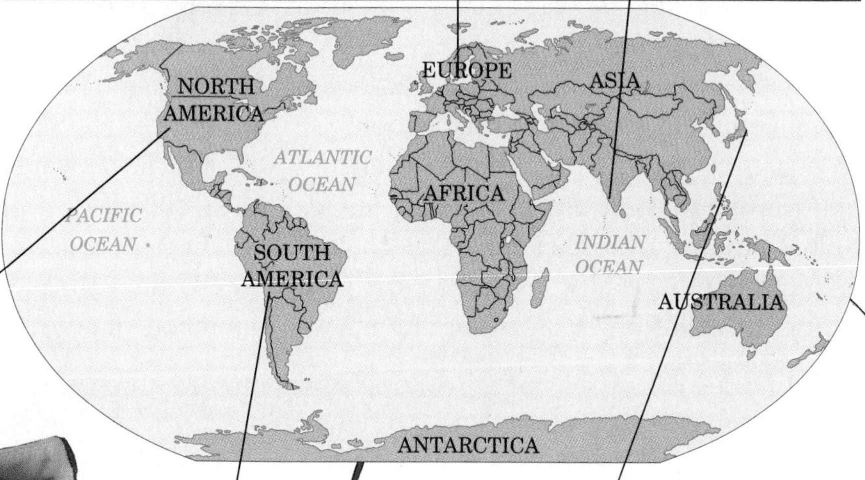

➤ *Where do some of your favorite goods come from? Many watches come from Switzerland, and Japan exports personal stereos. Your high-tops might have been made in the United States.*

NORTH AMERICA

EUROPE

ASIA

ATLANTIC OCEAN

AFRICA

PACIFIC OCEAN

SOUTH AMERICA

INDIAN OCEAN

AUSTRALIA

ANTARCTICA

Wool from Peru

Conclusion

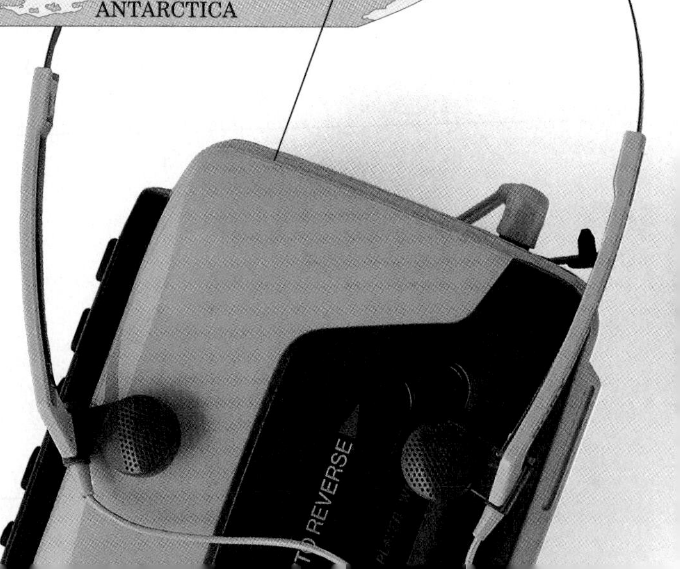

A Look Forward

An important concern across the world today is the need to protect the environment. Astronaut Neil Armstrong once said, "the earth itself is a spacecraft. . . . If you're going to run a spaceship you've got to be pretty cautious about how you use your resources . . . and how you treat your spacecraft." In other words, people have to take care of the earth to continue to live here. When Armstrong walked on the moon in 1969, he noted how beautiful and fragile the earth looked.

The first people who came to North America, Native Americans, took good care of the earth. They knew the importance of the land. They respected the water, animals, and plants. Today, some people treat the earth carelessly. They dump paper, food, and other wastes on streets, in forests, and in rivers.

In the years ahead, we can be sure that the world will keep changing. One day people may finally learn to take care of the earth. They may solve many of today's problems. New problems will surely arise, though. Through it all, people will still hope and work for better lives.

◄ *In what ways might the world be a different place when today's fifth graders become grown-ups?*

REVIEW

1. **FOCUS** In what ways is the United States now linked to the rest of the world?

2. **ECONOMICS** How do imports and exports link nations of the world?

3. **CRITICAL THINKING** Airplanes and fax machines have helped people around the world learn more about each other. What are some other things that help connect people around the world? Why are these items important?

4. **ACTIVITY** Go to your closet and read the labels inside several pieces of clothing. Make a list of where each piece of clothing was made.

Conclusion Review

Reviewing Key Terms

alliance (p. 544)
arms race (p. 566)
assembly line (p. 549)
civil rights (p. 560)
Cold War (p. 566)
communism (p. 546)
Depression (p. 552)
dictator (p. 556)
Holocaust (p. 559)

nuclear arms (p. 566)
multicultural (p. 571)
New Deal (p. 553)
pacifist (p. 546)
progressive (p. 540)
stock (p. 551)
suffrage (p. 542)
superpower (p. 559)

A. On your own paper, write a sentence using each pair of key terms.
1. Depression, New Deal
2. dictator, Holocaust
3. Cold War, arms race
4. superpower, nuclear arms
5. progressives, suffrage

B. Write *True* or *False* for each statement. Then rewrite false statements to make them true.
1. Due to population losses, the United States is less multicultural than ever.
2. Before World War I, pacifists believed in forming alliances with European nations.
3. Communism is a political system that encourages individual ownership of businesses.
4. The assembly line increased the time workers spent making a product.
5. Stock is a share in a company.
6. Civil rights means expecting others to be polite to you.

Using Critical Thinking

1. Imagine Jane Addams is visiting a city today. What improvements might she see in the city? What conditions might she recognize from her own time?
2. Dr. Martin Luther King, Jr., said to millions of Americans, "I have a dream." What is your dream for the United States? Describe the way you would like the United States to be in the future. Do you think it is likely that this dream will come true in your lifetime? Explain.
3. In what ways have immigrants who have come to the United States in recent years contributed to the nation?

Preparing for Citizenship

1. **COLLECTING INFORMATION** Read a library book about the 1930s Depression, such as *Roll of Thunder, Hear My Cry* by Mildred Taylor. Make notes of what you find interesting. Then share your information with the class.
2. **ARTS ACTIVITY** During the 1920s, many inventions changed the way people lived. Think of an invention that would make your life easier. Present your invention to the class. You can draw a picture, draw a diagram, or make a model. Explain how the invention works when you show it to the class.
3. **COLLABORATIVE LEARNING** In a small group, plan and present a panel discussion about the pros and cons of extending the right to vote to all Americans over the age of sixteen.

Conclusion

Time/Space Databank

Declaration of Independence	576
Constitution	580
Minipedia	600
Canada	600
Exploration	601
Flag	602
Gettysburg Address	604
Immigration	605
Indian, American	606
Mexico	609
President of the United States	610
United States	611
Washington, George	613
Atlas	614
World: Political	614
World: Physical	616
United States: Overview	618
United States: Political	620
United States: Physical	622
North America: Political/Physical	624
United States: Population Density, 1980	625
United States: Time Zones	625
United States: Climate	626
United States: Vegetation	626
United States: Precipitation	627
United States: Land Use and Resources	627
Glossary of Geographic Terms	628
Gazetteer	630
Biographical Dictionary	633
Glossary	638

U.S. Custom House, 1805.

★ ★ ★ ★ ★ ★ ★ ★ ★

The Declaration of Independence

In Congress, July 4, 1776
The unaimous declaration of the thirteen united States of America

INTRODUCTION*

In the Declaration of Independence, the colonists explained why they were breaking away from Britain. They believed they had the right to form their own country.

When, in the course of human events, it becomes necessary for one people to dissolve the political bands which have connected them with another, and to assume, among the powers of the earth, the separate and equal station to which the laws of nature and of nature's God entitle them, a decent respect to the opinions of mankind requires that they should declare the causes which impel them to the separation.

BASIC RIGHTS

The opening part of the Declaration is very famous. It says that all people are equal. Everyone has certain basic rights that are unalienable. That means that these rights cannot be taken away. Governments are formed to protect these basic rights. If a government does not do this, then the people have a right to begin a new one.

We hold these truths to be self-evident: That all men are created equal, that they are endowed by their Creator with certain unalienable rights; that among these are life, liberty, and the pursuit of happiness; that, to secure these rights, governments are instituted among men, deriving their just powers from the consent of the governed; that whenever any form of government becomes destructive of these ends, it is the right of the people to alter or to abolish it, and to institute new government, laying its foundation on such principles, and organizing its powers in such form, as to them shall seem most likely to effect their safety and happiness. Prudence, indeed, will dictate that governments long established should not be changed for light and transient causes; and accordingly all experience hath shown that mankind are more disposed to suffer, while evils are sufferable, than to right themselves by abolishing the forms to which they are accustomed. But when a long train of abuses and usurpations, pursuing invariably the same object, evinces a design to reduce them under absolute despotism, it is their right, it is their duty, to throw off such government, and to provide new guards for their future security. Such has been the patient sufferance of these colonies; and such is now the necessity which constrains them to alter their former systems of government. The history of the present King of Great Britain is a history of repeated injuries and usurpations, all having in direct object the establishment of an absolute tyranny over these states. To prove this, let facts be submitted to a candid world.

Forming a new government meant ending the colonial ties to the king. The writers listed the wrongs of King George III to prove the need for their actions.

*Titles have been added to the Declaration to make it easier to read. These titles are not in the original document.

★ ★ ★ ★ ★ ★ ★ ★ ★

CHARGES AGAINST THE KING

He has refused his assent to laws, the most wholesome and necessary for the public good.

He has forbidden his governors to pass laws of immediate and pressing importance, unless suspended in their operation till his assent should be obtained; and, when so suspended, he has utterly neglected to attend to them.

He has refused to pass other laws for the accommodation of large districts of people, unless those people would relinquish the right of representation in the legislature, a right inestimable to them, and formidable to tyrants only.

He has called together legislative bodies at places unusual, uncomfortable, and distant from the depository of their public records, for the sole purpose of fatiguing them into compliance with his measures.

He has dissolved representative houses repeatedly, for opposing, with manly firmness, his invasions on the rights of the people.

He has refused for a long time, after such dissolutions, to cause others to be elected; whereby the legislative powers, incapable of annihilation, have returned to the people at large for their exercise; the state remaining, in the mean time, exposed to all the dangers of invasions from without and convulsions within.

He has endeavored to prevent the population of these states; for that purpose obstructing the laws for the naturalization of foreigners; refusing to pass others to encourage their migration hither, and raising the conditions of new appropriations of lands.

He has obstructed the administration of justice, by refusing his assent to laws for establishing judiciary powers.

He has made judges dependent on his will alone, for the tenure of their offices, and the amount of payment of their salaries.

He has erected a multitude of new offices, and sent hither swarms of officers to harass our people and eat out their substance.

He has kept among us, in times of peace, standing armies, without the consent of our legislatures.

He has affected to render the military independent of, and superior to, the civil power.

He has combined with others to subject us to a jurisdiction foreign to our constitution and unacknowledged by our laws, giving his assent to their acts of pretended legislation:

For quartering large bodies of armed troops among us;

For protecting them, by a mock trial, from punishment for any murders which they should commit on the inhabitants of these states;

For cutting off our trade with all parts of the world;

For imposing taxes on us without our consent;

For depriving us, in many cases, of the benefits of trial by jury;

Colonists said the king had not let the colonies make their own laws. He had limited the people's representation in their assemblies.

The king had made colonial assemblies meet at unusual times and places. This made going to assembly meetings hard for colonial representatives.

In some cases the king stopped the assembly from meeting at all.

The king stopped people from moving to the colonies and into new western lands.

The king prevented the colonies from choosing their own judges. Instead, he sent over judges who depended on him for their jobs and pay.

The king kept British soldiers in the colonies, even though the colonists had not asked for them.

The king and Parliament had taxed the colonists without their consent. This was one of the most important reasons the colonists were angry at Britain.

★ ★ ★ ★ ★ ★ ★ ★ ★ ★ ★ ★

For transporting us beyond seas, to be tried for pretended offenses;

For abolishing the free system of English laws in a neighboring province, establishing therein an arbitrary government, and enlarging its boundaries, so as to render it at once an example and fit instrument for introducing the same absolute rule into these colonies;

For taking away our charters, abolishing our most valuable laws, and altering fundamentally the forms of our governments.

For suspending our own legislatures, and declaring themselves invested with power to legislate for us in all cases whatsoever.

He has abdicated government here, by declaring us out of his protection and waging war against us.

He has plundered our seas, ravaged our coasts, burned our towns, and destroyed the lives of our people.

He is at this time transporting large armies of foreign mercenaries to complete the works of death, desolation, and tyranny already begun with circumstances of cruelty and perfidy scarcely paralleled in the most barbarous ages, and totally unworthy the head of a civilized nation.

He has constrained our fellow-citizens, taken captive on the high seas, to bear arms against their country, to become the executioners of their friends and brethren, or to fall themselves by their hands.

He has excited domestic insurrection among us, and has endeavored to bring on the inhabitants of our frontiers, the merciless Indian savages, whose known rule of warfare is an undistinguished destruction of all ages, sexes, and conditions.

RESPONSE TO THE KING

In every stage of these oppressions we have petitioned for redress in the most humble terms; our repeated petitions have been answered only by repeated injury. A prince, whose character is thus marked by every act which may define a tyrant, is unfit to be the ruler of a free people.

Nor have we been wanting in our attentions to our British brethren. We have warned them, from time to time, of attempts by their legislature to extend an unwarrantable jurisdiction over us. We have reminded them of the circumstances of our emigration and settlement here. We have appealed to their native justice and magnanimity; and we have conjured them, by the ties of our common kindred, to disavow these usurpations, which would inevitably interrupt our connections and correspondence. They, too, have been deaf to the voice of justice and of consanguinity. We must, therefore, acquiesce in the necessity which denounces our separation, and hold them, as we hold the rest of mankind, enemies in war, in peace friends.

The colonists felt that the king had waged war on them.

The king had hired German soldiers and sent them to the colonies to keep order.

The colonists said that they had asked the king to change his policies, but he had not listened to them.

★ ★ ★ ★ ★ ★ ★ ★ ★ ★ ★ ★

INDEPENDENCE

We, therefore, the representatives of the United States of America, in General Congress assembled, appealing to the Supreme Judge of the world for the rectitude of our intentions, do, in the name and by the authority of the good people of these colonies, solemnly publish and declare, that these United Colonies are, and of right ought to be, FREE AND INDEPENDENT STATES; that they are absolved from all allegiance to the British crown, and that all political connection between them and the state of Great Britain is, and ought to be, totally dissolved; and that, as free and independent states, they have full power to levy war, conclude peace, contract alliances, establish commerce, and do all other acts and things which independent states may of right do. And for the support of this declaration, with a firm reliance on the protection of Divine Providence, we mutually pledge to each other our lives, our fortunes, and our sacred honor.

The writers declared that the colonies were free and independent states, equal to the world's other states. They had the powers to make war and peace and to trade with other countries.

John Hancock

The signers pledged their lives to the support of this Declaration. The Continental Congress ordered the Declaration of Independence to be read in all the states and to the army.

NEW HAMPSHIRE
Josiah Bartlett
William Whipple
Matthew Thornton

MASSACHUSETTS
John Adams
Samuel Adams
Robert Treat Paine
Elbridge Gerry

NEW YORK
William Floyd
Philip Livingston
Francis Lewis
Lewis Morris

RHODE ISLAND
Stephen Hopkins
William Ellery

NEW JERSEY
Richard Stockton
John Witherspoon
Francis Hopkinson
John Hart
Abraham Clark

PENNSYLVANIA
Robert Morris
Benjamin Rush
Benjamin Franklin
John Morton
George Clymer
James Smith
George Taylor
James Wilson
George Ross

DELAWARE
Caesar Rodney
George Read
Thomas McKean

MARYLAND
Samuel Chase
William Paca
Thomas Stone
Charles Carroll of Carrollton

NORTH CAROLINA
William Hooper
Joseph Hewes
John Penn

VIRGINIA
George Wythe
Richard Henry Lee
Thomas Jefferson
Benjamin Harrison
Thomas Nelson, Jr.
Francis Lightfoot Lee
Carter Braxton

SOUTH CAROLINA
Edward Rutledge
Thomas Heyward, Jr.
Thomas Lynch, Jr.
Arthur Middleton

CONNECTICUT
Roger Sherman
Samuel Huntington
William Williams
Oliver Wolcott

GEORGIA
Button Gwinnett
Lyman Hall
George Walton

The Constitution of the United States

PREAMBLE
INTRODUCTION*

Introduction The Preamble states the purposes of the Constitution. The writers wanted to strengthen the national government and to secure peace for the United States.

We the people of the United States, in order to form a more perfect union, establish justice, insure domestic tranquility, provide for the common defense, promote the general welfare, and secure the blessings of liberty to ourselves and our posterity, do ordain and establish this Constitution for the United States of America.

ARTICLE 1
LEGISLATIVE BRANCH

SECTION 1. CONGRESS

Congress Section 1 gives Congress the power to make laws. Congress has two parts, the House of Representatives and the Senate.

All legislative powers herein granted shall be vested in a Congress of the United States, which shall consist of a Senate and House of Representatives.

SECTION 2. HOUSE OF REPRESENTATIVES

Election and Term of Members Citizens elect the members of the House of Representatives every two years.

Election and Term of Members *The House of Representatives shall be composed of members chosen every second year by the people of the several States, and the electors in each State shall have the qualifications requisite for electors of the most numerous branch of the State legislature.*

Qualifications Representatives must be at least 25 years old. They must have been United States citizens for at least seven years. They also must live in the state they represent.

Qualifications *No person shall be a representative who shall not have attained to the age of twenty-five years, and been seven years a citizen of the United States, and who shall not, when elected, be an inhabitant of that State in which he shall be chosen.*

Number of Representatives per State The number of representatives each state has is based on its population. The biggest states have the most representatives. Each state must have at least one representative.

Number of Representatives per State *Representatives and direct taxes shall be apportioned among the several States which may be included within this Union, according to their respective numbers,* which shall be determined by adding to the whole number of free persons, including those bound to service for a term of years, and excluding Indians not taxed, three-fifths of all other persons.** *The actual enumeration shall be made within*

---

* The titles of the Preamble, and of each article, section, clause, and amendment have been added to make the Constitution easier to read. These titles are not in the original document.

** Parts of the Constitution are printed in regular type rather than italics to show that they are not in force anymore. They have been changed by amendments or they no longer apply.

★ ★ ★ ★ ★ ★ ★ ★ ★

three years after the first meeting of the Congress of the United States, and within every subsequent term of ten years, in such manner as they shall by law direct. The number of representatives shall not exceed one for every thirty thousand, but each State shall have at least one representative; and until such enumeration shall be made, the State of New Hampshire shall be entitled to choose three, Massachusetts eight, Rhode Island and Providence Plantations one, Connecticut five, New York six, New Jersey Four, Pennsylvania eight, Delaware one, Maryland six, Virginia ten, North Carolina five, South Carolina five, and Georgia three.

Vacancies *When vacancies happen in the representation from any State, the executive authority thereof shall issue writs of election to fill such vacancies.*

Special Powers *The House of Representatives shall choose their speaker and other officers, and shall have the sole power of impeachment.*

SECTION 3. SENATE

Number, Term, and Selection of Members *The Senate of the United States shall be composed of two senators from each State, chosen by the legislature thereof, for six years; and each senator shall have one vote.*

Overlapping Terms and Filling Vacancies *Immediately after they shall be assembled in consequence of the first election, they shall be divided as equally as may be into three classes. The seats of the senators of the first class shall be vacated at the expiration of the second year, of the second class at the expiration of the fourth year, and of the third class at the expiration of the sixth year, so that one-third may be chosen every second year;* and if vacancies happen by resignation, or otherwise, during the recess of the legislature of any State, the executive thereof may make temporary appointments until the next meeting of the legislature, which shall then fill such vacancies.

Qualifications *No person shall be a senator who shall not have attained to the age of thirty years, and been nine years a citizen of the United States, and who shall not, when elected, be an inhabitant of that State for which he shall be chosen.*

President of the Senate *The Vice President of the United States shall be President of the Senate, but shall have no vote, unless they be equally divided.*

Other Officers *The Senate shall choose their other officers, and also a President pro tempore, in the absence of the Vice President, or when he shall exercise the office of President of the United States.*

Impeachment Trials *The Senate shall have the sole power to try all impeachments. When sitting for that purpose, they shall be on oath or affirmation. When the President of the United States is tried, the Chief Justice shall preside: and no person shall be*

Number, Term, and Selection of Members In each state, citizens elect two members of the Senate. This gives all states, whether big or small, equal power in the Senate. Senators serve six-year terms. According to the original Constitution, state legislatures choose the senators for their states. Today, however, people elect their senators directly. The Seventeenth Amendment made this change in 1913.

Qualifications Senators must be at least 30 years old and United States citizens for at least nine years. Like representatives, they must live in the state they represent.

President of the Senate The Vice President of the United States acts as the President, or chief officer, of the Senate. The Vice President votes only in cases of a tie.

Impeachment Trials If the House of Representatives impeaches an official with a crime, the Senate holds a trial. If two-thirds of the senators find the official guilty, then the person is removed from office. The only President ever impeached was Andrew Johnson in 1868. He was found not guilty.

convicted without the concurrence of two-thirds of the members present.

Penalties *Judgment in cases of impeachment shall not extend further than to removal from office, and disqualification to hold and enjoy any office of honor, trust or profit under the United States: but the party convicted shall nevertheless be liable and subject to indictment, trial, judgment and punishment, according to law.*

SECTION 4. ELECTIONS AND MEETINGS

Election of Congress *The times, places and manner of holding elections for senators and representatives shall be prescribed in each State by the legislature thereof; but the Congress may at any time by law make or alter such regulations, except as to the places of choosing senators.*

Annual Sessions *The Congress shall assemble at least once in every year, and such meeting shall be on the first Monday in December, unless they shall by law appoint a different day.*

SECTION 5. RULES OF PROCEDURE

Organization *Each house shall be the judge of the elections, returns and qualifications of its own members, and a majority of each shall constitute a quorum to do business; but a smaller number may adjourn from day to day, and may be authorized to compel the attendance of absent members, in such manner, and under such penalties as each house may provide.*

Rules *Each house may determine the rules of its proceedings, punish its members for disorderly behavior, and, with the concurrence of two-thirds, expel a member.*

Journal *Each house shall keep a journal of its proceedings, and from time to time publish the same, excepting such parts as may in their judgment require secrecy; and the yeas and nays of the members of either house on any question shall, at the desire of one-fifth of those present, be entered on the journal.*

Adjournment *Neither house, during the session of Congress, shall, without the consent of the other, adjourn for more than three days, nor to any other place than that in which the two houses shall be sitting.*

SECTION 6. PRIVILEGES AND RESTRICTIONS

Pay and Protection *The senators and representatives shall receive a compensation for their services, to be ascertained by law, and paid out of the treasury of the United States. They shall in all cases, except treason, felony and breach of the peace, be privileged from arrest during their attendance at the session of their respective houses, and in going to and returning from the same; and for any speech or debate in either house, they shall not be questioned in any other place.*

Restrictions *No senator or representative shall, during the time for which he was elected, be appointed to any civil office under the authority of the United States, which shall have been created, or the emoluments thereof shall have been increased during such time; and*

Election of Congress Each state decides where and when to hold elections. Today congressional elections are held in even-numbered years, on the Tuesday after the first Monday in November.

Annual Sessions The Constitution requires Congress to meet at least once a year. In 1933, the Twentieth Amendment moved the required meeting date of Congress to January 3.

Organization A quorum is the smallest number of members that must be present for an organization to hold a meeting. For each house of Congress, this number is the majority, or more than one-half, of its members.

Journal The Constitution requires each house to keep a record of its proceedings. *The Congressional Record* is published every day. It allows any person to look up the votes of his or her representative.

Pay and Protection Congress sets the salaries of its members, and they are paid by the federal government. No member can be arrested for anything he or she says while in office. This protection allows members to speak freely in Congress.

Restrictions Members of Congress cannot hold other federal offices during their terms. This rule protects the checks and balances system set up by the Constitution.

★　★　★　★　★　★　★　★　★

no person holding any office under the United States shall be a member of either house during his continuance in office.

SECTION 7. MAKING LAWS

Tax Bills *All bills for raising revenue shall originate in the House of Representatives; but the Senate may propose or concur with amendments as on other bills.*

Passing a Law *Every bill which shall have passed the House of Representatives and the Senate, shall, before it becomes a law, be presented to the President of the United States; if he approve he shall sign it, but if not he shall return it, with his objections to that house in which it shall have originated, who shall enter the objections at large on their journal, and proceed to reconsider it. If after such reconsideration two-thirds of that house shall agree to pass the bill, it shall be sent, together with the objections, to the other house, by which it shall likewise be reconsidered, and if approved by two-thirds of that house, it shall become a law. But in all such cases the votes of both houses shall be determined by yeas and nays, and the names of the persons voting for and against the bill shall be entered on the journal of each house respectively. If any bill shall not be returned by the President within ten days (Sundays excepted) after it shall have been presented to him, the same shall be a law, in like manner as if he had signed it, unless the Congress by their adjournment prevent its return, in which case it shall not be a law.*

Orders and Resolutions *Every order, resolution, or vote to which the concurrence of the Senate and House of Representatives may be necessary (except on a question of adjournment) shall be presented to the President of the United States; and before the same shall take effect, shall be approved by him, or being disapproved by him, shall be repassed by two-thirds of the Senate and House of Representatives, according to the rules and limitations prescribed in the case of a bill.*

SECTION 8. POWERS DELEGATED TO CONGRESS

Taxation *The Congress shall have power to lay and collect taxes, duties, imposts, and excises, to pay the debts and provide for the common defense and general welfare of the United States; but all duties, imposts and excises shall be uniform throughout the United States;*

Borrowing *To borrow money on the credit of the United States;*

Commerce *To regulate commerce with foreign nations, and among the several States, and with the Indian tribes;*

Naturalization and Bankruptcy *To establish a uniform rule of naturalization, and uniform laws on the subject of bankruptcies through the United States;*

Coins and Measures *To coin money, regulate the value thereof, and of foreign coin, and fix the standard of weights and measures;*

Counterfeiting *To provide for the punishment of counterfeiting the securities and current coin of the United States;*

Post Offices *To establish post offices and post roads;*

Tax Bills A bill is a proposed law. Only the House of Representatives can introduce bills that tax the people.

Passing a Law A bill must be passed by the majority of members in each house of Congress. Then it is sent to the President. If the President signs it, the bill becomes a law.

The President can also veto, or reject, a bill by not signing it. However, if each house of Congress repasses the bill by a two-thirds vote, it becomes a law. Passing a law after the President has vetoed it is called overriding a veto. This process is an important part of the checks and balances system set up by the Constitution.

Orders and Resolutions Congress can also pass orders and resolutions that have the same power as laws. Such acts are also subject to the President's veto.

Taxation Only Congress has the power to collect taxes.

Commerce Congress controls trade with foreign countries.

Naturalization and Bankruptcy Naturalization is the process by which a person from another country becomes a United States citizen. Congress decides the requirements for this procedure.

Copyrights and Patents Patents allow inventors to profit from their work by keeping control over it for a certain number of years. Congress grants patents to encourage scientific research.

Declaring War Only Congress can declare war on another country.

Militia Today the militia is called the National Guard. The National Guard often helps people after floods, tornadoes, and other disasters.

National Capital Congress makes the laws for Washington, D.C., the nation's capital.

Necessary Laws This clause allows Congress to make laws on issues, such as television or radio, that are not mentioned in the Constitution.

Slave Trade This clause was another compromise between the North and the South. It prevented Congress from regulating the slave trade for 20 years. Congress outlawed the slave trade in 1808.

Habeas Corpus A writ of habeas corpus requires the government to either charge a person in jail with a particular crime, or else let the person go free. Except in emergencies, Congress cannot deny the right of a person to a writ.

★ ★ ★ ★ ★ ★ ★ ★ ★

Copyrights and Patents *To promote the progress of science and useful arts by securing for limited times to authors and inventors the exclusive right to their respective writings and discoveries;*

Courts *To constitute tribunals inferior to the Supreme Court;*

Piracy *To define and punish piracies and felonies committed on the high seas, and offenses against the law of nations;*

Declaring War *To declare war, grant letters of marque and reprisal, and make rules concerning captures on land and water;*

Army *To raise and support armies, but no appropriation of money to that use shall be for a longer term than two years;*

Navy *To provide and maintain a navy;*

Military Regulations *To make rules for the government and regulation of the land and naval forces;*

Militia *To provide for calling forth the militia to execute the laws of the Union, suppress insurrections and repel invasions;*

Militia Regulations *To provide for organizing, arming, and disciplining the militia, and for governing such part of them as may be employed in the service of the United States, reserving to the States respectively the appointment of the officers, and the authority of training the militia according to the discipline prescribed by Congress;*

National Capital *To exercise exclusive legislation in all cases whatsoever, over such district (not exceeding ten miles square) as may, by cession of particular States and the acceptance of Congress, become the seat of the government of the United States, and to exercise like authority over all places purchased by the consent of the legislature of the State in which the same shall be, for the erection of forts, magazines, arsenals, dockyards, and other needful buildings; and*

Necessary Laws *To make all laws which shall be necessary and proper for carrying into execution the foregoing powers, and all other powers vested by this Constitution in the government of the United States, or in any department or officer thereof.*

SECTION 9. POWERS DENIED TO CONGRESS

Slave Trade The migration or importation of such persons as any of the States now existing shall think proper to admit, shall not be prohibited by the Congress prior to the year one thousand eight hundred and eight, but a tax or duty may be imposed on such importation, not exceeding ten dollars for each person.

Habeas Corpus *The privilege of the writ of habeas corpus shall not be suspended, unless when in cases of rebellion or invasion the public safety may require it.*

Special Laws *No bill of attainder or ex post facto law shall be passed.*

Direct Taxes *No capitation, or other direct, tax shall be laid, unless in proportion to the census or enumeration herein before directed to be taken.*

★ ★ ★ ★ ★ ★ ★ ★ ★

Export Taxes No tax or duty shall be laid on articles exported from any State.

Ports No preference shall be given by any regulation of commerce or revenue to the ports of one State over those of another; nor shall vessels bound to, or from, one State be obliged to enter, clear, or pay duties in another.

Regulations on Spending No money shall be drawn from the treasury, but in consequence of appropriations made by law; and a regular statement and account of the receipts and expenditures of all public money shall be published from time to time.

Titles of Nobility and Gifts No title of nobility shall be granted by the United States: and no person holding any office of profit or trust under them, shall, without the consent of the Congress, accept of any present, emolument, office, or title, of any kind whatever, from any king, prince, or foreign State.

SECTION 10. POWERS DENIED TO THE STATES

Complete Restrictions No State shall enter into any treaty, alliance, or confederation; grant letters of marque and reprisal; coin money; emit bills of credit; make anything but gold and silver coin a tender in payment of debts; pass any bill of attainder, ex post facto law, or law impairing the obligation of contracts, or grant any title of nobility.

Partial Restrictions No State shall, without the consent of the Congress, lay any imposts or duties on imports or exports, except what may be absolutely necessary for executing its inspection laws: and the net produce of all duties and imposts laid by any State on imports or exports, shall be for the use of the treasury of the United States; and all such laws shall be subject to the revision and control of the Congress.

Other Restrictions No State shall, without the consent of Congress, lay any duty of tonnage, keep troops, or ships of war in time of peace, enter into any agreement or compact with another State, or with a foreign power, or engage in war, unless actually invaded, or in such imminent danger as will not admit of delay.

ARTICLE II
EXECUTIVE BRANCH

SECTION 1. PRESIDENT AND VICE PRESIDENT

Term of Office The executive power shall be vested in a President of the United States of America. He shall hold his office during the term of four years, and, together with the Vice President, chosen for the same term, be elected as follows:

Electoral College Each State shall appoint, in such manner as the legislature thereof may direct, a number of electors, equal to the whole number of senators and representatives to which the State may be entitled in the Congress; but no senator or representative, or person holding an office of trust or profit under the United States, shall be appointed an elector.

Ports When regulating trade, Congress must treat all states equally. Also, states cannot tax goods traveling between the states.

Regulations on Spending Congress controls the spending of public money. This clause checks the President's power.

Complete Restrictions The Constitution prevents the states from acting like individual countries. States cannot make treaties with foreign nations. They cannot issue their own money.

Partial Restrictions States cannot tax imports and exports without approval from Congress.

Other Restrictions States cannot declare war. They cannot keep their own armies.

Term of Office The President has the power to carry out the laws passed by Congress. The President and the Vice President serve four-year terms.

The Electoral College A group of people called the Electoral College actually elect the President. The number of electors each state receives equals the total number of its representatives and senators.

Election Process Today electors almost always vote for the candidate who won the popular vote in their states. In other words, the candidate who wins the popular vote in a state also wins its electoral votes.

Time of Elections Today we elect our President on the Tuesday after the first Monday in November.

Qualifications A President must be at least 35 years old, a United States citizen by birth, and a resident of the United States for at least 14 years.

Vacancies If the President resigns, dies, or is impeached and found guilty, the Vice President becomes President.

Salary The President receives a yearly salary that cannot be increased or decreased during his or her term. The President cannot hold any other government positions while in office.

Oath of Office Every President must promise to uphold the Constitution. The Chief Justice of the Supreme Court usually administers this oath.

Election Process The electors shall meet in their respective States, and vote by ballot for two persons, of whom one at least shall not be an inhabitant of the same State with themselves. And they shall make a list of all the persons voted for, and of the number of votes for each; which list they shall sign and certify, and transmit sealed to the seat of the government of the United States, directed to the President of the Senate. The President of the Senate shall, in the presence of the Senate and House of Representatives, open all the certificates, and the votes shall then be counted. The person having the greatest number of votes shall be the President, if such number be a majority of the whole number of electors appointed, and if there be more than one who have such majority, and have an equal number of votes, then the House of Representatives shall immediately choose by ballot one of them for President; and if no person have a majority, then from the five highest on the list the said house shall in like manner choose the President. But in choosing the President, the votes shall be taken by States, the representation from each State having one vote; a quorum for this purpose shall consist of a member or members from two-thirds of the States, and a majority of all the States shall be necessary to a choice. In every case, after the choice of the President, the person having the greatest number of votes of the electors shall be the Vice President. But if there should remain two or more who have equal votes, the Senate shall choose from them by ballot the Vice President.

Time of Elections. The Congress may determine the time of choosing the electors, and the day on which they shall give their votes; which day shall be the same throughout the United States.

Qualifications No person except a natural-born citizen, or a citizen of the United States at the time of the adoption of this Constitution, shall be eligible to the office of President; neither shall any person be eligible to that office who shall not have attained to the age of thirty-five years, and been fourteen years a resident within the United States.

Vacancies In case of the removal of the President from office, or of his death, resignation, or inability to discharge the powers and duties of the said office, the same shall devolve on the Vice President, and the Congress may by law provide for the case of removal, death, resignation, or inability, both of the President and Vice President, declaring what officer shall then act as President, and such officer shall act accordingly, until the disability be removed, or a President shall be elected.

Salary The President shall, at stated times, receive for his services a compensation, which shall neither be increased nor diminished during the period for which he shall have been elected, and he shall not receive within that period any other emolument from the United States, or any of them.

Oath of Office Before he enter on the execution of his office, he shall take the following oath or affirmation:—"I do solemnly swear

★ ★ ★ ★ ★ ★ ★ ★ ★

(or affirm) that I will faithfully execute the office of President of the United States, and will to the best of my ability, preserve, protect and defend the Constitution of the United States."

SECTION 2. POWERS OF THE PRESIDENT

Military Powers *The President shall be commander in chief of the army and navy of the United States, and of the militia of the several States, when called into the actual service of the United States; he may require the opinion, in writing, of the principal officer in each of the executive departments, upon any subject relating to the duties of their respective offices, and he shall have power to grant reprieves and pardons for offenses against the United States, except in cases of impeachment.*

Treaties and Appointments *He shall have power, by and with the advice and consent of the Senate, to make treaties, provided two-thirds of the senators present concur; and he shall nominate, and by and with the advice and consent of the Senate, shall appoint ambassadors, other public ministers and consuls, judges of the Supreme Court, and all other officers of the United States, whose appointments are not herein otherwise provided for, and which shall be established by law: but the Congress may by law vest the appointment of such inferior officers, as they think proper, in the President alone, in the courts of law, or in the heads of departments.*

Temporary Appointments *The President shall have power to fill up all vacancies that may happen during the recess of the Senate, by granting commissions which shall expire at the end of their next session.*

SECTION 3. DUTIES

He shall from time to time give to the Congress information of the State of the Union, and recommend to their consideration such measures as he shall judge necessary and expedient; he may on extraordinary occasions, convene both houses, or either of them, and in case of disagreement between them with respect to the time of adjournment, he may adjourn them to such time as he shall think proper; he shall receive ambassadors and other public ministers; he shall take care that the laws be faithfully executed, and shall commission all the officers of the United States.

SECTION 4. IMPEACHMENT

The President, Vice President and all civil officers of the United States, shall be removed from office on impeachment for, and conviction of, treason, bribery, or other high crimes and misdemeanors.

ARTICLE III
JUDICIAL BRANCH

SECTION 1. FEDERAL COURTS

The judicial power of the United States shall be vested in one Supreme Court, and in such inferior courts as the Congress may from time to time ordain and establish. The judges, both of the Supreme and inferior courts, shall hold their offices during good behavior, and

Military Powers The President is the leader of the country's military forces.

Treaties and Appointments The President can make treaties with other nations. However, treaties must be approved by a two-thirds vote of the Senate. The President also appoints Supreme Court Justices and ambassadors to foreign countries. The Senate must approve these appointments.

Duties The President must report to Congress at least once a year and make recommendations for laws. This report is known as the State of the Union Address. The President delivers it each January.

Impeachment The President can be forced out of office only if found guilty of particular crimes. This clause protects government officials from being impeached for unimportant reasons.

Federal Courts The Supreme Court is the highest court in the nation. It makes the final decisions in all of the cases it hears. Today nine judges sit on the Supreme Court. Congress also has the power to set up a system of lower federal courts. All federal judges hold their offices for as long as they live.

587

shall, at stated times, receive for their services, a compensation which shall not be diminished during their continuance in office.

SECTION 2. AUTHORITY OF THE FEDERAL COURTS

The Supreme Court One of the Supreme Court's most important jobs is to decide whether a law passed is constitutional. This power is another example of the checks and balances system in the federal government.

General Jurisdiction *The judicial power shall extend to all cases, in law and equity, arising under this Constitution, the laws of the United States, and treaties made, or which shall be made, under their authority;—to all cases affecting ambassadors, other public ministers and consuls;—to all cases of admiralty and maritime jurisdiction;—to controversies to which the United States shall be a party;—to controversies between two or more States;—between a State and citizens of another State; between citizens of different States;—between citizens of the same State claiming lands under grants of different States, and between a State, or the citizens thereof, and foreign states, citizens or subjects.*

The Supreme Court *In all cases affecting ambassadors, other public ministers and consuls, and those in which a State shall be party, the Supreme Court shall have original jurisdiction. In all the other cases before mentioned, the Supreme Court shall have appellate jurisdiction, both as to law and fact, with such exceptions, and under such regulations as the Congress shall make.*

Trial by Jury The Constitution guarantees everyone the right to a trial by jury. The only exception is in impeachment cases, which are tried in the Senate.

Trial by Jury *The trial of all crimes, except in cases of impeachment, shall be by jury; and such trial shall be held in the State where the said crimes shall have been committed; but when not committed within any State, the trial shall be at such place or places as the Congress may by law have directed.*

SECTION 3. TREASON

Definition People cannot be convicted of treason in the United States for what they think or say. To be guilty of treason, a person must rebel against the government by using violence or helping enemies of the country.

Definition *Treason against the United States shall consist only in levying war against them, or in adhering to their enemies, giving them aid and comfort. No person shall be convicted of treason unless on the testimony of two witnesses to the same overt act, or on confession in open court.*

Punishment *The Congress shall have power to declare the punishment of treason, but no attainder of treason shall work corruption of blood, or forfeiture except during the life of the person attainted.*

ARTICLE IV
RELATIONS AMONG THE STATES

SECTION 1. OFFICIAL RECORDS

Official Records Each state must accept the laws, acts, and legal decisions made by other states.

Full faith and credit shall be given in each State to the public acts, records, and judicial proceedings of every other State. And the Congress may by general laws prescribe the manner in which such acts, records, and proceedings shall be proved, and the effect thereof.

SECTION 2. PRIVILEGES OF THE CITIZENS

Privileges Citizens have all the rights of the citizens of whichever state they are in.

Privileges *The citizens of each State shall be entitled to all privileges and immunities of citizens in the several States.*

Return of a Person Accused of a Crime *A person charged in any State with treason, felony, or other crime, who shall flee from justice, and be found in another State, shall on demand of the executive authority of the State from which he fled, be delivered up, to be removed to the State having jurisdiction of the crime.*

Return of Fugitive Slaves *No person held to service or labor in one State, under the laws thereof, escaping into another, shall, in consequence of any law or regulation therein, be discharged from such service or labor, but shall be delivered up on claim of the party to whom such service or labor may be due.*

SECTION 3. NEW STATES AND TERRITORIES

New States *New States may be admitted by the Congress into this Union; but no new State shall be formed or erected within the jurisdiction of any other State; nor any State be formed by the junction of two or more States or parts of States, without the consent of the legislatures of the States concerned as well as of the Congress.*

Federal Lands *The Congress shall have power to dispose of and make all needful rules and regulations respecting the territory or other property belonging to the United States; and nothing in this Constitution shall be so construed as to prejudice any claims of the United States, or of any particular State.*

SECTION 4. GUARANTEES TO THE STATES

The United States shall guarantee to every State in this Union a republican form of government, and shall protect each of them against invasion; and on application of the legislature, or of the executive (when the legislature cannot be convened) against domestic violence.

ARTICLE V
AMENDING THE CONSTITUTION

The Congress, whenever two-thirds of both houses shall deem it necessary, shall propose amendments to this Constitution, or, on the application of the legislatures of two-thirds of the several States, shall call a convention for proposing amendments, which, in either case, shall be valid to all intents and purposes, as part of this Constitution, when ratified by the legislatures of three-fourths of the several States, or by conventions in three-fourths thereof, as the one or the other mode of ratification may be proposed by the Congress; provided that no amendments which may be made prior to the year one thousand eight hundred and eight shall in any manner affect the first and fourth clauses in the ninth section of the first article, and *that no State, without its consent, shall be deprived of its equal suffrage in the Senate.*

ARTICLE VI
GENERAL PROVISIONS

Public Debt *All debts contracted and engagements entered into, before the adoption of this Constitution, shall be as valid against the United States under this Constitution, as under the Confederation.*

Return of a Person Accused of a Crime If a person charged with a crime escapes to another state, he or she must be returned to the original state to go on trial. This act of returning someone from one state to another is called extradition.

New States Congress has the power to create new states out of the nation's territories. All new states have the same rights as the old states. This clause made it clear that the United States would not make colonies out of its new lands.

Guarantees to the States The federal government must defend the states from attacks by other countries and from rebellions.

Amending the Constitution An amendment to the Constitution may be proposed either by a two-thirds vote of each house of Congress or at the request of two-thirds of the states. To be ratified, or approved, an amendment must be supported either by three-fourths of the state legislatures or by three-fourths of special conventions held in each state.

Once an amendment is ratified, it becomes a part of the Constitution. Only a new amendment can change it. Amendments have allowed people to change the Constitution to meet the changing needs of the nation.

Federal Supremacy The Constitution is the highest law in the nation. Whenever a state law and a federal law are different, the federal law must be obeyed.

Oaths of Office All state and federal officials must promise to obey the Constitution.

Ratification The Constitution went into effect as soon as nine of the thirteen states approved it.

Each state held a special convention to debate the Constitution. The ninth state to approve the Constitution, New Hampshire, voted for ratification on June 21, 1788.

★ ★ ★ ★ ★ ★ ★ ★ ★

Federal Supremacy This Constitution, and the laws of the United States which shall be made in pursuance thereof; and all treaties made, or which shall be made, under the authority of the United States, shall be the supreme law of the land; and the judges in every State shall be bound thereby, anything in the constitution or laws of any State to the contrary notwithstanding.

Oaths of Office The senators and representatives before mentioned, and the members of the several State legislatures, and all executive and judicial officers, both of the United States, and of the several States, shall be bound by oath or affirmation to support this Constitution; but no religious test shall ever be required as a qualification to any office or public trust under the United States.

ARTICLE VII
RATIFICATION

The ratification of the conventions of nine States shall be sufficient for the establishment of this Constitution between the States so ratifying the same.

Done in Convention by the unanimous consent of the States present the seventeenth day of September in the year of our Lord one thousand seven hundred and eighty-seven and of the independence of the United States of America the twelfth. In witness whereof we have hereunto subscribed our names.

George Washington, President and deputy from Virginia

DELAWARE
George Read
Gunning Bedford, Junior
John Dickinson
Richard Bassett
Jacob Broom

MARYLAND
James McHenry
Daniel of St. Thomas Jenifer
Daniel Carroll

VIRGINIA
John Blair
James Madison, Junior

NORTH CAROLINA
William Blount
Richard Dobbs Spaight
Hugh Williamson

SOUTH CAROLINA
John Rutledge
Charles Cotesworth Pinckney
Charles Pinckney
Pierce Butler

GEORGIA
William Few
Abraham Baldwin

NEW HAMPSHIRE
John Langdon
Nicholas Gilman

MASSACHUSETTS
Nathaniel Gorham
Rufus King

CONNECTICUT
William Samuel Johnson
Roger Sherman

NEW YORK
Alexander Hamilton

NEW JERSEY
William Livingston
David Brearley
William Paterson
Jonathan Dayton

PENNSYLVANIA
Benjamin Franklin
Thomas Mifflin
Robert Morris
George Clymer
Thomas FitzSimmons
Jared Ingersoll
James Wilson
Gouverneur Morris

★　★　★　★　★　★　★　★　★

FIRST AMENDMENT (1791)*
BASIC FREEDOMS

Congress shall make no law respecting an establishment of religion, or prohibiting the free exercise thereof; or abridging the freedom of speech, or of the press; or the right of the people peaceably to assemble, and to petition the government for a redress of grievances.

SECOND AMENDMENT (1791)
WEAPONS AND THE MILITIA

A well-regulated militia being necessary to the security of a free State, the right of the people to keep and bear arms shall not be infringed.

THIRD AMENDMENT (1791)
HOUSING SOLDIERS

No soldier shall, in time of peace, be quartered in any house, without the consent of the owner, nor in time of war, but in a manner to be prescribed by law.

FOURTH AMENDMENT (1791)
SEARCH AND SEIZURE

The right of the people to be secure in their persons, houses, papers, and effects, against unreasonable searches and seizures, shall not be violated, and no warrants shall issue, but upon probable cause, supported by oath or affirmation, and particularly describing the place to be searched, and the persons or things to be seized.

FIFTH AMENDMENT (1791)
RIGHTS OF THE ACCUSED

No person shall be held to answer for a capital or otherwise infamous crime, unless on a presentment or indictment of a grand jury, except in cases arising in the land or naval forces, or in the militia, when in actual service in time of war or public danger; nor shall any person be subject for the same offense to be twice put in jeopardy of life or limb; nor shall be compelled in any criminal case to be a witness against himself, nor be deprived of life, liberty, or property, without due process of law; nor shall private property be taken for public use without just compensation.

SIXTH AMENDMENT (1791)
RIGHT TO A FAIR TRIAL

In all criminal prosecutions, the accused shall enjoy the right to a speedy and public trial, by an impartial jury of the State and district wherein the crime shall have been committed, which district shall have been previously ascertained by law, and to be informed of the nature and cause of the accusation; to be confronted with the witnesses against him; to have compulsory process for obtaining witnesses in his favor, and to have the assistance of counsel for his defense.

* The date beside each amendment is the year that the amendment was ratified.

Basic Freedoms The government cannot pass laws that favor one religion over another. Nor can it stop people from saying or writing whatever they want. The people have the right to openly gather and discuss problems they have with the government.

Weapons and the Militia This amendment was included to prevent the federal government from taking away guns used by members of state militias.

Housing Soldiers The army cannot use people's homes to house soldiers unless it is approved by law.

Search and Seizure This amendment protects people's privacy in their homes. The government cannot search or seize anyone's property without a warrant, or a written order, from a court. A warrant must list the people and property to be searched and give reasons for the search.

Rights of the Accused A person accused of a crime has the right to a fair trial. A person cannot be tried twice for one crime. This amendment also protects a person from self-incrimination, or having to testify against himself or herself.

Right to a Fair Trial Anyone accused of a crime is entitled to a quick and fair trial by jury. This right protects people from being kept in jail without being convicted of a crime. Also, the government must provide a lawyer for anyone accused of a crime who cannot afford to hire a lawyer.

Jury Trial in Civil Cases Civil cases usually involve two or more people suing each other over money, property, or personal injury. A jury trial is guaranteed in large lawsuits.

Bail and Punishment Courts cannot treat people accused of crimes in ways that are unusually harsh.

Powers Reserved to the People The citizens keep all rights not listed in the Constitution.

Powers Reserved to the States Any rights not clearly given to the federal government by the Constitution belong to the states or the people.

Suits Against States A citizen from one state cannot sue the government of another state in a federal court. Such cases are decided in state courts.

Election of the President and Vice President Under the original Constitution, each member of the Electoral College voted for two candidates for President. The candidate with the most votes became President. The one with the second highest total became Vice President.

The Twelfth Amendment changed this system. Members of the electoral college distinguish between their votes for President and Vice President. This change was an important step in the development of the two-party system. It allows each party to nominate its own team of candidates.

★   ★   ★   ★   ★   ★   ★   ★   ★

SEVENTH AMENDMENT (1791)
JURY TRIAL IN CIVIL CASES

In suits at common law, where the value in controversy shall exceed twenty dollars, the right of trial by jury shall be preserved, and no fact tried by a jury shall be otherwise reexamined in any court of the United States, than according to the rules of the common law.

EIGHTH AMENDMENT (1791)
BAIL AND PUNISHMENT

Excessive bail shall not be required, nor excessive fines imposed, nor cruel and unusual punishments inflicted.

NINTH AMENDMENT (1791)
POWERS RESERVED TO THE PEOPLE

The enumeration in the Constitution of certain rights shall not be construed to deny or disparage others retained by the people.

TENTH AMENDMENT (1791)
POWERS RESERVED TO THE STATES

The powers not delegated to the United States by the Constitution, nor prohibited by it to the States are reserved to the States respectively, or to the people.

ELEVENTH AMENDMENT (1795)
SUITS AGAINST STATES

The judicial power of the United States shall not be construed to extend to any suit in law or equity, commenced or prosecuted against one of the United States by citizens of another State, or by citizens or subjects of any foreign State.

TWELFTH AMENDMENT (1804)
ELECTION OF THE PRESIDENT AND VICE PRESIDENT

The electors shall meet in their respective States, and vote by ballot for President and Vice President, one of whom, at least, shall not be an inhabitant of the same State with themselves; they shall name in their ballots the person voted for as President, and in distinct ballots the person voted for as Vice President, and they shall make distinct lists of all persons voted for as President, and of all persons voted for as Vice President, and of the number of votes for each, which lists they shall sign and certify, and transmit sealed to the seat of government of the United States, directed to the President of the Senate;—The President of the Senate shall, in the presence of the Senate and House of Representatives, open all the certificates and the votes shall then be counted;—The person having the greatest number of votes for President shall be the President, if such number be a majority of the whole number of electors appointed; and if no person have such majority, then from the persons having the highest numbers not exceeding three on the list of those voted for as President, the House of Representatives shall choose immediately, by ballot, the President. But in choosing the President, the votes shall be taken by States, the representation from each State having one vote; a quorum for this purpose shall consist of a member or members from two-thirds of the States, and a majority of all the States shall be necessary to a choice. And if the House of Representatives shall not choose a President whenever the right of choice shall devolve upon them, before the fourth day of March next following, *then the Vice President shall act as President, as in the case of the death or other constitutional disability of the President. The person having the greatest number of votes as Vice President shall be the Vice President, if such number be a majority of the whole number of electors appointed, and if no person have a majority, then from the two highest numbers on the list, the Senate shall choose the Vice President; a quorum for the purpose shall consist of two-thirds of the whole number of senators, and a majority of the whole number shall be necessary to a choice. But no person constitutionally ineligible to the office of President shall be eligible to that of Vice President of the United States.*

THIRTEENTH AMENDMENT (1865)
END OF SLAVERY

SECTION 1. ABOLITION

Neither slavery nor involuntary servitude, except as a punishment for crime whereof the party shall have been duly convicted, shall exist within the United States, or any place subject to their jurisdiction.

SECTION 2. ENFORCEMENT

Congress shall have power to enforce this article by appropriate legislation.

FOURTEENTH AMENDMENT (1868)
RIGHTS OF CITIZENS

SECTION 1. CITIZENSHIP

All persons born or naturalized in the United States, and subject to the jurisdiction thereof, are citizens of the United States and of the State wherein they reside. No State shall make or enforce any law which shall abridge the privileges or immunities of citizens of the United States; nor shall any State deprive any person of life, liberty, or property, without due process of law; nor deny to any person within its jurisdiction the equal protection of the laws.

SECTION 2. NUMBER OF REPRESENTATIVES

Representatives shall be apportioned among the several States according to their respective numbers, counting the whole number of persons in each State, excluding Indians not taxed. But when the right to vote at any election for the choice of electors for President and Vice President of the United States, representatives in Congress, the executive and judicial officers of a State, or the

Abolition This amendment ended slavery in the United States. It was ratified right after the Civil War.

Citizenship This amendment defined citizenship in the United States. "Due process under law" means that no state can deny its citizens the rights and privileges they enjoy as United States citizens. The goal of this amendment was to protect the rights of the recently freed blacks.

Number of Representatives: This clause replaced the Three-Fifths Compromise in Article 1. Each state's representation is based on its total population. Any state denying its male citizens over the age of 21 the right to vote will have its representation in Congress decreased.

members of the legislature thereof, is denied to any of the male inhabitants of such State, being twenty-one years of age, and citizens of the United States, or in any way abridged, except for participation in rebellion, or other crime, the basis of representation therein shall be reduced in the proportion which the number of such male citizens shall bear to the whole number of male citizens twenty-one years of age in such State.

SECTION 3. PENALTY FOR REBELLION

Penalty for Rebellion Officials who fought against the Union in the Civil War could not hold public office in the United States. This clause tried to keep Confederate leaders out of power. In 1872, Congress removed this limit.

No person shall be a senator or representative in Congress, or elector of President and Vice President, or hold any office, civil or military, under the United States, or under any State, who, having previously taken an oath, as a member of Congress, or as an officer of the United States, or as a member of any State legislature, or as an executive or judicial officer of any State, to support the Constitution of the United States, shall have engaged in insurrection or rebellion against the same, or given aid or comfort to the enemies thereof. But Congress may by a vote of two-thirds of each house, remove such disability.

SECTION 4. GOVERNMENT DEBT

Government Debt The United States paid all of the Union's debts from the Civil War. However, it did not pay any of the Confederacy's debts. This clause prevented the southern states from using public money to pay for the rebellion or to pay citizens who lost their slaves.

The validity of the public debt of the United States, authorized by law, including debts incurred for payment of pensions and bounties for services in suppressing insurrection or rebellion, shall not be questioned. But neither the United States nor any State shall assume or pay any debt or obligation incurred in aid of insurrection or rebellion against the United States, or any claim for the loss or emancipation of any slave; but all such debts, obligations, and claims shall be held illegal and void.

SECTION 5. ENFORCEMENT

The Congress shall have power to enforce, by appropriate legislation, the provisions of this article.

FIFTEENTH AMENDMENT (1870) VOTING RIGHTS

SECTION 1. RIGHT TO VOTE

Right to Vote No state can deny its citizens the right to vote because of their race. This amendment was designed to protect the voting rights of blacks.

The right of citizens of the United States to vote shall not be denied or abridged by the United States or by any State on account of race, color, or previous condition of servitude.

SECTION 2. ENFORCEMENT

The Congress shall have power to enforce this article by appropriate legislation.

SIXTEENTH AMENDMENT (1913) INCOME TAX

Income Tax Congress has the power to tax personal incomes.

The Congress shall have power to lay and collect taxes on incomes, from whatever source derived, without apportionment among the several States, and without regard to any census or enumeration.

★ ★ ★ ★ ★ ★ ★ ★ ★

SEVENTEENTH AMENDMENT (1913)
DIRECT ELECTION OF SENATORS

SECTION 1. METHOD OF ELECTION

The Senate of the United States shall be composed of two senators from each State, elected by the people thereof, for six years; and each senator shall have one vote. The electors in each State shall have the qualifications requisite for electors of the most numerous branch of the State legislatures.

Direct Election of Senators In the original Constitution, the state legislatures elected the senators. This amendment gave citizens the power to elect their senators directly. It made senators more responsible to the people they represented.

SECTION 2. VACANCIES

When vacancies happen in the representation of any State in the Senate, the executive authority of such State shall issue writs of election to fill such vacancies: Provided, that the legislature of any State may empower the executive thereof to make temporary appointments until the people fill the vacancies by election as the legislature may direct.

SECTION 3. EXCEPTION

This amendment shall not be so construed as to affect the election or term of any Senator chosen before it becomes valid as part of the Constitution.

EIGHTEENTH AMENDMENT (1919)
BAN ON ALCOHOLIC DRINKS

SECTION 1. PROHIBITION

After one year from the ratification of this article the manufacture, sale, or transportation of intoxicating liquors within, the importation thereof into, or the exportation thereof from the United States and all territory subject to the jurisdiction thereof for beverage purposes is hereby prohibited.

Prohibition This amendment made it against the law to make or sell alcoholic beverages in the United States. This law was called Prohibition. Fourteen years later, the Twenty-First Amendment ended Prohibition.

SECTION 2. ENFORCEMENT

The Congress and the several States shall have concurrent power to enforce this article by appropriate legislation.

SECTION 3. RATIFICATION

This article shall be inoperative unless it shall have been ratified as an amendment to the Constitution by the legislatures of the several States, as provided in the Constitution, within seven years from the date of the submission hereof to the States by the Congress.

Ratification This amendment was the first one to include a time limit for ratification. To go into effect, the amendment had to be approved by three-fourths of the states within seven years.

NINETEENTH AMENDMENT (1920)
WOMEN'S SUFFRAGE

SECTION 1. RIGHT TO VOTE

The right of citizens of the United States to vote shall not be denied or abridged by the United States or by any State on account of sex.

Women's Suffrage This amendment gave the right to vote to all women 21 years of age and older.

SECTION 2. ENFORCEMENT

The Congress shall have power to enforce this article by appropriate legislation.

TWENTIETH AMENDMENT (1933)
TERMS OF OFFICE

SECTION 1. BEGINNING OF TERMS

Beginning of Terms The President and Vice President's terms begin on January 20 after being elected. The terms for senators and representatives begin on January 3. Before this amendment, an official defeated in a November election stayed in office until March.

The terms of the President and Vice President shall end at noon on the twentieth day of January, and the terms of senators and representatives at noon on the third day of January, of the years in which such terms would have ended if this article had not been ratified; and the terms of their successors shall then begin.

SECTION 2. SESSIONS OF CONGRESS

The Congress shall assemble at least once in every year, and such meeting shall begin at noon on the third day of January, unless they shall by law appoint a different day.

SECTION 3. PRESIDENTIAL SUCCESSION

Presidential Succession A President who has been elected but has not yet taken office is called the President-elect. If the President-elect dies, the Vice President-elect becomes President. If neither the President-elect nor the Vice President-elect can take office, then Congress decides who will act as President.

If, at the time fixed for the beginning of the term of the President, the President-elect shall have died, the Vice President-elect shall become President. If a President shall not have been chosen before the time fixed for the beginning of his term, or if the President-elect shall have failed to qualify, then the Vice President-elect shall act as President until a President shall have qualified; and the Congress may by law provide for the case wherein neither a President-elect nor a Vice President-elect shall have qualified, declaring who shall then act as President, or the manner in which one who is to act shall be selected, and such persons shall act accordingly until a President or Vice President shall have qualified.

SECTION 4. ELECTIONS DECIDED BY CONGRESS

The Congress may by law provide for the case of the death of any of the persons from whom the House of Representatives may choose a President whenever the right of choice shall have devolved upon them, and for the case of the death of any of the persons from whom the Senate may choose a Vice President whenever the right of choice shall have devolved upon them.

SECTION 5. EFFECTIVE DATE

Sections 1 and 2 shall take effect on the fifteenth day of October following the ratification of this article.

SECTION 6. RATIFICATION

This article shall be inoperative unless it shall have been ratified as an amendment to the Constitution by the legislatures of three-fourths of the several States within seven years from the date of its submission.

★ ★ ★ ★ ★ ★ ★ ★ ★

TWENTY-FIRST AMENDMENT (1933)
END OF PROHIBITION

SECTION 1. REPEAL OF EIGHTEENTH AMENDMENT

The eighteenth article of amendment to the Constitution of the United States is hereby repealed.

SECTION 2. STATE LAWS

The transportation or importation into any State, territory, or possession of the United States for delivery or use therein of intoxicating liquors, in violation of the laws thereof, is hereby prohibited.

SECTION 3. RATIFICATION

This article shall be inoperative unless it shall have been ratified as an amendment to the Constitution by conventions in the several States, as provided in the Constitution, within seven years from the date of submission hereof to the States by the Congress.

End of Prohibition This amendment repealed, or ended, the Eighteenth Amendment. It made alcoholic beverages legal once again in the United States. However, states can still control or stop the sale of alcohol within their borders.

TWENTY-SECOND AMENDMENT (1951)
LIMIT ON PRESIDENTIAL TERMS

SECTION 1. TWO-TERM LIMIT

No person shall be elected to the office of the President more than twice, and no person who has held the office of President, or acted as President, for more than two years of a term to which some other person was elected President shall be elected to the office of the President more than once. But this article shall not apply to any person holding the office of President when this article was proposed by the Congress, and shall not prevent any person who may be holding the office of President, or acting as President, during the term within which this article becomes operative from holding the office of President or acting as President during the remainder of such term.

SECTION 2. RATIFICATION

This article shall be inoperative unless it shall have been ratified as an amendment to the Constitution by the legislatures of three-fourths of the several States within seven years from the date of its submission to the States by Congress.

Two-Term Limit George Washington set a precedent that Presidents should not serve more than two terms in office. However, Franklin Roosevelt broke the precedent. He was elected President four times between 1932 and 1944. Some people feared that a President holding office for this long could become too powerful. This amendment limits Presidents to two terms in office.

TWENTY-THIRD AMENDMENT (1961)
PRESIDENTIAL VOTES FOR WASHINGTON, D.C.

SECTION 1. NUMBER OF ELECTORS

The District constituting the seat of government of the United States shall appoint in such manner as the Congress may direct:

A number of electors of President and Vice President equal to the whole number of senators and representatives in Congress to which the District would be entitled if it were a State, but in no event more than the least populous State; they shall be in addition to those appointed by the States, but they shall be considered, for the

Presidential Votes for Washington, D.C. This amendment gives people who live in the nation's capital a vote for President. Washington, D.C.'s electoral votes are based on its population. However, it cannot have more votes than the state with the smallest population. Today Washington, D.C. has three electoral votes.

purposes of the election of President and Vice President, to be electors appointed by a State; and they shall meet in the District and perform such duties as provided by the twelfth article of amendment.

SECTION 2. ENFORCEMENT

The Congress shall have power to enforce this article by appropriate legislation.

TWENTY-FOURTH AMENDMENT (1964)
BAN ON POLL TAXES

SECTION 1. POLL TAXES ILLEGAL

The right of citizens of the United States to vote in any primary or other election for President or Vice President, for electors for President or Vice President, or for senator or representative in Congress, shall not be denied or abridged by the United States or any State by reason of failure to pay any poll tax or other tax.

SECTION 2. ENFORCEMENT

The Congress shall have power to enforce this article by appropriate legislation.

TWENTY-FIFTH AMENDMENT (1967)
PRESIDENTIAL SUCCESSION

SECTION 1. VACANCY IN THE PRESIDENCY

In case of the removal of the President from office or of his death or resignation, the Vice President shall become President.

SECTION 2. VACANCY IN THE VICE PRESIDENCY

Whenever there is a vacancy in the office of the Vice President, the President shall nominate a Vice President who shall take office upon confirmation by a majority vote of both houses of Congress.

SECTION 3. DISABILITY OF THE PRESIDENT

Whenever the President transmits to the President pro tempore of the Senate and the speaker of the House of Representatives his written declaration that he is unable to discharge the powers and duties of his office, and until he transmits to them a written declaration to the contrary, such powers and duties shall be discharged by the Vice President as Acting President.

SECTION 4. DETERMINING PRESIDENTIAL DISABILITY

Whenever the Vice President and a majority of either the principal officers of the executive departments or of such other body as Congress may by law provide, transmit to the President pro tempore of the Senate and the speaker of the House of Representatives their written declaration that the President is unable to discharge the powers and duties of his office, the Vice President shall immediately assume the powers and duties of the office as Acting President.

Ban on Poll Taxes A poll tax requires a person to pay a certain amount of money to register to vote. These taxes were used to stop poor blacks from voting. This amendment made any such taxes against the law in federal elections.

Vacancy in the Vice Presidency If the Vice President becomes President, he or she may nominate a new Vice President. This nomination must be approved by both houses of Congress.

Disability of the President This section tells what happens if the President suddenly becomes ill or is seriously injured. The Vice President takes over as Acting President. When the President is ready to take office again, he or she must tell Congress.

★ ★ ★ ★ ★ ★ ★ ★ ★

Thereafter, when the President transmits to the President pro tempore of the Senate and the speaker of the House of Representatives his written declaration that no inability exists, he shall resume the powers and duties of his office unless the Vice President and a majority of either the principal officers of the executive departments or of such other body as Congress may by law provide, transmit within four days to the President pro tempore of the Senate and the speaker of the House of Representatives their written declaration that the President is unable to discharge the powers and duties of his office. Thereupon Congress shall decide the issue, assembling within 48 hours for that purpose if not in session. If the Congress, within 21 days after receipt of the latter written declaration, or, if Congress is not in session, within 21 days after Congress is required to assemble, determines by two-thirds vote of both houses that the President is unable to discharge the powers and duties of his office, the Vice President shall continue to discharge the same as Acting President; otherwise, the President shall resume the powers and duties of his office.

TWENTY-SIXTH AMENDMENT (1971)
VOTING AGE

SECTION 1. RIGHT TO VOTE

The right of citizens of the United States, who are eighteen years of age or older, to vote shall not be denied or abridged by the United States or by any State on account of age.

Right to Vote This amendment gave the vote to everyone 18 years of age and older.

SECTION 2. ENFORCEMENT

The Congress shall have power to enforce this article by appropriate legislation.

TWENTY-SEVENTH AMENDMENT (1992)
CONGRESSIONAL PAY RAISES

No law, varying the compensation for the services of the Senators and Representatives, shall take effect, until an election of Representatives shall have intervened.

Limits on Pay Raises This amendment prohibits a Congressional pay raise from taking effect during the current term of the Congress that voted for it.

Canada

The flag of Canada   The Canadian coat of arms

Facts in brief

Capital: Ottawa.
Official languages: English and French.
Area: 3,849,674 sq. mi. (9,970,610 km²), including 291,577 sq. mi. (755,180 km²) of inland water. *Greatest distances*—east-west, 3,223 mi. (5,187 km), from Cape Spear, Nfld., to Mount St. Elias, Y.T.; north-south, 2,875 mi. (4,627 km), from Cape Columbia on Ellesmere Island to Middle Island in Lake Erie. *Coastline*—151,485 mi. (243,791 km), including mainland and islands; Atlantic Ocean, 28,019 mi. (45,092 km); Arctic Ocean, 82,698 mi. (133,089 km); Hudson Bay, Hudson Strait, and James Bay, 24,786 mi. (39,890 km); Pacific Ocean, 15,985 mi. (25,726 km). *Shoreline*—Great Lakes, 5,251 mi. (8,452 km).
Elevation: *Highest*—Mount Logan, 19,524 ft. (5,951 m) above sea level. *Lowest*—sea level.
Population: *Estimated 1993 population*—27,719,000; density, 7 persons per sq. mi. (3 per km²); distribution, 77 per cent urban, 23 per cent rural. *1991 census*—27,296,859. *Estimated 1998 population*—28,387,000.
Chief products: *Agriculture*—beef cattle, milk, wheat, hogs, chickens, canola, eggs. *Fishing industry*—cod, lobster, salmon. *Forest industry*—spruce, pine, fir. *Manufacturing*—motor vehicles and parts; food products; chemicals; paper products; aluminum, steel, and other metals; electronic equipment; fabricated metal products; wood products; petroleum and coal products; printed materials; machinery. *Mining*—petroleum, natural gas, nickel, copper, gold, zinc, coal, iron ore, uranium.
National anthem: "O Canada."
National symbols: Maple leaf and beaver.
National holiday: Canada Day, July 1.
Money: *Basic unit*—dollar.

Important dates

A.D. 1000's Vikings sailed along the northeast coast, possibly establishing a temporary settlement.
1497 John Cabot of England landed on Canada's east coast. Britain laid claim to all of Canada.
1534 French explorer Jacques Cartier reached the Gulf of St. Lawrence and claimed the surrounding territory for France.
1610 Henry Hudson of England sailed into Hudson Bay.
1642 French missionaries founded Montreal.
1689-1763 A series of wars between British and French colonists ended with Britain's conquest of New France, the French empire in America.
1774 The Quebec Act gave French Canadians political and religious rights.
1867 The British North America Act established the Dominion of Canada.
1869 Louis Riel led the métis in the Red River Rebellion in Manitoba.
1870 The North West Territories (now Northwest Territories) was established.
1885 Riel led a métis revolt in Saskatchewan. The Canadian Pacific Railway (now CP Rail) spanned Canada.
1898 The Yukon area became a territory of Canada.
1914-1918 More than 600,000 Canadians served in World War I.
1920 Canada became a member of the League of Nations.
1931 The Statute of Westminster made Canada an independent nation.
1939-1945 More than a million Canadians served during World War II.
1945 Canada joined the United Nations (UN).
1949 Canada signed a treaty that set up the North Atlantic Treaty Organization (NATO).
1959 The St. Lawrence Seaway, a joint U.S.-Canadian project, opened.
1962 The Trans-Canada Highway, the country's first ocean-to-ocean road, was completed.
1964 A national pension plan was introduced.
1965 A new official Canadian flag flew for the first time on February 15.
1967 Canadians celebrated the 100th anniversary of Confederation with Expo 67, a world's fair in Montreal.
1969 The Official Languages Act required federal facilities to provide service in both French and English if 10 per cent of the people in an area speak either language.
1982 The Constitution Act ended British control over amendments to Canada's Constitution. The act included a new bill of rights.
1991 Canadian forces fought in the Persian Gulf War.

The provinces and territories of Canada

Provinces

Province	Capital	Area In sq. mi.	In km²	Rank in area	Population (1991 census)	Rank in pop.	Floral emblem	Date became province	Province abbr.
Alberta	Edmonton	255,287	661,190	4	2,545,553	4	Wild rose	1905	Alta.
British Columbia	Victoria	365,900	947,800	3	3,282,061	3	Pacific dogwood	1871	B.C.
Manitoba	Winnipeg	250,947	649,950	6	1,091,942	5	Pasqueflower	1870	Man.
New Brunswick	Fredericton	28,355	73,440	8	723,900	8	Violet	1867	N.B.
Newfoundland	St. John's	156,649	405,720	7	568,474	9	Pitcher plant	1949	Nfld.
Nova Scotia	Halifax	21,423	55,490	9	899,942	7	Trailing arbutus	1867	N.S.
Ontario	Toronto	412,581	1,068,580	2	10,084,885	1	White trillium	1867	Ont.
Prince Edward Island	Charlottetown	2,185	5,660	10	129,765	10	Lady's-slipper	1873	P.E.I.
Quebec	Quebec	594,860	1,540,680	1	6,895,963	2	White garden lily	1867	Que.
Saskatchewan	Regina	251,866	652,330	5	988,928	6	Prairie lily	1905	Sask.

Territories

Territory	Capital	Area In sq. mi.	In km²	Population (1991 census)	Floral emblem	Territory abbreviation
Northwest Territories	Yellowknife	1,322,910	3,426,320	57,649	Mountain avens	N.W. Ter. or N.W.T.
Yukon Territory	Whitehorse	186,661	483,450	27,797	Fireweed	Y.T.

Explorers of the great age of European discovery

Explorer	Nationality	Main achievements	Date
* Balboa, Vasco Núñez de	Spanish	Led expedition across Isthmus of Panama; sighted Pacific Ocean.	1513
* Cabeza de Vaca, Álvar Núñez	Spanish	Explored Gulf Plains from Texas to Mexico.	1528-1536
* Cabot, John	Italian	Sailed across the North Atlantic to what is now Canada.	1497-1498
* Cabot, Sebastian	Italian	Explored South American coast to the Río de la Plata.	1526-1530
* Cabral, Pedro Álvares	Portuguese	Reached Brazilian coast; sailed around Africa to India.	1500-1501
* Cartier, Jacques	French	Sailed up the St. Lawrence River.	1535
* Columbus, Christopher	Italian	Made four voyages to the West Indies and Caribbean lands.	1492-1504
* Coronado, Francisco de	Spanish	Explored the American Southwest.	1540-1542
* Cortés, Hernando	Spanish	Conquered Mexico.	1519-1521
* Da Gama, Vasco	Portuguese	First European to reach India by sea.	1498
* De Soto, Hernando	Spanish	Explored American Southeast; reached Mississippi River.	1539-1542
* Dias, Bartolomeu	Portuguese	First European to round the Cape of Good Hope.	1487-1488
* Drake, Sir Francis	English	First English explorer to sail all around the world.	1577-1580
* Frobisher, Sir Martin	English	Searched North American coast for a Northwest Passage.	1576-1578
* Magellan, Ferdinand	Portuguese	Commanded first globe-circling voyage, completed in 1522 after his death.	1519-1521
* Oñate, Juan de	Spanish	Explored American Southwest.	1598-1605
* Orellana, Francisco de	Spanish	Explored Amazon River.	1541
* Pizarro, Francisco	Spanish	Conquered Peru; founded Lima.	1531-1535
* Ponce de León, Juan	Spanish	Explored Florida.	1513
* Verrazano, Giovanni da	Italian	Searched for a Northwest Passage.	1524
* Vespucci, Amerigo	Italian	Sailed to the West Indies and South America.	1499-1504

*Has a separate biography in WORLD BOOK.

Famous explorers of North America

Explorer	Nationality	Main achievements	Date
* Bridger, James	American	Probably the first white person to reach Great Salt Lake.	1824-1825
* Champlain, Samuel de	French	Explored eastern coast of North America, and St. Lawrence River west to Lake Huron; reached Lake Champlain.	1603-1616
* Clark, William	American	Led an expedition across the Rocky Mountains to the Pacific Ocean with Meriwether Lewis.	1804-1806
Duluth, Sieur	French	Explored Lake Superior region.	1678-1687
* Frémont, John Charles	American	Explored the American West.	1842-1846
* Hennepin, Louis	Belgian	Explored upper Mississippi River region.	1680
* Hudson, Henry	English	Explored Hudson Bay, Hudson River, and Hudson Strait.	1609-1611
* Jolliet, Louis	French Canadian	Explored northern Mississippi River region with Jacques Marquette.	1673
* La Salle, Sieur de	French	Explored the Great Lakes region and tracked the Mississippi River to the Gulf of Mexico.	1679-1682
* La Vérendrye, Sieur de	French Canadian	Explored western Canada.	1731-1743
* Lewis, Meriwether	American	Led an expedition across the Rocky Mountains to the Pacific Ocean with William Clark.	1804-1806
* Mackenzie, Sir Alexander	Canadian	Explored western Canada; followed the Mackenzie River to the Arctic Ocean.	1789-1793
* Marquette, Jacques	French	Explored northern Mississippi River region with Louis Jolliet.	1673
* Pike, Zebulon	American	Explored Middle West and Rocky Mountain region.	1805-1807
* Radisson, Pierre Esprit	French	Explored Lake Superior and northern Mississippi River regions.	1659-1661
* Smith, Jedediah Strong	American	Explored Great Basin region; blazed trails across the Rocky Mountains to California and the Pacific Northwest.	1824-1829
* Thompson, David	Canadian	Explored western Canada.	1789-1812
* Tonti, Henri de	French	Explored the Great Lakes region and the Mississippi River with de La Salle.	1679-1682

*Has a separate biography in WORLD BOOK.

Famous space explorers

Explorer	Nationality	Main achievements	Date
* Aldrin, Edwin E., Jr.	American	Landed on the moon with Neil A. Armstrong.	1969
Anders, William A.	American	Orbited the moon with James A. Lovell, Jr., and Frank Borman.	1968
* Armstrong, Neil A.	American	First person to set foot on the moon.	1969
* Borman, Frank	American	Commanded the first space flight to orbit the moon.	1968
Crippen, Robert L.	American	Piloted the first space shuttle flight with John W. Young.	1981
* Gagarin, Yuri A.	Soviet	First person to travel in space.	1961
Leonov, Alexei A.	Soviet	First person to leave a spacecraft and float freely in space.	1965
* Lovell, James A., Jr.	American	Orbited the moon.	1968
* Tereshkova, Valentina V.	Soviet	First woman to travel in space.	1963
Young, John W.	American	Commanded the first space shuttle flight.	1981

*Has a separate biography in WORLD BOOK.

Excerpted from the Exploration article in *World Book*. Copyright © 1993 by World Book, Inc.

Flags in American history

The Viking flag of Leif Ericson was the first flag in North America, in the 1000's.

The Spanish flag carried by Columbus in 1492, *left,* combined the arms of Castile and Leon. Columbus' own flag, *right,* bore the initials F and Y for Ferdinand and Isabella (Ysabel).

This French flag was one of many flown in North America between 1604 and 1763.

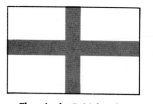

Flags in the British colonies. Britain's North American colonies began with Jamestown in 1607. At the left is a flag of England. The British flag, *right,* was adopted in 1606.

Dutch-East India Company flag of Henry Hudson flew in the New York area in 1609.

Russian-American Company flag flew at Russian settlements in Alaska in 1806.

The Continental Colors served as America's first national flag from 1775 to 1777.

The flag of 1777 had no official arrangement for the stars. The most popular design had alternating rows of 3, 2, 3, 2, and 3 stars. Another flag with 13 stars in a circle was rarely used.

The flag of 1795 had 15 stripes, as well as 15 stars, to stand for the 15 states.

New England flags. The Taunton Flag, *left,* was raised at Taunton, Mass., in 1774. The Bedford Flag, *above,* flown in 1775, bears the words *vince aut morire,* meaning *conquer or die.* The

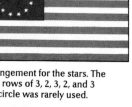

Rhode Island Flag, *above,* was carried in battle until 1781. The Bennington Flag, *right,* a variation of the original Stars and Stripes, may have flown during the Battle of Bennington in 1777.

Navy flags. American ships in New England waters flew a liberty tree flag, *left,* in 1775. Later that year, the Continental Navy began using a striped flag with a rattlesnake design.

Southern flags often had rattlesnake designs, as in the flag of Virginia's Culpeper Minute Men, 1775. William Moultrie's flag was flown by defenders of Charleston, S.C., in 1776.

Flags of the United States

The *Stars and Stripes* is the most popular name for the red, white, and blue national flag of the United States. No one knows where this name came from, but we do know the origin of several other names. Francis Scott Key first called the United States flag the *Star-Spangled Banner* in 1814 when he wrote the poem that became the national anthem. William Driver, a sea captain from Salem, Mass., gave the name *Old Glory* to the U.S. flag in 1824.

The Stars and Stripes stands for the land, the people, the government, and the ideals of the United States, no matter when or where it is displayed. Some other flags also stand for the United States, or its government, in certain situations. The *Navy Jack,* a blue flag with white stars, stands for the United States whenever it flies from a U.S. Navy ship. The stars, stripes, and colors of the U.S. flag appear in many federal and state flags.

The colors. The Continental Congress left no record to show why it chose red, white, and blue as the colors for the flag. But, in 1782, the Congress of the Confederation chose these same colors for the newly designed Great Seal of the United States. The resolution on the seal listed meanings for the colors. *Red* is for hardiness and courage, *white* for purity and innocence, and *blue* for vigilance, perseverance, and justice.

The stripes in the flag stand for the thirteen original colonies. The stripes were probably adopted from the flag of the Sons of Liberty, which had five red and four white stripes. The British Union Jack was added to show

Today's 50-star United States flag has the following dimensions: hoist (width) of flag, 1.0 unit; fly (length) of flag, 1.9; hoist of union, .5385 (7/13); fly of union, .76; width of each stripe, .0769 (1/13); and diameter of each star, .0616.

that the colonists did not at first seek full independence.

The stars. The resolution passed by Congress in 1777 stated that the flag should have 13 stars. But Congress did not indicate how the stars should be arranged. The most popular arrangement showed the stars in alternating rows of three, two, three, two, and three stars. Another version had 12 stars in a circle with the 13th star in the center. A flag with 13 stars in a circle is often associated with the period. But there is little evidence that such a design was used. There is also no historical basis for assigning each star to a particular state.

The flag of 1818 went back to 13 stripes, and had 20 stars for the 20 states. One design had four rows of five stars each. The Great Star Flag, *right,* formed the 20 stars in a large star.

The flag of 1861, used in the Civil War, had stars for 34 states, including the South.

The 48-star flag served as the national flag the longest of any flag, from 1912 to 1959.

Perry's flag in 1813 bore the last words of James Lawrence, a hero of the War of 1812.

Texas flags. A Texas flag that flew when Texas was part of Mexico, *left,* bore the date of Mexico's constitution. The Texas Navy Flag, *right,* had a lone star.

The Bear Flag flew over an independent California republic for a few months in 1846.

  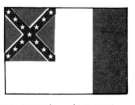

Confederate flags. The Stars and Bars, *left,* adopted in 1861, had stars for 7 seceding states. It looked too much like the U.S. flag, so troops carried a battle flag, *above.* It had stars for 11 states and for secession governments in Kentucky and Missouri, as did the flag of 1863, *above.* This looked too much like a flag of truce, so a red bar was added in 1865, *right.*

Gettysburg Address

Detail of a lithograph (1905); Granger Collection.

Abraham Lincoln delivered the Gettysburg Address four months after the historic Civil War battle was fought.

Gettysburg Address is a short speech that United States President Abraham Lincoln delivered during the Civil War at the site of the Battle of Gettysburg in Pennsylvania. He delivered the address on Nov. 19, 1863, at ceremonies to dedicate a part of the battlefield as a cemetery for those who had lost their lives in the battle. Lincoln wrote the address to define for the people of the Northern States the purpose in fighting the war. His simple and inspired words rank among the best remembered in American history.

Lincoln wrote five different versions of the speech. He wrote most of the first version in Washington, D.C., and probably completed it at Gettysburg. He probably wrote the second version at Gettysburg on the evening before he delivered his address. He held this second version in his hand during the address. But he made several changes as he spoke. The most important change was to add the phrase "under God" after the word "nation" in the last sentence.

Historians are reasonably sure they know what Lincoln actually said in his speech at Gettysburg. Several reporters attended the ceremonies and took down his words as he spoke. Although the reports vary somewhat, they all include the phrase "under God." Lincoln added that phrase to the three versions of the address that he wrote after the ceremonies at Gettysburg.

Lincoln wrote the final version of the address—the fifth written version—in 1864. This version also differed somewhat from the speech he actually gave, but it was the only copy he signed. It is carved on a stone plaque in the Lincoln Memorial.

Many false stories have grown up about this famous speech. One story says that the people of Lincoln's time did not appreciate the speech. But Edward Everett, the principal speaker at the dedication, wrote to Lincoln: "I should be glad if I could flatter myself that I came as near to the central idea of the occasion in two hours as you did in two minutes." Many newspapers also immediately recognized the nobility of Lincoln's brief remarks.

Gabor S. Boritt

Two versions of the Gettysburg Address

Lincoln wrote five different versions of his famous Gettysburg Address. The fifth version, *below left,* is the only one he signed. The version at the right differs slightly from all five of the written versions but is probably closer to what Lincoln actually said at Gettysburg. It is based on the shorthand notes of a reporter who heard Lincoln deliver the speech.

Four score and seven years ago our fathers brought forth on this continent, a new nation, conceived in Liberty, and dedicated to the proposition that all men are created equal.

Now we are engaged in a great civil war, testing whether that nation, or any nation so conceived and so dedicated, can long endure. We are met on a great battlefield of that war. We have come to dedicate a portion of that field, as a final resting place for those who here gave their lives that that nation might live. It is altogether fitting and proper that we should do this.

But, in a larger sense, we can not dedicate—we can not consecrate—we can not hallow—this ground. The brave men, living and dead, who struggled here, have consecrated it, far above our poor power to add or detract. The world will little note, nor long remember what we say here, but it can never forget what they did here. It is for us the living, rather, to be dedicated here to the unfinished work which they who fought here have thus far so nobly advanced. It is rather for us to be here dedicated to the great task remaining before us—that from these honored dead we take increased devotion to that cause for which they gave the last full measure of devotion—that we here highly resolve that these dead shall not have died in vain—that this nation, under God, shall have a new birth of freedom—and that government of the people, by the people, for the people, shall not perish from the earth.

Four score and seven years ago our fathers brought forth upon this continent a new nation, conceived in Liberty, and dedicated to the proposition that all men are created equal.

Now we are engaged in a great civil war, testing whether that nation or any nation so conceived and so dedicated can long endure. We are met on a great battlefield of that war. We are met to dedicate a portion of it as the final resting place of those who here gave their lives that that nation might live. It is altogether fitting and proper that we should do this.

But in a larger sense we cannot dedicate—we cannot consecrate—we cannot hallow this ground. The brave men living and dead who struggled here have consecrated it far above our poor power to add or detract. The world will little note nor long remember what we say here, but it can never forget what they did here. It is for us, the living, rather to be dedicated here to the unfinished work that they have thus far so nobly carried on. It is rather for us to be here dedicated to the great task remaining before us—that from these honored dead we take increased devotion to that cause for which they here gave the last full measure of devotion—that we here highly resolve that the dead shall not have died in vain—that the nation shall, under God, have a new birth of freedom—and that governments of the people, by the people, and for the people, shall not perish from the earth.

Immigration is the act of coming to a foreign country to live. The act of leaving one's country to settle in another is called *emigration*. Immigrants who flee their country because of persecution, war, or such disasters as famines or epidemics are known as *refugees* or *displaced persons* (DP's).

Most people find it extremely difficult to pull up roots in their native land and move to a strange country. But throughout history, countless millions of people have done so. The heaviest immigration worldwide took place from the early 1800's to the Great Depression—the economic hard times of the 1930's. During that period, about 60 million people moved to a new land. Most of them came from Europe. More than half emigrated to the United States. Other destinations included Canada, Argentina, Brazil, Australia, New Zealand, and South Africa.

Today, the availability of fast, safe, and cheap transportation helps make migration easier in many parts of the world. Asia is replacing Europe as the major immigrant-sending area. The United States remains the chief receiving nation.

Number of legal immigrants admitted to the United States annually

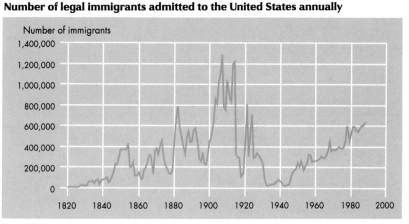

Number of immigrants

Legal immigration to the United States has varied in a wavelike pattern. These ups and downs have occurred in response both to economic and political conditions in the United States and in the major immigrant-sending nations. Statistics on legal immigration have been kept since 1820.

Source: U.S. Immigration and Naturalization Service.

Major immigration movements to the United States

Who	When	Number	Why
Irish	1840's and 1850's	About 1½ million	Famine resulting from potato crop failure
Germans	1840's to 1880's	About 4 million	Severe economic depression and unemployment; political unrest and failure of liberal revolutionary movement
Danes, Norwegians, and Swedes	1870's to 1900's	About 1½ million	Poverty; shortage of farmland
Poles	1880's to 1920's	About 1 million	Poverty; political repression; cholera epidemics
Jews from eastern Europe	1880's to 1920's	About 2½ million	Religious persecution
Austrians, Czechs, Hungarians, and Slovaks	1880's to 1920's	About 4 million	Poverty; overpopulation
Italians	1880's to 1920's	About 4½ million	Poverty; overpopulation
Mexicans	1910 to 1920's 1950's to 1980's	About 700,000 About 2 million	Mexican Revolution of 1910; low wages and unemployment Poverty; unemployment
Cubans	1960's to 1980's	About 700,000	Communist take-over in 1959
Dominicans, Haitians, and Jamaicans	1970's and 1980's	About 900,000	Poverty; unemployment
Vietnamese	1970's and 1980's	About 500,000	Vietnam War (1957-1975); Communist take-over

Source: U.S. Immigration and Naturalization Service.

Excerpted from the Immigration article in *World Book.* Copyright © 1993 by World Book, Inc.

Indian ways of life

The Indians had many ways of life. This chart shows some details of tribal life in the 11 major Indian culture areas. It pictures Indian clothing, buildings and shelters, and crafts and weapons.

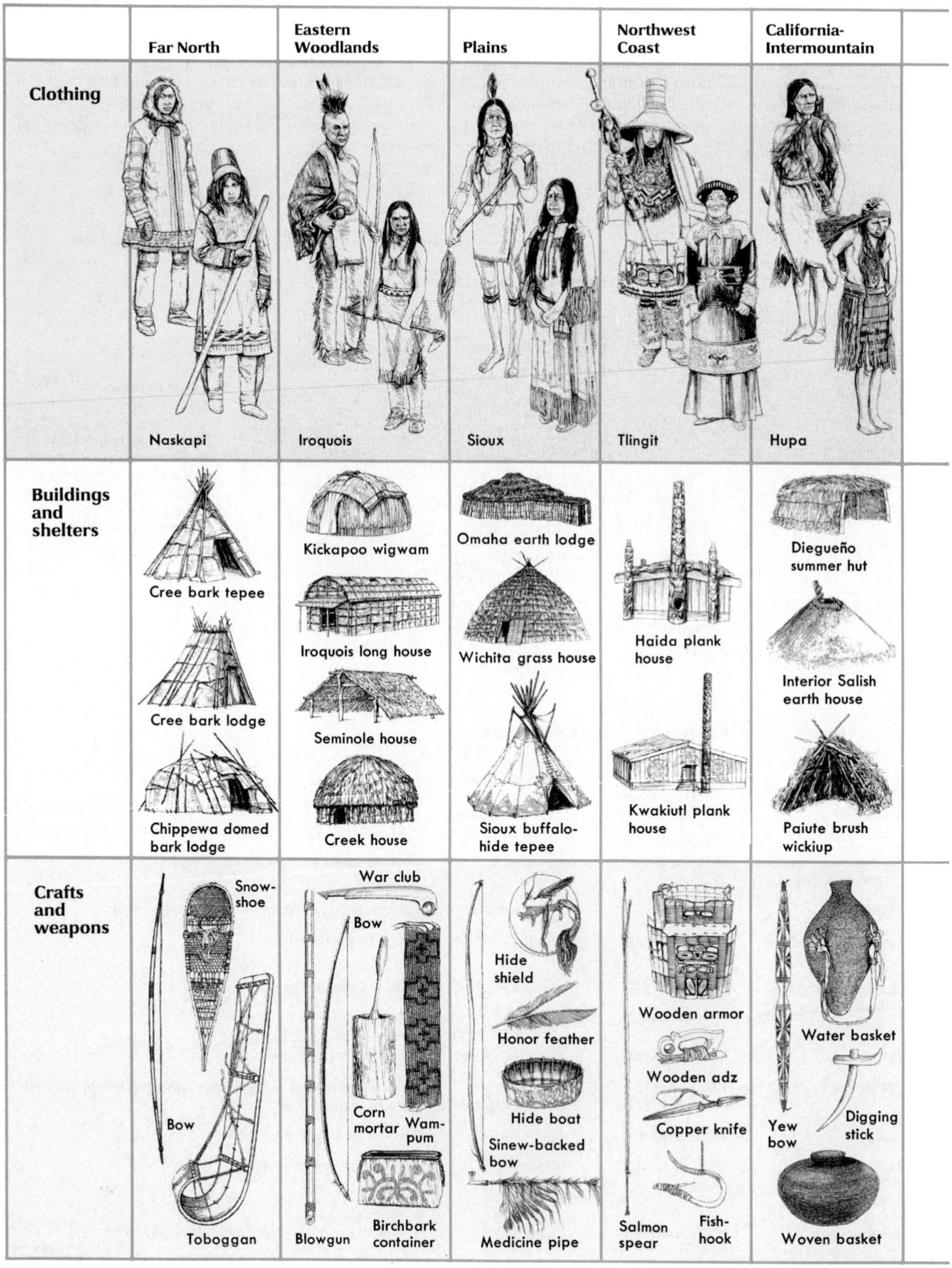

	Far North	Eastern Woodlands	Plains	Northwest Coast	California-Intermountain	
Clothing	Naskapi	Iroquois	Sioux	Tlingit	Hupa	
Buildings and shelters	Cree bark tepee / Cree bark lodge / Chippewa domed bark lodge	Kickapoo wigwam / Iroquois long house / Seminole house / Creek house	Omaha earth lodge / Wichita grass house / Sioux buffalo-hide tepee	Haida plank house / Kwakiutl plank house	Diegueño summer hut / Interior Salish earth house / Paiute brush wickiup	
Crafts and weapons	Snowshoe / Bow / Toboggan	War club / Bow / Corn mortar / Wampum / Blowgun / Birchbark container	Hide shield / Honor feather / Hide boat / Sinew-backed bow / Medicine pipe	Wooden armor / Wooden adz / Copper knife / Salmon spear / Fishhook	Water basket / Yew bow / Digging stick / Woven basket	

WORLD BOOK illustrations by Anthony Saris

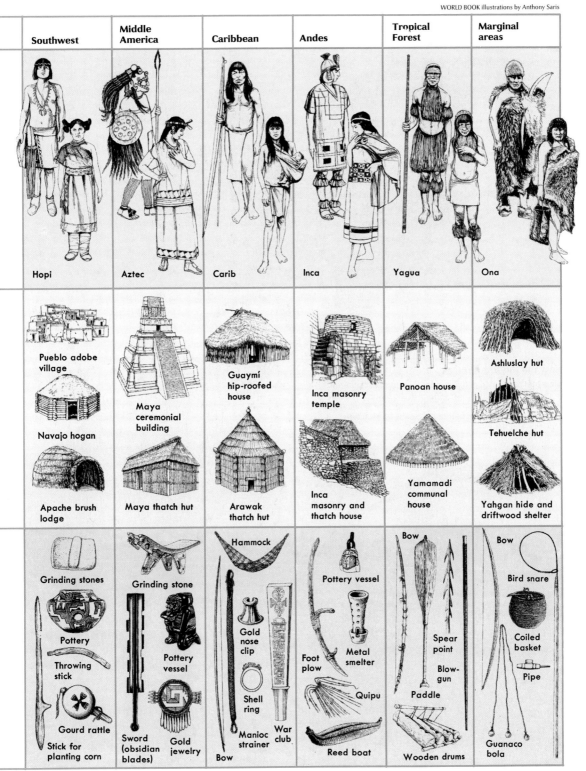

Southwest	Middle America	Caribbean	Andes	Tropical Forest	Marginal areas
Hopi	Aztec	Carib	Inca	Yagua	Ona
Pueblo adobe village / Navajo hogan / Apache brush lodge	Maya ceremonial building / Maya thatch hut	Guaymí hip-roofed house / Arawak thatch hut	Inca masonry temple / Inca masonry and thatch house	Panoan house / Yamamadi communal house	Ashluslay hut / Tehuelche hut / Yahgan hide and driftwood shelter
Grinding stones / Pottery / Throwing stick / Gourd rattle / Stick for planting corn	Grinding stone / Pottery vessel / Sword (obsidian blades) / Gold jewelry	Hammock / Gold nose clip / Shell ring / Manioc strainer / War club / Bow	Pottery vessel / Foot plow / Metal smelter / Quipu / Reed boat	Bow / Spear point / Blow-gun / Paddle / Wooden drums	Bow / Bird snare / Coiled basket / Pipe / Guanaco bola

Copyright © 1990 by World Book, Inc.

Indian, American

Where the Indians lived

The Indians of North and South America formed hundreds of tribes with many different ways of life. The location of many major tribes is shown below. Scholars divide the various tribes into groups of similar tribes that they call *culture areas.* Each culture area is shown as a different color.

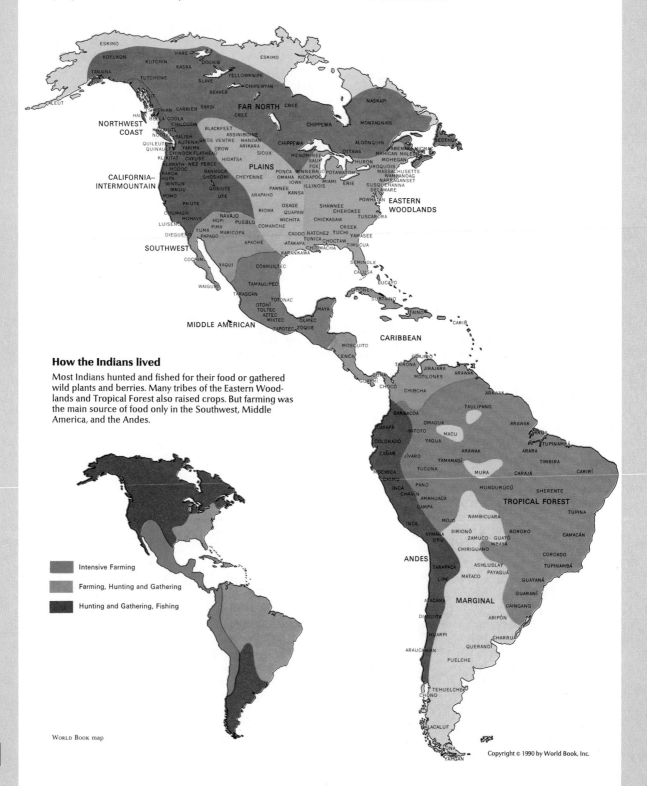

How the Indians lived

Most Indians hunted and fished for their food or gathered wild plants and berries. Many tribes of the Eastern Woodlands and Tropical Forest also raised crops. But farming was the main source of food only in the Southwest, Middle America, and the Andes.

Intensive Farming

Farming, Hunting and Gathering

Hunting and Gathering, Fishing

Flag Research Center

Mexico's flag, adopted in 1821, features a version of the country's coat of arms. The green stands for independence, white for religion, and red for union.

Coat of arms. A legend says the Aztec Indians built their capital Tenochtitlan (now Mexico City) where they saw an eagle perched on a cactus and devouring a snake.

Facts in brief

Capital: Mexico City.
Official language: Spanish.
Official name: *Estados Unidos Mexicanos* (United Mexican States).
Area: 756,067 sq. mi. (1,958,201 km²). *Greatest distances*—north-south, 1,250 mi. (2,012 km); east-west, 1,900 mi. (3,060 km). *Coastline*—6,320 mi. (10,170 km).
Elevation: *Highest*—Orizaba (Citlaltépetl), 18,701 ft. (5,700 m) above sea level. *Lowest*—near Mexicali, 33 ft. (10 m) below sea level.
Population: *Estimated 1993 population*—94,545,000; density, 125 persons per sq. mi. (48 per km²), distribution, 73 per cent urban, 27 per cent rural. *1980 census*—66,846,833. *Estimated 1998 population*—103,994,000.
Chief products: *Agriculture*—bananas, beans, beef cattle, chickens and eggs, coconuts, corn, cotton, mangoes, milk, oranges, potatoes, sorghum, soybeans, sugar cane, tomatoes, wheat. *Fishing*—anchovies, oysters, sardines, shrimp, tuna. *Forestry*—chicle, ebony, mahogany, pine, rosewood. *Manufacturing*—automobiles, beer, cement, chemicals, clothing, fertilizers, iron and steel, household appliances, processed foods, wood pulp and paper. *Mining*—barytes, copper, fluorite, gold, iron ore, lead, manganese, natural gas, petroleum, salt, silver, sulfur, zinc.
National anthem: "Himno Nacional de México" ("National Anthem of Mexico").
National holidays: Independence Days, September 15 and 16.
Money: *Basic unit*—peso.

Important dates in Mexico

c. 2000 B.C. Village life developed in the Valley of Mexico.
c. A.D. 250-900 Great Indian civilizations thrived during the Classic Period.
c. 900-1200 The Toltec empire controlled the Valley of Mexico.
1325 (according to legend) The Aztec founded Tenochtitlán (now Mexico City).
1519-1521 Hernando Cortés conquered the Aztec empire for Spain.
1810 Miguel Hidalgo y Costilla began the Mexican struggle for independence.
1821 Mexico won independence.
1824 Mexico became a republic.
1836 Texas won independence from Mexico.
1846-1848 The United States defeated Mexico in the Mexican War, and won much Mexican territory.
1855 A liberal government under Benito Juárez began a period of reform.
1863 French troops occupied Mexico City.
1864 Maximilian of Austria became emperor of Mexico.
1867 Liberal forces led by Benito Juárez regained power.
1876-1880 and **1884-1911** Porfirio Díaz ruled Mexico as dictator.
1910-1911 Francisco I. Madero led a revolution that overthrew Díaz.
1914 United States forces occupied Veracruz.
1917 A revolutionary constitution was adopted.
1920 The government began making revolutionary social and economic reforms.
1929 The National Revolutionary Party was formed.
1934 The government began a major program of land distribution to farmers.
1938 Mexico took over foreign oil-company properties.
1942-1945 Mexico's industries expanded rapidly during World War II to supply the Allies with war goods.
1953 Women received the right to vote in all elections.
1968 The Summer Olympic Games were held in Mexico City.
1970's Major new petroleum deposits were discovered on the Gulf of Mexico coast.
1985 Two earthquakes struck south-central Mexico, killing about 7,200 people.

States and Federal District of Mexico

States

Name	Area In sq. mi.	In km²	Population	Capital	Name	Area In sq. mi.	In km²	Population	Capital
Aguascalientes	2,112	5,471	684,247	Aguascalientes	Oaxaca	36,275	93,952	2,650,232	Oaxaca
Baja California					Puebla	13,090	33,902	4,068,038	Puebla
Norte	26,997	69,921	1,388,476	Mexicali	Querétaro	4,420	11,449	952,875	Querétaro
Baja California					Quintana Roo	19,387	50,212	393,398	Chetumal
Sur	28,369	73,475	315,095	La Paz	San Luis Potosí	24,351	63,068	2,020,715	San Luis Potosí
Campeche	19,619	50,812	592,933	Campeche					
Chiapas	28,653	74,211	2,518,679	Tuxtla	Sinaloa	22,520	58,328	2,367,567	Culiacán
Chihuahua	94,571	244,938	2,238,542	Chihuahua	Sonora	70,291	182,052	1,799,646	Hermosillo
Coahuila	57,908	149,982	1,906,119	Saltillo	Tabasco	9,756	25,267	1,299,507	Villahermosa
Colima	2,004	5,191	419,439	Colima	Tamaulipas	30,651	79,384	2,266,677	Ciudad Victoria
Durango	47,560	123,181	1,384,518	Durango					
Guanajuato	11,773	30,491	3,542,103	Guanajuato	Tlaxcala	1,550	4,016	665,606	Tlaxcala
Guerrero	24,819	64,281	2,560,262	Chilpancingo	Veracruz	27,683	71,699	6,658,946	Jalapa
Hidalgo	8,036	20,813	1,822,296	Pachuca	Yucatán	14,827	38,402	1,302,600	Mérida
Jalisco	31,211	80,836	5,198,374	Guadalajara	Zacatecas	28,283	73,252	1,251,531	Zacatecas
México	8,245	21,355	11,571,111	Toluca					
Michoacán	23,138	59,928	3,377,732	Morelia					
Morelos	1,911	4,950	1,258,468	Cuernavaca					
Nayarit	10,417	26,979	846,278	Tepic					
Nuevo León	25,067	64,924	3,146,169	Monterrey					

Federal District

Name	In sq. mi.	In km²	Population	Capital
Federal District	571	1,479	19,150,275	Mexico City

Source for population figures: 1988 estimates.

Compiled from the Mexico article in *World Book*. Copyright © 1993 by World Book, Inc.

The Presidents of the United States

President	Born	Birthplace	Political party	Age at inauguration	Served	Died	Age at death
1. George Washington	Feb. 22, 1732	Westmoreland County, Va.	None	57	1789-1797	Dec. 14, 1799	67
2. John Adams	Oct. 30, 1735	Braintree, Mass.	Federalist	61	1797-1801	July 4, 1826	90
3. Thomas Jefferson	Apr. 13, 1743	Albemarle County, Va.	Democratic-Republican	57	1801-1809	July 4, 1826	83
4. James Madison	Mar. 16, 1751	Port Conway, Va.	Democratic-Republican	57	1809-1817	June 28, 1836	85
5. James Monroe	Apr. 28, 1758	Westmoreland County, Va.	Democratic-Republican	58	1817-1825	July 4, 1831	73
6. John Quincy Adams	July 11, 1767	Braintree, Mass.	Democratic-Republican	57	1825-1829	Feb. 23, 1848	80
7. Andrew Jackson	Mar. 15, 1767	Waxhaw settlement, S.C. (?)	Democratic	61	1829-1837	June 8, 1845	78
8. Martin Van Buren	Dec. 5, 1782	Kinderhook, N.Y.	Democratic	54	1837-1841	July 24, 1862	79
9. William H. Harrison	Feb. 9, 1773	Berkeley, Va.	Whig	68	1841	Apr. 4, 1841	68
10. John Tyler	Mar. 29, 1790	Greenway, Va.	Whig	51	1841-1845	Jan. 18, 1862	71
11. James K. Polk	Nov. 2, 1795	near Pineville, N.C.	Democratic	49	1845-1849	June 15, 1849	53
12. Zachary Taylor	Nov. 24, 1784	Orange County, Va.	Whig	64	1849-1850	July 9, 1850	65
13. Millard Fillmore	Jan. 7, 1800	Locke, N.Y.	Whig	50	1850-1853	Mar. 8, 1874	74
14. Franklin Pierce	Nov. 23, 1804	Hillsboro, N.H.	Democratic	48	1853-1857	Oct. 8, 1869	64
15. James Buchanan	Apr. 23, 1791	near Mercersburg, Pa.	Democratic	65	1857-1861	June 1, 1868	77
16. Abraham Lincoln	Feb. 12, 1809	near Hodgenville, Ky.	Republican, Union	52	1861-1865	Apr. 15, 1865	56
17. Andrew Johnson	Dec. 29, 1808	Raleigh, N.C.	Union†	56	1865-1869	July 31, 1875	66
18. Ulysses S. Grant	Apr. 27, 1822	Point Pleasant, Ohio	Republican	46	1869-1877	July 23, 1885	63
19. Rutherford B. Hayes	Oct. 4, 1822	Delaware, Ohio	Republican	54	1877-1881	Jan. 17, 1893	70
20. James A. Garfield	Nov. 19, 1831	Orange, Ohio	Republican	49	1881	Sept. 19, 1881	49
21. Chester A. Arthur	Oct. 5, 1829	Fairfield, Vt.	Republican	51	1881-1885	Nov. 18, 1886	57
22. Grover Cleveland	Mar. 18, 1837	Caldwell, N.J.	Democratic	47	1885-1889	June 24, 1908	71
23. Benjamin Harrison	Aug. 20, 1833	North Bend, Ohio	Republican	55	1889-1893	Mar. 13, 1901	67
24. Grover Cleveland	Mar. 18, 1837	Caldwell, N.J.	Democratic	55	1893-1897	June 24, 1908	71
25. William McKinley	Jan. 29, 1843	Niles, Ohio	Republican	54	1897-1901	Sept. 14, 1901	58
26. Theodore Roosevelt	Oct. 27, 1858	New York, N.Y.	Republican	42	1901-1909	Jan. 6, 1919	60
27. William H. Taft	Sept. 15, 1857	Cincinnati, Ohio	Republican	51	1909-1913	Mar. 8, 1930	72
28. Woodrow Wilson	Dec. 29, 1856	Staunton, Va.	Democratic	56	1913-1921	Feb. 3, 1924	67
29. Warren G. Harding	Nov. 2, 1865	near Blooming Grove, Ohio	Republican	55	1921-1923	Aug. 2, 1923	57
30. Calvin Coolidge	July 4, 1872	Plymouth Notch, Vt.	Republican	51	1923-1929	Jan. 5, 1933	60
31. Herbert C. Hoover	Aug. 10, 1874	West Branch, Iowa	Republican	54	1929-1933	Oct. 20, 1964	90
32. Franklin D. Roosevelt	Jan. 30, 1882	Hyde Park, N.Y.	Democratic	51	1933-1945	Apr. 12, 1945	63
33. Harry S. Truman	May 8, 1884	Lamar, Mo.	Democratic	60	1945-1953	Dec. 26, 1972	88
34. Dwight D. Eisenhower	Oct. 14, 1890	Denison, Tex.	Republican	62	1953-1961	Mar. 28, 1969	78
35. John F. Kennedy	May 29, 1917	Brookline, Mass.	Democratic	43	1961-1963	Nov. 22, 1963	46
36. Lyndon B. Johnson	Aug. 27, 1908	near Stonewall, Tex.	Democratic	55	1963-1969	Jan. 22, 1973	64
37. Richard M. Nixon	Jan. 9, 1913	Yorba Linda, Calif.	Republican	56	1969-1974		
38. Gerald R. Ford‡	July 14, 1913	Omaha, Nebr.	Republican	61	1974-1977		
39. Jimmy Carter	Oct. 1, 1924	Plains, Ga.	Democratic	52	1977-1981		
40. Ronald W. Reagan	Feb. 6, 1911	Tampico, Ill.	Republican	69	1981-1989		
41. George H. W. Bush	June 12, 1924	Milton, Mass.	Republican	64	1989-1993		
42. Bill Clinton	Aug. 19, 1946	Hope, Ark.	Democratic	46	1993-		

†The Union Party consisted of Republicans and War Democrats; Johnson was a War Democrat.
‡Inaugurated Aug. 9, 1974, to replace Nixon, who resigned that same day.

Each President has a separate biography and picture in *World Book*.

Symbols of the United States include the American flag and the Great Seal. The eagle holds an olive branch and arrows, symbolizing a desire for peace but the ability to wage war. The reverse side bears the Eye of Providence, representing God, and a pyramid dated 1776.

Facts in brief

Capital: Washington, D.C.
Form of government: Republic. For details, see **United States, Government of the.**
Area: 3,618,770 sq. mi. (9,372,571 km²), including 79,481 sq. mi. (205,856 km²) of inland water but excluding 60,788 sq. mi. (157,440 km²) of Great Lakes and Lake Saint Clair and 13,942 sq. mi. (36,110 km²) of coastal water. *Greatest distances excluding Alaska and Hawaii*—east-west, 2,807 mi. (4,517 km); north-south, 1,598 mi. (2,572 km). *Greatest distances in Alaska*—north-south, about 1,200 mi. (1,930 km); east-west, about 2,200 mi. (3,540 km). *Greatest distance in Hawaii*—northwest-southeast, about 1,610 mi. (2,591 km). *Extreme points including Alaska and Hawaii*—northernmost, Point Barrow, Alaska; southernmost, Ka Lae, Hawaii; easternmost, West Quoddy Head, Me.; westernmost, Cape Wrangell, Attu Island, Alaska. *Coastline*—4,993 mi. (8,035 km), excluding Alaska and Hawaii; 12,383 mi. (19,929 km), including Alaska and Hawaii.
Elevation: *Highest*—Mount McKinley in Alaska, 20,320 ft. (6,194 m) above sea level. *Lowest*—In Death Valley in California, 282 ft. (86 m) below sea level.
Physical features: *Longest river*—Mississippi, 2,348 mi. (3,779 km). *Largest lake within the United States*—Michigan, 22,300 sq. mi. (57,757 km²). *Largest island*—island of Hawaii, 4,038 sq. mi. (10,458 km²).
Population: *Estimated 1993 population*—256,300,000; density, 71 persons per sq. mi. (27 per km²); distribution, 74 per cent urban, 26 per cent rural. *1990 census*—249,632,692. *Estimated 1998 population*—264,082,000.
Chief products: *Agriculture*—beef cattle, chickens, corn, cotton, eggs, hogs, milk, soybeans, wheat. *Fishing industry*—crabs, salmon, shrimp. *Manufacturing*—airplanes, broadcasting equipment, cameras, computers and computer parts, fabricated metal products, gasoline, guided missiles, industrial chemicals, industrial machinery, motor vehicles, paper, pharmaceuticals, plastics, printed materials, processed foods, steel. *Mining*—coal, natural gas, petroleum.
Flag: Adopted June 14, 1777.
Motto: *In God We Trust,* adopted July 30, 1956.
National anthem: "The Star-Spangled Banner," adopted March 3, 1931.
Bird: Bald eagle, adopted June 20, 1782.
Flower: Rose, adopted Oct. 7, 1986.
Money: *Basic unit*—dollar.

Important dates

1492 Christopher Columbus sailed from Spain to the Western Hemisphere. Europeans honored him as the discoverer of America.
1497 John Cabot made the first voyage to North America for England.
1513 Ponce de León of Spain began exploring Florida, seeking the Fountain of Youth.
1540-1542 Francisco Coronado of Spain explored the American Southwest.
1565 Spaniards founded St. Augustine, Fla., the oldest city in what is now the United States.
1607 About 100 colonists founded Jamestown, the first permanent British settlement in North America.
1619 Virginia established the House of Burgesses, the first representative legislature in America.
1620 The Pilgrims founded Plymouth Colony, the second permanent British settlement in North America.
1624 The Dutch established the settlement of New Netherland.
1636 Harvard—the first college in the colonies—was founded.
1638 People from Sweden established the settlement of New Sweden.
1647 Massachusetts established the first colonial public school system.
1649 Maryland passed the first religious toleration act in North America.
1664 England took control of New Netherland and New Sweden.
1704 *The Boston News-Letter,* the first successful colonial newspaper, began publication.
1763 Britain defeated France in the French and Indian War and gained control of eastern North America.
1763 Britain stationed a standing army in North America and prohibited colonists from settling west of the Appalachian Mountains.
1765 The British Parliament passed the Stamp Act, taxing newspapers, legal documents, and other printed matter in the colonies.
1770 British troops killed American civilians in the Boston Massacre.
1773 Colonists staged the Boston Tea Party, dumping British tea into Boston Harbor.
1774 The Intolerable Acts closed Boston Harbor and included other steps to punish the colonists.
1774 The First Continental Congress met to consider action against the British.
1775 The Revolutionary War between the colonists and the British began.
1776 The colonists adopted the Declaration of Independence and formed the United States of America.
1781 The Americans defeated the British at Yorktown, Va., in the last major battle of the Revolutionary War.
1783 The Treaty of Paris officially ended the Revolutionary War.
1787 The Founding Fathers wrote the Constitution.
1790's The first U.S. political parties developed.
1800 Washington, D.C., became the national capital.
1803 The Louisiana Purchase almost doubled the size of the United States.
1811 Work began on the National Road, which—when completed—linked the East and the Midwest.
1812-1814 The United States and Great Britain fought the War of 1812.
1820 The Missouri Compromise ended a slavery dispute.
1823 The Monroe Doctrine warned Europeans against interference in Western Hemisphere affairs.
1825 The Erie Canal opened, providing a water route from the Atlantic Ocean to the Great Lakes.
1832 South Carolina threatened secession over a tariff.
1846 Britain ceded the southern part of the Oregon Country to the United States.
1848 Victory in the Mexican War gave the United States vast new territory in the West.
1848 The discovery of gold in California triggered the Gold Rush.

Compiled from articles on the United States in *World Book.* © Copyright 1993 by World Book, Inc.

United States

1850 The Compromise of 1850 temporarily ended a national crisis over the slavery question.

1854 Passage of the Kansas-Nebraska Act led to nationwide turmoil over the slavery issue.

1860 Pony express riders began carrying mail from St. Joseph, Mo., to the Far West.

1861-1865 The North and the South fought each other in the Civil War.

1863 The Emancipation Proclamation declared freedom for all slaves in Confederate-held territory.

1865 The 13th Amendment outlawed slavery.

1867 The United States bought Alaska from Russia.

1868 The House of Representatives impeached President Andrew Johnson, but the Senate did not remove him from office.

1898 The United States defeated Spain in the Spanish-American War.

1913 The 16th Amendment gave the federal government the power to levy an income tax.

1917-1918 The United States fought in World War I.

1920 The U.S. Senate rejected American participation in the League of Nations.

1920 The U.S. Census showed that, for the first time, the majority of Americans lived in urban areas.

1920 The 18th Amendment, prohibiting the sale of alcoholic beverages nationwide, became effective; the 19th Amendment gave women complete suffrage.

1929 The stock market crash brought financial ruin to thousands of investors.

1930's The United States suffered through the Great Depression.

1933 President Franklin D. Roosevelt began the New Deal program to try to end the depression.

1941-1945 The United States fought in World War II.

1945 An American airplane dropped the first atomic bomb used in warfare on Hiroshima, Japan.

1945 The United States became a charter member of the United Nations (UN).

1947 President Truman announced the Truman Doctrine, which pledged American aid to nations threatened by Communism.

1950 Senator Joseph R. McCarthy gained national fame by charging that Communists had infiltrated the federal government.

1950-1953 The United States fought in the Korean War.

1954 The Supreme Court ruled compulsory segregation in public schools unconstitutional.

1955 Martin Luther King, Jr., began organizing a movement to protest discrimination against blacks.

1957 The Soviet Union launched Sputnik I—the first space satellite—causing the United States to place more emphasis on space research.

1962 The Soviet Union removed missiles from Cuba, ending a threat of war with the United States.

1964 Congress passed a flood of important civil rights laws.

1965 American combat troops entered the Vietnam War.

1969 Astronaut Neil A. Armstrong became the first person to set foot on the moon.

1973 The United States removed its last ground troops from Vietnam. The war ended in 1975.

1974 Richard M. Nixon became the first American President to resign from office.

1976 The United States celebrated its bicentennial.

1986 The U.S. spacecraft Challenger exploded, and all seven crew members were killed.

1987 The United States celebrated the bicentennial of the signing of the U.S. Constitution.

1991 U.S. armed forces helped defeat Iraq in the Persian Gulf War.

612

The United States after the Revolutionary War

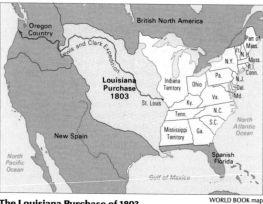

The Louisiana Purchase of 1803

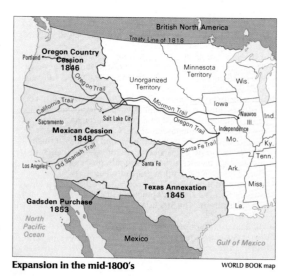

Expansion in the mid-1800's

Compiled from articles on the United States in *World Book.* Copyright © 1990 by World Book, Inc.

1st President of
the United States 1789-1797

Washington
1st President
1789-1797
No political
party

J. Adams
2nd President
1797-1801
Federalist

John Adams
Vice President
1789-1797

Oil painting on canvas (1796) by Gilbert Stuart; Jointly owned by the National Portrait Gallery, Smithsonian Institution, and the Museum of Fine Arts, Boston

Washington, George (1732-1799), won a lasting place in American history as the "Father of our Country." For nearly 20 years, he guided his country much as a father cares for a growing child.

In three important ways, Washington helped shape the beginning of the United States. First, he commanded the Continental Army that won American independence from Great Britain in the Revolutionary War. Second, Washington served as president of the convention that wrote the United States Constitution. Third, he was elected the first President of the United States.

The people of his day loved Washington. His army officers would have made him king if he had let them. From the Revolutionary War on, his birthday was celebrated each year throughout the country.

Washington lived an exciting life in exciting times. As a boy, he explored the wilderness. When he grew older, he helped the British fight the French and Indians. Many times he was nearly killed. As a general, he suffered hardships with his troops in the cold winters at Valley Forge, Pa., and Morristown, N.J. He lost many battles, but led the American army to final victory at Yorktown, Va. After he became President, he successfully solved many problems in turning the plans of the Constitution into a working government.

Washington went to school only until he was about 14 or 15. But he learned to make the most of all his abilities and opportunities. Washington's remarkable patience and his understanding of others helped him win people to his side in times of hardship and discouragement.

There are great differences between the United States of Washington's day and that of today. The new nation was small and weak. It stretched west only to the Mississippi River and had fewer than 4,000,000 people. Most people made their living by farming. Few children went to school. Few men or women could read or write. Transportation and communication were slow. It took Washington 3 days to travel about 90 miles (140 kilometers) from New York City to Philadelphia, longer than it now takes to fly around the world. There were only 11 states in the Union when Washington became President and 16 when he left office.

Important dates in Washington's life

1732	(Feb. 22) Born in Westmoreland County, Virginia.
1749	Became official surveyor for Culpeper County, Virginia.
1751	Went to Barbados Island, British West Indies.
1753	Carried British ultimatum to French in Ohio River Valley, as a major.
1754	Surrendered Fort Necessity in the French and Indian War, as a colonel.
1755	(July 9) With General Edward Braddock when ambushed by French and Indians.
1755-1758	Commanded Virginia's frontier troops, as a colonel.
1759	(Jan. 6) Married Mrs. Martha Dandridge Custis.
1774	Elected delegate to First Continental Congress.
1775	Elected delegate to Second Continental Congress.
1775	(June 15) Elected commander in chief of Continental Army.
1781	(Oct. 19) Victory at Yorktown.
1787	(May 25) Elected president of the Constitutional Convention.
1789	Elected first President of the United States.
1792	Reelected President of the United States.
1796	(Sept. 19) Published *Farewell Address,* refusing a third term.
1798	(July 4) Commissioned lieutenant general and commander in chief of new United States Army.
1799	(Dec. 14) Died at Mount Vernon at age 67.

Excerpted from the George Washington article in *World Book.* Copyright © 1993 by World Book, Inc.

WORLD: *Political*

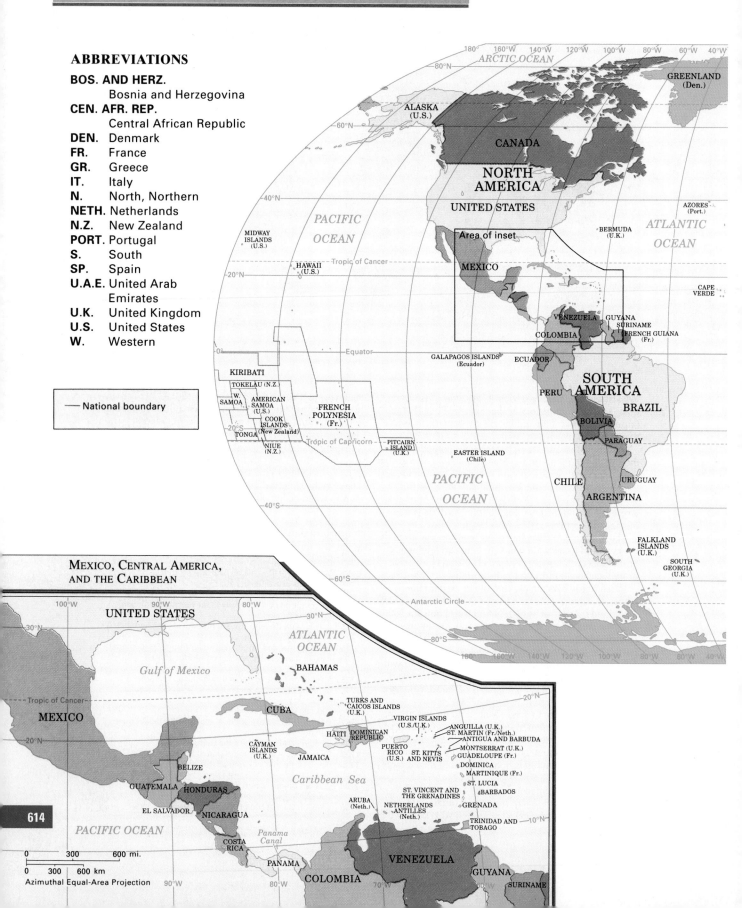

ABBREVIATIONS

BOS. AND HERZ.
Bosnia and Herzegovina
CEN. AFR. REP.
Central African Republic
DEN. Denmark
FR. France
GR. Greece
IT. Italy
N. North, Northern
NETH. Netherlands
N.Z. New Zealand
PORT. Portugal
S. South
SP. Spain
U.A.E. United Arab
Emirates
U.K. United Kingdom
U.S. United States
W. Western

—— National boundary

ARCTIC OCEAN

GREENLAND
(Den.)

ALASKA
(U.S.)

CANADA

NORTH
AMERICA

UNITED STATES

AZORES
(Port.)

PACIFIC
OCEAN

ATLANTIC
OCEAN

BERMUDA
(U.K.)

MIDWAY
ISLANDS
(U.S.)

HAWAII
(U.S.)

Tropic of Cancer

Area of inset

MEXICO

CAPE
VERDE

VENEZUELA GUYANA
SURINAME
COLOMBIA FRENCH GUIANA
(Fr.)

KIRIBATI

TOKELAU (N.Z.)
W.
SAMOA AMERICAN
SAMOA
(U.S.)
COOK
ISLANDS
(New Zealand)
TONGA
NIUE
(N.Z.)

FRENCH
POLYNESIA
(Fr.)

GALAPAGOS ISLANDS
(Ecuador)

ECUADOR

SOUTH
AMERICA

PERU

BRAZIL

BOLIVIA

Equator

Tropic of Capricorn

PITCAIRN
ISLAND
(U.K.)

EASTER ISLAND
(Chile)

PACIFIC
OCEAN

PARAGUAY

CHILE

URUGUAY

ARGENTINA

FALKLAND
ISLANDS
(U.K.)

SOUTH
GEORGIA
(U.K.)

Antarctic Circle

MEXICO, CENTRAL AMERICA, AND THE CARIBBEAN

UNITED STATES

ATLANTIC
OCEAN

Gulf of Mexico

BAHAMAS

Tropic of Cancer

MEXICO

CUBA

TURKS AND
CAICOS ISLANDS
(U.K.)

VIRGIN ISLANDS
(U.S./U.K.)
ANGUILLA (U.K.)
ST. MARTIN (Fr./Neth.)
ANTIGUA AND BARBUDA
MONTSERRAT (U.K.)
GUADELOUPE (Fr.)

CAYMAN
ISLANDS
(U.K.)

HAITI DOMINICAN
REPUBLIC

PUERTO
RICO ST. KITTS
(U.S.) AND NEVIS

JAMAICA

DOMINICA
MARTINIQUE (Fr.)

ST. LUCIA

BELIZE

Caribbean Sea

GUATEMALA HONDURAS

ST. VINCENT AND
THE GRENADINES

BARBADOS

EL SALVADOR NICARAGUA

ARUBA
(Neth.)

NETHERLANDS
ANTILLES
(Neth.)

GRENADA

COSTA
RICA

PACIFIC OCEAN

Panama
Canal

TRINIDAD AND
TOBAGO

PANAMA

VENEZUELA

COLOMBIA

GUYANA

SURINAME

0   300   600 mi.

0   300   600 km

Azimuthal Equal-Area Projection

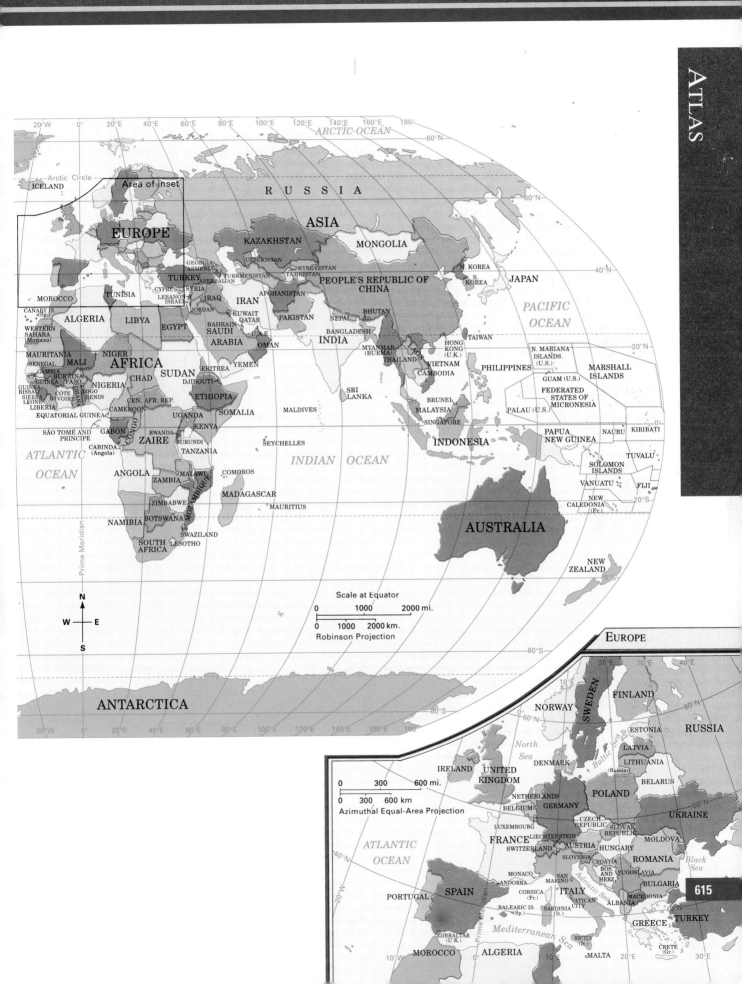

ARCTIC OCEAN
80°N

Arctic Circle
ICELAND
Area of inset

R U S S I A
60°N

EUROPE
ASIA
KAZAKHSTAN
MONGOLIA
40°N

GEORGIA
ARMENIA
UZBEKISTAN
KYRGYZSTAN
TURKMENISTAN
TAJIKISTAN
N. KOREA
TURKEY
AZERBAIJAN
S. KOREA
JAPAN
CYPRUS SYRIA
LEBANON
ISRAEL
IRAQ
IRAN
AFGHANISTAN
PEOPLE'S REPUBLIC OF
CHINA
MOROCCO
TUNISIA
JORDAN
KUWAIT
PACIFIC
OCEAN
CANARY IS.
(Sp.)
ALGERIA
LIBYA
EGYPT
SAUDI
ARABIA
BAHRAIN
QATAR
U.A.E.
OMAN
PAKISTAN
NEPAL
BHUTAN
BANGLADESH
INDIA
TAIWAN
HONG
KONG
(U.K.)
20°N
WESTERN
SAHARA
(Morocco)
MAURITANIA
NIGER
YEMEN
MYANMAR
(BURMA)
THAILAND
LAOS
VIETNAM
CAMBODIA
N. MARIANA
ISLANDS
(U.S.)
MARSHALL
ISLANDS
SENEGAL
MALI
AFRICA
SUDAN
ERITREA
DJIBOUTI
SRI
LANKA
GUAM (U.S.)
GAMBIA
BURKINA
FASO
CHAD
PHILIPPINES
FEDERATED
STATES OF
MICRONESIA
GUINEA
BISSAU
GUINEA
NIGERIA
CEN. AFR. REP.
ETHIOPIA
MALDIVES
BRUNEI
PALAU (U.S.)
0°
SIERRA
LEONE
LIBERIA
CÔTE
D'IVOIRE
TOGO
BENIN
CAMEROON
UGANDA
SOMALIA
MALAYSIA
SINGAPORE
EQUATORIAL GUINEA
KENYA
SÃO TOMÉ AND
PRINCIPE
GABON
RWANDA
BURUNDI
SEYCHELLES
INDONESIA
PAPUA
NEW GUINEA
NAURU
KIRIBATI
ATLANTIC
ZAIRE
TANZANIA
INDIAN OCEAN
TUVALU
OCEAN
CABINDA
(Angola)
ANGOLA
ZAMBIA
MALAWI
COMOROS
SOLOMON
ISLANDS
VANUATU
FIJI
ZIMBABWE
MOZAMBIQUE
MADAGASCAR
NEW
CALEDONIA
(Fr.)
20°S
NAMIBIA
BOTSWANA
MAURITIUS
AUSTRALIA
SWAZILAND
SOUTH
AFRICA
LESOTHO

N
W E
S

Scale at Equator
0   1000   2000 mi.
0   1000   2000 km.
Robinson Projection

NEW
ZEALAND

60°S

ANTARCTICA
80°S

20°W   0°   20°E   40°E   60°E   80°E   100°E   120°E   140°E   160°E

Prime Meridian

SWEDEN
FINLAND
NORWAY
60°N

North
Sea
ESTONIA
DENMARK
LATVIA
LITHUANIA
(Russia)
IRELAND
UNITED
KINGDOM
BELARUS
NETHERLANDS
POLAND
0   300   600 mi.
BELGIUM
GERMANY
0   300   600 km
Azimuthal Equal-Area Projection
LUXEMBOURG
CZECH
REPUBLIC
UKRAINE
50°N
FRANCE
LIECHTENSTEIN
SLOVAK
REPUBLIC
MOLDOVA
ATLANTIC
OCEAN
SWITZERLAND
AUSTRIA
HUNGARY
SLOVENIA
CROATIA
ROMANIA
Black
Sea
MONACO
SAN
MARINO
BOS.
AND
HERZ.
YUGOSLAVIA
ANDORRA
BULGARIA
CORSICA
(Fr.)
ITALY
MACEDONIA
PORTUGAL
SPAIN
VATICAN
CITY
ALBANIA
615
BALEARIC IS.
(Sp.)
SARDINIA
(It.)
Adriatic Sea
TURKEY
GREECE
SICILY
(It.)
CRETE
(Gr.)
GIBRALTAR
(U.K.)
Mediterranean Sea
MOROCCO
ALGERIA
MALTA
20°E
30°E

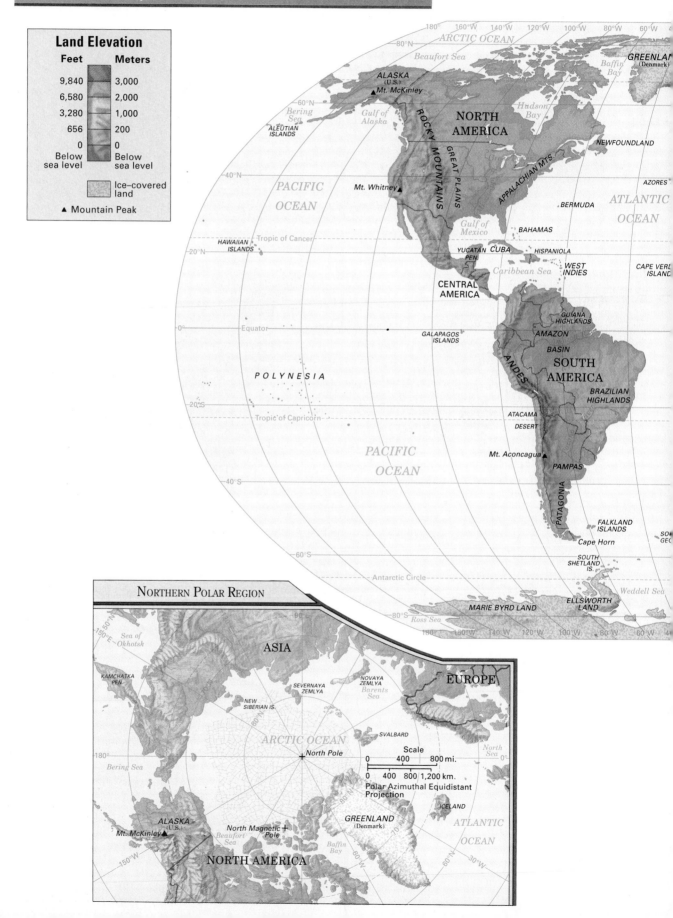

Land Elevation

Feet		Meters
9,840		3,000
6,580		2,000
3,280		1,000
656		200
0		0
Below sea level		Below sea level

Ice-covered land

▲ Mountain Peak

ARCTIC OCEAN

Beaufort Sea

Baffin Bay

GREENLAND (Denmark)

ALASKA (U.S.)
▲ Mt. McKinley

Bering Sea

Gulf of Alaska

ROCKY MOUNTAINS

NORTH AMERICA

Hudson Bay

NEWFOUNDLAND

ALEUTIAN ISLANDS

PACIFIC OCEAN

Mt. Whitney ▲

GREAT PLAINS

APPALACHIAN MTS.

AZORES

ATLANTIC OCEAN

BERMUDA

Gulf of Mexico

BAHAMAS

YUCATAN PEN.

CUBA

HISPANIOLA

Tropic of Cancer

HAWAIIAN ISLANDS

Caribbean Sea

WEST INDIES

CAPE VERDE ISLANDS

CENTRAL AMERICA

Equator

GALAPAGOS ISLANDS

GUIANA HIGHLANDS

AMAZON BASIN

SOUTH AMERICA

P O L Y N E S I A

ANDES

BRAZILIAN HIGHLANDS

Tropic of Capricorn

ATACAMA DESERT

PACIFIC OCEAN

Mt. Aconcagua ▲

PAMPAS

PATAGONIA

FALKLAND ISLANDS

SOUTH GEORGIA

Cape Horn

SOUTH SHETLAND IS.

Antarctic Circle

Weddell Sea

MARIE BYRD LAND

ELLSWORTH LAND

Ross Sea

NORTHERN POLAR REGION

Sea of Okhotsk

ASIA

KAMCHATKA PEN.

SEVERNAYA ZEMLYA

NOVAYA ZEMLYA

Barents Sea

EUROPE

NEW SIBERIAN IS.

SVALBARD

North Sea

ARCTIC OCEAN

North Pole

Scale

0   400   800 mi.

0   400 800 1,200 km.

Polar Azimuthal Equidistant Projection

Bering Sea

ICELAND

ATLANTIC OCEAN

ALASKA (U.S.)
▲ Mt. McKinley

North Magnetic + Pole

Beaufort Sea

GREENLAND (Denmark)

Baffin Bay

NORTH AMERICA

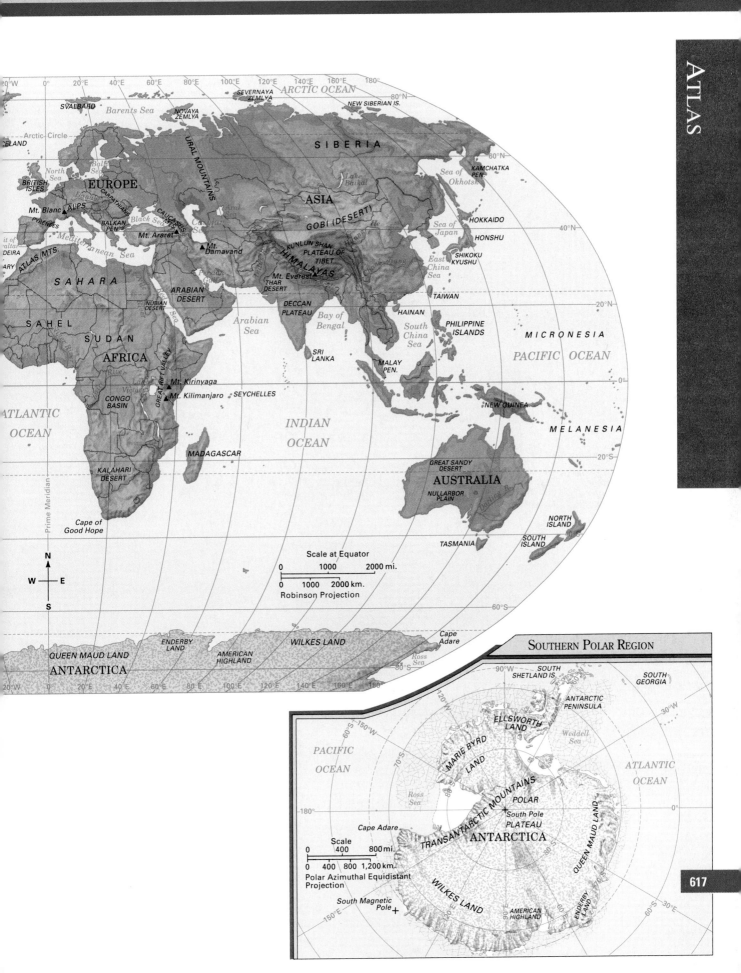

20°W 0° 20°E 40°E 60°E 80°E 100°E 120°E 140°E 160°E 180°

ARCTIC OCEAN

SVALBARD
SEVERNAYA ZEMLYA
NOVAYA ZEMLYA
NEW SIBERIAN IS.
80°N

Arctic Circle
ICELAND
Barents Sea

North Sea
BRITISH ISLES
Baltic Sea
URAL MOUNTAINS
SIBERIA
60°N
KAMCHATKA PEN.
Lake Baikal
Sea of Okhotsk

EUROPE
Mt. Blanc ALPS
CARPATHIANS
CAUCASUS MTS.
ASIA
Sea of Japan
HOKKAIDO
40°N
HONSHU

PYRENEES
BALKAN PEN.
Black Sea
Mt. Ararat
Caspian Sea
Mt. Damavand
GOBI (DESERT)
KUNLUN SHAN
PLATEAU OF TIBET
HIMALAYAS
SHIKOKU KYUSHU

it of Gibraltar
DEIRA
Mediterranean Sea
ATLAS MTS.
ARY
SAHARA
ARABIAN DESERT
NUBIAN DESERT
THAR DESERT
Mt. Everest
DECCAN PLATEAU
East China Sea
TAIWAN
20°N

SAHEL
SUDAN
Arabian Sea
Bay of Bengal
HAINAN
South China Sea
PHILIPPINE ISLANDS
MICRONESIA
PACIFIC OCEAN

AFRICA
Red Sea
SRI LANKA
MALAY PEN.
0°

ATLANTIC OCEAN
Mt. Kirinyaga
CONGO BASIN
GREAT RIFT VALLEY
Mt. Kilimanjaro
SEYCHELLES
Lake Victoria
INDIAN OCEAN
NEW GUINEA
MELANESIA

MADAGASCAR
GREAT SANDY DESERT
20°S

KALAHARI DESERT
AUSTRALIA
NULLARBOR PLAIN
Darling R.
NORTH ISLAND

Prime Meridian
Cape of Good Hope
Scale at Equator
0 1000 2000 mi.
TASMANIA
SOUTH ISLAND
40°S

N
W E
S
0 1000 2000 km.
Robinson Projection

60°S

ENDERBY LAND
WILKES LAND
Cape Adare
Ross Sea
80°S
QUEEN MAUD LAND
AMERICAN HIGHLAND
ANTARCTICA
20°W 0° 20°E 40°E 60°E 80°E 100°E 120°E 140°E 160°E 180°

SOUTHERN POLAR REGION

90°W
SOUTH SHETLAND IS.
SOUTH GEORGIA
ANTARCTIC PENINSULA
30°W

PACIFIC OCEAN
ELLSWORTH LAND
MARIE BYRD LAND
Weddell Sea
ATLANTIC OCEAN

Ross Sea
TRANSANTARCTIC MOUNTAINS
POLAR PLATEAU
South Pole
0°

Cape Adare
180°
ANTARCTICA
QUEEN MAUD LAND

Scale
0 400 800 mi.
WILKES LAND

0 400 800 1,200 km.
Polar Azimuthal Equidistant Projection
AMERICAN HIGHLAND
ENDERBY LAND
60°S 30°E

South Magnetic Pole +
150°E

617

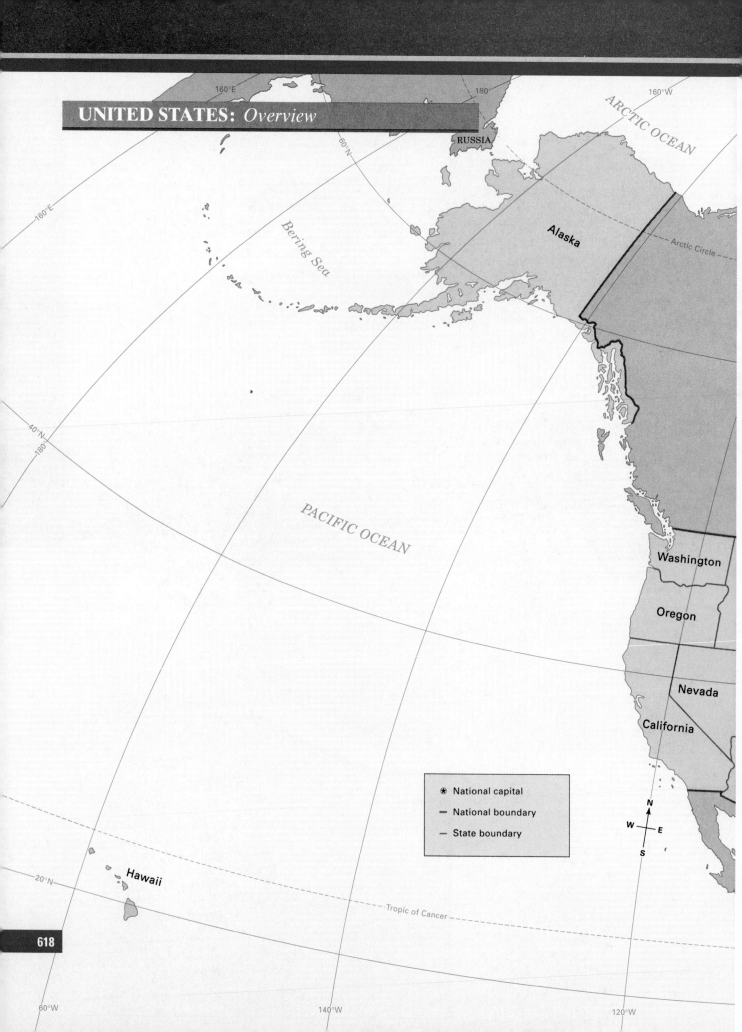

ARCTIC OCEAN

160°E

180°

160°W

RUSSIA

60°N

Alaska

Arctic Circle

Bering Sea

160°E

40°N

180°

PACIFIC OCEAN

Washington

Oregon

Nevada

California

⊛ National capital

— National boundary

— State boundary

N

W   E

S

20°N

Hawaii

Tropic of Cancer

60°W

140°W

120°W

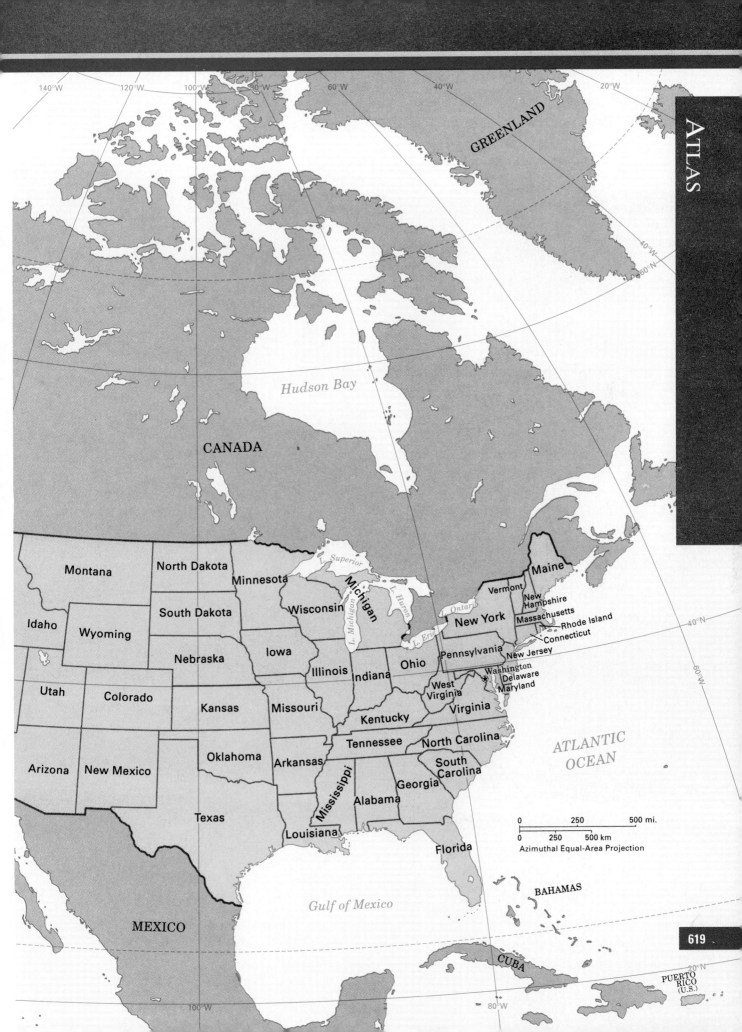

GREENLAND

CANADA

Hudson Bay

Montana
North Dakota
Minnesota
L. Superior
Michigan
Maine
Vermont
New Hampshire
Idaho
Wyoming
South Dakota
Wisconsin
L. Michigan
L. Huron
L. Ontario
New York
Massachusetts
Rhode Island
Connecticut
Nebraska
Iowa
Illinois
Indiana
Ohio
L. Erie
Pennsylvania
New Jersey
Utah
Colorado
Kansas
Missouri
West Virginia
Washington
Delaware
Maryland
Virginia
Kentucky
Arizona
New Mexico
Oklahoma
Arkansas
Tennessee
North Carolina
ATLANTIC OCEAN
Mississippi
Alabama
Georgia
South Carolina
Texas
Louisiana
Florida

0   250   500 mi.
0   250   500 km
Azimuthal Equal-Area Projection

MEXICO

Gulf of Mexico

BAHAMAS

619

CUBA

PUERTO RICO (U.S.)

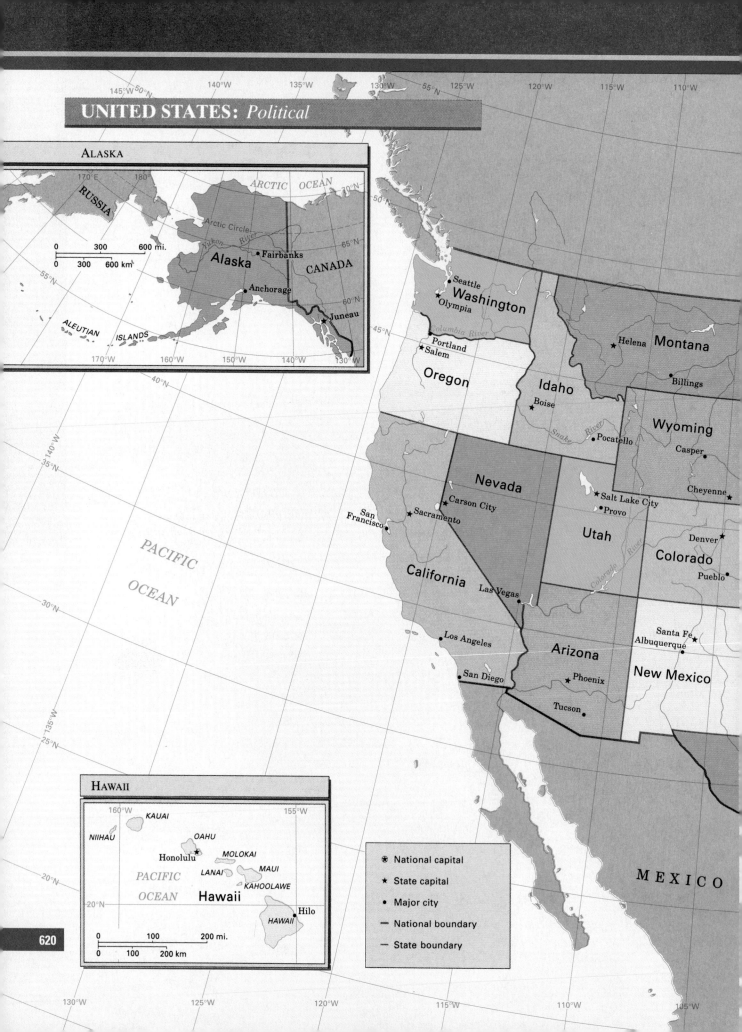

UNITED STATES: *Political*

ALASKA

RUSSIA

ARCTIC OCEAN

Arctic Circle

Yukon River

Alaska

• Fairbanks

CANADA

• Anchorage

• Juneau

ALEUTIAN ISLANDS

0   300   600 mi.
0   300   600 km

170°E   180°   70°N   65°N   60°N   55°N

170°W   160°W   150°W   140°W   130°W

PACIFIC

OCEAN

HAWAII

KAUAI

NIIHAU

OAHU

Honolulu ★

MOLOKAI

LANAI

MAUI

KAHOOLAWE

PACIFIC

OCEAN

Hawaii

HAWAII

Hilo •

0   100   200 mi.
0   100   200 km

160°W   155°W

Washington
Seattle •
★ Olympia

Columbia River

Portland •
★ Salem

Oregon

Idaho
★ Boise

Snake River

Montana
★ Helena
• Billings

Wyoming
Casper •
Cheyenne ★

Nevada
★ Carson City

San
Francisco •

• Sacramento

Salt Lake City ★
• Provo

Utah

Denver •
Colorado
Pueblo •

California

Las Vegas •

• Los Angeles

Colorado River

Arizona

Santa Fe ★
Albuquerque ★

New Mexico

San Diego •

★ Phoenix

Tucson •

MEXICO

Legend

⊛ National capital

★ State capital

• Major city

— National boundary

— State boundary

620

145°W 50°N   140°W   135°W   130°W   55°N   125°W   120°W   115°W   110°W

40°N   35°N   140°W   135°W   130°W   30°N   125°W   25°N   120°W   20°N   115°W   110°W   105°W

50°N   45°N

CANADA

North Dakota
Bismarck ★
Fargo ●

Minnesota
St. Paul ★
Minneapolis ●

South Dakota
Pierre ★
Sioux Falls ●

Lake Superior

Michigan
Lake Huron

Wisconsin
Milwaukee ●
Madison ★

Lansing ★
Detroit ●

Lake Michigan

Lake Ontario

Lake Erie

Maine
Augusta ★

Vermont
Montpelier ★
Burlington ●

New Hampshire
Concord ★
Portland ●

Albany ★

Massachusetts
Boston ★
Providence ★

Rhode Island

New York
New York ●
Hartford ★
New Haven ●

Connecticut

Iowa
Sioux City ●
Des Moines ★

Nebraska
Omaha ●
Lincoln ★

Platte River
Missouri River

Illinois
Chicago ●
Springfield ★

Indiana
Indianapolis ★

Ohio
Cleveland ●
Columbus ★

Pennsylvania
Harrisburg ★
Pittsburgh ●

New Jersey
Trenton ★

Philadelphia ●
Wilmington ●

Delaware
Dover ★

Baltimore ●
Washington ●
Annapolis ★

Maryland

Kansas
Topeka ★
Wichita ●

Arkansas River

Missouri
Kansas City ●
Jefferson City ★
St. Louis ●

Louisville ●
Frankfort ★

Kentucky
Evansville ●

West Virginia
Charleston ●

Virginia
Richmond ●
Norfolk ●

Ohio River

Oklahoma
Tulsa ●
Oklahoma City ★
Fort Smith ●
Little Rock ★

Arkansas

Tennessee
Nashville ★
Memphis ●

North Carolina
Raleigh ★
Charlotte ●

South Carolina
Columbia ★
Charleston ●

Mississippi River

Texas
Dallas ●
Austin ★
Houston ●

Red River

Louisiana
Greenville ●
Jackson ★
Baton Rouge ★
New Orleans ●

Mississippi

Alabama
Birmingham ●
Montgomery ★

Georgia
Atlanta ★
Savannah ●

Tallahassee ★

Florida
Tampa ●
Miami ●

ATLANTIC OCEAN

BAHAMAS

Gulf of Mexico

N
W — E
S

CUBA

0   200   400 mi.

0   200   400 km

Albers Equal-Area Projection

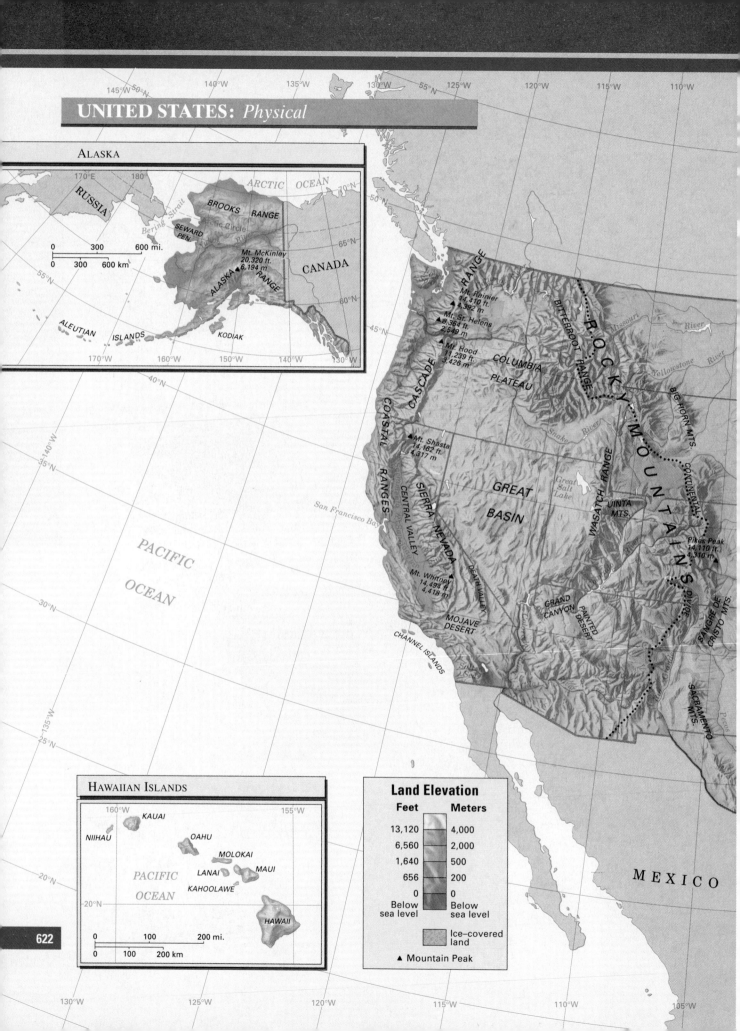

ALASKA

RUSSIA

ARCTIC OCEAN

BROOKS RANGE

Arctic Circle

Bering Strait

SEWARD PEN.

CANADA

Mt. McKinley
20,320 ft.
6,194 m

ALASKA RANGE

ALEUTIAN ISLANDS

KODIAK

| 0 | 300 | 600 mi. |
| 0 | 300 | 600 km |

PACIFIC

OCEAN

HAWAIIAN ISLANDS

KAUAI

NIIHAU

OAHU

MOLOKAI

LANAI   MAUI

KAHOOLAWE

PACIFIC
OCEAN

HAWAII

| 0 | 100 | 200 mi. |
| 0 | 100 | 200 km |

CANADA

COASTAL RANGE

Mt. Rainier
14,410 ft.
4,392 m

Mt. St. Helens
8,364 ft.
2,549 m

Mt. Hood
11,239 ft.
3,426 m

CASCADE

COLUMBIA

PLATEAU

BITTERROOT RANGE

Missouri   River

Yellowstone   River

Snake   River

BIG HORN MTS.

R O C K Y   M O U N T A I N S

Mt. Shasta
14,162 ft.
4,317 m

CENTRAL VALLEY

COASTAL RANGES

SIERRA NEVADA

San Francisco Bay

GREAT

BASIN

Great
Salt
Lake

WASATCH RANGE

UINTA
MTS.

CONTINENTAL

Pikes Peak
14,110 ft.
4,310 m

Mt. Whitney
14,494 ft.
4,418 m

DEATH VALLEY

MOJAVE
DESERT

GRAND
CANYON

PAINTED
DESERT

DIVIDE

SANGRE DE
CRISTO MTS.

CHANNEL ISLANDS

SACRAMENTO
MTS.

Pecos

M E X I C O

Land Elevation

Feet	Meters
13,120	4,000
6,560	2,000
1,640	500
656	200
0	0
Below sea level	Below sea level

Ice-covered
land

▲ Mountain Peak

622

CANADA

G R E A T

P L A I N S

Lake of
the Woods

MESABI
RANGE

Lake Superior

Lake
Huron

Lake Michigan

Lake Erie

Lake Ontario

St. Lawrence River

WHITE
MTS.
▲ Mt. Washington
6,288 ft.
1,917 m

ADIRONDACK
MTS.

CATSKILL
MTS.

NANTUCKET

MARTHA'S
VINEYARD

LONG ISLAND

Delaware
Bay

Chesapeake Bay

BLACK
HILLS
BADLANDS

Red River

Mississippi River

Des Moines River

SAND HILLS

CENTRAL PLAINS

Platte River

Missouri River

Missouri River

PLATEAU

Susquehanna River

ALLEGHENY

APPALACHIAN MOUNTAINS

FALL LINE

ATLANTIC COASTAL PLAIN

ATLANTIC

OCEAN

Arkansas River

OZARK
PLATEAU

CUMBERLAND PLATEAU

BLUE RIDGE MTS.

▲ Mt. Mitchell
6,684 ft.
2,037 m

LLANO
ESTACADO

OUACHITA
MOUNTAINS

Red River

Arkansas River

EDWARDS
PLATEAU

Brazos River

Colorado River

Sabine River

Red River

Ohio River

Tennessee River

Alabama River

GULF COASTAL PLAIN

Galveston
Bay

Mobile
Bay

Pensacola
Bay

Tampa
Bay

Lake
Okeechobee

BAHAMAS

N
W · E
S

EVERGLADES

Gulf of Mexico

FLORIDA KEYS

CUBA

623

0   200   400 mi.
0   200   400 km
Albers Equal-Area Projection

NORTH AMERICA: Political/Physical

ASIA

ARCTIC OCEAN

EUROPE

Bering Sea

Bering Strait

Beaufort Sea

QUEEN ELIZABETH ISLANDS

ELLESMERE ISLAND

GREENLAND (Denmark)

Baffin Bay

BROOKS RANGE

Yukon River

BANKS ISLAND

ALASKA RANGE
•Fairbanks

VICTORIA ISLAND

BAFFIN ISLAND

•Anchorage

Gulf of Alaska

KODIAK ISLAND

Great Bear Lake

Mackenzie River

ALEXANDER ARCHIPELAGO

Labrador Sea

QUEEN CHARLOTTE ISLANDS

Great Slave Lake

LAURENTIAN SHIELD

UNGAVA PENINSULA

Arctic Circle

COAST MOUNTAINS

Hudson Bay

LABRADOR

VANCOUVER ISLAND

ROCKY

•Edmonton

CANADA

NEWFOUNDLAND

Vancouver

Puget Sound

•Calgary

Lake Winnipeg

PRINCE EDWARD ISLAND

CAPE BRETON ISLAND

Seattle

•Winnipeg

Quebec•

Portland

MOUNTAINS

•Montreal

Ottawa•

Boston

San Francisco

COAST RANGES

SIERRA NEVADA

Salt Lake City

BLACK HILLS

Minneapolis

Missouri River

Milwaukee

L. Superior

Lake Michigan

Lake Huron

Toronto

Lake Ontario

Lake Erie

New York

Cape Cod

ATLANTIC OCEAN

Chicago

Detroit

Cleveland

Philadelphia

Baltimore

Denver

Omaha

Indianapolis

St. Louis

Louisville

APPALACHIAN MTS.

Washington

Los Angeles

MOJAVE DESERT

Kansas City

Wichita

Ohio River

Nashville

Charlotte

Cape Hatteras

San Diego

GRAND CANYON

UNITED STATES

BERMUDA (U.K.)

Phoenix

Red

River

Atlanta

Fort Worth•

Birmingham

Ciudad Juárez

Austin•

Houston

Jacksonville

Cape Canaveral

Tropic of Cancer

Chihuahua

San Antonio

New Orleans

PACIFIC OCEAN

BAJA CALIFORNIA

Gulf of California

Monterrey

Mississippi River

Miami

Nassau

BAHAMAS

Cabo San Lucas

MEXICO

PLATEAU OF MEXICO

Gulf of Mexico

Havana

CUBA

SIERRA MADRE OCCIDENTAL

SIERRA MADRE ORIENTAL

San Juan

VIRGIN ISLANDS (U.S., U.K.)

ANGUILLA (U.K.)

ANTIGUA AND BARBUDA

Guadalajara•

Mexico City

Veracruz

Santiago de Cuba

DOMINICAN REPUBLIC

PUERTO RICO (U.S.)

ST. KITTS NEVIS

GUADELOUPE (Fr.)

MARTINIQUE (Fr.)

Puebla

YUCATÁN PENINSULA

CAYMAN ISLANDS (U.K.)

Port-au-Prince

HAITI

Santo Domingo

DOMINICA

Roseau

ST. LUCIA

Castries

Acapulco

ISTHMUS OF TEHUANTEPEC

JAMAICA

Kingston

Kingston

ST. VINCENT AND THE GRENADINES

BARBADOS

Bridgetown

Belmopan

BELIZE

NETHERLANDS ANTILLES (Neth.)

GRENADA

St. George's

Port of Spain

GUATEMALA

HONDURAS

Caribbean Sea

ARUBA (Neth.)

TRINIDAD AND TOBAGO

Guatemala City

Tegucigalpa

San Salvador

NICARAGUA

EL SALVADOR

MOSQUITO COAST

Managua

Lago de Nicaragua

COSTA RICA

San José

ISTHMUS OF PANAMA

Panama City

PANAMA

SOUTH AMERICA

Equator

Legend

⊛ National capital

• Major city

— National boundary

0   400   800 mi.

0   400   800 km

Azimuthal Equal-Area Projection

624

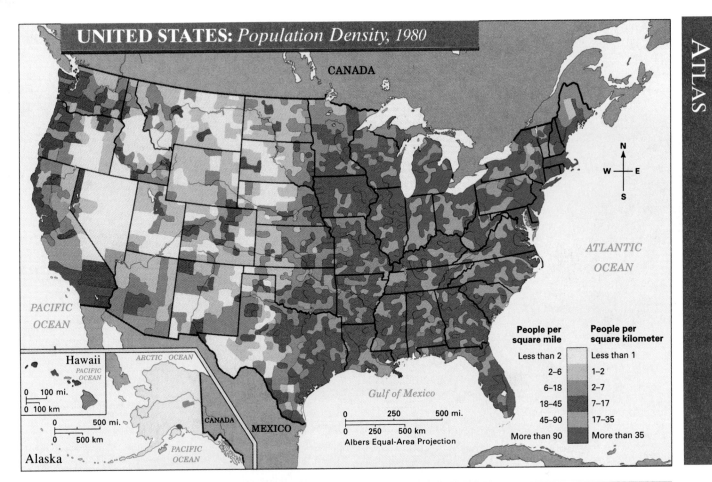

UNITED STATES: *Population Density, 1980*

CANADA

PACIFIC OCEAN

ATLANTIC OCEAN

Hawaii

ARCTIC OCEAN

PACIFIC OCEAN

0 100 mi.
0 100 km

0 500 mi.
0 500 km

Alaska

CANADA

MEXICO

Gulf of Mexico

0 250 500 mi.
0 250 500 km
Albers Equal-Area Projection

People per square mile	People per square kilometer
Less than 2	Less than 1
2–6	1–2
6–18	2–7
18–45	7–17
45–90	17–35
More than 90	More than 35

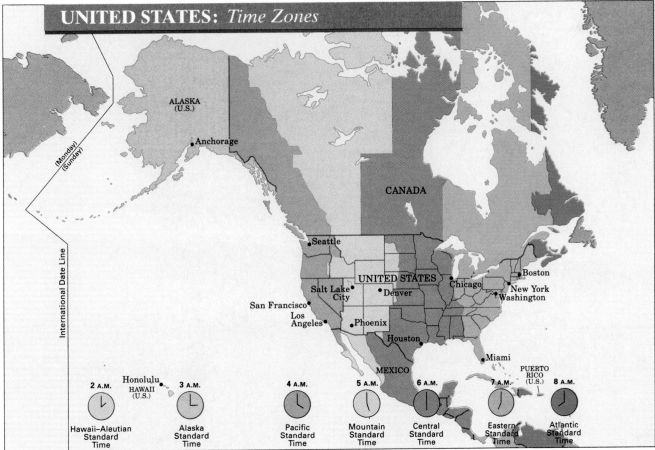

UNITED STATES: *Time Zones*

ALASKA (U.S.)

Anchorage

International Date Line

(Monday)
(Sunday)

CANADA

Seattle

Salt Lake City

Denver

Chicago

Boston

New York
Washington

UNITED STATES

San Francisco

Los Angeles

Phoenix

Houston

Miami

MEXICO

PUERTO RICO (U.S.)

2 A.M.
Honolulu
HAWAII (U.S.)
Hawaii–Aleutian Standard Time

3 A.M.
Alaska Standard Time

4 A.M.
Pacific Standard Time

5 A.M.
Mountain Standard Time

6 A.M.
Central Standard Time

7 A.M.
Eastern Standard Time

8 A.M.
Atlantic Standard Time

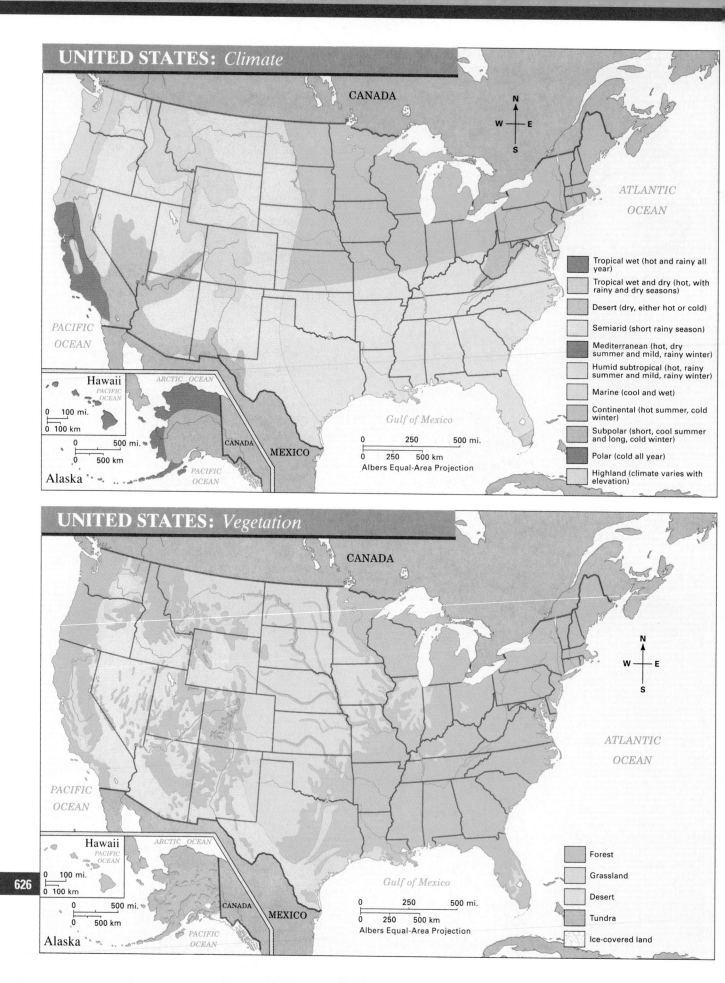

UNITED STATES: *Climate*

CANADA

ATLANTIC OCEAN

PACIFIC OCEAN

Gulf of Mexico

Hawaii
PACIFIC OCEAN
ARCTIC OCEAN
0   100 mi.
0   100 km

0   500 mi.
0   500 km
CANADA
MEXICO
PACIFIC OCEAN

Alaska

0   250   500 mi.
0   250   500 km
Albers Equal-Area Projection

- Tropical wet (hot and rainy all year)
- Tropical wet and dry (hot, with rainy and dry seasons)
- Desert (dry, either hot or cold)
- Semiarid (short rainy season)
- Mediterranean (hot, dry summer and mild, rainy winter)
- Humid subtropical (hot, rainy summer and mild, rainy winter)
- Marine (cool and wet)
- Continental (hot summer, cold winter)
- Subpolar (short, cool summer and long, cold winter)
- Polar (cold all year)
- Highland (climate varies with elevation)

UNITED STATES: *Vegetation*

CANADA

ATLANTIC OCEAN

PACIFIC OCEAN

Gulf of Mexico

Hawaii
PACIFIC OCEAN
ARCTIC OCEAN
0   100 mi.
0   100 km

0   500 mi.
0   500 km
CANADA
MEXICO
PACIFIC OCEAN

Alaska

0   250   500 mi.
0   250   500 km
Albers Equal-Area Projection

- Forest
- Grassland
- Desert
- Tundra
- Ice-covered land

UNITED STATES: *Precipitation*

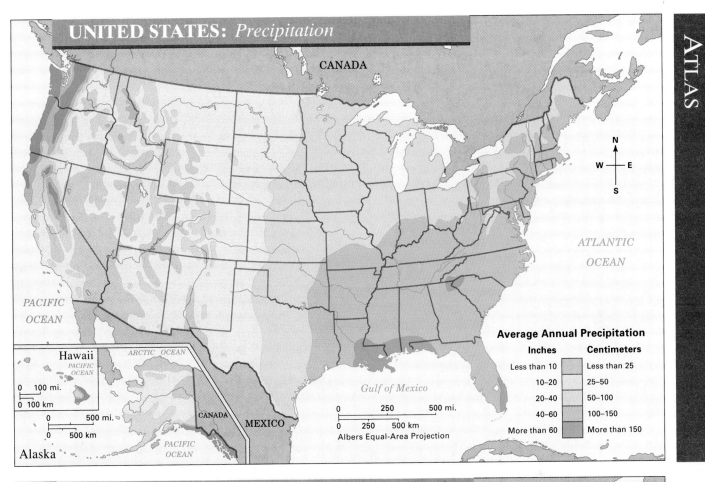

Average Annual Precipitation

Inches	Centimeters
Less than 10	Less than 25
10–20	25–50
20–40	50–100
40–60	100–150
More than 60	More than 150

Hawaii

Alaska

0   250   500 mi.
0 250 500 km
Albers Equal-Area Projection

UNITED STATES: *Land Use and Resources*

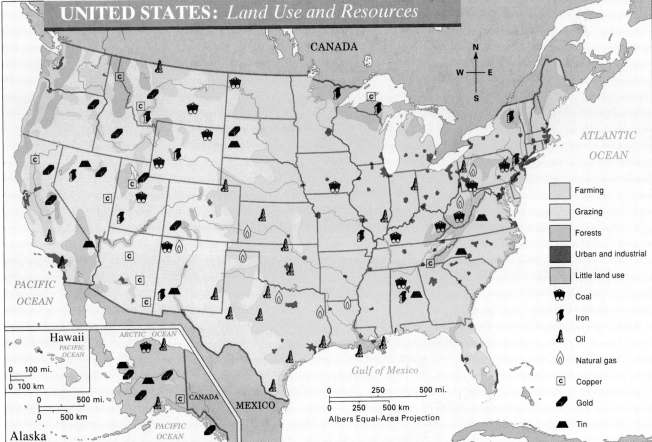

Farming
Grazing
Forests
Urban and industrial
Little land use
Coal
Iron
Oil
Natural gas
C Copper
Gold
Tin

Hawaii

Alaska

0   250   500 mi.
0 250 500 km
Albers Equal-Area Projection

627

GLOSSARY OF GEOGRAPHIC TERMS

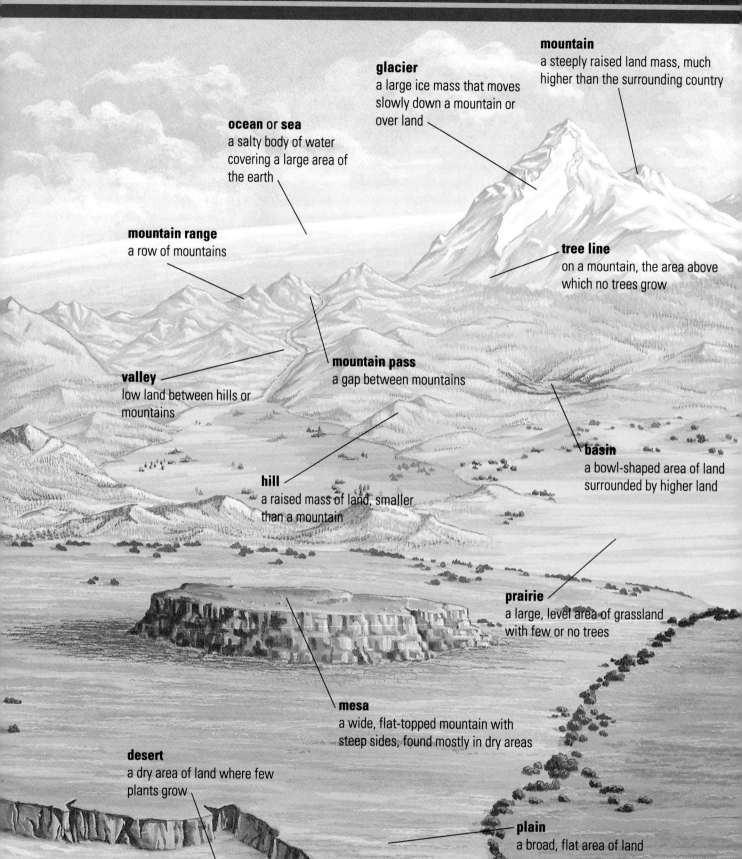

mountain
a steeply raised land mass, much
higher than the surrounding country

glacier
a large ice mass that moves
slowly down a mountain or
over land

ocean or **sea**
a salty body of water
covering a large area of
the earth

tree line
on a mountain, the area above
which no trees grow

mountain range
a row of mountains

mountain pass
a gap between mountains

valley
low land between hills or
mountains

basin
a bowl-shaped area of land
surrounded by higher land

hill
a raised mass of land, smaller
than a mountain

prairie
a large, level area of grassland
with few or no trees

mesa
a wide, flat-topped mountain with
steep sides, found mostly in dry areas

desert
a dry area of land where few
plants grow

plain
a broad, flat area of land

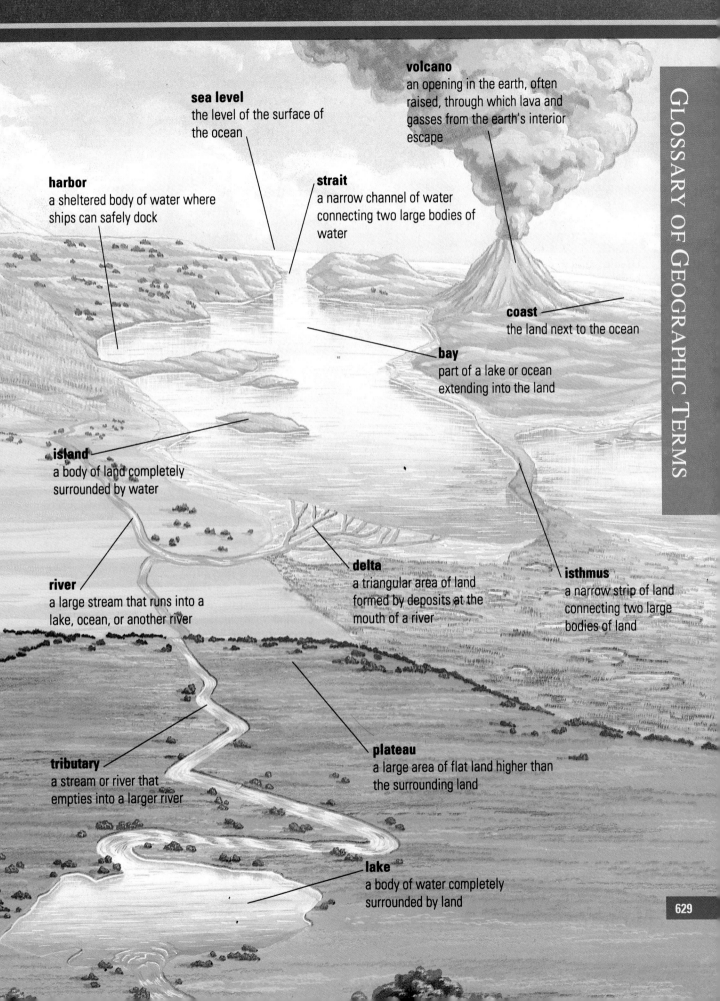

volcano
an opening in the earth, often raised, through which lava and gasses from the earth's interior escape

sea level
the level of the surface of the ocean

strait
a narrow channel of water connecting two large bodies of water

harbor
a sheltered body of water where ships can safely dock

coast
the land next to the ocean

bay
part of a lake or ocean extending into the land

island
a body of land completely surrounded by water

delta
a triangular area of land formed by deposits at the mouth of a river

isthmus
a narrow strip of land connecting two large bodies of land

river
a large stream that runs into a lake, ocean, or another river

tributary
a stream or river that empties into a larger river

plateau
a large area of flat land higher than the surrounding land

lake
a body of water completely surrounded by land

This Gazetteer will help you locate many of the places discussed in this book. Latitude and longitude given for large areas of land and water refers to the centermost point of the area; latitude and longitude of rivers refers to the river mouth. The page number tells you where to find each place on a map.

PLACE	LAT.	LONG.	PAGE
A			
Albany (capital of New York, on Hudson R.)	43°N	74°W	**209**
Appalachian Mts. (range stretching from Maine to Alabama)	37°N	82°W	**5**
Atlanta (capital of Georgia)	34°N	84°W	**424**
Augusta (city in Georgia on Savannah R.)	33°N	82°W	**51**
B			
Bering Strait (waterway connecting Arctic Ocean and Bering Sea)	65°N	170°W	**624**
Boonesborough (fort in Kentucky; founded by Daniel Boone in 1775; south of present-day Lexington)	37°N	85°W	**342**
Boston (capital and largest city in Massachusetts)	42°N	71°W	**139**
Bristol (city in England)	51°N	3°W	**199**
Buffalo (city in western New York; on Lake Erie and Niagara R.)	43°N	79°W	**424**
C			
Canada (country bordering U.S. on north)	50°N	100°W	**36**
Cape Cod (peninsula in southeastern Massachusetts between Cape Cod Bay and the Atlantic Ocean; landing place of Pilgrims on the *Mayflower*)	41°N	70°W	**139**
Catskill Mts. (part of the Appalachian Mts. in New York)	42°N	75°W	**97**
Charleston (port city in South Carolina on Atlantic Ocean)	33°N	80°W	**272**
Chesapeake Bay (between Virginia and Maryland; about 190 miles long)	39°N	77°W	**133**
Chicago (city in Illinois on Lake Michigan; third largest U.S. city)	42°N	88°W	**5**
Cincinnati (city in Ohio; on Ohio R.)	39°N	85°W	**424**
Cleveland (largest city in Ohio; on Lake Erie)	42°N	82°W	**424**

PLACE	LAT.	LONG.	PAGE
Colorado Plateau (in New Mexico and Arizona)	36°N	109°W	**36**
Columbia R. (forms Washington-Oregon border)	46°N	124°W	**375**
Concord (city in Massachusetts near Boston, site of early Revolutionary War battle)	42°N	71°W	**272**
Connecticut R. (longest in New England)	41°N	72°W	**139**
Cumberland Gap (pass through the Appalachian Mts. in Tennessee)	36°N	83°W	**342**
D			
Delaware R. (in New York and Delaware)	39°N	75°W	**209**
Detroit (largest city in Michigan)	42°N	83°W	**425**
District of Columbia (site of U.S. capital)	39°N	77°W	**G4**
E			
El Paso (city on the Rio Grande in Texas)	32°N	106°W	**375**
England (island country in Europe; largest unit of the United Kingdom of Great Britain and Northern Ireland)	52°N	2°W	**120**
Erie Canal (artificial waterway in New York; 525 miles long)	43°N	79°W	**342**
F			
Fort Sumter (site of first Civil War battle)	33°N	80°W	**468**
France (country in southeastern Europe)	47°N	1°E	**523**
G			
Germany (country in Europe)	52°N	9°E	**427**
Grand Banks (fishing area off Newfoundland)	47°N	56°W	**130**
Grand Canyon (deep canyon in Arizona formed by the Colorado R.)	36°N	112°W	**622**
Great Britain (England, Scotland, and Wales)	57°N	0°W	**199**

PLACE	LAT.	LONG.	PAGE
Great Lakes (five freshwater lakes between U.S. and Canada)	45°N	83°W	**88**
Great Plains (large, flat, dry area in western U.S.)	45°N	104°W	**36**
Gulf of Mexico (body of sea-water along southern U.S. and Mexico)	25°N	94°W	**5**

H

PLACE	LAT.	LONG.	PAGE
Hudson R. (in New York; named for explorer Henry Hudson)	41°N	74°W	**209**

I

PLACE	LAT.	LONG.	PAGE
Ireland (country in Europe)	54°N	13°W	**523**
Italy (country in southern Europe; bordered by the Adriatic and Mediterranean Seas)	44°N	11°E	**523**

J

PLACE	LAT.	LONG.	PAGE
James R. (in central Virginia; flows into Chesapeake Bay)	43°N	97°W	**165**
Jamestown (first permanent English settlement in America; founded in 1607 on the shore of the James R. in Virginia)	37°N	78°W	**165**
Japan (island country off east coast of Asia)	37°N	134°E	**523**

L

PLACE	LAT.	LONG.	PAGE
Lake Erie (one of the five Great Lakes)	42°N	81°W	**342**
Lake Huron (one of the five Great Lakes)	45°N	83°W	**342**
Lake Michigan (one of the five Great Lakes)	43°N	87°W	**342**
Lake Ontario (one of the five Great Lakes)	44°N	79°W	**342**
Lake Superior (one of the five Great Lakes)	48°N	89°W	**342**
Lexington (city near Boston; site of first Revolutionary War battle)	42°N	71°W	**272**
London (capital and most populated city in England)	52°N	0°W	**199**
Los Angeles (largest city in California)	34°N	118°W	**5**

PLACE	LAT.	LONG.	PAGE
Louisiana Territory (western half of Mississippi R. basin; purchased by U.S. in 1803 from France)	37°N	92°W	**302**

M

PLACE	LAT.	LONG.	PAGE
Mexico (country bordering U.S. to the south)	24°N	104°W	**371**
Mexico City (capital of Mexico)	19°N	99°W	**371**
Mississippi River (longest river in the U.S., flows into the Gulf of Mexico)	29°N	89°W	**5**
Missouri R. (flows from Montana to Missouri; tributary of the Mississippi R.)	39°N	90°W	**5**

N

PLACE	LAT.	LONG.	PAGE
Netherlands (provinces united under leadership of largest province, also called Holland; in western Europe)	52°N	6°E	**120**
New Amsterdam (founded by Dutch settlers in 1624; now New York City)	41°N	74°W	**144**
Newfoundland (island in Atlantic Ocean off coast of Canada)	48°N	57°W	**120**
New Netherland (Dutch North American colony in present New York, New Jersey, and Connecticut)	41°N	74°W	**144**
New Orleans (largest city in Louisiana; on Mississippi R.)	30°N	90°W	**5**
New York City (largest city in U.S.)	41°N	74°W	**209**
Nogales (city in southern Arizona)	31°N	111°W	**15**
Norfolk (city in southeastern Virginia)	37°N	76°W	**424**
North America (continent of which U.S. is a part)	48°N	100°W	**G1**
Northwest Territory (land north of Ohio R., west of Pennsylvania, east of Mississippi R.)	41°N	85°W	**302**

O

PLACE	LAT.	LONG.	PAGE
Oakland (city in California)	38°N	122°W	**51**
Ohio R. (in Pennsylvania and Ohio)	37°N	89°W	**342**

PLACE	LAT.	LONG.	PAGE
Oregon Territory (also Oregon Country; area from Rocky Mts. to Pacific Ocean)	45°N	120°W	**375**

P

PLACE	LAT.	LONG.	PAGE
Philadelphia (city in Pennsylvania; location of Constitutional Convention)	40°N	75°W	**272**
Pittsburgh (second largest city in Pennsylvania)	40°N	80°W	**342**
Plymouth (town in Massachusetts; site of the first Pilgrim settlement)	41°N	71°W	**139**
Portsmouth (city in southeastern Rhode Island)	42°N	71°W	**139**
Portsmouth (city in New Hampshire)	43°N	71°W	**184**
Portugal (country in western Europe)	38°N	8°W	**523**
Potomac R. (in West Virginia and Virginia)	38°N	76°W	**144**
Providence (capital of Rhode Island)	42°N	71°W	**139**

Q

PLACE	LAT.	LONG.	PAGE
Quebec (capital of Quebec Province, Canada; site of first successful French settlement in North America)	47°N	71°W	**130**

R

PLACE	LAT.	LONG.	PAGE
Richmond (capital of Virginia)	38°N	78°W	**424**
Rio Grande (river that forms the Texas-Mexico border)	26°N	97°W	**375**
Rocky Mts. (longest mountain range in the U.S.)	50°N	114°W	**36**

S

PLACE	LAT.	LONG.	PAGE
Sacramento (capital of California)	39°N	122°W	**51**
Salem (city in northeastern Massachusetts)	43°N	71°W	**184**
Salt Lake City (capital and largest city in Utah)	41°N	112°W	**375**
San Antonio (city in central Texas; site of the Alamo)	29°N	99°W	**375**
San Francisco (city in northern California)	38°N	122°W	**51**
San Diego (city in southern California)	33°N	117°W	**51**

PLACE	LAT.	LONG.	PAGE
Santa Fe (capital of New Mexico)	35°N	106°W	**375**
Saratoga (city in New York; site of Revolutionary War battle)	43°N	75°W	**272**
Savannah (oldest city in Georgia)	32°N	81°W	**272**
Spain (country in Europe)	40°N	5°W	**523**
St. Lawrence R. (forms part of Canada-U.S. boundary)	49°N	67°W	**274**
St. Louis (largest city in Missouri; on Mississippi R.)	39°N	90°W	**424**
Strait of Magellan (waterway from the Atlantic Ocean to the Pacific Ocean; near the tip of S. America)	53°S	69°W	**123**

T

PLACE	LAT.	LONG.	PAGE
Texas (southern state)	31°N	99°W	**G6**
Trenton (capital of New Jersey)	40°N	75°W	**51**

V

PLACE	LAT.	LONG.	PAGE
Valley Forge (George Washington's winter camp in 1777; near Philadelphia, Pennsylvania)	40°N	75°W	**272**
Vicksburg (western Mississippi city, on Mississippi River)	32°N	91°W	**G8**

W

PLACE	LAT.	LONG.	PAGE
Washington, D.C. (capital of the U.S.)	39°N	77°W	**G4**
West Indies (islands stretching 2,500 miles; in the Caribbean Sea)	19°N	79°W	**111**
Williamsburg (colonial capital of Virginia)	37°N	77°W	**165**

Y

PLACE	LAT.	LONG.	PAGE
Yorktown (in Virginia; site of last battle of Revolutionary War)	37°N	77°W	**272**

This dictionary lists many of the important people introduced in this book. The page number refers to the main discussion of that person in the book. A page reference in italics indicates an illustration. For more complete references see the Index.

Pronunciation Key

This chart presents the pronunciation key used in this Biographical Dictionary and in the Glossary beginning on page 638.

Spellings	Symbol	Spellings	Symbol	Spellings	Symbol
pat	ă	kick, cat, pique	k	thin	th
pay	ā	lid, needle	l	this	*th*
care	âr	mum	m	cut	ŭ
father	ä	no, sudden	n	urge, term, firm, word, heard	ûr
bib	b	thing	ng		
church	ch	pot, horrid	ŏ	valve	v
deed, milled	d	toe	ō	with	w
pet	ĕ	caught, paw, for	ô	yes	y
bee	ē	noise	oi	zebra, xylem	z
life, phase, rough	f	took	ŏŏ	vision, pleasure, garage	zh
gag	g	boot	ōō		
hat	h	out	ou	about, item, edible, gallop, circus	ə
which	hw	pop	p		
pit	ĭ	roar	r	butter	ər
pie, by	ī	sauce	s		
pier	îr	ship, dish	sh	Primary stress ´	
judge	j	tight, stopped	t	Secondary stress ˏ	

A

Adams, Abigail 1744–1818, American First Lady, wife of John (p. 284).

Adams, John 1735–1826, 2nd U.S. President, 1797–1801 (p. 319).

Adams, John Quincy 1767–1848, 6th U.S. President, 1825–1829 (p. 444).

Adams, Samuel 1722–1803, American Revolutionary leader (p.250).

Addams, Jane 1860–1935, American social reformer; shared Nobel peace prize, 1931 *(p. 540)*.

Alcott, Louisa M. 1832–1888, American author (p. 480).

Argall, Samuel 1572?–1626, English colonial governor of Virginia (p.63).

Armstrong, Neil 1930– , American astronaut; first person to walk on the moon *(p. 570)*.

Attucks (ăt´ əks), **Crispus** 1723?–1770, African American victim of Boston Massacre, 1770 *(p.249)*.

Austin, Stephen F. 1793–1836, leader in fight for Texas' independence from Mexico (p. 371).

B

Bacon, Nathaniel 1647–1676, English-born colonist; led Bacon's revolution (p. 165).

Balboa, Vasco Núñez de 1475–1517, Spanish discoverer of the Pacific Ocean (p. 114).

Baltimore, Lord *See* Calvert, George.

Banneker, Benjamin 1731–1806, African American scientist (p. 331).

Benavides (bā nä-vē´*th*äs), **Santos**, rallied Mexican American support for Confederacy *(p. 481)*.

Berkeley, William 1606–1677, English colonial governor of Virginia (p. 163).

Bethune (bĭ-thōōn´), **Mary McLeod** 1875–1955, American educator (p. 555).

Black Hawk or **Ma-ka-tae-mish-kia-kiak** 1767–1838, American Indian (Sauk) leader *(p. 365)*.

Bodmer, Karl 1809–1893, Swiss artist; traveled in U.S. with Prince Maximilian, 1833 (p. 70).

Boone, Daniel 1734–1820, American frontiersman; helped settle Kentucky *(p. 357)*.

Booth, John Wilkes 1838–1865, American actor; assassin of President Abraham Lincoln (p. 492).

Boudinot (bōō´d´nō), **Elias** 1803?–1839, published Cherokee newspaper (p. 364).

Bowie (bōō´ĭ), **Jim (James)** 1796?–1836, American soldier; died at the Alamo (p. 372).

Bradford, William 1590–1657, governor of Plymouth colony (p. 139).

Breckenridge, John 1821–1875, U.S. Vice President, 1857–1861 (p. 464).

Brown, John 1800–1859, U.S. abolitionist (p. 450).

Burgoyne (bər-goin´), **John** 1722–1792, British general defeated in American Revolution (p. 270).

Burnaby, Andrew 1732–1812, English preacher; wrote about the Middle Colonies (p. 213).

Bush, George H. W. 1924– , 41st U.S. President, 1989–1993 (p. 570).

C

Cabot, John (Giovanni Caboto) 1450?–1498, Italian–born explorer in English service (p. 121).

Calhoun, John 1782–1850, U.S. Vice President, 1825–1832 (p. 448).

Calvert, George, Lord Baltimore 1580?–1632, granted territory to found Maryland, 1632 (p. 135).

Carter, James (Jimmy) Earl, Jr. 1924– , 39th U.S. President, 1977–1981 (p. 570).

Cartier, Jacques 1491–1557, French explorer (p. 119).

Champlain (shăm-plān´), **Samuel de** 1567?–1635, French explorer (p. 131).

Charles I 1600–1649, king of England, 1625–1649 (p. 142).

Charles II 1630–1685, king of England, 1660–1685 (p. 144).

Chávez (chä´vĕs´), **Cesar Estrada** 1927– , American agricultural labor leader (p. 564).

Clark, William 1770–1838, American explorer of the Northwest (p. 353).

Clay, Henry 1777–1852, American statesman (p. 477).

Clemens, Samuel *See* Twain, Mark

Cleveland, Grover 1837–1908, 22nd and 24th U.S. President, 1885–1889, 1893–1897 (p. 520).

Clinton, Henry 1738?–1795, English general in American Revolutionary War (p. 272).

Clinton, William (Bill) J. 1946– , 42nd U.S. President, 1993– *(p. 539)*.

Columbus, Christopher or **Cristoforo Colombo** 1451–1506, Italian navigator, under Spanish employ; his voyages led to European awareness of the Americas *(p. 110)*.

Coolidge, (John) Calvin 1872–1933, 30th U.S. President, 1923–1929 (p. 548).

Cooper, Peter 1791–1883, American manufacturer, inventor, and philanthropist (p. 422).

Copley, John Singleton 1738–1815, American portrait painter (p. 239).

Corbin, Margaret 1751–1800, American Revolutionary heroine (p. 269).

Cornwallis, Charles 1738–1805, British general in Revolutionary War (p. 273).

Coronado, Francisco 1510?–1554, Spanish explorer and colonial administrator (p. 115).

Cortéz, Hernán 1485–1547, Spanish explorer (p. 114).

Crazy Horse or **Tashunca-Uitco** 1849?–1877, Oglala Sioux leader; victor at Little Big Horn (p. 506).

Crockett, Davey 1786–1836, American frontiersman; Tennessee Congressman (p. 372).

Cullen, Countee 1903–1946, American poet (p. 549).

Custer, George Armstrong 1839–1876, commanded U.S. troops at Little Big Horn, defeated, killed, 1876 (p. 506).

D

Davis, Jefferson 1808–1889, President of the Confederacy, 1861–1865 (p. 483).

de Soto, Hernando 1496?–1542, Spanish explorer (p. 115).

Dewey, John 1859–1952, American educator (p. 541).

Dias, Bartholomeu 1450?–1500, Portuguese navigator; discovered Cape of Good Hope (p. 110).

Díaz, Bernal 1492?–1581, Spanish explorer (p. 114).

Douglas, Stephen 1813–1861, American legislator (p. 463).

Douglass, Frederick 1817?–1895, African American anti-slavery leader (p. 436).

Drake, Francis 1540?–1596, English naval hero and explorer (p.121).

Du Bois (dōō bois´), **William Edward Burghardt (W.E.B.)** 1868–1963, American educator and writer (p.542).

Duryea (dŏŏr´ yā), **Charles E.** 1861–1938 and **J. Frank,** 1869–1967, brothers; pioneer U.S. automobile manufacturers (p. 503).

E

Edwards, Jonathan 1703–1758, American preacher of Great Awakening (p. 195).

Eisenhower, Dwight D. 1890-1969, 34th U.S. President, 1953–1961 (p. 560).

Elizabeth I 1533–1603, queen of England, 1558–1603 (p. 121).

Equiano, Olaudah 1745?–1797, African brought to America as a slave in 1700s (p. 167).

F

Ferdinand II 1452–1504, ruled Spain, 1474–1504, with Isabella (p. 110).

Ford, Gerald R. 1913– , 38th U.S. President, 1974–1977 (p. 570).

Ford, Henry 1863–1947, American automobile manufacturer (p. 549).

Fox, George 1624–1691, English Quaker religious leader (p. 145).

Franklin, Benjamin 1706–1790, American statesman, scientist (p. 297).

Frémont, John C. 1813–1890, American soldier, explorer, and politician *(p. 456)*.

Fulton, Robert 1765–1815, American inventor (p. 325).

G

Gadsden, James 1788–1858, American diplomat, politician, and railroad promoter (p. 375).

Gage, Thomas 1721–1787, English general and colonial administrator (p. 268).

Gama, Vasco da 1460?–1524, Portuguese explorer who sailed around tip of Africa (p. 110).

Garrison, William Lloyd 1805–1879, American abolitionist (p. 437).

Garvey, Marcus 1887–1940, Jamaican-born, U.S.-based social activist; leader of "Back to Africa" movement (p. 543).

Gates, Horatio 1727?–1806, American Revolutionary general (p. 272).

George II 1683–1760, king of England, 1727–1760 *(p. 239)*.

George III 1738–1820, king of England during the American Revolution, 1760–1820 (p. 262).

Grant, Ulysses S. 1822–1885, 18th U.S. President, 1869–1877; Union general (p. 471).

Greeley, Horace 1811–1872, American journalist and politician (p. 434).

Greenhow, Rose O'Neal 18--?–1863, Confederate spy *(p. 481)*.

H

Hakluyt, Richard 1552–1616, English geographer (p. 133).

Hamilton, Alexander 1757–1804, American statesman; killed by Aaron Burr in duel (p. 316).

Harding, Warren G. 1865–1923, 29th U.S. President, 1921–1923 (p. 548).

Hargreaves, James 1722?–1778, English inventor of the spinning jenny (p. 423).

Harrison, Benjamin 1833–1901, 23rd U.S. President, 1889–1893 (p. 540).

Harrison, William Henry 1773–1841, 9th U.S. President, 1841 (p. 360).

Hastie, William 1904–1976, first African American federal district judge, 1936 (p. 555).

Hayes, Rutherford B. 1822–1893, 19th U.S. President, 1877–1881 *(p. 499)*.

Henry, Patrick 1736–1799, American Revolution leader; famous orator (p. 253).

Henry the Navigator 1394–1460, prince of Portugal, patron of navigational studies *(p. 109)*.

Henry VIII 1491–1547, king of England, 1509–1547 (p. 139).

Henson, Josiah 1789–1883, slave who escaped to Canada; published autobiography (p. 407).

Hicks, Edward 1780–1849, American painter (p. 211).

Hitler, Adolf 1889–1945, Austrian-born Nazi dictator of Germany during World War II (p. 556).

Hoover, Herbert C. 1874–1964, 31st U.S. President, 1929–1933 (p. 552).

Houston, Sam 1793–1863, President of Republic of Texas (p. 373).

Hudson, Henry 1565?–1611, English explorer (p. 120).

Hughes, (James) Langston 1902–1967, American author and poet *(p. 549)*.

Hurston, Zora Neale 1901–1960, American writer (p. 549).

Hussein, Saddam 1937–   , President and dictator of Iraq, 1979– ; defeated in Gulf War, 1991 (p. 573).

Hutchinson, Anne 1591–1643, English-born American colonist and religious leader (p. 193).

I

Inouye, Daniel 1924–   , Japanese–American war hero; U.S. Senator from Hawaii, 1963– *(p. 564)*.

Isabella 1451–1504, Queen of Castile and Aragon; sponsored Christopher Columbus (p. 110).

J

Jackson, Andrew 1767–1845, 7th U.S. President, 1829–1837, called "Old Hickory" (p. 413).

James I 1566–1625, ruled England, 1603–1625 (p. 162).

James II 1633–1701, ruled England, 1685–1688 (p. 144).

Jay, John 1745–1829, American diplomat; signed treaty with England (p. 274).

Jefferson, Thomas 1743–1826, 3rd U.S. President, 1801–1809 *(p. 262)*.

Johnson, Andrew 1808–1875, 17th U.S. President, 1865–1869 *(p. 497)*.

Johnson, James Weldon 1871–1938, American author, lawyer, diplomat (p. 549).

Johnson, Lyndon B. (LBJ) 1908–1973, 36th U.S. President, 1963–1969 (p. 565).

K

Kay, John 1733–1764, English inventor (p. 423).

Kennedy, John F. (JFK) 1917–1963, 35th U.S. President, 1961–1963; assassinated *(p. 538)*.

King, Martin Luther, Jr. 1929–1968, American civil rights leader, assassinated *(p. 562)*.

Knox, Henry 1750–1806, American revolutionary soldier and public official *(p. 317)*.

L

Lee, Ann 1736–1784, "Mother Ann," English founder of American Shakers (p. 435).

Lee, Richard Henry 1732–1794, American revolutionary leader (p. 264).

Lee, Robert E. 1807–1870, Confederate general; (p. 477).

Lewis, Meriwether 1774–1809, American explorer (p. 353).

Lincoln, Abraham 1809–1865, 16th U.S. President, 1861–1865 assassinated *(p. 443)*.

Lindbergh, Charles A. 1902–1974, American pilot, first solo flight across Atlantic 1927 (p. 548).

Longstreet, James 1821–1904, Confederate general (p. 489).

M

Madison, Dolley 1768–1849, American First Lady, wife of James *(p. 322)*.

Madison, James 1751–1836, 4th U.S. President, 1809–1817 (p. 297).

Magellan, Ferdinand 1480?–1521, Portuguese navigator, killed circumnavigating the globe (p. 114).

Malcolm X. *See* X, Malcolm.

Marshall, James 1810–1885, American pioneer; first to find gold in California (p. 384).

Marshall, Thurgood 1908–1993, first African American justice of U.S. Supreme Court, 1967–1991 *(p. 560)*.

Massasoit 1580?–1661, Wampanoag Indian leader who negotiated peace with Pilgrims (p. 142).

Mather, Cotton 1663–1728, American clergyman and author (p. 194).

McKay, Claude 1890–1948, American writer (p. 549).

McKinley, William 1843–1901, 25th U.S. President, 1897–1901; assassinated (p. 540).

Means, Russell 1940– , American Indian activist *(p. 538)*.

Meir, Golda 1898–1978, Israeli Prime Minister (p. 522).

Mercator, Gerardus 1512–1594, Flemish geographer and mathematician (p. 45).

Montezuma II (mŏn´tə –zoō´mə) or **Moctezuma** 1466?–1520, last Aztec emperor of Mexico (p. 115).

Monroe, James 1758–1831, 5th U.S. President, 1817–1825 (p. 352).

Morris, Gouverneur 1752–1816, American diplomat and political leader *(p. 299)*.

Mott, Lucretia 1793–1880, American social reformer (p. 438).

N

Napoleon Bonaparte 1769–1821, French general and emperor (p. 352).

Nixon, Richard M. 1913– , 37th U.S. President, 1969–1974; resigned from office, 1974 (p. 568).

North, Frederick 1732–1792, English prime minister, 1770–1782 (p. 254).

Novello, Antonia Coello 1944– , Hispanic-American Surgeon General, 1991 (p. 539).

O

Oñate (ô–nyä´tĕ), **Juan de** 1549?–1624, Spanish explorer, conquistador (p. 128).

P

Paine, Thomas 1737–1809, English-born American author of *Common Sense* (p. 263).

Parker, Ely Samuel or **Hasanoanda** 1828–1895, Seneca Iroquois leader; first Indian to serve as U.S. Commissioner of Indian Affairs, 1869 *(p. 481)*.

Parks, Rosa 1913– , her actions sparked Montgomery bus boycott and civil rights gains *(p. 561)*.

Penn, William 1644–1718, Quaker leader; founded Commonwealth of Pennsylvania *(p. 146)*.

Perkins, Frances 1882–1965, first woman Cabinet member, Secretary of Labor 1933–1945 (p. 555).

Philip II 1527–1598, king of Spain, 1556–1598 (p. 128).

Pickett, George E. 1825–1875, Confederate general (p. 489).

Pike, Zebulon 1779–1813, American army officer and explorer *(p. 356)*.

Pitt, William 1708–1778, British statesman (p. 244).

Pocahontas 1595?–1617, American Indian princess *(p. 162)*.

Polk, James K. 1795–1849, 11th U.S. President, 1845–1849 (p. 374).

Powell, John Wesley 1834–1902, American geologist and explorer (p. 30).

Powhatan 1550?–1618, American Indian chief (p. 162).

Ptolemy 2nd century A.D. Greek astronomer and geographer (p. 110).

R

Raleigh, Sir Walter 1552?–1618, English navigator, colonizer (p. 133).

Reagan, Ronald 1911– , 40th U.S. President, 1981–1989 (p. 570).

Red Cloud 1822–1909, leader of Sioux and Cheyenne, 1866; deposed by U.S. (p. 504).

Revels, Hiram Rhodes 1827–1901, U.S. Senator from Mississippi, 1870–1901 (p. 497).

Revere, Paul 1735–1818, American revolutionary patriot; silversmith (p. 261).

Rolfe, John 1585–1622, English colonist (p. 161).

Roosevelt, (Anna) Eleanor 1884–1962, American humanitarian, wife of Franklin (p. 553).

Roosevelt, Franklin D. (FDR) 1882–1945, 32nd U.S. President, 1933–1945, died in office *(p. 552)*.

Roosevelt, Theodore (Teddy) 1858–1919, 26th U.S. President, 1901–1909 *(p. 536)*.

S

Sacajawea (săk´ə-jə–wē´a) 1788?–1812, Shoshone Indian guide for Lewis and Clark (p. 356).

Samoset 1590?–1653, American Indian chief and friend to Pilgrims at Plymouth (p. 142).

Scott, Dred 1795?–1858, African American slave involved in Supreme Court case (p. 462).

Scott, Winfield 1786–1866, U.S. general (p. 374).

Seattle 1786?–1866, American Indian leader (p. 389).

Sequoyah (sĭ-kwoi´ə) 1770?–1843, Cherokee leader and scholar (p. 363).

Shays, Daniel 1747?–1825, leader of Shays's Rebellion (p. 296).

Slater, Samuel 1768–1835, English-born textile pioneer in America (p. 423)

Sherman, William Tecumseh 1820–1891, Union general (p. 491).

Sitting Bull 1834?–1890, Hunkpapa–Dakota leader; won battle of Little Big Horn, 1876 (p. 506).

Smith, John 1580?–1631, English adventurer, mapmaker, colonist, explorer, and author (p. 158).

Smith, Joseph 1805–1844, American Mormon religious leader (p. 387).

Squanto (skwăn´tō) 1580?–1622, Pawtuxet Indian who aided Plymouth colony (p. 142).

Stanford, Leland 1824–1893, American politician, financier, and railroad promoter (p. 516).

Stanton, Elizabeth Cady 1815–1902, American feminist and social reformer (p. 285).

Stowe, Harriet Beecher 1811–1880, author of powerful antislavery novel, *Uncle Tom's Cabin (p. 443).*

Sutter, John Augustus 1803–1896, immigrant pioneer; found gold in California, 1848 (p. 383).

T

Taft, William H. 1857–1930, 27th U.S. President, 1909–1913 (p. 540).

Taney, Roger B. 1777–1864, American jurist involved in Dred Scott decision (p. 463).

Taylor, Zachary 1784–1850, 12th U.S. President, 1849–1850 (p. 374).

Tecumseh *(teh KUHM suh)* 1768–1813, Shawnee chief (p. 360).

Travis, William Barret 1809–1836, commander of the Texans in battle of the Alamo (p. 373).

Trollope, Frances *(TRAHL uhp)* 1780–1863, English author on American manners (p. 324).

Truman, Harry S 1884–1972, 33rd U.S. President, 1945–1953 (p. 560).

Truth, Sojourner 1797–1883, American abolitionist and feminist *(p. 438).*

Tubman, Harriet 1820–1913, American abolitionist (p. 451).

Turner, Nat 1800–1831, American leader of slave revolt (p. 405).

Twain, Mark (pen name of **Samuel Clemens**) 1835–1910, American author, creator of the characters Tom Sawyer and Huckleberry Finn (p. 34).

Tweed, William Marcy 1823–1878, American politician; "Boss Tweed" of New York (p. 525).

V

Verrazano (věr´ə-zä´nō), **Giovanni da** 1485?–1528? Italian navigator, explorer (p.119).

Vespucci (věs-pōō´chē), **Amerigo** 1454–1512, Italian navigator, explorer, mapmaker (p. 114).

Voltaire (vōl-târ´) 1694–1778, French writer (p. 216).

W

Washington, Booker T. 1856–1915, American educator *(p. 542).*

Wayne, Anthony 1745–1796, American Revolutionary general (p. 362).

Weaver, Robert C. 1907– , American statesman, served under three presidents (p. 555).

Webster, Noah 1758–1843, lexicographer; compiled first American usage dictionary (p. 308).

Weems, Mason 1759–1825, American clergyman; biographer of G. Washington *(p. 306).*

Wells, Ida B. 1862–1931, American civil rights activist; writer, journalist *(p. 536).*

Wesley, John 1703–1791, British founder of Methodism (p. 330).

West, Benjamin 1738–1820, American painter (p. 224).

White, John ?–1593?, English painter and cartographer in America (p. 132).

Whitefield, George 1714–1770, British religious leader (p. 195).

Whitney, Eli 1765–1825, American inventor of cotton gin (403).

Williams, Roger 1603?–1683, English preacher in America; founded Rhode Island (p. 193).

Wilson, (Thomas) Woodrow 1856–1924, 28th U.S. President, 1913–1921 (p. 547).

Winslow, Edward 1595–1655, founder and later governor Plymouth colony, Massachusetts (p. 138).

Winthrop, John 1588–1649, Puritan leader of Massachusetts Bay Colony (p. 180).

Wolfe, James 1727–1759, British army officer, defeated French in Quebec (p. 245).

X

X, Malcolm (born **Malcolm Little**) 1925–1965, African American activist; assassinated *(p. 538).*

Y

York, Duke of *See* James II.

Young, Brigham 1801–1877, American Mormon leader; led trek to Utah (p. 387).

GLOSSARY

See page 633 for a chart presenting the **pronounciation key** used in this Glossary.

A

abolitionist (ăb´ə -lĭsh´ə-nist) a person who wanted to abolish, or do away with, slavery (p. 406).

agriculture (ăg´rĭ-kŭl´chər) the science and business of farming (p. 83).

alliance (ə-lī´əns) a formal pact of mutual help between nations (p. 544).

amendment (ə-mĕnd´mənt) a statement added to the Constitution (p. 303).

annex (ə-nĕks´) to take a new area into an existing country (p. 373).

apprentice (ə-prĕn´tĭs) a person working for a skilled worker in order to learn the skill (p. 187).

archives (är´kīvz´) a collection of important records about a place, person, or organization (p. 64).

arms race (ärmz rās) a competition between nations to have the most weapons (p. 566).

artifact (är´tə-făkt´) an object made by humans, especially one of historical interest (p. 68).

assassinate (ə-săs´ə-nāt´) to murder for a political reason (p. 492).

assembly (ə-sĕm´blē) citizens gathered to debate and decide (p. 240).

assembly line (ə-sĕm´blē līn) manufacturing method in which each worker does one part of the process as the product moves from person to person (p. 549).

B

blockade (blŏ-kād´) to close off an area to travel or trade (p. 478).

boycott (boi´kŏt´) to refuse to buy, sell, or use an item in order to force a change (p. 249).

Bureau of Indian Affairs (byŏor´ō ŭv ĭn´dē-ən ə-fâr´z) a U.S. government agency established in 1824 with authority to make treaties and regulate trade with the Indians (p. 364).

C

Cabinet (kăb´ə-nĭt) the President's council made up of the heads of government departments (p. 316).

camp meeting (kămp mē´tĭng) a large religious gathering held outdoors or in a tent, often lasting several days (p. 330).

canal (kə-năl´) a waterway made by humans and used for shipping, travel, or irrigation (p. 346).

cartographer (kär-tŏg´rə-fər) a mapmaker (p. 35).

cash crop (kăsh krŏp) a product grown for sale and not for the farmer's own use (p. 173).

checks and balances (chĕks ənd băl´əns-əz) a system in which each branch of government—legislative, executive, or judicial—keeps the others from misusing their power (p. 301).

chronology (krə-nŏl´ə-jē) the arrangement of events in time order (p. 61).

civil disobedience (sĭv´əl dĭs´ə-bē´dē-əns) refusal to obey certain laws that one regards as unjust (p. 193).

civil rights (sĭv´əl rītz) the individual freedoms of each citizen (p. 560).

civilian (sĭ-vĭl´yən) a person who is not a member of the armed forces (p. 285).

claim (klām) a formal request to own a tract of public land; or the tract of land as staked out (p. 382).

Cold War (kōld wôr) the political and military contest, without actual fighting, between the U.S. and USSR (p. 566).

colonization (kŏl´ə-nĭ-zā´shən) the process of starting a colony or colonies by sending settlers to a new place, usually a distant one (p. 129).

colony (kŏl´ə-nē) a territory under the rule of another country, usually a distant one (p. 111).

common (kŏm´ən) a large public pasture in the center of a town (p. 183).

common school (kŏm´ən skōōl) a public elementary school in which students of all ages and abilities sat together and studied in the same room (p. 333).

communism (kŏm´yə-nĭz´əm) the social and political system under which there is no private property and there are no social classes (p. 546).

compromise (kŏm´prə-mīz´) to settle an argument by each side giving up some demands (p. 300).

Confederacy (kən-fĕd´ər-ə-sē) the eleven states that seceded from the United States in 1860–1861; also called the Confederate States of America (p. 466).

confederation (kən-fĕd´ə-rā´shən) a group of states or nations united for a common goal (p. 95).

constitution (kŏn´stĭ-tōō´shən) the basic law and plan for governing a country or state (p. 287).

contagious disease (kən-tā´jəs dĭ-zēz´) an illness that tends to spread from one person to another (p. 121).

cotton gin (kŏt´n jĭn) a machine that cleans cotton by separating the seeds from the fibers (p. 403).

council (koun´səl) a group of people called together to give advice (p. 163).

covenant (kŭv´ə-nənt) an agreement with God; an agreement between two persons (p. 181).

culture (kŭl´chər) the attitudes, beliefs, and customs of a group of people that are passed from one generation to another (p. 6).

D

delegate (dĕl´ĭ-gāt´) one person chosen to act for a group; a representative or agent (p. 262).

democracy (dĭ-mŏk´rə-sē) rule by the majority; a system of government in which the people rule, either directly or through elected representatives (p. 191).

Depression (dĭ-prĕsh´ən) a very bad economic period in the 1930s with few jobs and much suffering (p. 552).

descendant (dĭ-sĕn´dənt) a person who is born to particular parents, grandparents, and more distant ancestors (p. 13).

dictator (dĭk´tā´tər) a leader with complete power over a country (p. 556).

dissenter (dĭ-sĕn´tər) a person who disagrees with an accepted idea or refuses to follow certain beliefs (p. 193).

diversity (dĭ-vûr´sĭ-tē) variety; the condition of being different or varied (p. 214).

draft (drăft) a call to military service that is not voluntary (p. 486).

duty (dōō´tē) a tax paid on goods brought into a country (p. 200).

E

emancipation (ĭ-măn´sə-pā´shən) the act of freeing people from oppression or slavery (p. 482).

empathy (ĕm´pə-thē) an understanding of other people's feelings, actions, and situations (p. 71).

encomienda (ĕn-kō´mē-ĕn´də) large tracts of land owned by wealthy Spanish settlers in North America; some included Indian villages and their inhabitants (p. 129).

epoch (ĕp´ək) a period of time, especially one that is remarkable in some way (p. 82).

equality (ĭ-kwŏl´ĭ-tē) the state of having the same rights, privileges, and responsibilities (p. 264).

ethnic custom (ĕth´nĭk kŭs´təm) a practice of a certain cultural group that is passed from one generation to another (p. 19).

evidence (ĕv´ĭ-dəns) something that proves a belief; something that indicates what happened (p. 58).

exodus (ĕk´sə-dəs) many people leaving at the same time (p. 505).

expedition (ĕk´spĭ-dĭsh´ən) an organized journey with a specific purpose, such as exploration (p. 110).

export (ĕk´spôrt´) a product grown or manufactured in one country and sold to another (p. 168).

F

factory (făk´tə-rē) a building or group of buildings in which products are manufactured (p. 423).

fault (fôlt) a break or crack in the earth's crust (p. 52).

federal (fĕd´ər-əl) relating to a central government (p. 293).

Federalist (fĕd´ər-ə-lĭst) a member of a political party led by Alexander Hamilton that supported a strong federal government (p. 319).

fort (fôrt) a place of defense; a permanent army post (p. 131).

forty-niner (fôr´tē-nī´nər) a California gold seeker named for 1849, when gold-rush fever peaked (p. 385).

free state (frē stāt) one of the states north of the Ohio River where slavery was not allowed (p. 445).

G

geography (jē-ŏg´rə-fē) the study of the earth and its features and of life on the earth, including the relationship between people and their environment (p. 31).

ghetto (gĕt´ō) a part of a city where members of a minority group are forced to live because of poverty or social prejudice (p. 532).

glacier (glā´shər) a huge mass of ice moving slowly over land (p. 81).

Great Awakening (grāt ə-wā´kən-ĭng) the Puritan religious movement of the early 1700s, characterized by an awakening of interest in spiritual matters (p. 195).

Great Plains (grāt plānz) the grasslands of the central United States (p. 504).

H

hemisphere (hĕm´ĭ-sfîr´) half the earth: the Northern or Southern hemisphere; the Eastern or Western hemisphere (p. 42).

hero (hîr´ō) a person admired for strength, noble purpose, or brave actions (p. 307).

historian (hĭ-stôr´ē-ən) a person who studies the events of the past (p. 59).

historical map (hĭ-stôr´ĭ-kəl măp) a map that gives information about a historical period (p. 52).

history (hĭs´tə-rē) the study of what happened in the past; a record of past events (p. 59).

Holocaust (hŏl´ə-kôst´) the mass killing of Jewish people by Nazi Germany (p. 559).

House of Burgesses (hous ŭv bûr´jĭs-z) a lawmaking body in colonial Virginia (p. 161).

I

immigrant (ĭm´ĭ-grənt) a person who leaves his or her own country to live permanently in another (p. 13).

import (ĭm´-pôrt) a product brought into a country for sale or use (p. 242).

impressment (ĭm-prĕs´mənt) the act of seizing people and forcing them into military service (p. 322).

indentured servant (ĭn-dĕn´chərd sûr´vənt) a person who agreed to provide five to seven years of unpaid labor in return for free passage across the ocean, food, clothing, and shelter (p. 160).

independence (ĭn´dĭ-pĕn´dəns) the state of being free of the influence, guidance, or control of others; state of being free of political control or rule (p. 262).

Industrial Revolution (ĭn-dŭs´trē-əl rĕv´ə-lōō´shən) a period of great social and economic change that began in the late 1700s, when steam, oil, and electricity began to replace human and animal power and when products began to be made in factories by machines (p. 422).

inflation (ĭn-flā´shən) the problem of rapidly rising prices (p. 484).

interpret (ĭn-tûr´prĭt) to explain the meaning or importance of something (p. 59).

investor (ĭn-vĕs´tôr) a person who provides money for a business, usually to gain income or make a profit (p. 134).

J

journal (jûr´nəl) a personal record of experiences kept on a regular basis (p. 70).

L

labor union (lā´bər yōōn´yən) an organization formed by workers to obtain better wages and working conditions (p. 519).

landlord (lănd´lôrd´) the owner of land, houses, or apartments that are rented to tenants (p. 227).

latitude (lăt´ĭ-tōōd´) the distance north or south of the equator, expressed in degrees (p. 44).

legislature (lĕj´ĭ-slā´chər) a governmental body made up of persons elected to make laws (p. 294).

life expectancy (līf ĭk-spĕk´tən-sē) The number of years a person is expected to live, as predicted by statistics (p. 158).

long house (lông hous) a long wooden house in which several Iroquois families lived together (p. 95).

longitude (lŏn´jĭ-tōōd´) the distance east or west of the Prime Meridian expressed in degrees (p. 44).

Louisiana Purchase (lōō-ē´zē-ăn´ə pûr´chĭs) land between the Mississippi River and the Rocky Mountains that the United States purchased from France in 1803 (p. 352).

Loyalist (loi´ə-lĭst) an American who remained faithful to the British government during the Revolution (p. 269).

M

mechanization (mĕk´ə-nĭz-ā´-shən) using machines to do work; equipping factories with machines (p. 518).

meetinghouse (mē´tĭng-hous´) a large building used by the Puritans as a gathering place for religious services, celebrations, and town meetings (p. 182).

merchant (mûr´chənt) a person whose business is buying and selling goods for profit (p. 198).

meridian (mə-rĭd´ē-ən) one of a series of imaginary lines that run north and south from the North Pole to the South Pole and measure distance east and west of the prime meridian (p. 44).

mesa (mā´sə) a flat-topped hill or mountain with steep sides, common in the southwestern United States (p. 86).

middle class (mĭd´l klăs) a social and economic class made up of people who are neither rich nor poor (p. 532).

migrate (mī´grāt´) to move from one country or region to another (p. 378).

militia (mə-lĭsh´ə) a nonprofessional army made up of citizens who serve during emergencies (p. 260).

mission (mĭsh´ən) a place, usually including a church and a school, that is established for religious and humanitarian purposes (p. 130).

Monroe Doctrine (mən-rō´ dŏk´trĭn) a statement by President Monroe opposing European interference in the Americas and U.S. interference in Europe (p. 323).

Mormon (môr´mən) a member of the Church of Jesus Christ of Latter-day Saints, founded in 1830 by Joseph Smith (p. 387).

mound (mound) a large, steep platform built for protection, burial, or religious purposes (p. 90).

multicultural (mŭl´tĭ-kŭl´chər-əl) enjoying the heritage of many ethnic groups in one nation (p. 571).

N

nationalism (năsh´ə-nə-lĭz´əm) devotion to the interests or culture of a particular nation; emphasis on national rather than international goals (p. 321).

nativism (nā´tĭ-vĭz´əm) the policy of favoring native-born inhabitants over immigrants, especially in America in the 1800s (p. 527).

navigable (năv´ĭ-gə-bəl) broad and deep enough for a ship to pass through (p. 209).

navigate (năv´ĭ-gāt´) to plan and control the course of a ship or aircraft (p. 107).

New Deal (nōō dēl) the programs and policies of President Franklin D. Roosevelt to fight the economic depression of the 1930s (p. 553).

nomad (nō´măd´) one of a group of people who move with their flocks and herds as the seasons change to find water and pasture (p. 390).

Northwest Passage (nôrth-wĕst´ păs´ĭj) a legendary water route through North America; Europeans in the 1500s believed it would lead to China (p. 119).

nuclear arms (nōō´ klē-ər ärmz) weapons using atomic energy (p. 566).

O

oral history (ôr´əl hĭs´tə-rē) information about the past gathered from interviews with people (p. 65).

ordinance (ôr´dn-əns) a law or regulation, especially one made by a city or town (p. 344).

overseer (ō´vər-sē´ər) a person who directed the work of the slaves (p. 408).

P

pacifism (păs´ə-fĭz´əm) opposition to war and violence; the belief that war is the wrong way to solve differences between nations (p. 145).

pacifist (păs´ə-fĭst) a person who thinks war is wrong (p. 546).

parallel (păr´ə-lĕl´) one of a series of imaginary east-west lines that circle the globe and measure distance north and south of the equator (p. 43).

Parliament (pär´lə-mənt) the lawmaking body of England, consisting of the House of Lords and the House of Commons (p. 200).

patriotism (pā´trē-ə-tĭz´əm) love and loyal support for one's country (p. 309).

patroon system (pə-trōōn´ sĭs´təm) a plan of the Dutch West India Company for colonizing New Netherland, which included New York; any member of the company who brought 50 families over could have a large tract of land; he would rule over the settlers, who would farm the land (p. 227).

physical map (fĭz´ĭ-kəl măp) a map that shows land and water features, such as mountains and lakes (p. 50).

Pilgrim (pĭl´grəm) one of the English Puritans who founded the colony of Plymouth in New England in 1620 (p. 139).

pioneer (pī´ə-nîr´) one of the first persons to explore or settle a region (p. 341).

plain (plān) a broad area of flat, open land (p. 371).

plantation (plăn-tā´shən) a large farm where one crop is grown. A plantation includes the home of the owner and residences for workers (p. 161).

pluralism (plŏŏr´ə-lĭz´əm) the existence within a society of a number of different ethnic, racial, religious, and social groups (p. 6).

political party (pə-lĭt´ĭ-kəl pär´tē) a group organized to promote candidates for political office (p. 319).

politics (pŏl´ĭ-tĭks) the activities of governments (p. 244).

popular sovereignty (pŏp´yə-lər sŏv´ər-ĭn-tē) the belief that the power or authority in a nation rests with its people (p. 453).

potlatch (pŏt´lăch´) a ceremony among the American Indians of the northwest Pacific coast in which the host distributes gifts (p. 89).

precedent (prĕs´ĭ-dənt) an action or decision used later as an example for similar cases (p. 316).

prejudice (prĕj´ə-dĭs) an unfavorable opinion formed without knowledge of the facts (p. 21).

primary source (prī´mĕr´ē sôrs) information about events recorded at the time of those events (p. 64).

profit (prŏf´ĭt) the money made by a business after all the expenses have been met (p. 134).

progressive (prə-grĕs´ĭv) a social reformer (p. 540).

projection (prə-jĕk´shən) a way of drawing the curved surface of the earth on a flat map (p. 45).

propaganda (prŏp´ə-găn´də) the spread of ideas, often in a biased or one-sided form, to win support for a particular cause (p. 249).

Puritan (pyŏŏr´ĭ-tn) a member of a Protestant group in England and the American colonies. Puritans believed in simple creeds and ceremonies, strict discipline, and high moral standards (p. 139).

Q

Quakers (kwā´kərs) or Religious Society of Friends, founded about 1652, believing in equality and pacifism (p. 145).

R

racism (rā´sĭz´əm) the idea that one's own race or ethnic group is superior to another (p. 146).

ratify (răt´ə-fī´) consent to officially; to make valid (p. 293).

rebel (rĕb´əl) a person who uses force to oppose a government or another authority; a rebel is someone who rebels (rĭ-bĕlz´) (p. 165).

Reconstruction (rē´kən-strŭk´shən) the period after the Civil War when the federal government controlled the former Confederate states (p. 496).

reform (rĭ-fôrm´) to change for the better (p. 436).

region (rē´jən) an area with certain characteristics —such as physical features, language, or climate— that set it apart from surrounding areas (p. 35).

registration (rĕj´ĭ-strā´shən) the act of signing up officially; for example, to enroll in a class or to vote in an election.

repeal (rĭ-pēl´) to officially cancel or to do away with a law or tax (p. 248).

representative (rĕp´rĭ-zĕn´tə-tĭv) an elected member of a lawmaking body in a government, acting for the people in a certain geographical area (p. 161).

republic (rĭ-pŭb´lĭk) a nation in which political power lies with the citizens, who elect leaders and representatives (p. 268).

Republican (rĭ-pŭb´lĭ-kən) a member of a political party led by Thomas Jefferson that became what is now the Democratic party (p. 319).

revolution (rĕv´ə-lōō´shən) the overthrow of a government by force (p. 268).

S

salutary neglect (săl′yə-tĕr′ē nĭ-glĕkt′) Britain's policy, which proved salutary, or helpful, of neglecting its North American colonies and not collecting taxes from them (p. 239).

secede (sĭ-sēd′) to withdraw formally, especially as a group, from an organization or country (p. 448).

secessionist (sĭ-sĕsh′-ə-nist) a person who believes in the right of a state to secede, especially those Southerners who wanted to withdraw from the Union (p. 465).

Second Great Awakening (sĕk′ənd grāt ə-wā′kən-ing) a religious movement of the 1830s and 1840s characterized by a rebirth of interest in spiritual matters (p. 434).

segregation (sĕg′rĭ-gā′shən) the policy of keeping people of different races apart (p. 499).

self-interest (sĕlf′ĭn′trĭst) concern about how an issue affects one personally; a selfish regard for one's own interests over those of others (p. 515).

separation of powers (sĕp′ə-rā′shən ŭv pou′ərz) the division of responsibilities among the branches of the government, giving each branch a different job (p. 302).

Separatist (sĕp′ər-ə-tĭst) a person belonging to a Protestant church that had left the Church of England (p. 139).

Shaker (shā′kər) the common name for a religious sect called the United Society of Believers (p. 435).

sharecropper (shâr′krŏp′ər) one of the poor southern farmers who rented land and gave part of the crops to the owner (p. 414).

slave state (slāv stāt) one of the states south of the Ohio River where slavery was allowed (p. 445).

slavery (slā′və-rē) an inhuman system in which people are owned as property. Slaves work without pay and have no rights (p. 167).

slum (slŭm) a crowded section of a city, with run-down housing and poor living conditions (p. 432).

smuggle (smŭg′əl) to move goods secretly and unlawfully to avoid paying a duty (p. 200).

spiritual (spĭr′ĭ-chōō-əl) a religious song of slaves, often expresses hope for a better life (p. 410).

strike (strīk) to refuse to work until certain demands, such as higher wages, are met (p. 519).

stock (stŏk) the share of control that a business exchanges with a person, called an investor, who puts in money (p. 550).

suffrage (sŭf′rĭj) the right to vote (p. 542).

superpower (sōō′pər-pou′ər) a nation stronger than other nations; the United States is a superpower (p. 559).

surplus (sûr′pləs) an extra amount (p. 324).

T

tax (tăks) money, or occasionally property, that people pay to their government (p. 130).

technology (tĕk-nŏl′ə-jē) the tools, machines, and methods used to manufacture things or used in other ways to improve people's lives (p. 105).

tenant farmer (tĕn′ənt fär′mər) a farmer who works land that is owned by someone else and pays rent either in cash or in a share of the crops (p. 227).

tenement (tĕn′ə-mənt) a low-rental apartment building, overcrowded and run down (p. 429).

textile (tĕks′tīl′) fabric; woven cotton or wool (p. 325).

tolerance (tŏl′ər-əns) willingness to respect beliefs or practices different from one's own (p. 214).

township (toun′shĭp′) an area of land measuring 36 square miles (p. 293).

treaty (trē′tē) a formal written or spoken agreement, especially between nations (p. 211).

tributary (trĭb′yə-tĕr′ē) a stream or small river that flows into a larger river (p. 346).

U

Underground Railroad (ŭn′dər-ground′rāl′rōd′) a series of secret escape routes used by slaves fleeing from the South to free states and Canada (p. 451).

Union (yōōn′yən) the United States of America, especially during the Civil War (p. 445).

utopian community (yōō-tō′pē-ən kə-myōō′nĭ-tē) a planned perfect community where people hoped to live together in peace and harmony (p. 435).

V

veto (vē′tō) to reject a law passed by a lawmaking body, preventing it from going into effect (p. 240).

W

walking city (wôkĭng sĭt′ē) a community with no public transportation (p. 430).

War Hawk (wôr hôk) a senator or congressman who favored war with Britain in 1812 (p. 322).

Italic numbers refer to pages on which illustrations appear.

A

Abbot, Abiel, 402, 405, 412, 414
Abbott, John, 332
Abolitionists, 406, 436–438, 482
  southern response to, 452–453
A.D., understanding, 99
Adams, Abigail, *258,* 284–285, 332
Adams, John, 58–59, 250, *258, 262,*
  264–265, 284, 308, 319, 332, *613*
Adams, John Quincy, 364, 444
Adams, Samuel, 250
Addams, Jane, 540, 542
Adventures of Huckleberry Finn,
  The (Twain), 416
Africa, 167–171, 174–175, 410–411
African Americans. *See also names*
  of individuals, such as, Douglass,
  Frederick
  in American Revolution, *269,* 272,
    286–287
  citizenship, 496
  civil rights and, 560–563
  in Civil War, *474, 480*
  education, 495
  free community of, 330–331
  music, 537, 550
  officeholders, 497
  and Progressivism, 542–543
  and racism, 542–543
  and Reconstruction, 494–495,
    497–499
  religion of, 331
  and slavery, 167–171
  and voting rights, 498, 563
  in world wars, 547, 560
Africa, West, culture of, 170–171
Akan, 170–171
Alabama, 66, 91, 307, 363
Alamo, Battle of the, 372, 373
Alaska, 37
Albany, N.Y. 121, 270
Alcott, Louisa May, 480–481
Algonquin Indians, 52, 132–133, 135,
  159, 184–185, 193
  and Puritans, 184–185
  and Virginia, 164–166
America, naming of, 114
American Anti–Slavery Society, 451
American Dictionary of the English
  Language, (Webster), 308, 309
American Indians. *See* Native
  Americans
American Red Cross, 307
American Revolution
  African Americans in, 269, 286–287
  beginning of, 260–261
  French allies in, 272–273
  Native Americans in, 270, 286–287
  northern battles of, 269–272
  price increases during, 285–286
  soldiers in, 268–269, *271*
  southern battles of, 272–273

  women's role in, 269, 284–286
American River, 383
American Spelling–Book, (Webster),
  308–309
Amish, 217
Anasazi Indians, 31, *52, 79,* 87–88,
  92, 99
Anglicanism. *See* Church of England
Ann, Mother, 435
Anthony, Susan B., 542
Antietam, Battle of, 479
Antislavery movement. *See* Aboli-
  tionists
Apache Indians, 390
Appomattox Courthouse, Va.,
  474, 491
Apprenticeship, 187, 220–221
Arbella (ship), 142, 180, 182
Archaic epoch, 82–83
Argall, Samuel, 63–65
Arizona, 12, 30, 33, 79
Arkansas, 476
Armstrong, Neil, 538, 570, 573
Art, as historical evidence, 62
Articles of Confederation, *272,*
  293–294, 297
Artifacts, 68–69
  understanding, 69
Asante, 170–171
Asian Americans, *3,* 17, 19–21, 542,
  557. *See also* Chinese Ameri-
  cans; Japanese Americans
Assemblies, in colonies, 240
Astrolabe, *107,* 108
Athens, Greece, 498
Atlanta, Ga., 491
Atomic bombs, 537, 559
Attucks, Crispus, 249, *250*
Augusta, Ga., 50, *51*
Austin, Stephen F., 371
Austria-Hugary, 545
Aztecs, 83, 90, 99, 115

B

Bacon, Elizabeth, 163
Bacon, Nathaniel, 155, 163, 165–166
Bacon's Rebellion, 165–166
Balboa, Vasco Núñez de, 114
Ball, Charles, 169, 412
Bakersfield, Calif., 46–47
Banjo Lesson, The (Tanner), 417
Baltimore, Md., 135
Banneker, Benjamin, *2,* 331
Baptists, 217, 330
Barbados, 135
Barrio, 15–16
Barrio Boy (Galarza), 12
Barton, Clara, 307
B.C., understanding, 99
Bear Flag Republic, 384
Belcher, Andrew, 198

Benavides, Santos, *481*
Benet, Rosemary and Stephen, 341
Benin, 171
Bering Strait, 81
Beringian epoch, 81–83
Berkeley, William, 163–166
Berry, Erick, 276
Bethune, Mary McLeod, 555
Bill of Rights, 303, 591–592
Blacks. *See* African Americans
Blackfoot Indians, *71,* 390
Black Hawk, 365
Black Hawk War, 365
Blegen, Theodore C., 426
Bodmer, Karl, 70–71
Book of Mormon, 387
Boone, Daniel, 340–342, 347, 357
Boone, Rebecca, 341, 347, 357
Boonesborough, Kentucky, *347*
Booth, John Wilkes, 492
Boston, Mass., 28, 58–61, 142,
  178, 203
Boston Massacre, 58–61, 249–250
Boston Tea Party, 250–252
Boudinot, Elias, 266, 364
Bowie, Jim, 372–373
Boycott, 249
Bradford, William, 139
Breckinridge, John, 464
Breed's Hill, Battle of, 268
Britain. *See* England; Great Britian
British East India Company, 250
British Empire, 238–240
Brook Farm, Mass., 436
Brown, John, 450, 455, 464
Brown, Thaddeus, 260
Budd, Benjamin, 292
Budd, Rachel, 292
Bull Run, Battle of, 477
Bunker Hill, Battle of, 268
Bureau of Indian Affairs, 364, 391
Burgoyne, John, 270, 272
Burnaby, Andrew, 213–214, 238
Bush, George, G14, 565, 570
Byrd, William, 404–405, 412

C

Cabinet, establishment of, 316
Cabot, John, 121, 131
Cahokia, Miss., 88, 89–90, 99
Cahokia Indians, 89–90
Cajuns, 4, 6
Calhoun, John, 448–449, 457
California, 20, 53, 375, 447
  gold rush in, 383–387, 397
  mining towns in, 386
  Native Americans, 384, 386
  under Spain and Mexico, 384
Californios, 384
Calvert, George, 135
Cambridge, Mass., 142

Camp meetings, 330, 415, 434–435
Canada, 600
Canals, 346, 424–425
Canassateego, 219
Cape Cod, *139,* 140
Caravel, 107
Caribbean, The. *See* West Indies
Carnegie, Andrew, 517
Carolina colony, 173
"Carrying the Running–Aways,"
    458–461
Carter, James Earl, Jr., (Jimmy) 565, 570
Cartier, Jacques, 119
Cartographers, 35
Cash crop, 173
Catholic Church. *See* Roman
    Catholic Church
Cause and effect, understanding, 376
Cayuga Indians, 97–98, 270
Central America, *15, 19, 614*
Central Pacific Railroad, 516
Champlain, Samuel de, 131
Change, citizenship and, 498
Chang Heng, 43
Charles I, 135, 139, 142, 166
Charles II, 144–147, 211, 214
Charleston, S.C., 412
    battle of, 272–273
Chávez, César, 564
Checks and balances, 301–302
Cherokee Indians, 341, 363, 390, 481
    folktale of, 84–85
    and Trail of Tears, 364–365, 391
Cherokee Phoenix (Boudinot), 364
Chert, 89
Chesapeake Bay, 134, 478
Chesapeake Indians, 134
Cheyenne Indians, 390
Chibchas, 115
Chicago, Ill., *8*
Chickasaw Indians, 4, 363–364, 390
Child labor laws, 421, 520, 541
Children
    and apprenticeship, 187
    and factory work, 519, 541
    among Puritans, 186–189
China, 20, *327,* 385
Chinese Americans, *3,* 13, 17, 19–21
Chipewyan Indians, 83
Choctaw Indians, 4, 363, 390
    removal of, 364
Cholera, 392
Christianity, and exploration,
    105–107, 122, 126
Church of England, 139, 181, 330
Cincinnati, Ohio, *420,* 430–433
Cities
    growth of, 325–327, 531–532
    immigration and, 428
    middle class flight from, 533
    northern: life in, 428–433, 540
    population growth in, 428, 432

Citizenship, 498
Civil disobedience, 193
Civil rights, 496, 560–563
Civil Rights Act of 1964, 563
Civil War, 476–477, 479–481,
    483–489, 491–493
Clark, William, 338, 353–356, 360
Clay, Henry, 447–449, 457
Cleveland, Grover, 520
Climate, 37, 93
Clinton, Henry, 272
Clinton, William (Bill), G14, *539,* 570
Cluster diagrams, *334–335*
Cohen, Barbara, 22
Cold War, 538, 565–566
Colonialism, understanding, 146
Colonies. *See also specific colonies*
    daily life in, 196–197
    divisions among, 237–238
    government in, 240
    as part of British Empire, 238–240
    taxation of, 248–250
    unity among, 252–253
Colonization, 129, 146
    Dutch, 144
    English, 132–135, 138–147, 154–162
    French, 127, *130,* 131
    Spanish, 128–130
Colorado, 86, 356
Columbus, Christopher, 103, 110–114
Comanche Indians, *390*
Committees of Correspondence, 250
Common, 183
Common schools, 333
Common Sense (Paine), 263, *272*
Communism, 546, 566–567
Compass, *102, 106*
Compass rose, *G3,* G4, 47, *105*
Compromise, understanding, 448
Compromise of 1850, 449
*Concessions to the Province of
    Pennsylvania* (Penn), 212
Concord, Mass., 258, 261, *272*
Conestoga Indians, 236
Confederacy, 443, 466, 476, 487,
    491–492. *See also* Union
Confederation among Iroquois, 95
Congo, 171
Congregationalism, 181, 330
Congress, organization of, 300–301
Connecticut, 144, 292
Constitution, 290, 297–303
    amendments to, 303. *See also* Bill
        of Rights
    and civil rights, 562–563
    "necessary and proper" clause, 317
    ratification of, 302–303
    text of, 580–599
Contagious disease, 121–122
Continental Army, *259,* 268–269
Continental Congresses, 252–253,
    262–263, 272, 293

Continents, 42, 81
Cooper, Peter, 422
Corbin, John, 269
Corbin, Margaret, 269
Cornwallis, Charles, 273–274
Coronado, Francisco, 115
Cortés, Hernán, 114–115
Cotton, 400–401, 403–404
Cotton, John, 191
Cotton gin, *400,* 403–404
Covenant, 181
Craftspeople, 200–201
Crazy Horse, 506–507
Creek Indians, 87, 91–92, 99, 341, *390*
    removal of, 364
Creoles, 6
Crèvecoeur, Michel Jean de, 2, 292
Critical thinking skills
    artifacts: interpreting information,
        69
    B.C. and A.D.: timelines, 99
    cause and effects, 376
    climate: observing seasons, 93
    cluster diagrams, 334
    group projects, 439
    how to outline, 275
    identifying fact and opinion, 304
    interpreting political cartoons,
        254
    latitude and longitude, 48
    line graphs, 148
    map directions, 123
    map making: using landmarks, 358
    map symbols, 521
    oral reports, 467
    point of view, 457
    reference books, 9
    scale: choosing maps, 18
    symbols: interpreting flow lines,
        174
    tables, comparing, 229
    understanding, 254
    visuals: comparing art and photos,
        62
Crockett, Davy, 372–373 350–351
Cross–staff, *102*
Crow Indians, *390*
Crusades, 105–106
Cuba, *15*
Cuffe, Paul, *330*
Culture, 6
    and pluralism, 6, 18
    understanding, 18
Cumberland Gap, *338, 340–341*
Curry, John Steuart, *450*
Custer, George Armstrong, 502, 507

D

Daughters of Liberty, 248
Davis, Jefferson, 443, 466, 483, 487
"Davy Crockett," 350–351

Dawes, Billy, 261
Dawkins, Henry, *236, 245*
Declaration of Independence,
    263–265, 272
  text of, 576–579
Delaware Indians, 147, 219, 245
  treaty with Pennsylvania, 211–212
Delaware River, 208–209
Delaware (state), 144
Delegates, 262
Democracy, 191, 498
Democratic Party, 456
Demographic change, understand-
    ing, 392
DeMonte, Claudia, 19
Denmark, *143*
Denning, William, *152*
Depression. *See* Great Depression
Derby, Elias, 328
De Soto, Hernando, 115
Detroit, Mich., 363
Diamond, William, 260
Dias, Bartholomeu, 110–111
Díaz, Bernal, 114, 118
DiLucente, Nicolette, 525
Discrimination, 542–543. *See also*
    Prejudice; Racism
Dissent, understanding, 192
Dixieland music, 4
Dongan, Thomas, 212
Douglas, Stephen, 453–456, 463–464
Douglass, Frederick, 436–437, 451, 463
Drake, Francis, 121, 203
Drayton, John G., *403*
Drayton, Michael, 68
Dred Scott decision, 463
Dreiser, Theodore, 530
Du Bois, W.E.B., 536, *542,* 543, 549
Dutch East India Company, 120
Dutch Reformed Church, 219
Duties (taxes), 200, 240, 248–249
Duwamish Indians, 389
Dyer, Mary, 194

E

Earth, *41,* 570
Earthquakes, 51–52
Economy, 324, 572
Education. *See* Public schools.
Edwards, Jonathan, 195
Eisenhower, Dwight D., 560, 565
El Paso, Tex., 129, *130*
Elections, presidential, 319, 322, 323,
    382, 413, 443, 464–465, 487, 499,
    539, 568
Elizabeth I, 121, 138
Ellis Island, 13, 23
Emancipation Proclamation, 482
Emerson, John, 462
Empathy, 71–72
Encomiendas, 129

Encyclopedias, using, 9
England, 57, 65, 139, 146, 154. *See
    also* Great Britain
  and Middle Colonies, 143–147
  and New England, 138–142
  and South, 132–135, 154–166
  exploration of New World, 121
Episcopal Church, 330
Epochs, 82
Equality, understanding, 264
Equator, 42, *43, 93*
Equiano, Olaudah, 167, 172
Erie Canal, 346, 424–425
Ethnic custom, 19–20
Ethnic diversity, 8. *See also* Pluralism
Europe
  map of, *615*
  world view of, 104–105
Expansion, understanding, 114
Exploration, 105–106, 109–115,
    120–121, 601
  impact on Native Americans,
    121–122
  money for, *116,* 117
  of North America, 118–121, 601
  of space, 601
  and spread of disease, 121–122
  technology and, 105–108
  weapons and, 108
Exports, 168

F

Fact and opinion, 304–305
Factories
  development of, 423
  mechanization of, 518
  women in, 423–424
  working in, 519–520
Fallen Timbers, Battle of, 362
Fall-line cities, 50–51
Families, changes in by 1800s, 332
Farming
  and economic changes, 324, 328
  harvest time, *226–227*
  in the Middle Colonies, 224–228
  post-Revolution changes in,
    324–325
  in the South, 415
  and standard of living, 225–226
  and trade, 324–325
Fault, 52
Fault-line cities, *51, 52*
Federalist party, 319
Ferdinand of Aragon, 102–103, 107,
    110–111, 116–117
Finley, James B., 435
First Amendment, 303
Flags, 309, *602,* 603
Florida, 39, *66,* 129
Flow lines, 174–175
Flying shuttle, 423

Fodorovich, Anna, 524
Folktales, 84–85
Ford, Gerald R., 560, 565, 570
Ford, Henry, 549
Ford, Mary Theodosia, *400*
Fordham, Elias Pym, 329
Foreign policy. *See* Monroe Doc-
    trine; *and presidents by name*
Fort Kearney, 49
Fort Laramie, meeting of Indians
    and government, 393
Fort McHenry, *323*
Fort Stanwix, Treaty of, 287, 361
Fort Sumter, shelling of, 466
Forty-niners, 385–387
Fourteenth Amendment, 496
Fowler, Amy, 345–346
Fox, George, 145
Fox Indians, 363, 365
France, *327, 352*
  colonization of New World, 127,
    130, 131
  exploration of New World, 119–120
  rivalry with Britain, 242–245
  role in American Revolution,
    272–273
Francis Ferdinand, Archduke, 545
Franklin, Benjamin, 220–223, 228,
    234, 236, 238, 240, 262, 266, 274,
    297–298, *299,* 308
Free states, 445–446
Freedmen's Bureau, *475,* 495
Freeman, Elizabeth, *331*
Frémont, John C., *456*
French and Indian War. *See* Seven
    Years' War
French Revolution, 317–318
Friends, Society of. *See* Quakers
Fritz, Jean, 220
Frontier
  and Indians, 349
  life on, 345–349
  pioneers on, 341–349
  stations, 347
  understanding, 348
Frontiersmen, 342–344
Fugitive Slave Law, 449
Fulton, Robert, 315, 325
Fur trade, 131, 148–149
  control by Iroquois, 208, 212

G

Gadsden Purchase, 375
Gage, Thomas, 268
Galarza, Ernesto, 12, 14–16, 21
Gama, Vasco da, 110–111, 118
Garrison, William Lloyd, 406, 437, 451
Gates, Horatio, 272
Gavin, Anna Maria, 528–529
General Historie of Virginia, A
    (Smith), *64*

Geography, 31
  cultural features, 31–32
  and environmental change, 33
  and movement, 32–33
  physical features, G15, 31–32, 36–38
George II, *239*
George III, 254, 262–263, 265, 270
Georgia, 91, 363
Germany, *143,* 237, 330, 428
Gettysburg, Battle of, 489
Gettysburg Address, 489–490, 604
Ghettos, 532
Ghost Dance religion, 507
Glaciers, 81–82
Globe, G9, G10, 42–44. *See also*
  Grids; Latitude; Longitude;
  Projections
Gold rush, 383–387
Goode's projection, 46
Gooseberries to Oranges, 22–25
Government, formation of, 287,
  292–294
Grand Banks, 131
Grand Canyon, 30–33
Grant, Ulysses S., 474, 479, 490–491,
  499
Graphic organizers, understanding,
  334–335
Grasse, Admiral de, 273
Gray Panthers, *539*
Great Awakening, 195. *See also*
  Second Great Awakening
Great Britain. *See also* England
  claims on Oregon, 282
  colonial trade with, 238–239
  rivalry with France, 242–245
Great Compromise, 300–301
Great Depression, 537, 552–555
Great Salt Lake, 388
Great Seal of the U.S., 308–309
Greeley, Horace, 434
Green Corn Dance, 91
Greene, Asa, 430
Greenhow, Rose O'Neal, *481*
Grenada, 135
Grids, map, G8, 43–44
Group projects, understanding, 439
Guadalupe Hidalgo, Treaty of, 375,
  384, 388
Guam, 146

H

Hakluyt, Richard, 133
Hamilton, Alexander, 297, 316–319,
  334–335
Hamilton, Virginia, 458
Harding, Warren G., 546
Hargreaves, James, 423
Harlem, 547, 549–550

Harpers Ferry, Va., 464
Harrison, William Henry, 360–363
Harvard College, 189
Hastie, William, 555
Hawaii, *37,* 556
Hawley, Gideon, 243
Hayes, Rutherford B., *475,* 499
Haynes, Lemuel, *331*
Heap, George, 228
Heemskerk, Egbert van, 145
Hemispheres, G9, 42–43
Heng, Chang, 43
Henry, Marguerite, 224
Henry, Patrick, *235,* 253
Henry the Navigator, 109–110
Henry VIII, 121, 138–139
Henson, Josiah, 407, 412
Heroes and heroism, 307–308
  and nationalism, 321
  understanding, 307
Hewes, George 247, 250
Hiawatha, legend of, 98–99
Hicks, Edward, *211, 215*
Hiroshima, Japan, 537, 559
Hispanic Americans, 481, *539,* 564.
  See also Mexican Americans;
  *and names of individuals such
  as* Benavides, Santos
  and gold rush, 386
Historian, job of, 59–60, 63–68, 70–73
Historical evidence, 58–60, 62
Historical maps, 52–53
Historical perspective, understand-
  ing, 60
History. *See also* Oral history; Pri-
  mary sources
  current events and, 72–73
  definitions of, 59
  reasons for studying, 70–73
Hitler, Adolf, 556
Holocaust, 558–559
Homestead Act, 488
Hoover, Herbert, 552
Hopi Indians, 129, 136–137
Hornbooks, *187,* 189
House of Burgesses, 161, 163–164
House of Representatives, 300
Houston, Sam, 373
"How the Turtle Beat the Rabbit"
  (folktale), 84–85
Howard University, 495
Huckleberry Finn. *See Adventures
  of Huckleberry Finn, The*
Hudson, Henry, 120–121
Hudson River, 121, 208–210
Hughes, Langston, 549–550
Hull House, 540, 542
Hunkpapa Indians, 507
Huron Indians, 243–244
Hutchinson, Anne, 191–195

I

Ibo, 170
Illinois, 348, 365, 462, 493
Imago Mundi, 116
Immigrants, 10–16
  lives of, *502,* 506, 508–515, 524–526
  and politics, 525
  and racism, 527
  treatment of, 428–429
Immigration, 13, 427–428, 528–529,
  571, 605
  after Civil War, *502,* 523–525
  laws to control, 527, 529
  and pluralism, 16
  reasons for, 14
Immigration Act of 1965, 570, 571
Impressment, 322
Incas, 115
Indentured servants, 160
  Africans as, 172–173
Independence, Mo., 49, 378
Independence Day, 309
Indiana, 346, 360–363, 365
Indians. *See* Native Americans; *spe-
  cific peoples*
Industrial Revolution, 422–425, 493
Interdependence, understanding, *40*
Intolerable Acts, 252
Investors, 134
Iowa, 39, 365
Ireland, 330, 427–428
Iroquois Nation, 94–98, 208, 212, 245
  in American Revolution, 270,
  286–287
  Dutch trade with, 144, 212
  loss of lands by, 219
  religion in, 97
  in Seven Years' War, 244
Irving, Washington, 210, 304–305
Isabella of Castile, 102–103, 107,
  110–111, 116–117
Ishigaki, Eitaro, *553*

J

Jackson, Andrew, 364–365, 413–416
James I, 134, 161–162
James II, 144
James River, 157, 162
Jamestown, 65, 133–135, 140, 155–162
Japanese Americans, 13
  during World War II, 557
Jay, John, 274
Jazz, 537, 550
Jefferson, Thomas, 72, 114, *262,*
  264–265, 294, 304, 308, *314,*
  316–319, 320–322, 334–335,
  352–354, 356–357, 410, 447
  presidency of, 320–322

Jews, 8, 13–14, 22–25, 146, 207, 217, 524, 558
Johnson, Andrew, 496–497
Johnson, Annabel and Edgar, 388
Johnson, Anthony, 172–173
Johnson, Lyndon B., 560, 565, 567, 570
Johnson, Richard, 173
Jones, Betty, 411
Journals, 70–71
Journey to Pennsylvania (Mittelberger), 14

K

Kalm, Peter, 208–210, 214, 219
Kansas, 356, 450
  slavery vote in, 453, 455
  statehood for, 455–456
Kansas Indians, 390
Kansas-Nebraska Act, 453–456
Kay, John, 423
Kennedy, John F., 348, *538,* 560, 565
Kentucky, 341, 344, 345–349
Kickapoo Indians, 361, 363
Kimmel, Husband E., 556
King, Martin Luther, Jr., 192, *538,* 561–564
King, Rufus, 446
Knight, Amelia Stewart, 377
Knox, Henry, *317*
Knox, John, 330
Ku Klux Klan, 498, 505
Kuhn, Maggie, *539*

L

Labor unions, 519–520, 553
Land, disputes over, 292–294
Landforms. *See* Geography
Landmarks, use in mapmaking, 358–359
Language
  differences among colonies, 237
  and pluralism, 20
  and regions, 39
Larcom, Lucy, 424
Las Casas, Bartolomé de, 116
Lateen sail, 107
Latitude, *G2,* G9, 38, *43,* 44
  understanding, 48
Latrobe, John, 422
Lee, Ann, 435
Lee, Richard Henry, 264
Lee, Robert E., 474, 477, 479, 489, *490,* 491
Levy, Harriette Lane, 8
Lewis and Clark expedition, 338, 353–356
Lewis, Meriwether, 338, 353–356, 378
Lexington, Battle of, 260–261, *272*

Lexington, Ky., 346, 349
Liberator, (newspaper), 406, 437, 451
Life expectancy, 158
Lincoln, Abraham, *443,* 456, 463–466, 467, 478, 482, 487–492, 604
  election of, 464–465
Lincoln-Douglas debates, 463–464
Lindbergh, Charles, 548
Line graphs, understanding, 148–149
Literature, as history, 68
Little Big Horn, Battle of, 502, 506–507
Little Turtle, 360
Livingston, Robert R., *262*
Location, 32
London, England, 94
Long house, 95
Longitude, *G2,* G9, 38, 43–44
  understanding, 48
Lord, Bette Bao, 17, 19–20
Los Angeles, Calif., 8
Louisiana, 4–6, 127
Louisiana Purchase, 338, 352–357
Lovell, Jim, 41–42
Lowell, Mass., 423
Loyalists, 266–267, 269, 272, 286
Ludington, Sybil, 276–283
Luther, Martin, 330
Lutherans, 217, 330

M

Madison, Dolley, 304–305, *322*
Madison, James, 297, 303–305
  presidency of, 322–323
Magellan, Ferdinand, 114, 123
Maine, 119, 212, 447
Makah Indians, 87–89
Malcolm, John, 247
Malcolm X. *538, 562–563*
Malcolmson, Anne, 350
Mandan Indians, 355–356
Mandeville, John, 104
Map directions, understanding, 123
Mapmaking, understanding, 38, 358–359
Maps
  choosing of, 202–203
  direction on, 47, 123
  historical, 52–53
  inset, *G2,* G7
  physical, G11, 50–52
  and projections, G10, 45–46
  purposes of, G12–G14, 46
  scale on, *G3,* G6, 46–47, 202–203
  symbols on, *G3,* 174–175, 521
  titles and legends on, *G2–G3,* G5, 46
Marshall, James, 384–385
Marshall, Thurgood, 560
Maryland, 293, 479
  settlement of, 135

Massachusetts, 139–140, 182, 203, 295–296, 421
Massachusetts Bay Colony
  founding of, 139, 142
  religious conflict in, 191–194
Massasoit, 138, 142, 193
Mather, Cotton, 194
May, John, *346*
Mayflower (ship), 139–140, 571
Mayflower Compact, 140
McGuffey's Reader, 526
Meadowcroft, Enid LaMonte, 333
Means, Russell, 538
Mechanization, understanding, 518
Meetinghouses, 179, 182–183
Meir, Golda, 522
Mercator projection, *G10, 45–46*
Merchants, 198–201
Meridians, *42,* 43–44. *See also* Prime meridian
Merrimack (ship), 478–479
Mesa Verde, 86–87
Methodists, 330
Meuse-Argonne, Battle of, 546–547
Mexican Americans, *3,* 12, 21, 481, 545, 554–555
  during World War II, 557
Mexican War, 373–375, 384
Mexico, 12, 14–15, 19, 33, 128, 133
  facts about, 609
  and Texas land grants, 371–372
Miami Indians, 360–361
Michigan, 212, 363
Middle class, growth of, 532–533
Middle Colonies
  cultural diversity in, 206–207, 213–219
  English settlement in, 143–147
  farming in, 224–227
  geography of, 208–210
  immigration to, 216–218
  standard of living in, 225–227
  trade of, 225–226
  urban growth in, 227–228
Migration
  across Bering land bridge, 81–82
  decisions about, 394–395
  to Oregon, 377–382, 395
  to Utah, 387–388
Militia, colonial, 260, 262
Minipedia, 600–613
Minnesota, 383
Minnetaree Indians, *70*
Minorities. *See specific groups*
Minuit, Peter, 52
Minutemen, 258–261
Missions, 129–130
Mississippians, 79, 87, 89–90, 99
Mississippi River, *79, 89,* 127, 338, 353, 363, 365, 478
Missouri, 348, 357, 378, 462
  statehood for, 446–447

Missouri Compromise, 443–447
Mittelberger, Gottlieb, 14, 225
Mohawk Indians, 98, 270
Molasses Act, 240, 248–249
Money
    and Continental Congress, 262, *263*
    after Revolution, 295–296
Monitor (ship), *478*, 479
Monroe, James, 323, 352, 444
Monroe Doctrine, 323
Montezuma, 115
Montgomery, Ala., 561
    bus boycott, 560, 561
Montreal, Canada, 119
Moody, Eleazar, 187
Morgan, Edmund, 64
Mormons, 368, 387
Morris, Gouverneur, *299*
Mott, Lucretia, 438, 542
Mounds, 90
Music
    Cajun, 4
    Dixieland, 4
    instruments, *7*, 410–411
    and slaves, 410–411
    zydeco, 4

N

NAACP (National Association for
    the Advancement of Colored
    People), *536*, 543
Nagasaki, Japan, 537, 559
Napoleon I, 352
Natchez Indians, 4
National bank, 317
National Era (magazine), 452
National Geographic Society, 31, 46
Nationalism
    after War of 1812, 323
    understanding, 321
National Road, 346
Native Americans, *2*, 13, 78–101,
    498, 542. *See also names of
    individuals and groups, such as*
    Crazy Horse; Seneca Indians
    in American Revolution, 270,
        286–287
    ancestors of, 82–83
    and diseases, 219, 392
    and frontier settlers, 349, 391–392
    impact of exploration on, 121–122
    Indian Self–Determination Law,
        564
    locations of (map), *390*, *608*
    loss of lands, 52–53, 164–166, 219,
        344, 360–365, 389
    and Northwest Territory, 294
    and Pennsylvania colonists, 147,
        211–212
    removal treaties and, 364–365
    and reverence for land, 389–390

in Seven Years' War, 243–246
    treaties with, 361–362, 389, 393
    ways of life of, 84, 390–391, 606–608
Nativism, 527
Navajo Indians, *390*
Navigation, 108
Navigation Acts, 200, 239–240
Nazi party, 556–558
Nebraska, *379*, 453, 508–515
Nematanew, 162
Netherlands, 139
    colonization of New World, *143*, 144
    exploration of New World, 120–121
New Amsterdam, *133*, 143–144
New Deal, 537, 553–556
New England, 198–201
    English settlement of, 138–142
    Puritan life in, 186–190, *192*, 195
New England Primer, 189
New Harmony, Ind., 436
New Jersey, 39, 144
New Jersey Plan, 300
New Mexico
    early exploration of, 129
    Spanish settlement of, *126*, 129–130
New Netherland, 127, 144, 217
New Orleans, La., 4–6, 39, 325, 353
New York City, *8*, 39, *50*, 52, 121,
        143, 228, 425, 428–429, *432*, 433.
    See also New Amsterdam
    British capture of, 269
New York (state), *127*, 144, 203, 212,
        227–228. *See also* New Nether-
        land
Nez Perce Indians, 356, *390*
Nicolls, Richard, 144
Nineteenth Amendment, 542–543
Nixon, Richard M., 560, 565, 568, 570
Nogales, Ariz., 12, 15
Norfolk, Va., burning of, 263
North. *See* Union
North, Frederick, 254
North America (map), *624*
North American Indians, 606–607
North Bridge, Battle of, 261
North Carolina, *18*, 119, *126*,
        132–134, 237, 476
Northrup, George W., *383*
Northup, Solomon, 408–409, 412
Northwest Ordinance, 333, 344
    and slavery, 344, 445
Northwest Passage, 119
Northwest Territory, 293–295
Notes on the Federal Convention
    (Madison), 305
Novello, Antonia, *539*
Nuclear arms, 566

O

O'Dell, Scott, 160
Oglala Sioux, 504, 506–507

Ohio, 346, 361, 363, 365, 420,
        430–433, 493
Ohio River, 344–346
Oklahoma, 364–365, 391
Old Northwest, *342. See also*
    Northwest Territory
Olive Branch Petition, 262–263
Oliver, Andrew, 248
Olmsted, Frederick Law, 415
Oñate, Cristobal de, 128
Oñate, Juan de, 128–129
Oneida Indians, *97*, 98
Onondaga Indians, 98, 270
Oral history, 65, 68
Oregon, *369*, 395
    migration to, 377–382
    statehood for, 382
Oregon Trail, 378–381, 395
Orphan for Nebraska, An (Talbot),
        508–515
Overseers, 408–409

P

Paine, Thomas, 263, 266, 269, 318
Paiute Indians, *33*, *390*
Paleo-Indian epoch, 82–83
Palos, Spain, 110
Parallels, 43–44. *See also* Latitude
Paris, Treaty of, 245, 272, 274
Parke, Robert, 217, 225–227
Parker, Ely Samuel, 481
Parker, John, 260
Parker, Jonas, 260–261
Parks, Rosa, 307, 561
Parliament, 199–200
Paterson, William, 300
Patriotism, 309
Pawnee Indians, *390*
Pawtucket, R.I., 423
Paxton Boys, 286–287
Pearl Harbor, Hawaii, 556
Penn, William, 145–147, 206,
        211–212, 214–216, 218–219
Pennsylvania, 493
    constitution of , 287
    farming in, 225–227
    founding of, 145–147
    and Quakers, 214–215
    relations with Indians, 211–212
Percy, George, 156–157
Perot, H. Ross, G14
Perry, David, 241–242
Philadelphia, Pa., 217,
        228, 236–237, 252–253, 269, 291,
        297–298, 329
Philip II, 128
Phoenix, Arizona, *3*
Photographs, as historical evidence,
        62
Pike, Zebulon, 356–357, 368
Pikes Peak, *356*, 357, 368

Pilgrims, 138–142
Pioneers, *29,* 341–342, 346–349, 505–506. *See also* Frontier
Pitcairn, John, 261
Pitcher, Molly, 307, 309
Pitt, William, 244
Pittsburgh, Pa., 345, 425
Plains Indians, 70–72, 390–393, 504–507. *See also specific groups*
   and conflict with settlers, 391–393
Plantations, 161–162, 171, 403–404
   owners of, 404–405
   slaves on, 405–412
Pluralism, 6, 8
   benefits of, 17–20
   challenges of, 20–21
   and culture, 18
   and language, 20
   and prejudice, 21
Plymouth Colony, 65, 138–142
Pocahontas, 159, 162
Point of view, understanding, 457
Pokanoket Indians, 193
Poland, 321
Poles, 42–44
Political cartoons, *253,* 254–255
Political parties, 318–319
Politics, 244
   boss system, 525
   and immigrants, 525
   Iroquois study of, 244
Polk, James K., 374, 382
Pollard, Anne, *178*
Polo, Marco, 106–107
Pope, John, *346*
Popular sovereignty, 453
Port cities, growth of, 325–327
Portsmouth, R.I., 194
Portugal, exploration of New World, 109–110
Postarchaic epoch, 82–83, 99
Potawatomi Indians, 361, 363
Potlatch ceremony, 89
Pottawatomie Creek massacre, 455
Poverty
   and immigration, 429
   after Revolution, 328
   in the South, 413–415
Powell, John Wesley, 30–33
Powhatan, 134, 159, 162
Prejudice. *See also* Discrimination; Racism
   and African Americans, 330–331, 542–543
   in California gold fields, 386–387
   and immigrants, 527
   and pluralism, 21
Presbyterians, 330
Prescott, Samuel, 261
Presidents, facts about, 610
Primary sources, 63–68, 72
Prime meridian, *42, 43*

Printing press, 106
Proclamation of 1763, 245–246, 341–342
Progressives, 540–541
Projections, G10, 45–46
Promontory Point, Utah, 516
Propaganda, 249–250
Prophet, the, 362–363
Prophetstown, Ind., 362–363
Ptolemy, 110
Public schools, 315, 333, 541
   and puritans, 187, 189
Pueblo Indians, *31*
Pueblos, 129
Puerto Rico, 558
Pullman Company, 519–520
Puritans, 139, 142, 178
   beliefs of, 180–181, 184–185
   children, 186–189
   communities of, 182–183
   crafts of, 183–184
   and dissenters, 193–194
   family life of, 189–190
   relationship with land, 183–189
   and witchcraft, 194

Q

Quackenbush, Robert, 143
Quakers, 145–147, 329
   antislavery beliefs of, 206, 450
   ideals of, 214–215
   pacifism of, 145, 211
   persecution by Puritans, 192, 194
Quebec, Battle of, 244–245
Quebec, settlement of, 131

R

Racism, 146, 527. *See also* Discrimination; Prejudice
   and African Americans, 542–543
   and immigrants, 527
Railroads, 425,503, 516–517
Raleigh, Walter, *126,* 133–134
Randolph, Edmund, 300, 302, 304, *317*
Rankin, John, 458–461
Reagan, Ronald, 565, 570
Reconstruction, 494–499
Red Cloud, 504
Reference books, understanding, 9
Regions, 35
   and climate, 37
   and geography, 36–37
   and groups of people, 37–39
   identification of, 35–36
   and interdependence, 40
   of United States, 36–40
Religion. *See also specific religions*
   of African Americans, 331
   divisions among colonies, 238

   in early 1800s, 329–330
   and English colonization, 139
   freedom of, 193
   and government, 191–192
   and prejudice against immigrants, 429
Renney, William, *269*
Reports, understanding, 467
Representative government, 161, 268, 287
Republican form of government, 268, 287
Republican party (Jefferson), 319
Republican Party (modern), 456, 487
Revels, Hiram, 475, *497*
Revere, Paul, 60–61, 261, 307
Revolution, definition of, 268
Revolutionary War. *See* American Revolution
Reynolds, Anna, 371
Rhode Island, 39, 193–194
   establishment of, 193, 330
Rice plantations, 173
Richmond, Virginia, 50, *51,* 253, 478, 491, *493*
Riley, Isaac, 407
"Rip Van Winkle" (Irving), 210
Rivers, navigability of, 209
Roanoke Island, 132
   colony on, 132, 134
Robinson, Arthur, 45–46
Robinson projection, *44,* 45
Rochambeau, Jean Baptiste, 273
Rock 'n' roll, 538
Rolfe, John, 154, 161–162
Roman Catholic Church, 180, 330
   in Maryland, 135
   and Spanish colonization, 129–130
Roosevelt, Eleanor, 553
Roosevelt, Franklin, *537,* 552–555
Roosevelt, Theodore, *536,* 541
Royall, Anne, 329
Rutledge, John, *299*

S

Sacajawea, 354, 356
Sacramento, Calif., 12
Sagres, Portugal, 109
Sailors, 201
St. Augustine, Fla., 129
St. Lucia, 135
Salem, Mass., 194, *201,* 328
Salt Lake City, Utah, 388
Salutary neglect, 239–240, 252
Samoset, *142*
Sampson, Deborah, 269
San Andreas Fault, 52
San Antonio, Tex., 372–373
San Francisco, Calif., 8, 46–47, 51–52, 383, 386, 387
San Jacinto River, Texas, 373

San Salvador, 111
Santa Anna, Antonio Lopez de, 372–373
Santo Domingo, 352
Saratoga, Battle of, 272
Sauk Indians, 363, 365, 391
Savannah, Ga., 272
Scale, understanding, G6, 202–203
Schoolcraft, Mrs. Henry, 402–403, 412, 414
School of Good Manners, The (Moody), 187
Schools, public. *See* Public schools
Schuylkill River, 218
Scott, Dred, 462–463
Scott, Winfield, 374
Scurvy, 118
Seattle, Chief, 389
Seattle, Wash., 389
Sebron, Hyppolite, 432
Secessionists, 465
Second Great Awakening, 434–435
    and antislavery movement, 436–437
    and women, 435
Sedition Act, 319
Segregation, 499, 562
Seminole Indians, *390*
Senate, 300
Seneca Falls Declaration, 438
Seneca Indians, *57,* 97–98, 270, 481
    in Seven Years' War, 243–244
Separation of powers, 301–302
Separatists, 139
Sequoyah, 363, *364*
Seven Years' War, 235, 241–246, 341
    results of, 245–246
Sextant, 32
Shakers, 435–436
Sharecroppers, 414, 495
Shawnee Indians, 245, 322, 340, 341, 360–363
Shays, Daniel, 296
Shays's Rebellion, 295, 296
Sherman, Roger, *262,* 300
Sherman, William Tecumseh, 491
Shoshone Indians, 354, 356, *390*
Sierra Leone, 287
Sinners in the Hands of an Angry God (Edwards), 195
Sioux Indians, 390–391, *393,* 504, 506–507. *See also* Oglala Sioux
Sitting Bull, 507
Slater, Samuel, 420, 423
Slater's Mill, 423
Slavery
    and auctions, 407
    beginnings of, 167–119
    defense of by small farmers, 416
    and Lincoln–Douglas debates, 463–464
    northern attacks on, 405–406

and Northwest Ordinance, 344, 445
    outlawing by Mexico, 372
    on plantations, 405–406
    resistance by slaves, 412
    in southern colonies, 167–173
    southern defense of, 405–406
    and statehood: compromises over, 447–449
    understanding, 168
Slaves
    and African traditions, 410–411
    and Constitutional Convention, 300–301
    culture of, 410–411
    emancipation of, 482, 493, 494
    escape by, 412, 454
    harsh treatment of, 409
    house slaves, 409
    life of, 408–412
    and music, 410–411
    and Northwest Territory, 294
    and overseers, 408–409
    rebellions by, 405–406, 412
    and religion, 410
Slave states, 445
Slave trade, 169–172
    outlawing of, 301, 400
Smallpox, 122, 219, 392
Smith, John, 64, 140, *157,* 158–159
Smith, Joseph, 387
Smuggling, 200
Social class, understanding, 414
Social needs, understanding,
Social Security, 552, 554–555
Somme River, Battle of, 545
Sons of Liberty, 248
South. *See also* Confederacy
    in Civil War, 476–479
    life on small farms, 415
    poverty in, 328, 413–414
South Carolina, 237, 272–273, *465,* 466
South Dakota, 507
Southwest Indians, 607
Soviet Union, *15,* 559, 565–569
Spain
    colonization, 128–130
    exploration, 110–115
Speare, Elizabeth George, 186
Spinning jenny, 423
Spirituals, 410–411
Squanto, 142
Stamp Act, 234, 248–249
Standard of living, in the Middle Colonies, 225–227
Standish, Myles, 141
Stanford, Leland, 516
Stanton, Elizabeth Cady, 285, 438, 542
"Star Spangled Banner," *323*
Statehood, requirements for, 294, 344

Statue of Liberty, 15, *472–473*
Steamboats, 315, 325
Stearns, Junius B., 300
Steel industry, 517–518
Steendam, Jacob, 217
Stock Market Crash, 537, 550–551
Stowe, Harriet Beecher, *443,* 451–452
Strauss, Levi, 387
Strikes, 519–520
Stuyvesant, Peter, 144
Suburbs, 533
Sugar Act, 248–249
Sumner, Charles, 494–495
Superpowers, 559, 565–566
Supreme Court, 300, 364, 560
Susquehannock Indians, 163
Sutter, John, 384–385, 387
Sutter's Mill, 383–385
Sweden, 330
Sybil Ludington's Ride (Berry), 276–283

T

Tables, understanding, 229
Talbot, Charlene Joy, 508
Tamanend, *147*
Taney, Roger, 463
Tanner, Henry Ossawa, 417
Tarring and feathering, 247–248
Tau-gu, *33*
Taxation
    of colonies, 248–250
    understanding, 252
Taylor, Zachary, 374
Tea Act, 250
Technology, and exploration, 105, 107–108
Tecumseh, 360–363
Tenements, 429
Tennessee, 344, 476
Tenochtitlan, 83, 114
Tewa culture, 87
Texas, 370, 447
    annexation vote, 373
    independence of, 373
    settlement of, 371–372
    statehood for, 373–374
Thirteenth Amendment, 493–494
Ticonderoga, Battle of, 241–242
Timelines, using, 99
Tippecanoe, Battle of, 362–363
Tobacco, 65, 154, 173, *327*
    establishment in Virginia, 161–162
To Be a Slave (Jones), 411
Tolerance, 214
    understanding, 216
Tourtillott, Jane Gould, 379
Townshend, Charles, 248
Townshend Duties, 248–249
Township system, 294

Trade
  and exploration, 105–106
  global, 572
  in New England, 198–201
  Parliament control of, 199–200
Trail of Tears, 364–365, 391
Transportation
  in cities, 432, 502
  developments in, 424–425
  and modern technology, 571
Travis, William, 373
Trenton, New Jersey, 50, *51*
Trollope, Frances, 324, 430
Truman, Harry S., 556, 559, 560, 565
Trumbull, John, 262
Truth, Sojourner, 438
Tubman, Harriet, *451*
Turner, Nat, 405–406, 412
Tuskegee Institute, 66
Twain, Mark, 34, 388, 416
Tweed, William, 525

U

Uncle Tom's Cabin (Stowe), *443*,
  451–452
Underground Railroad, 451, 454,
  458–461
Union, in Civil War, 476–479
Unions. *See* Labor unions
United States. *See also names of
    specific states*
  climate (map), *626*
  daily life in, 308–309, 329–333
  facts about, 611–612
  flags of, 309
  holidays of, 309
  land use and resources (map), *627*
  naming of, 114
  overview (map), *618–619*
  physical (map), *622–623*
  pluralism, in, 8
  political (map), *620–621*
  population density, 1980 (map),
    625
  precipitation (map), *627*
  regions of, *36*, 37–40
  time zones (map), *625*
  vegetation (map), *626*
Upson, Theodore, 476
Utah, 55
  migration to, 387–388
  statehood for, 388
Ute Indians, *390*
Utopian communities, 435–436

V

Valley Forge, 269, 272
Vandalia, Ill., 346
Vermont, *37, 181*

Verrazano, Giovanni da, 119
Versailles, Treaty of, 547
Vespucci, Amerigo, 114
Veto power
  and colonial governors, 240
Vicksburg, Battle of, 490
Vienna, Austria, *19*
Vietnam War, 538, 566–569
Virginia, *127, 155,* 166, 212, 237
  settlement of, 134–135, 156–162
Virginia Company, 64–65, 139, 156,
  160–162
Virginia Plan, 300, 304
Visuals, understanding, 62
Voltaire, 216
Voting rights. *See also* Women's
    suffrage
  for blacks, 563

W

Wallace, Linda, 73
Wall Street, 143
Wampanoag Indians, 142
Wampum, *98*
War Hawks, 322
War of 1812, 322–323
Washington, Booker T., *542,* 543
Washington, D.C., 291, 320
  burning of by British, 322
Washington, George, 246, *259, 262,*
  269–270, *272,* 273–274, *290,* 297,
  298, 306–307, 311, 330, 613
  presidency of, 316–318
Wayne, Anthony, 362
Weaver, Robert C., 555
Webster, Noah, 308–309
Weems, Mason, 306
Wells, Ida, *536,* 542–543
Wesley, John, 330
West, Benjamin, 224
West, Rebecca, 379
West Africa. *See* Africa, West
West Indies, English settlement of,
  135
West Virginia, 346
Wetherill, Richard, 86
What's the Big Idea, Ben Franklin?
  (Fritz), 220–223
Wheatley, Phillis, *235*
Wheeling, W. Va., 346
Whipper, William, *442*
Whitaker, Alexander, 156
White, John, 132–134
Whitefield, George, 195
White Hall, 403
Whitney, Eli, 400, 403–404
Wied, Prince Maximilian of, 70–71
Wilderness Road, 340–342, 344, 346
Williams, Roger, 192–195, 330
Wilson, James, *299,* 302

Wilson, Woodrow, 540, 541, 544,
  546–547, 548
Winslow, Edward, 138
Winthrop, John, 142, 180, 182
  views on democracy, 191
Wisconsin, 348, 462
Witchcraft, 194
Wolfe, James, *244,* 245
Women. *See also names of individ-
    uals, such as* Bethune, Mary
    McLeod; Roosevelt, Eleanor
  and abolitionist movement,
    437–438
  in American Revolution, 284–286
  in Civil War, 480, 481, 484, 485
  in Continental Army, 269
  equal rights movement, 437–438,
    563
  and factory work, 423–424
  in Iroquois Nation, 95–97
  in Puritan religious practice,
    191–194
  and religious revival, 435
  in World War II, 557
Women's suffrage, 542–543
Wonders of the Invisible World, The,
  (Mather), *194*
Wong, Elizabeth, 20–21
Wood, Grant, 306
Worcester, Mass., 203
World
  physical (map), *616–617*
  political (map), *614–615*
World War I, 536, 544–547
World War II, 537, 556–559
Wounded Knee, S. Dak., 502,
  507
Wyalusing Indians, 236
Wyandot Indians, 361
Wyoming, *379, 381,* 390, 393, 542

Y

Yakima Indians, *390*
Yellowstone National Park, 72–73
York, Duke of. *See* James II
Yorktown, Battle of, 258, *272,*
  273–274
Young, Brigham, 387–388

Z

Zane's Trace, 346
Zanzibar, *327*
Zuñi Indians, 129, 137
Zydeco music, 4

Credits (continued from page iv)

Illustrations

Literature border design by Peggy Skycraft

Maps

Photographs

RJB (bc). **30–31** © David Hiser, TIB. **31** © Jerry Jacka Photography. **32** © Jerry Jacka Photography. **33** BET. **37** © Karl Hentz, TIB (l); © Don King, TIB (r). **38** RJB (tr,bl,br). **39** RJB (l); © John Schekler (r). **40** SuperStock. **41** NASA/Science Source, Photo Researchers, Inc. **45** RJB. **47** Private Collection. **49** Northwestern University Library, RJB. **50** © New York City Transit Authority (l); RJB (r). **52** © Ernest Braun, Comstock. **56** GC (l); The Shelburne Museum (b). **56–57** University of Oregon. **57** Smithsonian Institution (r); American Numismatic Society (b). **58** RJB. **59** © The Bostonian Society (l); Boston Parks and Recreation Department (r). **60** LC, Laurie Platt Winfrey (tr); The Newberry Library, Chicago (b). **61** Boston Public Library. **62** California State Library (t); © Peter Newark's Western Americana (b). **63** New York Public Library, Newsweek Books (l,c); American Numismatic Society (r). **65** Jamestown-Yorktown Foundation. **66** LC (l); Smithsonian Institution, Art Resource (br). **66–67** RJB. **67** RJB (tl,tc,c,br); Old Sturbridge Village (tr). **68** AR (l); LC (r). **69** RJB (t, b). **70** New York Public Library. **71** Joslyn Art Museum (tl); LC (c); Smithsonian Institution (r). **72** Jim Peaco, © Yellowstone National Park (l, r); © Yellowstone National Park (c). **73** Bozeman Daily Chronicle, RJB (l); RJB (r). **75** Glenbow Archives. **76–77** © Jerry Jacka Photography. **78** © Jerry Jacka Photography (tl); Southwest Museum, Los Angeles, (c,b). **78–9** Comstock. **79** Art Resource. **81** © NASA, Grant Heilman Photography, Inc. **83** © Smithsonian Institution. **86** © Comstock. **87** © P. Hollembeak, American Museum of Natural History (r); RJB (b). **88** © Art Wolfe, Allstock. **89** © Sharon Gerig, Tom Stack & Associates (l); RJB (r). **90** Ohio Historical Society (t); © Gary Irving, TSW. (b). **91** RJB (t); © Richard & Mary Magruder, TIB (b). **92** © Kathleen O'Donnell, Stockphotos, Inc. **94** © Benn Mitchell, TIB. **95** © W.A. Banaszewski, Finger Lake Images. **97** RJB (t,b). **98** The New York State Museum. **102** Robert Harding Picture Library (l); AR (r); **102–3** GC **105** British Museum (t); New York Public Library, Map Division (r). **106** Galdiano Museum, AR (l); GC (r). **107** Science Museum, Florence, AR (c); RJB (b). **109** Bibliotheque Nacionale. **110** Biblioteca Nacional, Madrid (t); Naval Museum, Pegli, AR (b). **111** GC. **112** Randolph Goodlett, Pittsburgh Aqua Zoo. **112–13** RJB. **113** RJB. **115** Laurie Platt Winfrey, Inc. (t); Biblioteca Escorial, Newsweek Books (c). **116** British Museum, Michael Holford (c); © David Manso Martin, Prado (bl,bc); American Numismatic Society (br). **117** NASA. **119** New York Hispanic Society (t); New York Public Library, Rare Book Division (b). **120** GC. **121** Ovieda, Historia Natural. **122** Biblioteca Medicea Laurenziana, Italy. **126** National Portrait Gallery, London (t); American Numismatic Society (r); © Doug Keats (b). **127** Laurie Platt Winfrey, Inc. **128** Archivo de Indias, Seville, Laurie Platt Winfrey, Inc. **129** British Museum, The Bridgeman Art Library. **131** The Plimoth Plantation (t,b). **132** New York Public Library, Newsweek Books. **134** GC (tl); New York Public Library, Rare Book Room (tr); The Jamestown-Yorktown Foundation (bc,bl). **135** Ashmolean Museum, Oxford. **137** Northwestern University Library, RJB. **140** © Farrell Grehan, Photo Researchers, Inc. **141** The Pilgrim Society, Plymouth, Massachusetts (tl,tr,cl,br); RJB (bl). **142** American Antiquarian Society (l); The New England (r). **143** LC. **145** Atwater-Kent Museum (c); British Museum (b); **146** Historical Society of Pennsylvania. **147** Historical Society of Pennsylvania. **149** © Dan D. Briere, SuperStock. **152–53** Private Collection. **154** Laurie Platt Winfrey, Inc. (t); Colonial Williamsburg (c); RJB (br). **154–55** © David King Gleason. **156** New York Public Library, Rare Book Division. **157** Colonial National Historical Park (t); Colonial Williamsburg (b). **158** Virginia State Library and Archives. **158–59** Jamestown-Yorktown Foundation. **159** LC. **160** Colonial Williamsburg Foundation. **161** © John Colwell, Grant Heilman Photography, Inc. (t); Smithsonian Institution (c). **162** National Portrait Gallery, Art Resource. **163** BET. **164** RJB (t); LC (b). **166** GC. **167** GC. **168** RJB (t,b). **169** New York Public Library. **170** Museum of African Art, Newsweek Books (t); © Aldo Tutino, Smithsonian Institution, Art Resource (b). **171** Nelson Gallery-Atkins Museum (Nelson Fund) (tr); The Metropolitan Museum of Art (c); Colorphoto Hinz Allschwil-Basil (b). **172** GC. **173** GC (l); Rice Council for Market Development (b). **178** Massachusetts Historical Society (tl); The Newberry Library, Chicago (r); Plimouth Plantation (b). **179** Henry Ford Museum and Greenfield Village. **180** American Antiquarian Society. **181** © F.B. Grunzweig, F Stop Pictures (tl); © Homer Sykes, Woodfin Camp & Associates (tr); © Massachusetts Historical Society (b). **183** SuperStock (c); LC (b). **187** The Fine Arts Museum of San Francisco (t); The Henry Francis du Pont Winterthur Museum (b). **189**

GC (l,lc,rc,r). **190** Mystic Seaport, Mystic, Connecticut (t); Smithsonian Institution (c). **191** The Newberry Library, Chicago. **192** Northwind Picture Archives. **193** © John Jenkins III (c); RJB (b). **194** GC. **195** Ipswich Historical Society, Ipswich, Massachusetts. **196** RJB. **197** Mark Sexton, Essex Institute (c); RJB (b). **198** RJB. **200** St. Louis Art Museum. **201** Miniature Dining Room, 1720, Turner-Ingersoll House, Salem, Mass., Workshop of Mrs. James Ward Thorne. Gift of Mrs. James Ward Thorne, 1942.483. © 1988 The Art Institute of Chicago (t); The Metropolitan Museum of Art (c). **202** TIB. **206** LC (tl,cl). **206–7** New-York State Historical Association, Cooperstown, New York. **207** Philadelphia Museum of Art. **209** © TIB. **210** RJB. **211** Yale University Art Gallery. **213** The Henry Francis du Pont Winterthur Museum. **214** The Metropolitan Museum of Art, Rogers Fund, 1914. (14.26) (t); National Gallery of Art (c); Philadelphia Museum of Art (b). **215** Colonial Williamsburg. **216** Library Company of Philadelphia. **217** © Jerry Irwin, Photo Researchers, Inc. (l,r). **219** Haverford College Library. **224** Smithsonian Institution (l); Philidelphia Museum of Art (r). **225** Princeton University Library (t); The Shelburne Museum (c). **226** Colonial Williamsburg (tr); © Vic Kumma, Quiet Valley Living Historical Farm (tl). **227** © Vic Kumma, Quiet Valley Living Historical Farm (tl); John Deere Museum (r); RJB (l). **228** Historical Society of Pennsylvania. **232–233** LC. **234** Colonial Williamsburg (l); The White House Collection (r). **235** Virginia Historical Society (t); GC (b). **236** New York Public Library, Prints Division. **238** The Bostonian Society. **239** The Museum of Fine Arts, Boston (l); American Numismatic Society (c); Smithsonian Institution, Straub Collection (r). **240** Colonial Williamsburg. **241** © Continental Insurance. **243** Breton Littlehales, © National Geographic Society. **244** North Wind Picture Archives (c); Private Collection (b). **245** LC, Laurie Platt Winfrey, Inc. **246** New York Public Library. **247** Laurie Platt Winfrey, Inc. **248** GC (l); LC; Newsweek Books (r). **250** Historical Pictures Service, Inc., Chicago (t); GC (b). **251** RJB (t,bl); GC (c), © Vic Kumma, Quiet Valley Living Historical Farm (bc,br). **252** Historical Pictures Service, Inc., Chicago (l,r). **253** Brown University Library, Laurie Platt Winfrey, Inc. **255** The John Carter Brown Library, Brown University. **257** LC. **258** Mrs. John Adams; Gilbert Stuart; National Gallery of Art, Washington; Gift of Mrs Robert Homans (l); PHOTRI (c); The National Archives (c); The Henry Francis du Pont Winterthur Museum (r). **260** The Concord Museum (l,r). **261** GC. **262** Architect of the Capitol. **263** American Numismatic Society (tl); GC (tr). **264** LC. **265** Private Collection (l); RJB (r). **266** © Vic Kumma, Quiet Valley Living Historical Farm (l); The Concord Museum (r). **267** Essex Institute, Salem, Massachusetts. **268** Guilford Courthouse National Military Park. **269** Capitol, State of South Carolina (t); Rhode Island Historical Society (c). **270** RJB (t); LC (b). **274** The National Archives (l,c). **282** The Concord Museum. **284** GC. **286** LC. **290** Joseph Szaszfai, Yale University Art Gallery (l); PHOTRI (r). **291** Laurie Platt Winfrey, Inc. (l); © Jonathan Wallen Photography, The National Archives (r). **294** © Harald Sund, TIB (l); The National Archives (r). **296** GC. **298** © Daniel S. Brody, Stock Boston (t); © Erich Hartmann, Magnum Photos (c); Independence National Historic Park Collection (b). **299** Independence National Historic Park Collection (b); GC (c); The National Archives (b). **300** Virginia Museum of Art. **305** Historical Pictures Service, Inc. **306** Amon Carter Museum, Fort Worth, Texas. **307** BET (t); NASA (b). **308** © G. Glander, F.P.G. International (tl); GC (tr); RJB (b). **309** BET (l); The New-York Historical Society (r). **312–13** Private Collection. **314** The White House Collection (tl); William L. Clements Library (c); GC (bl). **315** The New-York Historical Society. **316** Sally Anderson-Bruce (t,c). **317** CP. **318** British Museum, Newsweek Books (t); The New-York Historical Society (bl,br). **320** GC. **321** RJB. **322** Pennsylvania Academy of Fine Arts. **323** Smithsonian Institution (t); © Jane Iverson, National Gallery of Art (b). **325** RJB. **326** RJB (c,b). **326–27** RJB (t); Museum of the City of New York (c). **327** RJB (r,b). **328** The Henry Francis du Pont Winterthur Museum (l); The Peabody Museum of Salem (c). **330** New York Public Library. **331** Massachusetts Historical Society (t); The Museum of Art, Rhode Island School of Design (b). **332** © Henry E. Peach, Old Sturbridge Village (t); National Gallery of Art (b). **333** RJB (c,r). **334** Columbia University, Newsweek Books. **335** The White House Collection. **338** © William Strode Associates (tl); The Newberry Library, Chicago (bl); Laurie Platt Winfrey, Inc. (br). **338–39** LC. **339** Henry Ford Museum and Greenfield Village. **340** © William Strode Associates. **340–41** © William Strode Associates. **345** GC. **346** State Historical Society of Wisconsin. **347** ©

William Strode Associates (t,c). **348** NASA. **349** The Shelburne Museum (l); RJB (r); GC (cl,cr). **352** James Monroe Memorial Library. **353** The National Archives. **354** Amon Carter Museum, Fort Worth, Texas (t); Missouri Historical Society (bl). **354–55** American Philosophical Society. **355** Peabody Museum, Harvard University (t); American Philosophical Society (b); Harper Horticulture Slide Library (r). **356** Independence Hall, Philadelphia (l); © Spencer Swanger, Tom Stack & Associates (r). **357** Massachusetts Historical Society. **359** Gerold Wunderlich & Co., Inc. **360** Field Museum of Natural History. **360–61** RJB. **362** LC. **363** Museum of the American Indian. **364** The National Portrait Gallery (l); New York Public Library, Rare Book Division (r). **365** GC. **368** The Newberry Library, Chicago (t); CP (b). **369** The Newberry Library, Chicago (tl); Oakland Museum, History Department (bl); © David Hizer, Photographers Aspen (cr). **370** Barker Texas History Center (l); © David Muench, David Muench Photography (r); **372** Museo de Historia, Chapultepec. **373** Gallery of the Republic, Austin, Texas (t); Chicago Historical Society (b). **374** © Henry Grosinsky, Time-Life Books (tl,tr); © Henry B. Beville, Time-Life Books (b). **377** Denver Public Library. **378** Denver Public Library. **379** Henry Ford Museum and Greenfield Village. **380** © Vic Kumma, Quiet Valley Living Historical Farm (bl); © Jeff Foott, Tom Stack & Associates (br). **380–81** Daughtridge Collection, Chicago, RJB. **381** © Jake Rajs, TIB (t); RJB (r); © Tom Stack & Associates (bl). **382** Oregon Historical Society. **383** Minnesota Historical Society (l); Oakland Museum, History Department (r). **384** California State Library. **385** Oakland Museum, History Department. **386** Wells Fargo Bank & Union Trust Co. **387** © Levi Strauss & Co. **388** The Massillon Museum. **389** GC. **391** Joslyn Art Museum (l,r). **392** Smithsonian Institution. **393** The Newberry Library, Chicago. **394** © Linda Borcover. **395** © Photo Researchers, Inc. (cl); © Peter Miller/TIB (cr); RJB (b). **398–99** Collection of Wiliam Gladstone. **400** Carolina Art Association (t); Boston Athenaeum (c); The National Archives (b). **400–1** The Museum of Fine Arts, Boston. **401** The Shelburne Museum. **402** © Grayson L. Matthews. **403** Magnolia Plantation (t); RJB (c). **404** Private Collection. **406** New York Public Library. **407** William R. Perkins Library, Duke University (l); Charleston Museum (c,r). **408** © Hillel Burger, Peabody Museum, Harvard University (t); CP (b). **409** © Louie Psihoyos, 1984, Contact Press Images, Inc. **410–11** © Susan Roach (t); RJB (b). **411** RJB (tr,tc,br). **412** GC. **413** Historical Society of Pennsylvania. **415** Methodist Publishing House, Nashville, Tennessee, RJB (t); © Colonial Williamsburg (b). **417** Hampton University Museum. **420** The Cincinnati Historical Society (t); Smithsonian Institution (b). **420–21** Historical Society of Pennsylvania. **421** CP. **422** Smithsonian Institution. **423** The Pilgrim Society, Plymouth, Massachusetts (t); Rhode Island Historical Society (b). **424** Museum of American Textile History (l,c); GC (r). **426** GC. **428** RJB. **429** Smithsonian Institution (t); Museum Purchase with Los Angeles County Funds, Los Angeles County Museum of Art. **431** RJB (tl,bl,br); The Cincinnati Historical Society (tr,cr). **432** Laurie Platt Winfrey, Inc. **433** GC (l); The Shelburne Museum (r). **434** Disciples of Christ Historical Society. **435** GC (t); RJB (b). **436** State of Illinois, Department of Conservation (t); LC (b). **437** GC (t); RJB (b). **438** Sophia Smith Collection, Smith College, Northampton, Massachusetts (l); CP (r). **439** RJB. **442** The New York State Historical Association, Cooperstown (l); GC (r). **443** Chicago Historical Society (t); LC (b); Museum of the Confederacy, Richmond, Virginia.(r). **444** GC. **448** Office of the Architect of the Capitol (t); RJB (b). **450** State House, Topeka. **451** GC (t); Northwestern University Library, RJB (b). **452** ©1984 Louie Psihoyos, Contact Press Images Inc. (tr,bl,br). **453** © 1984 Louie Psihoyos, Contact Press Images (l); State Historical Society of Wisconsin (r). **456** Ontario County Historical Society. **457** RJB. **459** RJB. **462** *Leslie's Illustrated*, September 17th, 1858 (l); GC (r). **463** GC. **464** LC. **465** New York Public Library (t); © Larry Sherer, Museum of the Confederacy (l); Museum of the Confederacy (r). **468** Albert S. Reynold, Arizona Pioneers' Historical Society Library (c); Light Impressions (b). **469** Pioneer Memorial Museum (t); Valentine Museum (c); State Historical Society of Wisconsin (b). **470** New York Public Library (l); Chicago Historical Society (r). **471** LC. **472—473** © Ted Russel, TIB. **474** Chicago Historical Society (l); Museum of the City of New York, Gift of Mrs. J. West Roosevelt (r); Museum of the City of New York (c). **475** Gil Gonzolez, Rutherford B. Hayes Foundation (b); Chicago Historical Society (t). **476** LC. **477** *The Civil War: Tenting Tonight*, photograph by Larry Sherer, © 1984, Time-Life Inc. (l); *The Civil War: Struggle for Tennessee*, photograph by Larry Sherer, ©1985, Time-Life Inc. (r); Mississippi State Historical Museum (tl). **478** BET (b), CP (inset). **479** National Archives (l); Museum fo the Confederacy (r). **480** Louis Plummer, Smithsonian Institution (l). Chicago Historical Society (r) **481** Historical Pictures (tc); Institute of Texan Cultures (tr); LC (b). **482** GC. **483** Birmingham Museum of Art. **484** LC. **485** Smithsonian Institution. **486** LC. **487** LC (t); Ohio Historical Society (b). **488** Robert Frerck, TSW. **489** GC. **490** National Portrait Gallery, Washington DC, Art Resource, NY (t); SEF, Art Resource, NY (b). **491** Detroit Public Library, Burton Historical Collection. **492** Ford's Theatre National Historic Site, National Park Service (tl), CP (tr); Louis A. Warren, Lincoln Library & Museum. **493** National Archives (l); BET (r). **494** Southern Historical Collection. **495** GC (l); LC (r); Schomburg Center for Research in Black Culture (t). **496** GC. **497** CP (b); Historical Pictures, Stock Montage, Inc. (t). **498** GC. **499** BET. **500** RJB. **502** Smithsonian Institution. **505** Brown Brothers (b); National Museum of American Art, Art Resource (t). **506** BET (b); South Dakota Art Museum Collection (t). **507** CP. **515** RJB.**516** Mississippi Department of Archives and History. **517** Bethlehem Steel Company. **518** RJB. **519** LC (tl); ©Jeff Perkell/The Stock Market (tc, tr); Northwestern University, RJB (b). **520** RJB (l); ACTWU/Labor Unity (r). **522** Statue of Liberty National Monument, Metaform (l); LC (r). **524** GC (t); Los Angeles Museum of Natural History (b). **525** The New-York Historical Society (l); RJB (r). **526** GEO/Eastman House (tl); GC (tr);RJB (bl, br). **527** New York Public Library, Prints Division. **528** © Alfred Stieglitz, The Collection of the Estate of Alfred Stieglitz. **529** CP (t); © Alvis Upitis, TIB (b). **530** RJB (l); Chicago Historical Society (r). **532** New York Public Library. **533** Chicago Historical Society. **536** Brown Brothers (tr); LC (tl, bl); National Archives (bc); AL (br). **537** AL (bl); CP (br); Otto Hagel, ©Time Warner, Inc. (cl); LC (tl, tr); GC (c); BET (r). **538** AP/Wide World (bc); BET (cl, bl); AL (t); Paul Conklin, Time Magazine (c); PHOTRI (cr). **539** Dept. of Health and Human Services (bl); PHOTRI (tr); AP/Wide World (c, tc, br); © George Mars Cassidy/TSW (tl). **540** Chicago Historical Society. **541** BET. **542** BET. **543** BET. **544** CP. **545** RJB. **546** CP. **547** Brown Brothers. **548** CP (b); AL (t). **549** BET. **550** BET. **552** FPG International. **553** CP (l); LC (c); AL (r). **554** AL (t); LC (b). **555** RJB. **556** Brown Brothers. **557** BET. **558** National Archives (t, b); AL (c). **559** National Archives. **560** BET. **561** Joan Sydlow/FPG International (r); AP/Wide World (l). **562** © Danny Lyon, Magnum (t); BET (c); Brown Brothers (b). **565** BET. **566** BET. **567** BET. **568** SuperStock (both). **569** AL. **570** © Cliff Fuelner, TIB (t); SuperStock (b). **571** © J.P. Laffront/SYGMA. **573** © Lawrence Migdale.